W9-CEA-380

FORENSIC
PSYCHOLOGY

FORENSIC PSYCHOLOGY

Second Edition

Joanna Pozzulo, Carleton University

Craig Bennell, Carleton University

Adelle Forth, Carleton University

PEARSON

Prentice
Hall

Toronto

Library and Archives Canada Cataloguing in Publication

Pozzulo, Joanna
  Forensic psychology / Joanna Pozzulo, Craig Bennell, Adelle Forth.—2nd ed.

Includes bibliographical references and index.
ISBN 978-0-13-205176-7

1. Forensic-psychology—Textbooks.   I. Forth, Adelle Elizabeth, 1961–   II. Bennell, Craig   III. Title.

RA1148.P69 2008   614'.15   C2007-904761-0

ISBN-13: 978-0-13-205176-7
ISBN-10: 0-13-205176-1

Vice President, Editorial Director: Gary Bennett
Acquisitions Editor: Ky Pruesse
Marketing Manager: Judith Allen
Developmental Editor: Patti Altridge
Production Editor: Tara Tovell/Amanda Wesson
Copy Editor: Tara Tovell
Proofreader: Joe Zingrone
Production Coordinator: Janis Raisen
Composition: Integra
Permissions and Photo Research: Sandy Cooke
Art Director: Julia Hall
Cover Design: Kerrin Hands
Interior Design: Julia Hall
Cover Image: Getty Images, iStock Photo/composite by Kerrin Hands

For permission to reproduce copyrighted material, the publisher gratefully acknowledges the copyright holders listed on pages 457–458, which are considered an extension of this copyright page.

Statistics Canada information is used with the permission of Statistics Canada. Users are forbidden to copy the data and redisseminate them, in an original or modified form, for commercial purposes, without permission from Statistics Canada. Information on the availability of the wide range of data from Statistics Canada can be obtained from Statistics Canada's Regional Offices, its World Wide Web site at http://www.statcan.ca, and its toll-free access number 1-800-263-1136.

1 2 3 4 5   11 10 09 08 07

Printed and bound in the United States of America.

Brief Contents

Chapter 1   An Introduction to Forensic Psychology   1

Chapter 2   Police Psychology   27

Chapter 3   The Psychology of Police Investigations   56

Chapter 4   Deception   90

Chapter 5   Eyewitness Testimony   125

Chapter 6   Child Victims and Witnesses   159

Chapter 7   Juries: Fact Finders   189

Chapter 8   The Role of Mental Illness
in Court   220

Chapter 9   Sentencing and Parole in Canada: Practices and Public
Opinions   249

Chapter 10   Domestic Violence and Sexual Offenders   276

Chapter 11   Homicidal and Psychopathic Offenders   307

Chapter 12   Risk Assessment   337

Chapter 13   Assessment and Treatment of Young, Female, and
Aboriginal Offenders   370

Detailed Contents

Preface   xiii

1   An Introduction to Forensic Psychology   1

What Is Forensic Psychology?   2
The Roles of a Forensic Psychologist   3
The Forensic Psychologist as Clinician   3

Box 1.1   Differences among Other Forensic Disciplines   5

The Forensic Psychologist as Researcher   5
The Forensic Psychologist as Legal Scholar   6
The Relationship between Psychology and Law   6
Psychology and the Law   7
Psychology in the Law   7
Psychology of the Law   7
The History of Forensic Psychology   8
Early Research: Eyewitness Testimony and Suggestibility   8
Early Court Cases in Europe   10
Advocates of Forensic Psychology in North America   10
Forensic Psychology in Other Areas of the Criminal Justice System   11
Landmark Court Cases in the United States   12

Box 1.2   Influential Canadian Court Cases in the History of Forensic Psychology   13

Psychological Theories of Crime   14

Box 1.3   Biological and Sociological Theories of Crime   15

Signs of a Legitimate Field of Psychology   18
Modern-Day Debates: Psychological Experts in Court   18

Box 1.4   Canadian Researcher Profile: Dr. James Ogloff   19

The Functions of the Expert Witness   20
The Challenges of Providing Expert Testimony   20
Criteria for Accepting Expert Testimony   22

Box 1.5   The Case of *R. v. McIntosh and McCarthy* (1997): Potential Problems with the *Mohan* Criteria   24

2   Police Psychology   27

Police Selection   28
A Brief History of Police Selection   28
The Police Selection Process   30

Box 2.1   Validation and Police Selection   31

The Validity of Police Selection Instruments   33

Box 2.2   Situational Tests Used in Assessment Centres   37

Police Discretion   37
Why Is Police Discretion Necessary?   38
Areas Where Police Discretion Is Used   39
Factors That Influence Police Discretion   42

Box 2.3   The Case of *Ernst v. Quinonez et al.* (2003)   43

Controlling Police Discretion   43

Box 2.4   The National Use-of-Force Model in Canada   45

Police Stress   46
Sources of Police Stress   46
Consequences of Police Stress   49

Box 2.5   Canadian Researcher Profile: Dr. Robert Loo   51

Preventing and Managing Police Stress   51

3   The Psychology of Police Investigations   56

Police Interrogations   57
The Reid Model of Interrogation   58
Potential Problems with the Reid Model of Interrogation   60
Interrogation Practices and the Courts   62
Recent Changes to Interrogation Procedures   63

Box 3.1   When the Police Go Too Far: The Case of *R. v. Hoilett* (1999)   63

Recent Changes to Interrogation Procedures   63
False Confessions   64
The Frequency of False Confessions   65
Different Types of False Confessions   65

Box 3.2   False Confession in a Child-Abuse Case   67

Interrogative Suggestibility and Compliance   68

**Box 3.3   Using the Gudjonsson Compliance
and Suggestibility Scales   69**

Studying False Confessions in the Lab   70
The Consequences of Falsely Confessing   72
Criminal Profiling   73
What Is a Criminal Profile?   73
The Origins of Criminal Profiling   74

**Box 3.4   The RCMP's Violent Crime Linkage
Analysis System (VICLAS)   75**

How Is a Criminal Profile Constructed?   76
Different Types of Profiling Methods   76
The Validity of Criminal Profiling   78
Other Types of Profiling   82
Geographic Profiling   82

**Box 3.5   Canadian Researcher Profile:
Dr. Kim Rossmo   83**

Racial Profiling   85

Box 3.6   A Canadian Example of Racial Profiling   85

4   Deception   90
The Polygraph Technique   91
Applications of the Polygraph Test   91
Types of Polygraph Tests   92
Validity of Polygraph Techniques   95
Can the Guilty Learn to Beat the Polygraph?   98

**Box 4.1   Seeing through the Face of
Deception   98**

Scientific Opinion: What Do the Experts Say?   99

**Box 4.2   Canadian Researcher Profile:
Dr. Christopher Patrick   100**

Admissibility of Polygraph Evidence   101
Impact of Polygraph Evidence on Jurors   102
Brain-Based Polygraph Techniques   102
Vocal and Nonverbal Behaviour Cues to Lying   104

**Box 4.3   Brain Fingerprinting: Evidence
for a New Deception-Detection
Technology?   105**

Can You Detect Deception through
Voice-Stress Analysis?   107
Verbal Cues to Lying   107
Are Some People Better at Detecting
Deception?   107

Box 4.4   Detecting High-Stakes Lies   109

Deception in Witnesses   110
Deception in Children   111
Assessment of Malingering and Deception   112
Disorders of Deception   112
Explanatory Models of Malingering   114
How to Study Malingering   115
Malingered Psychosis   116

Box 4.5   Ethics of Deception Research   117

Box 4.6   Being Sane in Insane Places   118

Malingered Amnesia   121

5   Eyewitness Testimony   125
**Eyewitness Testimony: The Role
of Memory   126**
How Do We Study Eyewitness Issues?   127
The Laboratory Simulation   127
Recall Memory   129
Interviewing Eyewitnesses   129
The Leading Question—The Misinformation Effect   130
**Procedures That Help Police Interview
Eyewitnesses   132**
Hypnosis   132
The Cognitive Interview   133

**Box 5.1   How the Cognitive Interview
Components Are Implemented with
Witnesses   133**

Recall Memory Following a Long Delay   135
Can Traumatic Memories Be Forgotten?   135

Box 5.2   Delayed Memory Goes to Court   135

**Box 5.3   Delayed Prosecutions of Historic
Child Sexual Abuse   137**

Recall of the Culprit   138
Quantity and Accuracy of Descriptions   138
Recognition Memory   139
Lineup Identification   139

**Box 5.4   Canadian Researcher Profile:
Dr. R.C.L. Lindsay   144**

Use of Surveillance Recordings for Identification   145
Voice Identification   146
Are Several Identifications Better than One?   147
Are Confident Witnesses Accurate?   147
Estimator Variable Research in Recognition
Memory   148

Expert Testimony on Eyewitness Issues   151
Public Policy Issues and Guidelines   152

Box 5.5   A Case of Wrongful Conviction   154

6   Child Victims and Witnesses   159
History   160
Recall for Events   160

Box 6.1   The Martensville Babysitting Case   161

Free Recall versus Directed Questioning   161
Why Are Children More Suggestible Than Adults?   162
Anatomically Detailed Dolls   163
Other Techniques for Interviewing Children   164
Recall for People   169
Describing the Culprit   169
Factors Affecting Children's Person Descriptions   169
Recognition   170
Lineup Procedure and Identification Rates   170
Testifying in Court   172
Preparing Children to Testify   173

Box 6.2   Questions for a Competency Inquiry   173

Courtroom Accommodations   175

Box 6.3   Canadian Researcher Profile:
           Professor Nicholas Bala   176

Child Maltreatment   177

Box 6.4   Corporal Punishment: Discipline or
           Physical Abuse?   177

Box 6.5   A Case of Neglect or Forgetfulness?   178

Box 6.6   One of the Worst Cases of Physical Abuse
           in Canada's History   180

Risk Factors Associated with Child Maltreatment   180
Short-Term and Long-Term Effects of Physical Abuse   181
Short-Term and Long-Term Effects of Sexual Abuse   182

Box 6.7   Luring Children over the Internet   183

Child Custody and Access   184
Legal History of Custody and Access   184
Factors Related to Divorce   185

7   Juries: Fact Finders   189
Jury Selection in Canada   190
The Cases Heard by Juries   190
Jury Selection   191

Box 7.1   Ontario's and British Columbia's Criteria
           for Serving on a Jury   192

Juror Payment   193
Are Lawyers Able to Select Favourable Jurors?   193
Scientific Jury Selection   193
Characteristics and Responsibilities of Juries
in Canada   195
Representativeness   195
Impartiality   195

Box 7.2   Balancing a Jury by Race   196

Box 7.3   Canada's Most Famous Partial Juror   197

Box 7.4   Cases Allowing a Challenge
           for Cause   199

Jury Functions   199

Box 7.5   The Pig Farmer Goes to Court   200

Box 7.6   Two Cases of Jury Nullification   201

How Do We Study Juror and Jury
Behaviour?   202
Post-Trial Interviews   203
Archives   203
Simulation   203
Field Studies   204
Reaching a Verdict   204
Listening to the Evidence   205
Disregarding Inadmissible Evidence   206
Judge's Instructions   207
Jury Decision-Making Models   208
Deliberations   210
The Final Verdict   210
Predicting Verdicts   211
Demographic Variables   211
Personality Traits   212
Attitudes   213
Defendant Characteristics   213
Victim Characteristics   213
Expert Testimony   214

Box 7.7   Canadian Researcher Profile:
           Dr. Regina Schuller   216

8   The Role of Mental Illness
       in Court   220
Presumptions in Canada's Legal System   221
Fitness to Stand Trial   221
Raising the Issue of Fitness   222
How Many Defendants Are Referred for Fitness
Evaluations?   222
Who Can Assess Fitness?   223
Fitness Instruments   223

Distinguishing between Fit and Unfit
Defendants   224

Box 8.1   Fitness Instruments   225

How Is Fitness Restored?   227

**Box 8.2   Canadian Researcher Profile:
Dr. Ron Roesch   228**

**Box 8.3   Mentally Ill but Competent to Make
Treatment Decisions?   229**

What Happens after a Finding of Unfitness?   229
Mental State at Time of Offence   230

**Box 8.4   Sportscaster Shot Dead by Patient
with a Mental Illness   233**

Raising the Issue of Insanity   234
Assessing Insanity   235
What Happens to a Defendant Found
NCRMD?   235
Automatism   237

**Box 8.5   A Gas Company, a Tire Company,
and a Case of Automatism   238**

Box 8.6   Can Insults Lead to Automatism?   239

How Do NCRMD and Automatism Differ?   239
Intoxication as a Defence   240
Defendants with Mental Disorders   240
Why Are There Such High Rates of Mental Illness
in Offender Populations?   241
Dealing with Offenders Who Are Mentally Ill   241
Bias against Mentally Ill Offenders   242
Are People with Mental Illnesses Violent?   242
Types of Offences Committed by People with
Mental Illnesses   243
Recidivism Rates and People with Mental
Illnesses   244
Treatment of Offenders with Mental Disorders   244
**A New Court for the Mentally Ill: The Mental
Health Courts   245**
Are Mental Health Courts Effective?   245

**9   Sentencing and Parole in Canada:
Practices and Public Opinions   249**
**The Structure of the Canadian Court
System   250**
Sentencing in Canada   252
The Purposes of Sentencing   253
The Principles of Sentencing   254
Sentencing Options in Canada   254

Box 9.1   Sentencing Options in Canada   255

Factors That Affect Sentencing Decisions   256
Sentencing Disparity   257
Sentencing Guidelines in Canada   260
Are the Goals of Sentencing Achieved?   261

**Box 9.2   The Death Penalty in Canada:
Were We Right to Abolish It?   263**

What Works in Offender Treatment?   264
Parole in Canada   265
Parole Decision Making   266

**Box 9.3   Myths and Realities Concerning
Parole Decision Making   267**

Types of Parole   268
Research on the Effectiveness of Parole   269
**Public Attitudes toward Sentencing
and Parole   270**

**Box 9.4   Canadian Researcher Profile:
Professor Julian V. Roberts   270**

Factors That Influence Public Opinion   272

**10   Domestic Violence and Sexual
Offenders   276**
Domestic Violence   276
The Conflict Tactics Scale   277

Box 10.1   Husband Battering Does Exist   278

Intimate Partners: A Risky Relationship   279
Theories of Intimate Violence   280
Why Do Battered Women Stay?   281

**Box 10.2   Woman's Best Friend: Pet Abuse
and Intimate Violence   283**

A Heterogeneous Population: Typologies of Male
Batterers   284
Criminal Justice Response   285
Does Treatment of Male Batterers Work?   286
Sexual Offenders   288
Nature and Extent of Sexual Violence   288
Definition of Sexual Assault   289
Rape Myths   289
Effects of Rape   289

**Box 10.3   Sexual Assault: Discounting
Rape Myths   290**

Classification of Sexual Offenders   291
Rapist Typologies   291

Is Resisting a Sexual Attack a Good Idea?   293
Child Molester Typologies   293
Theories of Sexual Aggression   294
Adolescent Sexual Offenders   295

Box 10.4   Canadian Researcher Profile:
            Dr. Vernon Quinsey   296

Female Sexual Offenders   296
Assessment and Treatment of Sexual Offenders   298
Effectiveness of Psychological Treatment of Sexual
Offenders   301

Box 10.5   Relapse Prevention with Sexual
            Offenders   302

11   **Homicidal and Psychopathic
     Offenders   307**
Homicidal Offenders   308
Filicide: When Parents Kill   309
Mothers Who Kill   310
Infanticide and Mental Illness   310

Box 11.1   From Devotion to Depression:
            Mothers Who Kill   311

Fathers Who Kill   312
Youth Who Kill   313
Spousal Killers   313
Bimodal Classification of Homicide   315
Multiple Murder: What Is Known   316
Serial Murderers: The Ultimate Predator   317
Mass Murderers   321

Box 11.2   Canada's Deadliest Mass Murder   322

The Psychopath   323
Assessment of Psychopathy   323

Box 11.3   Canadian Researcher Profile:
            Dr. Robert Hare   324

Psychopathy and Antisocial Personality Disorder   325
Psychopathy and Violence   326

Box 11.4   Clifford Olson: A Predatory Psychopath
            327

Psychopathy and Sexual Violence   328
Psychopathy and Treatment   328
Psychopathy in Youth   329

Box 11.5   Psychopathy Label: The Potential
            for Stigma   330

Psychopathy: Nature versus Nurture?   332

Does Family Matter?   332
Psychopathy and Law Enforcement   333
What Makes Them Tick?: Cognitive and Affective
Models of Psychopathy   333

12   **Risk Assessment   337**
What Is Risk Assessment?   338
**Risk Assessments: When Are They
Conducted?   339**
Civil Setting   339
Criminal Settings   340
Types of Prediction Outcomes   341
The Base Rate Problem   342
A History of Risk Assessment   343
Methodological Issues   344
Judgment Error and Biases   345
Approaches to the Assessment of Risk   346

Box 12.1   Dr. Death: A Legendary (Notorious)
            Forensic Psychiatrist   347

Types of Predictors   348

Box 12.2   Canadian Researcher Profile:
            Dr. Christopher Webster   349

Important Risk Factors   349
Dispositional Factors   350
Historical Factors   352
Clinical Factors   353
Contextual Factors   354

Box 12.3   Risk Factors Relating to Stalking   355

**Risk-Assessment Instruments and
Predictive Accuracy   355**
Actuarial Instruments   356
Structured Professional Judgment Schemes   358
Can We Predict Specific Types of Violence?   361
Spousal Assault   361
Sexual Violence   362
Current Issues   363
Where Is the Theory?   363

Box 12.4   Coping-Relapse Model of Criminal
            Recidivism   364

What about Protective Factors?   365
Are Decision Makers Using the Scientific
Research?   365
Why Do Some Individuals Stop Committing
Crimes?   366

Box 12.5   Why Do High-Risk Violent Offenders
            Stop Offending?   367

13 Assessment and Treatment of Young, Female, and Aboriginal Offenders 370

Young Offenders 371
Historical Overview 371
Youth Crime Rates 374
Assessment of Young Offenders 375

Box 13.1 Do Youthful Offenders Get Away with Murder? 375

Rates of Behaviour Disorders in Youth 376
Trajectories of Youthful Offenders 376
Theories to Explain Antisocial Behaviour 377

Box 13.2 Canadian Researcher Profile: Dr. Richard Tremblay 378

Risk Factors 379
Protective Factors 381
Treatment 382
Female Offenders 383
Historical Overview 383
Rates 384
Theories of Female Criminality 385
What Do We Know about Female Offenders? 386
Victimization Rates 387

Risk Factors 388
Battered Women Who Kill 389

Box 13.3 The Breaking Point: When Battered Women Kill 390

Treatment 392
Aboriginal Offenders 394
Historical Overview 394

Box 13.4 The Gladue Court 395

Rates 395
Risk Factors 397
Treatment 399

Box 13.5 The Okimaw Ohci Healing Lodge 401

Is an End to Aboriginal Overrepresentation in Sight? 402

Glossary 406
References 414
Credits 457
Case and Legislation Index 459
Name Index 461
Subject Index 468

Preface

We remember the day that the three of us gathered in Adelle's office to lament our teaching assignment: an introductory course in forensic psychology. Not that we weren't interested in teaching the course, but we worried about not having an undergraduate Canadian textbook on the subject. Given the need to discuss the law when studying forensic psychology, a text based on U.S. or British law would not do. We decided to write a Canadian forensic psychology textbook that was directed at Canadian undergraduates, a comprehensive book with as much Canadian content as possible.

The second edition of *Forensic Psychology* incorporates many new developments by theorists and researchers. For example, we discuss theories of women offending and the cognitive and affective processing deficits of psychopathy. In addition, chapters have been reorganized and new sections have been added, reflecting areas of interest to students and instructors. You will also find increased coverage on domestic violence and sexual offending, with a profile of a prominent Canadian researcher in this area. As well, a new chapter dedicated to homicide offending, including multiple murderers and the assessment, treatment, and etiology of psychopathy, has been added. All chapters have been updated to reflect the expanding field of forensic psychology, including recent changes to Canadian legislation. With the interest of the reader in mind, we have added new boxes to highlight provocative Canadian cases and cutting-edge research. *Forensic Psychology* is designed primarily for use in undergraduate courses, although graduate students and practitioners may find the comprehensive and up-to-date summary of key areas a useful resource.

We have taken a broad-based perspective that incorporates both experimental and clinical topics. The text covers topics that might otherwise be discussed in traditional social and cognitive psychology courses—including eyewitness testimony, jury decision making, and police procedures—as well as topics that are clinical in nature and might otherwise be discussed in traditional personality or abnormal psychology courses—such as the meaning of being unfit to stand trial, mentally disordered offenders, and psychopathy. Our goal is to present the important ideas, issues, and research in a way that students will understand and enjoy, and in some cases find useful in their professional careers. We hope that the academic community will find this textbook a valuable teaching tool that provides a comprehensive and current coverage of forensic psychology.

DISTINGUISHING FEATURES

The pedagogical aids are designed to promote student learning and assist instructors in presenting key material. Important features include the following:

- **Learning Objectives and End-of-Chapter Summaries.** Each chapter starts with a list of learning objectives to guide students' learning of the material and closes with a summary linked to the learning objectives.

- **Vignettes.** Chapter-opening vignettes provide students with a context for the key concepts they will encounter in each chapter. These engaging vignettes present real-world scenarios in which students, or people they know, could potentially find themselves.

- **Boxes.** Boxed features within the chapters provide interesting asides to the main text. Some detail current Canadian cases and legal rulings, while others highlight "hot" topics in the news that have not yet been the subject of much psychological research. These boxes will develop students' consciousness of current issues and hopefully spark some research ideas.

■ **Profiles of Canadian Researchers.** To expose students to the varied and excellent research in forensic psychology being conducted by Canadians, each chapter includes a profile of a key Canadian researcher whose work is relevant to the chapter topic. These profiles highlight educational background, current position, and research interests, along with a little about the researcher's personal life, so students realize they are people too.

■ **Research Methodology.** Research methodology specific to forensic topics is described in the relevant chapters, with the goal of helping students understand how studies in forensic psychology are conducted.

■ **Research Studies.** Data reported in original studies is cited throughout the textbook, often in graph or table form for easy interpretation. Diagrams of psychological models and flow charts demonstrate key processes that occur through the criminal justice system.

■ **Theoretical Perspectives.** In Chapter 1, we describe some general theories of criminal behaviour. More focused theories that provide accounts for specific topic areas are discussed in each of the subsequent chapters. The discussion of the various theories emphasizes a multidisciplinary approach, showing the interplay among cognitive, biological, and social factors in understanding the different forensic psychology areas.

■ **Law.** *Forensic Psychology* provides the student with information on current Canadian law relevant to the psychological issues discussed. At times, Canadian law is contrasted with U.S. and/or British law; however, it is important to remember that the emphasis is on Canadian case law, statutes, regulations, and so on. We do not provide full coverage of law that is not Canadian, so students who are interested in the laws of other countries should refer to other resources.

■ **Discussion Questions.** Several discussion questions are offered at the end of each chapter. Instructors can assign these questions for group discussion, or students can use the questions to examine their comprehension and retention of the chapter material. We hope these questions will inspire critical thought in students.

■ **Key Terms and Glossary.** Throughout the chapters, key words with which students in forensic psychology should be familiar appear in bold type and are defined in marginal notes. These key terms and their definitions are also provided in a glossary at the end of the book for easy reference.

SUPPLEMENTS FOR INSTRUCTORS

The following supplements specific to *Forensic Psychology*, Second Edition, can be downloaded by instructors from a password-protected location on Pearson Education Canada's online catalogue (**vig.pearsoned.ca**). Contact your local sales representative for further information.

■ **Instructor's Manual.** The instructor's manual is a comprehensive resource that provides chapter outlines, class activities, and summaries of select cases cited. We hope our colleagues will use the textbook and instructor's manual as a foundation that they can build on in the classroom lecture.

- **Test Item File.** This test bank, offered in Microsoft Word format, contains multiple-choice and short-answer questions. Each question is classified according to difficulty level and is keyed to the appropriate page number in the textbook.
- **PowerPoint Presentations.** PowerPoint slides highlight the key concepts in each chapter of the text.

SUPPLEMENTS FOR STUDENTS

For the second edition of *Forensic Psychology*, a customized study guide is available. Contact your local Pearson Education sales representative for details.

In addition, students can visit Pearson Education Canada's Criminology Resource Site at **www.pearsoned.ca/criminology** for information about the study of criminology and careers in criminology, supplementary information, and links to other resources.

ACKNOWLEDGMENTS

This book would never have come to fruition had we not been mentored by outstanding forensic researchers. Joanna Pozzulo is indebted to Rod Lindsay at Queen's University for his unfailing support, his rich insights, and his commitment to academic excellence that she aspires to achieve. Craig Bennell is grateful to David Canter at the University of Liverpool for providing a stimulating intellectual environment in which to study and for teaching him how to think critically. Adelle Forth wishes to express her admiration, respect, and gratitude to Robert Hare at the University of British Columbia, who nurtured her interest in the area of psychopathy and who has provided consistent support and guidance. These researchers continue to be a source of inspiration to us.

We would like to acknowledge that the forensic program at Carleton University, of which we are part, would not exist without Don Andrews. He has been instrumental in guiding the forensic field both locally and internationally. Also, our colleagues Shelley Brown, Kevin Nunes, and Ralph Serin have contributed to our program and our thinking of forensic issues.

We are thankful to the pre-eminent researchers we profiled in this textbook for giving us their time and insight into their life. Specifically, Nick Bala, Bob Hare, Rod Lindsay, Robert Loo, Jim Ogloff, Christopher Patrick, Vern Quinsey, Julian Roberts, Ron Roesch, Kim Rossmo, Regina Schuller, Richard Tremblay, and Christopher Webster. All have made significant contributions to the field of forensic psychology.

We would like to thank the reviewers who provided us with exceptional feedback that allowed us to make the textbook stronger. Reviewers include the following:

Mike Woodworth, UBC Okanagan

J. Thomas Dalby, University of Calgary

Deborah Connolly, Simon Fraser University

Brent Snook, Memorial University of Newfoundland

Stephen Hart, Simon Fraser University

Tracey Curwen, Nipissing University

Janne Holmgren, Mount Royal College

David Nussbaum, University of Toronto

Abe Worenklein, Concordia University

Alison Kerr, York University

We have tried to incorporate as many of the suggestions as possible, but of course we were restricted in terms of page length. In the end, we feel this second edition provides excellent breadth and good depth.

We thank our many undergraduate and graduate students who over the years have challenged our thinking and who have influenced the ideas expressed in this book. A number of students have provided countless hours of editorial support: Carolyn Barnes, Heather Clark, Shevaun Corey, Julie Dempsey, Jillian Flight, Alberta Girardi, Shannon Gottschall, Diana Grech, Natalie Jones, Bonny-Jean Klemm, Caleb Lloyd, Tamara Melnyk, Melissa Pagliaro, Erin Robertson, and Angela Stevens. Their help with tracking down references and legal cases was greatly appreciated, and their insights and suggestions were invaluable.

We would like to thank the great staff at Pearson Education Canada. Ky Pruesse (executive acquisitions editor) and Patti Altridge (developmental editor) deserve special mention—this book would not exist without their enthusiasm, expertise, and dedication. Tara Tovell (copy editor), Amanda Wesson (production editor), Sandy Cooke (photo researcher), and Joe Zingrone (proofreader) also played important roles in making *Forensic Psychology*, Second Edition, become a reality.

Finally on a personal note, Joanna Pozzulo would like to thank her family for their unending love and support through the hardest of times. She also would like to thank Craig and Adelle for being great collaborators and dear friends. Craig Bennell would like to thank his wife Cindy for her love, patience, and support during the long hours of writing, and his son Noah for making him always remember what is most important. Adelle Forth would like to thank her partner, colleague, and friend, John Logan, for his insights, suggestions, and feedback that improved the book, as well as his understanding and support while preparing the book.

Chapter 1
An Introduction to Forensic Psychology

Learning Objectives

- Provide a narrow and a broad definition of forensic psychology.

- Describe the differences between clinical and experimental forensic psychology.

- List the three ways in which psychology and the law can interact.

- Describe three major psychological theories of crime.

- List the criteria used in Canada to decide when expert testimony is admissible.

Jennifer Chen is an undergraduate university student who wants to become a forensic psychologist. She has just finished watching her favourite movie, *The Silence of the Lambs*. In fact, Jennifer always seems to be watching movies like this. If she's not watching movies, Jennifer's watching television shows like *CSI* or reading the latest true crime book. Fortunately, Jennifer's neighbour works as a probation officer and she has come into regular contact with forensic psychologists. This neighbour has repeatedly told Jennifer that forensic psychology isn't what you see in the movies. Jennifer finally decides to find out for herself what forensic psychology is all about and enrols in a course, much like the one you are currently taking. Throughout the course, Jennifer learns more about the field of forensic psychology. It turns out that her neighbour was correct, but what Jennifer learns in the course makes her even more confident that she has chosen the right career path.

Although you may not appreciate it yet, **forensic psychology** is all around us. Every time you turn on the television or pick up the paper, there are news stories that relate directly to the field of forensic psychology. Hollywood has also gotten in on the act. More and more often, blockbuster movies focus on issues that are also related directly to the field of forensic psychology—whether it is profiling serial killers, selecting jury members, or determining someone's sanity. Unfortunately, the way in which the popular media portray forensic psychology is usually inaccurate. Although forensic psychologists often carry out the sorts of tasks you see depicted in the movies, the way in which they carry them out is very different from (and certainly less glamorous than) the typical Hollywood image. One of our primary goals throughout this book is to provide you with a more accurate picture of what forensic psychology is and to encourage you to think more critically about the things you see and hear in the media.

Forensic psychology: A field of psychology that deals with all aspects of human behaviour as it relates to the law or legal system

Gene Hackman's role as a jury consultant in Grisham's *Runaway Jury* relates to a task that forensic psychologists are involved in. Much of what is seen in this Hollywood movie is an exaggeration of what actually occurs in jury selection.

WHAT IS FORENSIC PSYCHOLOGY?

So, if Hollywood hasn't gotten it right, what exactly is forensic psychology? On the surface, this seems like a relatively simple question to answer, and it is undoubtedly an important question to ask. When being introduced to a new field of psychology, as you are now, one of the first questions you probably ask yourself is, "What am I going to be studying?" Although providing a clear and comprehensive definition of the discipline is obviously a logical way to begin a textbook on forensic psychology, this task is far more difficult than it seems because there is no generally accepted definition of the field (Brigham, 1999). Indeed, experts in this area don't even agree on what the field should be called, let alone how it should be defined (Ogloff, 2002). For example, you will often see forensic psychology being referred to as legal psychology or criminological psychology.

Much of the ongoing debate about how forensic psychology should be defined centres on whether the definition should be narrow or broad (Brigham, 1999). A narrow definition of forensic psychology would focus on certain aspects of the field while ignoring other, potentially important, aspects. For example, a narrow definition of forensic psychology might focus on applied aspects while ignoring the experimental research that many psychologists (who refer to themselves as forensic psychologists) conduct. This appears to be how many leading psychologists prefer to define the discipline (e.g., Otto & Heilbrun, 2002). Indeed, even the major professional associations in this area, such as the American Board of Forensic Psychology (ABFP) and the American Psychology-Law Society (AP-LS), define the field in a narrow fashion. These associations have defined forensic psychology as "the professional practice by psychologists within the areas of *clinical psychology, counseling psychology, neuropsychology, and school psychology, when they are engaged regularly as experts* and represent themselves as such, in an activity *primarily intended to provide professional psychological expertise to the judicial system*" (emphasis added; ABFP & AP-LS, 1995, p. 6).

Thus, according to the ABFP and AP-LS definition, any psychologist who provides expertise to the judicial system but happens to *work in an area of psychology outside the scope of their definition*, such as social psychology, would not technically be doing work in the area of forensic psychology. In addition, any psychologist who spends all of his or her time conducting what appears to be forensic-related research—for example, studying whether brain damage leads to criminal behaviour—in one of the prescribed areas of psychology (in this case, neuropsychology), but *does not provide professional expertise to the judicial system on a regular basis*, would not be considered a forensic psychologist. For reasons such as these, many psychologists have problems with using narrow definitions to define the field of forensic psychology.

By their very nature, broad definitions of forensic psychology are less restrictive than narrow definitions. One of the most commonly cited examples of a broad definition of forensic psychology is the one proposed by Bartol and Bartol (2006). They define the discipline as "(a) the research endeavour that examines aspects of human behaviour directly related to the legal process . . . and (b) the professional practice of psychology within, or in consultation with, a legal system that embraces both civil and criminal law" (p. 3). Thus, unlike the narrow definition of forensic psychology provided above, which focuses solely on the *application* of psychology to the legal system, this definition does not restrict forensic psychology to applied issues. It also focuses on the *research* that is required to inform applied practice in the field of forensic psychology.

Throughout this textbook, we adopt a broad definition of forensic psychology. Although we will often focus on the application of psychological knowledge to various aspects of the Canadian legal system, our primary goal is to demonstrate that this application of knowledge must always be based on a solid grounding of psychological research. In line with a broad definition of forensic psychology, this research frequently originates in areas of psychology that are often not obviously connected with the forensic area, such as social, cognitive, and developmental psychology. The fact that forensic psychology is such an eclectic field is just one of the reasons why it is such an exciting area of study.

THE ROLES OF A FORENSIC PSYCHOLOGIST

What is consistent across the various definitions of forensic psychology is that individuals who call themselves forensic psychologists are always interested in issues that arise at the intersection between psychology and the law. What typically differs across the definitions is the particular focus the forensic psychologist takes. For example, by looking at the definitions provided above, it is clear that forensic psychologists can take on the role of clinician or researcher. In reality, however, these roles are not mutually exclusive and one individual can take on more than one role. Indeed, some of the best-known forensic psychologists, many of whom will be profiled in this book, are both clinicians *and* researchers, while others are clinicians, researchers, *and* legal scholars. Since we will continually touch upon these various roles throughout the upcoming chapters, we will briefly clarify what each role entails.

The Forensic Psychologist as Clinician

Clinical forensic psychologists are broadly concerned with mental health issues as they pertain to the legal system (Otto & Heilbrun, 2002). This can include both research and practice in a wide variety of settings, such as schools, prisons, hospitals, and so forth. For

Clinical forensic psychologists: Psychologists who are broadly concerned with the assessment and treatment of mental health issues as they pertain to the law or legal system example, clinical forensic psychologists are often concerned with the assessment and treatment of persons with mental disorders within the context of the law. On the research side, a frequent task for the clinical forensic psychologist might involve the validation of an assessment tool that has been developed to predict the risk of an offender being violent (e.g., Kropp & Hart, 2000). On the practical side, a frequent task might involve the assessment of an offender to assist the parole board in making an accurate determination of whether that offender is likely to pose a risk to the community. Other issues that clinical forensic psychologists are interested in may include, but are certainly not limited to, the following:

- Divorce and child custody mediation
- Determinations of criminal responsibility (insanity) and competency to stand trial
- Providing expert testimony on questions of a psychological nature
- Personnel selection (e.g., for law enforcement agencies)
- Conducting critical incident stress debriefings
- Designing and conducting treatment programs for offenders

As in the United States, a clinical forensic psychologist in Canada must be a licensed clinical psychologist who has specialized in the forensic area. The educational requirements to obtain a licence vary across provinces and territories, but some form of graduate-level training is always required. In Alberta, Saskatchewan, Newfoundland and Labrador, New Brunswick, and Nova Scotia, the requirement is a master's degree in psychology, while in British Columbia, Manitoba, Ontario, Prince Edward Island, and Quebec, a doctoral degree in psychology is required. The forensic specialization typically takes the form of an intense period of supervised practice after the completion of the required degree, in an applied forensic setting of some kind under the watchful eye of an experienced clinical supervisor. The last step of the licensing process is a comprehensive exam, which often involves an oral component.

One of the most common questions that undergraduate students ask is, "What is the difference between forensic psychology and **forensic psychiatry**?" In fact, many people, including those in the media, confuse these two fields. To some extent in Canada, clinical forensic psychology and forensic psychiatry are more similar than they are different and, as a result, it is often difficult to separate them clearly. For example, both clinical forensic psychologists and forensic psychiatrists are trained to assess and treat individuals experiencing mental health problems who come into contact with the law, and you will see psychologists and psychiatrists involved in every component of the criminal justice system. In addition, clinical forensic psychologists and forensic psychiatrists often engage in similar sorts of research (e.g., developing causal models of violent behaviour).

However, there are also important differences between the two fields. Probably the most obvious difference is that psychiatrists, including forensic psychiatrists, are medical doctors who can prescribe medication. Therefore, forensic psychiatrists undergo training that is quite different from the training clinical forensic psychologists receive, and this leads to several other distinctions between the fields. For example, in contrast to a psychiatrist's general reliance on a medical model of mental illness, psychologists tend to view mental illness more as a product of an individual's physiology, personality, and environment. See Box 1.1, which looks at some other important forensic-related disciplines that are often confused with the field of forensic psychology.

Forensic psychiatry: A field of medicine that deals with all aspects of human behaviour as it relates to the law or legal system

Differences among Other Forensic Disciplines

Nowadays, people are being bombarded by media portrayals of various forensic disciplines, beyond just forensic psychology and forensic psychiatry. Although this does much to promote the respective specialties, it can also be the source of a lot of confusion. Listed below are brief descriptions of just a few forensic specialty areas. Each of these disciplines is sometimes confused with forensic psychology.

■ *Forensic anthropology*. Forensic anthropologists examine the remains of deceased victims to determine key facts about them such as their gender, age, appearance, and so forth.

■ *Forensic linguistics*. Forensic linguists examine the spoken and written word in an attempt to assist criminal investigators. For example, they can assess the language in suicide notes to determine whether the notes are fake or genuine.

■ *Forensic chemistry*. Forensic chemists study the chemical aspects of crime scenes, which can include an analysis of paint particles, dyes, fibres, and other materials.

■ *Forensic ondontology*. Forensic ondontologists study the dental aspects of criminal activity, which can include identifying deceased victims through dental records and determining whether bite marks were made by an adult or child.

■ *Forensic pathology*. Forensic pathologists examine the remains of dead bodies in an attempt to determine the time and cause of death through physical autopsy.

■ *Forensic entomology*. Forensic entomologists are concerned with how insects can assist with criminal investigations. For example, they can help determine when someone died based on an analysis of insect presence (e.g., different types of insects will be present on a corpse at different points in time) and/or insect development (e.g., certain insects who are attracted to corpses soon after death develop in predictable, set cycles).

Source: Decaire, 2004.

The Forensic Psychologist as Researcher

A second role for the forensic psychologist is that of experimenter, or researcher. As we have indicated above, although this role does not necessarily have to be separate from the clinical role, it often is. As with clinical forensic psychologists, **experimental forensic psychologists** are concerned with mental health issues as they pertain to the legal system, and they can be found in a variety of criminal justice settings. However, researchers in the forensic area are usually concerned with much more than just mental health issues. Indeed, they can be interested in any research issue that relates to the law or legal system. The list of research issues that are of interest to this type of forensic psychologist is far too long to present here, but they include the following:

Experimental forensic psychologists: Psychologists who are broadly concerned with the study of human behaviour as it relates to the law or legal system

■ Examining the effectiveness of risk assessment strategies

■ Determining what factors influence jury decision making

■ Developing and testing better ways to conduct eyewitness lineups

■ Evaluating offender and victim treatment programs

■ Studying the impact of questioning style on memory recall

■ Examining the effect of stress management interventions on police officers

Not only do clinical forensic psychologists differ from experimental forensic psychologists in terms of what they do, but they also differ in terms of their training. The forensic psychologist who is interested primarily in research will have undergone Ph.D. level graduate training in one of many different types of experimental graduate programs (and no internship is typically required). Only some of these graduate programs will be devoted solely to the study of forensic psychology. Others will be programs in social psychology, cognitive psychology, or developmental psychology, although the program will have a faculty member associated with it who is conducting research in a forensic area. Regardless of the type of graduate program chosen, the individual's graduate research will be focused primarily on a topic related to forensic psychology (e.g., the malleability of child eyewitness memory). As can be seen in the short list of topics provided above, research in forensic psychology is eclectic and requires expertise in areas such as memory processing, decision making, organizational issues, and so on. This is one of the reasons why training for experimental forensic psychology is more varied than the training for clinical forensic psychology.

The Forensic Psychologist as Legal Scholar

A third role for the forensic psychologist, which is far less common than the previous two but no less important, is that of legal scholar. Because this role is less common, we will not deal with it as much throughout this textbook, but it is important to discuss it briefly, especially given the recent focus on this role in Canada. Much of this focus resulted from the formation of two initiatives at Simon Fraser University (SFU) in Burnaby, B.C. The first of these was SFU's Psychology and Law Program, originally established in 1991. More recently, this program has partnered with the University of British Columbia to allow students to obtain both their Ph.D. in psychology as well as their L.L.B. in law. This program produces forensic psychologists in North America who are much more informed about the legal process and the legal system than was the case previously. The second initiative was the formation, also in 1991, of the Mental Health, Law, and Policy Institute (MHLPI) at SFU. The purpose of the MHLPI is to "promote interdisciplinary collaboration in research and training in areas related to mental health law and policy" (MHLPI, 2007). According to Brigham (1999), forensic psychologists in their role as legal scholars "would most likely engage in scholarly analyses of mental health law and psychologically oriented legal movements," whereas their applied work "would most likely center around policy analysis and legislative consultation" (p. 281).

THE RELATIONSHIP BETWEEN PSYCHOLOGY AND LAW

Not only is forensic psychology a challenging field to be in because of the diversity of roles that a forensic psychologist can play, but it is also challenging because forensic psychology can be approached from many different angles. One of the most interesting ways of thinking about these various angles has been proposed by Craig Haney, a professor of psychology at the University of California, Santa Cruz. Haney (1980) suggests there are three primary ways in which psychology and the law can relate to each other. He calls these relationships **psychology *and* the law**, **psychology *in* the law**, and **psychology *of* the law**. Throughout this textbook, we will focus on the first two relationships, psychology and the law and psychology in the law. Clinical and experimental forensic psychologists are typically involved in these areas much more often than in the third. Psychology of the law

Psychology and the law: The use of psychology to examine the operation of the legal system

Psychology in the law: The use of psychology in the legal system as that system operates

Psychology of the law: The use of psychology to examine the law itself is largely the domain of the legal scholar role and, therefore, we will only touch on it very briefly.

Psychology and the Law

In this relationship, "psychology is viewed as a separate discipline [to the law], examining and analysing various components of the law [and the legal system] from a psychological perspective" (Bartol & Bartol, 1994, p. 2). Frequently, research that falls under the category of psychology *and* the law examines assumptions made by the law or our legal system, asking questions such as, Are eyewitnesses accurate?; Do certain interrogation techniques cause people to falsely confess?; Are judges fair in the way they hand down sentences?; and Is it possible to accurately predict whether an offender will be violent when released from prison? When working within the area of psychology and the law, forensic psychologists attempt to answer these sorts of questions and communicate their findings to the legal community. Much of forensic psychology deals with this particular relationship. Therefore, research issues that fall under the general heading of "psychology and the law" will be thoroughly discussed throughout this textbook.

Psychology in the Law

Once a body of psychological knowledge exists in any of the above-mentioned areas of study, that knowledge can be used in the legal system by psychologists, lawyers, judges, and others. As the label indicates, psychology *in* the law involves the use of psychological knowledge in the legal system (Haney, 1980). As with psychology and the law, psychology in the law can take many different forms. It might consist of a psychologist in court providing expert testimony concerning some issue of relevance to a particular case. For example, the psychologist might testify that, based on his or her understanding of the psychological research, the eyewitness on the stand may have incorrectly identified the defendant from a police lineup. Alternatively, psychology in the law might consist of a police officer using his or her knowledge of psychology in an investigation. For example, the officer may base his questioning strategy during an interrogation on his knowledge of various psychological principles that are known to be useful for extracting confessions. Many of the research applications that we focus on in this textbook fit nicely with the label "psychology in the law."

Psychology of the Law

Psychology *of* the law involves the use of psychology to study the law itself (Haney, 1980), and it addresses questions such as, What role should the police play in domestic disputes?; Does the law reduce the amount of crime in our society?; and Why is it important to allow for discretionary decision making in the Canadian criminal justice system? Although often not considered a core topic in forensic psychology, there does appear to be a growing interest in the area of psychology of the law. The challenge in this case is that, to address the sorts of questions posed above, a set of skills from multiple disciplines (e.g., criminology, sociology, law) is often important and sometimes crucial. The new focus in North America and elsewhere on the role of forensic psychologist as legal scholar will no doubt do much to assist in this endeavour, and we are confident that in the future more research in the area of forensic psychology will focus on issues surrounding psychology of the law.

THE HISTORY OF FORENSIC PSYCHOLOGY

Now that we have defined the field of forensic psychology and discussed the various roles that forensic psychologists can play, we will turn to a discussion of where the field came from and where it is currently headed. Forensic psychology, when it is broadly defined, has a relatively short history, dating back roughly to the late nineteenth century. In the early days, this type of psychology was actually not referred to as forensic psychology and most of the psychologists conducting research in the area did not identify themselves as forensic psychologists. However, their research formed the building blocks of an emerging field of psychology that continues to be strong today. See Figure 1.1 for a timeline of some significant dates in the history of forensic psychology.

Early Research: Eyewitness Testimony and Suggestibility

In the late nineteenth century, research in the area of forensic psychology was taking place in both North America and Europe, though as indicated above, it wasn't being referred to as forensic psychology at the time. Some of the first experiments were those of James McKeen Cattell (who is perhaps better known for his research in the area of intelligence testing) at Columbia University in New York. Cattell, a previous student of Wilhelm Wundt, who developed the first psychology laboratory in Leipzig, Germany, was one of the major powerhouses of psychology in North America. After developing an expertise in the study of human cognitive processes while in Leipzig, Cattell conducted some of the first North American experiments looking at what would later be called the psychology of eyewitness testimony (e.g., Cattell, 1895). Cattell would ask people to recall things they had witnessed in their everyday life (e.g., "In which direction do apple seeds point?"), and he found that their answers were often inaccurate.

At around the same time, a number of other psychologists began studying eyewitness testimony and suggestibility (see Ceci & Bruck, 1993, for a review). For example, the famous French psychologist Alfred Binet conducted numerous studies in which he showed that the testimony provided by children was highly susceptible to suggestive questioning techniques. In a study discussed by Ceci and Bruck (1993), Binet (1900) presented children with a series of objects for a short period of time (e.g., a button glued to poster board). After viewing an object, some of the children were told to write down everything that they saw while others were asked questions. Some of these questions were direct (e.g., "How was the button attached to the board?"), others were mildly leading (e.g., "Wasn't the button attached by a thread?"), and still others were highly misleading (e.g., "What was the colour of the thread that attached the button to the board?"). As found in numerous studies since this experiment, Binet demonstrated that asking children to report everything they saw (i.e., free recall) resulted in the most accurate answers and that highly misleading questions resulted in the least accurate answers.

Shortly after Binet's study, a German psychologist named William Stern also began conducting studies examining the suggestibility of witnesses (Ceci & Bruck, 1993). The

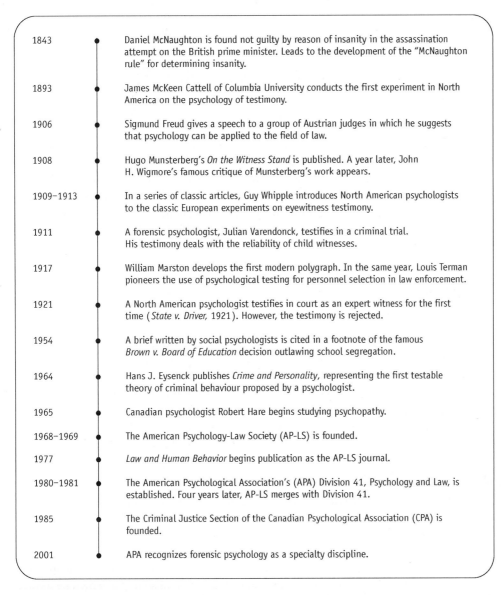

1843	Daniel McNaughton is found not guilty by reason of insanity in the assassination attempt on the British prime minister. Leads to the development of the "McNaughton rule" for determining insanity.
1893	James McKeen Cattell of Columbia University conducts the first experiment in North America on the psychology of testimony.
1906	Sigmund Freud gives a speech to a group of Austrian judges in which he suggests that psychology can be applied to the field of law.
1908	Hugo Munsterberg's *On the Witness Stand* is published. A year later, John H. Wigmore's famous critique of Munsterberg's work appears.
1909–1913	In a series of classic articles, Guy Whipple introduces North American psychologists to the classic European experiments on eyewitness testimony.
1911	A forensic psychologist, Julian Varendonck, testifies in a criminal trial. His testimony deals with the reliability of child witnesses.
1917	William Marston develops the first modern polygraph. In the same year, Louis Terman pioneers the use of psychological testing for personnel selection in law enforcement.
1921	A North American psychologist testifies in court as an expert witness for the first time (*State v. Driver*, 1921). However, the testimony is rejected.
1954	A brief written by social psychologists is cited in a footnote of the famous *Brown v. Board of Education* decision outlawing school segregation.
1964	Hans J. Eysenck publishes *Crime and Personality*, representing the first testable theory of criminal behaviour proposed by a psychologist.
1965	Canadian psychologist Robert Hare begins studying psychopathy.
1968–1969	The American Psychology-Law Society (AP-LS) is founded.
1977	*Law and Human Behavior* begins publication as the AP-LS journal.
1980–1981	The American Psychological Association's (APA) Division 41, Psychology and Law, is established. Four years later, AP-LS merges with Division 41.
1985	The Criminal Justice Section of the Canadian Psychological Association (CPA) is founded.
2001	APA recognizes forensic psychology as a specialty discipline.

Figure 1.1 Some Important European and North American Developments in the History of Forensic Psychology

Sources: Bartol and Bartol, 2004; Brigham, 1999.

"reality experiment" that is now commonly used by eyewitness researchers to study eyewitness recall and recognition can, in fact, be attributed to Stern. Using this research paradigm, participants are exposed to staged events and are then asked to recall information about the event. In one of Stern's experiments, participants were exposed to a scenario that involved two students arguing in a classroom setting until one of the students drew a revolver (Stern, 1910). As was the case with Binet, Stern found that eyewitness testimony can often be incorrect, and he was perhaps the first researcher to demonstrate that a person's level of emotional arousal can have an impact on the accuracy of that person's testimony.

Early Court Cases in Europe

Around the time that this research was being conducted, psychologists in Europe also started to appear as expert witnesses in court. Unsurprisingly, much of the testimony that they were providing dealt with issues surrounding the accuracy of eyewitness testimony. For example, in 1896, Albert von Schrenck-Notzing was probably the first expert witness to provide testimony in court on the effect of pretrial publicity on memory. The case took place in Munich, Germany, and involved a series of three sexual murders. The court case attracted a great deal of attention from the press of the time, and Schrenck-Notzing testified that this extensive pretrial press coverage could influence the testimony of witnesses by causing what he called "retroactive memory falsification" (Bartol & Bartol, 2006). This referred to a process whereby witnesses confuse actual memories of events with the events described by the media. Schrenck-Notzing supported his expert testimony with laboratory research, and this research is very much in line with what we know about the effects of pretrial publicity from more recent studies (e.g., Ogloff & Vidmar, 1994).

Following this case, Julian Varendonck, a Belgian psychologist, was called on to be an expert witness in a 1911 case involving the murder of a young girl, Cecile. Ceci and Bruck (1993) describe the case:

> Two of Cecile's friends who had played with her on the day of her murder were awakened that night by Cecile's mother to ask of her whereabouts. One of the children replied that she did not know. Later that night, she led the police to the spot where the children had played, not far from where Cecile's body was found. In the next month, the two children were repeatedly interviewed by authorities who asked many suggestive questions. The children quickly changed their original testimony of not knowing about Cecile's actions on the day of her murder. They provided details of the appearance of the murderer as well as his name. Because of an anonymous letter, the police arrested the father of one of the playmates for the murder of Cecile. On the basis of the details of the case, Varendonck was convinced of the defendant's innocence. He quickly conducted a series of studies with the specific intent of demonstrating the unreliability of children's testimony. (p. 406)

According to Ceci and Bruck (1993), in one of his studies, Varendonck (1911) asked a group of children to describe a person who had supposedly approached him in front of the children earlier that morning. Although this person did not exist, Varendonck was able to demonstrate, in line with more recent studies, that many of the children were easily led by suggestive questioning. Based on these findings, Varendonck concluded to the court that the testimony provided by the children in this case was likely to be inaccurate and that, as a group, children are very prone to suggestion.

Advocates of Forensic Psychology in North America

Although it was not until years later that psychologists began testifying on similar issues in North America, psychology in North America was making great strides in other areas of the criminal justice system. Perhaps one of the most important landmarks was the publication in 1908 of Hugo Munsterberg's *On the Witness Stand* (Munsterberg, 1908). Another student of Wilhelm Wundt, Munsterberg is considered by many to be the father of forensic psychology. Coming from Germany to Harvard University in 1892, he quickly established a name for himself (Brigham, 1999). In his book, Munsterberg argued that psychology had much to offer the legal system. Through a collection of his essays, he discussed how psychology could assist with issues involving eyewitness testimony, crime detection, false confessions, suggestibility, hypnotism, and even crime prevention.

Unfortunately, he presented his ideas in a way that led to heavy criticism from the legal profession. This is unsurprising given the way in which he wrote. Consider the following quotation from the introduction to his book:

> The lawyer and the judge and the juryman are sure that they do not need the experimental psychologist. They do not wish to see that in this field pre-eminently applied experimental psychology has made strong strides. . . . They go on thinking that their legal instinct and their common sense supplies them with all that is needed and somewhat more . . . if the time is ever to come when even the jurist is to show some concession to the spirit of modern psychology, public opinion will have to exert some pressure. (Munsterberg, 1908, pp. 10–11)

Munsterberg's biggest critic was John Henry Wigmore, a well-respected law professor at Northwestern University in Chicago. Wigmore is known for many things, most notably his *Treatise on Evidence*, which is a critical examination of the laws of evidence. In the field of forensic psychology, however, what Wigmore is most commonly known for is his ruthless critique of Munsterberg's book. Through a series of fabricated "transcripts," Wigmore (1909) put Munsterberg on "trial," where he was sued, and found guilty of "claiming more than he could offer" (Brigham, 1999, p. 276). Wigmore criticized Munsterberg for the lack of relevant research publications to back up his claims and, more generally, for the lack of applied research in the field of forensic psychology as a whole. Due perhaps in large part to Wigmore's comprehensive attack on Munsterberg's work, North American psychologists working in areas that we would now define as forensic psychology were largely ignored by the legal profession for a long period of time. However, according to some, Munsterberg was still instrumental in pushing North American psychologists into the legal arena (Bartol & Bartol, 2006).

The father of forensic psychology, Hugo Munsterberg, is best known for his controversial book *On the Witness Stand*, which many people believe pushed North American psychologists into the legal arena.

Forensic Psychology in Other Areas of the Criminal Justice System

After the publication of Munsterberg's controversial book, forensic psychology in North America gradually caught up to what was happening in Europe. Not only was more research being conducted in the area by psychologists, but this research was also being practically applied in a wide range of criminal justice settings. For example, as Bartol and Bartol (2004) highlight, forensic psychologists were instrumental in establishing the first clinic for juvenile delinquents in 1909, psychologists began using psychological testing for law enforcement selection purposes in 1917, and 1919 saw the first forensic assessment laboratory (to conduct pretrial assessments) set up in a U.S. police agency. After these events, psychologists in the United States began to be more heavily involved in the judicial system as well, starting with the case of *State v. Driver* in 1921.

Landmark Court Cases in the United States

Unlike their European counterparts who had provided expert testimony in courts as early as the late nineteenth century, the first time this happened in the United States was 1921 (*State v. Driver*, 1921). However, according to Bartol and Bartol (2006), the *Driver* case was only a partial victory for forensic psychology. This West Virginia case involved the attempted rape of a young girl and the court accepted expert evidence from a psychologist in the area of juvenile delinquency. However, the court rejected the psychologist's testimony that the young girl was a "moron" and, therefore, could not be believed. In its ruling the court stated, "It is yet to be determined that psychological and medical tests are practical, and will detect the lie on the witness stand" (quoted in Bartol & Bartol, 2006, pp. 11–12).

A number of more recent U.S. court cases are also enormously important in the history of forensic psychology. Perhaps the best-known case is that of *Brown v. Board of Education* (1954). This case challenged the constitutionality of segregated public schools (Benjamin & Crouse, 2002). Opponents of school segregation argued that separating children based on their race creates feelings of inferiority, especially among African-American children. On May 17, 1954, the U.S. Supreme Court agreed. In the Court's ruling, Chief Justice Earl Warren stated,

> Segregation of White and colored children in public school has a detrimental effect upon the colored children. The impact is greater when it has the sanction of the law, for the policy of separating the races is usually interpreted as denoting the inferiority of the Negro group. A sense of inferiority affects the motivation of the child to learn. Segregation with the sanction of law, therefore, has a tendency to retard the educational and mental development of Negro children and to deprive them of some of the benefits they would receive in a racially integrated school system. Whatever may have been the extent of psychological knowledge [in previous court cases] this finding is amply supported by modern authority. (Benjamin & Crouse, 2002, p. 39)

Beyond the obvious social importance of this ruling, it is important in the field of forensic psychology because of a footnote that was attached to the last sentence of the ruling, the famous footnote 11. The modern authority that the U.S. Supreme Court was referring to in this ruling was research in the social sciences demonstrating the detrimental effect of segregation. At the top of the list of seven references included in footnote 11 was the work of Kenneth Clark, an African-American psychologist who taught psychology at City College in New York City. This was the first time that psychological research was cited in a U.S. Supreme Court decision and some have argued that this validated psychology as a science (e.g., Benjamin & Crouse, 2002).

The last court case that we will discuss here is *Jenkins v. United States* (1962). The trial involved charges of breaking and entering, assault, and intent to rape, with the defendant, Jenkins, pleading not guilty by reason of insanity. Three clinical psychologists were presented by the defendant, each of them supporting an insanity defence on the basis that the defendant was suffering from schizophrenia at the time of the crimes. At the conclusion of the trial, the judge instructed the jury to disregard the testimony from the psychologists because "psychologists were not qualified to give expert testimony on the issue of mental disease" (American Psychological Association, 2007). The case was appealed. As part of the appeal, the American Psychological Association provided a report to the court stating their view that clinical psychologists are competent to provide opinions concerning the existence of mental illness. On appeal, the court reversed the conviction and ordered a new trial, stating that "some psychologists are qualified to render expert testimony on mental disorders . . . the determination of a psychologist's competence to render an expert opinion . . . must depend upon the nature and extent of his knowledge and not simply on the claim to the title 'psychologist'" (American Psychological Association, 2007). This decision helped to increase the extent to which psychologists could contribute directly to the legal system as expert witnesses.

Although the landmark U.S. court cases we have discussed so far have been fundamental in shaping forensic psychology, there are also numerous Canadian court cases that have been influential. A brief discussion of some of these cases is provided in Box 1.2. We will provide a more detailed discussion of some of the cases in the relevant chapters (where we focus on research relating to these rulings).

Box 1.2

Influential Canadian Court Cases in the History of Forensic Psychology

Some influential Canadian cases of particular interest to forensic psychologists include the following:

- *R. v. Hubbert (1975)*. The Ontario Court of Appeal states that jurors are presumed to be impartial (i.e., unbiased) and that numerous safeguards are in place within the Canadian judicial system to ensure this (e.g., limitations can be imposed on the press in terms of what they can report before the start of a trial).

- *R. v. Sophonow (1986)*. The Manitoba Court of Appeal overturns the murder conviction of Thomas Sophonow due to errors in law, many of which related to problems with the eyewitness evidence collected by the police as part of their investigation.

- *R. v. Lavallee (1990)*. The Supreme Court of Canada (SCC) sets guidelines for when, and how, expert testimony should be used in cases involving battered women syndrome. Since this ruling, expert testimony in cases of battered women who kill has increased.

- *Wenden v. Trikha (1991)*. The Alberta Court of Queen's Bench rules that mental health professionals have a duty to warn a third party if they have reasonable grounds to believe that their client intends to seriously harm that individual.

- *R. v. Swain (1991)*. The SCC makes a ruling that results in changes to the insanity defence standard in Canada, including the name of the defence, when the defence can be raised, and for how long insanity acquittees can be detained.

- *R. v. Levogiannis (1993)*. The SCC rules that children are allowed to testify in court behind screens that prevent them from seeing the accused.

- *R. v. Mohan (1994)*. The SCC establishes formal criteria for determining when expert testimony should be admitted into court.

- *R. v. Williams (1998)*. The SCC formally acknowledges that jurors can be biased by numerous sources, ranging from community sentiment on a particular issue to direct involvement with a case (e.g., being related to the accused).

- *R. v. Gladue (1999)*. The SCC rules that prison sentences are being relied on too often by judges as a way of dealing with criminal behaviour, especially for Aboriginal offenders, and that other sentencing options should be considered.

- *R. v. Oickle (2000)*. The SCC rules that police interrogation techniques, which consist of various forms of psychological coercion, are acceptable and that confessions extracted through their use can be admissible in court.

Psychological Theories of Crime

In addition to the increased use of psychologists in the criminal justice system, the mid-twentieth century saw a proliferation of psychological theories of crime, in both Europe and North America. This is not to say there weren't psychological theories of crime (or theories from other disciplines) proposed before this time, but there was a renewed interest in attempts to explain criminal behaviour during this period. We cannot adequately cover all of the psychological theories of crime in this one chapter. In fact, it would take more than this entire book to do justice to the topic. Instead, we will focus on three specific theories that can be categorized generally under the headings of **psychoanalytic theories**, **learning theories**, and **personality theories**. For a more detailed discussion of these theories, you can refer to Akers and Sellers (2003). In addition, see Box 1.3 for a brief discussion of theories of crime from other disciplines.

Psychoanalytic Theories and Crime The development of psychoanalytic theory can be attributed to Sigmund Freud. However, although Freud had much to say about many psychological issues, it seems he had relatively little to say about crime or criminals. His involvement in the field of forensic psychology appears to have been restricted to a speech he gave to a group of Austrian judges in 1906, in which he advocated the use of psychology in the legal system. In that speech he suggested that "the task for the therapist . . . is the same as that of the examining magistrate. We have to uncover the hidden psychical material. . . . [T]o do this we have to invent a number of detective devices, some of which it seems that you gentlemen of the law are now about to copy from us" (Freud, 1906/1959, p. 108). In terms of psychoanalytic theories of crime, these can be attributed to several of Freud's followers. Most of these theories have several things in common. They take the position that it is primarily dynamic internal forces within people that account for their criminal behaviour, and they argue that early childhood events and experiences are crucial for understanding crime (Hollin, 1989).

There are, in fact, many different psychoanalytic theories of crime—far too many to discuss here. Therefore, we will focus on just one, John Bowlby's **theory of maternal deprivation**. Bowlby (1944) argued that the early separation of a child from his or her mother prevents effective social development from taking place. Without effective social development, Bowlby hypothesized that children will experience long-term problems in developing positive social relationships and will instead develop antisocial behaviour patterns. In large part, Bowlby's theory is based on his study of juvenile delinquents. In support of his theory, Bowlby (1944) found that a far greater number of juvenile delinquents experienced early separation from their mothers compared with a nondelinquent control group. Researchers have criticized Bowlby's theory of maternal deprivation on multiple fronts, ranging from problems with his original control group to inadequate assessment procedures (Feldman, 1977; Morgan, 1975). However, since the time when these criticisms were first levied against the theory, numerous studies have indicated that negative early childhood experiences can indeed influence the development of antisocial behaviour (e.g., Waschbusch, Porter, Carrey, Kazmi, Roach, & D'Amico, 2004).

Learning Theories and Crime As with psychoanalytic theories of crime, there are also many different learning theories that have been proposed to explain the development and maintenance of criminal behaviour (Hollin, 1989). However, here too there are threads that bind the various theories together. In this case, all learning theories are based upon

---

Psychoanalytic theories: Theories that attempt to explain criminal conduct by focusing on dynamic internal forces within people and the importance of early childhood events and experiences

Learning theories: Theories that attempt to explain criminal conduct by focusing on principles of conditioning (e.g., being rewarded for criminal behaviour)

Personality theories: Theories that attempt to explain criminal conduct by focusing on the personality makeup of offenders

Theory of maternal deprivation: Theory that early separation from one's mother plays a role in the development of antisocial behaviour

Box 1.3

Biological and Sociological Theories of Crime

In addition to psychological theories of crime, a variety of biological and sociological theories of crime have also been proposed throughout the past century. Below are brief descriptions of some of the best-known theories.

Biological Theories of Crime

- *Sheldon's (1949) constitutional theory.* Sheldon proposed that crime is largely a product of an individual's body build, or somatotype, which is assumed to be linked to an individual's temperament. According to Sheldon, endomorphs (obese) are jolly, ectomorphs (thin) are introverted, and mesomorphs (muscular) are bold. Sheldon's studies indicated that, due to their aggressive nature, mesomorphs were more likely to become involved with crime.

- *Jacobs, Brunton, Melville, Brittan, and McClemont's (1965) chromosomal theory.* Jacobs and her colleagues proposed that chromosomal irregularity is linked to criminal behaviour. A normal female has two X chromosomes, whereas a normal male has one X and one Y chromosome. However, it was discovered that there were men with two Y chromosomes, which, it was proposed, made them more masculine and, therefore, more aggressive. According to Jacobs and her colleagues, this enhanced aggressiveness would result in an increased chance that these men would commit violent crimes.

- *Mark and Ervin's (1970) dyscontrol theory.* Mark and Ervin proposed that lesions in the temporal lobe and limbic system result in electrical disorganization within the brain, which can lead to a dyscontrol syndrome. According to Mark and Ervin, symptoms of this dyscontrol syndrome can include outbursts of sudden physical violence, impulsive sexual behaviour, and serious traffic violations.

Sociological Theories of Crime

- *Merton's (1938) strain theory.* Merton proposed that crime is largely a product of the strain felt by certain individuals in society (typically from the lower class) who have restricted access to legitimate means, such as education, of achieving valued goals of success. Merton argued that, while some of these individuals will be happy with the lesser goals that are achievable, others will turn to illegitimate means, such as crime, in an attempt to achieve the valued goals.

- *Sutherland's (1939) differential association theory.* Sutherland proposed that criminal behaviour is learned through social interactions in which people are exposed to values that can either be favourable or unfavourable to violations of the law. More specifically, Sutherland maintained that a person is likely to become involved in criminal activity when he or she learns more values (i.e., attitudes) that are favourable to violations of the law than values that are unfavourable to it.

- *Hirschi's (1969) social control theory.* Hirschi proposed that individuals possess certain bonds with society and that the strength and quality of these bonds control their behaviour (including the likelihood that they will exhibit criminal behaviour). Hirschi focused on four bonds in particular: attachment to others (e.g., teachers), commitment to conventional values (e.g., reputation), involvement in conventional activities (e.g., school), and belief in a societal value system (e.g., respect for the law). If these bonds weaken for some reason (e.g., children start to perform poorly in school and, as a result, begin to dislike teachers), individuals are more likely to become involved in criminal activity.

principles of conditioning, which speculate that a person's behaviour, including criminal behaviour, is learned and maintained by its consequences (Skinner, 1974). By extension, these theorists also generally agree that criminal behaviour can be eliminated, or at least reduced, by modifying these consequences. Indeed, as you will see in Chapter 9, this principle is largely what guides our sentencing practices in North America. Many people believe that, if the negative consequences of committing crime are increased to a point at which they far outweigh the rewards, criminal activity will decrease. As in the previous section, we will focus on just one of the many learning theories that have had a significant impact on forensic psychology—**social learning theory**, as formulated by Albert Bandura.

Social learning theory extends learning theory as defined by psychologists such as B.F. Skinner (1974) in that it recognizes that learning through consequences can come from many different sources. Not only can learning occur from the consequences that result from an individual's own behaviour, but it can also occur by observing the consequences experienced by others. In fact, according to social learning theorists, it is largely through our observations of others that we learn how to perform the observed behaviours (Bandura, 1977).

As it relates to criminal behaviour, observational learning can take place through three primary contexts: the family, peer groups, and cultural symbols, such as television shows (Bandura, 1973). Thus, an individual's antisocial behaviour is largely viewed as a function of his or her exposure to antisocial behaviour on the part of others, especially when the individual has observed antisocial behaviour being rewarded. In support of this theory, there is now a wealth of research to suggest that interacting with antisocial individuals can predict future antisocial behaviour (e.g., Andrews & Bonta, 2006). In addition, the most recent research looking at the effects of exposure to violence on television suggests that this exposure also predicts aggressive and violent behaviour (e.g., Bushman & Huesmann, 2006).

As with psychoanalytic theories of crime, social learning theories are not without their critics. One of the most commonly voiced criticisms is that social learning theory cannot explain the fact that many people are exposed to antisocial role models and yet not all of these people go on to commit crimes (Nietzel, 1979). However, others have argued that learning theories do in fact provide the means to explain such findings. Hollin (1989), for example, points out that learning theories consist of a variety of explanations for this finding, such as vicarious punishment, or seeing others suffer the negative consequences of being caught for their crimes. As you will see in upcoming chapters, there are some problems with Hollin's argument that still need to be addressed, since we now have substantial evidence that observing others getting punished (e.g., by seeing them get long-term prison sentences) does not have the deterrent effect many social learning theorists would predict.

Personality Theories and Crime Finally, according to some theorists, individuals who get involved in crime do so primarily because of their personality makeup. More specifically, personality theorists suggest that criminals have either developed, or inherited, a personality (i.e., a set of underlying stable traits) that differentiates them in some way from law-abiding citizens. There are numerous theories that attempt to explain the connection between personality and crime, but none have been as influential as the biosocial theory of crime proposed by Hans J. Eysenck, the famous personality psychologist. It is believed that Eysenck's theory represents the first testable theory of criminal behaviour proposed by a psychologist (Bartol & Bartol, 2004). As a result, this theory deserves special mention in a textbook such as this one and we will focus our discussion on it.

Eysenck's theory of crime, which is explained thoroughly in his book *Crime and Personality*, is one of the few that focuses on biological, social, and individual factors. According to Eysenck (1977), the three major dimensions that make up all of our personalities are **extroversion** (E), **neuroticism** (N), and psychoticism (P). Most of Eysenck's research dealt primarily with E and N, so we will focus on these two constructs here. Each

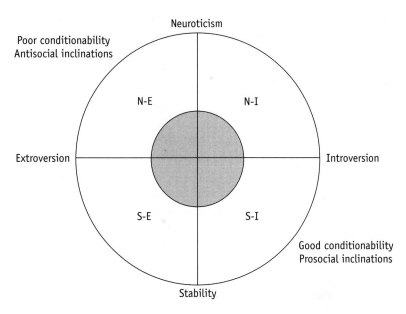

Figure 1.2 Eysenck's Model of Personality and Its Relationship to Conditionability and Crime

Source: Adapted from Hollin, 1989.

of these personality constructs is thought to fall along a continuum. The E construct is represented by high extroversion at one end of the continuum and high introversion at the other end. The N construct is represented by high neuroticism at one end of the continuum and high stability at the other end. Eysenck assumed that everybody's personality makeup falls somewhere on the two-dimensional diagram shown in Figure 1.2. However, because most people will not exhibit the extremes of either continuum, it is assumed that the majority of us will be located somewhere in the shaded area.

In addition, Eysenck also believed that some individuals are born with cortical and autonomic nervous systems (ANS) that affect their ability to learn from the consequences of their behaviour. More specifically, Eysenck believed extroverts are cortically underaroused and therefore continually seek out stimulation. Introverts, conversely, are assumed to be cortically overaroused and therefore continually avoid stimulation. Similarly, Eysenck believed that neurotic individuals have an overreactive ANS, which causes strong reactions to unpleasant stimuli. Highly stable individuals, however, are assumed to have a stable ANS.

This theory's relevance to the formation and maintenance of criminal behaviour becomes clear when we consider how Eysenck relates personality to people's ability to learn from the consequences of their behaviour, especially the negative consequences experienced in childhood as part of the socialization and conscience-building process. According to Eysenck (1977), high-E individuals condition less efficiently than high-I individuals. Compared with introverts, extroverts require more intense stimulation to achieve the same level of cortical arousal and they are, therefore, less responsive to the negative consequences of their actions and more difficult to socialize. Likewise, high-N individuals condition less effectively than high-S individuals because of the unpleasant effects of anxiety that neurotic individuals experience and, therefore, they are also more difficult to socialize. Thus, due to their poor conditionability, it is assumed that high-E/high-N individuals will have strong antisocial inclinations. Conversely, low-E/low-N individuals will have strong prosocial inclinations.

A lot of research has examined Eysenck's theory of crime, much of it using the Eysenck Personality Questionnaire to measure and contrast the various personality constructs in matched offender and nonoffender groups. Much of this research supports Eysenck's original assertions that offender samples often score higher on E and N (see Hollin, 1989, for a summary of this research). For example, in McGurk and McDougall's (1981) study of delinquents and nondelinquents, evidence emerged for high-E/low-N and low-E/high-N individuals in both groups. The supposedly antisocial high-E/high-N individual was only found in the delinquent group, and the supposedly prosocial low-E/low-N individual was only found in the nondelinquent group. However, despite some general level of support for Eysenck's theory, it is often criticized because it cannot explain how all crime emerges, the empirical evidence linking conditioning and socialization is weak, and the theory relies on a model of personality (the classic trait model, as discussed in Chapter 3) that is often challenged (Hollin, 1989).

Signs of a Legitimate Field of Psychology

Although the field of forensic psychology has perhaps not come as far as many forensic psychologists would have hoped in its relatively short history, it has now become a recognized and legitimate field of study within psychology. Indeed, forensic psychology now appears to have many of the markings of an established discipline. As highlighted by Schuller and Ogloff (2001), this is reflected in numerous ways. First, there are a growing number of high-quality textbooks in the area that provide the opportunity to teach students about forensic psychology. This is particularly so in the United States. Second, there are now a large number of academic journals dedicated to various aspects of the field, and more mainstream psychology journals are beginning to publish research from the forensic domain at a regular rate. Third, a number of professional associations have now been developed to represent the interests of forensic psychologists and to promote research and practice in the area. The largest of these associations is the AP-LS, in which Canadian forensic psychologists have played a crucial role (one of these individuals, Dr. James Ogloff, is profiled in Box 1.4). Other countries have developed similar professional associations. In Canada, for example, forensic psychologists can belong to the Criminal Justice Section of the Canadian Psychological Association (CPA). Lastly, new training opportunities in forensic psychology, at both the undergraduate and graduate level, are being established in North America (some in Canada), and existing training opportunities are being improved.

MODERN-DAY DEBATES: PSYCHOLOGICAL EXPERTS IN COURT

Since the field of forensic psychology has become more widely accepted, forensic psychologists have increasingly been asked to provide expert testimony in court. The variety of topics that forensic psychologists testify about is very broad indeed, including competency

Box 1.4

Canadian Researcher Profile: Dr. James Ogloff

James Ogloff entered the University of Calgary intending to major in commerce and to go on to complete a law degree. His career plan was to become a corporate lawyer. While majoring in commerce, during his second year he was required to complete an undergraduate course in social sciences. Viewing this as a largely useless requirement, he opted to complete Introduction to Psychology in an inter-session course in the summer "to get it over with." Much to his surprise, he ended up being captivated with psychology, so much so that the following fall semester, he ended up dropping out of his commerce courses and transferring to psychology. At that time, his interests were in the area of child psychology. Soon, though, his longstanding interests in law re-emerged and he completed his undergraduate research on the topic of eyewitness memory and hypnosis. Dr. Ogloff entered graduate school in clinical psychology, obtaining his M.A. at the University of Saskatchewan. While there, he spent a great deal of time at the Regional Psychiatric Centre, a secure prison hospital, where he trained, conducted research, and did clinical work. Although he was working in the forensic psychology area, he still felt the need to learn more about the law.

With a desire to learn more about the law and how it relates to psychology, Dr. Ogloff went on to attend the Law/Psychology program at the University of Nebraska at Lincoln. The University of Nebraska had established the first program that offered a combined law degree and Ph.D. in

psychology. He completed his Juris Doctor in Law, with distinction, and had a short stint of legal practice while still a student. He completed his Ph.D. in psychology, doing his doctoral research in the area of jury understanding of the insanity defence. His interest in this area was spawned by John Hinckley Jr.'s attempted assassination of President Ronald Reagan. John Hinckley Jr. was found "not guilty by reason of insanity" and the verdict initiated a great deal of controversy regarding the use of the insanity defence in the United States. Numerous reforms were initiated—including changing the wording of the defence in many states with the intention to limit the number of people found "not guilty by reason of insanity." Curiously, though, no one had conducted research to determine whether varying the insanity defence standards produced changes in jury verdicts. Dr. Ogloff's research showed that even fairly dramatic changes to the insanity defence standards did not produce differences in verdicts by simulated jurors.

Following graduate school, Dr. Ogloff began his academic career at Simon Fraser University, where he eventually became the University Endowed Professor of Law and Forensic Psychology. He helped to develop, and served as director of, the Program in Law and Forensic Psychology at Simon Fraser University. He also held an appointment as Adjunct Professor of Law at the University of British Columbia, where he taught classes in mental health law and the psychology of litigation.

Dr. Ogloff has continued his research in the area of the comprehension of legal instructions, though his more recent work has focused more generally on jurors' comprehension of judges' legal instructions. In addition to his continued interest in jury research and judicial instructions, most of his research and scholarly writing has been in the areas of offenders with mental illnesses, training in law and psychology, the assessment of risk for violence, and professional ethics.

In 2001, Dr. Ogloff left Simon Fraser University to assume the position of Foundation Professor of Clinical Forensic Psychology at Monash University in Melbourne, Australia. He is also Director of Psychological Services for the Victorian Institute of Forensic Mental Health. As well, he has established and directs the Centre for Forensic

(continued)

(continued)

Behavioural Science, a research, training, and consultation institute. In addition to his other work, he has shown a commitment to professional associations in psychology. He has served as the president of the Canadian Psychological Association and the president of the American Psychology-Law Society. Currently, he is the president-elect of the Australian and New Zealand Association of Psychiatry, Psychology and Law and he is the chair of the College of Forensic Psychologists in Australia.

Although he enjoys his work, Dr. Ogloff's real joy in life comes from his relationship with his wife, Kathleen, to whom he has been married for 23 years. They have three young children who keep them very busy. Aleksandra (14 years), Andrew (12 years), and Karena (9 years) have taken to life in Australia very well. Most of their spare time is spent enjoying family activities, spending summers at the beach, and travelling when they have the opportunity.

to stand trial, custody issues, malingering and deception, the accuracy of eyewitness identification, the effects of crime on victims, and the assessment of dangerousness. In order for forensic psychologists to increase the extent to which they can contribute to the judicial system in this way, it is important for them to become more knowledgeable about the law and the legal system (Ogloff & Cronshaw, 2001). This includes becoming more aware of what the role of an expert witness is, the various ways in which psychology and the law differ from one another, and the criteria that courts consider when determining whether psychological testimony should be admitted.

The Functions of the Expert Witness

According to Ogloff and Cronshaw (2001), an expert witness generally serves one of two functions. One is to provide the court with information that assists them in understanding a particular issue, and the other is to provide the court with an opinion. Understanding these functions is important because they are what separate the **expert witness** from other witnesses who regularly appear in court (e.g., eyewitnesses). To be clear on this issue, in contrast to other witnesses in court, who can testify only about what they have directly observed, expert witnesses can provide the court with their personal opinion on matters relevant to the case and they are often allowed to draw inferences based on their observations (Ogloff & Cronshaw, 2001). These opinions and inferences must always fall within the limits of expert witnesses' areas of expertise, which they typically get through specialized training and experience, and the testimony must be deemed reliable and helpful to the court. In addition, it is important to point out that, when providing testimony to the courts, the expert witness is supposed to be there as an educator to the judge and jury, not as an advocate for the defence or the prosecution.

Expert witness: A witness who provides the court with information (often an opinion on a particular matter) that assists the court in understanding an issue of relevance to a case

The Challenges of Providing Expert Testimony

Providing expert testimony to the courts in an effective way is not a simple task. This probably explains why in the past few years numerous manuals have been published for the purpose of assisting expert witnesses with the task of preparing for court (e.g., Brodsky, 1991, 1999). Even judges have provided suggestions on how forensic psychologists can increase their chances of being effective witnesses in court (e.g., Saunders, J.W.S., 2001). In large part, these difficulties arise because of the inherent differences (often conflicts) that exist between the fields of psychology and law. Numerous individuals have discussed these differences, but we will focus on one particular attempt to describe them.

According to Hess (1987, 1999), psychology and law differ along at least seven different dimensions:

1. *Knowledge.* Knowledge gain in psychology is accomplished through cumulative research. In the law, knowledge comes through legal precedent, logical thinking, and case law.

2. *Methodology.* Methodological approaches in psychology are predominantly **nomothetic**. In other words, the goal is to uncover broad patterns and general trends through the use of controlled experiments and statistical methods. In contrast, the law is **idiographic** in that it operates on a case-by-case basis.

   Nomothetic: An attempt to understand something by uncovering broad patterns and general trends

3. *Epistemology.* Psychologists assume that it is possible to uncover hidden truths if the appropriate experiments are conducted. Truth in the law is defined subjectively and is based on who can provide the most convincing story of what really happened.

   Idiographic: An attempt to understand something by examining the specific details of individual cases

4. *Criteria.* In terms of a willingness to accept something as true, psychologists are cautious. To accept a hypothesis, results must be replicated, and conservative statistical criteria are used. The law decides on what is true based on a single case and criteria that are often more lenient.

5. *Nature of law.* The goal in psychology is to describe how people behave. Law, however, is prescriptive. It tells people how they should behave.

6. *Principles.* Good psychologists always consider alternative explanations for their findings. Good lawyers always convince the judge and jury that their explanation of the findings is the only correct explanation.

7. *Latitude.* The behaviour of the psychologist when acting as an expert witness is severely limited by the court. The law imposes fewer restrictions on the behaviour of lawyers (though they are also restricted in numerous ways).

Understanding these differences is important because they help us to appreciate why the courts are often so reluctant to admit testimony provided by psychological experts. For example, after considering how psychology and the law differ with respect to their methodological approach, it may not be surprising that judges often have difficulty seeing how psychologists can assist in court proceedings. Indeed, numerous legal scholars have questioned whether the general patterns and trends that result from a nomothetic psychological approach should ever be used in court. As Sheldon and Macleod (1991) state:

> The findings derived from empirical research are used by psychologists to formulate norms of human behaviour. From observations and experiments, psychologists may conclude that in circumstance X there is a likelihood that an individual . . . will behave in manner Y. . . . [N]ormative data of this sort are of little use to the courts. The courts are concerned to determine the past behaviour of accused *individuals*, and in carrying out that function, information about the past behaviour of *other individuals* is wholly irrelevant. (emphasis added, p. 815)

Currently, little attempt has been made to understand these differences between psychology and law, or their implications for the field of forensic psychology. Once we gain such an understanding, perhaps forensic psychologists will be in a better position to assist the courts with the decisions they are required to make. We believe that research conducted by forensic psychologists, particularly in their role as legal scholars, will greatly assist in this endeavour. This research will also increase our understanding of the criteria the courts use for determining the conditions under which they will accept expert testimony from psychologists.

Criteria for Accepting Expert Testimony

In order for a forensic psychologist to provide expert testimony in court, he or she must meet certain criteria. In the United States, criteria of one sort or another have been in place since the early twentieth century. In fact, until quite recently, the admissibility of expert testimony in the United States was based on a decision handed down by the courts in *Frye v. United States* (1923). Frye was being tried for murder and the court rejected his request to admit the results from a polygraph exam he had passed. On appeal, the court also rejected requests to allow the polygraph expert to present evidence on Frye's behalf (Bartol & Bartol, 1994). In the ruling, the court spoke specifically to the issue of when expert testimony should be admitted into court. The court indicated that, for novel scientific evidence to be admissible in court, it must be established that the procedure(s) used to arrive at the testimony is generally accepted in the scientific community. More specifically, the court stated, "while courts will go a long way in admitting expert testimony deduced from a well-recognized scientific principle or discovery, the thing from which the deduction is made must be sufficiently established to have gained general acceptance in the particular field in which it belongs" (*Frye v. United States*, 1923, p. 1).

General acceptance test:
A standard for accepting expert testimony, which states that expert testimony will be admissible in court if the basis of the testimony is generally accepted within the relevant scientific community

This criterion came to be called the "**general acceptance test**," and although it formed the basis of admissibility decisions in the United States for a long time, it is heavily criticized. The major criticism centres on the vagueness of terms such as "general acceptance" and "the particular field in which it belongs" and whether trial judges are able to make appropriate determinations of what these terms mean. As just one example of where problems might emerge, consider a defence lawyer who would like to have a criminal profiler provide testimony in court. How should the trial judge decide whether the profiler used generally accepted profiling techniques? If the courts turned to the profiling community (typically consisting of specially trained law enforcement personnel) to make this determination, the answer would most likely be far more favourable than if they had asked forensic psychologists who conduct research in the area of criminal profiling (e.g., Alison, Bennell, Mokros, & Ormerod, 2002). So, whom should the judge turn to and believe? In what "particular field" does criminal profiling belong?

This issue of vagueness was addressed more recently in the U.S. Supreme Court decision handed down in *Daubert v. Merrell Dow Pharmaceuticals, Inc.* (1993), when more specific admissibility criteria were set. Daubert sued Merrell Dow because he believed a morning sickness drug his mother ingested while pregnant, which was produced by the company, led to his birth defects. At trial, Merrell Dow presented experts who provided evidence that the use of the drug Bendectin does not result in birth defects. In turn, Daubert provided evidence from experts who claimed that Bendectin could lead to birth defects. The state court and the appeal court both rejected the testimony provided by Daubert's experts on the basis that the methods they used to arrive at their results were not generally accepted by the scientific community. On appeal before the U.S. Supreme Court, Daubert's lawyers challenged the state and appeal courts' interpretation of "general acceptance."

In addressing this issue, the U.S. Supreme Court stated that, for scientific evidence to be admitted into court, it must (1) be provided by a qualified expert, (2) be relevant, and (3) be reliable (meaning scientifically valid). To assist judges in making the decision as to whether evidence is in fact valid, the U.S. Supreme Court laid out four specific criteria, now commonly referred to as the **Daubert criteria**. These criteria suggest that scientific evidence is valid if:

1. The research has been peer reviewed.
2. The research is testable (i.e., falsifiable through experimentation).
3. The research has a recognized rate of error.
4. The research adheres to professional standards.

More recently, in the case of *Kumho Tire Company v. Carmichael* (1999), the U.S. Supreme Court ruled that the *Daubert* criteria apply to all expert testimony, not just scientific testimony.

Similar criteria are currently being used in Canada. The rules for admissibility in Canada were laid out in *R. v. Mohan* (1994). Mohan was a pediatrician charged with sexually assaulting several of his teenage female patients. At trial, Mohan wanted to provide expert testimony from a psychiatrist who was prepared to testify that the typical offender in such a case would be a pedophile and, in his opinion, Mohan was not a pedophile. The trial judge ruled that the testimony was inadmissible and, on appeal before the Supreme Court of Canada, the court agreed and established the standard for admitting expert testimony in Canada.

The standard is now referred to as the **Mohan criteria** and it includes four admissibility criteria, some of which are similar to the *Daubert* criteria:

1. The evidence must be relevant, in that it makes a fact at issue in the case more or less likely.
2. The evidence must be necessary for assisting the trier of fact (i.e., the testimony must be about something that goes beyond the common understanding of the court).
3. The evidence must not violate any rules of exclusion (e.g., the testimony must not relate to whether a witness is telling the truth).
4. The testimony must be provided by a qualified expert, which is typically determined through training, experience, and research.

Although these criteria probably make the judge's job of deciding when to admit expert testimony easier, they do not eliminate all possible problems. In large part, this is because the criteria are still highly subjective and rely heavily on the discretion of the judge. An example of one potential problem is illustrated by the case of *R. v. McIntosh and McCarthy* (1997), discussed in Box 1.5 on page 24, in which a judge decided that testimony relating to the accuracy of eyewitness testimony was common knowledge and, as

Daubert criteria: A standard for accepting expert testimony, which states that scientific evidence is valid if the research upon which it is based has been peer reviewed, is testable, has a recognized rate of error, and adheres to professional standards

Mohan criteria: A standard for accepting expert testimony, which states that expert testimony will be admissible in court if the testimony is relevant, necessary for assisting the trier of fact, does not violate any exclusionary rules, and is provided by a qualified expert

Box 1.5

The Case of *R. v. McIntosh and McCarthy* (1997): Potential Problems with the *Mohan* Criteria

R. v. McIntosh and McCarthy (1997) is an important court case for forensic psychologists who want to act as expert witnesses in the area of eyewitness testimony. The case deals with the crimes of Owen McIntosh and Paul McCarthy, who were charged with attempted murder, robbery, and firearms offences (Peters, 2001). The robbery and shooting took place at a dry cleaner. During the investigation, two eyewitnesses came forward. One witness was the Chinese owner of the dry cleaner; the other was a Caucasian bystander. Both McIntosh and McCarthy are black men. At trial, the defence lawyer wanted to submit testimony provided by an expert in the area of eyewitness memory. The expert was Dr. Dan Yarmey, a professor of psychology at the University of Guelph, and his proposed testimony was going to deal with "factors present at the time of the robbery that would impair the witnesses' ability to make an accurate identification, the problem with cross-racial identification, the quality of memory recall for perceived events of different time spans, the influence of 'post event information' on memory, [and] the validity of the photographic lineup" (Peters, 2001, p. 103).

Although a large amount of research addresses each of these various points, the trial judge and the Ontario Court of Appeal judge ruled that Dr. Yarmey's testimony was inadmissible according to the *Mohan* criteria. One of the main problems raised about the testimony (there were several others) was that it did not go beyond the common understanding of the jurors and would, therefore, not assist them in their deliberations (Yarmey, 2001). The Court of Appeal judge stated, "This opinion evidence is directed to instructing the jurors that all witnesses have problems in perception and recall with respect to what occurred during any given circumstance that is brief and stressful. Accordingly, Dr. Yarmey is not testifying to matters that are outside the normal experience of the trier of fact: he is reminding the jury of the normal experience" (*R. v. McIntosh and McCarthy*, 1997, para. 20). The problem with this decision is that it was most likely wrong. As argued by Yarmey and Jones (1983), although jurors may have opinions about eyewitness testimony, "they do not necessarily have sufficient knowledge to interpret and evaluate correctly the many variables that affect its reliability" (p. 14).

When psychologists have specifically examined the issue of whether lay opinions about eyewitness testimony match the general findings from the research literature, the degree of match is often quite low, at least for certain issues. More important for *R. v. McIntosh and McCarthy* (1997) is that many of the issues that seem to be beyond the common understanding of jurors were contentious issues in that particular case. For example, research has clearly demonstrated that potential jurors have misconceptions about the effect of viewing time on eyewitness accuracy, the fairness of police lineups, the accuracy of cross-racial identifications, and the impact of violence on identification accuracy (Yarmey & Jones, 1983). Clearly, these sorts of findings need to be considered by the courts when they are deciding whether to admit expert testimony and, to a large extent, forensic psychologists can assist with this task by making it clear that such research does in fact exist.

a result, inadmissible (Yarmey, 2001). Most of the research in the area of eyewitness accuracy indicates that the judge was most likely wrong in this case. This highlights the need not only to conduct high-quality research in the area of forensic psychology, but also to get that research into the hands of the legal community. As you will see as you read through this textbook, much of the high-quality research already exists, but on the whole, forensic psychologists have not done a great job at transferring this research to the legal community.

SUMMARY

1. Forensic psychology can be defined in a narrow or broad fashion. Narrow definitions focus only on the clinical *or* experimental aspects of the field, whereas broad definitions are less restrictive and encompass both aspects.

2. Forensic psychologists can play different roles. Clinical forensic psychologists are primarily interested in mental health issues as they pertain to law. Experimental forensic psychologists are interested in studying any aspect of human behaviour that relates to the law (e.g., eyewitness memory, jury decision making, risk assessment).

3. Psychology can relate to the field of law in three ways. Psychology and the law refers to the use of psychology to study the operation of the legal system. Psychology in the law refers to the use of psychology within the legal system as it operates. Psychology of the law refers to the use of psychology to study the legal system itself.

4. The mid-twentieth century saw a number of psychological theories of crime being proposed. Psychodynamic theories, such as Bowlby's theory of maternal deprivation, place a heavy emphasis on the internal dynamics of the offender and early childhood experiences. Learning theories, such as Bandura's social learning theory, place a heavy emphasis on how offenders learn to commit crime through a process of direct and indirect reinforcement. Personality theories, such as Eysenck's biosocial theory of crime, place a heavy emphasis on how offenders' personalities differ from those of law-abiding citizens.

5. Expert witnesses differ from regular witnesses in that expert witnesses can testify about their opinions, whereas other witnesses can only testify as to what they know to be fact. In Canada, the criteria for determining whether an expert's testimony will be admitted into court relate to whether the testimony (1) is relevant, (2) goes beyond the common understanding of the court, (3) does not violate any exclusionary rules, and (4) comes from a qualified expert.

Key Concepts

clinical forensic psychologists 3

Daubert criteria 23

experimental forensic psychologists 5

expert witness 20

extroversion 16

forensic psychiatry 4

forensic psychology 1

general acceptance test 22

idiographic 21

learning theories 14

Mohan criteria 23

neuroticism 16

nomothetic 21

personality theories 14

psychoanalytic theories 14

psychology and the law 6

psychology in the law 6

psychology of the law 6

social learning theory 16

theory of maternal deprivation 14

Discussion Questions

1. You are sitting on a panel of experts that has been charged with the task of redefining the field of forensic psychology. In your role as a panel member, you have to consider whether forensic psychology should be defined in a narrow or broad fashion. What are some of the advantages and disadvantages of adopting a narrow definition? What are some of the advantages and disadvantages of adopting a broad definition? Decide what type of definition you prefer and explain why.

2. The majority of forensic psychologists have no formal training in law. Do you think this is appropriate given the extent to which many of these psychologists are involved in the judicial system?

3. You have just been hired as a summer intern at a law office. One of your tasks is to assist in preparing for a high-profile murder case that has attracted a great deal of media attention. One of the lawyers has found out that you've taken this course and she wants to know whether the extensive pretrial press coverage the crime has received will make it difficult to find impartial jurors. Design a study to determine whether this is likely to be the case.

4. You have just read about Bandura's social learning theory and how it relates to crime. Although you think the theory is interesting, you can't help but notice that there are a lot of people who are exposed to antisocial role models, sometimes for extended periods of time, and yet not all these people go on to become criminals. What factors can you think of to explain this?

5. It took much longer for forensic psychology to become an established field of study in North America than in Europe. Why do you think this was the case?

6. Put yourself in the shoes of an expert witness. You are supposed to act as an educator to the judge and jury, not as an advocate for the defence or for the prosecution. To what extent do you think you could do this? Why or why not?

7. One criterion that must be met in Canada in order for expert evidence to be considered admissible is that it must go beyond the common understanding of the court. A friend of yours taking this class believes that research in the field of forensic psychology does not offer anything that goes beyond the common knowledge of judges and jurors. How would you convince him that he is wrong? Give specific examples.

Readings

Hess, A.K., & Weiner, I.B. (Eds.). (2006). *The handbook of forensic psychology* (3rd edition). New York: John Wiley & Sons.

Ogloff, J.R.P. (Ed.). (2002). *Taking psychology and law into the 21st century*. New York: Kluwer Academic.

Roesch, R., Hart, S.D., & Ogloff, J.R.P. (Eds.). (1999). *Psychology and law: The state of the discipline*. New York: Kluwer Academic.

Websites

APA Division 41: The American Psychology-Law Society
www.unl.edu/ap-ls

CPA: Criminal Justice Section
www.cpa.ca/sections/criminaljustice

Chapter 2
Police Psychology

Learning Objectives

- Outline the major steps in developing a valid police selection procedure.

- Describe the various instruments that are used to select police officers.

- Define what is meant by the term *police discretion*.

- List some key decisions in policing that require the use of discretion.

- Outline some of the major sources and consequences of stress in policing.

- Describe various strategies for dealing with police stress.

Officer James Leyton receives a call over his patrol car radio indicating that a domestic dispute has just been reported. According to the report, neighbours heard screaming and what sounded like a gunshot coming from a house. Officer Leyton and his partner arrive at the location and approach the front door of the residence, where they can hear arguing. They knock on the door, which is opened by a young girl. The girl is crying as she tells the officers that her mom and dad are in the kitchen fighting. As Officer Leyton approaches the kitchen, he sees a man and a woman. The man is obviously upset. Based on what Officer Leyton overhears, it appears as though the woman has caught the husband cheating on her and is threatening to divorce him and move away with their child. At this point, the man reaches for a gun on the kitchen counter and tells his wife he will kill her if she ever leaves. The husband points the gun at the wife, but before any shots are fired, Officer Leyton shoots the husband in the chest. Officer Leyton radios for an ambulance and the husband is taken to the hospital, where he dies from his injuries.

The scenario described above raises many questions about police officers and the nature of the work they do. For example, we might ask whether Officer Leyton is well suited to deal with this sort of situation (e.g., is he the type of person who can think clearly under pressure?). If he is not, why was he able to successfully graduate from the police academy? Alternatively, we might question whether Officer Leyton made an appropriate choice when he decided to shoot the husband. More specifically, was there anything else he could have done (e.g., use pepper spray on the husband) to de-escalate the situation before he had to use lethal force? Finally, we might be interested in how Officer Leyton will deal with the death of the husband. Will he be able to shrug off the incident and return to his duties or will he require support (e.g., in the form of psychological counselling)? This chapter will provide some of the answers to these questions by examining a number of issues in the area of police psychology, including police selection, police discretion, and police stress.

POLICE SELECTION

Consider the following excerpt from the City of Vancouver Police Department's recruitment web page:

> On any given day, our police officers respond to burglar alarms, console victims of traumatic events, and assist people in getting their lives back on track. They collect and log evidence at crime scenes, apprehend dangerous criminals, and testify in court. . . . Our police officers are skilled in investigation and interviewing techniques. . . . Our officers must have a sound knowledge of modern policing methods, and they must learn and memorize portions of the Criminal Code, the Motor Vehicle Act, other federal and provincial statutes, and our own departmental policies and procedures. . . . At crime scenes, officers must pay close attention to detail and make observations on suspects and the crime scene itself. . . . Often, they must visualize and recall an event after the fact so they can document it accurately, possibly for court purposes. . . . Reflecting the physical demand of policing, our officers know the importance of maintaining a high level of fitness. . . . In addition to knowing arrest and control tactics, our officers are trained to handle and care for a variety of firearms and to operate police vehicles in emergency situations. . . . Police officers must sometimes deal with people who are intoxicated, high on drugs, or mentally unstable. (City of Vancouver Police Department, 2007)

As this excerpt clearly indicates, police work is a complex, demanding, stressful, and potentially dangerous occupation. It requires intelligent, creative, patient, ethical, and hard-working individuals. The job may not be for everyone and, therefore, it is important for all those involved to ensure that the individuals who are accepted for the job have the highest potential for success. The purpose of police selection is to ensure this happens (Ash, Slora, & Britton, 1990). This requires the use of valid **police selection procedures** that allow police agencies to effectively screen out applicants who possess undesirable characteristics or select applicants who possess desirable characteristics (Fabricatore, 1979). These characteristics may relate to a variety of personal features, including (but not limited to) an applicant's physical fitness, cognitive abilities, personality, and performance on various job-related tasks.

Police selection procedures: A set of procedures used by the police to either screen out undesirable candidates or select in desirable candidates

A Brief History of Police Selection

The task of selecting appropriate police officers is not a new one for police agencies, nor is it a new phenomenon in the world of psychology. Indeed, psychologists have been involved in police selection since the early twentieth century. In what is considered one of the earliest examples, Lewis Terman, in 1917, used the Stanford-Binet intelligence test to assist with police selection in California (Terman, 1917). Terman tested the intelligence of 30 police and firefighter applicants, which led him to recommend a minimum IQ score of 80 for future applicants. Following this, attempts were made to use personality tests to predict police performance in the mid-twentieth century. For example, in the 1940s, police recruits in the Los Angeles Police Department (LAPD) were tested using the Humm-Wadsworth Temperament Scale, which was found to predict job success with a reasonably high level of accuracy (Humm & Humm, 1950). By the mid-1950s, psychological and psychiatric screening procedures of police applicants became a standard part of the selection procedure in several major police forces (Reiser, 1982).

In the 1960s and 1970s, major changes to police selection procedures took place in the United States, primarily as a result of two major events. In 1967, the U.S. president's Commission on Law Enforcement and Administration of Justice recommended that police forces adopt a higher educational requirement for police officers, obviously implying that intelligence is a core characteristic of successful officers. In 1973, the National Advisory Commission on Criminal Justice Standards and Goals in the United States recommended that police agencies establish formal selection processes, which would include the use of tests to measure the cognitive abilities and personality features of applicants (Ho, 1999). Since that time, police selection has indeed become more formalized, with police forces using a wide range of selection procedures, as indicated in Table 2.1 (Cochrane, Tett, & Vandecreek, 2003).

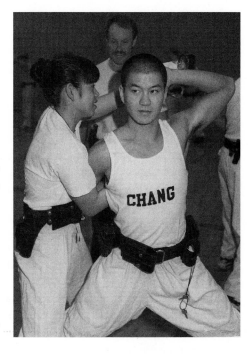

A police recruit undergoing physical training

Table 2.1 U.S. Police Agency Selection Procedures

Selection Procedure	Percentage of Police Agencies*
Background checks	99.4
Medical exams	98.7
Selection interviews	98.1
Personality tests	91.6
Drug testing	88.4
Physical agility tests	80.0
Polygraph tests	65.8
Recommendation letters	46.5
Cognitive ability tests	46.5

*These data represent responses from 155 U.S. police agencies that responded to a survey sent out by Cochrane et al., 2003.

Source: Adapted from Cochrane et al., 2003.

Although police selection research is not as common in Canada as it is in the United States, many of the same selection procedures are used in both countries. For example, all Canadian police agencies currently conduct background checks of their applicants and require medical exams (Forcese, 1999). In addition, most Canadian police agencies use a range of cognitive ability and personality tests in their selection process, such as the RCMP's Police Aptitude Test and the Six Factor Personality Questionnaire, which measures conscientiousness. In general, the same selection procedures are used by police agencies across Canada, although there are some slight differences across provincial and territorial boundaries. For example, while some police agencies, such as the Edmonton Police Service, use polygraph tests for selection purposes, other police forces (e.g., the Hamilton Police Service) do not.

The Police Selection Process

Regardless of whether a police agency decides to adopt a screening-out approach or a selecting-in approach, the general stages a force must go through to develop a valid selection process are the same (Gowan & Gatewood, 1995). In general terms, there are two separate stages to this process. Stage one is referred to as the job analysis stage. Here, the agency must define the knowledge, skills, and abilities (KSAs) of a "good" police officer. Stage two is referred to as the construction and validation stage. In this stage, the agency must develop an instrument for measuring the extent to which police applicants possess these KSAs. A crucial part of this stage also requires that the agency determine the instrument's validity, or the extent to which the scores on the instrument actually relate to measures of actual, on-the-job police performance.

Job analysis: A procedure for identifying the knowledge, skills, and abilities that make up a good police officer

Conducting a Job Analysis As indicated above, a **job analysis** involves a procedure to identify and define the KSAs that make a good police officer. An organizational psychologist, working in conjunction with a police agency, frequently conducts the job analysis. These psychologists can use a range of techniques for identifying relevant KSAs, including survey methods and observational techniques. At other times, a job analysis can be conducted more informally, simply by asking members of a police agency to list the range of qualities they feel is essential for their job. Each of these approaches has certain advantages and disadvantages. However, for the moment, we will focus on some common problems that emerge when conducting any sort of job analysis in the policing context.

One of the major problems that can be encountered is that the KSAs of a good police officer may not be stable over time, making it difficult to determine what the selection procedures should actually be testing for. For example, Pugh (1985a, 1985b) found that, at two years of service, police officers who were enthusiastic and fit in well were rated as the best officers, while at four years of service, officers who were stable and responsible were given the highest performance ratings. A potential explanation for this problem, and a problem in its own right, is the fact that different types of police officers, or different policing jobs, will be characterized by different KSAs. For example, Ainsworth (1993) draws attention to the fact that the KSAs that describe the ideal street-level police officer will not be the same KSAs that describe the ideal police administrator. Thus, as police officers move up through the ranks into supervisory or administrative positions, it should not be surprising to see relevant KSAs changing along the way.

Another problem with conducting a job analysis is that individuals may disagree over which KSAs are important. For example, if you were to ask a group of street-level police officers and a group of senior police administrators to define the characteristics of a good police officer, the answers could be quite different (though some similarities might also be expected). To illustrate this point, consider a survey in which Ainsworth (1993) asked street-level police officers to list the qualities they thought were essential for effective policing. Topping their list was a sense of humour. In contrast, this personal quality is rarely, if ever, found to be important when police administrators are asked to list the essential qualities for effective policing. When this is done, the most important KSAs typically relate to cognitive skills (Sanders, 2003).

Despite these problems, there does appear to be some agreement, even across police officers of varying ranks, on what type of person is "right for the job" (Sanders, 2003). For example, regardless of how the job analysis is conducted, the following KSAs are typically viewed as essential: honesty, reliability, sensitivity to others, good communication skills, high motivation, problem-solving skills, and being a team player.

Constructing and Validating Selection Instruments Recall that the goals in stage two of the police selection process are (1) to develop a selection instrument for measuring the extent to which police applicants possess relevant KSAs (construction) and (2) to ensure that this instrument relates to measures of police performance (validation). The measure of validation that we are most interested in is referred to as predictive validity, which is our ability to use a selection instrument to predict how applicants will perform in the future. Box 2.1 presents a more thorough discussion of predictive validity.

Box 2.1

Validation and Police Selection

There are many different types of validation measures, and each refers to something slightly different. The most common validation measure used in police selection focuses on predictive validity, in which the goal is to determine if there is a relationship between scores obtained from a selection instrument and measures of job performance (Gowan & Gatewood, 1995). In the policing context, predictive validity involves collecting data from police applicants using a selection instrument, such as scores on a test of decision making under stress. Then, the results on this test are compared with a measure of job performance, such as performance scores provided by supervisors. If the selection data accurately predict job performance, then the selection instrument is said to have predictive validity.

A selection instrument's predictive validity can be determined by calculating validity coefficients, which range from +1.00 to −1.00. These coefficients indicate the strength and direction of the relationship between the scores from a selection instrument and ratings of job performance. If a selection instrument is shown to have a validity coefficient near +1.00, then a very strong positive relationship exists, indicating that, as performance on the selection instrument increases, ratings of job performance also increase (see Figure 2.1 on page 32). Conversely, if a selection instrument is shown to have a validity coefficient near −1.00, a very strong negative relationship exists: as performance on the selection instrument increases, ratings of job performance decrease (see Figure 2.2 on page 32). Any value between these two extreme values represents an intermediate level of predictive validity.

(continued)

(*continued*)

Figure 2.1 A Positive Relationship between Scores on a Selection Instrument and Job Performance Ratings

Figure 2.2 A Negative Relationship between Scores on a Selection Instrument and Job Performance Ratings

Note that validity coefficients of + 1.00 and − 1.00 both represent high levels of predictive validity, even if the values are not what we would expect. For example, it seems unlikely that measures of decision-making performance under stress would relate negatively to the job performance of police officers, but if they did, we could still use those measures to predict job performance. We would simply predict that people who make poor decisions under stress make great police officers!

Researchers have identified a number of major problems with validation research in the area of police selection. Arguably, the most serious problem relates to how we measure the performance of police officers (Hargrave & Hiatt, 1987). This is a crucial issue to address, since it will have a direct impact on the validity of any selection instrument. Unfortunately, no answer currently exists. This is not to say that a variety of performance measures do not exist. Indeed, researchers have used several measures as indicators of job performance, including the number of times an officer is tardy, the number of complaints against an officer, the number of commendations received by an officer, graduation from training academy, academy exam scores, performance ratings by supervisors, performance ratings by peers, and so forth. The problem is that there is no evidence to suggest that one of these measures is any better than another, and even police agencies do not agree on how to define good performance (Falkenberg, Gaines, & Cordner, 1991). Furthermore, research suggests that a different picture of performance can emerge depending on what measure is used. For example, measures of performance during training often do not generalize to on-the-job performance (Kleinman & Gordon, 1986) and ratings by different individuals (e.g., peers versus supervisors) are often contradictory (Gardner, Scogin, Vipperman, & Varela, 1998).

The Validity of Police Selection Instruments

Now that we have discussed some of the problems with constructing and validating police selection instruments, we will describe some of the instruments that are currently in use and present some research on their validity. Although some of these instruments might be new to you, there are many others, such as the selection interview, that you will be familiar with. We will focus our attention here on three specific selection instruments, including the selection interview, psychological tests, and the assessment centre.

The Selection Interview The **selection interview** is one of the most common selection instruments used by the police. Typically, selection interviews take the form of a semi-structured interview. In a semi-structured interview, the interviewer has a preset list of questions that are asked of each applicant, thus ensuring a more objective basis for comparing applicants (Gowan & Gatewood, 1995). One of the main goals of the selection interview is to determine the extent to which the applicant possesses the KSAs that have been deemed important in a job analysis. These qualities may differ from agency to agency and, as indicated above, they may depend on the job being applied for. The criteria evaluated by the RCMP's Regular Member Selection Interview include a continuous learning orientation, interpersonal skills, service orientation, personal effectiveness and flexibility, thinking skills, leadership, and oral communication (RCMP, 2007).

Surprisingly, given its frequent use as a selection instrument, the results from research that has examined the validity of the interview for police selection are somewhat mixed. Although some research does indicate that selection interviews can be used in a relatively accurate fashion to predict job performance (e.g., Hargrave & Hiatt, 1987), other research suggests that basing police selection decisions on interviews can be potentially problematic (e.g., Doerner, 1997). These findings accord well with the general research literature from the field of organizational psychology, where mixed results regarding the predictive validity of the selection interview are also reported (McDaniel, Whetzel, Schmidt, & Maurer, 1994).

Despite the fact that some research suggests that interviews might provide information that is predictive of job performance, many police researchers remain cautious about their use. To understand why, one need only look at the degree to which different interviewers disagree on their ratings of various attributes when interviewing the same applicant. For example, Doerner (1997) examined the level of inter-rater reliability between interviewers who were interviewing the same applicant (where a score of +1.00 indicates total agreement between interviewers and a score of −1.00 indicates

Selection interview: In recruiting police officers, an interview used by the police to determine the extent to which an applicant possesses the knowledge, skills, and abilities deemed important for the job

Table 2.2 Measures of Inter-Rater Reliability

Attribute of Interviewee	Interviewers					
	1 and 2	**1 and 3**	**1 and 4**	**1 and 5**	**1 and 6**	**1 and 7**
Appearance	0.55*	0.14	0.58*	−0.25	0.50*	0.18
Self-confidence	0.06	0.30	0.43*	0.55	0.45*	0.63
Self-expression	0.27	0.42	0.27	0.26	0.15	0.69*
Understanding	0.85*	0.03	0.67*	0.46	0.35*	0.47
Comprehension	0.47	0.56	0.24	0.14	0.42*	0.59
Background	0.38	0.72*	0.38*	−0.28	0.26	0.70*
Overall impression	0.45	0.38	0.37*	0.00	0.30	0.52
N (number of interviews)	15	10	22	10	28	10

*Denotes a significant finding.

Source: Adapted from Doerner, 1997.

total disagreement). As illustrated in Table 2.2, Doerner found that the majority of inter-rater reliability measures were relatively low. This was the case across a number of different interviewer pairs, who were assessing a range of personal attributes. Indeed, of the 42 comparisons Doerner made, only 14 were found to be statistically significant, and most of these came from only one pair of interviewers. Given such findings, the validity of the interview technique as a method for selecting police officers must be called into question, and it should continue to be used with caution.

Psychological Tests In addition to the selection interview, psychological tests are also commonly used by police agencies to select suitable officers (Cochrane et al., 2003). Some of these tests have been developed to measure cognitive abilities, whereas others have been designed to assess an applicant's personality. In addition, some of these tests have been developed with police selection in mind, whereas others have been developed in other contexts, such as the mental health field. As with other selection instruments, there are still many unanswered questions when it comes to the use of psychological tests. However, there seems to be general agreement among police researchers that psychological tests are useful in deciding whether a person possesses certain attributes, and it is believed that this knowledge can be helpful in selecting applicants to become police officers.

Cognitive ability tests:
Procedure for measuring verbal, mathematical, memory, and reasoning abilities

Cognitive Ability Tests A wide variety of **cognitive ability tests** are available for police use. Although each test may emphasize something slightly different, they are typically used to measure verbal, mathematical, memory, and reasoning abilities. Such tests are used regularly when selecting police officers in Canada. Indeed, if you were to apply to the RCMP today, part of the selection procedure would require you to take the RCMP Police Aptitude Test (RPAT). The RPAT consists of 114 multiple-choice questions designed to evaluate an applicant's potential aptitude for police work. More specifically, the test measures seven core skills that are considered essential in performing the duties of a police officer: written composition, comprehension, memory, judgment, observation, logic, and computation.

In general, the reliance on cognitive ability tests for police selection purposes is supported by empirical research. However, these tests tend to be better at predicting performance during police academy training compared with future on-the-job performance (Gowan & Gatewood, 1995). For example, Hirsh, Northrop, and Schmidt (1986) conducted a meta-analysis of 40 validation studies involving cognitive ability tests. They found average validity coefficients of 0.36 and 0.13 for predicting training success and on-the-job performance, respectively. One reason why Hirsh and his colleagues suggest they did not get higher scores for on-the-job performance is that personality variables may also play a role in determining job success, above and beyond one's cognitive abilities. Thus, it is worthwhile describing some of the personality tests used for police selection and the degree of validity associated with each.

Personality Tests There are a number of different personality tests used for police selection, but only two of the most commonly used tests will be discussed here. Perhaps the most common test is an assessment instrument known as the **Minnesota Multiphasic Personality Inventory** (MMPI), now in its second version. According to Cochrane et al. (2003), of the 155 U.S. police agencies that responded to their survey, 71.9% of them indicated that the MMPI-2 was the personality test they used most often for selection purposes. Interestingly, the MMPI, originally designed in the 1940s, was not developed for selecting police officers. Neither was the MMPI-2. Rather, this assessment instrument was developed as a general inventory for identifying people with psychopathological problems. Currently, the MMPI-2 consists of 567 true-false questions that attempt to identify psychopathological problems including depression, paranoia, schizophrenia, and others.

The validity of the original MMPI for selection purposes in the policing context has been reviewed extensively. However, there is still little in the way of research on the MMPI-2, with a few notable exceptions (e.g., Weiss, Davis, Rostow, & Kinsman, 2003). The research that does exist suggests that the MMPI and the MMPI-2 are associated with significant, but moderate, levels of predictive accuracy (Sanders, 2003). For example, studies have reported positive validity coefficients between MMPI and MMPI-2 scores and several job performance indicators, including performance at the police academy, supervisor ratings of job performance, and the number of disciplinary actions taken against an officer. In part, the moderate levels of predictive validity associated with the MMPI tests may be due to the fact that they were never developed as selection instruments. If this is true, it may be that personality tests developed for police selection purposes will be associated with higher levels of predictive validity. In fact, this does appear to be the case, as indicated by studies examining the **Inwald Personality Inventory** (IPI).

Unlike the MMPI tests, the IPI was developed specifically for the law enforcement community. According to Inwald (1992), the creator of the IPI, the purpose of this selection instrument is to identify police applicants who are most suitable for police work by measuring their personality attributes and behaviour patterns. The instrument consists of 310 true-false questions that measure factors such as stress reactions, interpersonal difficulties, and alcohol and other drug use. According to several researchers, the IPI appears to be more predictive of police officer performance than the MMPI. For example, in one study, Scogin, Schumacher, Gardner, and Chaplin (1995) compared the MMPI, the IPI, and the Shipley Institute of Living Scale (SILS), a brief intellectual screening device, on their ability to predict seven different job performance indicators—supervisor ratings,

Minnesota Multiphasic Personality Inventory: An assessment instrument for identifying people with psychopathological problems

Inwald Personality Inventory: An assessment instrument used to identify police applicants who are suitable for police work by measuring their personality attributes and behaviour patterns verbal reprimands, written reprimands, vehicular reprimands, citizen complaints, an overall composite of negative indicators, and an overall composite of positive recognitions.

The participants in the study were 82 trainees at the University of Alabama Law Enforcement Academy. Each participant completed the three selection instruments during the first week of academy training. One year following their graduation from the academy, each participant's police agency was contacted to obtain job performance indicators. The results found that the IPI was a slightly better predictor of on-the-job performance in the one-year follow-up period than both the MMPI and SILS. More specifically, the MMPI and the SILS could accurately predict only one of the seven performance indicators (supervisor ratings). The IPI, on the other hand, was able to predict three of the seven indicators (supervisor ratings, citizen complaints, and the overall composite of negative indicators). In addition, combining the MMPI and IPI scores did not appreciably improve predictive power over that observed with the IPI alone. As the authors of this study indicate, the one-year follow-up used in this study might not have been long enough for sufficient positive and negative on-the-job behaviour to occur. However, the results of this study do provide some preliminary evidence that the IPI performs slightly better than the MMPI under certain conditions.

Assessment Centres The last selection procedure we will discuss is the **assessment centre**, a procedure that is growing in popularity in Europe and North America (Lowry, 1996). An assessment centre is a facility at which the behaviour of police applicants can be observed in a number of different ways by multiple observers (Pynes & Bernardin, 1992). The primary selection instrument used within an assessment centre is the **situational test**, which involves simulations of real-world policing tasks. Trained observers evaluate how applicants perform during these tasks, and the performance appraisals are used for the purpose of selection.

The situational tests used in assessment centres attempt to tap into the KSAs identified as part of a job analysis. For example, the assessment centre evaluated by Pynes and Bernardin (1992) was based on a job analysis that identified eight core skill sets deemed crucial for effective policing: directing others, interpersonal skills, perception, decision making, decisiveness, adaptability, oral communication, and written communication. Based on these skill sets, four assessment exercises were developed, which allowed the applicants to be evaluated across the range of relevant KSAs (see Box 2.2). For example, as is probably clear from the description in Box 2.2, the domestic disturbance exercise requires excellent interpersonal skills in order to excel.

Although there is not a great deal of research examining the validity of assessment centres for police selection, some research does suggest that situational tests have moderate levels of predictive validity. For example, Pynes and Bernardin (1992) examined the scores given to each applicant across the four simulation exercises. These scores were then compared with training academy performance and future on-the-job performance. Training academy performance included scores on written exams as well as on simulation tasks. On-the-job performance was based on rating scales provided by supervisors for judgment, dependability, work initiative, quality of work, appearance, cooperation, knowledge of work, and public contacts. Overall assessment centre performance correlation coefficients were 0.14 and 0.20 for training academy performance and future on-the-job performance, respectively. Each of these validity coefficients was statistically significant.

Assessment centre: A facility in which the behaviour of police applicants can be observed in a number of situations by multiple observers

Situational test: A simulation of a real-world policing task

Situational Tests Used in Assessment Centres

■ *Work simulation exercise.* For the first five minutes of this 60-minute exercise, applicants view videotaped instructions that explain the content of the videos and the procedures they are to follow. The exercise comprises ten video units. Each unit consists of a one-minute animation depicting illegal activity in progress that a police officer might come across while on routine patrol. After each unit is shown, the applicants are given three minutes to answer multiple-choice and true-false questions. Each questionnaire is designed to evaluate the applicant's ability to identify possible law violations, as well as his or her ability to recommend appropriate courses of action consistent with policy.

■ *Domestic disturbance exercise.* Each applicant is given 15 minutes of this 35-minute exercise to meet with two people involved in a domestic dispute. The applicant is expected to intervene in the dispute as a police officer and resolve it. At the end of the 15 minutes,

the applicant is given 20 minutes to complete an incident report.

■ *Homeowner complaint.* Each applicant is given 15 minutes of this 35-minute exercise to speak to a homeowner who reported an incident of vandalism. At the 10-minute mark, the assessment centre administrator hands the applicant a dispatch bulletin directing the applicant to respond to a high-priority call. The applicant is required to terminate the interaction with the homeowner as quickly as possible to respond to the next call. Responding to this call constitutes the end of the homeowner exercise. The applicant is given 20 minutes to complete an incident report.

■ *Witness probing exercise.* Each applicant has 20 minutes to interview two people who witnessed an armed robbery in a liquor store. The applicant is then given 20 more minutes to complete an incident report.

Source: Pynes & Bernardin, 1992.

POLICE DISCRETION

As indicated by job analyses, many of the qualities deemed necessary for success as a police officer have to do with the applicant being adaptable, having common sense, possessing effective decision-making skills, and being a good problem solver (Sanders, 2003). In large part, these qualities are necessary because police officers are required to use discretion in much of their daily work (Walma & West, 2002). **Police discretion** can be defined in numerous ways, but McKenna (2002) has perhaps stated it best:

> Police discretion is the term that represents the critical faculty that individual officers must possess that will allow them to differentiate and discriminate between those circumstances that require absolute adherence to the letter of the law and those occasions when a degree of latitude is justified, based on the officer's knowledge, experience, or instinct. (p. 118)

Police discretion: A policing task that involves discriminating between circumstances that require absolute adherence to the law and circumstances where a degree of latitude is justified

To appreciate the extent to which the police use discretion, consider the following decisions that need to be made routinely by police officers:

■ What street should I patrol tonight?

■ Should I stop that vehicle for a traffic violation?

■ What level of force is required to achieve my objective?

■ Should I run after that suspect or wait for backup?

- Should I call an end to this investigation?
- Should I take this person to a psychiatric hospital or the police station?

The list of scenarios requiring some degree of police discretion is endless and, therefore, police discretion is a topic of major concern to researchers. More specifically, researchers are interested in whether police discretion is really necessary, the sorts of situations in which discretion is used, the factors that influence police decision making in these situations, and ways of controlling the inappropriate use of police discretion. Each of these issues will be examined in this section.

Why Is Police Discretion Necessary?

Although some individuals and interest groups believe that police officers should always enforce the law, police officers clearly do not (and perhaps cannot) do this all the time. Indeed, police officers have great latitude in how they apply the law (McKenna, 2002). But is this discretion necessary? What good are laws if they are only applied under certain conditions? The typical answers that researchers offer for such questions are based on the fact that it is impossible to establish laws that adequately encompass all the possible situations an officer can encounter and, therefore, a degree of discretion is inevitable. For example, Walma and West (2002) argue that,

> No manual or rule book can take into consideration every possible situation a police officer may face in doing his or her daily duties. No supervisor can follow a police officer around to monitor every decision he or she makes. As a result, police officers are entrusted with the discretion to apply their training and fulfill their duties in the manner they think is best. (p. 165)

In addition to this explanation, there are many other arguments for why police discretion is a necessary part of modern-day policing. For example, Sheehan and Cordner (1989) have provided the following important reasons for police discretion:

- A police officer who attempts to enforce all the laws all the time would be in the police station and in court all the time and, thus, of little use when serious problems arise in the community.
- Legislatures pass some laws that they clearly do not intend to have strictly enforced all the time.
- Legislatures pass some laws that are vague, making it necessary for the police to interpret them and decide when to apply them.
- Most law violations are minor in nature, such as driving slightly over the posted speed limit, and do not require full enforcement of the law.
- Full enforcement of all the laws all the time would alienate the public and undermine support for the police.
- Full enforcement of all the laws all the time would overwhelm the criminal justice system, including the prisons.
- The police have many duties to perform with limited resources. Good judgment must, therefore, be used in establishing enforcement priorities.

However, it should be stressed that by accepting police discretion as an inevitable part of policing, we as a society must be prepared to deal with the consequences. Although the arguments put forward by researchers like Sheehan and Cordner (1989) highlight some obvious advantages of police discretion, there are also potential disadvantages. For police discretion to be advantageous, officers must exercise discretion in a nondiscriminatory manner (Walma & West, 2002), and unfortunately this does not always happen (see Chapter 3 for a discussion of racial profiling). Despite the fact that all members of Canadian society have their rights protected under the Charter of Rights and Freedoms, the police do, on occasion, use their discretion inappropriately.

Areas Where Police Discretion Is Used

Having now established that there are a variety of rationales for police discretion, it is important that we consider some of the situations in which it is used. As indicated above, there are relatively few decisions that a police officer has to make that do not require at least some degree of discretion. However, there are several domains that are worthy of a more in-depth discussion, including encounters with youths, offenders with mental illnesses, domestic violence, and use-of-force situations.

Youth Crime According to Siegal and Senna (1994), as the "initial gatekeepers" to the juvenile justice system, police officers have a great deal of discretion when dealing with young offenders. Common police responses to youth crime include formal arrests, police cautions, community referrals, and family conferences. Indeed, one study suggests that approximately 30% to 40% of youth crime is handled informally by police officers or through referrals to community services (Office of Juvenile Studies and Delinquency Prevention, 1992).

In Canada, police officers are actively encouraged to use discretion when dealing with youth crime (Department of Justice Canada, 2007a). This encouragement appears to be the result of a growing belief that formal sentences are probably not the most effective response for dealing with many young offenders. Indeed, one common view is that custodial sentences make matters worse by putting young offenders into a situation in which they are forced to interact and associate with other, often more serious, offenders. Instead, community-based intervention strategies that involve family members, teachers, social workers, and the police are thought to be more useful (Department of Justice Canada, 2007a). In addition, to instill values of responsibility and accountability in young offenders, greater attention is now being paid to restorative justice options, in which the youth is made to repay the victim.

A movement toward informal processing of youths is evident in some recent programs established in Canada. For example, the Sparwood Youth Assistance Program (SYAP), which began in 1995, provides young offenders in Sparwood, B.C., an opportunity to be dealt with outside the formal court system. This intervention program is based in the community and involves the young person's family and the community as a whole. An integral part of the program is the **resolution conference**, in which the offender and his or her family are brought together with the victim and the police in an attempt to come up with a plan to (1) compensate the victim, (2) penalize the youth, (3) provide support to the youth's family, and (4) establish a monitoring scheme to ensure the youth complies with the program (SYAP, 2007). For our purposes here, one of the most important aspects of the program is that it relies almost entirely on the discretion of the police.

Resolution conference: Involves an offender and his or her family coming together with the victim and the police in an attempt to solve a problem

Not only is it up to the police to decide whether the program is suitable for the offender, it is also up to them to determine whether the program is working. If, in their view, the program is not having the intended effect, they can use their discretion to pursue a more serious course of action.

Offenders with Mental Illnesses As is the case with young offenders, police officers frequently come into contact with offenders with mental illnesses. According to Teplin (2000), several factors have increased the likelihood of these encounters. Primary among these factors is the recent movement toward de-institutionalizing individuals who have a mental illness. In an attempt to ensure these encounters are dealt with effectively, formal policies are often put in place that specify how police officers should deal with offenders who have mental illnesses. These policies typically instruct police officers to apprehend the individual whenever he or she poses a danger to self or others or is causing some other kind of serious disturbance (Teplin, 2000). However, although these policies provide the police with the legal power to intervene, police officers must still rely on their discretion to choose the most appropriate action.

When police officers encounter an individual with a mental illness who is creating a disturbance, there are three options available to them: (1) they can transport that person to a psychiatric institution of some kind, (2) they can arrest the person and take him or her to jail, or (3) they can resolve the matter informally (Teplin, 2000). Although this decision may not seem difficult, in practice it is. In fact, when faced with such an encounter, police officers have to consider numerous issues. For example, as Teplin (2000, p. 9) states, "emergency hospitalization often is fraught with bureaucratic obstacles and the legal difficulties of obtaining commitment for treatment . . . many psychiatric programs will not accept everyone, particularly those considered dangerous, those who also have substance abuse disorders, or those with numerous previous hospitalizations." As a result, police officers may be forced to take actions that are not in the best interest of the offender, such as taking the individual to jail.

Unfortunately, research indicates that this is often what happens. For example, Bittner (1967) found that, when police officers encounter offenders with mental illnesses, psychiatric referrals are made only in the absence of other alternatives. More recently, Teplin (1986) reported a similar finding. In her study, police officers typically resolved encounters with offenders who had a mental illness in an informal fashion (72% of cases), with arrests and emergency hospitalization occurring much less frequently (16% and 12% of cases, respectively).

The limited options that are often available to the police when they are dealing with mentally ill offenders can mean that these offenders become criminalized (Teplin, 1984). In other words, individuals who would have typically been treated within the mental health system are now dealt with by the criminal justice system. This criminalization process appears to be at work in a study reported by Teplin (2000), which involved 506 police–offender encounters, 147 of which resulted in an arrest. As you can see in Table 2.3, the probability of being arrested if you are an offender in Teplin's study is much greater for suspects exhibiting signs of mental illness compared with other individuals. More specifically, 14 of the 30 suspects with a mental illness (47%) in this study were arrested, compared with only 133 of the 476 other suspects (28%). These figures raise many difficult questions. For example, do these figures reflect the discriminatory use of discretion on the part of the police or do they reflect the fact that mentally ill offenders

Table 2.3 Mental Illness and the Likelihood of Being Arrested

		Presence of a Mental Illness		
		No	**Yes**	**Total**
	No	343 (72%)	16 (53%)	359 (71%)
Arrest	**Yes**	133 (28%)	14 (47%)	147 (29%)
	Total	476 (94%)	30 (6%)	506 (100%)

Source: Adapted from Teplin, 2000.

commit more serious crimes? Alternatively, could it be that these figures simply reflect the fact that the hands of the police are often tied, with arrests being one of the few options available to ensure that individuals with mental illnesses remain free from harm? To know what these figures actually mean, more systematic research clearly needs to be conducted.

✹Domestic Violence Another area in which police officers have a great deal of discretion is in their response to domestic disputes. Historically, domestic violence by a husband against his wife was often ignored by the police. However, in the 1960s and 1970s people became more aware of victim needs in domestic violence situations, and numerous individuals and interest groups began pushing for a more aggressive policy of arrest (Melton, 1999).

According to Melton (1999), this push was helped along by a number of factors. First, several lawsuits were successfully brought against U.S. police departments that had failed to arrest offenders of domestic violence. Second, domestic violence research began being conducted, with some of this research suggesting that arrests had a deterrent effect on offenders of domestic violence. Eventually, pro-arrest policies were put in place in many police agencies, both in Canada and in the United States, and new government legislation was enacted. An example of such legislation in Canada is B.C.'s Violence Against Women in Relationships Policy (British Columbia Ministry of Attorney General, 2004), which attempts to ensure a strong criminal justice response to domestic violence.

However, even with new policies and legislation in place, there are still a range of responses available to police officers when faced with domestic disputes. As a result, the police must still use their discretion to decide on the best course of action. For example, Melton (1999) indicates that arrest rates range from 12% to 40% of all cases of domestic violence seen by the police, with other responses being used in the remainder of cases. These other options regularly include mediation (e.g., talking to the victim), community referrals (e.g., recommending the couple seek professional help), and separation (e.g., asking one of the participants to leave). Indeed, some studies indicate that separation is used as an intervention strategy as often as arrests are used, if not more often. In addition, Melton (1999) argues that, in many domestic violence cases, the police still decide to do nothing at all.

Use-of-Force Situations Perhaps the topic that has received the most attention when it comes to police discretion is the use of force, particularly lethal force, by the police. Highly publicized cases of police use of force, such as the 1991 Rodney King incident in the United States, have done much to fuel this debate. Police officers are granted the right to use force—in fact, they are required to use force—to protect the general public and themselves (Walma & West, 2002). However, police officers can only use force that is necessary to suppress a situation, and only to the extent that is necessary to accomplish this goal. When a police officer uses force for any other purpose, or in excess of what is needed, that officer has made inappropriate use of his or her discretionary power. When this happens, the result can be deadly. It can also be very costly for the police, who may have to deal with potential lawsuits.

In Canada, the authority to use force is laid out in our Criminal Code (Walma & West, 2002). For example, Section 25 of the Criminal Code states that "Everyone who is required by law to do anything in the administration of enforcement of the law . . . is, if he acts on reasonable grounds, justified in doing what he is required or authorized to do and in using as much force as is necessary for that purpose." However, problems arise in use-of-force situations due to the ambiguity of terms such as "reasonable grounds" and "as is necessary." Indeed, there are many examples in which people disagree on these terms, which is what often leads to lawsuits. When this happens, we must turn to our judicial system to resolve the problem. In many cases, the court will decide that the force used by the police was inappropriate (as in the case described in Box 2.3). This could be because the use of force was viewed as unnecessary, in excess of what was needed, or based on factors that should not have been taken into account, such as the race of the suspect. In other cases, the courts find police use of force appropriate and justifiable.

Fortunately, police use of force is a relatively rare phenomenon. As MacDonald, Manz, Alpert, and Dunham (2003) state, "Whether measured by use-of-force reports, citizen complaints, victim surveys, or observational methods, the data consistently indicate that only a small percentage of police–public interactions involve use of force" (p. 120). Recently, for example, the Police Public Contact Survey developed by the U.S. Bureau of Justice Statistics found that only 1.5% of people who come into contact with the police either experience force first-hand or are threatened by the use of force (U.S. Bureau of Justice Statistics, 2005). Furthermore, when the police do decide to use force, it is often the minimal amount of force necessary (Adams, 1999), and it is typically in response to a resistant suspect (Alpert & Dunham, 1999).

Factors That Influence Police Discretion

Much research in the area of police discretion has focused on identifying factors that influence police decision making, particularly the decision to make arrests. A number of factors have now been identified as having a reasonably consistent impact. For example, according to Walker and Katz (2001), a police officer is more likely to make an arrest in the following situations:

■ The crime is more serious, such as an indictable offence rather than a summary offence.

■ The evidence is strong, as when eyewitnesses are available.

■ The victim asks for an arrest to be made.

■ The victim and offender are strangers to each other.

■ The suspect is resistant or disrespectful to the officer.

The Case of *Ernst v. Quinonez et al.* (2003)

In *Ernst v. Quinonez et al.* (2003) the court examined the methods used by the defendants to arrest the plaintiff, Edward Ernst. The plaintiff and his friend, Jason Steves, drove up to Niagara Falls, Ontario, from their home in Buffalo, New York. After leaving a nightclub, the pair decided to drive Steves's vehicle up and down a street that was known to be a popular tourist area. While stopped at a red light, Steves proceeded to squeal his tires. A nearby police officer observed the incident, approached the vehicle, and asked Steves for his licence and registration. Steves retrieved some papers from his vehicle but could not locate the requested documentation. Noticing that the appropriate documentation was in Steves's hand, the police officer reached into the vehicle to take it. At this time, Steves put his car into gear and began to drive away with the police officer still halfway in his car. The officer yelled for Steves to stop the vehicle, as did the plaintiff. The plaintiff also attempted to reach the brake pedal of the car but was unable to do so. Eventually, the vehicle stopped and the police officer pulled Steves out of his car.

At this time, an unidentified uniformed officer approached the plaintiff, ordered him out of the vehicle, handcuffed him, and informed him he was under arrest. While the plaintiff was handcuffed, the unidentified officer knelt on the plaintiff's shoulder and neck to prevent him from moving. At this point, several other officers arrived at the scene. One of these officers pulled the plaintiff from the ground and wrapped his arm around the plaintiff's neck to drag him to the hood of the vehicle. While the plaintiff was being dragged, another of the defendants punched Ernst in the stomach numerous times. According to videotape of the incident captured by an onlooker, the plaintiff did not show any sign of resisting the police officers.

Among the plaintiff's allegations was that the defendants assaulted him. All of the defendants were required to describe and justify the actions they took in dealing with the situation. Throughout the hearing, the defendants explained it was their belief they acted reasonably in response to the situation. For example, in responding to why he put his arm around the plaintiff's neck, the defendant who was responsible claimed that, when he lifted the plaintiff off the ground, the plaintiff stiffened his back and was thus being uncooperative. In order to get control of Ernst, the defendant testified that he "grabbed Ernst by the front of the shirt . . . he had to reach over Ernst's shoulder in order to do this as [he] was standing slightly behind Ernst" (*Ernst v. Quinonez et al.*, 2003, para. 26). Likewise, another defendant claimed the plaintiff attempted to kick and spit at him and, as a result, he "punched Ernst with a closed fist in the upper chest area once" (para. 31).

Largely by analyzing the videotape of the incident, the judge found that the amount of force used by the defendants on the plaintiff was far more than was necessary. The defendants were convicted for assault and false arrest and imprisonment. The plaintiff was awarded a total of $38 300 in damages.

Other factors, such as the race of the victim and offender, and the neighbourhood environment in which the offence took place, are also known to have an impact on arrest decisions (Fyfe, 1981; Smith, Visher, & Davidson, 1984).

Controlling Police Discretion

In an attempt to ensure that police officers exercise their discretion appropriately, a number of organizations have established guidelines that allow police discretion to be controlled. As indicated by Walma and West (2002), the Charter of Rights and Freedoms can, in a sense, be seen as a guideline to control police discretion because it makes clear that all people should be treated fairly and equally. In addition, specific codes of conduct for police officers have been developed that also help control the use of discretion (Walma & West, 2002). For example, in Canada, one section of the Police Services Act states that police officers commit misconduct if they fail to treat or protect a person without discrimination. Another method for controlling police discretion is the enactment of government legislation to deal with a particular problem. As indicated previously, B.C.'s Violence Against Women in Relationships Policy is an example of such legislation.

In this section, we will deal specifically with methods for controlling inappropriate police discretion in use-of-force situations. One reason for focusing on such situations is the public's widespread interest in this area. The other reason is that numerous attempts have been made, in Canada particularly, to develop innovative approaches for controlling the abuse of force by the police. One approach is the development of administrative policies within police agencies that are specifically meant to control the use of force by police officers. A related approach is the development of models (the most common being the **use-of-force continuum**) to help guide a police officer's decision-making process in use-of-force situations.

Use-of-force continuum: A model that is supposed to guide police officer decision making in use-of-force situations by providing the officer with some guidance as to what level of force is appropriate given the suspect's behaviour and other environmental conditions

Departmental Policies

Departmental policies for restricting use of force by police officers are not new. Research on the effectiveness of these policies is also not new. For example, Fyfe (1979) examined the impact of use-of-force policies put in place by the New York Police Department (NYPD) in 1972. These policies were meant to decrease the use of lethal force by NYPD officers and Fyfe's study indicated just that. Not only did the frequency of police shooting decrease in New York from 1971 to 1975, but the numbers of officers injured and killed during the same period also decreased. Similar findings have been reported in several other U.S. cities, indicating that departmental policies can effectively restrict the use of inappropriate force (e.g., Geller & Scott, 1992). However, White (2001) draws attention to the fact that restrictive use-of-force policies do not always have the desired impact, and that other factors can minimize their effect. For instance, he has argued that the philosophies of senior police officers can often outweigh departmental polices. As White put it, if the police leadership has a "bust their heads" philosophy, departmental policies will likely not have their intended effect (p. 135).

The Use-of-Force Continuum

Although use-of-force continuums may not directly restrict the use of force by police officers in the same way that departmental policies do, they may indirectly control force by ensuring that officers carefully assess and evaluate potential use-of-force situations when deciding what course of action to take. In the words of Walma and West (2002, p. 67),

> The theory behind the continuum is that, in order to subdue a suspect, the officer must be prepared to use a level of force that is one step higher than that used by the suspect in resisting the officer. There is no need for the officer to move up the continuum of force step by step since it is certainly unlikely that the suspect will do so. Once the suspect displays his or her level of resistance, the officer must react with subduing force. If, however, the officer moves to a level of force that is disproportionate to the force offered by the suspect, the officer is open to the accusation of using excessive force.

Thus, use-of-force continuums control police officer actions in the sense that they encourage them to use only what force is necessary to deal adequately with a situation.

In Canada, a lot of time and energy has been put into developing a national use-of-force model. Recently, the Canadian Association of Chiefs of Police (CACP) has approved such a model, which is described more fully in Box 2.4 (CACP, 2007). It is

Box 2.4

The National Use-of-Force Model in Canada

In order to provide guidelines to police officers with regard to what level of force is reasonable under various circumstances, Canadian police agencies have developed a National Use-of-Force Model (see Figure 2.3). The model represents the process by which a police officer assesses, plans, and responds to use-of-force situations (CACP, 2007, p. 11):

The assessment process begins in the centre of the graphic [in Figure 2.3] with the situation confronting the officer. From there, the assessment process moves outward and addresses the subject's behaviour and the officer's perception and tactical considerations. Based on the officer's assessment of the conditions represented by these inner circles, the officer selects from the use of force options contained within the model's outer circle. After the officer chooses a response option, the officer must continue to assess, plan and act to determine if his or her actions are appropriate and/or effective or if a new strategy should be selected. The whole process should be seen as dynamic and constantly evolving until the situation is brought under control.

Figure 2.3 The National Use-of-Force Model

(continued)

(continued)

Even with this model, the decisions a police officer has to make when deciding whether to use force are not easy. For example, according to the CACP (2007), a police officer will have to consider, among many other factors, whether the incident is occurring in a public place, whether there is enough light to assess the situation properly, whether the location poses a risk to him or her or the subject, whether the subject is alone, whether the subject is intoxicated, and so on. This must occur at the same time the officer is considering the subject's behaviour and the officer's own ability to deal with the situation. Based on this assessment, the police officer must then develop a plan that involves selecting what he or she feels to be an appropriate response. As indicated in the outermost ring of the diagram, there are five basic options. Officer presence is the least forceful option, followed by verbal and nonverbal communication, physical control, intermediate weapons, and, finally, use of lethal force. As the CACP (2007) notes, there is an approximate correspondence between the graphic's depiction of a subject's behaviour and the options available to the officer. For example, if a suspect is exhibiting potentially lethal behaviour, it may be necessary for the police officer to use lethal force.

hoped that this model will have its intended effect of assisting Canadian police officers with their decision making in use-of-force situations and in educating others on the subject.

POLICE STRESS

Many police psychologists, as well as police officers and their families, consider policing to be one of the most stressful occupations (Anshel, 2000). After our discussion of some of the dangerous situations police officers encounter, you will likely come to a similar conclusion yourself. Even if policing is not considered one of the most stressful occupations, we can all probably agree that police officers are exposed to many stressful events. Not only has research demonstrated that this is the case, but it has also indicated that these stressful events can have a negative impact on police officers and their families, as well as the organizations they work for (Brown & Campbell, 1994). In this section, we will discuss some of the sources of police stress and examine the potential consequences. In addition, we will focus on what can be done to prevent and manage police stress.

Sources of Police Stress

As Finn and Tomz (1996) make clear, "different officers are likely to perceive different events as stressful, depending on their individual background, personalities, expectations, law enforcement experience, years on the job, type of law enforcement work they perform, and access to coping resources" (p. 6). However, research suggests that there are a number of common sources of police stress (Abdollahi, 2002). Although the labelling of these categories may differ depending on what article or book you read, the major sources of police stress tend to include organizational stressors, occupational stressors, criminal justice stressors, and public stressors. Finn and Tomz (1996) have provided a reasonably comprehensive list of specific stressors that fall into each of these categories, a partial listing of which is presented in Table 2.4.

Table 2.4 Sources of Police Stress

1. **Organizational Stressors**
   - *Lack of career development*. In most police agencies, there is little room for advancement, regardless of the performance of the officer.
   - *Excessive paperwork*. The need for duplicate forms of every police transaction is often questioned.

2. **Occupational Stressors**
   - *Irregular work schedule*. Shift work is disruptive to the personal lives of most police officers.
   - *Human suffering*. Officers are constantly exposed to the inequities and brutalities of life.

3. **Criminal Justice Stressors**
   - *Ineffectiveness of the corrections system*. Officers are alarmed by the recidivism rate of criminals who seem to be perpetually "on the street" rather than incarcerated.
   - *Unfavourable court decisions*. Many court decisions are viewed by officers as unfairly increasing the difficulty of police work.

4. **Public Stressors**
   - *Distorted press accounts*. Reports of incidents are often inaccurate and perceived as derogatory by officers, whether or not the inaccuracy is intentional.
   - *Ineffectiveness of referral agencies*. The ineffectiveness of social service agencies frustrates officers who view these agencies as their only source of assistance.

Source: Adapted from Finn & Tomz, 1996.

Although the majority of people assume that **occupational stressors** are the most stressful for police officers, officers indicate that they experience a degree of stress for each of the stressors described in Table 2.4. In fact, many police researchers believe they have evidence to show that **organizational stressors** more strongly affect officers than occupational stressors (Finn & Tomz, 1996). Such claims are backed up by anecdotal evidence. For example, according to the wife of an officer who ended up resigning due to stress, "My husband came home more screwed up with department problems than with anything he ever encountered on the streets" (Finn & Tomz, 1996, p. 7).

Surveys of police officers also indicate that, while occupational stressors are clearly some of the most stressful events that an officer will ever experience, organizational stressors can also be stressful, as can stressors related to responses from the criminal justice system and the general public. For example, Taylor and Bennell (2006) recently asked 154 full-time officers employed by a police agency in Ontario to fill out the Operational Police Stress Questionnaire and the Organizational Police Stress Questionnaire, both of which were developed by McCreary and Thompson (2006). More specifically, police officers were asked to rank each of the 40 stressors included on these surveys from 1 to 7, with a score of 1 indicating that the event caused them no stress at all in the previous six months and a score of 7 indicating that the event caused them a lot of stress in the previous six months. For illustrative purposes, the ten highest-ranked stressors across the two surveys are provided in Table 2.5 on page 48. As you can see from the results, many of the highest-ranked events

Occupational stressors: In policing, stressors relating to the job itself

Organizational stressors: In policing, stressors relating to organizational issues

Although occupational stressors, such as police shootings, can cause a great deal of stress for many police officers, organizational stressors, such as perceptions of inadequate departmental support, can also result in harmful levels of stress.

are actually organizational stressors (e.g., the feeling that different rules apply to different people), although a number of occupational stressors (e.g., fatigue) also rank very high.

In addition to the categories of stressors presented in Table 2.4, a number of researchers have proposed that there are certain personality features that police officers can possess that may contribute to their experience of stress. For example, in Abdollahi's (2002) review of police stress research, she indicates that there is now enough evidence to suggest that low levels of self-confidence and low levels of optimism are associated with increased stress levels among police officers. Furthermore, she suggests that high levels of cynicism, authoritarianism, and type-A personality features are also associated with increased stress.

Table 2.5 The Ten Highest-Ranked Police Stressors

The feeling that different rules apply to different people (4.78)*

Fatigue (4.47)

Feeling like you always have to prove yourself to the organization (4.41)

Inconsistent leadership style (4.36)

Dealing with the court system (4.17)

Bureaucratic red tape (4.14)

Not enough time available to spend with friends and family (4.09)

Shift work (4.04)

Finding time to stay in good physical condition (3.98)

Perceived pressure to volunteer free time (3.91)

*Numbers in brackets are means out of 7.

Source: Adapted from Taylor & Bennell, 2006.

Consequences of Police Stress

When a police officer experiences a potentially life-threatening situation, the acute stress reactions that the officer experiences can have serious repercussions that last long after the actual event. (See Table 2.6 for examples of stress reactions that police officers typically experience during shooting encounters.) Likewise, constant exposure to other police stressors, particularly organizational stressors, can affect police officers on a more chronic basis (McCraty, Tomasino, Atkinson, & Sundram, 1999). Without an effective prevention or management strategy (at both the individual and the organizational level) to deal with police stressors, police officers, their families, and the organizations they work for will suffer in numerous ways. The general consequences of police stress have been categorized by Brown and Campbell (1994) into physical health problems, psychological and personal problems, and job performance problems. See Table 2.7 on page 50 for a summary of possible consequences of police stress that fall into each of these categories.

Physical Health Problems One of the major consequences of police stress is the impact it can have on an officer's physical health. As McCraty et al. (1999) explain, constant exposure to acutely stressful events can result in the chronic activation of the body's stress response systems to a point where physiological breakdown occurs. The result of such a breakdown can take many different forms. For example, research by Franke, Collins, and Hinz (1998) has suggested that police officers are more than twice as likely as people in other occupations to develop cardiovascular disease. In addition, Kroes, Margolis, and Hurrell (1974) reported that more than 32% of the police officers they examined experienced digestive disorders, which is significantly higher than the prevalence rate in the civilian population. Finally, in a large-scale study of 2376 police officers, Violanti, Vena, and Marshall (1986) found that rates of death due to cancer were significantly higher

Table 2.6 Typical Reactions Experienced by Police Officers during Shooting Encounters

Sounds diminished (84%)

Tunnel vision (79%)

Responded on auto-pilot with little or no conscious thought (74%)

Heightened visual clarity (71%)

Viewed the incident in slow motion (62%)

Memory loss for parts of the event (52%)

Memory loss for their own behaviour (46%)

Dissociation (e.g., sense of detachment from the situation) (39%)

Intrusive, distracting thoughts (26%)

Memory distortions (e.g., saw something that did not actually happen) (21%)

Temporary paralysis (7%)

*Numbers in brackets are the percentage of officers (out of 157 participants) who experienced the reaction.
Source: Adapted from Artwhohl, 2002.

Table 2.7 Possible Consequences of Police Stress

Physical Health Problems	Psychological and Personal Problems	Job Performance Problems
High blood pressure	Depression and anxiety	Low morale
Cardiovascular disease	Aggression	Tardiness
High cholesterol	Post-traumatic stress disorder	Absenteeism
Stomach ulcers	Drug and alcohol abuse	Early retirement
Respiratory problems	Suicide	Reduced productivity
Skin problems	Domestic violence	Reduced efficiency
Weight gain	Separation and divorce	Citizen complaints
Diabetes	Extramarital affairs	Turnover
Death	Burnout	Hostile interactions

Source: Adapted from Brown & Campbell, 1994.

among police officers than among the general population. However, the limited amount of research in the area makes it difficult to determine how many of these health problems are due to the stressful events police officers are exposed to and how many of them are due to the lifestyle habits adopted by police officers (Abdollahi, 2002).

Psychological and Personal Problems Psychological and personal problems, including depression, post-traumatic stress disorder, drug and alcohol abuse, marital problems, and suicide, can also emerge when police officers are exposed to stressful situations. However, it should be noted that, as in the case of physical health problems, the research in this area can often be contradictory and, therefore, caution must be used when interpreting the results of any single study. For example, although numerous studies have suggested that alcohol use may be particularly problematic among police officers (e.g., Violanti, Marshall, & Howe, 1985), Alexander, Innes, Irving, Sinclair, and Walker (1991) found that alcohol consumption by police officers was not statistically greater than consumption rates found for firefighters, prison officers, or nurses. Similarly, although some researchers have found indications of burnout among police officers (e.g., Anson & Bloom, 1988), other researchers have failed to find significant levels of burnout. Of particular interest is the work of Dr. Robert Loo, who has failed to find indications of serious police burnout among Canadian police managers (Loo, 1994). See Box 2.5 for a profile of Dr. Loo.

Job Performance Problems Job performance problems are the third major category of stress consequences. Often as a direct result of the physical and psychological problems discussed above, the way a police officer performs on the job can suffer greatly. As with other stress reactions, impaired job performance can take many forms, including a decrease in work efficiency and productivity, increased absenteeism and tardiness, and early retirement. Although these consequences may not seem as serious as the physical and psychological problems caused by police stress, from an organizational perspective they certainly are significant. For example, consider the problem of absenteeism due to illness. According to one newspaper article from the late 1980s, it was estimated that each

Canadian Researcher Profile: Dr. Robert Loo

For many years, Dr. Robert (Bob) Loo was a professor of human resource management and organizational studies at the University of Lethbridge in Alberta. Before joining the University of Lethbridge in 1989, Dr. Loo had an active managerial career dating back to the 1960s. For example, Dr. Loo has acted as program evaluation manager in the Public Service Commission of Canada, he was the manager of the Officer Selection Research Program in the Canadian Forces, and he was a project manager and research scientist in the Systems Division at Bell-Northern Research. Of particular interest here is the fact that Dr. Loo served as the first manager of Psychological Services in the RCMP from 1982 to 1987. Dr. Loo's roles in this position were many and varied. For example, he was responsible for staffing the

psychology positions being used to deliver psychological services to RCMP officers, for evaluating these psychological services, and for coordinating psychological services within special duty areas, such as the undercover drug program.

Although many of Dr. Loo's research interests over the years focused more generally on management issues (e.g., health-care management), he still actively conducted research on various topics related to police psychology. His research in this area included post-shooting police stress, police suicide, the use of drugs by the police, women in policing, and psychological aspects of police selection. One of Dr. Loo's most recent studies is an impressive meta-analysis of police suicide rates (Loo, 2003). By summarizing suicide data from many different countries over an extended period of time, he was able to show a variety of interesting patterns in the data that had remained largely hidden until his study. For example, in contrast to popular thinking, the results from his meta-analysis indicate that suicide rates for police in North America are not significantly different from the suicide rates found in comparable male populations around the globe.

During the years preceding Dr. Loo's retirement, *Maclean's* magazine consistently identified him as one of the most popular professors at the University of Lethbridge. Retirement is providing Dr. Loo with time to pursue his other interests, such as hiking and snowshoeing in the Rockies. His retirement is also allowing him to be more active in human rights through his involvement with Amnesty International and Anti-Slavery International.

year in England and Wales the police service lost approximately 1.6 million working days through sickness, some of which can undoubtedly be attributed to stress (*The Guardian*, October 28, 1988). Similar statistics are unavailable in Canada, but if they come even close to this figure, job performance problems due to stress certainly require attention.

Preventing and Managing Police Stress

Most police officers and police agencies have now recognized the need to prevent and manage negative reactions to stressful events. Indeed, over the last 20 years, formal stress programs have been set up in most agencies to combat the effects of police stress. A variety of strategies are included in these programs, including informal support networks, physical fitness programs, professional counselling services, family assistance programs, and special assessments following exposure to critical events such as shootings or accidents (Brown & Campbell, 1994). A thorough discussion of each of these strategies is beyond the scope of this chapter, but such a discussion can be found in Brown and Campbell (1994). Here, we will simply focus on one particular strategy—training police officers to use effective coping strategies.

The Impact of Effective Coping Strategies Police stress is not only a result of being exposed to stressful events. It is also a result of the poor coping skills that some police officers use when faced with these events (Anshel, 2000). Many coping strategies are maladaptive and can lead to further, more serious problems for the police officer. For example, in a study of Canadian police officers, Burke (1993) found that officers who coped with stress by using alcohol, other drugs, anger, or withdrawal were more likely to suffer from health problems and further stress than were officers who used more adaptive coping strategies. Thus, one potential method for preventing and managing stress at the level of the individual police officer is to teach officers how to use adaptive coping strategies. As Anshel (2000) points out, this may be a particularly useful approach because "although police officers often cannot control the sources of job-related stress, their effective use of coping strategies following unpleasant events is controllable" (p. 377). Furthermore, this intervention has been shown to have a significant and positive impact, not only on the health and general well-being of police officers, but also on how they deal with stressful events in the future (McCraty et al., 1999).

To appreciate the kind of impact that such an intervention program can have, we will focus on a study by McCraty et al. (1999). This study was designed to examine the potential impact of teaching police officers **adaptive coping skills**. To carry out their study, the researchers recruited 65 participants from seven police agencies in California, and these participants were randomly split into two groups—an experimental (i.e., trained) group and a control (i.e., untrained) group. The entire study took place over a 16-week period. The experimental group received training between week 5 and week 16 on how to use adaptive coping skills, while the control group received no such training. Various measures of stress were collected at the start of the study, at a five-week, pre-training point during two simulated scenarios (a building search scenario and a high-speed pursuit scenario), and at a 16-week, post-training point during another simulated scenario (a domestic dispute scenario). Measures of performance were also collected for every participant during each of the scenarios (with the expectation that performance scores would be higher for the experimental group in the 16-week, post-training domestic dispute scenario).

The training provided to the experimental group between week 5 and week 16 was part of the HeartMath stress management program (McCraty et al., 1999). This program includes numerous techniques for recognizing and reducing stress. Some of the training teaches police officers how to use general stress-relieving techniques. For example, they are taught how to communicate with others more effectively, because ineffective communication is a primary cause of stress. Other techniques are more specific, such as Freeze-Frame®, which is a technique in which officers are taught to "consciously disengage from negative mental and emotional reactions as they occur by shifting their attention to the area of the heart, then self-generating a positive or neutral feeling" (p. 6).

The results from this study indicate that teaching police officers how to use adaptive coping skills improves their performance on job-related tasks. For example, with regard to

Adaptive coping skills: Skills that allow people to deal more effectively with stressful events

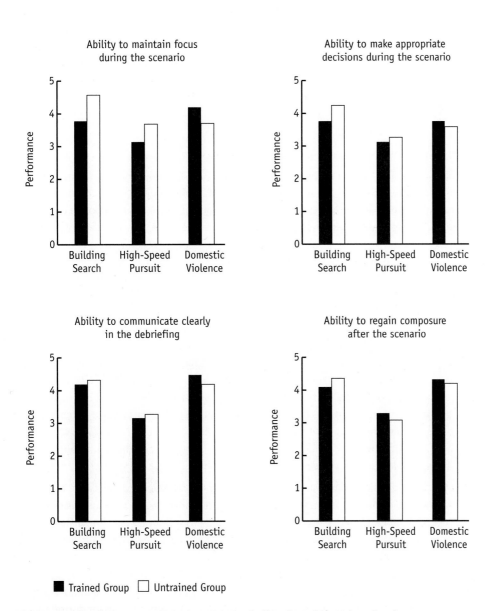

Figure 2.4 Performance Improvements Following Adaptive Coping Skills Training*

*Training took place for participants in the experimental group between the building search/high-speed pursuit scenario (during week 5) and the domestic violence scenario (during week 16).

Source: Adapted from McCraty et al., 1999; © 1999 Institute of Heart Math.

post-training performance during the week 16 domestic violence scenario, Figure 2.4 indicates that participants in the trained group scored higher than the untrained group on all performance measures (McCraty et al., 1999). The results also indicate that the use of adaptive coping skills has a more general impact on the well-being of officers. For example, participants in the trained group exhibited considerable reduction over time across a range of stress symptoms, including anger, distress, depression, sadness, and fatigue, while showing significant improvements in peacefulness and vitality. Likewise, the trained group reported fewer problems over time with sleeplessness, anxiety, and indigestion. Findings such as these strongly support the use of training programs like this one for reducing general stress reactions in police officers and for increasing their ability to perform well under pressure.

SUMMARY

1. The development of a useful police selection process requires two major steps: (1) an analysis of the knowledge, skills, and abilities that are required for the job and (2) the construction and validation of selection instruments that measure these qualities and compare them with job performance.

2. Some of the most common police selection procedures are semi-structured interviews, psychological tests, and the use of assessment centres.

3. Police discretion refers to the power that police officers have to decide which laws apply to a given situation and whether or not to apply them. Many view police discretion as an inevitable part of police work and, so long as it is used in an unbiased manner, police discretion can be very useful.

4. Nearly every decision that a police officer has to make requires some degree of discretion. However, four of the most commonly studied areas of police discretion deal with youth crime, offenders with mental illnesses, domestic violence, and use-of-force situations. A major effort has been made in Canada to develop policies to guide police decision making in each of these areas. One example is the National Use-of-Force Model, which provides guidelines to police officers with regard to what level of force is reasonable under various circumstances.

5. Policing is considered by many to be one of the most stressful occupations. Sources of stress include organizational stressors, occupational stressors, criminal justice stressors, and public stressors. These stressors can lead to serious physical health problems, psychological and personal problems, and job performance problems if they are not dealt with appropriately.

6. In order to combat the negative effects of stress, police forces are developing and using a variety of prevention and management strategies. One strategy that looks particularly promising involves teaching police officers how to use adaptive coping skills when faced with stressful events.

Key Concepts

adaptive coping skills 52

assessment centre 36

cognitive ability tests 34

Inwald Personality Inventory 35

job analysis 30

Minnesota Multiphasic Personality Inventory 35

occupational stressors 47

organizational stressors 47

police discretion 37

police selection procedures 28

resolution conference 39

selection interview 33

situational test 36

use-of-force continuum 44

Discussion Questions

1. You are a member of a community group that has been put together to provide your local police agency with recommendations regarding police selection criteria. What do you, as a community citizen, feel are the most important characteristics of a good police officer? Do you think these characteristics should be considered when police forces select police officers? Why or why not?

2. Given the problems with interviews for selecting good employees, do you think they should be used for police officer selection? Why or why not?

3. Members of police forces have rated sense of humour an important characteristic of an effective police officer. As a researcher in the area of police psychology, what problems might you encounter when developing a situational test to determine whether police applicants have a good sense of humour?

4. Imagine you are a police officer who encounters a well-dressed woman walking down the street who is obviously intoxicated. What would you do? Would you arrest her and take her to jail, or would you drive her home? What factors would you consider when making your decision? Would your decision have been different if you encountered an older man who was dressed in dirty and ripped clothes? Why or why not?

5. You are a police officer who has just received a call over your radio about a domestic violence situation. You arrive at the scene to find a woman and a man arguing. The woman has a bloody nose and it is clear the man is the person who hit her. The woman pleads with you not to arrest the man, stating that it was her fault she got hit. What would you do and why?

6. Your friend has been a police officer for five years. He constantly talks to you about the stress he feels, but rarely does he raise any issues about occupational stressors. Instead, he seems most upset with his organization. Why do you think organizational stressors make such a big impact on police officers?

7. What sorts of things could you do as a police psychologist to help the police officer in question 6 deal with his stress? What do you think his police force could do, as an organization, to prevent and manage his stress?

Readings

Blau, T.H. (1994). *Psychological services for law enforcement.* New York: John Wiley & Sons.

Brown, J.M., & Campbell, E.A. (1994). *Stress and policing: Sources and strategies.* New York: John Wiley & Sons.

Walma, M.W., & West, L. (2002). *Police powers and procedures.* Toronto: Emond Montgomery Publications Limited.

Websites

RCMP Recruitment Web Page
www.rcmp-grc.gc.ca/recruiting/index_e.htm

Police Stress Site
www.police-stress.com/index.htm

Chapter 3
The Psychology of Police Investigations

Learning Objectives

- Describe the Reid model of interrogation and summarize the rationale for its use.

- Outline three potential problems with the Reid model of interrogation.

- Differentiate among false, retracted, and disputed confessions.

- Define the three major types of false confessions.

- Explain why the police use criminal profiling and outline three potential problems with its use.

- Describe two other types of profiling that are used by the police.

Mark Jackson was arrested for shooting a man inside a convenience store. Upon his arrest, he was taken to the police station for questioning. Over the course of a 24-hour period, Mark was interrogated on five separate occasions. The last interrogation took place at 2:00 A.M. Although Mark stated he was exhausted, he was told the interrogation would not take long and that it was best to get things over with. In reality, the interrogation lasted for more than three hours.

Initially, Mark maintained that, although he was at the store on the day of the shooting, he had nothing to do with the crime. However, throughout his interrogations the police challenged him, stating they had hard evidence proving he was the killer. This evidence not only included a security video but several eyewitnesses. None of this evidence actually existed. In addition, the police minimized the seriousness of the crime, stating that the victim was a known drug dealer who "had it coming" and that Mark "did everyone a favour."

Over the course of his interrogations, the police continually pressured Mark to stop denying his involvement in the crime and said that if he told the truth "all of this would end." Finally, during his last interrogation, Mark admitted to the shooting. The case went to court and Mark was convicted, largely on the basis of his confession. Months later, it was discovered that he had not committed the crime. Mark Jackson had confessed to a crime he had nothing to do with.

As seen in Chapter 2, forensic psychology plays an important role in many aspects of police work. One element we have yet to discuss, however, is psychology's role in criminal investigations, such as the Mark Jackson investigation described above. Many people are aware that psychology is used in criminal investigations, and recent movies and television shows have done much to promote this fact. However, as you will see throughout this chapter, psychology played an important role in the investigative process long before Hollywood became interested in the topic, and it continues to do so today.

Psychologists have identified a number of key investigative tasks where psychology is particularly relevant. One of these tasks relates to the collection and evaluation of investigative information—information that is often obtained from suspects. Another relates to investigative decision making, especially decisions that require an in-depth understanding of criminal behaviour. This chapter will focus on how psychology contributes to these tasks by looking first at how the police interrogate suspects, and some possible consequences of their interrogation practices, and then by examining the practice of profiling the characteristics of criminals based on the way they commit their crimes.

POLICE INTERROGATIONS

Confession evidence is often viewed as "a prosecutor's most potent weapon" (Kassin, 1997, p. 221). In some countries, people may be convicted solely on the basis of their confession, although in Canada and the United States, a confession usually has to be backed up by some other form of evidence (Gudjonsson, 2003). Regardless of whether corroborative evidence is required, it is a well-established fact that people who confess to a crime are more likely to be prosecuted and convicted than those who do not. Indeed, some legal scholars have gone so far as to claim that a confession makes other aspects of a trial unnecessary, because "the real trial, for all practical purposes, occurs when the confession is obtained" (McCormick, 1972, p. 316). Given the importance of confession evidence, it should come as no surprise that, although one of the goals of a **police interrogation** is to gain information that furthers the investigation, such as the location of important evidence, the other goal is to obtain a confession from the suspect (Kassin, 1997).

Being interrogated by the police for the purpose of extracting a confession is often considered to be inherently coercive. Imagine yourself being interrogated for the very first time. You would probably be in an environment that is foreign to you, faced with one, possibly two, police officers whom you have never met. You would know little of what the police officers are going to do to you and would have no one to turn to for support. Even if you were innocent of the crime in question, the situation would no doubt be an extremely intimidating one. In large part, this is due to the fact that the police interrogators are part of a system that gives them certain powers over you, the suspect (Gudjonsson, 2003).

There is no question that police interrogations were coercive in the past. Consider police tactics in the mid-twentieth century, for example, when whipping was occasionally used to obtain confessions (e.g., *Brown v. Mississippi*, 1936). Or consider a more recent episode occurring in the 1980s, where New York City police officers jolted a suspect with a stun gun in order to extract a confession (Huff, Rattner, & Sagarin, 1996). Although these overt acts of physical coercion have become much less frequent with time, they have been replaced with more subtle, psychologically based interrogation techniques (Leo, 1992), such as lying about evidence, promising lenient treatment, and implying threats to loved ones. Although not all interrogators use these

Police interrogation: A process whereby the police interview a suspect for the purpose of gathering evidence and obtaining a confession strategies, police officers often view these techniques as a necessary evil in order to obtain confessions from guilty persons. Indeed, leading authorities in the field of interrogation training openly state that, because offenders are typically reluctant to confess, they must often be tricked into doing so (Inbau, Reid, Buckley, & Jayne, 2001).

The extent to which some police officers use trickery and deceit in their interrogations has been made clear by Wakefield and Underwager (1998, p. 428):

> Police freely admit deceiving suspects and lying to induce confessions. Police have fabricated evidence, made false claims about witnesses to a crime, and falsely told suspects whatever they thought would succeed in obtaining a confession. They have lied about the suspect's culpability, assuring him that his behaviour was understandable and not really blameworthy, or telling him that if he described what happened, the victim could be helped. They have falsely told suspects that they had physical evidence such as footprints, fingerprints, or semen, that a co-defendant had confessed, that the weapon used in the crime had been found, that the suspect failed a lie detector, and that there was medical proof of sexual molestation.

Police officers around the world often receive specialized training in exactly how to extract confessions from suspects. Depending on where this training is provided, different approaches are taught. For example, as discussed later in this chapter, police officers in

A police officer interrogating a suspect

England are trained to use interrogation techniques that are far less coercive than those used in North America (Kassin & Gudjonsson, 2004; Sear & Williamson, 1999). This is primarily because courts in England have begun to recognize some of the potential problems associated with coercive interrogation practices, such as increasing the likelihood of false confessions (Meissner & Russano, 2003).

Before moving on to discuss these potential problems and exploring some possible ways they can be prevented, let us look closely at the format of police interrogations as they typically take place across North America.

The Reid Model of Interrogation

The most common interrogation training program offered to U.S. and Canadian police officers is based on a book written by Inbau et al. (2001) called *Criminal Interrogation and Confessions*. Within this manual, the authors describe the now-famous **Reid model** of interrogation, a technique originally developed by John E. Reid, a polygrapher from Chicago (Meissner & Russano, 2003).

Reid model: A nine-step model of interrogation used frequently in North America to extract confessions from suspects

At a general level, the Reid model consists of a three-part process. The first stage is to gather evidence related to the crime and to interview witnesses and victims. The second stage is to conduct a nonaccusatorial interview of the suspect to assess any evidence of deception (i.e., to determine whether the suspect is lying when they say they are innocent). The third stage is to conduct an accusatorial interrogation of the suspect (if he or she is perceived to be guilty) in which a nine-step procedure is implemented, with the primary objective being to secure a confession (Inbau et al., 2001).

This nine-step procedure in stage three consists of the following steps:

1. The suspect is immediately confronted with his or her guilt. If the police do not have any evidence against the suspect at this time, this fact can be hidden and, if necessary, the interrogator can pretend that such evidence exists.

2. Psychological themes are then developed that allow the suspect to justify, rationalize, or excuse the crime. For example, a suspected rapist may be told that the victim must have been asking for it.

3. Any statements of denial by the suspect are interrupted by the interrogator to ensure the suspect does not get the upper hand in the interrogation.

4. The interrogator overcomes the suspect's objections to the charges to a point at which the suspect becomes quiet and withdrawn.

5. Once the suspect has become withdrawn, the interrogator ensures that the suspect does not tune out of the interrogation by reducing the psychological distance between the interrogator and the suspect, such as by physically moving closer to the suspect.

6. Sympathy and understanding are then exhibited by the interrogator and the suspect is urged to come clean. For example, the interrogator might try to appeal to the suspect's sense of decency.

7. The suspect is offered face-saving explanations for the crime, which makes self-incrimination easier to achieve.

8. Once the suspect accepts responsibility for the crime (typically by agreeing with one of the face-saving explanations), the interrogator develops this admission into a full confession.

9. Finally, the interrogator gets the suspect to write and sign a full confession.

The Reid model of interrogation is based on the idea that suspects do not confess to crimes they have committed because they fear the potential consequences that await them if they do (Inbau et al., 2001). In addition, their fear of the potential consequences is not sufficiently outweighed by their internal feelings of anxiety associated with remaining deceptive (i.e., by maintaining they did not commit the crime in question). The goal of the Reid model, therefore, is to reverse this state of affairs, by making the consequences of confessing more desirable than the anxiety related to the deception (Gudjonsson, 2003). It is assumed that the consequences of confessing and the anxiety of remaining deceptive can be manipulated by the interrogator through the use of psychologically based techniques, such as the minimization and maximization techniques described below (Jayne, 1986). For example, many believe that providing the suspect with a way to rationalize his or her behaviour can reduce the perceived consequences of confessing. Conversely, focusing on feelings of guilt can increase the anxiety associated with deception.

Techniques used in the Reid model of interrogation can be broken down into two general categories. These categories are often referred to by different names, including friendly and unfriendly techniques, Mutt and Jeff techniques, and minimization and maximization techniques. You will probably know them as good cop–bad cop techniques. Throughout this chapter, the labels *minimization* and *maximization* will be used to refer to the categories, since these terms are the most commonly accepted.

Minimization techniques refer to "soft sell" tactics used by police interrogators that are designed to "lull the suspect into a false sense of security" (Kassin, 1997, p. 223). These tactics include the use of sympathy, excuses, and justifications. For example, when the interrogator in the opening scenario suggested to Mark Jackson that the victim "had it coming" because he was a drug dealer, and that Mark "did everyone a favour" by shooting the victim, that interrogator was using minimization techniques. In contrast to minimization techniques, **maximization techniques** refer to "scare tactics" that interrogators often use "to intimidate a suspect believed to be guilty" (Kassin, 1997, p. 223). This intimidation is typically achieved by exaggerating the seriousness of the offence and by making false claims about evidence the police supposedly have. The use of the nonexistent eyewitnesses in the opening scenario is an example of such a scare tactic.

Potential Problems with the Reid Model of Interrogation

Because the Reid model of interrogation is used so extensively in North America, it has been the subject of much research. This research indicates that a number of potential problems are associated with the technique. Three problems in particular deserve our attention. The first two relate to the ability of investigators to detect deception (Memon, Vrij, & Bull, 2003) and to biases that may result when an interrogator believes, perhaps incorrectly, that a suspect is guilty (Kassin, Goldstein, & Savitsky, 2003). The third problem has to do with the coercive nature of certain interrogation practices and the possibility that these practices will result in false confessions (Ofshe & Leo, 1997). We will discuss the first two problems here and reserve our discussion of false confessions for the next section of this chapter.

Detecting Deception   A more thorough discussion of **deception detection** will be provided in Chapter 4, so our discussion here will be limited to how deception detection relates to police interrogations. The issue of whether investigators are effective deception detectors is an important one, especially when using the Reid model of interrogation, because the actual interrogation of a suspect begins only after an initial interview has allowed the interrogator to determine whether the suspect is guilty (Inbau et al., 2001). The decision to commence a full-blown police interrogation, therefore, relies on an accurate assessment of whether the suspect is being deceptive when he or she claims to be innocent.

As you will see in Chapter 4, there is currently very little research available to suggest that police officers, or anyone else for that matter, can detect deception with any degree of accuracy (e.g., Memon et al., 2003). This often appears to be true even after people receive specialized training (Köhnken, 1987), although there is a recent exception to this in Canada, where one specific training program has been shown to increase lie detection accuracy amongst parole officers (Porter, Woodworth, & Birt, 2000). As a result, it seems likely that the decision to interrogate a suspect when using the Reid model of interrogation will often be based on an incorrect determination that the suspect is guilty (Kassin et al., 2003).

There are, of course, procedural safeguards in place to protect an individual during the transition into the interrogation phase of the Reid model (Kassin & Gudjonsson, 2004). Most notably in the United States are an individual's *Miranda* rights (*Miranda v. Arizona,*

1966). As most readers will know from numerous television series, *Miranda* rights include a right to silence and a right to counsel, and it is only when suspects knowingly and voluntarily waive these rights that their statements can be used as evidence against them (Kassin & Gudjonsson, 2004). In other countries, including Canada, suspects have similar rights (e.g., in Canada, rights of suspects are included in the Charter of Rights and Freedoms). Research, however, has demonstrated that *Miranda*-type rights may not provide the protection that they are assumed to provide.

One significant problem is that many individuals do not understand the rights that are read to them. Particularly vulnerable populations in this regard appear to include young people and those with impaired intellectual capacity (Fulero & Everington, 2004; Oberlander & Goldstein, 2001). Another problem is that police officers occasionally use techniques to overcome the potential obstacles posed by requiring waivers to *Miranda*-type rights. For example, police in some jurisdictions have been found to minimize the importance of the *Miranda* process and to use rapport-building techniques in an attempt to increase compliance (Leo, 1996a). What is now clear is that both of these problems result in a large number of individuals waiving their *Miranda* rights, particularly people who are actually innocent of the crime in question (Leo, 1996b). While it is not yet completely understood why innocent people waive these rights, it appears that this decision relates to feelings of reassurance that accompany innocence, which in turn is associated with perceptions that interrogating officers will be able to "see" when an individual is actually innocent (Kassin & Gudjonsson, 2004). As already demonstrated, empirical research that is described above indicates that this is unlikely to be true.

Investigator Bias The second problem with the Reid model of interrogation occurs during the actual interrogation and results from the fact that, when the police begin their interrogation, they already believe the suspect to be guilty. The problem here is that when people form a belief about something before they enter a situation, they often unknowingly seek out and interpret information in that situation in a way that verifies their initial belief (Kassin et al., 2003). A recent study by Kassin et al. (2003) demonstrates some of the potential dangers that can result from this particular form of **investigator bias**.

In a mock interrogation study, the researchers had students act as interrogators or suspects. Some of the interrogators were led to believe that the suspect was guilty of a mock crime (finding a hidden key and stealing $100 from a locked cabinet), while others were led to believe that the suspect was innocent. In reality, some of the suspects were guilty of the mock crime whereas others were innocent. Interrogators were instructed to devise an interrogation strategy to use on the suspects, and the suspects were told to deny any involvement in the crime and to convince the interrogator of their innocence. The interrogation was taped, and a group of neutral observers then listened to the tape and were asked questions about the interrogator and the suspect.

A number of important results emerged from this study:

Investigator bias: Bias that can result when police officers enter an interrogation setting already believing that the suspect is guilty

1. Interrogators with guilty expectations asked more questions that indicated their belief in the suspect's guilt. For example, they would ask, "How did you find the key that was hidden behind the DVD player?" instead of "Do you know anything about the key that was hidden behind the DVD player?"

2. Interrogators with guilty expectations used a higher frequency of interrogation techniques compared with interrogators with innocent expectations, especially at the outset of the interrogation.

3. Interrogators with guilty expectations judged more suspects to be guilty, regardless of whether the suspect was actually guilty.

4. Interrogators indicated that they exerted more pressure on suspects to confess when, unbeknownst to them, the suspect was innocent.

5. Suspects had fairly accurate perceptions of interrogator behaviour (i.e., innocent suspects believed their interrogators were exerting more pressure).

6. Neutral observers viewed interrogators with guilty expectations as more coercive, especially against innocent suspects, and they viewed suspects in the guilty expectation condition as more defensive.

In sum, these findings indicate that "investigative biases led to coercive and pressure-filled interrogations that, in turn, caused suspects to appear more 'defensive' and 'guilty' even when they were not guilty of the crime being investigated" (Meissner & Russano, 2003, p. 57).

Interrogation Practices and the Courts

The decision to admit confession evidence into court rests on the shoulders of the trial judge. Within North America, the key issues a judge must consider when faced with a questionable confession are whether the confession was made voluntarily and whether the defendant was competent when he or she provided the confession (Wakefield & Underwager, 1998). The reason for using these criteria is that involuntary confessions and confessions provided when a person's mind is unstable are more likely to be unreliable.

What is meant by "voluntary" and "competent" is not always clear, which is why debate continues over the issue. What does seem clear, however, is that confessions resulting from overt forms of coercion will not be admitted in court. As Kassin (1997) states, "A confession is typically excluded if it was elicited by brute force; prolonged isolation; deprivation of food or sleep; threats of harm or punishment; promises of immunity or leniency; or, barring exceptional circumstances, without notifying the suspect of his or her constitutional rights" (p. 221).

Conversely, confessions that result from more subtle forms of psychological coercion are regularly admitted into court, in both Canada and the United States. For example, in the recent Canadian case of *R. v. Oickle* (2000), Richard Oickle confessed to seven counts of arson occurring in and around Waterville, Nova Scotia, between 1994 and 1995. The confession was obtained after a police interrogation in which several questionable interrogation techniques were used. These tactics included exaggerating the infallibility of a polygraph exam, implying that psychiatric help would be provided if the defendant confessed, minimizing the seriousness of the crimes, and suggesting that a confession would spare Oickle's girlfriend from having to undergo a stressful interrogation. After considering whether Oickle's confession was voluntarily given, the trial judge deemed the confession admissible and convicted him on all counts. The Court of Appeal subsequently deemed the confession evidence inadmissible and entered an acquittal. On appeal before the Supreme Court of Canada, a ruling was handed down, which stated that Oickle's confession was properly admitted by the trial judge, and therefore his conviction should stand, despite the interrogation techniques employed by the police. So, if these sorts of interrogation practices are condoned

Box 3.1

When the Police Go Too Far: The Case of *R. v. Hoilett* (1999)

Hoilett was arrested for sexual assault in Toronto at 11:25 P.M. on November 28, 1997. At the time of his arrest, Hoilett was under the influence of alcohol and crack cocaine. He was taken to the police station and placed in a cell. At 1:24 A.M. on November 29, police officers came to Hoilett's cell to remove his clothing in order for them to be forensically - examined. All of his clothing was taken, including his underwear, shoes, and socks, and he was left naked in his cell with just a metal bed to sit on for one-and-a-half hours.

At 3:06 A.M., Hoilett was awakened and given some light clothes, but no underwear, and shoes that did not fit. When he asked for a tissue to wipe his nose, the police officers did not provide him with one. Hoilett was then taken from his cell to be interrogated. The interviewing officer was aware that Hoilett had consumed alcohol and crack cocaine that evening but believed the suspect was not impaired during the interrogation, only tired, which was why he kept nodding off. Although Hoilett was detained and under arrest, the interviewing officer testified that "the reason he proceeded with the interview at that hour . . . was because he was not sure he would have another opportunity to do so" (*R. v. Hoilett*, 1999, para. 5).

Hoilett made an incriminating statement to the police at this time, and the trial judge ruled that the statement was made voluntarily and knowingly and, therefore, it was admissible. In his ruling, the trial judge recognized and openly disapproved of the inhumane conduct demonstrated by the police in this case. However, the judge concluded that the free will of the defendant was not affected by this treatment, and Hoilett was convicted on one count of sexual assault.

On appeal before the Ontario Court of Appeal, the court pointed out that, in reaching his conclusion that Hoilett's confession was voluntary, "the trial judge made no reference to . . . the accused's testimony where he said that his decision to speak was influenced by how cold he was and that he needed a tissue, and that the officers suggested these things could be made available to him after the interrogation" (para. 23). The Court of Appeal went on to state that "virtually everyone would have their . . . will to say no to the police significantly influenced by . . . receiving inhumane treatment . . ." (para. 25).

Referring to whether Hoilett was competent at the time he made his statement, the Court of Appeal added that there was substantial evidence he was not (e.g., Hoilett was awakened and interviewed at 3:06 A.M., he stated he was tired, and on several occasions the interrogators had to ask him whether he was awake).

As a result of their findings, the Ontario Court of Appeal reversed the decision of the trial judge, ruled that the statement of the accused was involuntary, and ordered that a new trial be held.

by the court, what sorts of practices are not? Box 3.1 provides a brief account of another recent Canadian case, *R. v. Hoilett* (1999), in which the Ontario Court of Appeal did rule that the defendant's confession was involuntary and therefore should not have been admitted at his trial. This ruling gives some indication as to how far Canadian police officers can go with their coercive interrogation tactics before it is considered too far by the courts.

Recent Changes to Interrogation Procedures

Due to the potential problems that can result from using coercive interrogation tactics, police agencies in several countries have recently introduced changes to their procedures. Perhaps more than anywhere else, these changes have been most obvious in England, where courts have restricted the use of many techniques found in the Reid model of interrogation (Gudjonsson, 2003).

Over the last 20 years, police agencies in England have gone through several phases of change in an attempt to reduce oppressive interrogation practices. Currently, these agencies use the so-called PEACE model to guide their interrogations (PEACE is an acronym for *planning* and *preparation*, *engage* and *explain*, *account*, *closure*, and *evaluation*). According to Meissner and Russano (2003), this model provides an inquisitorial framework within which to conduct police interrogations (compared with the accusatorial framework used in the Reid model) and is based on an interview method known as conversation management, which encourages information gathering more than securing a confession. In fact, police agencies in England have all but abandoned the term "interrogation" in favour of "investigative interviewing" to get away from the negative connotations associated with North American–style interrogation practices. Although little research has been conducted to examine the impact of this new model, some research indicates that a decrease in the use of coercive interrogation tactics does not necessarily result in a substantial reduction in the number of confessions that can be obtained (Meissner & Russano, 2003).

Although North American police agencies appear more hesitant to modify their interrogation techniques, video-recording interrogations is a growing practice. For example, according to Kassin (1997), approximately one third of all large police agencies in the United States video-record at least some interrogations, and 97% of police agencies that have video-recorded confessions have found the videos useful. In addition, since various court rulings in the mid-1990s (e.g., *R. v. Barrett*, 1993), the video-recording of interrogations by the police has become common practice in Canada. Video-recording police interrogations seems a wise move for a variety of reasons. For example, White (1997) suggests that, by video-recording an interrogation, the police can protect themselves against false allegations of coercive practices, suspects can be assured they will not be subjected to interrogation methods that potentially lead to false confessions, and the courts can make more informed judgments about the appropriateness of police tactics. However, recent research suggests that we must be cautious with the use of video cameras in this context. Indeed, even something as subtle as the camera angle (e.g., whether the camera is focused solely on the suspect versus the suspect and the interrogator) has been shown to have a significant impact on mock juror verdicts regarding guilt or innocence (Lassiter, Geers, Handley, Weiland, & Munhall, 2002). Part of the problem is that in suspect-only videos (which appear to be the standard in parts of Canada) it is difficult to determine the degree of coercion that is being used to extract the confession.

FALSE CONFESSIONS

False confession: A confession that is either intentionally fabricated or is not based on actual knowledge of the facts that form its content

Perhaps the biggest problem that people have with the use of coercive interrogation tactics is that these techniques can contribute to the likelihood of suspects making **false confessions** (Kassin & Gudjonsson, 2004). False confessions can be defined in a number of ways. However, Ofshe (1989) provides a definition that appears to be well accepted. He suggests that a confession should be considered false "if it is elicited in response to a demand for a confession and is either intentionally fabricated or is not based on actual knowledge of the facts that form its content" (p. 13). When false confessions do occur, they should be taken seriously, especially considering the weight that juries put on confessions when determining the guilt or innocence of a defendant (Kassin & Sukel, 1997).

Research indicates that when people have been wrongfully convicted of a crime, a false confession is often to blame. For example, Scheck, Neufeld, and Dwyer (2000) discovered that, in the 70 cases of wrongful convictions they examined, 21% included confession evidence that was later found to be false.

Before moving on to examine the extent of this problem, it is important to define two additional terms that are often confused with false confessions: **retracted confessions** and **disputed confessions**. Retracted confession consists of an individual declaring that the confession he or she made is false (regardless of whether it actually is or not) (Gudjonsson, 2003). Disputed confessions, however, are confessions that are disputed at trial. This does not necessarily mean the confession is false or that it was retracted. Instead, disputed confessions may arise due to legal technicalities, or because the suspect disputes the confession was ever made (Gudjonsson, 2003).

Retracted confession: A confession that the confessor later declares to be false

Disputed confession: A confession that is later disputed at trial

The Frequency of False Confessions

Most researchers readily admit that no one knows how frequently false confessions are made. The major problem is that in most cases it is almost impossible to determine whether a confession is actually false. The fact that a confession is coerced does not mean the confession is false, just as a conviction based on confession evidence does not mean the confession is true (Kassin, 1997). As a result of this problem, researchers come up with drastically different estimates of how frequently false confessions occur. For example, the incidence of self-reported false confessions amongst prison inmates has been found to vary from 0.6% (Cassell, 1998) to 12% (Gudjonsson & Sigurdsson, 1994). Regardless of the exact number, most researchers believe there are enough cases to treat the issue very seriously.

Different Types of False Confessions

One thing researchers do agree on is that there are different types of false confessions. While several different typologies exist for classifying false confessions (e.g., Gudjonsson, 2003; McCann, 1998), the most common typology still appears to be the one proposed by Kassin and Wrightsman (1985), which states that false confessions consist of voluntary false confessions, coerced-compliant false confessions, and coerced-internalized false confessions.

Voluntary False Confessions
Voluntary false confessions occur when someone voluntarily confesses to a crime he or she did not commit without any elicitation from the police. Research has indicated that people voluntarily false confess for a variety of reasons. For example, Gudjonsson (1992) suggests that such confessions may arise out of (1) a morbid desire for notoriety, (2) the person being unable to distinguish fact from fantasy, (3) the need to make up for pathological feelings of guilt by receiving punishment, or (4) a desire to protect somebody else from harm (which may be particularly prevalent among juveniles).

Voluntary false confession: A false confession that is provided without any elicitation from the police

Although it may seem surprising, many highly publicized cases do result in voluntary false confessions. Perhaps the most famous case was the kidnapping and murder of Charles Lindbergh's baby son. Charles Lindbergh was famous for being the first pilot to fly solo across the Atlantic Ocean in 1927. On March 1, 1932, Charles Lindbergh Jr., at the age of 20 months, was kidnapped. Two-and-a-half months later, the decomposed body of the baby was found with a fractured skull. It is estimated that some 200 people falsely confessed to the kidnapping and murder (Note, 1953). In the end, only one man was convicted for the crime, a German immigrant named Bruno Richard Hauptman, who was executed for the crime in 1936 despite his repeated claims of being innocent. To this day, questions are still raised about Hauptman's guilt (e.g., Jones, 1997).

Coerced-Compliant False Confessions

Coerced-compliant false confessions are those in which the suspect confesses to a crime, even though the suspect is fully aware that he or she did not commit it. This type of false confession is perhaps the most common (Gudjonsson & MacKeith, 1988). Unlike voluntary false confessions, these confessions are caused by the use of coercive interrogation tactics on the part of the police, such as the maximization techniques described earlier. Specifically, coerced-compliant confessions may be given so the suspect can (1) escape further interrogation, (2) gain a promised benefit, or (3) avoid a threatened punishment (Gudjonsson, 1992).

As with voluntary false confessions, there are a number of reported cases of coerced-compliant false confessions. For example, the 1993 movie *In the Name of the Father* starring Daniel Day-Lewis is based on such a case. Gerry Conlon, along with three other Irishmen, falsely confessed to bombing two pubs in Surrey, England, as a result of coercive police interrogations. The coercive tactics included making up false evidence and threatening to harm members of Conlon's family unless he confessed. Conlon and his acquaintances were subsequently convicted and sent to prison but were later released (Gudjonsson, 2003). Box 3.2 provides an example of a recent coerced-compliant false confession that occurred in Canada.

Coerced-compliant false confession: A confession that results from a desire to escape a coercive interrogation environment or gain a benefit promised by the police

A plea for help in the famous Lindbergh baby kidnapping case. It is estimated that 200 people falsely confessed to the kidnapping and murder of 20-month-old Charles Lindbergh, Jr.

Box 3.2

False Confession in a Child-Abuse Case

In the case *R. v. M.J.S.* (2000), M.J.S. was accused of aggravated assault on his baby son (J.S.) and, after supplying the police with a written confession, was charged with the crime. But was M.J.S. responsible for the crime, or was this a case of a coerced-compliant false confession?

J.S. was one to three months old at the time the abuse was supposed to have happened. The boy had been admitted to the hospital for a suspected chest infection and vomiting problems. While in the hospital, X-rays were taken, and it was later discovered that the baby had several rib fractures. The injuries were unusual for a baby so young, leading the baby's pediatrician to notify child welfare. The testimony of an expert suggested that the most likely cause of the fractures was that the baby was shaken.

A police investigation was begun. Both M.J.S and his wife cooperated with the police throughout the investigation. On four occasions, the police interrogated the accused. During these interrogations, the police used techniques similar to those used in the Reid model of interrogation, which eventually led the accused to confess. Fortunately, all of the interrogations were videotaped, which provided the courts with a means to determine whether the confession was coerced.

Much of the interrogation consisted of developing various psychological themes to justify the crime. For example, one of the interrogating officers stated, "No doubt it was probably accidental on your part. . . . I don't believe it was intentional. . . . Children's bones are so fragile. . . . You made a mistake" (*R. v. M.J.S.*, para. 16). In addition, every time the accused denied his involvement in the crime, the

officers interrupted with statements such as, "We are beyond that point—we know you did it" (para. 19).

The officers also lied to the accused, stating they had talked to everyone else who might have been involved with the incident and they were all cleared. This had not happened. Furthermore, the interviewing officers appealed to the accused's sense of honour and decency, and stressed how much better he would feel if he confessed. For example, one officer stated, "You'll be able to say to yourself . . . I'm going to sleep tonight, knowing that I told the truth" (para. 20). Still denying his involvement in any wrongdoing, the accused was presented with threatening statements. One interrogator stated, "If you run from this mistake, your family disintegrates, your family falls apart. . . . If you want your kids to be raised in a foster home, or adopted somewhere, that is a decision that you have to make" (para. 25).

In ruling on the confession evidence, the judge stated that the alleged confession in this case was extracted by threats and implied promises. The judge decided that the techniques employed by the investigators were coercive and that the accused confessed to the crime in order to escape the oppressive atmosphere created by the interrogations. The judge concluded by stating, "This case is a classic illustration of how slavish adherence to a technique can produce a coerced-compliant false 'apology' [confession] even from an accused who has denied 34 times that he did anything wrong when caring for his child" (para. 45). As a result of these findings, the confession evidence was deemed inadmissible.

Coerced-Internalized False Confessions The third, and perhaps the most bizarre, type of false confession proposed by Kassin and Wrightsman (1985) is the **coerced-internalized false confession**. Here, individuals recall and confess to a crime they did not commit, usually after they are exposed to highly suggestible questions, such as the minimization techniques described earlier in the chapter (Gudjonsson, 2003). In contrast to the coerced-compliant false confessor, however, these individuals actually end up believing they are responsible for the crime. According to Gudjonsson (1992), there are several vulnerability factors associated with this type of false confession, including (1) a history of substance abuse or some other interference with brain function, (2) the inability of people to detect discrepancies between what they

Coerced-internalized false confession: A confession that results from suggestive interrogation techniques, whereby the confessor actually comes to believe he or she committed the crime observed and what has been erroneously suggested to them, and (3) factors associated with mental state, such as severe anxiety, confusion, or feelings of guilt.

Perhaps the most frequently cited case of a false confession falls under the heading of a coerced-internalized false confession (Ofshe & Watters, 1994). The case involves Paul Ingram, who, in 1988, was accused by his two adult daughters of committing crimes against them, crimes that included sexual assault, rape, and satanic ritual abuse that involved slaughtering newborn babies. As if some of these allegations were not strange enough, Ingram confessed to the crimes after initially being adamant he had never committed them. In addition, he was eventually able to recall the crimes in vivid detail despite originally claiming he could not remember ever abusing his daughters. Ingram ended up pleading guilty to six counts of rape and was sentenced to 20 years in prison. In prison, Ingram came to believe he was not guilty of the crimes he confessed to. After having initial appeals rejected, Ingram was released from prison on April 8, 2003.

Many people feel that Ingram falsely confessed to the crimes he was sentenced for. Supporters of this position typically draw on two related pieces of evidence (see Olio & Cornell, 1998, for evidence to the contrary). First, it is known that Ingram was exposed to highly suggestive interrogation techniques that have been shown to adversely influence people's memory of events. For example, over the course of five months, Ingram took part in 23 interrogations in which he was instructed (on some of these occasions) to visualize scenes of satanic cult activity that he could not remember (Wrightsman, 2001). Second, a psychologist hired to evaluate the case, Dr. Richard Ofshe from the University of California, concluded that Ingram had been brainwashed into believing he was responsible for the crimes (Ofshe & Watters, 1994). To demonstrate this belief, Ofshe conducted an experiment in which he presented Ingram with a fabricated scenario: that Ingram had forced his son and daughter to have sex together while he watched (Olio & Cornell, 1998). According to Olio and Cornell (1998), phase 1 of the experiment consisted of Ofshe asking Ingram if he could remember the incident (Ingram indicated that he could not). Ofshe then instructed Ingram to use the same visualization techniques he had used during his previous interview sessions. The next day, Ingram informed Ofshe he could now remember the incident and he produced a written confession providing details of his involvement. In phase 2 of the experiment, Ofshe pressured Ingram to retract his confession, but Ingram was not willing to do so.

Interrogative Suggestibility and Compliance

As we have already mentioned, the major difference between coerced-compliant and coerced-internalized false confessions is that coerced-compliant false confessors are fully aware that they are not responsible for the crimes they are confessing to. Research indicates that two psychological characteristics play a key role in these two types of confessions—compliance and suggestibility. **Compliance** refers to a tendency to go along with demands made by people perceived to be in authority, even though the person may not agree with them (Gudjonsson, 1989). **Suggestibility** refers to the tendency to accept (i.e., internalize) information communicated during questioning (Gudjonsson, 1984). Dr. Gisli Gudjonsson, from the Institute of Psychiatry in London, has developed standardized scales for measuring both compliance and suggestibility.

Compliance: A tendency to go along with demands made by people perceived to be in authority, even though the person may not agree with them

Suggestibility: A tendency to accept information communicated during questioning

The Gudjonsson Compliance Scale The Gudjonsson Compliance Scale (GCS) is a self-report questionnaire consisting of 20 true-false questions that tap into two aspects of compliance: a person's eagerness to please others and a person's desire to avoid conflict and confrontation with people (Gudjonsson, 1989). For example, the section measuring a person's eagerness to please others includes questions such as, "I try hard to do what is expected of me" and "I generally believe in doing as I am told." In contrast, the section measuring a person's desire to avoid conflict and confrontation includes questions such as, "I give in easily to people when I am pressured" and "I tend to give in to people who insist that they are right" (Gudjonsson, 2003).

Although the GCS has not been the subject of much research, there is some evidence that it is useful for identifying suspects who can be characterized as compliant. For example, Gudjonsson (1989) compared the GCS scores for "resisters" (suspects who did not confess even though there was evidence they were guilty) with "false confessors" (suspects who retracted confessions they had previously made). The results suggested that the former group had significantly lower GCS scores than the latter group, providing one possible reason that these individuals performed the way they did during their police interrogations (a practical example of this scale in use is presented in Box 3.3).

The Gudjonsson Suggestibility Scale The Gudjonsson Suggestibility Scale (GSS1) measures two distinct types of interrogative suggestibility (Gudjonsson, 1984). First, it measures susceptibility to give in to leading questions, which is known as **yield**. It also measures the tendency to alter answers after being put under pressure by an interviewer, which is known as **shift**. This scale is based on a short story, which is read to a subject. The subject is then asked to recall details from the story. The subject is asked 20 questions, 15 of which are misleading (trial 1). Next, the subject is told that he or she has made a number of errors in answering the questions (even if no errors have been made),

Gudjonsson Compliance Scale: A scale developed by Gisli Gudjonsson that is used to measure a person's level of compliance

Gudjonsson Suggestibility Scale: A scale developed by Gisli Gudjonsson that is used to measure a person's level of suggestibility

Yield: The extent to which people who are completing the Gudjonsson Suggestibility Scale give in to leading questions

Shift: The extent to which people who are completing the Gudjonsson Suggestibility Scale alter their answers when put under pressure by the interviewer

Box 3.3

Using the Gudjonsson Compliance and Suggestibility Scales

Gudjonsson (2003) describes the following case of the Birmingham Six. In November 1974, two pubs in Birmingham, England, were bombed by the Irish Republican Army (IRA), killing 21 people. Six Irishmen were arrested for the bombings and interrogated. Two of the suspects did not sign any confession, and the other four did sign a confession. Although the defendants argued that the police had beaten their confessions out of them, their confessions were admitted as evidence in court and the six men were convicted. They were imprisoned until 1990, at which time they were released based on new evidence.

Thirteen years after their interrogation, Gudjonsson was asked to assess all six defendants. Part of the assessment protocol included the GCS and GSS1. Figure 3.1 on page 70 indicates that the six men differed dramatically in their level of compliance and suggestibility. Two of the defendants scored very high on both scales, two scored very low, and two scored in the middle. Interestingly, the two defendants who scored lowest on the scales were the same two men who did not sign a written confession in 1974. Gudjonsson (2003) is careful to point out that there is no way to know what the defendants' compliance and suggestibility scores were in 1974. Nevertheless, it is intriguing that these scores correspond so well with the behaviour exhibited by the Birmingham Six in their original police interrogations.

(continued)

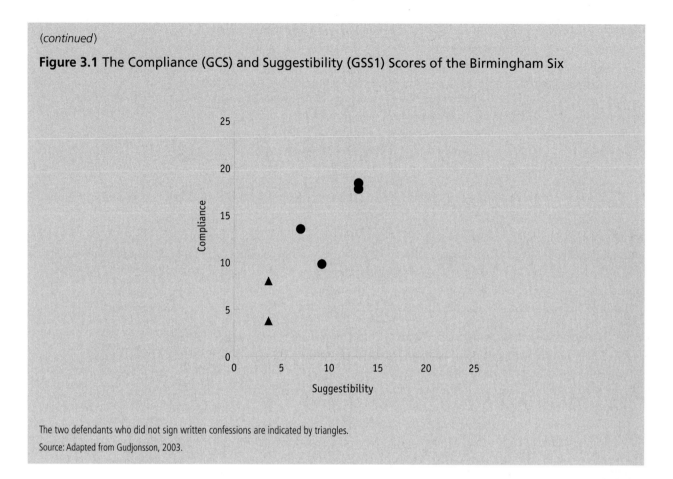

(continued)

Figure 3.1 The Compliance (GCS) and Suggestibility (GSS1) Scores of the Birmingham Six

The two defendants who did not sign written confessions are indicated by triangles.

Source: Adapted from Gudjonsson, 2003.

that it is necessary to ask all the questions again, and that the subject should try to be more accurate (trial 2). The extent to which the subject gives in to the misleading questions on the first trial is scored as *yield*. Any change in answers between the first and second trial is scored as *shift*. Yield and shift are added together to make up the total suggestibility score.

Research has indicated that the GSS1 is a potentially important diagnostic tool for assessing the degree to which a suspect can be characterized as suggestible. In a study similar to what was done with the GCS, Gudjonsson (1984) compared the GSS1 scores for resisters and false confessors and, as hypothesized, found that resisters had significantly lower GSS1 scores than did false confessors. Research has also been conducted to examine the various correlates of interrogative suggestibility. Many of these correlations are consistent with what would be expected. For example, certain forms of anxiety correlate positively with suggestibility (as anxiety increases, suggestibility increases), while intelligence correlates negatively (as intelligence increases, suggestibility decreases) (Gudjonsson, 2003).

Studying False Confessions in the Lab

It is obviously difficult to study if, and how, false confessions occur. Even in the research laboratory it is not an easy task because of obvious ethical constraints (Kassin & Kiechel, 1996). Nowadays, no university ethics committee would allow research participants to be led to believe they had committed crimes of the sort that Paul Ingram was accused of. As a result, researchers have attempted to develop innovative laboratory paradigms that allow them to study the processes that may cause false confessions to occur without putting their participants at risk. One such paradigm was proposed by Dr. Saul Kassin and his student.

In their study, Kassin and Kiechel (1996) tested whether individuals would confess to a crime they did not commit. They had participants take part in what they thought was a reaction time study. A co-conspirator read a list of letters out loud to a participant who had to type these letters into a computer. However, before each session began, the participant was warned that if he or she hit the ALT key on the keyboard while typing in the letters, all the data would be lost. Sixty seconds after beginning the task, the computer automatically crashed, which brought the head researcher into the lab with accusations that the participant had hit the key.

Kassin and Kiechel were specifically interested in how two factors would affect participant reactions to the allegations. Participant vulnerability (defined as the participant's certainty concerning his or her own innocence) was manipulated by varying the speed that participants had to type. In the "not vulnerable" condition, letters were read at a rate of 43 letters per minute; in the "vulnerable" condition, letters were read at a rate of 67 letters per minute. The researchers also varied whether false evidence was presented. In the "no false evidence" condition, the co-conspirator stated she did not see what happened; in the "false evidence" condition, she stated she saw the participant hit the ALT key. The results from the study are presented in Table 3.1.

To measure the degree to which participants complied with the allegations, the researchers presented each participant with a written confession and recorded how many participants signed it. As indicated in Table 3.1, many participants accepted responsibility for the crime despite the fact they were innocent, particularly the vulnerable participants presented with false evidence. To measure the degree to which participants internalized their confession, the researchers recorded comments made by participants to another co-conspirator outside the lab who asked them what had happened. If the participant accepted blame for the crime, he or she was recorded as exhibiting **internalization**. As indicated in Table 3.1, many participants also internalized their confession. Again, this was especially true for vulnerable participants presented with false evidence. Finally, to measure the degree to which participants made up details to fit with their confession, known as **confabulation**, the researchers brought the participant back into the lab, read the list of letters again, and asked the participant to try to reconstruct where things had

Internalization: Accepting that something suggested to you is true

Confabulation: Making things up

Table 3.1 Compliance, Internalization, and Confabulation in Kassin and Kiechel's Study

	No False Evidence (No Witness)		False Evidence (Witness)	
	Not Vulnerable (Slow Pace)	Vulnerable (Fast Pace)	Not Vulnerable (Slow Pace)	Vulnerable (Fast Pace)
Compliance	35%	65%	89%	100%
Internalization	0%	12%	44%	65%
Confabulation	0%	0%	6%	35%

Source: Adapted from Kassin and Kiechel, 1996.

gone wrong. As indicated in Table 3.1, vulnerable participants presented with false evidence were once again found to be particularly susceptible to confabulation.

In sum, these findings suggest that it is possible to demonstrate, under laboratory conditions, that people can admit to acts they are not responsible for and come to believe in their guilt to such a point that they can reconstruct details of an act that never occurred (Kassin & Kiechel, 1996). However, whether these findings can be generalized to actual police interrogations, in which people are falsely confessing to much more serious events that may ultimately lead to unwanted penalties, is clearly open to debate. Indeed, given the triviality of their mock crime and the fact that the false confessor suffered no negative consequences, even Kassin and Kiechel raise this issue about their findings. More recent research is helping to clarify this issue. For example, Horselenberg, Merckelbach, and Josephs (2003) were able to replicate Kassin and Kiechel's findings even when false confessions were directly linked to financial loss on the part of the confessor. However, studies being conducted in this area are still far from being realistic. Perhaps in the future, forensic psychologists will find a way to conduct laboratory studies of false confessions that are not so problematic in this regard.

The Consequences of Falsely Confessing

There are at least two major consequences of a false confession. The most obvious consequence is the impact on the individual making the confession, in particular if the confession is admitted as evidence in court. As mentioned previously, research indicates that false confessions do sometimes lead people to be convicted for crimes they did not commit (Leo & Ofshe, 1998). This finding has led some researchers to examine the impact that coerced confessions have on jurors.

In one study, Kassin and Sukel (1997) presented participants with transcripts of a mock murder trial. One group of participants received a transcript in which the defendant immediately confessed to the police during questioning (the low-pressure condition). A second group of participants received a transcript in which the defendant was coerced into confessing by having his hands cuffed behind his back and being threatened by the interrogator (the high-pressure condition). A third group of participants received a transcript in which the defendant never confessed to the murder (the control condition). The results of the study indicate that those participants presented with a confession obtained in the high-pressure condition recognized the confession was involuntary and said it would not affect their decisions. However, when actual verdicts were examined across the three groups, the presence of a confession was found to significantly increase the conviction rate, even for those participants in the high-pressure condition. Thus, not only can people be convicted of crimes they did not commit based on their false confession, but this can happen even when the confession appears to have been obtained through coercive interrogation tactics.

A second consequence of false confessions that is not as commonly recognized is usually caused by people voluntarily confessing to crimes they did not commit. Although such a confession no doubt has consequences for the false confessor, it also has unappreciated consequences for the police and, therefore, the public. When somebody volunteers a false confession, the police are diverted down a false trail that may waste valuable time, time that could be used to identify and apprehend the real offender. Howitt (2002) provides an example of this happening in the Yorkshire Ripper serial murder investigation that took place in England during the 1970s. At one point in the investigation, the police were sent several tape recordings supposedly from the Ripper himself. Howitt states that senior police officers on the case, believing the tapes to be genuine, used up valuable resources investigating the tapes. However, the tapes were not genuine, and these actions probably delayed the eventual arrest of Peter Sutcliffe and allowed further murders to take place.

CRIMINAL PROFILING

In order for the police to be able to conduct their interrogations, they need to have a viable suspect in custody. In some instances, the identification of probable suspects is relatively straightforward, because in many crimes the victim and the offender know each other and there is often a clear motivation for the crime, such as passion, greed, or revenge. But what about those crimes in which it is more difficult to identify a suspect, crimes in which the victim and offender are strangers and there is no clear motive? In these cases, the police often rely on unconventional investigative techniques, such as **criminal profiling**.

Criminal profiling: An investigative technique for identifying the major personality and behavioural characteristics of an individual based upon an analysis of the crimes he or she has committed

WHAT IS A CRIMINAL PROFILE?

There is no single definition of criminal profiling (Alison, Bennell, Mokros, & Ormerod, 2002). Indeed, there is still little agreement as to what the technique should even be called. Numerous terms are used to describe the technique, including criminal profiling, psychological profiling, offender profiling, and investigative profiling (Wilson, Lincoln, & Kocsis, 1997). However, the definition proposed by John Douglas and his former colleagues from the Federal Bureau of Investigation (FBI) fairly accurately describes them all: profiling is "a technique for identifying the major personality and behavioural characteristics of an individual based upon an analysis of the crimes he or she has committed" (Douglas, Ressler, Burgess, & Hartman, 1986, p. 405).

Although criminal profiling is now used in a range of contexts, it is most commonly used in cases of serial homicide and rape (Holmes & Holmes, 2002). In particular, profiling is thought to be most applicable in cases in which extreme forms of psychopathology are exhibited by the offender, including sadistic torture and ritualistic behaviour (Geberth, 1990). Criminal profiling was originally intended to help the police identify the criminal in these sorts of cases, either by narrowing down a list of suspects or by providing new lines of inquiry. However, criminal profiling is now used for a number of purposes including the following (Homant & Kennedy, 1998):

■ To help set traps to flush out an offender

■ To determine whether a threatening note should be taken seriously

■ To give advice on how best to interrogate a suspect

■ To tell prosecutors how to break down defendants in cross-examination

Although every criminal profile will undoubtedly be different in terms of the information it contains, some of the most common personality and behavioural characteristics that profilers try to predict include the offender's age, sex, race, level of intelligence, educational history, hobbies, family background, residential location, criminal history, employment status, psychosexual development, and post-offence behaviour (Holmes & Holmes, 2002). Often these predictions are made by forensic psychologists and psychiatrists who have either clinical or research experience with offenders (Wilson et al., 1997). In North America, however, the majority of profilers are experienced and specially trained law enforcement officers (Rossmo, 2000).

The Origins of Criminal Profiling

Criminal profiling is usually thought to have been developed by agents from the FBI in the 1970s. However, there are numerous examples of profiling techniques being used long before that time (Canter, 2000). Woodworth and Porter (1999), for example, suggest that the documented history of profiling can be traced back at least to the publication of the *Malleus Maleficarum*, "a text from the late 1400s written by contractors to the Catholic Church for the purpose of accurately identifying and eradicating witches" (p. 243). According to these researchers, this was one of the first systematic approaches for identifying and making inferences about the characteristics of supposedly guilty individuals. Beyond this example, there are other early instances of profiling techniques, which were often used for the specific purpose of inferring the background characteristics of an unknown offender from the behaviours he or she exhibited at the crime scene. The investigation that you may be most familiar with is the famous case of Jack the Ripper (Harrison, 1993).

Early Attempts at Criminal Profiling In 1888, a series of murders were committed in the east end of London, around an area known as Whitechapel. The victims were all women, and all were mutilated by the offender. At one point, the unknown offender sent a letter to the newspapers, and at the end of it he signed his name, Jack the Ripper (Holmes & Holmes, 2002). A police surgeon involved with the investigation of the murders engaged in a form of criminal profiling. As Woodworth and Porter (1999, p. 244) reveal,

> Dr. George Phillips attempted to create a reconstruction of various crime scenes and describe the wounds of the victims for the purpose of gaining a greater insight into the offender's psychological make-up. In particular, Phillips believed that a circumspect examination of the wound patterns of murder victims could provide clues about both the behaviour and personality of the offender who committed the crimes.

This is probably one of the first times that criminal profiling was used in a criminal investigation. Unfortunately, it assisted little, evidenced by the fact that we still have no idea who Jack the Ripper actually was.

Another well-known case, often cited as an example of how accurate some profilers can be, is the case of New York City's Mad Bomber. Starting in 1940, an unknown offender began detonating bombs in public places around New York (Wrightsman, 2001). Stumped, the New York City Police Department turned to a local forensic psychiatrist, Dr. James Brussel, to assist with the case. By examining the actions of the bomber, Brussel began to develop a profile of the unknown offender. Dr. Brussel's profile included characteristics such as the following: the offender would be a middle-aged male, he would suffer from paranoia, he would be pathologically self-centred, he would be reasonably educated, he would be unmarried and possibly a virgin, he would be Roman Catholic, and he would wear buttoned-up double-breasted suits (Turvey, 2002). In 1957, almost 17 years after the bombings started, the police finally arrested George Metesky. Metesky fit most of the characteristics that Dr. Brussel had profiled, even down to the double-breasted suit he wore to the police station (Holmes & Holmes, 2002). Metesky was subsequently sent to a mental institution for the criminally insane. He was released in 1973 and died in 1994.

The FBI and Beyond The next big milestone in the history of criminal profiling was the development of a criminal profiling program at the FBI in the 1970s (Turvey, 2002). Not only was this the first time that profiles were produced in a systematic way by a law enforcement agency, but it was also the first time that training was provided in how to construct criminal profiles. Subsequent to the development of the FBI's Behavioral Sciences Unit in 1972, the National Center for the Analysis of Violent Crime was opened for the purpose of conducting research in the area of criminal profiling and providing formal guidance to police agencies around the United States that were investigating serial crimes, in particular serial murder. Similar units have now sprung up in police agencies around the world, including Canada, Germany, and England. These outfits typically provide operational support to police agencies in cases in which profiling may be useful, and many conduct their own research into criminal profiling. See Box 3.4 for an example of how the RCMP has been moving the criminal profiling field forward.

VICLAS: The Violent Crime Linkage Analysis System, which was developed by the RCMP to collect and analyze information on serious crimes from across Canada

Linkage blindness: An inability on the part of the police to link geographically dispersed serial crimes committed by the same offender because of a lack of information sharing among police agencies

Box 3.4

The RCMP's Violent Crime Linkage Analysis System (VICLAS)

In recent years, the RCMP has played a pivotal role in developing the field of criminal profiling. In large part, they have been able to do this by drawing on the best of modern computer technology. One of the RCMP's most significant advances has been the development in the mid-1990s of an automated system for linking serial crimes, the Violent Crime Linkage Analysis System, or **VICLAS**. One of the biggest problems the police encounter when they are faced with a possible crime series is **linkage blindness**, which refers to an inability on the part of the police to link geographically dispersed serial crimes committed by the same offender because of a lack of communication among police agencies (Egger, 2002). VICLAS was developed, in part, to prevent such linkage blindness.

The backbone of VICLAS is a booklet that police officers fill out. The questions in this booklet are supposed to capture crucial behavioural information on crimes of a serious nature. These crimes include motiveless homicides, sexual assaults, missing persons, and nonparental abductions (Collins,

Johnson, Choy, Davidson, & Mackay, 1998). The booklet contains more than 200 questions about the offender's behaviour, the victim, and any forensic information that is available. This information is then entered into a computer and downloaded into a centralized database where it is carefully compared with other crimes. Specially trained VICLAS analysts determine if there are any possible crime linkages. If any potential links are identified, the crimes are highlighted as a series and the relevant police agencies are notified and encouraged to share information (Collins et al., 1998).

According to Woodworth and Porter (1999), as of the year 2000, "there were more than 30 000 cases in the system, and although there are no official statistics on its success rate, there were 3200 known linkages" (p. 253). These encouraging results, in addition to anecdotal evidence that suggests the system holds promise, have earned VICLAS a reputation as one of the best crime linkage analysis systems in existence (Collins et al., 1998). Police from around the world, including agencies in England, Australia, and Germany, are currently using VICLAS to help solve their serial crimes.

Investigative Psychology Since the early 1990s, some of the most important advances in the area of criminal profiling have been made by David Canter, the founder of a relatively new field of psychology that he has named *investigative psychology*. The origins of this field can be traced back to Canter's involvement in the John Duffy (a.k.a., Railway Rapist) rape/murder case. Canter was called in by Scotland Yard (the London, England, police force) to provide a profile of the unknown offender, and in doing so, he drew on his knowledge of human behaviour that he had gained as an academic psychologist (especially in the area of environmental psychology) (Canter, 1994). Since that early successful contribution, Canter has spent the last 20 years developing the field of profiling into a scientific practice with his colleagues at the Centre for Investigative Psychology (CIP) at the University of Liverpool (Canter, 2000). The CIP has also made countless contributions to other areas of investigative psychology (e.g., investigative interviewing) (Canter & Alison, 1999).

How Is a Criminal Profile Constructed?

Once a crime series has been detected, warranting a criminal profile, profilers must go through a process of profile construction. Despite the fact that profiling has been used regularly by the police since the 1980s, very little is actually known about this process. Indeed, the descriptions of the profiling process provided by researchers and profilers are incredibly vague. For example, in a now-classic study of criminal profiling, Pinizzotto and Finkel (1990) describe the process of profiling as an equation in the form: WHAT + WHY = WHO. The WHAT of the crime refers to the material that profilers collect at the start of an investigation, such as crime scene photos, autopsy reports, and descriptions of victims. The WHY of the crime refers to the motivation for the crime and each crime scene behaviour. The WHO of the crime refers to the actual profile that is eventually constructed once the WHAT and the WHY components have been determined.

Obviously, although this conceptual model may make sense at a general level, it is much too vague to be useful. As Pinizzotto and Finkel (1990) themselves point out, the model "does not tell us precisely how . . . the profiler gets from the WHAT to the WHY, or from the WHY to the WHO" (p. 217). Other conceptual models have also been produced, particularly by profilers from the FBI, but these models also lack the degree of specificity required to truly understand the process by which a criminal profile is constructed (e.g., Douglas & Burgess, 1986). Undoubtedly, part of the problem with providing such detail is that profiling is still viewed primarily as an art, not a science (Homant & Kennedy, 1998). Although some are making an effort to change this (e.g., Canter, 2000; Hicks & Sales, 2006), profiling is currently based to a large extent on the profiler's experience and intuition (Douglas & Olshaker, 1995). As a result, asking a profiler to provide specific details of how he or she constructs a criminal profile may be similar to asking Picasso to explain how he painted.

Different Types of Profiling Methods

Deductive criminal profiling: Profiling the background characteristics of an unknown offender based on evidence left at the crime scenes by that particular offender

Although it is not clear how criminal profilers construct their profiles, it is evident that they can draw on different types of profiling methods. Specifically, two approaches can be used by profilers: the deductive profiling method and the inductive profiling method. **Deductive criminal profiling** involves the prediction of an offender's background characteristics generated from a thorough analysis of the evidence left at the crime scenes by that particular offender (Holmes & Holmes, 2002). This deductive method of profiling largely relies on logical reasoning. This is indicated in an example provided by Canter (2000), in which the victim of an unidentified assailant noticed that the offender had short fingernails on his right hand and long fingernails on his left hand. According to Canter, "Somebody with specialist knowledge suggested that this was a characteristic of people who are serious guitar players. It was therefore a reasonable deduction that the assailant was somebody who played the guitar" (p. 24). The primary disadvantage of this profiling method is that the underlying logic of the argument can sometimes be faulty. Take the prediction we just described. Although the argument appears to be logical, it is in fact wrong. The offender in this case did not play the guitar at all. Instead, the reason he had short fingernails on his right hand was that he had a job repairing old tires.

In contrast to deductive profiling, **inductive criminal profiling** involves the prediction of an offender's background characteristics generated from a comparison of that particular offender's crimes with similar crimes committed by other, known offenders. This method is based on the premise that "if certain crimes committed by different people are similar, then the offenders must also share some common personality traits" (Holmes & Holmes, 2002, p. 5). The inductive method of profiling relies largely on a determination of how likely it is an offender will possess certain background characteristics given the prevalence of these characteristics among known offenders who have committed similar crimes. An example of the inductive profiling method is provided by Aitken et al. (1996), who developed a statistical profile of a murderer of children. Based on their analysis of similar crimes committed by known offenders, they predicted that there was a probability of .96 that the offender would know the victim, a probability of .92 that the offender would have a previous criminal conviction, a probability of .91 that the offender would be single, a probability of .79 that the offender would live within 8 kilometres of the crime scene, and a probability of .65 that the offender would be under the age of 20. In this case, the profile turned out to be very accurate.

In contrast to deductive profiling, the major problem with the inductive method of profiling is with sampling issues (Turvey, 2002). The key problem is that it will never be possible to have a representative sample of serial offenders from which to draw profiling conclusions. That is, if we encounter a serial crime with behaviours A, B, and C, but no crimes in our database have behaviours A, B, and C, how do we construct an accurate profile? One reason for this problem is that many offenders are never caught for their crimes and, therefore, these offenders can never be included in a database of solved offences.

The Organized-Disorganized Model Many profilers today use an inductive profiling approach developed by the FBI in the 1980s. This model was developed largely through interviews with incarcerated serial murderers and has come to be called the **organized-disorganized model** (Hazelwood & Douglas, 1980). The model suggests that an offender's crime scene can be classified as either organized or disorganized (see Table 3.2 on page 78). Organized crime scene behaviours reflect a well-planned and controlled crime, while disorganized behaviours reflect an impulsive crime, which is chaotic in nature. Similarly, an offender's background can be classified as either organized or disorganized (see Table 3.3 on page 78). Organized background characteristics reflect a methodical individual, while disorganized characteristics reflect a disturbed individual, who is usually suffering from some form of psychopathology. The basic idea is that, when encountering a disorganized crime scene, the investigator should

Inductive criminal profiling: Profiling the background characteristics of an unknown offender based on what we know about other solved cases

Organized-disorganized model: A profiling model used by the FBI that assumes the crime scenes and backgrounds of serial offenders can be categorized as *organized* or *disorganized*

Table 3.2 Organized and Disorganized Crime Scene Behaviours

Organized Behaviours	Disorganized Behaviours
Planned offence	Spontaneous offence
Use of restraints on the victim	No restraints used on the victim
Ante-mortem sexual acts committed	Post-mortem sexual acts committed
Use of a vehicle in the crime	No use of a vehicle in the crime
No post-mortem mutilation	Post-mortem mutilation
Corpse not taken	Corpse (or body parts) taken
Little evidence left at the scene	Evidence left at the scene

Source: Adapted from Ressler et al., 1986.

profile the background characteristics of a disorganized offender, and likewise for organized crime scenes and organized background characteristics. Although little research has examined whether the organized-disorganized model actually works, the research that does exist raises serious doubts (e.g., Canter, Alison, Alison, & Wentink, 2004). Indeed, even the FBI has refined this model to account for the many offenders who display mixtures of organized and disorganized features (Douglas, Burgess, Burgess, & Ressler, 1992).

The Validity of Criminal Profiling

Because the police frequently use profiling, it is important to consider whether the technique is actually reliable and valid. The view of some researchers is that profiling is generally accepted as a useful investigative technique (e.g., Homant & Kennedy, 1998), but others are more cautious (e.g., Alison et al., 2002). Many profilers claim they have experienced much success with their profiles, but these claims are typically based on personal observations, not empirical research (Woodworth & Porter, 1999). The few empirical studies that do exist suggest that profiling may be beneficial, but not necessarily for the reasons we might expect.

Table 3.3 Organized and Disorganized Background Characteristics

Organized Characteristics	Disorganized Characteristics
High intelligence	Low intelligence
Skilled occupation	Unskilled occupation
Sexually adequate	Sexually inadequate
Lives with a partner	Lives alone
Geographically mobile	Geographically stable
Lives and works far away from crimes	Lives and works close to crimes
Follows crimes in media	Little interest in media
Maintains residence and vehicle	Does not maintain residence or vehicle

Source: Adapted from Ressler et al., 1986.

For example, in one of the most comprehensive evaluation studies, Copson (1995) found that profiles were viewed as operationally useful by 82.6% of the police officers he surveyed, but only 2.7% of that sample said that this was because the profile led to the identification of the offender. Most of the police officers indicated that profiling was useful because it either furthered their understanding of the case (60.9%) or it reassured them of their own judgments about the offender (51.6%).

Despite the relatively high figures indicating that criminal profiling may be useful, the practice is still often criticized. Three criticisms in particular have received attention from researchers:

1. Many forms of profiling are based on a theoretical model of personality that lacks strong empirical support.

2. Many profiles contain information that is so vague and ambiguous they can potentially fit many suspects.

3. Professional profilers may be no better than untrained individuals at constructing accurate criminal profiles.

Let's now look at each of these criticisms in turn.

Does Profiling Have a Strong Theoretical Base?

There seems to be general agreement that most forms of profiling, including the FBI's organized-disorganized approach, rely on a **classic trait model** of personality that was popular in psychology before the 1970s (Alison et al., 2002). In this model, the primary determinants of behaviour are stable, internal traits (Mischel, 1968). These traits are assumed to result in the expression of consistent patterns of behaviour over time and across situations. In the criminal context, this consistency is thought to persist across an offender's crimes and into the offender's noncriminal lifestyle, thus allowing him or her to be accurately profiled (Homant & Kennedy, 1998). Thus, an offender characterized by a trait of "organization" is expected to exhibit organized behaviours across his or her crimes (e.g., the offender will consistently plan the crimes, use restraints, and use weapons), as well as in his or her noncriminal life (e.g., the offender will be highly intelligent, sexually adequate, and geographically mobile) (Alison et al., 2002).

Classic trait model: A model of personality that assumes the primary determinants of behaviour are stable, internal traits

Although some researchers believe this classic trait model provides a solid basis for criminal profiling (e.g., Homant & Kennedy, 1998), other researchers disagree (e.g., Alison et al., 2002). Those who disagree draw on research from the field of personality psychology, which demonstrates that traits are not the only (or even primary) determinant of behaviour (Cervone & Shoda, 1999). Rather, situational influences are also known to be very important in shaping our behaviour, and some researchers argue that there is no reason to suspect that serial offenders will be any different (Bennell & Canter, 2002; Bennell & Jones, 2005). From a profiling perspective, the impact of various situational factors (e.g., an extremely resistant victim, being interrupted during a crime, or having a bad day at work) may create behavioural inconsistencies across an offender's crimes, and between different aspects of his or her life, making it very difficult to create an accurate profile.

Those who believe the classic trait model forms a strong basis for criminal profiling also acknowledge the "checkered past" that this model has experienced (e.g., Homant & Kennedy, 1998). However, these individuals refer to instances in which behavioural consistency has been found in the noncriminal context and highlight the fact that higher levels of behavioural consistency typically emerge when we examine pathological populations (Pinizzotto & Finkel, 1990). Assuming that most serial offenders do in fact fall into this pathological population, these supporters argue that the level of behavioural consistency that they express may be adequate to develop accurate criminal profiles. Clearly, more empirical research dealing with this issue is required before any firm conclusions can be made. Until then, the debate over the validity of criminal profiling will continue.

What Is the Impact of Ambiguous Profiles? Another common criticism of criminal profiling is that many profiles are so ambiguous that they can fit many suspects. If one of the goals of profiling is to help prioritize potential suspects, this concern clearly needs to be addressed. To examine this issue, Alison, Smith, Eastman, and Rainbow (2003) examined the content of 21 profiling reports and found that almost one-quarter (24%) of all the profiling opinions provided in these reports could be considered ambiguous (i.e., the opinion could be interpreted differently by different people). Of more direct relevance to the ambiguity criticism, however, is an interesting follow-up study conducted by Alison, Smith, and Morgan (2003), in which they examined whether ambiguous profiles could in fact be interpreted to fit more than one suspect.

Alison et al. (2003) provided details of a genuine crime to two groups of forensic professionals, including senior police detectives. The crime involved the murder of a young woman. Each group of participants was then provided with a criminal profile constructed for this case by the FBI. They were asked to read the profile and compare it to the description of a suspect. Unbeknownst to the participants, each group was provided with a different suspect description. One group was provided with the description of the genuine offender, while the other group was provided with a suspect constructed by the researchers, who was different from the genuine offender on a number of key points. For example, the genuine offender had no previous criminal convictions whereas the bogus offender had several previous convictions for assault and burglary. After comparing the profile with their suspect, each participant was asked to rate the accuracy of the profile and to state if (and why) he or she thought the profile would be operationally useful.

Despite the fact that each group received different suspect descriptions, both groups of participants rated the profile as fairly accurate, with no significant difference between the groups. In addition, both groups viewed the profile as generally useful and indicated they thought it would allow the police to narrow down the list of potential suspects and develop new lines of inquiry. This study, therefore, provides preliminary support for the criticism that ambiguous profiles can in fact be interpreted to fit more than one suspect, even when those suspects are quite different from one another. However, although such a finding could have serious implications, we must be careful in interpreting these results. For example, it would be important to know how closely the profile used in this study matches the typical criminal profile provided in the field. In addition, it should be emphasized that this study is far from realistic. For example, the crime scene details and suspect descriptions provided to the participants in this study contained much less information than would be the case in an actual police investigation. Until a more realistic study is conducted, it is difficult to know what the practical implications of the study are, but it does raise some very interesting and potentially important questions.

How Accurate Are Professional Profilers? The last criticism that we will deal with here is the possibility that professional profilers may be no more accurate in their profiling predictions than individuals who have received no specialized training. In early writings on criminal profiling, claims were even made that profilers may be no better than bartenders at predicting the characteristics of unknown offenders (Campbell, 1976). If this is in fact the case, the police must consider how much weight they will put on statements made by professional profilers. Unlike the previous two criticisms, this issue has been examined on numerous occasions and the results have been mixed (Kocsis, 2003; Pinizzotto & Finkel, 1990). In other words, profilers are sometimes found to be more accurate than other groups when asked to construct profiles under laboratory conditions, but at other times they are found to be no more accurate.

In a fairly representative study, Kocsis, Irwin, Hayes, and Nunn (2000) compared profile accuracy across five groups of individuals: profilers, psychologists, police officers, students, and psychics. All participants were provided with the details of a genuine crime, which they were asked to review. The participants were then given a series of questionnaires that dealt with various aspects of the offender's background, including his or her physical characteristics, cognitions related to the offence, pre- and post-offence behaviours, social history, and personality characteristics. The participants' task with these questionnaires was to select the alternatives that best described the unknown offender. Accuracy was determined for each group by comparing the responses from the participants with the correct answers. The results from this study are presented in Table 3.4, which indicates the mean number of questions that each group got correct for each subset of characteristics.

As you can see from this table, professional profilers were the most accurate when it came to profiling cognitive processes (e.g., degree of planning) and social history (e.g., marital status). Therefore, they have received the highest total accuracy score, which is an aggregate score for all subsets of characteristics, excluding personality predictions. On the other hand, psychologists were the most accurate when it came to profiling physical characteristics (e.g., offender age), offence behaviours (e.g., degree of control), and personality features (e.g., temperament). When the results of the four nonprofiler groups were combined, Kocsis et al. found that the combined score of the nonprofiler groups was lower than the profilers, leading them to conclude that "the collective skills of profilers are superior to the individual skills represented by each of the comparison groups" (p. 325). This result has recently been endorsed by other researchers who have reanalyzed the data using sophisticated statistical techniques (Snook, Eastwood, Gendreau, Goggin, & Cullen, 2007). However, given the preliminary nature of these sorts of studies, the marginal accuracy differences

Table 3.4 Comparing Profilers, Psychologists, Police Officers, Students, and Psychics*

Measure	Profilers	Psychologists	Police	Students	Psychics
Cognitions	3.20	2.27	2.49	2.03	2.60
Physical	3.60	3.63	3.43	3.42	2.80
Offence	4.00	4.03	3.09	3.64	3.65
Social	3.00	2.63	2.60	2.94	2.25
Total	13.80	12.57	11.60	12.03	11.30
Personality	24.60	34.03	22.03	26.84	27.70

*Numbers refer to the mean number of correct questions. The number of correct questions that participants could have predicted was 7 for cognitions, 6 for physical characteristics, 7 for offence behaviours, and 10 for social history (total accuracy is, therefore, out of 30). Kocsis and colleagues did not provide information relating to the total number of correct predictions for personality characteristics.
Source: Adapted from Kocsis et al., 2000.

between groups, and the fact that other researchers have sometimes found little support for the accuracy of professional profilers, it seems likely that the debate over whether professional profilers can provide more accurate profiles than untrained individuals will continue (Bennell, Jones, Taylor, & Snook, 2006).

OTHER TYPES OF PROFILING

In addition to criminal profiling, two other forms of profiling are commonly used by the police: geographic profiling and racial profiling. As we shall see, the widespread use of racial profiling has recently been a hot topic in the news.

Geographic Profiling

Geographic profiling: An investigative technique that uses crime scene locations to predict the most likely area where an offender resides

Geographic profiling is used frequently by the police to help them investigate serial crimes more efficiently. In simple terms, geographic profiling uses crime scene locations to predict the most likely area where the offender resides (Rossmo, 2000). As is the case with criminal profiling, geographic profiling is used most often in cases of serial homicide and rape, though it has also been used in cases of serial robbery, arson, and burglary. Geographic profiling is used primarily for prioritizing potential suspects. This is accomplished by rank ordering the suspects based on how close they live to the predicted home location, so the suspect who lives closest to the predicted home location would be focused on first (Rossmo, 2000). This is an important task, considering the number of suspects who can enter a serial crime investigation. For example, in the Green River serial murder case in Washington State, which was solved in 2001, the police collected more than 18 000 suspect names (Rossmo, 1995).

The basic assumption behind geographic profiling is that most serial offenders do not travel far from home to commit their crimes and, therefore, it should be possible to make a reasonably accurate prediction about where an offender lives. Fortunately for the geographic profiler, research supports this assumption. Perhaps surprisingly, it turns out that serial offenders tend to be consistent in their crime site selection choices, often committing their crimes very close to where they reside (Rossmo, 2000). Indeed, even many of the most bizarre serial killers commit their crimes close to home (Canter, Coffey, Huntley, & Missen, 2000). For travelling offenders, geographic profiling is typically not a useful investigative strategy but, for the majority of serial offenders who do commit their crimes locally, a number of profiling strategies can be used (Snook, Zito, Bennell, & Taylor, 2005).

One of the first cases in which geographic profiling techniques were used was the case of the Yorkshire Ripper in England. After five years of unsolved murders, an advisory team was set up to review the investigation. Although some on the investigative team felt the offender lived in a different part of the country from where the crimes were happening (due largely to one of the voluntary false confessions discussed earlier), the advisory team believed the offender was a local man. To provide support for this claim, the advisory team constructed a type of geographic profile (Kind, 1987). They plotted the 17 Ripper murders onto a map and calculated the centre of gravity for the points. That is, by adding up the x-y coordinates for each crime and dividing by the 17 crimes, they could calculate the x-y coordinate for the centre of gravity. In this case, the centre of gravity was near Bradford, a city close to where the majority of the murders had taken place. When Peter Sutcliffe was eventually arrested for the crimes, he was found to reside in a district of Bradford.

During the 1990s, a number of individuals built computerized **geographic profiling systems** that could assist with the profiling task. One of these individuals was Dr. Kim Rossmo, who is profiled in Box 3.5. The locations of linked crime sites are input into these systems and are represented as points on a map. The systems then perform calculations using mathematical models of offender spatial behaviour, which reflect the probability that the offender lives at particular points in the area where the offences have taken place. Every single location on the map is assigned an overall probability and these

Geographic profiling systems: Computer systems that use mathematical models of offender spatial behaviour to make predictions about where unknown serial offenders are likely to reside

Box 3.5

Canadian Researcher Profile: Dr. Kim Rossmo

Dr. Kim Rossmo had been a police officer with the Vancouver Police Department for 16 years when he became the first Canadian police officer to get his Ph.D. in criminology. At Simon Fraser University in Burnaby, B.C., Rossmo began his doctoral studies with Paul Brantingham, a well-known environmental criminologist. Drawing on his background in mathematics and his experience as a streetwise police officer, Rossmo decided to take what was known about offender spatial behaviour from fields like environmental criminology and put them to practical use by developing an investigative tool for predicting where unknown serial offenders are likely to live.

After years of research, Rossmo developed an approach he called geographic profiling and designed a computer system named Rigel, which is now one of the most sought-after investigative tools by police agencies around the world. Dr. Rossmo is regularly called in to assist with serial crime investigations by the RCMP, the FBI, and Scotland Yard. Based on his most recent estimation, he has consulted on over 200 cases, ranging from murders to bombings to

robberies. One of his most recent cases was the high-profile Washington sniper case, which proved to be a particularly interesting and difficult case for geographic profiling because of the transient nature of the suspects.

After working as a detective inspector in charge of the Geographic Profiling Section of the Vancouver Police Department for a number of years, Dr. Rossmo moved on to serve a two-year term as the director of research for the prestigious Police Foundation in Washington, D.C. Dr. Rossmo now calls Texas State University home, where he directs the Center for Geospatial Intelligence and Investigation in the Department of Criminal Justice.

In addition to his ongoing consultancy work, Dr. Rossmo continues to conduct research on geographic profiling and is expanding his focus to deal with other issues of importance. He is currently engaged in research projects exploring the spatial patterns of illegal border crossing, insurgency attacks, and terrorist planning. Recently, he completed a collaborative study using Rigel to study the foraging patterns of great white shark attacks off the coast of South Africa. This year, he plans to finish a book on criminal investigative failures and their causes. When asked where he sees the field going in the future, he replied that environmental criminology research has the potential to provide immediate solutions to problems in public safety and homeland security.

Dr. Rossmo has been the recipient of many awards for his achievements as a police officer and an academic, and he made an appearance as a character in the crime novel *Burnt Bones* by Michael Slade. He is the author of numerous articles and *Geographic Profiling*, the first book on the subject. This text provides an excellent example of how academic research can successfully be applied to real-world policing problems.

probabilities are designated a colour. For example, the top 10% of probabilities might be assigned the colour red, and so on. The eventual output is a coloured map, in which each colour band corresponds to the probability that the offender lives in the area (see Figure 3.2). The police use this map to prioritize their investigative activities. Geographic profilers also consider other factors that may affect an offender's spatial behaviour, such as the density of suitable victims in an area, but this probability map forms the basis of their prediction.

Whether these computerized geographic profiling systems are necessary for constructing accurate profiles, or whether less sophisticated and potentially more-cost effective alternatives are possible, is a question that has recently begun to be explored (see Bennell, Taylor, & Snook, 2007, for a review of this issue). For example, Snook, Taylor, and Bennell (2004) examined whether individuals trained to use simple **heuristics** (e.g., predicting that serial offenders will live close to the locations of the majority of their crimes) would make profiling predictions that are as accurate as computerized systems. In that study, they found that, even before any training, approximately 50% of participants made predictions that were as accurate as a computerized system. After training, there was

Heuristics: Simple general rules that can be used to make decisions and solve problems. In some instances, a reliance on heuristics can result in biased decisions. In other cases, heuristics can result in reasonably accurate decisions.

Figure 3.2 A Computerized Geographic Profile

The black dots represent the crime locations and the different coloured bands (represented here by different shades of grey) correspond to the probability that the offender resides in that particular geographic area. The high-priority search area in this case centres on the four crimes in the upper half of the map.

no difference between the average accuracy of the participants and the system, when accuracy was measured by calculating the distance between the actual and predicted home location. Such findings have resulted in a debate over the relative merits of various profiling approaches (e.g., Rossmo, 2005), and research is currently being conducted in an attempt to resolve this debate.

Racial Profiling

Recently, it has also become clear that the police engage in another form of profiling—**racial profiling**. Unlike criminal profiling or geographic profiling, racial profiling refers to any police-initiated action that relies on the race or ethnicity of an individual, rather than that individual's criminal behaviour (Ramirez, McDevitt, & Farrell, 2000). According to Harris (1999a), one of the most common forms of racial profiling is the police practice of stopping and searching vehicles (for drugs and weapons usually) because the driver does not "match" the vehicle he or she is driving (see Box 3.6 for a Canadian example).

Racial profiling: Police-initiated action that relies on the race or ethnicity of an individual, rather than that individual's criminal behaviour

Due to some high-profile cases (e.g., *Wilkins v. Maryland State Police*, 1999), racial profiling is beginning to get more attention from researchers, the police, and the media. This attention appears to be warranted, at least in certain cases, given the results of

---

Box 3.6

A Canadian Example of Racial Profiling

On November 1, 1999, Decovan "Dee" Brown, a young black man and then Toronto Raptors basketball player, was arrested in Toronto for driving a motor vehicle while under the influence of alcohol (*R. v. Brown*, 2002). Before he was stopped, Brown was speeding slightly in his Ford Expedition. At trial, Brown's lawyer alleged that "Mr. Brown was arbitrarily stopped by the investigating officer because of racial profiling rather than for driving at a speed slightly in excess of the posted speed limit" (*R. v. Brown*, 2002, para. 2). According to Brown's lawyer, "the arrest . . . was based on the stereotypical assumption that young black men who are driving expensive motor vehicles obtained them by crime or are implicated in recent criminal activity" (para. 2).

Despite the fact that the defence had evidence to support their allegation that the police officer in this case had used racial profiling, the trial judge dismissed it, indicating that he found the allegations "nasty" and "malicious" (*R. v. Brown*, 2002, para. 2). In addition, the judge's remarks made during sentencing referred to his "distaste for the matters that were raised during the course of the trial"

(para. 20), and he suggested that the defendant "might extend an apology to the officer because [the judge was] satisfied the allegations [were] completely unwarranted" (para. 20).

On appeal, the Ontario Supreme Court stressed that judges "must be particularly vigilant in their efforts to impartially determine applications like this one" (*R. v. Brown*, 2002, para. 18). The court also indicated that "judges must be particularly sensitive to the need to . . . be fair to all Canadians of every race, religion, nationality and ethnic origin" (para. 19). On Brown's appeal, the Ontario Supreme Court ruled that many of the judge's comments to Brown and his lawyer during the trial were completely inappropriate and that the trial judge did not appear to understand the importance of some of the evidence. For example, the Court stated that for a judge to regard an application as distasteful "is materially inconsistent with the duty of a judge to hear and determine the application with an open mind" (para. 20). Ultimately, the Ontario Supreme Court ruled that the appeal by Brown should be allowed and a new trial was ordered.

---

recent public surveys. These surveys confirm that the majority of U.S. citizens believe the police actively engage in racial profiling. This seems to be the case regardless of the respondent's race. For example, a 1999 Gallup Poll indicated that 56% of whites and 77% of blacks believe that racial profiling is pervasive (Gallup Poll, 1999). What appears to differ by race, however, is the percentage of people who believe they have been the target of racial profiling. For example, results from the same Gallup Poll indicate that only 6% of white men believe they have been stopped by the police based on their race alone, versus 42% of black men, and this percentage increases further for black men between the ages of 18 and 34.

Anecdotal accounts and empirical research also confirm that racial profiling is practised by some U.S. police agencies (Ramirez et al., 2000). For example, Lamberth (1999) conducted an analysis of police stop and searches in Maryland. Using data from the Maryland State Police, he compared the drivers who were stopped and searched along a major highway in Maryland with those who were actually violating traffic laws. According to Harris (1999b), who discussed Lamberth's study in some detail, approximately 74% of Lamberth's "law violator" sample consisted of white individuals while only 17.5% were black individuals. More important, a staggering 79.2% of the drivers who were stopped and searched were black. Studies in other countries provide similar findings (Home Office, 1998).

Of course, the possibility exists that such behaviour simply reflects an accurate perception on the part of the police that members of some minority groups are more likely to be involved in illegal activity. Existing research, however, often does not support this assumption. In Lamberth's (1999) study, for example, he found that a similar percentage of black and white drivers who were stopped and searched were actually found with drugs in their possession (28.4% and 28.8%, respectively) (cited by Harris, 1999b). Other research also supports these findings (Fitzgerald, 1999). It appears, therefore, that racial profiling is not a valid police procedure in certain police jurisdictions, and some U.S. police forces have started to implement policies in an attempt to reduce the use of this sort of profiling.

What is the situation in Canada? As in the United States, there certainly have been allegations of racial profiling being used by Canadian police agencies—most notably the Toronto Police Service—and these allegations have led to a frenzy of newspaper articles (e.g., Blatchford, 2003; Fowlie, 2004; Rankin, Quinn, Shephard, Simmie, & Duncanson, 2002). Unfortunately, the same cannot be said about published research articles. In fact, there is, as of yet, little empirical research in Canada that examines the issue of racial profiling, and efforts to remedy this situation are often hindered by the fact that Canadian police agencies often do not collect the sort of data (e.g., race statistics) that is required to conduct such research. The relatively small amount of research that does exist on the topic is difficult to interpret (Gabor, 2004; Melchers, 2003; Wortley & Tanner, 2005), making it virtually impossible to determine whether, and to what degree, this form of profiling is actually used in Canada. Currently, it seems safe to say that the general perception is that racial profiling does exist in Canada, at least to some degree, and that, even if it does not, the perception that it exists by minority groups is cause for serious concern (Ontario Human Rights Commission, 2007).

SUMMARY

1. The police attempt to achieve two goals when conducting interrogations: to gain information that furthers the investigation and to obtain a confession from the suspect. Police officers in North America use the Reid model of interrogation to interrogate suspects. This model advocates the use of psychologically based interrogation tactics to break down a suspect's resistance to telling the truth. The tactics used in the Reid model of interrogation can be broken down into minimization and maximization techniques.

2. The three potential problems with the Reid model of interrogation are (1) the inability of police officers to accurately detect deception, (2) biases that result from presuming a suspect is guilty, and (3) an increased likelihood that suspects will make false confessions.

3. False confessions must be differentiated from retracted confessions and disputed confessions. A false confession is one that is either intentionally fabricated or is not based on actual knowledge of the facts in a case. A retracted confession is simply an individual's statement that his or her confession is false. A disputed confession is one that is disputed at trial, often because of a legal technicality or because the suspect disputes the confession was ever made.

4. There are three types of false confessions, each having its own set of vulnerability factors. Voluntary false confessions occur when someone voluntarily confesses to a crime he or she did not commit without any elicitation from the police. Coerced-compliant false confessions are those in which the suspect confesses to a crime, even though the suspect is fully aware that he or she did not commit it. Coerced-internalized false confessions consist of individuals confessing to a crime they did not commit—and subsequently coming to the belief they committed the crime—usually after they are exposed to highly suggestible questions.

5. Criminal profiling is used frequently by the police in serial crime investigations. They use it for prioritizing suspects, developing new lines of inquiry, setting traps to flush out offenders, determining whether an offender's actions should be taken seriously, giving advice on how to interrogate suspects, and developing courtroom strategies. Despite its widespread use, criminal profiling is often criticized. One major criticism centres on the lack of a strong theoretical base underlying the approach. A second criticism relates to the fact that many profiles contain ambiguous information and this may cause problems when police officers are asked to interpret the profile. A third criticism is that professionally trained profilers may be no better than other individuals at constructing accurate profiles.

6. The police also use two other types of profiling. Geographic profiling is defined as any technique that uses crime scene locations to predict the most likely area where the offender resides. Racial profiling refers to any police-initiated action that relies on the race or ethnicity of an individual, rather than that individual's criminal behaviour.

Key Concepts

classic trait model 79

coerced-compliant false confession 66

coerced-internalized false confession 67

compliance 68

confabulation 71

criminal profiling 73

deception detection 60

deductive criminal profiling 76

disputed confession 65

false confession 64

geographic profiling 82

geographic profiling systems 83

Gudjonsson Compliance Scale 69

Gudjonsson Suggestibility Scale 69

heuristics 84

inductive criminal profiling 77

internalization 71

investigator bias 61

linkage blindness 76

maximization techniques 60

minimization techniques 60

organized-disorganized model 77

police interrogation 57

racial profiling 85

Reid model 58

retracted confession 65

shift 69

suggestibility 68

VICLAS 76

voluntary false confession 65

yield 69

Discussion Questions

1. Imagine that you are a criminal profiler and have been called in by the police to give them advice on how to conduct a police interrogation. In particular, they want to know how far they can go to get a confession from a suspect, while at the same time making sure the confession will be admissible in court. What advice would you give to them?

2. Many police agencies now video-record their interrogations, thus presenting potential advantages for the police, suspects, and the courts. Do you see any potential problems with using this procedure? What are some other possible ways to minimize the problems that result from modern-day interrogation practices?

3. Because the Reid model of interrogation can increase the degree to which people falsely confess to crimes, people seem to agree that it should not be used with particular individuals (e.g., those who have a severe learning disability). However, few police agencies have policies in place to indicate when it is not appropriate to use the Reid model. Put yourself in the role of a police psychologist and develop a set of recommendations for when the technique should and shouldn't be used.

4. Researchers are now using laboratory-based studies in an attempt to understand the processes involved when people confess to crimes they did not commit. Do you think this is problematic? Why or why not?

5. You are a criminal profiler who uses the inductive approach to profiling. You encounter a series of crimes in which the offender consistently attacks elderly women in their apartments at night. How would you go about constructing a profile in this case? What sorts of problems would a deductive profiler have with your profile? How could you attempt to counter some of the arguments?

6. A number of studies have found that people view ambiguous criminal profiles as accurate even when they are asked to rate their accuracy against different suspects. Researchers

have claimed that this occurs because people are able to creatively re-interpret ambiguous profiles to make them fit any number of potential suspects. What other factors could contribute to this finding?

7. Geographic profiling works in large part because offenders commit most of their crimes close to home. Why do you think offenders do this?

Readings

Gudjonsson, G.H. (2003). *The psychology of interrogations and confessions: A handbook.* West Sussex, UK: John Wiley & Sons.

Hicks, S.J., & Sales, B.D. (2006). *Criminal profiling: Developing an effective science and practice.* Washington, DC: American Psychological Association.

Kassin, S.M., & Gudjonsson, G.H. (2004). The psychology of confessions: A review of the literature and issues. *Psychological Science in the Public Interest, 5,* 33–67.

Websites

The Homepage of the Reid Model of Interrogation
www.reid.com/index.html

Police Interrogations and Confessions
www.williams.edu/Psychology/Faculty/Kassin/research/confessions.htm

Criminal Profiling Site
www.corpus-delicti.com

Chapter 4
Deception

Learning Objectives

- Describe the different types of polygraph tests.

- List the three types of studies used to examine the accuracy of the polygraph.

- Describe the most common types of errors made by the Control Question Test (CQT) and the Guilty Knowledge Test (GKT).

- Describe physiologically based alternatives to the polygraph, including event-related brain potentials and functional brain-imaging techniques, and state their pros and cons.

- Outline the vocal and nonvocal characteristics of deception.

- Define malingering and list the three explanatory models of malingering.

- Differentiate among the types of studies used to examine malingering.

- Indicate how you might detect that someone has malingering psychosis and amnesia.

Dimitri Adonis is in trouble. He is a suspect in a vicious attack that occurred outside a popular nightclub. He was seen driving away from the scene of the attack. He has been asked by the police to take a polygraph exam. On the date of the first scheduled test, he tells the polygraph examiner that he has a bad cold. The police examiner asks him to come back the following week to take the exam. At the next exam, his numerical score is −10. The police examiner informs him of his deceptive scoring and attempts to obtain a confession from him about his role in the attack. Dimitri maintains that he is innocent and the polygraph must be wrong.

How do we know whether someone is telling the truth or lying? A person may lie to the police about his or her involvement in a crime, lie to a psychologist about psychological symptoms, or lie to a probation officer by claiming to be following conditional release requirements. Several techniques have been developed to try to answer this question. As seen in Chapter 3, police attempt to detect whether or not someone is telling them the truth during an interrogation. Psychologists have participated in the development and testing of a variety of techniques to detect deception. In this chapter, we focus on several issues associated with deception, including the use of the polygraph and alternatives to the polygraph, the relationship between verbal and nonverbal cues to deception, the use of deception by children, and methods for detecting the malingering of mental disorders.

THE POLYGRAPH TECHNIQUE

Physiological measures have long been used in an attempt to detect deception. For example, at one time the Chinese forced suspects to chew on dry rice powder and then to spit it out. If the powder was dry, the suspect was judged to be lying (Kleinmuntz & Szucko, 1984). The rationale for this technique was that anxiety causes a person's mouth to be dry. A person telling the truth would not be anxious and, therefore, would not have a dry mouth. In contrast, a person lying would be anxious and would have a dry mouth. Polygraphy relies on the same underlying principle: deception is associated with physiological change. The origins of modern polygraphy date from 1917 when William Marston, a Harvard psychologist also trained as a lawyer, developed a systolic blood pressure test (Iacono & Patrick, 1999) and attempted to use this physiological response as evidence for a person's innocence (see Lykken, 1998). Marston's testimony was rejected by the courts in *Frye v. United States* (1923) because they felt the test had not gained acceptance by the scientific community, foreshadowing the debate associated with physiological measures that continues to the present day.

A **polygraph** (the word is a combination of two Greek words, *poly* = "many," and *grapho* = "write") is a device for recording an individual's autonomic nervous system responses. Measurement devices are attached to the upper chest and abdomen to measure breathing. The amount of sweat on the skin is measured by attaching electrodes to the fingertips. Sweat changes the conductance of the skin, which is known as the galvanic skin response. Finally, heart rate is measured by a partially inflated blood pressure cuff attached to an arm. Each of these measures is amplified and can be printed out on paper or stored in a computer to be analyzed. In a forensic context, a polygraph is used to measure a person's physiological responses to questions asked by an examiner.

Polygraph: A device for recording an individual's autonomic nervous system responses

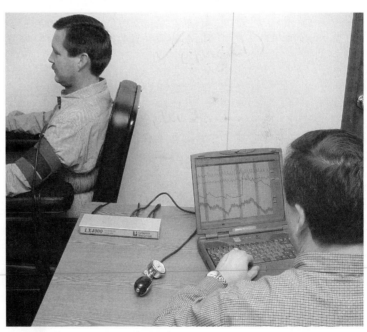

In Canada, polygraph training is provided by the Canadian Police College. In the United States, there are independent polygraph schools that can be accredited by the American Polygraph Association. The polygraph course at the Canadian Police College is restricted to police officers. The college offers a 12-week intensive course that covers the various techniques, interviewing practices, and scoring.

A suspect being given a polygraph test

Applications of the Polygraph Test

Polygraph tests are used for a range of purposes. In Canada, they are often used by the police to help in their criminal investigations. The police may ask a suspect to take a polygraph test as a means to resolve the case. If the suspect fails the polygraph test, that person may be pressured to confess, thereby giving the police incriminating evidence. Although not common, police may ask alleged victims of crimes to take a polygraph test to help verify whether a crime has occurred. Insurance companies may request a polygraph test to verify the claims of the insured. More recently, the polygraph has been used in the United States to assess and monitor sexual offenders on probation. **Polygraph disclosure tests** are used to uncover information about an offender's past behaviour. Polygraph tests are also used to determine whether the offender is violating the conditions of probation or used to test for evidence of risky behaviour, such as sexual fantasies about children.

The most widespread applications of polygraph testing in the United States were for the periodic testing of employees to identify those engaged in theft or using drugs at work and for the screening of prospective employees to weed out those with criminal tendencies or substance-abuse problems. However, the Employee Polygraph Protection Act of 1988 restricted private companies from using the polygraph for these purposes and limited the use of the polygraph to specific investigations of job-related wrongdoing. Nonetheless, governmental agencies in the United States and Canada still use the polygraph as a general screening tool. For example, some police departments require applicants to take a polygraph test, and the Canadian Security Intelligence Service (CSIS) also requires that its potential employees take a polygraph test in order to assess "the candidate's reliability and loyalty."

Types of Polygraph Tests

The polygraph does not detect lies per se, since the physiological states associated with lying share much in common with many other states, including anxiety, anger, embarrassment, and fear. Instead, polygraph tests rely on measuring physiological responses to different types of questions. Some questions are designed to elicit a larger physiological response in guilty individuals than in those who are innocent. The three main types of polygraph tests are reviewed below.

The Relevant/Irrelevant Test First developed in 1917 by William Marston and later refined by John Larson (1921) for use in criminal investigations, the **Relevant/Irrelevant Test** includes only two types of questions: relevant questions concerning the crime in question (e.g., Did you steal the rare gold coin?) and irrelevant questions that are unrelated to the crime (e.g., Is today Monday?). If an individual's physiological responses were larger to relevant questions than to irrelevant questions, this would be interpreted as a pattern consistent with deceptiveness. The major problem with this test is that nearly everyone responds more to the relevant questions than to the irrelevant questions. This test is no longer used in law enforcement. However, for employee screening, a version of this test called the Relevant/Irrelevant technique is used. In these tests, potential and current employees are asked about such areas as drug use, antisocial acts, rule breaking, and honesty.

The Control Question Test The **Control Question Test** (CQT) is the most commonly used test to investigate criminal acts. The typical CQT includes a pretest interview, followed by a series of questions administered while the suspect's physiological responses are measured (usually three separate question sequences are asked). The polygraph examiner then scores the charts and ends the CQT with a post-test interview in which the test results are discussed.

Polygraph disclosure tests: Polygraph tests that are used to uncover information about an offender's past behaviour

Relevant/Irrelevant Test: Type of polygraph test that includes relevant questions concerning the crime being investigated and irrelevant questions that are unrelated to the crime

Control Question Test: Type of polygraph test that includes irrelevant questions that are unrelated to the crime, relevant questions concerning the crime being investigated, and control questions concerning the person's honesty and past history prior to the event being investigated

A critical component of this technique is the pretest interview. During the pretest interview, the polygraph examiner develops the control questions, learns about the background of the suspect, and attempts to convince the suspect of the accuracy of the polygraph test. The examiner will do this by quoting very high accuracy rates and conducting a stimulation test. For example, the suspect will pick a card with a number on it from a deck of cards, and the examiner will determine the number by examining the polygraph chart. The deck of cards is rigged so the examiner knows which card the suspect picked.

The examiner then asks ten questions to be answered with either "yes" or "no." Table 4.1 provides an example of a typical question series used in a CQT. Three types of questions are asked. Irrelevant questions, referring to the respondent's identity or personal background (e.g., Is your first name Beatrice?) are included as a baseline but are not scored. Relevant and control questions establish guilt or innocence. Relevant questions deal with the crime being investigated (e.g., "On June 12, did you stab your ex-wife?"). Control questions are designed to be emotionally arousing for all respondents and typically focus on the person's honesty and past history prior to the event being investigated (e.g., "Before the age of 45, did you ever try to seriously hurt someone?"). Polygraph examiners assume they can detect deception by comparing reactions to the relevant and control questions. Guilty suspects are assumed to react more to relevant questions than control questions. In contrast, innocent suspects are assumed to react more to control questions than relevant questions. The reasoning behind these assumptions is that innocent people know they are telling the truth about the relevant question so they will react more strongly to general questions about their honesty and past history.

Examiners in the past used global scoring, incorporating all available information—including physiological responses, the suspect's demeanour during the examination, and information in the case file—to make a decision about the guilt or innocence of the suspect. Most examiners now numerically score the charts to ensure that decisions are based

Table 4.1 Typical Question Series Used in a Control Question Test	
Type of Question	**Questions**
Irrelevant	Do you understand that I will be asking only questions we have discussed before?
Irrelevant	Do you live in Canada?
Control	Between the ages of 18 and 28, did you ever deliberately plan to physically hurt someone?
Relevant	Did you stab Petunia Bottoms on the night of March 10?
Irrelevant	Is your first name Craig?
Control	Prior to 2003, did you ever verbally threaten to hurt anyone?
Relevant	Did you use a knife to stab Petunia Bottoms?
Irrelevant	Were you born in November?
Control	During the first 28 years of your life, did you ever do anything illegal?
Relevant	On March 10, did you participate, in any way, in the stabbing of Petunia Bottoms?

solely on the physiological responses. For each control/relevant pair, a score is assigned for each separate physiological measure. A +1 to +3 is assigned if the response to the control question is larger (the larger the difference, the higher the score). If the response for the relevant question is larger than that for the control question, a score between −1 and −3 is assigned. A 0 is assigned if the responses to the questions are identical. A total score is obtained by summing these scores across the physiological measures and the tests, with a positive score of +5 or greater indicating a truthful outcome, a negative score of more than −5 indicating a deceptive outcome, and scores between +5 and −5 considered inconclusive. During the post-test interview, the examiner tells the suspect the outcome, and if the outcome is deceptive the examiner attempts to elicit a confession.

Several psychologists have questioned the underlying rationale of the CQT (Cross & Saxe, 2001; Furedy, 1996; Iacono & Patrick, 2006). Imagine yourself being falsely accused of a serious crime and taking a polygraph exam. Being innocent, you might react more strongly to questions about a crime that you could get punished for (i.e., relevant questions) than about vague questions concerning your past behaviour (i.e., control questions). In contrast, guilty suspects might actually respond more to control questions because they are novel or because they believe they have other crimes to hide. In addition, the guilty suspect may no longer react to the crime-relevant questions because he or she may have been asked repeatedly about it. The validity of the CQT is discussed later in the chapter.

The Guilty Knowledge Test Developed by Lykken (1960), the **Guilty Knowledge Test** (GKT) does not assess deception but instead seeks to determine whether the suspect knows details about a crime that only the person who committed the crime would know. The general form of the GKT is a series of questions in multiple-choice format. Each question has one correct option (often called the *critical option*) and four options that are foils—alternatives that could fit the crime but that are incorrect. A GKT question in the context of a homicide might take the following form: "If you were the one who robbed the bank, then you will know what was used as a weapon. Was the weapon (a) a knife, (b) an axe, (c) a shotgun, (d) a revolver, or (e) a rifle?" The guilty suspect is assumed to display a larger physiological response to the correct option than to the incorrect options. An innocent person, conversely, who does not know the details of the crime, will not have a larger physiological response to the correct option than to any of the other options.

Underlying the GKT is the principle that people will react more strongly to information they recognize as distinctive or important than to unimportant information. Suspects who consistently respond to critical items are assumed to have knowledge of the crime. The likelihood that an innocent person with no knowledge of the crime would react most strongly to the critical alternative is one in five for each question. If ten questions are asked, the odds that an innocent person will consistently react to the critical alternative are exceedingly small (less than 1 in 10 000 000).

The most common physiological response measured when administering the GKT is palmar sweating (i.e., galvanic skin response measured in the palm of the hand). In recent years, two other responses have been studied in the lab. Preliminary research suggests that response times to questions can accurately identify participants with guilty knowledge (Seymour, Seifert, Shafto, & Mosmann, 2000). Some researchers have also investigated using eye blinks as an index of guilty knowledge (Fukuda, 2001; Thonney, Kanachi, Sasaki, & Hatayama, 2005).

Guilty Knowledge Test: Type of polygraph test designed to determine if the person knows details about a crime

Although the GKT is not used routinely by law enforcement in Canada or the United States, it is used regularly in a limited number of other jurisdictions, such as Israel and Japan (Ben-Shakhar & Furedy, 1990). Iacono and Patrick (1999) suggest two reasons for the lack of widespread acceptance of the GKT. First, since polygraph examiners believe in the accuracy of the CQT, they are not motivated to use the more difficult-to-construct GKT. Second, in order to use the GKT, there must be salient features of the crime only known to the perpetrator. If details of a crime appear in the media, the crime-related details given cannot be used to construct a GKT.

Validity of Polygraph Techniques

Types of Studies How is the accuracy of polygraph tests assessed? Accuracy is determined under ideal circumstances by presenting information known to be true and false to an individual and measuring his or her corresponding physiological responses. In practice, studies assessing the validity of polygraph techniques vary in how closely they are able to achieve this ideal. Studies of the validity of polygraph techniques can be classified into three types: laboratory, field, and field-analogue studies.

In laboratory studies, volunteers (often university students) simulate criminal behaviour by committing a mock crime. Volunteers come to a laboratory and are randomly assigned to one of two conditions: committing a mock crime or not committing a mock crime. The main advantage of these studies is that the experimenter knows **ground truth** (i.e., who is truly guilty or innocent). In addition, laboratory studies can also compare the relative merits of different types of polygraph tests and control for variables such as the time between crime and polygraph exam. However, because of the large motivational and emotional differences between volunteers in laboratory studies and actual suspects in real-life situations, the results of laboratory studies may have limited application to real-life situations. In laboratory studies, guilty participants cannot ethically be given strong incentives to "beat" the polygraph, and both guilty and innocent participants have little to fear if they "fail" the polygraph exam.

Field studies involve real-life situations and actual criminal suspects, together with actual polygraph examinations. Field studies often compare the accuracy of "original" examiners to "blind" evaluators. Original examiners conduct the actual evaluation of the suspect. Blind evaluators are provided only with the original examiner's charts and given no information about the suspect or case. Original examiners are exposed to extra-polygraph cues—information about the case in addition to that obtained via the polygraph—such as the case facts and the behaviour of the suspect during the examination. Although polygraph examiners are taught to ignore these cues, Patrick and Iacono (1991) found that examiners are nonetheless significantly influenced by these cues.

The largest problem with field studies is establishing ground truth. Indicators of guilt, such as physical evidence, eyewitness testimony, or DNA evidence, may not always be available. In such situations, truth is more difficult to establish. To deal with this problem, two additional ways of establishing ground truth have been developed: judicial outcomes and confessions. Judicial outcomes are problematic because some people are falsely convicted and some guilty people are not convicted. Confessions are also problematic. Although rare, some people may falsely confess. More significant, however, is the problem that confessions are often not independent from the polygraph examiner's decisions.

Ground truth: As applied to polygraph research, the knowledge of whether the person is actually guilty or innocent

Confessions are often elicited because a person fails a polygraph exam. Moreover, cases in which a guilty suspect beats the polygraph are not included in research studies. Thus, reliance on confessions to establish ground truth likely inflates polygraph accuracy rates (Iacono & Patrick, 2006). Most field studies have used confessions to establish ground truth.

The last type of study is the field-analogue study. In this type of study, the act of deception is freely committed by an individual, it is independently known which individuals committed the act, the individuals are concerned about the outcome of the polygraph test, and the polygrapher does not know the proportion of guilty and innocent individuals in the sample. One concern that is raised when conducting such studies is whether the practice is ethical. Is it fair to use such extreme deception? An example of a field-analogue polygraph study by Ginton, Daie, Elaad, and Ben-Shakhar (1982) is described next.

Polygraph Tests: Accurate or Not? The accuracy of the polygraph for detecting lies is controversial. Numerous laboratory studies have assessed the accuracy of the CQT and GKT (see Iacono & Patrick, 1999, for a review). However, as pointed out above, there are problems when relying on typical mock crime scenarios to estimate real-life accuracy. As a consequence, only field and field-analogue assessments of the CQT will be described here. The situation concerning the GKT is different. Since the GKT is almost never used in Canada or the United States, no relevant North American data are available. Thus, we will describe assessments of the GKT based on laboratory and field studies done in Israel.

Although the CQT has been investigated for more than 30 years, its ability to accurately measure deception remains controversial (Furedy, 1996; National Research Council, 2003). Most of the studies have used confessions to classify suspects as guilty or innocent, and as noted above, there are problems with using this as the criterion. Most guilty suspects (84% to 92%) are correctly classified as guilty (Patrick & Iacono, 1991; Raskin, Honts, & Kircher, 1997). However, the picture for innocent suspects is less optimistic, with accuracy rates ranging from 55% to 78% (Honts & Raskin, 1988; Patrick & Iacono, 1991). Many of the innocent suspects were classified as inconclusive. Between 9% and 24% of innocent suspects were falsely identified as guilty. Such a high false-positive rate indicates that innocent people respond more to relevant than control questions, suggesting that the premise underlying the CQT does not apply to all suspects.

Table 4.2 presents data from several field studies comparing the accuracy of the original examiner with the blind evaluators. The accuracy rates of the original examiner are

Table 4.2 Field Studies of the Control Question Test*						
Study	**Guilty Condition**			**Innocent Condition**		
	Guilty	*Innocent*	*Inconclusive*	*Guilty*	*Innocent*	*Inconclusive*
Honts &	92%	8%	0%	0%	91%	9%
Raskin (1988)	(92%)	(8%)	(0%)	(15%)	(62%)	(23%)
Patrick &	98%	0%	2%	8%	73%	19%
Iacono (1991)	(92%)	(2%)	(6%)	(24%)	(30%)	(46%)

*Blind examiners' results appear in parentheses.

higher than the accuracy of the blind evaluator, especially for innocent suspects. For example, Patrick and Iacono (1991) examined the accuracy of original examiner opinions to blind scoring for 37 innocent verified cases. The hit rate (in this context, cases classified as innocent when actually innocent, excluding inconclusives) for original examiners was 90%, compared with 55% for blind scorers. The main reason original examiners are more accurate than blind examiners is that the original examiners appear to be using extra-polygraph cues (such as the attitude of the suspect, other evidence about the case, and verbal cues), whereas blind chart evaluators have access only to polygraph information. Additional research is needed to confirm the source of these extra-polygraphic cues used by examiners.

Ginton et al. (1982) evaluated the CQT in a field-analogue study in which 21 police officers attending a police course served as participants. Given the opportunity to cheat on an aptitude test, seven officers cheated while scoring their tests. After several days had elapsed, the officers were told that some of them were suspected of cheating on the test. All 21 officers were asked to take a polygraph test to prove they had not cheated. Two guilty and one innocent officer refused. In addition, three of the other guilty officers confessed to cheating prior to the polygraph test. The 15 remaining officers—two who had cheated and 13 who had not—were administered a polygraph test. The rate of correct identifications using blind evaluators was quite low—only 1 of the 2 guilty officers and 7 out of the 13 innocent officers were correctly identified. After the polygraph exam, all the officers were told they had participated in a study and that the results would be used only for research purposes. Two important issues are raised by this type of research. First, to surmount the limited emotional impact typical of laboratory studies, Ginton and colleagues used a realistic event to create a meaningful and high-impact emotional effect in their participants. Second, deception is typically required in order to produce the required emotional effect. The researchers argued they needed to use deception in order to provide a more real-life test of the polygraph.

Not all research is critical of the CQT, however. Several studies indicate that the accuracy of the CQT can be enhanced by using objective scoring methods (Gordon et al., 2006; Kircher & Raskin, 1988) and that these methods can generalize from laboratory to field settings (Pollina, Dollins, Senter, Krapohl, & Ryan, 2004). Kircher and Raskin (1988) used a computer to numerically score mock-crime polygraph measures and obtained an accuracy of 93%, compared to 89% accuracy for a human using a similar algorithm. Gordon et al. (2006) compared three scoring algorithms in a blind test of deception detection. Depending on the algorithm used, accuracy ranged from 100% to 72% when "inconclusives"—cases unable to be classified as deceptive or truthful—were classified as errors (accuracy was 100% for all three algorithms when inconclusives were not considered errors). These results suggest that polygraph data has the potential to provide useful information on deception if the information is analyzed appropriately. Pollina et al. (2004) compared polygraph data obtained from participants in mock-crime settings to data obtained in actual criminal investigations. Although differences were found in the polygraph measures in the two settings, classification accuracy for the laboratory and field participants was not significantly different, suggesting that results from laboratory CQT studies can be applied profitably to field polygraph situations.

Mock-crime laboratory studies evaluating the GKT indicate that it is very effective at identifying innocent participants (hit rates of up to 95%) and slightly less effective at identifying guilty participants (hit rates between 76% and 85%) (Gamer, Rill, Vossel, & Gödert, 2005; Iacono & Patrick, 1988; Jokinen, Santilla, Ravaja, & Puttonen, 2006; Lykken, 1998). A meta-analysis of 80 GKT studies examined what factors are associated with higher accuracies (Ben-Shakhar & Elaad, 2003). Correct outcomes were better in studies that included motives to succeed, verbal response to alternatives, five or more questions, and in laboratory mock-crime studies. Two published field studies, both done in Israel, have assessed the accuracy of the GKT. Elaad (1990) found that 98% of innocent suspects were correctly classified, but only 42% of guilty suspects were correctly classified. Elaad, Ginton, and Jungman (1992) measured both respiration and skin conductance and found that 94% of innocent and 76% of guilty suspects were correctly classified.

Based on the research described above, the GKT appears to be vulnerable to false-negative errors (falsely classifying guilty suspects as innocent), whereas the CQT is vulnerable to false-positive errors (falsely classifying innocent suspects as guilty). See Box 4.1 for a new way of measuring deception.

Can the Guilty Learn to Beat the Polygraph?

Countermeasures: As applied to polygraph research, techniques used to try to conceal guilt

Is it possible to use **countermeasures** to beat the polygraph? There are websites that describe the best ways to beat the polygraph. Honts, Raskin, and Kircher (1994) showed that 30 minutes of instruction on the rationale underlying the CQT was sufficient for community volunteers to learn how to escape detection in a mock-crime study. Participants were told to use either physical countermeasures (e.g., biting their tongue or pressing their toes on the floor) or mental countermeasures (e.g., counting backward by 7 from a number greater than 200) when asked a control question during the polygraph

---

Box 4.1

Seeing through the Face of Deception

If you travel by air, you will be asked questions such as the following:

- "Did you pack your bags?"
- "Did you ever leave your bags unattended?"
- "Has anyone you don't know asked you to carry something on board?"

Technologies that can provide a rapid, accurate assessment of deceit are becoming more and more important.

Pavlidis, Eberhardt, and Levine (2002) examined whether high-definition thermal imaging of the face could be used to detect deceit. Thermal imaging measures the amount of facial warming, which is linked to regional blood flow. Imaging can be done quickly without the individual even knowing his or her facial temperature is being measured. Pavlidis and colleagues wanted to know whether facial warming was associated with deception. Individuals were randomly assigned to commit a mock crime (stab a mannequin and rob it of $20) or to a control condition in which they had no knowledge of the crime. Use of thermal imaging (in particular around the eyes) correctly classified 6 of the 8 guilty participants and 11 of the 12 innocent participants. This accuracy rate was similar to a polygraph exam administered to participants that correctly classified 6 of 8 guilty and 8 of 12 innocent participants. In the future, when ticket agents or customs officers ask you questions, they may be paying more attention to your facial temperature than to your answers.

exam. Both countermeasures worked, with 50% of the guilty suspects beating the polygraph test. In addition, the polygraph examiners were not able to accurately detect which participants had used the countermeasures.

Iacono, Cerri, Patrick, and Fleming (1992) investigated whether anti-anxiety drugs would allow guilty subjects to appear innocent on the GKT. Undergraduate students were divided into one innocent group (who watched a noncrime videotape) and four guilty groups. Participants in the guilty groups watched a videotaped crime and then were given one of three drugs (Diazepam, meprobamate, or propranolol) or a placebo prior to being administered a GKT. None of the drugs had an effect on the accuracy of the GKT. In addition, the polygraph examiner was able to identify 90% of the participants receiving drugs.

Can psychopaths beat the polygraph? Psychopaths pose a potential challenge to polygraphy as they are described as being skilled at lying and have a limited capacity for anxiety or guilt (Cleckley, 1976). In addition, research has found that psychopaths do not display anticipatory anxiety to threatening events (Hare, 2003). Two laboratory mock-crime studies have assessed psychopathic and nonpsychopathic offenders using the CQT (Patrick & Iacono, 1989; Raskin & Hare, 1978), and a more recent investigation recorded P300 amplitudes of event-related potentials (ERPs) among groups of psychopaths and nonpsychopaths (Miller & Rosenfeld, 2004). Patrick and Iacono (1989) attempted to ensure an incentive for taking the task seriously by using a "group contingency threat." Offenders were told that if they failed the polygraph, none of the participants would obtain a bonus for participating and that their names would be made available to the other offenders. (In fact, all participants received their bonus and the names of those who failed were not revealed.) Blind scoring of the charts obtained correct classification for 87% of the guilty and 57% for the innocent participants (excluding inconclusives). Both psychopaths and nonpsychopaths were detected at the same rate. Comparable results were obtained by Miller and Rosenfeld (2004) using P300 amplitudes. The P300 is measured using scalp electrodes and is a positive deflection in voltage that occurs about 300 milliseconds after a stimulus is presented. Miller and Rosenfeld were able to use the P300 to correctly identify 92% in the high-psychopathy group and 100% in the low-psychopathy group. (Further information about ERPs is found in the section "Brain-Based Polygraph Techniques," later in this chapter.) Whether or not psychopaths would be able to beat the polygraph during an actual field examination has never been investigated. Dr. Christopher Patrick, who conducted this research, is profiled in Box 4.2 on page 100.

Scientific Opinion: What Do the Experts Say?

Most knowledgeable scientists are skeptical about the rationale underlying the CQT and its accuracy. Iacono and Lykken (1997) conducted a survey of 195 members of the Society for Psychophysiological Research and 168 elected Fellows of the General Psychology Divisions of the American Psychological Association. Table 4.3 on page 101 presents the results from selected questions. Across both organizations, members considered the CQT neither scientifically sound nor suitable for evidence in court. In contrast, the GKT was viewed as being based on sound scientific principles. Survey respondents also believed that the CQT can be circumvented by easily learned countermeasures. However, it is important to note dissenting opinions on the validity of the CQT. Researchers such as

Box 4.2

Canadian Researcher Profile: Dr. Christopher Patrick

Dr. Christopher Patrick is the Starke R. Hathaway Distinguished Professor and Director of Clinical Training in the Department of Psychology at the University of Minnesota. Dr. Patrick is president of the Society for the Scientific Study of Psychopathy and editor of the *Handbook of Psychopathy* (Guilford Press, 2006). He has conducted research in numerous areas relevant to forensic psychology, including emotion and temperament in psychopathy, markers and mechanisms of disinhibitory (externalizing) psychopathology, effects of alcohol and other drugs on affective processing, and psychophysiological methods for detecting deception.

Dr. Patrick first became interested in forensic issues as an undergraduate at the University of Calgary, where he majored in psychology and minored in criminology. As a graduate student at the University of British Columbia, he was strongly influenced by two faculty members doing forensic research: Dr. Robert Hare, whose research focused on criminal psychopaths, and Dr. William Iacono, who was doing work on the detection of deception. Dr. Patrick was able to merge these two areas of interest in his doctoral research, which investigated lie detection in psychopathic and nonpsychopathic incarcerated offenders.

What maintains Dr. Patrick's interest in conducting research is the opportunity to address important unanswered questions and the associated process of discovery. For example, as a young researcher conducting his dissertation research, he was inspired by the unique opportunity he had to interview real-life offenders and investigate whether experienced polygraph examiners could detect which offenders had committed a staged crime. His favourite study is one in which he applied a new paradigm for the study of human emotion—the affect modulated startle paradigm—to a sample of incarcerated psychopaths (Patrick, Bradley, & Lang, 1993). This study sparked renewed interest among psychopathy researchers in the role of emotional processes in this disorder, and the study's basic finding has been replicated by several researchers around the world. The study also served as a foundation for much of Dr. Patrick's subsequent research investigating the underlying facets of psychopathy. The two samples he has most often studied are incarcerated offenders and university students. Since joining the faculty of the University of Minnesota in 1999, he has also worked with large samples of adolescent and adult twins recruited from the greater Twin Cities community.

Dr. Patrick believes future forensic psychology researchers should have a strong foundation in basic scientific principles along with specific methodological expertise in domains such as psychometrics, multivariate analysis, psychophysiology, brain imaging, or behavioural/molecular genetics. The course he most enjoys teaching at the undergraduate level is "Psychopaths and Serial Killers." Dr. Patrick plays guitar in two blues/rock bands, and he is an avid surfer (although his surfing activities have declined since moving to Minnesota) and reader of literary fiction (favourite novels include *Underworld* by Don DeLillo and *Continental Drift* by Russell Banks). He has been married for 25 years and is the proud father of one daughter, Sarah Kathryn, age 14. Dr. Patrick recently co-authored a chapter with his daughter entitled "Exploring the Dark Side: Harry Potter and the Psychology of Evil" for the anthology *The Psychology of Harry Potter* (BenBella Books, 2007).

Kircher and Raskin (1988) argue that the CQT can provide valid information about deception if used appropriately.

More recently, the United States National Research Council (NRC) established a panel of 14 scientists and four staff to review the validity of the polygraph (NRC, 2003). In a comprehensive report, the committee concluded the following:

Table 4.3 Scientific Opinion about the Polygraph

Question	Percent Who Agree	
	SPR	APA
CQT is based on scientifically sound theory	36	30
GKT is based on scientifically sound theory	77	72
Would advocate admitting a failed CQT as evidence in court	24	20
Would advocate admitting a passed CQT as evidence in court	27	24
Reasonable to conclude that an individual who fails 8 out of 10 GKT items has guilty knowledge	72	75
CQT can be beaten by increased response to control questions	99	—
Criminals and spies likely to beat a CQT	—	92

Source: Iacono & Lykken, 1997.

- "The theoretical rationale for the polygraph is quite weak, especially in terms of differential fear, arousal, or other emotional states that are triggered in response to relevant and comparison questions" (NRC, 2003, p. 213).

- "The existing validation studies have serious limitations. Laboratory test findings on polygraph validity are not a good guide to accuracy in field settings. They are likely to overestimate accuracy in field practice, but by an unknown amount" (p. 210).

- "In summary, we were unable to find any field experiments, field quasi-experiments, or prospective research-oriented data collection specifically designed to assess polygraph validity and satisfying minimal standards of research quality" (p. 115).

- "What is remarkable, given the large body of relevant research, is that claims about the accuracy of the polygraph made today parallel those made throughout the history of the polygraph: practitioners have always claimed extremely high levels of accuracy, and these claims have rarely been reflected in empirical research" (p. 107).

Despite scientists' negative view of it, the CQT is still used by law enforcement as an investigative tool. To understand why, we only have to know that whatever its actual validity, the polygraph will cause many suspects to confess, thereby providing resolution of the criminal investigation.

Admissibility of Polygraph Evidence

Polygraph results were first submitted as evidence in court in the United States in *Frye v. United States* (1923). James Frye was denied the opportunity to have the results of a polygraph test conducted by William Marston admitted as evidence. This ruling led to the requirement that a technique must obtain "general acceptance" by the relevant scientific community before it can be admitted as evidence. This precedent was replaced by a new admissibility standard which required courts to render scientific decisions (*Daubert v. Merrell Dow Pharmaceuticals*, 1993) and was later extended to non-scientific experts who could provide unique specialized information to the court (*Kumho Tire Co. Ltd. v. Carmichael*, 1999). Some states permit the admission of polygraph evidence if there is a prior agreement between prosecuting and defence lawyers. In a recent decision, the United States Supreme Court (*U.S. v. Scheffer*, 1998) rejected the admissibility of the polygraph because of the belief that polygraph evidence will usurp the role of the jury as determinant of the credibility of a witness. Justice Thomas ruled: "Jurisdictions, in promulgating rules of evidence, may legitimately be concerned about the risk that juries will give excessive weight to the opinions of the polygrapher, clothed as they are in scientific expertise and at times offering, as in respondent's case, a conclusion about the ultimate issue in the trial" (p. 422).

Polygraph evidence is not admissible in Canadian courts of law. The same concerns that have been raised by U.S. courts have been a focus of concern in Canadian courts. In *R. v. Beland* (1987), the Supreme Court of Canada ruled that polygraph evidence should not be admitted to help determine whether or not a person is telling the truth. They referred to the polygraph as being falsely imbued with the "mystique of science," thus causing jurors to weight polygraph evidence more than it deserves when determining the verdict. Internationally, the Western Australian Court of Criminal Appeal came to a similar decision (*Mallard v. The Queen*, 2003).

Impact of Polygraph Evidence on Jurors

Do jurors regard polygraph evidence with an aura of infallibility? Recent studies have shown that polygraph evidence has a limited effect on jurors and their verdicts (Myers, Latter, & Abdollahi-Arena, 2006; Myers, Rosol, & Boelter, 2003; Spanos, Myers, DuBreuil, & Pawlak, 1992–1993). For example, Myers and colleagues (2006) approached individuals in various airports and train stations in California, and presented them with a mock transcript of a sexual assault trial. Participants were randomly assigned to one of three groups: no polygraph evidence, evidence of a passed polygraph test, or evidence of a failed polygraph test. Presence of polygraph evidence did not influence verdicts. Although polygraph evidence may not affect a jury's decision in a laboratory study, we must be careful before generalizing these findings to real-life criminal cases. Consider a rape case in which the outcome depends on the credibility of the victim versus the suspect. In many such cases, the crux of the case is whether or not the victim consented. If both parties appear to be credible, but one enhances his or her claim by passing a polygraph test, the jury might be swayed by this information. Future research is needed to investigate the effect of polygraph testimony as a function of the extent and quality of other evidence.

BRAIN-BASED POLYGRAPH TECHNIQUES

Event-related brain potentials: Brain activity measured by placing electrodes on the scalp and electrical patterns related to presentation of a stimulus are recorded

In the past decade, researchers have attempted to use brain-based responses to detect deception. **Event-related brain potentials** (ERPs) are a type of brain-based response that has been investigated for detecting deception. ERPs are measured by placing electrodes on the scalp and noting changes in electrical patterns related to presentation of a stimulus. ERPs reflect underlying electrical activity in the cerebral cortex. One type of ERP that has shown promise is known as the P300. This ERP occurs in response to significant stimuli that occur infrequently. When using GKT procedures, guilty suspects should respond to such crime-relevant events with a large P300 response, compared to non-crime-relevant events. No difference in P300 responses to crime-relevant and irrelevant events should be observed in innocent suspects. One of the advantages of ERPs is that they have been proposed as a measure resistant to manipulation.

(However, Rosenfeld, Soskins, Bosh, & Ryan, [2004], have obtained results suggesting that participants who are knowledgeable about ERPs can evade detection.)

Several studies have been conducted to assess the validity of the P300 as a guilt detector (e.g., Abootalebi, Moradi, & Khalilzadeh, 2006; Allen & Iacono, 1997; Farwell & Donchin, 1991; Rosenfeld, Angell, Johnson, & Qian, 1991; Rosenfeld, Nasman, Whalen, Cantwell, & Mazzeri, 1987) and as a detector of feigned memory loss (Allen, 2002; Allen, Iacono, & Danielson, 1992; Rosenfeld, Sweet, Chuang, Ellwanger, & Song, 1996). Farwell and Donchin (1991) conducted one of the first studies on the use of the P300 to detect the presence of guilty knowledge. The study consisted of two experiments. In the first experiment, participants role-played one of two espionage scenarios, which involved the exchange of information with a foreign agent, during which they were exposed to six critical details (e.g., the colour of the agent's hat). In the second experiment, participants were asked about details of minor offences they had committed in their day-to-day lives. In the first experiment, using P300 as the measure, 18 of 20 participants were correctly classified in the guilty condition, and 17 of 20 were correctly classified in the innocent condition. In experiment two, all four of the guilty participants were correctly classified, and three of the four innocent participants were correctly classified. Although the results look impressive, there are several limitations to this study. First, guilty participants reviewed the crime-relevant details just prior to taking the GKT. In addition, there were no aversive consequences linked to performance in this study. Finally, the sample size, especially in experiment two, was very small. Abootalebi and colleagues (2006) recently reported lower detection rates than previously reported (e.g., Rosenfeld et al., 1991) when employing the P300-GKT paradigm, with correct identification ranging from 74% to 80%, depending on the approach. In summary, although the P300 has shown potential for detecting deception, its application remains limited to laboratory settings.

Other brain responses have also been tested with some success in the laboratory, including the N400 response (Boaz, Perry, Raney, Fieschler, & Shuman, 1991) and the contingent negative variation (Fang, Liu, & Shen, 2003). Like the P300, however, application of these additional brain responses remains limited to laboratory settings.

More recently, researchers have begun to investigate the cognitive processes used when people are deceptive. Johnson, Barnhardt, and Zhu (2004) recorded ERPs while participants made truthful and deceptive responses about words they had been told to memorize. The results revealed different patterns of brain activity when a person was being truthful versus deceptive. When participants made deceptive responses, they showed activity in the medial frontal cortex (more specifically the anterior cingulate cortex). This area of the brain plays an important role when the person is deciding between conflicting responses.

Investigators have also begun to use functional magnetic resonance imaging (fMRI) to determine which areas of the brain are associated with deception (Ganis, Kosslyn, Stose, Thompson, & Yurgelun-Todd, 2003; Langleben et al., 2002). For example, Ganis

Measuring brain activity during a deception task

and colleagues (2003) examined which brain areas were activated when someone told a spontaneous or rehearsed lie. Lies that were part of a story and that had been rehearsed repeatedly produced a higher level of activation in the right anterior frontal cortex than did spontaneous isolated lies. In contrast, spontaneous isolated lies produced a higher level of activation in the anterior cingulate and posterior visual cortices. These findings and others indicate that brain-imaging techniques can differentiate which parts of the brain are involved in lying and can even indicate which areas are associated with different types of lying. A limitation of this research, however, is that it is typically based on averaging fMRI data across multiple participants, which constrains its use for detecting deception in individuals. More recent research has employed fMRI to detect deception at the individual level (Kozel et al., 2005; Langleben et al., 2005) and found increased prefrontal and parietal activity when someone is lying. Kozel and colleagues (2005) note that, in order to better treat and diagnose patients, this methodology is important for examining the neurological factors of disorders for which deception plays a prominent role (e.g., malingering or psychopathy).

Iacono and Patrick (2006) provide a comprehensive review of these brain-based methods for detecting deception. Box 4.3 describes the case of Terry Harrington, a man convicted of murder who attempted to use the results of brain-based deception testing to prove his innocence.

Vocal and Nonverbal Behaviour Cues to Lying

Another method of deception detection is through the analysis of vocal characteristics and nonverbal behaviours. The underlying assumption is the same as that for polygraphy: the act of deception produces a physiological change compared with telling the truth. The argument here is that it is more difficult for people to control aspects of their nonverbal behaviour than their verbal behaviour (DePaulo & Kirkendol, 1989). The typical experiment involves one group of participants (called the "message source") who are told to provide either true or deceptive messages. For example, DePaulo, Lassiter, and Stone (1982) asked participants to honestly describe people they liked and disliked. They also asked participants to describe the same people dishonestly (i.e., to pretend to like the person they disliked and vice versa). Another group of participants was asked to detect when the message source participants were truthful or deceptive. Participants who were instructed to focus their attention on the message source participants' tone of voice were more successful at detecting deception than those participants given no special instructions.

Researchers have also assessed facial cues and other nonverbal cues to deception. For example, Ekman and Friesen (1974) showed student nurses a film of an ocean scene and videotaped them describing what they were seeing and how they felt while watching the film. They also watched a gruesome medical training film (e.g., the amputation of a hand or a severe industrial burn) and were videotaped while pretending that the film they were watching was pleasant. In order to motivate the nurses watching the gruesome film, the researchers told them that to be successful in nursing, they would have to be able to mask feelings when dealing with unpleasant events. Ekman and Friesen found that the nurses focused on controlling their facial expressions when attempting to deceive. Observers who watched videotapes of the nurses attempting to deceive were more likely to detect deception when they were shown a videotape of the nurses' bodies (with the faces blacked out) than when shown a videotape of their faces. Subsequent research on whether

Box 4.3

Brain Fingerprinting: Evidence for a New Deception-Detection Technology?

The case that put brain fingerprinting in the news was *State v. Harrington* (2003). On July 22, 1977, retired police officer John Schweer was shot and killed while working as a security guard for a car dealership in Iowa. Seventeen-year-old Terry Harrington and Curtis McGhee were arrested for the murder. At his trial, Terry Harrington claimed he was not at the crime scene and several witnesses testified that Harrington had been at a concert on the night of the murder. The prosecution's key witness was another teenager, Kevin Hughes, who testified that he was with Harrington and McGhee the night of the murder. According to Hughes, the three teenagers decided to steal a car. They went to the car dealership. Hughes testified that he waited in the car while Harrington, who first removed a shotgun from the trunk, and McGhee went around a building at the car dealership. Hughes claims he heard a gunshot and Harrington and McGhee came running back to the car. Hughes testified that Harrington had stated he had just shot a cop. Both Terry Harrington and Curtis McGhee were convicted of first-degree murder and sentenced to life in prison without the possibility of parole.

Throughout his 25 years of imprisonment, Terry Harrington maintained his innocence, but all his attempts to appeal his conviction were unsuccessful. From his prison cell, Harrington heard about a new technology that might help his case. He contacted Lawrence Farwell, a cognitive psychophysiologist and head of Brain Fingerprinting Laboratories. On April 18 and 25, 2000, Farwell came to the Iowa State Penitentiary to test Harrington to determine if he had knowledge of the crime scene and of details about his alibi (the concert he claims he attended). Farwell measured the amplitude of Harrington's P300 brain potential to irrelevant and relevant crime scene and concert details. According to Farwell, Harrington's lack of P300 response to crime-relevant details indicated that Harrington had not participated in the murder. In contrast, Harrington showed a prominent P300 to alibi-relevant information.

Harrington's case received national attention in December 2001 when the CBS show *60 Minutes* featured Farwell's research and his testing of Harrington. In March of 2002, Harrington's lawyer submitted a report to the Supreme Court of Iowa describing the results of Farwell's testing.

Although the results of the brain fingerprinting were entered as evidence, the judges relied on other evidence to overturn the murder conviction. During the hearing, three of the prosecution witnesses recanted their testimony. Kevin Hughes stated that he had made up the story about what happened the night of the murder. Hughes claimed that he lied to obtain the $5000 reward being offered about the murder and to avoid being charged with the crime. In addition, the police failed to turn over all the police reports to Harrington's defence lawyer. These reports documented the police investigation of an alternative suspect. On February 26, 2003, the Supreme Court of Iowa overturned the murder conviction of Terry Harrington and the case was remanded for a new trial. On October 24, 2003, the Pottawattamie County Attorney announced that he was dropping the murder charges against Terry Harrington.

---

nonverbal cues can be used as an indicator of deception is mixed (Vrij, 1998). Those engaging in deception tend to move their hands or arms and feet or legs more than those telling the truth. However, other nonverbal behaviours such as gaze aversion, smiling, and self-manipulation (e.g., rubbing one's hands) are not reliable indicators of deception.

If a liar is not feeling excited, scared, or guilty, or when the lie is easy to fabricate, behavioural cues to deception will likely not be present. In a study of everyday lying, DePaulo, Kashy, Kirkendol, Wyer, and Epstein (1996) found that both college students and community members practised deception daily. Most of the deception was not considered serious and the participants reported they were not concerned or worried about being caught. Participants lied about their opinions, feelings, achievements, reasons for doing things, and possessions. Most of the lies were told for psychological reasons, such as protecting the liar from embarrassment. For example, "I told her Ted and I still liked each other when really I don't know if he likes me at all." The reason this person lied was "because I'm ashamed of the fact that he doesn't like me anymore."

If people are under stress, it is possible to detect deceit by paying attention to signs of emotions, which are seen as micro facial expressions (Ekman, 1992; Frank & Ekman, 1997). In addition, DePaulo and colleagues (DePaulo, LeMay, & Epstein, 1991; Forrest & Feldman, 2000; Vrij, 2000) have found that high-stakes lies are easier to detect than low-stakes lies.

Strömwall, Hartwig, and Granhag (2006) explored the role of stress by creating a realistic deception scenario using experienced police officers, employing long interrogations, and generating suspects who were motive-driven and had adequate time to prepare their deception. Participants were offered $30 to tell a biographical story to a police officer, and were randomly instructed to be honest or deceitful. To create motivation and higher risk, participants were offered an additional $20 if they were able to convince the officer that they were being truthful. While liars felt more anxious and stressed during the task when compared to truth-tellers, no differences in nonverbal behaviours were observed. For verbal strategies, the majority of truth-tellers claimed to "keep it real" (50%) whereas liars would "keep it simple" (46.7%). (For more on verbal cues to lying, see the next section).

Table 4.4 describes the types of vocal and nonvocal indicators used to detect deception. The vocal indicator that has been most strongly associated with deception is voice

---

Table 4.4 Vocal and Nonvocal Characteristics of Deception

Vocal Characteristics

- Speech fillers (frequency of saying "ah" or "umm")
- Speech errors (word or sentence repetition, sentence change, sentence incompletion, or slips of the tongue)
- Pitch of voice (changes in pitch)
- Rate of speech (number of words spoken in a specific time period)
- Speech pauses (length of silence between question asked and answer given; number of noticeable pauses in speech)

Nonvocal Characteristics

- Gaze aversion (avoiding looking at the face of conversation partner or interviewer)
- Smiling (frequency of smiles or laughs)
- Blinking (frequency of eye blinks)
- Fidgeting (scratching head, playing with jewellery)
- Illustrators (gestures to modify or supplement what is being said)
- Hand/finger movements
- Leg or foot movements
- Body movements
- Shrugs (frequency of shoulders raised in an "I-don't-know"–type gesture)
- Head movements (nods or shakes head)
- Shifting positions

Source: Adapted from Vrij, 1998.

pitch. Liars tend to speak in a higher-pitched voice than those telling the truth. Most studies have found increased use of speech disturbances ("ah," "umm") and a slower rate of speech during deception (DePaulo et al., 1982; Fiedler & Walka, 1993; Sporer & Schwandt, 2006). However, if you ask participants only to conceal information or instruct them on what they should lie about, deception is associated with fewer speech disturbances and a faster speech rate (Vrij, 1995). In summary, it appears that cognitively more difficult lies (lies in which you have to fabricate an answer) may be associated with one pattern of speech disturbances, whereas cognitively simpler lies (lies in which you must conceal something) may be associated with a different pattern of speech disturbances.

Can You Detect Deception through Voice-Stress Analysis?

You can purchase a voice-stress analysis system which its sellers claim can be used to detect inaudible "microtremors of the vocal muscle" that are associated with heightened stress. Companies advertise them as "hand-held lie detectors" to be used to see whether your partner, boss, friend, or mechanic is lying to you. According to a review conducted by the U.S. National Research Council, current voice-stress analysis technology is of little or no use (NRC, 2003).

Verbal Cues to Lying

In a comprehensive meta-analysis, DePaulo and colleagues (2003) coded 158 cues to deception from 120 samples of adults. Most of the verbal and nonverbal behaviours coded did not discriminate between liars and truth-tellers. One of the most reliable indicators was that liars provide fewer details than do truth-tellers. Liars also told less compelling accounts as compared with truth-tellers. For example, liars' stories were less likely to make sense (less plausible, lack logical structure, have discrepancies), were less engaging, and were less fluent than were truth-tellers' stories. Liars were also rated as less cooperative and more nervous and tense than truth-tellers. Finally, truth-tellers were more likely to spontaneously correct their stories and more likely to admit to a lack of memory than liars were. Deception cues were easier to detect when the liar was motivated to lie or when he or she was attempting to cover up a personal failing or a transgression.

Sporer and Schwandt completed two recent meta-analyses, which examined verbal cues (2006) and nonverbal cues (2007) to deception. Verbal indices that were positively associated with deception were pitch, response latency, and errors in speech, with length of description negatively associated with deception. For nonverbal behaviour, only 3 of 11 behaviours were negatively associated with deception: nodding, foot and leg movements, and hand movements.

Are Some People Better at Detecting Deception?

Across studies, the ability to distinguish lies from truth tends to be only slightly better than chance. For example, a meta-analysis by Kraut (1980) indicated the average accuracy rate was 57%. This poor performance in deception detection has been explained in two ways. First, people tend to rely on behaviours that lack predictive validity (Fiedler & Walka, 1993).

Truth-bias: The tendency of
people to judge more messages
as truthful than deceptive

Second, most people have a **truth-bias**. Truth-bias refers to the tendency of people to judge more messages as truthful than deceptive (Anderson, Ansfield, & DePaulo, 1999).

Several studies by Ekman and colleagues have investigated the abilities of diverse professional groups to detect deception. In the 1991 study by Ekman and O'Sullivan, forensic psychiatrists, customs agents, FBI agents, and judges all performed around chance levels in detecting deception. The only group that performed better than chance (64% correct) were U.S. Secret Service agents. About a third of Secret Service agents were 80% accurate or better. The most accurate participants were those who relied on multiple cues to assess credibility rather than on any one cue.

More recently, Ekman, O'Sullivan, and Frank (1999) showed professional groups videotaped speakers describing a true or false opinion. Both federal law-enforcement officers and clinical psychologists were able to detect deceit at above chance levels (around 70% correct). In a Canadian study, Porter, Woodworth, and Birt (2000) found that parole officers performed below chance levels (40% correct) at distinguishing videotaped speakers describing a truthful or fictitious stressful personal experience, such as an animal attack or a serious car accident. However, after attending a deception-detection workshop, they were significantly more accurate (77% correct). Thus, although detecting deception is difficult, it is possible to improve judgment accuracy through training.

In a recent review of 40 studies, Vrij (2000) found a 67% accuracy rate for detecting truths and a 44% accuracy rate for detecting lies. Table 4.5 presents the accuracy rates of "professional lie catchers." In most of the studies, the professional lie catchers were not very accurate at detecting deception. The results also showed that in most studies, truthful messages were identified with more accuracy than deceptive ones. Thus, even professional lie catchers have a truthfulness bias. One reason even professionals are not good at detecting lies is that they rely on the wrong cues. For example, Vrij and Semin (1996) found that 75% of police and customs officers believe that gaze aversion is a reliable indicator of deception,

Table 4.5 Accuracy Rates of Professional Lie Catchers

Study	Accuracy Rates		
	Truth	Lie	Total
DePaulo & Pfeifer, 1996 (Experienced police)*	64%	42%	52%
DePaulo & Pfeifer, 1996 (New police recruits)*	64%	42%	53%
Ekman & O'Sullivan, 1991 (Federal polygraphers)			56%
Ekman & O'Sullivan, 1991 (Police officers)			56%
Ekman & O'Sullivan, 1991 (Secret Service)			64%
Köehnken, 1987 (Police officers)	58%	31%	45%
Vrij, 1994 (Police detectives)	51%	46%	49%
Ekman et al., 1999 (Federal law-enforcement officers)	66%	89%	73%
Ekman et al., 1999 (Sheriffs)	56%	78%	67%
Porter et al., 2000 (Parole officers)	41%	47%	52%
Mann et al., 2004 (Police officers)	64%	66%	65%

*Accuracy rates for experienced police and new recruits were collapsed together.

but empirical research has not found it to be a reliable indicator of deception (Vrij, 1998). Mann, Vrij, and Bull (2004) examined police officers' ability to detect lies and truths told by suspects during police interrogations. These police officers were able to reach accuracy rates similar to more specialized law-enforcement groups, such as U.S. Secret Service agents (Ekman et al., 1999). There are two potential explanations for the higher-than-usual accuracy. First, the suspects were highly motivated to lie and research has shown that high-stakes lies are easier to detect than low-stakes ones. Second, the police are more familiar with the setting and type of individual they were judging, namely suspects. Box 4.4 looks at police detection of high-stakes lies.

Two factors one might think would be related to deception-detection ability are level of job experience and confidence in judgment. DePaulo and Pfeifer (1996) compared the proficiency of deception detection of university students, new police recruits, and experienced police officers. None of the groups were better than others at detecting deception; however, the experienced police officers reported being more confident in their decisions. This finding is consistent with more recent research (Ekman & O'Sullivan, 1991; Leach, Talwar, Lee, Bala, & Lindsay, 2004; Porter et al., 2000) indicating that neither level of experience nor confidence in deception-detection ability are associated with accuracy rates. For example, in a meta-analysis examining the relation between judges' accuracy at detecting deception and confidence in their judgments, DePaulo, Charlton, Cooper, Lindsay, and Muhlenbruck (1997) found that the average correlation was .04. Men were

Box 4.4

Detecting High-Stakes Lies

You are watching the news, and a mother is being interviewed outside her home, begging for the return of her two sons. She says that while stopped at a stop sign, a black man approached her car with a gun and demanded she get out of the car. Her two young sons were in the backseat. Frightened for her life, she got out of the car and the carjacker jumped into the car and drove off with the children in the back. Over the next nine days, she is often on the news pleading with the carjacker to return her sons. Your initial reaction is concern for the mother and hope that the children will be found unharmed. On the ninth day, the mother confesses to police that there was no carjacker, that she had driven her car to a local lake, left the car on the boat ramp in neutral, got out, and watched as the car slowly rolled into the lake and sank. The two children's bodies were found in the car, still in their car seats.

This is the true case of 23-year-old Susan Smith. Smith was convicted of first-degree murder of 3-year-old Michael and 14-month-old Alex. During the penalty phase of the trial, the assistant prosecutor, Keith Giese, stated, "We're going to go back over the nine days of lies, the nine days of deceit, the nine days of trickery, the nine days of begging this country to help her find her children, while the whole time they lay dead at the bottom of that lake" (Reuter, 1995).

Would you have been able to detect if Susan Smith was lying by what she said or by her behaviour during her numerous press conferences? Vrij and Mann (2001) asked a similar question. They asked 52 police officers to view videotaped press conferences of people who were asking the public's help in locating their missing relatives or the murderers of their relatives. Vrij and Mann asked the officers to determine who was lying and who was telling the truth. What they didn't tell the officers was that every video showed people who had actually been found guilty of killing their own relatives. The officers were not very accurate at detecting the deception. Moreover, accuracy was not related to age, years of police work, level of experience interviewing suspects, or confidence.

more confident than women were (even though men are not more accurate detectors) and the closer the relation between sender and judge (e.g., dating partner, friend versus stranger), the higher the confidence (but again, not the accuracy). The reason that confidence is unrelated to accuracy may be that people rely on cues they believe are related to deception and when they see these cues, their confidence increases. However, since the cues people believe are related to deception are often not valid, their accuracy tends to be poor.

Porter, Campbell, Stapleton, and Birt (2002) investigated several factors related to the ability to detect deceit, including characteristics of the judge (e.g., handedness, type of cues used, personality), characteristics of the target (e.g., attractiveness, gender), and modality of reports (e.g., audiovisual or audio only). The findings were intriguing. In university students, detection accuracy was highest when the judge was left-handed, the target was unattractive, the target and judge were of opposite genders, and if facial cues were relied on. Porter and colleagues interpreted the left-handed advantage as being due to left-handers relying more on right-hemisphere processes, which in turn may be associated with greater emphasis on processing facial cues rather than relying on other, less informative, cues. Attractive liars are assumed to be more readily believed due to the activation of stereotypes (i.e., attractive people are more likely to tell the truth). Gender differences may also arise via the activation of stereotypes.

Deception in Witnesses

Not all eyewitnesses are honest. Some may be deceitful for a variety of reasons. For example, imagine you are at the front of a line to get into a popular bar. A tough-looking biker pushes his way to the front of the line. The doorman refuses to allow the biker to enter. The biker pulls out a knife, stabs the doorman, and flees. You are worried about the potential consequences to you and your family if you identify the biker to the police. When the police ask you to identify the biker from a photo array that includes the perpetrator, you quickly state the person is not present. Research on deception by eyewitnesses is more limited compared with research on other types of deception. Recently, however, researchers have begun to study the types of choices and decision times associated with eyewitness deception.

Parliament and Yarmey (2002) showed 128 university students a videotaped crime of a man abducting a child. The students were randomly assigned to tell the truth and to accurately identify the perpetrator or to lie to protect the perpetrator. Participants were shown a photo lineup and asked to identify the perpetrator. Participants in the lie-to-protect group more often stated that the perpetrator was not present (in the target-present condition) and made their decision faster compared with the truthful group.

Judges in court are faced with the challenging task of assessing the credibility of witness testimony. In some cases, two witnesses will totally contradict each other. Judges rely on common sense, personal experience, and the demeanour of the witness to determine the credibility of a witness. Some judges have based their assessments of credibility on generalizations rather than on specific demonstrations of deception from an individual witness. For example, in the case *Foto v. Jones* (1974), the judge stated that the plaintiff was not a credible witness, giving the reason as, "I regret to have to say that too many newcomers to our country have as yet not learned the necessity of speaking the whole truth. . . . They have not learned that frankness is essential to our system of law and justice." The court of appeal concluded that judges should not use this type of information when determining credibility.

Judges often need to decide on the credibility of only two witnesses. In a case in Nova Scotia, a youth court judge needed to determine the credibility of a white police officer and a 15-year-old black defendant. During the youth court trial, the judge made a statement to the Crown attorney that "police officers were known to mislead the court in the past, that they had been known to overreact particularly to non-white groups." The trial judge placed more credibility on the youth's testimony and the youth was acquitted on the charge of unlawfully assaulting a police officer. The Crown attorney appealed to the Nova Scotia Court of Appeal, claiming that the trial judge was biased against the police officer and this influenced her assessment of his credibility. The appeal was successful and a new trial was ordered. The defence appealed to the Supreme Court of Canada (*R. v. S. [R. D.]*, 1997) and the Supreme Court set aside the Court of Appeal decision and upheld the youth court judge's acquittal.

Deception in Children

Each year in North America, an estimated 100 000 children testify as witnesses in criminal trials (Bruck, Ceci, & Hembrooke, 1998). Out of this large group of children, some will engage in deception. Several studies indicate that children will deny engaging in a prohibited behaviour. Like deception in adults, deception in children varies along several dimensions, including the likelihood of engaging in deception and the rationale for lying, such as to protect themselves or another person. However, striking differences also exist when deception is compared in children and adults. For example, children may lack the cognitive sophistication to understand how one lie may require additional lies in order to achieve a coherent story.

Polak and Harris (1999) provide a representative example of a study designed to assess deception in young children. They assigned three- and five-year-olds to two conditions. In the permission condition, children were told they were allowed to touch a toy guitar when the experimenter was absent. In the prohibition condition, they were told not to touch the toy guitar in the experimenter's absence. All the children in the permission condition touched the toy and admitted touching it. However, in the prohibition condition, 54% of the children touched the toy guitar. Of these children, 86% denied when asked if they had touched the toy.

In a second study, Polak and Harris (1999) examined children's ability to sustain a false claim. Children were told that a toy house contained a particular animal, such as a stuffed horse. In the prohibition condition, they were told not to look inside the house when the experimenter was absent. In the permission condition, they were told they could look. In both conditions, the animal inside the toy house was different from what they had been told—not a stuffed horse but a stuffed tiger. Children were asked if they had looked inside the house and were also asked to point to the picture of the animal that was inside. Children in the prohibition condition who wanted to mislead the experimenter had to first deny looking in the house and, to sustain this deception, had to feign ignorance about the animal inside (pointing to the animal the experimenter had told them was in the house—the stuffed horse). All the children in the permission condition looked inside the house and admitted doing so. However, 95% of the children in the prohibition condition peeked inside the house and of these, 84% denied having looked. Of those children denying, 75% identified the animal that was actually in the house. Thus, although denying wrongful behaviour is widespread in young children, it is difficult for them to sustain a coherent story as part of the deception.

Not all lies are considered to be negative. **White lies** are untruthful statements told with no malicious intent (Bok, 1978). For example, expressing gratitude for an unwanted gift is usually intended to spare the gift-giver psychological duress arising from the lack of appreciation for the gift by the recipient. In other words, the intent of white lies is to avoid hurting the feelings of the listener and to sidestep negative reactions from the listener if the speaker told the truth. Talwar and Lee (2002) examined white-lie-telling behaviour in three- to seven-year-olds using a reverse rouge task. In this task, before children are asked to take a photo of the experimenter, they are asked, "Do I look okay for the photo?" In the experimental condition, the experimenter had a large red dot on his nose; in the control condition, there was no dot. In the experimental condition, 55 of the 65 children (85%) told the experimenter that he looked okay. All the children who told a white lie to the experimenter admitted to the confederate (who looked at the photo with the children) that the experimenter did not look okay. When the confederate asked why they didn't tell him, about half of the children stated they did not know why or said that they had forgotten to tell. Another 17% said that they thought the mark was permanent, and 11% indicated they did not want to embarrass the experimenter. These results indicate that although some children have insight into their behaviour, it is not clear what motivates other children to tell a white lie.

Overall, the results from these studies and similar ones indicate that white-lie behaviours and lying to conceal a transgression emerge from age three onward. Although young children are capable of deception, they often fail to make their deception believable. Deception in young children may be "inadequate" because their cognitive systems have not developed either basic memory or attentional mechanisms, or because they lack metacognitive abilities that would allow them to understand what is required to maintain a believable deception. An important constraint of this research when considering it in the light of forensic settings is that motivation to deceive was relatively limited. It is possible that young children would be more effective liars if they were sufficiently motivated. In addition, research needs to be done to explore how an awareness of the consequences of telling a lie (i.e., white lies vs. lies that have more serious consequences, such as an accusation of sexual abuse) may affect lying behaviour in young children.

ASSESSMENT OF MALINGERING AND DECEPTION
Disorders of Deception

Deception may be a central component of some psychological disorders. The disorders described below vary on two dimensions: (1) whether the person intentionally or consciously produces the symptoms, and (2) whether the motivation is internal or external.

The *Diagnostic and Statistical Manual of Mental Disorders*, Fourth Edition (*DSM-IV*) (American Psychiatric Association [APA], 1994), diagnostic criteria for a **factitious disorder** include (1) physical or psychological symptoms that are intentionally produced,

White lies: Untruthful statements told with no malicious intent

Factitious disorder: A disorder in which the person's physical and psychological symptoms are intentionally produced and are adopted to assume the role of a sick person

(2) internal motivation to assume the sick role, and (3) an absence of external incentives. Eisendrath (1996) has suggested that patients with factitious disorders might be aware they are intentionally producing the symptoms, but they may lack insight into the underlying psychological motivation.

There are many different subtypes of factitious disorders, with most being rare. An example of a physical factitious disorder is **Munchausen syndrome**. In this syndrome the patient intentionally produces a physical complaint, such as abdominal pain, and constantly seeks physician consultations, hospitalizations, and even surgery to treat the nonexistent illness. In some cases patients will ingest poison or purposely infect wounds in order to maintain a patient role. This disorder often emerges by age 20, is difficult to treat, and is chronic in nature (APA, 1994). Meadow (1977) coined the term "Munchausen syndrome by proxy" (MBP) to describe cases in which parents or caregivers falsified symptoms in their children. A study by Rosenberg (1987) evaluated 117 reported cases of MBP and found 98% of the individuals were the biological mother of the child; in almost 9% of the cases, the child died. In a more recent review of this syndrome, Sheridan (2003) analyzed the characteristics of 451 MBP cases. Although the most common perpetrator was the child's biological mother (77%), other perpetrators were also identified (the father in 7% of cases). Most the victims were young (age four or younger), with 6% of the victims dying and 7% suffering long-term physical injuries. Nearly one-third (29%) of the perpetrators had some symptoms of Munchausen syndrome.

Munchausen syndrome: A rare factitious disorder in which a person intentionally produces a physical complaint and constantly seeks physician consultations, hospitalizations, and even surgery to treat the nonexistent illness

The two key components of **somatoform disorders** include (1) physical symptoms that cannot be explained by an underlying organic impairment, and (2) the symptoms are not intentionally produced. In this disorder, patients truly believe they have a physical problem and often consult with their physicians for treatment of their physical problems. There are several different subtypes of somatoform disorders, including somatization disorder (patient complains of eight or more physical symptoms) and conversion disorder (patient complains of numbness in a specific area that makes no anatomical sense). Somatoform disorders are rare and often co-occur with other disorders such as depression or anxiety (Gureje, Simon, Ustun, & Goldberg, 1997).

Somatoform disorders: A disorder in which physical symptoms suggest a physical illness but have no known underlying physiological cause and the symptoms are not intentionally produced

The two key components to **malingering** are that (1) the psychological or physical symptoms are clearly under voluntary control and (2) there are external motivations for the production of symptoms. People typically malinger mental illness for one of the following external motivations:

Malingering: Intentionally faking psychological or physical symptoms for some type of external gain

- A criminal may attempt to avoid punishment by pretending to be unfit to stand trial, to have a mental illness at the time of a criminal act, or to have an acute mental illness in order to avoid being executed.

- Prisoners or patients may seek drugs, or prisoners may want to be transferred to a psychiatric facility to do easier time or to escape.

- Malingerers may seek to avoid conscription to the military or to avoid certain military duties.

- Malingerers may seek financial gain from disability claims, workers' compensation, or damages from alleged injury.

- Malingerers may seek admission to a hospital to obtain free room and board.

Any psychiatric or physical disorder may be malingered. As new syndromes are developed, such as post-traumatic stress disorder, they provide new opportunities for people to attempt to malinger them. Malingering varies in terms of severity from benign (e.g., "Not tonight, honey; I have a headache.") to serious (e.g., "I heard a voice telling me to kill my neighbour, so I obeyed it.").

Individuals with factitious and somatoform disorders often encourage and even insist on having physical tests and invasive procedures, whereas malingerers will often refuse to cooperate with invasive procedures to determine the veracity of their symptoms. The incidence of malingering in the general population is unknown. Patients who malinger rarely admit it. Thus, individuals who successfully malinger are never included in the statistics. Moreover, mental health professionals are often reluctant to label a patient as a malingerer.

The prevalence rate of malingering is relatively high in forensic contexts. For example, Frederick, Crosby, and Wynkoop (2000) reported that 45% of patients evaluated for competency or mental state at the time of offence produced invalid psychological test profiles. Rogers, Ustad, and Salekin (1998) reported that 20% of emergency jail referrals feigned psychological symptoms. Rogers (1986) reported that 4.5% of defendants evaluated for mental state at the time of offence were definite malingerers and another 20% were suspected. Given these large numbers, it is clear that malingering should be considered in all forensic evaluations. Estimates of malingering psychological symptoms following personal injury range widely. For example, Lees-Haley (1997) reported that about 25% of personal injury claimants were feigning post-traumatic symptoms in an attempt to receive financial compensation.

The opposite of malingering is called **defensiveness**. Defensiveness refers to the conscious denial or extreme minimization of physical or psychological symptoms. Patients or offenders of this sort seek to present themselves in a favourable light. Minimization of physical and psychological symptoms varies both in degree and motivation. Some people might want to appear to be functioning well in order to meet an external need, such as being a fit parent, or an internal need, such as unwillingness to acknowledge they are a "patient." Degree of defensiveness can range from mild, such as downplaying a minor symptom, to outright denial of a more serious psychological impairment, such as denying hearing command hallucinations. Defensiveness is commonplace in evaluations of sex offenders. The majority of sex offenders either deny their sexual offending or greatly minimize the effect of their sexual offending (Barbaree, 1991).

Explanatory Models of Malingering

Based on the primary motives, Rogers (1990) described three explanatory models of malingering: pathogenic, criminological, and adaptational. The pathogenic model assumes that people are motivated to malinger due to an underlying mental disorder. According to this model, the patient attempts to gain control over his or her pathology by creating bogus symptoms. Over time, these patients experience more severe mental disorders and the true symptoms emerge. Little empirical support exists for this model.

The criminological model focuses on "badness"—"a bad person (Antisocial Personality Disorder), in bad circumstances (legal difficulties), who is performing badly (uncooperative)" (Rogers, 1997, p. 7). This is similar to the definition of malingering expressed in the *DSM-IV* (APA, 1994). According to this definition, malingering should be strongly suspected if two or more of the following factors are evident: (1) presence of antisocial personality disorder, (2) forensic assessment, (3) lack of cooperation, and (4) marked discrepancy between subjective complaints and objective findings. Like the pathogenic model, little empirical support exists for this model. No research indicates that persons with antisocial personality disorder are any more likely to malinger than are other offenders (Rogers, 1990). In addition, many different types of patients are uncooperative with evaluations, including those with eating disorders or substance-use problems. In contrast, some malingerers appear to be highly cooperative. Rogers (1990) found that *DSM-IV* indicators of malingering tended to overdiagnose malingering in a forensic sample.

According to the adaptational model, malingering is likely to occur when (1) there is a perceived adversarial context, (2) personal stakes are very high, and (3) no other viable alternatives are perceived. Research findings support this model in that there are higher rates of malingering in adversarial settings or when the personal stakes are high. This model provides the broadest and least pejorative explanation of malingering. Rogers, Sewell, and Goldstein (1994) asked 320 forensic psychologists to rate 32 items subdivided into pathogenic, criminological, and adaptational models on how important the item was to malingering. The adaptational model was rated the most important and the pathogenic model as the least important.

How to Study Malingering

Research comprises three basic designs: case study, simulation, and known groups. Each of these designs has its associated strengths and weaknesses. Although case studies are not used as often as they once were, they are useful for generating a wide variety of hypotheses that can be tested using designs with more experimental rigour. In addition, a case study is the only way to examine rare syndromes such as Munchausen-by-proxy syndrome.

Most research on malingering has used a **simulation design** (similar to polygraph laboratory studies). Participants are told to malinger a specific disorder and are typically compared with two groups: (1) a control group randomly selected from the same population as the malingerers and (2) a clinical comparison group representing the disorders or symptoms that are being feigned. These studies address whether measures can detect malingering in nonclinical samples. However, individuals with mental disorders may also malinger. Studies have begun to ask patients with mental disorders to feign a different mental disorder or to exaggerate the severity of their symptoms. These studies address how effectively participants with mental disorders can malinger. In an early study using a clinical sample, Rogers (1988) reported that nearly half of the psychiatric inpatients either did not remember or did not follow the instructions to malinger. In order to examine the relative efficacy of detection methods for disordered and non-disordered samples, the optimal simulation design would use four groups—nonclinical experimental, nonclinical-control, clinical-experimental, and clinical-control.

Simulation design: As applied to malingering research, people are told to pretend they have specific symptoms or a disorder

The primary strength of the simulation design is its experimental rigour. The main disadvantage is its limited generalizability to the real world. Simulation studies are often limited in their clinical usefulness because of the minimal levels of preparation and level of motivation by participants. Early studies used brief and nonspecific instructions, such as, "Appear mentally ill." Instructions are now becoming more specific, with some studies giving participants a scenario to follow: For example, "Imagine you have been in a car accident and you hit your head. You have decided to exaggerate the amount of memory problems you are having in order to obtain a larger monetary settlement from the car insurance company." In addition, participants may be given time to prepare.

Some studies have coached participants by providing information about genuine mental disorders or by telling them about detection strategies. Research suggests that telling participants about disorders does not help them, whereas information about detection strategies does help them avoid detection (Baer, Wetter, & Berry, 1995; Storm & Graham, 2000). In contrast, Bagby et al. (2002) found that providing students with information about validity scales designed to detect deception did not enhance their ability to feign successfully.

Ethical concerns have been raised about whether participants should be taught how to become skilled malingerers. Ben-Porath (1994) has argued that such research does not "appear to have sufficient scientific justification to make up for the potential harm that might be caused by publishing such a study" (p. 150). A survey of lawyers and law students indicates that about 50% would provide information about psychological testing, including whether the test had any validity scales to detect deception (Wetter & Corrigan, 1995). See Box 4.5 for a discussion of the conflict between ethics and research design when doing this type of research.

When individuals engage in malingering in applied settings, the stakes are often high. For example, they may obtain funding for a disability or avoid a harsher sentence. Both the type and magnitude of incentives are typically limited in simulation studies. Studies that use incentives often offer monetary rewards to malingerers for being successful. The magnitude of the incentive ranges from very modest (e.g., $5) to more substantial (e.g., having their name in a lottery with the chance of getting $100). Simulation studies have rarely used negative incentives. For example, the researcher could offer money for participating in a malingering study but take some of the money away if the participant is detected as unsuccessfully using deception.

Known-groups design: As applied to malingering research, it involves comparing genuine patients and malingers attempting to fake the disorder the patients have

Studies investigating malingering in applied settings would ideally use the known-groups design. The **known-groups design** involves two stages: (1) the establishment of the criterion groups (e.g., genuine patients and malingerers), and (2) an analysis of the similarities and differences between these criterion groups. The main strength of the known-groups design is its generalizability to real-world settings. Its chief limitation is the establishment of the criterion groups. Samples of the genuine patients likely include errors, and some of the classified malingerers may be genuine patients. Because of the difficulty with the reliable and accurate classification of criterion groups, this design is rarely used in malingering research.

Malingered Psychosis

How often people attempt to feign psychosis is unknown. Pope, Jonas, and Jones (1982) found 9 patients with factitious psychosis in a sample of 219 consecutive admissions to a forensic psychiatric hospital. They followed these patients for seven years, and none went on to develop a psychotic disorder, although all were diagnosed with either borderline personality disorder (a personality disorder defined by instability in mood, self-image, and interpersonal relationships) or histrionic personality disorder (a personality disorder defined by excessive emotionality and attention-seeking behaviours). The presence of malingering does not negate the possibility that other psychiatric illnesses or psychological disorders are present. In fact, the term *instrumental psychosis* was developed to identify patients (many with psychiatric histories) attempting to feign symptoms to secure special accommodations (Waite & Geddes, 2006). Cornell and Hawk (1989) reported that 8% of 314 consecutive psychiatric admissions were diagnosed as malingering psychotic symptoms

Box 4.5

Ethics of Deception Research

Simulation laboratory studies are often used to study the accuracy of detection measures. In order to make these experiments more similar to real-world situations, rewards are given for successful deception but punishment can be meted out for unsuccessful deception. In the studies described below, both positive and negative incentives were used to approximate real-life criminal investigation settings.

Psychopathy, Threat, and Polygraph Test Accuracy

The participants in a laboratory polygraph study by Patrick and Iacono (1989) were incarcerated Canadian male offenders. The experimenters wanted to "create a realistic threat context for the polygraph tests. . . . A failure to live up to group expectations can provoke responses much stronger than mere disapproval: Peer labeling in the prison environment frequently leads to ostracism, persecution, and physical brutality" (p. 348). Offenders were offered $10 for participating in the experiment and the potential of a $20 bonus. Offenders were told that if more than ten offenders were judged by the polygraph examiner as deceptive, no one would receive the $20 bonus. In order to increase the offenders' motivation, they were told that a list of the names of participants who failed would be made public.

Offenders were randomly assigned to commit or not commit a mock crime. The mock crime consisted of sneaking into the doctor's office and removing $20 from the pocket of the doctor's jacket. Each participant was given a polygraph test. It was clear that some of the participants were concerned about their test outcomes. For example, one offender stated, "I hope they [the other inmates] don't beat my head if I fail" (Patrick & Iacono, 1989, p. 353).

At the end of the study, all participants were given the $20 bonus and participants' polygraph test outcomes were not made public.

Detecting Deceit and Different Types of High-Stakes Lies

In a study of observers' ability to detect deception, Frank and Ekman (1997) used both positive and negative incentives to motivate their participants. Participants engaged in a mock crime, which involved stealing $50 from a briefcase. They were told they could keep this money if they were able to convince an interviewer they had not taken the money (positive incentive). However, they were also warned that if the interviewer judged them as lying, they would have to give back the $50 and would not get the $10 for participating in the study (negative incentive). Some participants were also told that if they were unsuccessful liars, they would have to sit on a metal chair in a cold, small, darkened room and listen to repeated blasts of 110 dB white noise for an hour (even more negative incentive). At the end of the experiment, all participants received their $10 and were told they did not need to face the additional punishment.

Researchers often have to balance ethical concerns with attempts to increase the validity of their research. In the two studies described here, deception was used to motivate the participants. Some researchers might consider that the level of deception borders on unethical, whereas others would argue that this level of deception is necessary to make the research meaningful. Researchers submit their research protocols to ethical committees for review to ensure the rights of participants are protected. Thus, although you may have some concerns about the level of deception, both of these studies were approved by ethical review.

by experienced forensic psychologists. Box 4.6 on page 118 describes one of the first studies of malingered psychosis.

What Are the Indicators of Malingered Psychosis?

Table 4.6 on page 119 provides a list of the potential indicators of malingered psychosis. Resnick (1997) provides a comprehensive description of these indicators. Malingerers often tend to overact, believing the more bizarre they are, the more psychotic they will appear. Early observers have also reported this. For example, Jones and Llewellyn (1917) stated the malingerer "sees less than the blind, he hears less than the deaf, and is more lame than the paralysed. . . . He . . . piles

Box 4.6

Being Sane in Insane Places

In 1973, David Rosenhan published a paper in the journal *Science* entitled "Being Sane in Insane Places." Rosenhan's goal was to investigate the accuracy of psychiatric diagnoses and the consequences of diagnostic labels. In the first part of his study, eight individuals with no history of a mental disorder tried to gain admission to several mental hospitals. Imagine you are one of the pseudo-patients taking part in Rosenhan's study. You go to your local hospital complaining that you have been hearing voices. When asked what the voices are saying, you reply that it is sometimes unclear but you think they are saying "empty," "hollow," and "thud." You state that you do not recognize the voice. Other than falsifying your name and occupation, everything else about your personal history is true. Like the actual eight pseudo-patients in the study, you also have no history of any serious pathology. To your surprise, you are immediately admitted to the psychiatric inpatient ward with a diagnosis of schizophrenia. Once you are admitted, you tell the staff that your auditory hallucinations have disappeared. Like the real pseudo-patients, you are feeling somewhat apprehensive about what might happen to you. You are cooperative and friendly toward staff and patients. When the staff member asks you how you are feeling, you answer, "I am fine." You follow the rules in the hospital and pretend to take the medication given to you. You have been told that you have to get out of the hospital on your own. So you try to convince the staff you are "sane." To deal with the boredom, you pace up and down the hall, engage staff and patients in conversation, and write extensive notes about your daily activities. The staff members do not question you about this behaviour, although the other patients on the ward comment on your note-taking and accuse you of being "a journalist or a professor."

In the actual experiment, pseudo-patients were hospitalized from 7 to 52 days. Staff failed to recognize the lack of symptoms in the pseudo-patients. Not one of the pseudo-patients was identified as "normal" by staff. As noted by Rosenhan (1973), "once a person is designated abnormal, all of his other behaviors are colored by that label" (p. 253). For example, the nurses interpret your pacing behaviour as a manifestation of anxiety and your note-taking as a behavioural manifestation of your pathology. Pseudo-patients' attempts to initiate conversations with staff were not very successful, since the staff would "give a brief response while they were on the move and with head averted, or no response at all" (Rosenhan, 1973, p. 255). An example of one conversation was,

[Pseudo-patient]: "Pardon me, Dr. X. Could you tell me when I am eligible for grounds privileges?"
[Physician]: "Good morning, Dave. How are you today?" (Moves off without waiting for a reply.) (p. 255)

This study raises concerns about the use of labels and how such labels can influence the meaning of behaviours. What are the consequences of psychiatric diagnoses? As stated by Rosenhan (1973), "A diagnosis of cancer that has been found to be in error is cause for celebration. But psychiatric diagnoses are rarely found to be in error. The label sticks, a mark of inadequacy forever" (p. 257).

symptom upon symptom and so outstrips madness itself" (p. 17). Malingerers are often willing to discuss their symptoms when asked, whereas actual patients with schizophrenia are often reluctant to discuss their symptoms. Some malingerers may attempt to control the assessment by behaving in an intimidating manner or accusing the clinician of not believing them. In an interview, a malingerer may be evasive when asked to provide details, take a long time to answer, or answer, "I don't know." Malingerers often report rare or atypical symptoms, blatant symptoms, or absurd symptoms that are usually not endorsed by genuine patients. For example, a person attempting to malinger psychosis may claim have seen "a large 60-foot Christ who told me to kill my mother."

Malingerers are more likely to report positive symptoms of schizophrenia such as delusions (a false belief that is persistently held) or hallucinations (a perceptual experience in

Table 4.6 Cues to Malingered Psychosis in Criminal Defendants

- Understandable motive for committing crime
- Presence of a partner in the crime
- Current crime fits pattern of previous criminal history
- Suspicious hallucinations
  - Continuous rather than intermittent
  - Vague or inaudible hallucinations
  - Hallucinations with no delusions
  - Inability to describe strategies to diminish voices
  - Claiming all command hallucinations are obeyed
  - Visual hallucinations in black and white
- Suspicious delusions
  - Abrupt onset or termination
  - Eagerness to discuss delusions
  - Conduct markedly inconsistent with delusions
  - Elaborate delusions that lack paranoid, grandiose, or religious themes
- Marked discrepancies in interview versus noninterview behaviour
- Sudden emergence of psychotic symptoms to explain criminal act
- Absence of any subtle signs of psychosis

Source: Adapted from Resnick, 1997.

absence of external stimulation), as compared with negative or subtle symptoms of schizophrenia, such as blunted affect, concreteness, or peculiar thinking. Both auditory and visual hallucinations are common in psychotic patients. When a person is suspected of malingering auditory hallucinations, he or she should be asked the vocal characteristics (e.g., clarity, loudness, duration), source (inside or outside of the head), characteristics (e.g., gender, familiar or unfamiliar voice, command), and response (insight into unreality, coping strategies, obeying them). Comparing genuine and feigned auditory hallucinations is one way to detect a malingerer. For example, actual patients often report coping strategies to make the "voices go away," such as watching TV, seeking out interpersonal contact, or taking medications (Kanas & Barr, 1984). The malingerer may report there is nothing that will make the voices go away. In other cases, malingerers may report atypical auditory command hallucinations (hallucinations telling people to act in a certain way), such as, "Go commit a sex offence" or "Rob, rob, rob."

Genuine visual hallucinations are usually of normal-sized people seen in colour, and remain the same if eyes are open or closed. Atypical visual hallucinations such as seeing "a green devil in the corner laughing" or "a dog that would change in size when giving messages" or seeing hallucinations in black and white only are indicative of malingering.

Assessment Methods to Detect Malingered Psychosis

Interview-Based Methods The Structured Interview of Reported Symptoms (SIRS) (Rogers, Bagby, & Dickens, 1992) was initially developed in 1985, and in the most recent version consists of 172 items that are scored from a structured interview. The items are organized into the following eight scales that represent different strategies that a person may employ when malingering:

- Rare symptoms (RS)—symptoms very infrequently endorsed by true patients
- Symptom combinations (SC)—pairings of symptoms that are uncommon
- Improbable or absurd symptoms (IA)—symptoms unlikely to be true, since they are rarely endorsed by true patients
- Blatant symptoms (BL)—items that are obvious signs of mental disorder
- Subtle symptoms (SU)—items that contain what most people consider everyday problems
- Selectivity of symptoms (SEL)—ratio of symptoms endorsed versus those not endorsed
- Severity of symptoms (SEV)—number of severe symptoms reported
- Reported versus observed symptoms (RO)—discrepancy between self-report and observable symptoms

The SIRS has been extensively validated using both simulation and known-groups designs, and research has consistently demonstrated differences in SIRS scores between honest and simulating samples, and between clinical samples and suspected malingerers (Rogers, 1997). Recently, a strong two-factor structure for the SIRS was established, and cross-validated among various mental health and forensic populations (Rogers et al., 2005). Two main dimensions emerged as important detection strategies: Spurious Presentation (SP) (reported symptoms unlikely to ever occur) and Plausible Presentation (PP) (symptoms that have been reported by actual patients). Examples of scales loading on the SP factor included bogus symptoms (IA, RS, SC), obvious symptoms (BL), and symptoms inconsistent with clinical observations (RO). Scales on the PP factor included exaggeration of less severe (SU) or mundane issues.

The Miller-Forensic Assessment of Symptoms Test (M-FAST) (Miller, 2001) was developed on 330 forensic patients and 216 undergraduate students, and was intended as a brief, structured interview (25 items, 10-minute administration) to provide clinicians with a valid and reliable measure for detecting feigned mental illness. The M-FAST contains nine content items that resemble SIRS scales, including unusual hallucinations, reported versus observed symptoms, contradictory symptoms, extreme symptoms, trigger questions, rare combinations, negative image, unusual symptom onset, and suggestibility. A number of recent studies suggest that the M-FAST is a useful, reliable tool for detecting malingering (Guy, Kwartner, & Miller, 2006; Guy & Miller, 2004; Jackson, Rogers, & Sewell, 2005; Miller, 2001, 2005). For instance, Jackson and colleagues (2005) found that the recommended cut-off score of 6 maximized negative predictive power (.91) with a correct classification rate of 86%. However, the M-FAST performed only moderately well when identifying malingerers, with a positive predictive power of just .74. The M-FAST is intended as a screening tool, and is not recommended to be used in isolation.

Self-Report Questionnaires The first attempt to develop a self-report test of malingering was the M test (Baeber, Marston, Michelli, & Mills, 1985). The M test is a 33-item true-false test designed to screen for malingering schizophrenia. Items include genuine schizophrenic symptoms and bogus symptoms, such as atypical hallucinations and extremely severe symptoms. Simulation studies have found that students feigning schizophrenia consistently score higher than control students and psychiatric inpatients on the M test (see Smith, 1997, for a review). However, using the known-group design has produced variable results. In some studies, suspected malingerers have been detected at moderate levels (70%) (Smith & Borum, 1992), whereas Hankins, Barnard, and Robbins (1993) found that only 31% of the malingerer group was correctly classified.

The most widely used personality inventory to assess nonoffenders and offenders is the Minnesota Multiphasic Personality Inventory (Hathaway & McKinley, 1942) or the MMPI-2 (Butcher, Dahlstrom, Graham, Tellegen, & Kaemmer, 1989). The MMPI includes several clinical scales to assess psychopathology but also includes several scales specifically designed to test "faking-bad" or malingering. For example, the items on the infrequency (F) scale from the MMPI and the Back F (F_B) scale from the MMPI-2 were selected to detect unusual or atypical symptoms and consist of items endorsed by less than 10% of a normative sample. Another scale often used to detect malingering is the Gough Dissimulation Scale (Ds) (Gough, 1950). This scale consists of 74 items and was developed to differentiate a group of truly neurotic patients from a sample of college students told to simulate neuroses.

A comprehensive meta-analysis of the MMPI/MMPI-2 and malingering found that the F and F_B scales were the most useful at detecting malingerers (Rogers, Sewell, Martin, & Vitacco, 2003). However, the optimal cut-off score to use varies across the samples studied. Across studies, the Ds scale was also considered effective at detecting malingerers. A study by Storm and Graham (2000) examined whether the MMPI-2 validity scales would be able to correctly classify college students who have been coached on malingering strategies, students told to malinger but given no coaching, and psychiatric inpatients. Some validity indicators were more susceptible to coaching whereas others, such as the Infrequency Psychopathology Scale, could still discriminate coached malingerers from psychiatric inpatients.

Malingered Amnesia

Memory problems are a common symptom in both forensic and clinical practice. Memory deficits may consist of an inability to recall specific, highly salient incidents from the past (i.e., **retrograde amnesia**) or an impaired ability to establish new memories (i.e., **anterograde amnesia**). For example, the murderer who claims to have no memory for what happened before or during the homicidal event would be suffering from retrograde amnesia. In contrast, the patient who has been injured in a car accident who claims not to "remember anything" may be suffering from anterograde amnesia. Offenders may claim amnesia for their criminal behaviour in order to avoid or reduce the punishment (Parwatikar, Holcomb, & Menninger, 1985).

Retrograde amnesia: Memory deficits consisting of an inability to recall specific, highly salient incidents from the past

Anterograde amnesia: Memory deficits consisting of an impaired ability to establish new memories

Assessment Methods to Detect Malingered Amnesia
Several measures have been developed to catch the potential malingerer. Often, these tests appear to be difficult, but they are actually simple enough that even brain-damaged individuals perform adequately. The assumption underlying these tests is that the person attempting to fake will "overplay" the role and fail on even simple tasks. Many of the tasks available examine the effects of feigned impairments of anterograde amnesia or the acquisition of new information. A number of different versions of the Symptom Validity Test (SVT) (Pankratz, 1988) have been developed to assess malingered amnesia. In these tests, patients are typically presented with 20 to 100 stimuli, such as words or shapes, and following the presentation they are asked which of two choices they saw previously. Chance responding would result in 50% correct. Individuals who demonstrate below

chance responding are presumed to be feigning amnesia, because in order to systematically select the incorrect answer, memory for the correct alternative must be retained.

The Test of Memory Malingering (TOMM) (Tombaugh, 1996) is a 50-item recognition test designed to identify true memory-impaired patients from malingerers. In this test, the person is shown 50 drawings for 3 seconds each, and then is given a forced-choice recognition task in which he or she must choose the drawing he or she just saw from a pair of drawings. People are given feedback about their correct and incorrect choices. Trial 2 repeats the recognition task and, after a delay of ten minutes, a retention trial is administered (same recognition test but no feedback). Five or more errors on Trial 2 or the retention trial indicate the person might be malingering a memory deficit. Using the cut-off of five on Trial 2, Rees, Tombaugh, Gansler, and Moczynski (1998) correctly classified 95% of the brain-injured patients and 100% of controls attempting to malinger memory deficits. In a review of the validity of the TOMM to detect feigned memory impairment, Tombaugh (2002) concludes that the TOMM meets the required standards for court admissibility.

O'Bryant and Lucas (2006) reported the positive and negative predictive values of the TOMM to be .98 and .78 respectively, thus suggesting a 98% probability that the instrument will correctly identify a suspected malingerer (a score < 45 on Trial 2 or the retention trial), but only a 78% probability that a non-malingerer will be identified, given a score above 45 on Trials 1 and 2. So, while the TOMM is highly specific, it has low sensitivity. Consequently, while honest individuals are unlikely to be misclassified as malingerers, those who feign symptoms may go undetected. Greve and Bianchini (2006) suggest that the low sensitivity of the TOMM may be the result of incomplete administration (e.g., the retention trial is administered only when given a positive Trial 2). These authors caution that the retention trial of the TOMM should be dropped only if an additional SVT is administered.

SUMMARY

1. The Relevant/Irrelevant Test includes only two tests of questions: relevant questions concerning the crime in question and irrelevant questions that are unrelated to the crime. The Control Question Test (CQT) is the most commonly used polygraph exam in North America. It consists of three types of questions: neutral, control (questions relating to past behaviours that are supposed to generate emotion), and relevant (questions relating to the crime being investigated). The Guilty Knowledge Test (GKT) probes for whether the suspect has knowledge about the details of a crime that only the guilty person would have. This test is rarely used in North America but is used in Israel and Japan.

2. Three types of designs have been used to assess the accuracy of polygraph tests: laboratory, field, and field-analogue studies. In laboratory studies, volunteers (often university students) simulate criminal behaviour by committing a mock crime. Field studies involve real-life situations and actual criminal suspects, together with actual polygraph examinations. In field-analogue studies the act of deception is freely committed by an individual, it is independently known which individuals committed the act, the individuals are concerned about the outcome of the polygraph test, and

the polygrapher does not know the proportion of guilty and innocent individuals in the sample.

3. The CQT is quite accurate at detecting guilt but is not very good at determining a suspect's innocence (i.e., it has a high false-positive rate). Original examiners' accuracy is higher than blind chart examiners' scores, suggesting the original examiners are using extra-polygraphic cues to aid in their decisions. The GKT is quite accurate in detecting innocence but is not very good at determining a suspect's guilt (i.e., it has a high false-negative rate).

4. Event-related brain potentials (ERPs) and brain-imaging techniques can be used to detect deception in laboratory settings. However, these techniques have not yet been used extensively in forensic settings.

5. Another method of attempting to detect whether someone is lying is through the analysis of verbal/vocal characteristics and nonverbal behaviours. The vocal indicator most strongly associated with deception is voice pitch. A nonverbal indicator of deception that has been found consistently across studies is that liars tend to move their hands, arms, feet, and legs less than truth tellers. A verbal characteristic associated with deception is that liars provide a more limited number of details in their deception compared to those telling the truth.

6. The two key components to malingering are that the psychological or physical symptoms are clearly under voluntary control and that there are external motivations for the production of symptoms. Malingering should be considered in any forensic evaluation. Three explanatory models of malingering have been proposed: pathogenic, criminological, and adaptational. Only the adaptational model has received empirical support.

7. Malingering research utilizes three basic designs: case study, simulation, and known groups. Each of these designs has its associated strengths and weaknesses. The most common is the simulation design.

8. Both interview-based methods and self-report questionnaires have been developed in order to detect whether someone is malingering a mental disorder or memory deficit.

Key Concepts

anterograde amnesia 121

Control Question Test 92

countermeasures 98

defensiveness 114

event-related brain potentials 102

factitious disorder 112

ground truth 95

Guilty Knowledge Test 94

known-groups design 116

malingering 113

Munchausen syndrome 113

polygraph 91

polygraph disclosure tests 92

Relevant/Irrelevant Test 92

retrograde amnesia 121

simulation design 115

somatoform disorders 113

truth-bias 108

white lies 112

Discussion Questions

1. You are a forensic psychologist and have been called in by the police to give them advice on how to conduct a study to assess the accuracy of their polygraph examiners. In particular, they want to know whether or not their examiners are using any extra-polygraphic cues in making their decisions about guilt or innocence. What advice would you give to the police?

2. You are conducting a study on deception in children. You want to know the role of age and why children lie. How would you elicit lying behaviour in the children and what variables would you measure?

3. You are a forensic psychologist hired to determine if a defendant is truly psychotic. What sorts of information would you base your assessment on? What clinical indicators would you look for?

4. Many of the studies designed to detect deception involve deceiving research participants. What ethical concerns have been raised? What types of studies should be allowed?

5. The Control Question Test is the polygraph test commonly used by police in North America. Do you think this test has sufficient validity for use by the police? Should it be admissible in court?

6. You recently got hired as a customs agent. Knowing what you do about nonvocal and vocal cues to deception, what cues would you be watching out for?

7. List the advantages and disadvantages to using simulation studies to study malingering of mental disorders.

Readings

DePaulo, B.M., Lindsay, J.J., Malone, B.E., Muhlenbruck, L., Charlton, K., & Cooper, H. (2003). Cues to deception. *Psychological Bulletin, 129,* 74–118.

Lykken, D.T. (1998). *A tremor in the blood: Uses and abuses of the lie detector.* New York: Plenum.

Rogers, R. (1997). *Clinical assessment of malingering and deception.* New York: Guilford Press.

Websites

American Polygraph Association
www.polygraph.org

Criticism of the Polygraph
www.antipolygraph.org

Chapter 5
Eyewitness Testimony

Learning Objectives

- Describe two categories of independent variables and three general dependent variables found in eyewitness research.

- Describe and explain the misinformation effect.

- Outline the components of the cognitive interview.

- Describe lineup procedures and how they may be biased.

- Summarize the debate surrounding expert testimony on eyewitness issues.

- Outline the recommendations for collecting eyewitness identification evidence.

Lucy Peluso went to the bank on her lunch hour. As she approached the teller, a man pushed her out of the way so that he could quickly exit the bank. Seconds later, Lucy found out that the man had robbed the teller. Lucy was an eyewitness. The police interviewed her along with the others in the bank. The witnesses were able to hear each other describe what they saw. Six months after the robbery, Lucy was asked to go to the police station to view a series of photographs. When she was asked whether the man who robbed the bank was pictured, Lucy very quickly pointed and said, "That's him, I'm certain."

Eyewitness evidence is one of the earliest and most widely studied topics in forensic psychology. As you read in Chapter 1, the German psychologist Albert von Schrenck-Notzing testified during a serial killer trial about the influence of pretrial media exposure on witnesses' memory. Today, both the police and the courts rely on eyewitness evidence. Eyewitness testimony is one of the most compelling types of evidence presented in criminal trials. Thus, information about the likelihood and types of mistakes made by eyewitnesses is vitally important in terms of justice. In this chapter, we will focus on how memory works when it comes to remembering in an eyewitness context. As well, we will examine the various factors and police procedures that can influence how accurate eyewitnesses can be.

EYEWITNESS TESTIMONY: THE ROLE OF MEMORY

A large part of eyewitness testimony rests on memory. The concept of memory can be viewed as a process involving several stages. The encoding stage occurs first, when you perceive and pay attention to details in your environment. For example, you are perceiving and paying attention when you look at a stranger's face and notice his big, bushy eyebrows. To some extent, the stranger's face and eyebrows have been encoded. The encoded information then passes into your short-term holding facility, known as your short-term memory. Your short-term memory has a limited capacity. Consequently, in order to make room for other, new information, information in your short-term memory passes into your longer-term holding facility, known as your long-term memory. Information from long-term memory can be accessed or retrieved as needed. For example, if you are asked to describe the stranger you saw, you will retrieve the information you stored in your long-term memory and report that the stranger had bushy eyebrows. It is important to remember that not every piece of information will go through all the memory stages and also there are factors that can affect each stage. For example, not all details from an event will be encoded; nor will all information in short-term memory move to long-term memory. Using our example of Lucy Peluso witnessing a bank robbery, consider the factors that are occurring to affect memory and retrieval.

Look at this scene for five seconds.

Lucy is filling out a deposit slip so she will be ready for the bank teller. She is not paying attention to her environment (factor: inattention). Unexpectedly, there is a brief interaction between her and an unfamiliar male (factors: unexpectedness; amount of time to view environmental details). Lucy is now a witness and she is interviewed with several other people in the bank by police (factor: hearing others describe the same environmental details she saw). The police officer asks Lucy a few, brief questions (factor: the wording of the questions). Lucy is called six months after the crime to examine a lineup (factors: the amount of time elapsed between having witnessed the event and having to retrieve the information; type of lineup procedure used). Lucy is confident when she identifies the culprit (factor: relation between confidence and accuracy). Figure 5.1 delineates the stages of memory.

As you may have figured out by now, memory is not like a video recording in which an identical representation of the event is stored and then can be played on request (Loftus, 1979b). Our memory can change each time we retrieve the event; some parts of the event may be embellished or guessed at because we cannot remember all the details. Often in our everyday life, our memory fallibilities are insignificant. For example, remembering that you bought a coffee at a Second Cup when actually it came from a Tim Hortons is harmless, most likely. In contrast, remembering whether the culprit was right- or left-handed may be critical if police are going to arrest the guilty suspect.

Eyewitness memory retrieval can be broadly partitioned into either recall or recognition memory. **Recall memory** refers to reporting details of a previously witnessed event or person. For example, describing what the culprit did and what the culprit

Recall memory: Reporting details of a previously witnessed event or person

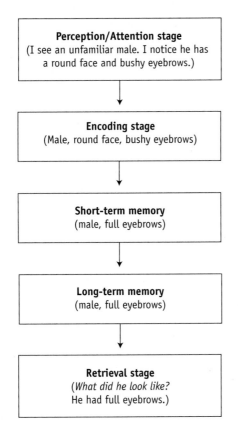

Figure 5.1 Stages of Memory

looked like are both recall tasks. In contrast, **recognition memory** refers to determining whether a previously seen item or person is the same as what is currently being viewed. For example, hearing a set of voices and identifying the culprit's voice or identifying clothing worn by the culprit during the crime are both recognition tasks.

Recognition memory:
Determining whether a previously seen item or person is the same as what is currently being viewed

HOW DO WE STUDY EYEWITNESS ISSUES?

Researchers interested in studying eyewitness issues can examine data from actual crimes. For example, they can use archival data such as police reports, or they can examine witnesses in naturalistic environments by accompanying police to crime scenes and interviewing witnesses after the police have done their job. Alternatively, they can conduct laboratory simulations. The laboratory simulation study is the most common paradigm used to study eyewitness issues.

The Laboratory Simulation

To study eyewitness memory using a laboratory simulation, an unknowing participant views a critical event, such as a crime, either through a slide sequence, video recording, or live. The participant is unaware that he or she will be questioned about the event until after the event is witnessed. Now witness, the participant is asked to describe what happened and the target/culprit involved. Following the descriptions of what was witnessed, the witness may be asked to examine a lineup. There can be many independent variables that are manipulated or examined; however, there are only three general dependent variables in eyewitness studies.

Independent Variables
Numerous independent variables can be manipulated or examined within the laboratory simulation. Wells (1978) has coined the terms *estimator variable* and *system variable* to help classify them. **Estimator variables** are those variables or factors that are present at the time of the crime and that cannot be changed. These can include the age of the witness, the amount of lighting, the presence of a weapon, and whether the witness was intoxicated. These are variables over which the criminal justice system *cannot* exert control. Thus, their effect on eyewitness accuracy can be estimated only after the crime. **System variables** are those variables or factors that can be manipulated to increase (or decrease) eyewitness accuracy, such as the type of procedure used by police to interview the witness or the type of lineup procedure used to present the suspect to the witness. These variables are under the control of the justice system. Both estimator and system variables can be manipulated in eyewitness laboratory studies.

Dependent Variables
The three general dependent variables in eyewitness studies are (1) recall of the event/crime, (2) recall of the culprit, and (3) recognition of the culprit.

Recall of the crime or culprit can take two formats. With **open-ended recall**, also known as a **free narrative**, witnesses are asked to either write or orally state all they remember about the event without the officer (or experimenter) asking questions. With this type of recall, the witness also may be asked to describe the culprit. With **direct question recall**, witnesses are asked a series of specific questions about the crime or the culprit. For example, the witness may be asked the colour of the getaway car or the length of the culprit's hair.

A witness's *recall* of the crime or culprit can be examined for the following:

- *The amount of information reported.* How many descriptors of the crime do witnesses report? How many descriptors of the culprit do witnesses report?
- *The type of information reported.* What is the proportion of peripheral details versus central details? What is the proportion of culprit details versus environment details?
- *The accuracy of information reported.* What is the proportion of correct descriptors reported? What is the proportion of omission errors (information the witness failed to report)? What is the proportion of commission errors (details falsely reported to be present)?

As for the recognition of the culprit, the typical recognition task is a lineup. A culprit **lineup** is a set of people presented to the witness, who in turn must identify the culprit if he or she is present. Another type of lineup takes the form of a set of voices, and the witness is asked to identify the culprit's voice. Clothing lineups, in which the witness examines clothing that may have been worn by the culprit, sometimes are also used.

A witness's *recognition* response can be examined for the following:

- *Accuracy of decision.* What is the rate of correctly identifying the culprit in the lineup? What is the rate of correctly stating that the culprit is not present in the lineup?
- *Types of errors made.* What is the rate of identifying an innocent person? What is the rate of stating that the culprit is not present when he or she is actually in the lineup?

RECALL MEMORY

The primary goal for an officer interviewing an eyewitness is to extract from the witness a complete and accurate report of what happened (Fisher, Geiselman, & Raymond, 1987; Jackson, Sijlbing, & Thiecke, 1996). Insufficient information may provide the officer with few leads to pursue, resulting in a case that will not be solved. In this situation, the culprit will remain free to commit further crimes. If inaccurate information is supplied, an officer may pursue innocent suspects, thus reducing the likelihood that the guilty person will be caught.

Now test your own recall. Without looking back at the crime scene photo on page 126, how many details can you remember?

Interviewing Eyewitnesses

Fisher et al. (1987) were curious about the techniques police were using to interview eyewitnesses. They analyzed 11 tape-recorded interviews from a police department in Florida. Eight different detectives, who averaged 10.5 years of experience each, conducted these interviews. The researchers found that there was a lot of variation in how the interviews were conducted. In general, however, the researchers found that the officers would introduce themselves, ask the eyewitnesses to report what they remembered using an open-ended format, and then ask the witnesses a series of direct questions to determine specific information, such as the age or height of the culprit. The officers usually ended the interview by asking the eyewitnesses if there was any additional information that they could remember.

Fisher et al. (1987) found that the police officers' approach limited their ability to collect complete and accurate information in a number of ways. First, the researchers found that police often interrupted eyewitnesses when they were providing an open-ended recall report. The police may limit the amount of information eyewitnesses have in their conscious memory by preventing them from speaking or distracting them with questions.

Second, police questioned eyewitnesses with very short, specific questions. This type of question format uses a more superficial level of concentration than open-ended questions and tends to result in very short answers. The other problem with short, specific questions is that a police officer may not ask a relevant question that would provide critical information. For example, the culprit may have a tattoo, but if the officer does not ask about tattoos, the eyewitness may not report this feature. Thus, the police officer may miss a descriptor that could help in narrowing the suspect pool and arresting the culprit.

Third, police officers tended to ask questions in a predetermined or random order that was inconsistent with the information that witnesses were providing at the time. For example, a police officer may have asked a question about the culprit's voice while the witness was describing the culprit's clothing. Mixing visual and auditory questions has been found to decrease recall by approximately 19% (Fisher & Price-Roush, as cited in Fisher et al., 1987). Lastly, officers tended to ask questions that are "leading" or suggestive, which can be very dangerous when trying to collect accurate information.

The Leading Question—The Misinformation Effect

Elizabeth Loftus, one of the most prominent researchers in the area of leading questions, has conducted many experiments demonstrating that a witness's recall report can be altered by the phrasing of a question. In one study, Loftus and Palmer (1974) had university students watch a videotape of a car accident. After viewing the accident, the participants were asked the identical question with a variation in one critical word, *hit*: "About how fast were the cars going when they *hit* each other?" *Hit* was replaced with either *smashed*, *collided*, *bumped*, or *contacted*. Even though all participants saw the same videotape, the speed reported by the participants varied depending on which critical word was used. Participants reported the highest rate of speed when the word *smashed* was used and lowest rates of speed when the words *bumped* and *contacted* were used.

The experiment did not end there. The researchers called participants back a week later and asked whether they had seen any broken glass. Participants who were questioned with the word *smashed* were more likely to recall seeing broken glass than were the other participants. However, there was no broken glass in the videotape. This study illustrates how the wording of a question can influence memory for the incident.

Loftus went on to demonstrate that simply introducing an inaccurate detail to witnesses could lead them to report that inaccurate detail when questioned later (Loftus, Altman, & Geballe, 1975). The **misinformation effect**, also called the **post-event information effect**, is a phenomenon in which a witness who is presented with inaccurate information after an event will incorporate that misinformation in a subsequent recall task (Loftus, 1975).

In one classic study, Loftus conducted four experiments demonstrating that how a question is worded can influence an eyewitness's recall at a later date. We'll discuss two of these experiments below.

These studies used a common method or paradigm to investigate the misinformation effect. Participants were exposed to an event via slides, video, or live action. They were then given a series of questions about the event, some of which contained misinformation. Later, the participants were asked a series of questions about the event, probing their response to the misinformation introduced. They were asked to respond from a forced-choice/multiple-choice set. That is, they were given a set of responses to choose from, with one response being correct, one response containing the misinformation, and one or two incorrect responses.

Experiment 1 Forty university students watched a three-minute film clip of a class being interrupted by eight demonstrators. Following the clip, participants were given 20 questions. Half of the participants were asked, "Was the leader of the four demonstrators who entered the classroom a male?" The remaining participants were asked, "Was the leader of the 12 demonstrators who entered the classroom a male?" All other questions were the same for the two groups. After a one-week delay, the participants were asked 20 new questions about the film. The critical question in this new set was, "How many demonstrators did you see entering the classroom?" The participants that were asked a question about 12 demonstrators reported seeing an average of almost 9 demonstrators (8.85). Those who were asked about four demonstrators reported seeing an average of 6.40 demonstrators. Thus, incorporating the number of demonstrators into

Misinformation effect:
Phenomenon where a witness who is presented with inaccurate information after an event will incorporate that misinformation in a subsequent recall task. Also known as the *post-event information effect*

Post-event information effect:
Phenomenon where a witness who is presented with inaccurate information after an event will incorporate that misinformation in a subsequent recall task. Also known as the *misinformation effect*

the question posed to witnesses affected the number of demonstrators witnesses recalled seeing later.

Experiment 2 One hundred and fifty university students watched a brief video of a car accident involving a white sports car. Participants then answered ten questions about the car accident. Half of the participants were asked, "How fast was the white sports car going when it passed the barn while travelling along the country road?" The remaining participants were asked, "How fast was the white sports car going while travelling along the country road?" A week later, all participants were asked ten new questions. The critical question was, "Did you see a barn?" No barn was shown in the videotape. For the first group who had the word barn embedded in the first set of questions, 17.3% stated they saw a barn. In contrast, 2.7% of participants in the no-barn group reported seeing a barn.

As you can see, the misinformation effect occurs using a number of different types of questions and methodology. But why does it occur?

Explaining the Misinformation Effect Many studies have demonstrated that a witness's report can include misinformation that was previously supplied (Cole & Loftus, 1979; Loftus, 1979a), and these have fuelled debates on how and why this phenomenon occurs (Loftus, Miller, & Burns, 1978; McCloskey & Zaragoza, 1985). Were witnesses' memories changed? Were the participants just going along with the experimenter (or guessing) and providing the answer they thought was wanted? Or maybe the witness had two memories, a correct one and an incorrect one, and could not remember where each memory came from. These are the three general positions that researchers have tried to advance or argue against, with each position having different implications for memory:

1. With changes in the methodology, some studies have found support for guessing or experimenter pleasing. Some witnesses will guess at the answer they think the experimenter wants, resulting in the misinformation effect. This explanation is known as the **misinformation acceptance hypothesis** (McCloskey & Zaragoza, 1985).

2. Some studies have found that witnesses can recall both memories—the original, accurate one and the inaccurate one. However, witnesses cannot remember where each memory came from. When asked to recall what was seen, the witness chooses the incorrect memory. This explanation is called the **source misattribution hypothesis** (Lindsay, 1994).

3. Loftus is perhaps the biggest proponent of the **memory impairment hypothesis**. This hypothesis refers to the original memory being replaced with the new, incorrect memory (Loftus, 1979b). The original memory is no longer accessible.

The debate on which explanation is responsible for the misinformation effect is far from over. Researchers continue to come up with different methodologies that point to alternative explanations. One issue that has been put to rest, though, is that the misinformation effect happens. The misinformation effect is a real phenomenon.

How can the misinformation effect happen in real life? A witness can be exposed to inaccurate information in a number of ways:

1. An officer may make assumptions about what occurred or what was witnessed and then inadvertently phrase a question consistent with his or her assumption. For example, the officer may ask the witness, "Did you see the gun?" rather than asking the more neutral question, "Did you see a gun?"

Misinformation acceptance hypothesis: Explanation for the misinformation effect where the incorrect information is provided because the witness guesses what the officer or experimenter wants the response to be

Source misattribution hypothesis: Explanation for the misinformation effect—where the witness has two memories, the original and the misinformation; however, the witness cannot remember where each memory originated or the source of each

Memory impairment hypothesis: Explanation for the misinformation effect where the original memory is replaced with the new, incorrect, information

2. There may be more than one witness, and the witnesses overhear each other's statements. If there are discrepancies between the witnesses, a witness may change his or her report to make it consistent.

3. A police officer may incorporate an erroneous detail from a previous witness's interview. For example, the officer may ask the witness, "What was the culprit with the scar wearing?" The witness may subsequently report that the culprit had a scar when in fact there was none.

PROCEDURES THAT HELP POLICE INTERVIEW EYEWITNESSES

Psychologists have been instrumental in developing procedures that can be beneficial at eliciting accurate information from witnesses.

Hypnosis

In some cases, eyewitnesses may be unable to recall very much that was witnessed, possibly because they were traumatized. With the help of hypnosis, they may be able to recall a greater amount of information. In a survey of ten forensic hypnosis experts, all felt that hypnosis could help witnesses to remember crime details (Vingoe, 1995). It is assumed that a person under hypnosis is able to retrieve memories that are otherwise inaccessible. A hypnotized witness may be able to produce a greater number of details than a nonhypnotized witness; this phenomenon is termed **hypnotically refreshed memory** (Steblay & Bothwell, 1994). Although most people can experience some effect of hypnosis, approximately 10% of the population cannot be hypnotized, and about 5% to 10% are highly suggestible (Hilgard, 1965). The ability to be hypnotized peaks in late childhood (Spiegel & Spiegel, 1987). A variety of factors can influence whether hypnosis can be induced:

- The degree of trust the witness places in the hypnotist
- The witness's willingness to be hypnotized
- The witness's belief in hypnosis
- The seriousness of the context for being hypnotized

According to Kebbell and Wagstaff (1998), two techniques that are often used in hypnosis are age regression and the television technique. With age regression, the witness goes back in time and re-experiences the original event. With the television technique, the witness imagines that he or she is watching an imaginary television screen with the events being played as they were witnessed. Further instructions stating that the eyewitness's memory will improve over time and in future sessions are provided once the witness has recalled the event. The witness is then awoken from the hypnosis.

Police are not interested in using hypnosis simply to collect *more* information—they are interested in collecting *accurate* information. For hypnosis to be useful in a forensic context, police need to know about the accuracy of the information recalled while under hypnosis.

Hypnotically refreshed memory: Where a hypnotized person is able to produce a greater number of details than a person who has not been hypnotized

Several reviews have examined the effectiveness of hypnosis in enhancing memory recall (e.g., Brown, Scheflin, & Hammond, 1998; Reiser, 1989; Steblay & Bothwell, 1994). These reviews find that individuals under hypnosis will provide more details, but those details are just as likely to be inaccurate as accurate (see also Fisher, 1995). The hypnotized individual seems to be more suggestible to subtle cues by the interviewer than under normal conditions. The difficulty with using hypnosis is not being able to differentiate between the accurate and inaccurate details. Witnesses recall both accurate and inaccurate details with the same degree of confidence (Sheehan & Tilden, 1984), and as we will see later, this confidence may be misleading.

The Canadian courts are aware of the difficulties with hypnotically induced recall and typically do not permit the use of information gained that way.

The Cognitive Interview

Given the limitations of hypnosis, researchers have developed an interview procedure based on principles of memory storage and retrieval called the **cognitive interview** (Geiselman et al., 1984). The cognitive interview can be used with eyewitnesses, but it is not a procedure recommended for use with unwilling participants such as suspects (see Chapter 3).

Cognitive interview: Interview procedure for use with eyewitnesses based on principles of memory storage and retrieval

The cognitive interview is based on four memory-retrieval techniques (see Box 5.1) to increase recall: (1) reinstating the context, (2) reporting everything, (3) reversing order, and (4) changing perspective.

Box 5.1

How the Cognitive Interview Components Are Implemented with Witnesses

Below are sample statements (from Geiselman, Fisher, MacKinnon, & Holland, 1986) that correspond to the cognitive interview memory-retrieval techniques:

1. *Reinstate the context:* "Try to reinstate in your mind the context surrounding the incident. Think about what the surrounding environment looked like at the scene, such as the room, the weather, and any nearby people or objects. Also think about how you were feeling at the time and think about your reactions to the incident" (p. 390).

2. *Report everything:* "Some people hold back information because they are not quite sure that the information is important. Please do not edit anything out of your report, report even things you think may not be important" (pp. 391–392).

3. *Recall the event in different orders:* "It is natural to go through the incident from beginning to end. However, you also should try to go through the events in reverse order. Or, try starting with the thing that impressed you the most in the incident and then go from there, going both forward in time and backward" (p. 391).

4. *Change perspectives:* "Try to recall the incident from different perspectives that you may have had or adopt the perspectives of others that were present during the incident. For example, try to place yourself in the role of a prominent character in the incident and think about what he or she must have seen" (p. 391).

It should be noted that changing perspectives has been criticized for eliciting erroneous information. If a witness is asked to imagine what he or she saw from a different perspective, the witness might report details that are made up or inaccurate.

Source: Geiselman et al., 1986.

In an initial study, Geiselman, Fisher, MacKinnon, and Holland (1985) compared the "standard" police interview, hypnosis, and the cognitive interview to determine differences in the amount and accuracy of information recalled by witnesses. Participants watched a police training film of a crime. Forty-six hours after viewing the film, each participant was interviewed with one of the procedures by experienced law enforcement professionals. Compared with the "standard" police interview and hypnosis, the cognitive interview produced the greatest amount of accurate information without an increase in inaccurate details.

Bekerian and Dennett (1993) reviewed 27 studies that tested the cognitive interview. Across the studies, the cognitive interview produced more accurate information than the alternatives, such as the "standard" police interview. Approximately a 30% increase in accurate information was obtained with the cognitive interview over other procedures, and there was an insignificant decrease in errors for the cognitive interview compared with other methods.

Over the years, Fisher and Geiselman (1992) expanded the cognitive interview into the **enhanced cognitive interview**, including various principles of social dynamics in addition to the memory retrieval principles used in the original cognitive interview. The additional components include the following:

Enhanced cognitive interview: Interview procedure that includes various principles of social dynamics in addition to the memory retrieval principles used in the original cognitive interview

1. *Rapport building.* An officer should spend time building rapport with the witness and make him or her feel comfortable and supported.

2. *Supportive interviewer behaviour.* A witness's free recall should not be interrupted; pauses should be waited out by the officer, who should express attention to what the witness is saying.

3. *Transfer of control.* The witness, not the officer, should control the flow of the interview; the witness is the expert—that is, the witness, not the officer, was the person who saw the crime.

4. *Focused retrieval.* Questions should be open-ended and not leading or suggestive; after free recall, the officer should use focused memory techniques to facilitate retrieval.

5. *Witness-compatible questioning.* An officer's questions should match the witness's thinking; if the witness is talking about clothing, the officer should be asking about clothing.

The enhanced cognitive interview, the original cognitive interview, and the standard police interview have been compared (Memon & Bull, 1991). Both cognitive interviews produced more accurate information, without an increase in inaccurate information, than standard interviews. Significant differences between the two cognitive interviews have not been found (Köehnken, 1995). The question remains as to which components are responsible for the increase in accurate information (Kebbell & Wagstaff, 1998).

The cognitive interview has been tested in the United Kingdom with different-aged participants, including younger adults (age 17 to 31), older adults (age 60 to 74), and older-older adults (age 75 to 95) (Wright & Holliday, 2007). Compared with a "standard" police interview conducted in the United Kingdom, the cognitive interview increased the amount of accurate "person," "action," "object," and "surrounding" details for each age group without increasing the amount of inaccurate information recalled.

Although some officers in Canada have been trained to conduct cognitive interviews, some are reluctant to use it, stating that it requires too much time to conduct and that the appropriate environment is not always available. However, trained officers report that they use some of the cognitive interview components on a regular basis when interviewing witnesses.

RECALL MEMORY FOLLOWING A LONG DELAY

Is it possible to forget a traumatic event such as abuse, only to recall it many years later? This question is at the centre of a heated debate about memory repression. Some argue that childhood sexual abuse memories are so traumatic for some individuals that they repress them in their unconscious. It is only as adults, and through the help of therapy, that they come to recall the abuse, through what are known as recovered memories. Others argue that it is only through therapy and the use of suggestive techniques that clients come to believe that they were sexually abused as children when in fact they were not; such recollections are known as false memories. Loftus is among the proponents of this second group. **False memory syndrome** was a term coined to describe a client's false belief that he or she was sexually abused as a child. Clients may have no memories of this abuse until they enter therapy to deal with some other psychological problem such as depression or substance abuse (Read, 1999). See Box 5.2 for a case involving "delayed" memory.

False memory syndrome: Term to describe clients' false beliefs that they were sexually abused as children, having no memories of this abuse until they enter therapy to deal with some other psychological problem such as depression or substance abuse

Can Traumatic Memories Be Forgotten?

Perhaps the greatest point of contention regarding false memory syndrome is whether traumatic memories can be completely forgotten only to be remembered many years later.

Box 5.2

Delayed Memory Goes to Court

On October 2, 1992, a 48-year-old teacher, Michael Kliman, from Richmond, B.C., was arrested and charged with the sexual abuse of two female students. The complainants (A and B) were in their late 20s when they made the allegations, but the abuse allegedly occurred in 1975, when the complainants were in Grade 6.

The complaints alleged that Kliman would take each of them out of class three or four times a week for up to 20 minutes at a time. It was alleged that Kliman would bring them to a small room in the school where he would sexually fondle them or they would fondle him. In addition, one of the complainants claimed that when she was on a class camping trip in Grade 7, Kliman took her to his tent and raped her. Both complainants alleged that they suffered from dissociative amnesia—that is, memory loss of an event because of the trauma of the event.

Both A and B testified that they had no memory of the abuse until many years later. A stated that she recovered the repressed memory after she was admitted to a hospital psychiatric ward for an eating disorder when she was 19. B stated that she recalled the past events after she was questioned by police following A's claim.

In A's hospital record for anorexia, Mr. Kliman's name was not mentioned. A testified that while she worked at an insurance company she was sexually abused/harassed by a superior. She also testified that she was repeatedly abused and stalked by a man between October 1990 and December 1991. She consulted a therapist as a result of this abuse in February 1991. The therapist specialized in adult survivorship of childhood sexual abuse, post-trauma reactions, dissociation, and memory. At the time A sought therapy, she had no memory of abuse at her elementary

(continued)

(continued)

school. It was during the course of this therapy that *A* first identified Mr. Kliman as an abuser.

B was sexually abused by a foster brother and neighbour when she was 11 years old. She has a continuous memory of this abuse. *B* had no memory of abuse by Mr. Kliman until interviewed by the police officer following up *A*'s allegation of abuse.

Dr. John Yuille and Dr. Elizabeth Loftus were called in to discuss memory and dissociative amnesia. The experts reached somewhat differing conclusions. Dr. Loftus noted that at present there is no scientific evidence to support the notion that several incidents of traumatic sexual abuse could cause memory of the events to be lost. She also testified that the use of leading questions and suggestive interviewing techniques could contaminate

memory. Dr. Yuille testified that there is literature, including some of his work, that supports the notion of dissociative amnesia.

Mr. Kliman was tried three times. In the first trial, the jury convicted him. The decision was appealed and the court of appeal set aside the conviction because of inadequate disclosure. In the second trial, the jury was unable to reach a unanimous verdict. In the third trial, Mr. Kliman was acquitted on all counts. The trial judge noted that there were many improbabilities about the details of the complainants' testimony that made it difficult to believe, aside from the memory issues. For example, it is hard to imagine how Mr. Kliman could excuse himself from class several times a week for 15 to 20 minutes at a time.

Source: *R. v. Kliman*, 1998.

In a study by Porter and Birt (2001), university students were asked to describe their most traumatic experience and their most positive experience. A number of different experiences were reported in each condition. Approximately 5% of their sample of 306 participants reported sexual assault or abuse as their most traumatic experience. The majority of these participants stated that they had consciously forced the memory out of their minds rather than never having a memory of it. Proponents of the false memory argument contend that not having any memory of abuse is different from preferring not to think about it. When there is absolutely no memory of abuse, and it is only through the use of suggestive techniques that the abuse is remembered, many argue that these memories should be interpreted cautiously.

Lindsay and Read (1995) suggest five criteria to consider when trying to determine the veracity of a recovered memory:

1. *Age of complainant at the time of the alleged abuse.* It is unlikely that anyone would have a memory (of abuse or otherwise) prior to age two.

2. *Techniques used to recover memory.* Techniques such as hypnosis and guided imagery heighten suggestibility and encourage fantasy.

3. *Similarity of reports across interview sessions.* Do the reports become increasingly more fantastic, or are they similar?

4. *Motivation for recall.* Is the client experiencing other psychological distress and wanting an answer to explain such feelings?

5. *Time elapsed since the alleged abuse.* It may be more difficult to recall abuse that occurred 25 years ago than two years ago.

Historic child sexual abuse (HCSA): Allegations of child abuse having occurred several years, often decades, prior to when they are being prosecuted

Although some may "recover" memories of abuse and others never truly forget this traumatic experience, the courts are seeing a number of cases where there has been a *delay in reporting* the abuse. See Box 5.3 for a discussion regarding the phenomenon of *historic child sexual abuse.*

Box 5.3

Delayed Prosecutions of Historic Child Sexual Abuse

Courts are having to deal with a relatively new phenomenon known as **historic child sexual abuse (HCSA)**—that is, allegations of child abuse having occurred several years, often decades, prior to the time at which they are being prosecuted (Connolly & Read, 2006). It should be noted that the vast majority of these cases involve memories of abuse that have been *continuous*. The alleged victim does not claim to have ever "forgotten" the abuse. From the results of a national survey in the United States, Smith, Letourneau, Saunders, Kilpatrick, Resnick, and Best (2000) found that 47% of adults who reported having been abused as children delayed reporting the abuse for over five years. Even more intriguing is that approximately 27% of this sample noted that they reported the abuse for the first time on the survey. Being male seems to be a reliable predictor of delayed reporting (Finkelhor, Hotaling, Lewis, & Smith, 1990).

In Canada (as well as the United Kingdom, Australia, and New Zealand) there is no time limit during which a victim must report the sexual abuse. Connolly and Read (2006) examined 2064 criminal complaints of HCSA in Canada with the objective of describing these criminal prosecutions. "Historic" abuse was defined as abuse in which the last offence occurred two or more years prior to the time of trial. Connolly and Read (2006) stated that the "typical" HCSA case had the following characteristics:

> The complainant is probably female. On average, she was 9 years old when the abuse began, 12 years old when it ended, and 26 years old at trial. She is unlikely to be reported to have been in therapy, and she is very likely to report continuous memory for the offence. Her abuser is more likely than not to be a male relative and he is on average 23 years older than her. On average, he was 33 years old when the abuse began, 36 years old when it ended and 51 years old at trial. In the majority of cases, the complainant reports repeated abuse that was sustained over an average period of almost 4 years. A threat is probably not reported to have accompanied the abuse, but if one is reported, it is likely to be against the complainant's or her family's physical safety. (p. 424)

Read, Connolly, and Welsh (2006) examined the factors that predicted the verdicts in actual HCSA cases between 1980 and 2002 in Canada. Four hundred and sixty-six cases were heard before a jury (434 cases resulted in a guilty verdict). Six hundred and forty-four cases were heard by judge alone (442 cases resulted in a guilty verdict). In each case, the complainant was 19 years old or younger when the alleged offence began, and two or more years had elapsed from the end of the alleged offence to the trial date. Eleven independent variables were examined: (1) length of delay, (2) age of complainant at the time the alleged abuse began, (3) repressed memory testimony, (4) involvement in therapy, (5) expert testimony, (6) frequency of alleged abuse, (7) intrusiveness of alleged abuse, (8) duration of alleged abuse, (9) presence of threat, (10) complainant's gender, and (11) relationship of accused to complainant. The following are the researchers' results, for both jury trials and judge-alone trials:

Results for Jury Trials

In 93% of the HCSAs prosecuted before a jury, a guilty verdict was reached. Guilty verdicts were lower with older-aged complainants (Mage = 12.67) than with younger-aged complainants (Mage = 9.52 years). Fewer guilty verdicts were obtained when experts provided an opinion for one side or the other, but not when there was an expert on each side. Surprisingly, when an expert testified on behalf of the Crown, fewer guilty verdicts were obtained than when there was no expert testifying. An expert testifying for the defence also resulted in somewhat fewer convictions than when there was no expert. When the abuse was accompanied by threats (i.e., physical and/or emotional), guilty verdicts were more likely than when there were no threats. Also, guilty verdicts were higher for defendants who had a familial relationship with the complainant rather than a community connection to the complainant. Other independent variables did not differ significantly in their influence on the verdict.

Results for Judge-Alone Trials

In approximately 69% of the HCSAs prosecuted before a judge alone, a guilty verdict was reached. The increase in likelihood of acquittal corresponded with the increase in length of delay. The average delay period was 14.98 years for acquittals as compared to an average delay of 12.36 years for guilty verdicts. Guilty verdicts were more likely when a claim of repression was made than when no repression claim was made by the complainant. Guilty verdicts were more likely with more intrusive sexual abuse than with less intrusive sexual abuse, such as sexual exposure or sexual touching. Judges were more likely to reach a guilty verdict when the defendant was a family member rather than someone in the community. When the defence had an unchallenged expert testify, guilty verdicts were less likely than if no expert testified.

RECALL OF THE CULPRIT

Along with a description of what happened, the witness will be asked to describe the culprit's appearance. Perusal of newspapers and news broadcasts find that descriptions are vague and apply to many. For example, a culprit may be described as white, male, between five-foot-nine and six feet tall, with short, brown hair. Think of how many people you know who fit this description.

Quantity and Accuracy of Descriptions

Research examining culprit descriptions provided by witnesses finds that descriptions are limited in detail and accuracy (Sporer, 1996). Lindsay, Martin, and Webber (1994) examined descriptions provided by adults in real and staged crimes. Witnesses to staged crimes reported an average of 7.35 descriptors. In contrast, witnesses to real crimes reported significantly fewer descriptors—3.94 on average. Hair and clothing items were commonly reported descriptors.

In a study examining real-life descriptions, Van Koppen and Lochun (1997) conducted an archival review of official court records examining descriptions of culprits from 400 robberies. Data were coded from 1300 witnesses and 1650 descriptions of culprits were analyzed. Consistent with anecdotal evidence, witnesses provided few descriptors. On average, witnesses reported eight descriptors. The researchers found that sex and height were the items most often reported. Witnesses were correct 100% of the time when identifying the sex of the culprit. Unfortunately, sex is not a great discriminator. Only 52% of witnesses were accurate when identifying the height of the culprit.

Yarmey and Yarmey (1997) examined person and clothing descriptors provided by a sample of 603 participants. Accuracy ranged dramatically across the various descriptors (see Figure 5.2).

Figure 5.2 Descriptor Accuracy as a Function of Item Recalled

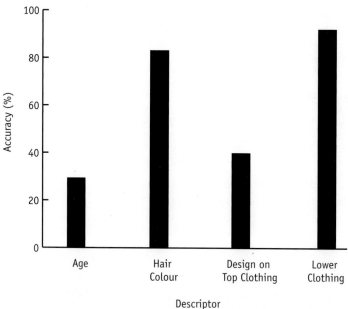

Accuracy was highest for hair colour and the type of clothing worn below the waist. Wagstafff, MacVeigh, Boston, Scott, Brunas-Wagstaff, and Cole (2003) also found that hair colour and hairstyle were reported most accurately. Yarmey, Jacob, and Porter (2002) found that witnesses had difficulty correctly reporting weight (27% accuracy), eye colour, (24% accuracy), and type of footwear (13% accuracy).

As you can see, culprit descriptions are limited in quantity and accuracy, which, in turn, limits their usefulness to the police in their investigation. Given the strides psychologists have made in other areas of police procedure, such as interviewing techniques, it would be worthwhile for psychologists to develop a technique or procedure that could be used to increase the amount and accuracy of witnesses' descriptions of culprits.

In one such attempt to increase the amount of descriptive information about an unfamiliar other, Kask, Bull, and Davies (2006) examined the effectiveness of having a "standard" for witnesses to use when answering questions about the target person. Participants saw an unfamiliar person interact with one of three experimenters. For half of the participants, the experimenter posed questions about the target stranger in reference to himself or herself (i.e., the experimenter functioned as a "standard" by which to be used as a reference). For example, when the experimenter was used as a "standard," he or she would ask the participant, "My hair is this long; how long was his hair?" For the participants in the no-standard condition, the experimenter would ask the participant, "How long was his hair?" Unfortunately, the researchers found that the use of a "standard" did not help witnesses to recall accurate person information. However, a "standard" did aid somewhat when it came to recalling descriptors that are not typically remembered well (e.g., appearance of eyes, nose, or mouth).

RECOGNITION MEMORY

As defined at the beginning of the chapter, recognition memory involves determining whether a previously seen item or person is the one that is currently being viewed. A witness's recognition memory can be tested in a number of ways:

- live lineups or photo arrays
- video surveillance records
- voice identification

Lineup Identification

"It's number 5; I'll never forget that face!" The typical method used to gain proof about the identity of the culprit is to conduct a lineup identification, in which a witness views a group of possible suspects and determines whether one is the culprit.

Why Conduct a Lineup? A critical distinction needs to be made between the terms *suspect* and *culprit*. A **suspect** is a person the police "suspect" committed the crime. However, a suspect may be guilty or innocent of the crime in question. In contrast, a **culprit** is the guilty person who committed the crime.

A lineup identification reduces the uncertainty of whether a suspect is the culprit beyond the verbal description provided (Wells, 1993). A witness identifying the suspect increases the likelihood that the suspect is the culprit. In contrast, not identifying the suspect decreases the likelihood that the suspect is the culprit.

Suspect: A person the police "suspect" committed the crime, who may be guilty or innocent for the crime in question

Culprit: The guilty person who committed the crime

An alternative view of a lineup identification is that it provides police with information about the physical similarity between the lineup member chosen and the culprit (Navon, 1990). Police will have some notion of what the culprit looks like based on the person selected from the lineup.

Lineup Distractors

In addition to placing a suspect in a lineup, other lineup members may be included. These members are called **foils** or **distractors**, and they are known to be innocent of the crime in question. Police can use two types of strategies to decide on the physical appearance of the lineup distractors. A similarity-to-suspect strategy matches lineup members to the suspect's appearance. For example, if the suspect had brown hair, blue eyes, and a moustache, then each lineup member would have these characteristics. A difficulty with this strategy, however, is that there are many physical features that could be matched, such as width of eyebrows, length of nose, thickness of lips, and so on. If taken to the extreme, this strategy would produce a lineup of clones—everyone would look exactly like the suspect, making it virtually impossible to identify the culprit. In contrast, a match-to-description strategy sets limits on the number of features that need to be matched. With this strategy, distractors are matched only on the items that the witness provided in his or her description. For example, if a witness stated that the criminal had brown hair, blue eyes, a round face, and no facial hair, then those would be the features on which each lineup member is matched.

Lindsay et al. (1994) noted that some general characteristics that might not be mentioned would need to be included to produce a "fair" lineup. A **fair lineup** is one in which the suspect does not stand out from the other lineup members. For example, if skin colour was not mentioned, then a lineup could be constructed with one white face (the suspect) and five black faces. Thus, the lineup would be unfair or biased. Some characteristics, such as sex and race, are known as default values and should be matched even if not mentioned in the witness's description.

Also, in order to avoid a biased lineup, Luus and Wells (1991; Wells, Rydell, & Seelau, 1993) suggest that if a feature is provided in the witness's description but does not match the suspect's appearance, then the distractors should match the suspect's appearance on that feature. For example, if the culprit is described as having brown hair but the suspect has blond hair, then the distractors should have blond hair.

Estimating Identification Accuracy

When we are interested in finding out how often witnesses will make an accurate (or inaccurate) identification decision, we need to create the condition when police have arrested the right person, the guilty suspect. We also need to create the condition when police have arrested the wrong person, an innocent suspect. Thus, we create two lineups in our research. One lineup—the **target-present lineup**—contains a picture of the culprit. In the other lineup—the **target-absent lineup**—we substitute the culprit's picture with another photo. Identification decisions are different with each type of lineup. See Table 5.1 for the types of identification decisions possible as a function of type of lineup.

Three types of identification decisions can occur with a target-present lineup. The witness can identify the guilty suspect, which is a correct identification. If the witness identifies a foil, that is a foil identification. In addition, the witness may state that the culprit is not present, which is a false rejection.

Three types of identification decisions can occur with a target-absent lineup. The witness can state that the culprit is not present, which is a correct rejection. The witness can identify a foil, which is a foil identification. The witness can also identify an innocent

Table 5.1 Possible Identification Decisions as a Function of Lineup Type

Type of Lineup	Identification Decision				
	Correct Identification	False Rejection	Foil Identification	Correct Rejection	False Identification
Target-present	X	X	X	Not possible	Not possible
Target-absent	Not possible	Not possible	X	X	X

Source: Wells, 1993.

suspect, in which case the witness makes a false identification. Sometimes, researchers will not make a distinction between false identifications and foil identifications from a target-absent lineup and will refer to these two errors simply as false positives.

Identification Decision Implications The only correct decision with a target-present lineup is to make a correct identification. The only correct decision with a target-absent lineup is to make a correct rejection. The other decisions with each type of lineup are errors and have different implications for the witness and the justice system (Wells & Turtle, 1986):

- A foil identification (with either a target-present lineup or a target-absent lineup) is a known error to the police, so the person identified will not be prosecuted. The witness, however, may be perceived as having a faulty memory. Moreover, the other details provided by this witness may be viewed with some skepticism because a known recognition error was made.

- A false rejection is an unknown error and may result in the guilty suspect going free and possibly committing further crimes.

- A false identification also is an unknown error in real life and may result in the innocent suspect being prosecuted and convicted for a crime he or she did not commit. Moreover, with a false identification, the real criminal remains free to commit further crimes. False identifications may be the most serious type of identification error a witness can make.

Live Lineups or Photo Arrays? Most often, police will use a set of photographs rather than live persons to assemble a lineup (Turtle, Lindsay, & Wells, 2003). *Photo array* is the term used for photographic lineups. Photo arrays are more common than lineups for a number of reasons:

- They are less time-consuming to construct. The police can choose foils from their mug shot (pictures of people who have been charged with crimes in the past) files rather than find live persons.

- They are portable. The police are able to bring the photo array to the witness rather than have the witness go to the police department.

- The suspect does not have the right to counsel being present when a witness looks at a photo array. This right is present with live lineups.

- Because photos are static, the police need not worry that the suspect's behaviour may draw attention to himself or herself, thus invalidating the photo array.

- A witness may be less anxious examining a photo array than a live lineup.

An alternative to photographs or live lineups is to use video-recorded lineups. Advantages to video lineups include the ability to enlarge faces or focus on particular features. Also, lineup members can be paused to demonstrate a specific body position. In a study by Cutler, Fisher, and Chicvara (1989), they found that correct identification and correct rejection rates did not differ across live and video-recorded lineups. However, this conclusion needs to be tempered given the limited research on the topic and the small number of participants in the study.

Lineup Presentation Procedures Lineups can be presented in different formats or with different procedures to the witness. Perhaps most common is the procedure known as the **simultaneous lineup** (Wells, 1993). The simultaneous procedure presents all lineup members at one time to the witness. Wells (1993) suggested that this procedure encourages the witness to make a **relative judgment**, whereby lineup members are compared with each other and the person who looks most like the culprit is identified.

An alternative lineup procedure is the **sequential lineup**. This lineup procedure involves presenting the lineup members serially to the witness. The witness must make a decision as to whether the lineup member is the culprit before seeing the next lineup member (Lindsay & Wells, 1985). Also, with the sequential procedure, a witness cannot ask to see previously seen photos and the witness is unaware of the number of photos to be shown. Wells (1993) suggested that the sequential procedure reduces the likelihood that the witness *can* make a relative judgment. Instead, witnesses may be more likely to make an **absolute judgment**, whereby each lineup member is compared with the witness's memory of the culprit and the witness decides whether it is the culprit.

Lindsay and Wells (1985) compared the identification accuracy rate achieved with the simultaneous and sequential lineup procedures. University students witnessed a video-taped theft and were asked to identify the culprit from six photographs. Half the students saw a target-present lineup and the other half of students saw a target-absent lineup. Across target-present and -absent conditions, the lineups were either presented using a simultaneous procedure or a sequential procedure. See Figure 5.3 for identification rates according to lineup procedure.

Correct identification (target-present lineups) rates did not differ across lineup procedures. However, correct rejection rates were significantly different across lineup procedures. Only 42% of the participants made a correct rejection with a simultaneous lineup, whereas 65% of the participants made a correct rejection with a sequential lineup. In other words, if the culprit was not included in the lineup, witnesses were more likely to correctly indicate that he or she was not present if they were shown a sequential lineup than a simultaneous lineup. The higher correct rejection rate with the sequential procedure compared with the simultaneous procedure has been replicated numerous times (Steblay, Dysart, Fulero, & Lindsay, 2001). In real life, the sequential lineup could decrease false identifications. The sequential lineup is the procedure used in some Canadian jurisdictions, such as Ontario, and some U.S. states, such as New Jersey. Recent research, however, has called into question the "sequential superiority effect" (McQuinston-Surrett, Malpass, & Tredoux, 2006). The researchers suggest that when certain methodological factors are considered, the simultaneous procedure produces

Simultaneous lineup: A common lineup procedure that presents all lineup members at one time to the witness

Relative judgment: Witness compares lineup members to each other and the person that looks most like the culprit is identified

Sequential lineup: Alternative lineup procedure where the lineup members are presented serially to the witness and the witness must make a decision as to whether the lineup member is the culprit before seeing another member. Also a witness cannot ask to see previously seen photos and is unaware of the number of photos to be shown.

Absolute judgment: Witness compares each lineup member to his or her memory of the culprit to decide whether the lineup member is the culprit

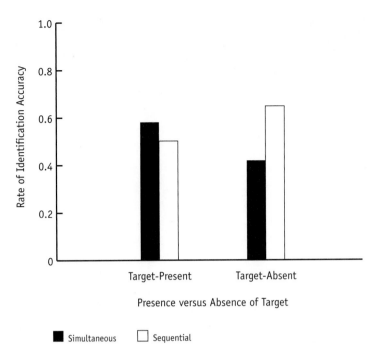

Figure 5.3 Identification Accuracy as a Function of Lineup Procedure
Source: Lindsay & Wells, 1985.

similar correct rejection rates as the sequential procedure without a drop in correct identifications. Thus, the debate continues.

Dr. Rod Lindsay has been a key researcher in the area of lineup identification. See Box 5.4 on page 144 to read about him and his research.

An alternative identification procedure to the lineup is a **showup**. This procedure shows one person to the witness: the suspect. The witness is asked whether the person is the culprit. Although an absolute judgment is likely with a showup, it has a number of other difficulties, making it a less-than-ideal procedure. Both courts and researchers have argued (*Stovall v. Denno*, 1967; Wells, Leippe, & Ostrom, 1979) that because there are no other lineup members shown, the witness is aware of whom the police suspect, and this knowledge may increase a witness's likelihood of making an identification that may be false.

Not everyone agrees with this view, however. In the early 1990s, a series of studies were conducted by Gonzalez, Ellsworth, and Pembroke (1993). They did not find false identifications to be higher with a showup than with a lineup. In fact, they found that witnesses were more likely to reject a showup than a lineup. Gonzalez et al. concluded that witnesses are more cautious with their decision making when presented with a showup rather than a lineup, and as a result will err on making a rejection rather than an identification. Yarmey, Yarmey, and Yarmey (1996), however, reached a different conclusion. They found that lineups produced lower false-identification rates than showups. In a recent meta-analysis comparing showups and lineups, Steblay, Dysart, Fulero, and Lindsay (2003)

Showup: Identification procedure that shows one person to the witness: the suspect

Box 5.4

Canadian Researcher Profile: Dr. R.C.L. Lindsay

Dr. Rod Lindsay recalls the fortuitous meeting that started his more than 30-year career researching eyewitness issues. While he was working in his office one day during his time as a graduate student at the University of Alberta, a new faculty member walked in and introduced himself as Gary Wells. It was January 1978 and Dr. Wells was looking for graduate students who would be interested in working on a research project he was planning. The project was examining jurors' perceptions of eyewitness identification. In 1979, this project was published in the *Journal of Applied Psychology*, and it would be one of the first in a long list of articles that would follow for Dr. Lindsay.

In the early 1980s, Dr. Lindsay joined the faculty at Queen's University, where he has continued conducting his eyewitness research. Dr. Lindsay describes his favourite research questions as those that can lead to real-world applications. He prefers to use experimental methodology to investigate the research questions that intrigue him. Although he respects surveys, case studies, and many other forms of methodology, he likes how a good experiment can answer a very specific and narrowly defined question such as, "Which of two lineup procedures will generate more accurate identifications?"

Dr. Lindsay's extensive eyewitness expertise has led him to the courts as an expert witness in a number of cases. Perhaps one of the most emotionally difficult cases for him was a Rwandan war-crime trial. The defendants were charged with 20 000 counts of murder in a single afternoon.

There have been two recent Canadian cases on which Dr. Lindsay consulted that he found professionally interesting and very frustrating. In one of the cases, a First Nations suspect was placed in a 12-person lineup in which no other lineup member was First Nations. In the other case, a Filipino suspect also was placed in a 12-person lineup; this time, all the other lineup members were First Nations! In each case, the court decided there was nothing wrong with the lineup—decisions that Dr. Lindsay did not agree with.

To deal with eyewitness issues on a practical level, Dr. Lindsay would like to see the Canadian government create something like the U.K.'s Home Office. Such an organization could take responsibility for researching police procedures, then decide on the best practices, and write and distribute this information through directives for law enforcement. Moreover, the courts would have the clout to back up a Home Office–type department by throwing out any evidence that resulted from procedures that did not meet the standards outlined.

In addition to informing the justice system on how to improve eyewitness evidence, Dr. Lindsay is committed to teaching and training future eyewitness researchers. He enjoys getting students excited about the eyewitness world: "If you love it, they will."

Eyewitness research is not the only thing Dr. Lindsay is passionate about. Often, he will escape the lab on a Friday afternoon only to re-emerge on Monday morning, having spent the time in between playing duplicate bridge and more duplicate bridge.

Dr. Lindsay has received numerous distinctions for his work. Most recently, in 2002, Dr. Lindsay's contribution to the eyewitness field was recognized by the Canadian Psychological Association, with the Career Award for Distinguished Contributions to the Application of Psychology.

found that false identifications were higher with showups than with lineups. Also, in an analysis of 271 actual police cases, the suspect was more likely to be identified in a field showup (76%) than in a photographic lineup (48%) (Behrman & Davey, 2001). These results are consistent with the notion that showups are suggestive. Further research is needed to understand the discrepancy in identification rates for showups across studies.

For now, there are only two acceptable uses of a showup. It may be used for deathbed identifications, when there is a fear that the witness will not be alive by the time a lineup is assembled (Wells, Malpass, Lindsay, Turtle, & Fulero, 2000). Also, police may use a showup if a suspect is apprehended immediately at or near the crime scene.

One other identification procedure that may precede a lineup identification is known as a **walk-by**. This identification occurs in a naturalistic environment. The police take the witness to a public location where the suspect is likely to be. Once the suspect is in view, the witness is asked whether he or she sees the culprit.

Walk-by: Identification procedure that occurs in a naturalistic environment. The police take the witness to a public location where the suspect is likely to be. Once the suspect is in view, the witness is asked whether he or she sees the culprit.

Lineup Biases Constructing a fair lineup is a challenging task. **Biased lineups** suggest who the police suspect and thereby who the witness should identify. In some way, the suspect stands out from the other lineup members in a biased lineup. The following biases have been investigated and found to increase false positives:

Biased lineup: A lineup that "suggests" who the police suspect and thereby who the witness should identify

1. *Foil bias.* The suspect is the only lineup member who matches the description of the culprit. For example, the suspect has a beard and moustache while the other lineup members are clean-shaven (Lindsay, Lea, & Fulford, 1991).

2. *Clothing bias.* The suspect is the only lineup member wearing similar clothing to that worn by the culprit. For example, the culprit was described as wearing a blue baseball cap. The suspect is wearing a blue baseball cap while the foils are not (Dysart, Lindsay, & Dupuis, 2006; Lindsay et al., 1991; Lindsay, Wallbridge, & Drennan, 1987).

3. *Instruction bias.* The police fail to mention to the witness that the culprit may not be present; rather, the police imply that the culprit is present and that the witness should pick him or her out (Malpass & Devine, 1981; Steblay, 1997).

What is wrong with this lineup?

Use of Surveillance Recordings for Identification

When you walk into a bank or convenience store (among other types of businesses), you may notice a video recorder located at the top corner of the wall. In the event that a crime occurs, the culprit is caught on video, creating a permanent record. Surely it would be easier to identify the culprit in this situation than if no recording existed.

In a related study, Kemp, Towell, and Pike (1997) had supermarket cashiers match credit card photos to the shopper. For half of the transactions, the shoppers presented a credit card that included their picture, while for the other transactions, they used cards that included someone else's picture. Overall, approximately 67% of the cashiers' decisions to accept or reject a card were correct. Errors were common, though. The researchers found that the cashiers falsely accepted more than 50% of the fraudulent cards. Thus, the ability to match a surveillance video to a culprit can be challenging. A number of factors may be critical for accurate identification decisions from surveillance tapes, such as lighting, view, and disguise.

Voice Identification

Perhaps one of the first and most prominent cases involving voice identification (or "ear-witness" identification) occurred in the United States in 1937. The infant son of Charles Lindbergh, a well-known doctor and aviator, was kidnapped and murdered (see Chapter 2). Lindberg identified Bruno Hauptmann's voice as the one he heard three years earlier when he paid the ransom. The kidnapper had said, "Hey, doctor, over here, over here." Hauptmann was convicted of kidnapping and murder. At the time, no studies on voice identification existed. Unfortunately, little has changed over the past 65 years, as very few studies have been conducted in this area.

In one study examining many key voice variables, Orchard and Yarmey (1995) had 156 university students listen to a taped voice of a mock kidnapper that varied in length—either 30 seconds or 8 minutes. The voice was varied such that the kidnapper either had a distinctive or nondistinctive voice. The researchers also varied whether the speaker spoke in a whisper or a normal tone. Voice-identification accuracy was tested using six-person voice lineups two days after the participants heard the taped voice. Here are some of the results:

- Identification accuracy was higher with longer voice samples.
- Whispering significantly decreased identification accuracy.
- Distinctiveness interacted with whispering, influencing identification accuracy.

Factors That Decrease Likelihood of Correct Voice Identification Other studies have found that the likelihood of a correct identification is decreased if a voice is changed by whispering or muffling, or through emotion (Bull & Clifford, 1984; Saslove & Yarmey, 1980). Orchard and Yarmey (1995) have stated that "when voices are disguised as whispers, or changed in tone between first hearing the perpetrator and the conduction of the voice lineup, identification evidence should be accepted with critical caution" (p. 259).

Kersholt, Jansen, Van Amelsvoort, and Broeders (2006) examined the question of whether the perpetrator and witness having different accents would affect voice identification. There was a trend for participants to be more accurate when the speaker had a familiar versus a different accent: 41% correct identifications versus 34% correct identifications respectively, and 56% correct rejections versus 35% correct rejections respectively.

In terms of target-voice position in a lineup, if the target voice occurs later in the lineup, correct identification decreases compared with an earlier presentation (Doehring & Ross, 1972). Cook and Wilding (1997) reported that when the target's face was visible when participants originally heard the voice at encoding, correct identification decreased greatly. Also, as the number of foils increased from four to eight voices, correct identification decreased (Clifford, 1980).

Are Several Identifications Better Than One?

If identification decisions for different pieces of evidence were combined, would the decision regarding the suspect's guilt be more accurate? Pryke, Lindsay, Dysart, and Dupuis (2004) conducted two experiments examining the usefulness of multiple independent lineups to identify a culprit: for example, having the participants identify the clothing worn by the culprit in one lineup and identify the culprit's face in another lineup. If both of these identification decisions are of the suspect, then the likelihood that the suspect is the culprit should be greater than if just one identification decision implicates the suspect. In the first experiment, following exposure to a live target, participants were shown a face lineup, then a voice lineup, and lastly a body lineup (Pryke et al., 2004). In the second experiment, a clothing lineup was added to the other three lineups. The researchers found that exposing witnesses to more than one lineup, each consisting of a different aspect of the suspect, increased the ability to determine the reliability of an eyewitness's identification of the suspect. Thus, the likelihood of the suspect's guilt increased as the number of independent identifications of the suspect increased by any one witness. This research presents an interesting avenue for future research, with many questions still unanswered. For example, are certain types of lineups more diagnostic of a suspect's guilt than others?

Are Confident Witnesses Accurate?

In a landmark U.S. Supreme Court Case in 1972 (*Neil v. Biggers*), the Court stated that the confidence of a witness should be taken as an indicator of accuracy. This assertion implies that witnesses who are certain in their identification of the culprit are likely to be accurate. Many studies, however, have investigated this relationship and found a different result (Cutler & Penrod, 1989a, 1989b; Penrod & Cutler, 1995; Sporer, Penrod, Read, & Cutler, 1995). Overall, there appears to be a small positive correlation between accuracy and confidence. There also are a number of moderator variables that can increase or decrease this relation.

Wells and his colleagues have investigated post-lineup identification feedback and its effect on the confidence–accuracy relationship (Bradfield, Wells, & Olson, 2002; Luus & Wells, 1994; Wells & Bradfield, 1998). In one study (Wells & Bradfield, 1998), after the witness made a lineup identification decision, the experimenter provided one of the following:

1. Confirming feedback: "Good, you identified the actual suspect."
2. Disconfirming feedback: "Actually, the suspect is number __."
3. No feedback.

Participants were asked to make a number of judgments following the feedback or lack thereof. Of key interest were the ratings the participants made regarding how confident they were that they identified the correct person on a 1-to-7-point scale in which 1 means not at all certain and 7 means totally certain. See Figure 5.4 on page 148 for the confidence ratings as a function of feedback condition.

Participants who were informed that they had identified the culprit reported significantly higher confidence ratings than did participants who received disconfirming

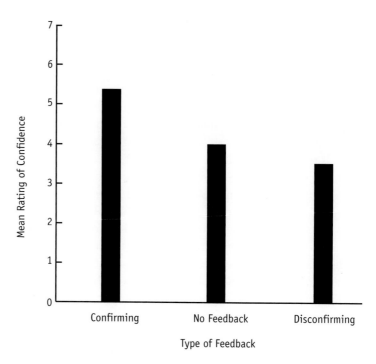

Figure 5.4 Mean Confidence Ratings as a Function of Feedback
Source: Wells & Bradfield, 1998.

feedback or no feedback. Thus, confidence can be manipulated and inflated, thereby affecting the confidence–accuracy relation.

Research also indicates that the more often you express a decision, the greater your confidence in subsequent reports (Shaw, 1996; Shaw & McClure, 1996). You can imagine that by the time a witness testifies in court, he or she has been interviewed many times. Consequently, the confidence the witness expresses in the courtroom may be inflated. Inflated confidence may be problematic given that it is an indicator used by fact finders (judges and juries) to assess accuracy. Wells, Small, Penrod, Malpass, Fulero, and Brimacombe (1998) have recommended that police ask witnesses for their confidence rating immediately following their identification decision prior to any feedback and that this rating be used in court. This rating may be more informative with regard to accuracy.

Estimator Variable Research in Recognition Memory

Three estimator variables have received much attention in eyewitness research: age, race, and weapon focus.

Age Differences in the ability to make correct identifications have *not* been found between younger and older adults. Although older adults (over age 60) are just as likely as younger adults to correctly identify the culprit from a target-present lineup, older adults are more likely to make an incorrect decision from a target-absent lineup than are younger adults (Wells & Olson, 2003). In other words, older adults make similar correct identifications but fewer correct rejections than do younger adults. This pattern of responding can also be found between children and young adults (see Chapter 6 for more on this topic).

Memon and Gabbert (2003) tested younger (age 18 to 30) and older (age 60 to 80) witnesses' identification abilities. A crime video was shown, and target-present and target-absent lineups were presented using either a simultaneous or sequential lineup. Younger and older witnesses did not differ in their correct identification rate with the simultaneous lineup or the sequential lineup. Greater correct identifications were obtained with the simultaneous lineup than with the sequential lineup for both groups. Older witnesses made fewer correct rejections with the simultaneous and the sequential lineup than did younger witnesses. Thus, older witnesses were more likely to make a false positive than were younger witnesses when shown a target-absent lineup, regardless of the procedure used. However, older witnesses made more correct rejections with a sequential lineup than with the simultaneous lineup (as did younger adults). This result replicates the superiority of the sequential lineup over the simultaneous lineup to reduce false positive responding found with younger adults in other studies. Overall, though, older adult witnesses may have more difficulty than younger adult witnesses in making correct rejection decisions.

Race The **cross-race effect**, also known as the **other-race effect**, is the phenomenon of witnesses remembering faces of people of their own race with greater accuracy than they remember faces of people of other races. In a meta-analysis, Meissner and Brigham (2001) examined 30 years of research, including almost 5000 participants, on the topic of cross-race identification. They found that own-race faces produced higher correct identifications and lower false positives than other-race faces. A number of explanations for this phenomenon have been suggested. Below are three of the more common explanations.

Cross-race effect: The phenomenon of witnesses remembering own-race faces with greater accuracy than faces from other races. Also known as the *other-race effect*.

Other-race effect: Phenomenon of witnesses remembering own-race faces with greater accuracy than faces from other races. Also known as the *cross-race effect*.

Attitudes One hypothesis to explain the other-race effect is based on attitudes. More specifically, people with less prejudicial attitudes may be more inclined to distinguish among members of other races. However, research to date does not support this explanation (Platz & Hosch, 1988; Slone, Brigham, & Meissner, 2000). Having said that, Meissner and Brigham (2001) do note that prejudicial attitudes may be related to the amount of contact a person has with other-race members, which, in turn, may help explain the other-race effect (see below).

Physiognomic Homogeneity An alternative hypothesis to explain the other-race effect suggests that some races have less variability in their faces—"they all look alike." This hypothesis has not received much empirical support either. Goldstein (1979) for example, examined Japanese, black, and white faces and did not find that one group was more similar across members than the others were. Although physical similarity may not explain the other-race effect, there are some features that may be more appropriate for discriminating among faces of certain races, such as hair colour (Deregowski, Ellis, & Shepherd, 1975; Shepherd, 1981; Shepherd & Deregowski, 1981). Thus, persons from other races may not pay attention or encode relevant features that distinguish between members of a particular race. For example, paying attention to hair colour for Asian faces may be less discriminating than hair colour for Caucasian faces. This explanation, however, does not seem adequate at explaining the cross-race phenomenon.

Interracial Contact Perhaps the hypothesis receiving the most attention examines the amount or type of contact people have had with other races. This hypothesis states that the more contact you have with other races, the better you will be able to identify them. In the 1970s, some researchers examined children and adolescents living in integrated neighbourhoods versus those living in segregated neighbourhoods. It was predicted that participants from integrated neighbourhoods would be better at recognizing other-race faces than would those living in segregated neighbourhoods. Some support for this prediction was found (Cross, Cross, & Daly, 1971; Feinman & Entwisle, 1976).

In another test of this hypothesis, Li, Dunning, and Malpass (as cited in Meissner & Brigham, 2001) examined the ability of white basketball "experts" (dedicated fans) and white basketball novices to recognize black faces. Given that the majority of U.S. professional basketball players are black, it was thought that the experts would have more experience distinguishing black faces because of their experience watching basketball. Indeed, the experts were better at identifying black faces than were the novices.

It is important to note that not all studies that have investigated interracial contact have found the predicted effect. For example, Ng and Lindsay (1994) examined university students from Canada and Singapore and the other-race effect was not completely supported.

A definitive conclusion on the contact hypothesis and how it factors into the other-race effect remains unclear. Further work in this area is needed.

Weapon Focus

Weapon focus is the term used to describe the phenomenon of a witness's attention being focused on the culprit's weapon rather than on the culprit (Steblay, 1992). The witness will remember less about the crime and culprit when a weapon is present than when no weapon is present. It is clear that this phenomenon occurs, but why it occurs is less clear. There have been two primary explanations for the weapon focus effect, namely arousal and unusualness.

Arousal

The cue-utilization hypothesis was proposed by Easterbrook (1959) to explain why a witness may focus on the weapon rather than other details. The hypothesis suggests that when emotional arousal increases, attentional capacity decreases. With limited attentional capacity, central details, such as the weapon, are more likely to be encoded than are peripheral details, such as the colour of the culprit's hair. There is some support for this hypothesis.

Unusualness

An alternative explanation for the weapon focus phenomenon has to do with unusualness, in that weapons are unusual and thus attract a witness's attention. Because a witness is not paying attention to and encoding other details, these other details are not remembered (Mitchell, Livosky, & Mather, 1998; Pickel, 1998). To follow this line of thinking, you would predict that not only weapons but also other objects might produce a "weapon focus" effect, if they were unusual for the situation.

Pickel (1999) conducted two experiments to investigate the unusualness explanation. In the first experiment, university students watched one of four videotapes in which a woman was approached by a man with a handgun. The scenarios differed in their location and the degree of threat posed to the witness. In one video, the interaction occurred at a baseball game in the stadium parking lot. In the other video, the interaction occurred at a shooting range. In the low-threat condition, the man kept the

Weapon focus: Term used to describe the phenomenon of a witness's attention being focused on the culprit's weapon rather than on the culprit

Cue-utilization hypothesis: Proposed by Easterbrook (1959) to explain why a witness may focus on the weapon rather than other details. The hypothesis suggests that when emotional arousal increases, attentional capacity decreases.

gun pointed to the ground. In the high-threat condition, the man pointed the gun at the woman. Participants provided less accurate descriptions of the man if he was carrying a gun in the parking lot rather than at the shooting range. The degree of threat did not influence the descriptions of the man. These data suggest that unusualness can produce the weapon focus phenomenon. However, it should be noted that identification of the target was not affected.

In the second experiment, a man was dressed as a police officer or a priest and was carrying a gun or cell phone. A gun would be usual for a police officer but unusual for a priest. However, neither the gun nor cell phone would be unusual for the officer. Witnesses should remember less about the priest if he was carrying a gun compared to a phone. Witnesses should remember roughly the same amount of information about the officer whether he carried a gun or phone. Indeed, Pickel found that witnesses reported a similar number of descriptors for the police officer regardless of what he was carrying. Furthermore, witnesses were more likely to describe the priest when he was carrying a phone than when he was carrying a gun. Once again, identification of the target was not affected.

Thus, there is some support for the unusualness explanation for the weapon focus effect. More research, however, is needed to definitively conclude why the weapon focus effect occurs.

EXPERT TESTIMONY ON EYEWITNESS ISSUES

Eyewitness testimony is an area for which experts may be able to provide the courts with data that can help the fact finders with their decision making. However, not all eyewitness experts agree as to whether there is sufficient reliability across eyewitness studies and whether it is appropriate to apply the results of laboratory simulations to the real world. An additional criticism lodged against the testimony of eyewitness experts is that the information provided is common sense and, therefore, not necessary for the fact finder.

Kassin, Tubb, Hosch, and Memon (2001; Kassin, Ellsworth, & Smith, 1989) surveyed researchers to determine which eyewitness issues they felt were reliable enough to provide expert testimony in court. Issues that were deemed sufficiently reliable included lineup procedures, interview procedures, and the confidence–accuracy relationship.

There are, however, some dissenters (e.g., Egeth, 1993; McCloskey & Egeth, 1983). In one critique, Ebbesen and Konecni (1997) argue that eyewitness experts are overconfident in their conclusions and have thus misled the courts about the validity, consistency, and generalizability of the data. The researchers take issue with the lack of theory in the eyewitness area, and argue that the studies are too far removed from real-world eyewitness situations to be useful in predicting how "actual" witnesses would behave. They outline a number of weaknesses in eyewitness research that should limit its usefulness to real-world application and experts testifying:

1. Studies examining the same issue produce different results.
2. Most of the studies use university students; real-life witnesses vary in age and other demographic variables.
3. Most studies allow a witness to view the culprit for approximately six seconds; in reality, witnesses may view the culprit for five or more minutes.

In defence of eyewitness research, Leippe (1995) noted that eyewitness research uses a number of methodologies and types of participants (see also Loftus, 1983). In addition, a number of studies are highly reliable. In support of the laboratory simulation using staged crimes, Wells (1993) asks, "If subjects believe that they are witnessing real crime, for instance, in what important way are they different from people who witness a real crime?" (p. 555). Perhaps the eyewitness field will always have critics on each side.

Currently, the Canadian justice system tends to limit, and might not allow, the testimony of eyewitness experts on these issues in court. For example, the Ontario Court of Appeal in *R. v. McIntosh and McCarthy* (1997) ruled not to permit expert testimony on eyewitness-identification issues. Other Canadian jurisdictions may feel bound to this decision and follow suit. It is unclear how the Canadian courts will respond to eyewitness experts providing testimony on the topic in the future.

PUBLIC POLICY ISSUES AND GUIDELINES

In a survey of commonly held beliefs by the public about eyewitness testimony, Leippe (1995; see also Brewer, Potter, Fisher, Bond, & Luszcz, 1999) found that the public makes several fundamental errors:

- Overestimating identification accuracy
- Not understanding the influence of situational factors on identification accuracy
- Not being aware of system variables that may lead to increases (or decreases) in identification accuracy

Furthermore, Yarmey (2001) has concluded that many results found with eyewitness studies are counterintuitive and contradict the common-sense beliefs of those in the community. A number of criminal cases involving eyewitness identification may have reached erroneous conclusions based on what we know about eyewitness identification. Examples include *R. v. Sophonow* (1986) in Canada, *Neil v. Biggers* (1972) in the United States, and *R. v. Turnball et al.* (1976) in the United Kingdom. Several reports dealing with eyewitness testimony have been commissioned in these three countries, including Brooks (1983), the Technical Working Group for Eyewitness Evidence (1999), and the *Devlin Report* (1976).

In the mid-1990s, then-U.S. Attorney General Janet Reno commissioned a set of guidelines for the collection and preservation of eyewitness evidence. She was prompted by the large body of empirical literature on eyewitness issues. In addition, the more sensational factor that caught her attention involved a review of DNA exoneration cases (Wells et al., 2000). According to Turtle et al. (2003), in more than 75% of DNA exoneration cases, the primary evidence used to convict was eyewitness identification. See Table 5.2 for some of the cases that involved mistaken identification.

Eyewitness researchers, along with police officers and lawyers, constituted the Technical Working Group for Eyewitness Evidence (1999) that was commissioned in the United States to respond to Janet Reno's request. They developed a national set of

Table 5.2 DNA Exoneration Cases

Name	Crime	Years in Prison	Evidence
Adams, Kenneth	Murder, rape	16	Witness I.D.*
Bloodsworth, Kirk	Murder, rape	9	Five witness I.D.s; Self-incriminating statements
Chalmers, Terry	Rape	8	Victim I.D.; Weak alibi
Cotton, Ronald	Rape	10.5	Victim I.D.; Similarity of shoes, flashlight
Jimmerson, Verneal	Murder	11	Witness I.D.
Rainge, Willie	Murder	18	Witness I.D.
Scruggs, Dwayne	Rape	7.5	Victim I.D.; similarity of boots
Smith, Walter	Rape	11	Victim I.D.
Toney, Steven	Rape	14	Victim I.D.; Witness I.D.
Web, Thomas	Rape	13	Victim I.D.
Williams, Dennis	Murder	18	Witness I.D.

*I.D. = identification.

Source: Wells et al., 1998.

guidelines known as *Eyewitness Evidence: A Guide for Law Enforcement*. The guide is divided into five stages of criminal investigation concerning eyewitness evidence:

1. Managing witnesses at the crime scene
2. Mug books and composites
3. Follow-up investigative interviews
4. Field identification
5. Lineup identifications

In terms of lineup identification, Wells et al. (1998) proposed that the guidelines be limited to four recommendations:

1. The person who conducts the lineup or photo array should not know which person is the suspect.
2. Eyewitnesses should be told explicitly that the criminal may not be present in the lineup and, therefore, witnesses should not feel that they must make an identification.
3. The suspect should not stand out in the lineup as being different from the foils based on the eyewitness' previous description of the criminal or based on other factors that would draw extra attention to the suspect.
4. A clear statement should be taken from the eyewitness at the time of the identification and prior to any feedback as to his or her confidence that the identified person is the actual criminal.

Kassin (1998) added one more rule for lineup identification. He stated that the entire lineup procedure should be recorded on video to ensure accuracy in the process. In particular, the lineup and the interaction between the officer and the witness should be on video so that lawyers, the judge, and the jurors can later assess for themselves whether the reports of the procedure made by police are accurate.

Parallel guidelines have also been developed in Canada. In the early 1980s, law professor Neil Brooks (1983) prepared Canadian guidelines entitled *Police Guidelines: Pretrial Eyewitness Identification Procedures*. In addition, psychologists (eyewitness researchers) were asked to consult in the preparation of these guidelines. Thirty-eight recommendations were made with the goal of increasing the reliability of eyewitness identification. These recommendations, however, have not always been followed.

One Canadian case involving poor police techniques in collecting eyewitness identification was that of Thomas Sophonow (*R. v. Sophonow*, 1986). Sophonow was convicted of murdering Barbara Stoppel in Winnipeg, Manitoba. Sophonow spent four years in prison for a murder that he did not commit. DNA evidence exonerated him 15 years later. Supreme Court Justice Peter Cory requested a public inquiry into the case. Forty-three recommendations were made, including these:

- The photo lineup procedure with the witness should be videotaped or audiotaped from the point the officer greets the witness to the completion of the interview.

- Officers should inform witnesses that it is just as important to clear innocent suspects as it is to identify guilty suspects.

- The photo lineup should be presented sequentially.

- Officers should not discuss a witness's identification decision with him or her.

See Box 5.5 to read more about the Sophonow case. It will be interesting to examine future cases to determine whether the recommendations from the inquiry are met.

A Case of Wrongful Conviction

On the evening of December 23, 1981, Barbara Stoppel was working as a waitress at the Ideal Donut Shop in Winnipeg, Manitoba. At about 8:45 P.M., several patrons found her in the women's washroom of the shop, where she had been strangled and was close to death. Barbara later died in hospital.

A number of eyewitnesses were available in this case. For example, Mrs. Janower worked at a drugstore in the same plaza as the doughnut shop. She went to the doughnut shop at about 8:20 P.M. She saw a man standing inside who had locked the door and headed toward the washroom. Mr. Doerksen was selling Christmas trees near

the doughnut shop. He chased a man who walked out of the doughnut shop when Barbara's body was found. Mr. McDonald sat in his parked truck as he waited for his wife to finish her shopping in the plaza. He could see into the doughnut shop and noticed a man talking to the waitress. He saw the man walk with the waitress to the back of the shop. He then came out to lock the front door of the doughnut shop. In addition to eyewitness accounts, police accumulated much physical evidence.

Police discovered that Thomas Sophonow was in Winnipeg visiting his daughter on the night Barbara Stoppel was murdered. Sophonow was forthcoming with

(continued)

(continued)

hair samples and so on. The police interview notes suggested that Sophonow might have been at the doughnut shop between 8:00 and 9:00 P.M. A few days later, Sophonow was interrogated for more than four hours. He was arrested in Vancouver and charged with Stoppel's murder on March 12, 1982.

Sophonow's first trial was a mistrial, but he was convicted in the second trial. The verdict was appealed, and the court of appeal overturned the guilty verdict from the second trial and ordered a new trial. After the third trial, the court of appeal overturned the guilty verdict and acquitted Sophonow. For the 15 years that followed, he sought his exoneration for the crime.

In 1998, the Winnipeg Police Service reopened the investigation of the murder of Stoppel. On June 8, 2000, it was announced that Sophonow was not responsible for the murder and that another suspect had been identified. The Manitoba government issued a news release stating that the attorney general had made an apology to Sophonow, as he had endured three trials and two appeals, and spent 45 months in jail for an offence he did not commit. An inquiry was ordered into the police investigation and court proceedings to determine if mistakes were made and whether compensation should be provided.

The following are some of the issues that may have contributed to Sophonow's wrongful conviction:

- Detective notes when interviewing Sophonow were not verbatim, and a misquote was recorded. For example, Sophonow stated, "I could not have been in Ideal Donut Shop," but the statement recorded was "I could have been in Ideal Donut Shop."

- Winnipeg police did not inform Sophonow that he could call a lawyer at any time or inform him that the statements he made could be used against him. Sophonow stated that he asked for a lawyer on several occasions during interrogation but the officers did not allow him to call one.

- Sophonow was strip-searched and a search of his anal cavity was done to determine if he was carrying any drugs, even though there was no reason to believe this

was the case. Sophonow felt that there was nothing he could say that the police would believe and felt it best to keep quiet.

- Mr. Doerksen was hypnotized and asked to describe the assailant. Mr. Doerksen called the police when he thought he saw the culprit at a hotel. This man was quickly exonerated. Mr. Doerksen also identified a reporter as the culprit, who was also quickly exonerated. Mr. Doerksen failed to identify Sophonow from a lineup that the police assembled. The sergeant conducting the lineup told Mr. Doerksen to consider number 7— Sophonow was number 7.

- Sophonow had an alibi that was not considered seriously. He had stopped at a Canadian Tire the night of the 23rd, spoke to a woman and her daughter waiting for their car repairs, went to a Safeway store, bought some red mesh stockings, and went to hospitals to deliver the stockings for Christmas. These events occurred around 8:00 P.M. and, given the timeline of the killing, ruled Sophonow out as the murderer.

- Terry Arnold lived near the doughnut shop and reportedly had a crush on Barbara. He fit the description and did not have an alibi. He was not fully investigated.

Dr. Elizabeth Loftus testified in the inquiry and noted a number of problems with the eyewitness evidence:

- When there is more than one witness, they can inadvertently influence each other.

- People under hypnosis are suggestible and often assume that what they retrieve under hypnosis is accurate, even though it may not be.

- The photo arrays shown to Mrs. Janower had Sophonow's picture stand out—his picture had a yellow background and his hat was off to the side, as was the suspect's hat in the composite drawing initially issued to the public. There also was a live lineup in which Sophonow stood out in terms of his height.

Source: R. v. Sophonow, 1986.

SUMMARY

1. Independent variables in the eyewitness area can be categorized as estimator or system variables. The effect of estimator variables on eyewitness accuracy can only be estimated after the crime. In contrast, system variables can be manipulated by the criminal justice system to increase (or decrease) eyewitness accuracy. The three dependent variables in the eyewitness area are recall of the event, recall of the culprit, and recognition of the culprit.

2. The misinformation effect is a phenomenon in which a witness who is presented with inaccurate information after an event will incorporate that misinformation into a subsequent recall task. This effect can occur as a result of a witness guessing what the officer wants the response to be. Alternatively, this effect can occur because a witness has two memories—one for the correct information and one for the incorrect information—but cannot accurately remember how he or she acquired each piece of information. The misinformation effect can also occur because the inaccurate information replaces the accurate information in memory.

3. The cognitive interview is based on four memory-retrieval techniques to increase recall: reinstating the context, reporting everything that comes to mind, recalling the event in different orders, and changing the perspective from which the information is recalled. In addition to these techniques, the enhanced cognitive interview includes five more techniques: building rapport, exhibiting supportive interviewer behaviour, transferring the control of the interview to the witness, asking for focused recall with open-ended questions, and asking the witness questions that match what the witness is recalling.

4. The simultaneous lineup, sequential lineup, showup, and walk-by are lineup procedures used by police to determine whether the suspect is the culprit. Biased lineups suggest who the police suspect and thereby who the witness should identify. In some way, the suspect stands out from the other lineup members in a biased lineup. Foil bias, instruction bias, and clothing bias have been investigated and shown to increase false-positive responding.

5. Not all eyewitness experts agree on the reliability of research findings and whether we can apply the results of laboratory simulations to the real world. An additional criticism lodged against the eyewitness expert testifying is whether the information provided is common sense and therefore not necessary for the fact finder.

6. Four rules were outlined to reduce the likelihood of false identification. First, the person who conducts the lineup should not know which member of the lineup is the suspect. Second, eyewitnesses should be told explicitly that the criminal may not be present in the lineup and, therefore, witnesses should not feel that they must make an identification. Third, the suspect should not stand out in the lineup as being different from the foils based on the eyewitness's previous description of the criminal or based on other factors that would draw extra attention to the suspect. Fourth, a clear statement should be taken from the eyewitness at the time of the identification (and prior to any feedback) as to his or her confidence that the identified person is the actual criminal.

Key Concepts

absolute judgment 142

biased lineup 145

cognitive interview 133

cross-race effect 149

cue-utilization hypothesis 150

culprit 139

direct question recall 128

distractors 140

enhanced cognitive interview 134

estimator variables 128

fair lineup 140

false memory syndrome 135

foils 140

free narrative 128

historic child sexual abuse (HCSA) 138

hypnotically refreshed memory 132

lineup 128

memory impairment hypothesis 131

misinformation acceptance hypothesis 131

misinformation effect 130

open-ended recall 128

other-race effect 149

post-event information effect 130

recall memory 126

recognition memory 127

relative judgment 142

sequential lineup 142

showup 143

simultaneous lineup 142

source misattribution hypothesis 131

suspect 139

system variables 128

target-absent lineup 140

target-present lineup 140

walk-by 145

weapon focus 150

Discussion Questions

1. Imagine you are a judge and are allowing an eyewitness psychological expert to testify. What factors would you consider appropriate for the expert to testify about? What factors would you disallow testimony on?

2. A neighbour informs you that she has just entered therapy to help understand why she is no longer happy in her marriage. She says the therapist feels she may have been abused as a child, even though she has no memory of it. She is uncertain whether to continue with the therapy and wonders whether, in fact, she could have been abused. What advice do you give her?

3. One of your friends is training to be a police officer. His training is almost complete, but he is worried that he has not received sufficient training on how to interview eyewitnesses. He asks whether you can describe some of the techniques you learned in your "forensic" class. Explain interview strategies to elicit complete and accurate recall, as well as the techniques that may hinder the process.

4. There has been a considerable amount of research on the misinformation effect. Design an experiment to test whether the misinformation effect also occurs if participants witness a violent crime.

5. Different types of lineup procedures are used by police. Describe these different types of procedures and distinguish among the types of identification decisions that can occur in both target-present and target-absent lineups.

6. A number of explanations have been proposed to account for the finding that witnesses remember the faces of people of their own race better than faces of people of other races. Which of these explanations do you think best accounts for this cross-race effect? Why?

7. Your friend works as a cashier at the 7-11. He was robbed while at work by someone who was armed with a sawed-off shotgun. He is upset because he could not provide the police with many details of the robber. How would you explain his lack of memory?

Readings

Doyle, J. (2005). *True witness: Cops, courts, science, and the battle against misidentification.* New York: Palgrave Macmillan.

Loftus, E.F., & Ketchum, K. (1991). *Witness for the defense.* New York: St. Martin's Press.

Schacter. D.L. (2002). *The seven sins of memory: How the mind forgets and remembers.* Boston, MA: Houghton Mifflin Company.

Scheck, B., Neufeld, P., & Dwyer, J. (2000). *Actual innocence: Five days to execution and other dispatches from the wrongly convicted.* New York: Doubleday.

Websites

The Association in Defence of the Wrongly Convicted
www.aidwyc.org

Dr. Gary Wells's Eyewitness Page
www.psychology.iastate.edu/faculty/gwells/homepage.htm

Chapter 6
Child Victims and Witnesses

Learning Objectives

- Differentiate between techniques that decrease versus increase the likelihood of accurate recall in child witnesses.

- Summarize children's ability to recall/describe people's appearances.

- Describe a lineup technique designed for children's identification.

- Outline the competency inquiry and courtroom accommodations available for child witnesses.

- Explain child maltreatment categories and related consequences.

- List the negative outcomes that are related to divorce for children.

Six-year-old Carrie Webber was attending the Nature Adventures Day Camp during her summer vacation. For some activities, children were able to scavenge in the small, wooded grounds on their own while supervisors walked around observing.

One day when Ms. Webber picked up her daughter, she noticed some scrapes on Carrie's knees. When Ms. Webber asked what happened, Carrie said, "I fell when the man helper touched my bum." When they arrived home, Ms. Webber questioned Carrie further, examined her, and noticed that Carrie's inner thighs were irritated. Immediately, Ms. Webber took Carrie to the hospital, where police were called.

Following an examination, the cause of the irritation could not be determined. Carrie was questioned by a police officer and a social worker about the events occurring at the camp. Fairly certain abuse had occurred, they launched a full investigation.

The "man helper" was identified as 25-year-old Jason Smith, one of the three male supervisors at the camp, who had been at the camp for two years. All children (ages six to eight) who had ever taken part in the camp's programs under Mr. Smith's supervision were interviewed. Social workers used anatomically detailed dolls with the reluctant children to help them to describe what Mr. Smith did to them. Many times, social workers had to describe what they thought happened and children were asked whether they agreed or disagreed. Some children were interviewed for six hours or more. Mr. Smith was charged with the sexual assault of seven children.

How do we interview children? Should we rely on children's memory? How does the criminal justice system view child witnesses/victims? These are some of the questions that we will explore in this chapter. We will focus on the historical legal context around children testifying in court, children's memory abilities, how best to tap into children's memory, and, lastly, we'll examine the various forms of child abuse.

HISTORY

The way in which child victims and witnesses have been viewed by the justice system has changed dramatically over the years. Some early views can be traced back to the Salem witch trials in 1692, when children claimed to have witnessed the defendants perform supernatural feats and other falsehoods (Ceci & Bruck, 1993). Several years following the execution of the defendants for witchcraft, some of the children recanted their testimonies. For the most part, the prevailing legal attitude toward child witnesses for the following 300 years was that of skepticism.

Research testing the validity of these negative attitudes toward child witnesses started in Europe in the early twentieth century. Reviews from this time seemed to conclude that young children were highly suggestible and had difficulty separating fact from fantasy, and thus were capable of providing inaccurate testimony, even if the testimony was of personal significance (Whipple, 1909, 1910, 1911, 1912). Unfortunately, little is known about the details of the research on which these conclusions were based. Also, the criminal justice system was not very interested in these reviews. As a result, few studies were conducted on children's competencies during the early and mid-twentieth century.

A flurry of research on children's witness abilities started in the 1970s and continues to this day. Ceci and Bruck (1993) outlined four factors that led to the renewed interest in child witnesses:

1. Expert psychological testimony was becoming more acceptable in the courtroom.
2. Social scientists were interested in research that could be applied to real-world problems.
3. Studies on *adult* eyewitness testimony were increasing.
4. The legal community became interested in behavioural science research regarding child witnesses.

This last point was in response to the increasing number of reported sexual and physical abuse cases where a child was a victim or witness. These cases, arising in both the United States and Canada, often involved numerous children and numerous defendants. Box 6.1 describes a Canadian case in which children were the primary victims and witnesses.

RECALL FOR EVENTS

Are children able to recall events accurately? How does their performance compare with the recall of adults? The Martensville case and others similar to it may suggest that children do not make very reliable witnesses, even about events they supposedly experienced. However, studies have found that children *are* capable of accurately recalling forensically relevant details of events (e.g., Ceci & Bruck, 1993). Moreover, children are capable of recalling much that is accurate. The challenge, of course, is determining when children are recalling accurately and when they are **fabricating**—making false claims. Research suggests that the accuracy of children's reporting is highly dependent on *how* they are asked to report.

Fabricating: Making false claims

Box 6.1

The Martensville Babysitting Case

In the fall of 1991 in Martensville, Saskatchewan, Ms. L. noticed a rash on her two-and-a-half-year-old daughter's bottom. Ms. L. suspected that child abuse had occurred at the babysitting service run by Linda Sterling. Following a medical examination of the child, a doctor concluded that the rash was not indicative of abuse.

The investigation continued, however, and several claims were made against Linda Sterling, her husband, Ronald, and her son Travis. The child in question was interviewed intensely and eventually stated that a man had touched her. Many more children were subsequently interviewed, some claiming that they had been confined in cages, penetrated with axe handles, forced to drink blood, whipped, and thrown naked into freezers. The children also claimed to have witnessed a ritual murder, a child's nipple being bitten off, a body dumped into an acid bath, and a dog stabbed to death.

Linda, Ronald, and Travis Sterling, along with one other woman and five other men, were arrested and charged. More than 40 charges, including sexual assault, sexual assault with a weapon, unlawful confinement, and intercourse with a minor, were laid against the Sterlings.

Dr. John Yuille from the University of British Columbia was an expert witness in the case. He noted that the interviews with the children were fraught with leading questions and that rewards were offered to children for giving the "right answer." Moreover, there was a lack of physical evidence consistent with the claims being made.

The investigation and trial spanned over two and a half years. Linda and Ronald Sterling were acquitted, while Travis was convicted on several of the charges. Eventually, six of eight convictions were overturned due to the inappropriate interview techniques that were used with the children.

Source: *R. v. Sterling*, 1995.

Free Recall versus Directed Questioning

When children are asked to report all they can remember, using a free narrative approach, their accuracy in reporting is comparable with adults' (Ceci & Bruck, 1993). Unfortunately, children tend to report very little information using a free narrative. Direct questions or probes, such as, "What else do you remember?" or "Tell me more about what you remember" are often necessary to elicit the required information. The dilemma arises when we consider the accuracy of direct questioning.

As we have seen with adult eyewitnesses in Chapter 5, when children are asked leading, direct questions, they are more likely to produce an erroneous response than when they are asked nonleading, direct questions (Roebers, Bjorklund, Schneider, & Cassel, 2002). Generally, older children are more resistant to leading questions than are younger children, and adults are even more resistant to leading questions (Ceci & Bruck, 1993).

Direct questions that require a yes/no response or use a forced-choice format are particularly problematic for preschoolers (Peterson & Biggs, 1997). For example, Peterson and Grant (2001) examined preschoolers' responses to yes/no and multiple-choice questions. In the first of two sessions, the experimenter interacted with the children for a few minutes. During this session, a second experimenter entered and the two had a disagreement over a crayon. In the second session that took place a week later, an experimenter whom the children had never met asked them questions about the appearance, actions, speech, and emotions of the two experimenters from the first session. Children were asked yes/no questions such as, "Did the woman knock over the crayons?" and multiple-choice questions with two options such as, "Did the woman wear a flowered hat or a straw hat?" The preschoolers demonstrated a bias toward saying yes to yes/no questions. They did not demonstrate a bias for multiple-choice questions; that is, children were just as likely to choose either of the two options. If neither of the options in the multiple-choice question was correct, children tended to respond with "I don't know." However, it should be noted that many children do not respond with "I don't know" if they do not know the answer to a question (as will be seen in a study described below). Thus, both yes/no questions and multiple-choice questions are not ideal for preschoolers if we are interested in accuracy.

Why Are Children More Suggestible Than Adults?

Generally, two directions have been taken to understand children's greater propensity toward suggestibility (Bruck & Ceci, 1999). One focus has investigated the "social characteristics" of the interview. It has been argued that children respond to interviewers in the manner they feel the interviewer desires, known as *social compliance*. The alternative area researchers have concentrated in to understand children's responding has been to investigate developmental changes in their cognitive or memory system.

Social Compliance It has been argued that children may respond to suggestive influences because they trust and want to cooperate with adult interviewers, even if the children do not understand or have the knowledge to answer the question. In a study by Hughes and Greive (1980), young children between five and seven were asked nonsensical questions such as, "Is milk bigger than water?" and "Is red heavier than yellow?" Even though these questions are illogical and do not have correct responses, many children provided a yes/no answer rather than saying, "I don't know." It should be noted, however, that although children may respond according to a suggestion provided, their memory for the actual event may remain intact, and, if later questioned, they may report the accurate response (even if asked in a nonsuggestive manner).

Changes to the Cognitive System Some research has found developmental differences in the ways children and adults encode, store, and retrieve memories (Brainerd & Reyna, 2004). Moreover, differences between children and adults have also been found in terms of forgetting and retention. Also related to memory is the notion that children "misattribute" where information came from (Parker, 1995). For example, children may report on an event that they *heard* about (e.g., through suggestive questioning from an interviewer) as it being something they experienced. Children may not remember that Ms. Z suggested that the event occurred, and, when later asked about it, children report the "suggestion," believing that the event actually occurred.

Currently, researchers believe that an interaction of social and cognitive factors is likely responsible to explain children's suggestibility and their reporting of false information. The content and format of questions posed to child witnesses should be considered carefully. Interviewers need to balance asking direct questions with the risk of obtaining false information. Many would recommend relying on free recall as much as possible to obtain accurate information.

Anatomically Detailed Dolls

If children have difficulty providing a verbal account of what they witnessed or experienced, props may be useful. When interviewing children suspected of being sexually abused, some mental health professionals may introduce **anatomically detailed dolls**. Just as the name implies, anatomically detailed dolls, sometimes like a "rag doll," are consistent with the male or female anatomy. Dolls may be of an adult male or female or a young male or female. The assumption underlying the use of these dolls is that children may have difficulty verbalizing what occurred, and in their play with the dolls they will demonstrate the events they experienced (Vizard & Trantor, 1988). Is this assumption correct, though? The research provides some contradictory results.

Anatomically detailed doll:
A doll, sometimes like a rag doll, that is consistent with the male or female anatomy

In a field study, Thierry, Lamb, Orbach, and Pipe (2005) examined the impact of anatomically detailed dolls on reports provided by 3- to 12-year-old alleged sexual abuse victims. The children were separated into two groups: younger (age 3 to 6) and older (age 7 to 12). The number of details provided were comparable in response to open-ended questions, whether or not dolls were used. When direct questions were posed, children 3 to 6 years old were more likely to use the dolls to re-enact what occurred than to report verbally. In contrast, 7 to 12 year olds provided more verbal details rather than use the dolls to report. Younger children were more likely to play with the dolls in a suggestive manner and to contradict details that were reported verbally. Overall, both younger and older children reported proportionally more "fantastic" details with the dolls than without.

In a laboratory study, DeLoache and Marzolf (1995) asked children aged three to five to describe an upsetting event that had occurred in their classroom. Some of the children were asked to re-enact the event with the use of anatomically detailed dolls and the others were asked to orally describe the event. Both groups of children provided a similar number of details. However, a greater proportion of inaccurate details were provided when children used the dolls than when they provided an oral description.

Anatomically detailed dolls being used in a therapy session

Contrary to the above results, Goodman, Quas, Batterman-Faunce, Riddlesberger, and Kuhn (1997) found that three- to ten year olds who had been touched during an examination were more likely to report such touching with dolls than when questioned orally. In another study, Saywitz, Goodman, Nicholas, and Moan (1991) interviewed five- and seven-year-old girls who had received a physical examination. For half the girls, a genital examination was included. In this study, many of the children failed to report genital touching when they were asked for a verbal report of their examination, or they failed to show on the dolls what had actually happened. However, when asked a direct question—such as "Did the doctor touch you here?"—many of the children correctly agreed. Children who had not received the genital examination never made false reports of genital touching in either the oral free recall or the doll-enactment conditions. For this group, very few errors were made when the experimenter pointed to the genital area of the doll and asked, "Did the doctor touch you here?"

Should Anatomically Detailed Dolls Be Used? The use of anatomically detailed dolls in the assessment of abuse is a controversial and hotly debated topic, and a number of difficulties have been identified (Koocher, Goodman, White, Friedrich, Sivan, & Reynolds, 1995). For example, no specifications or guidelines are available for manufacturers of these dolls. Consequently, wide variation exists and some mental health professionals even make their own dolls. Not only is there no standardization for what the dolls should look like, there also are no standard procedures for scoring the behaviours children exhibit when interacting with the dolls. Research is not available to answer how nonabused versus abused children play with the dolls. Moreover, it is not clear whether abused versus nonabused children play with the dolls differently. Thus, the use of anatomically detailed dolls for diagnosing sexual abuse should be undertaken cautiously.

Other Techniques for Interviewing Children

Although we can see that numerous challenges face the evaluator when trying to get at the truth during interviews with children, psychologists have developed techniques and protocols that may be useful.

Criterion-Based Content Analysis Criterion-based content analysis (CBCA) was developed in Germany by Udo Undeutsch to facilitate distinguishing truthful from false statements made by children (Stellar, 1989). It is part of a more comprehensive protocol called **statement validity analysis** (SVA). SVA consists of three parts: (1) a structured interview of the child witness; (2) a systematic analysis of the verbal content of the child's statements (CBCA); and (3) the application of the statement validity checklist.

For the first part of SVA, the child is interviewed without the use of leading questions. In the second part, the CBCA criteria are applied to the child's report to determine its truthfulness. The underlying assumption is that descriptions of memories of real events differ in quality and content from memories that are fabricated. The child's interview is scored on 18 items. For example, the evaluator will examine the logical structure of the account. Is it coherent? Do the different segments fit together? When a criterion is present in the report, it suggests truthfulness. In the last part of SVA, the statement validity checklist is applied. The statement validity checklist contains 13 criteria for other characteristics that might be indicative of truthfulness. For example, the evaluator will examine the language the child used and whether the depth of knowledge displayed is appropriate given the age of the child. Lastly, an overall evaluation decision is reached regarding the truthfulness of the report.

To evaluate the accuracy of CBCA, two types of studies have been used: simulations and field studies. Stellar (1989) described a simulation study John Yuille conducted in 1988 with children aged six to nine. In the study, a research assistant told each child participant that he or she would be asked to tell two stories—one that had happened to him or her and one that was made up but could have happened. After a couple of days, the children were interviewed. An SVA procedure was used when interviewing the child. Two blind evaluators then scored the children's interviews using the CBCA criteria. Table 6.1 illustrates the evaluators' classification decisions for children telling true and false stories. These data indicate that the majority of the children's stories were accurately classified; most of the true stories were classified as true and most of the false stories were classified as false.

Criterion-based content analysis: Analysis using criteria to distinguish truthful from false statements made by children

Statement validity analysis: A comprehensive protocol to distinguish truthful or false statements made by children containing three parts: a structured interview of the child witness, a systematic analysis of the verbal content of the child's statements (criterion-based content analysis), and the application of the statement valid-

Child's Story	Classification Decision		
	True	*False*	*Unclassified**
True	29	3	3
False	6	21	9

Table 6.1 Classification Decisions as a Function of Children's Story

*The story did not contain enough information to be scored.
Source: Stellar, 1989.

However, simulation studies have been criticized for lacking ecological validity in that they are different from the phenomena they are meant to generalize to in the real world. For example, the topics children discussed in Yuille's study are not comparable with accounts of child sexual abuse. As a result of these shortcomings, it has been suggested that researchers attempt to create situations that reflect child-sexual-abuse cases in order to make simulation studies as realistic as possible (Vrij, 2005).

At times, field studies are conducted because they have greater ecological validity than the simulation (but may fall short in other areas, such as truly knowing whether an event occurred as reported or not). In field studies, the experimenter must decide on the criteria to use to estimate if the statement provided by the child is true or false. For instance, the researcher may classify statements as false if there was no confession from the alleged perpetrator. Such criteria are problematic in that it is impossible to know if by using the criteria, the accurate classification is made. It is possible that the perpetrator did not confess to the allegation not because the abuse did not take place but rather because the perpetrator felt that he/she would not be found guilty if the only evidence was the child's statement.

Stellar (1989) described a field study conducted by Esplin, Boychuk, and Raskin in 1988 to evaluate the accuracy of the CBCA. Children aged three-and-a-half to 17 were interviewed using the SVA procedure. The criteria used to categorize alleged abuse cases as confirmed was whether there was a confession by the alleged offender and/or there was medical evidence clearly substantiating the allegation. In total, there were 20 cases of confirmed sexual abuse. The criteria used to categorize alleged abuse cases as unconfirmed were whether there was persistent denial by the alleged perpetrator, absence of medical evidence, dismissal of the case by the justice system, or other corroborating evidence, and a psychologist concluding sexual abuse was unlikely. In total, there were 20 cases of unconfirmed allegations of sexual abuse. Each case was subjected to CBCA scoring by a professional who had been trained to use the criteria and was blind to the initial categorization. Each interview received a total score for the CBCA criteria. The mean score for confirmed cases of sexual abuse was 24.8, and the mean score for unconfirmed sexual abuse cases was 3.6 (Stellar, 1989), indicating that the criteria were successful at distinguishing between true and false reports.

CBCA is not without its critics, however. For example, Ruby and Brigham (1997) suggest that the technique needs further research before it should be used in forensic cases. They note a number of difficulties with CBCA, such as inconsistencies with the number of criteria that need to be present to conclude truthfulness and the different decision rules for reaching a conclusion.

Research has shown that age of the interviewee is positively correlated with scores on the CBCA (e.g., Buck, Warren, Betman, & Brigham, 2002; Vrij, Akenhurst, Soukara, & Bull, 2002). Younger children do not possess the cognitive abilities and command of the language to provide as detailed statements as older children. As a result, truthful statements by younger interviewees may be judged as doubtful because the statements are missing certain CBCA criteria (Vrij, 2005).

Sporer (1997) focused his criticism on the atheoretical nature of CBCA. He pointed out that the psychological processes behind the differences in CBCA scores of genuine and fabricated accounts have not been specified. This is an important point, as without theoretical foundation, the boundaries of the instrument are unknown—that is, when differences in CBCA scores are likely to occur and under what circumstances they are unlikely to occur (Sporer, 1997, as cited in Vrij & Mann, 2006).

Typically, CBCA scores are calculated using a truth–lie classification, that requires the assessor to classify the statement as truthful or not based on his or her own interpretation of the statement. As a result, this method is highly subjective and does not ensure interrater reliability.

Nonetheless, SVA is being used in parts of Europe to distinguish between children's truthful and false reports. Recently, SVA has also been applied to adult statements to distinguish between truthful and false reports, and studies report great success (Parker & Brown, 2000).

Step-Wise Interview An alternative procedure for interviewing children that aims to keep false claims at a minimum is the **step-wise interview** developed by Yuille and his colleagues (e.g., Yuille, Hunter, Joffe, & Zaparniuk, 1993). This interview protocol consists of a series of "steps" designed to start the interview with the least leading and directive type of questioning, and then proceeding to more specific forms of questioning as necessary (see Table 6.2). The objective with this protocol is to provide the child with lots of opportunity to report using a free narrative before other types of questioning are used.

Lindberg, Chapman, Samsock, Thomas, and Lindberg (2003) have tested the step-wise procedure, along with a procedure they developed, the modified structured interview, and a procedure developed by Action for Child Protection in West Virginia that uses doll play. The three procedures are similar in terms of rapport building and the general question phases. The major difference is in terms of specific questioning. With the step-wise procedure, specific questioning occurs through progressively more focused questions and probes information obtained from the more general questions. With the modified structured interview, specific questioning occurs through the use of *who*, *what*, *where*, and *when* questions. With the Action for Child Protection procedure, specific questioning occurs through doll play.

To test these three procedures, children in Grades 1 and 2 watched a video of a mother hitting her son. The children were then randomly assigned to be interviewed using one of the three procedures. The interviewers were blind to what the children witnessed on the video. Interviews were transcribed and then coded for correct and incorrect statements. The results indicated that the procedure developed by the Action for Child Protection group was less effective than the other two, and the step-wise and modified interviews produced a comparable amount of information during the free-narrative portions. The modified procedure was superior to the step-wise or the Action for Child Protection procedure for *where* questions.

Table 6.2 The Step-Wise Interview

Step	Goal	How
1	Rapport building	Talk to the child about neutral topics, trying to make him or her feel comfortable.
2	Recall of two nonabuse events	Have the child describe two experienced events such as a birthday party and going to the zoo.
3	Explanation of truth	Explain truth in general and have the child agree to tell the truth.
4	Introduction of critical topic	Start with open-ended questions, such as, "Do you know why you are talking with me today?" Proceed to more specific questions if disclosure does not occur, such as, "Who are the people you like/don't like to be with?"
5	Free-narrative	Ask the child to describe what happened using a free narrative approach.
6	General questions	Ask questions based on what the child said, in a manner the child understands.
7	Specific questions (if necessary)	Follow up and clarify inconsistencies with more specific questions.
8	Interview aids (if necessary)	Have the child draw if he or she is not responding. Dolls may be introduced only after disclosure has occurred.
9	Conclude	Thank the child for helping and explain what will happen next.

Source: Yuille et al., 1993.

Overall, the step-wise procedure is consistent with what we know about children's recall abilities and how to elicit accurate information. The step-wise interview is the procedure most commonly used in Canada.

Narrative Elaboration In the United States, Saywitz and Snyder (1996) developed an interview procedure called **narrative elaboration**. With this procedure, children learn to organize stories into relevant categories:

- participants
- settings
- actions
- conversation/affective states
- consequences

Narrative elaboration: An interview procedure whereby children learn to organize their story into relevant categories—participants, settings, actions, conversation/affective states, and consequences

A card containing a line drawing is available for each category (see Figure 6.1 on page 168 for four of them). These visual cues help children remember to state all that they can. Children practise telling stories with each card before being questioned about the critical event. Then, they are asked for a free narrative about the critical event—for

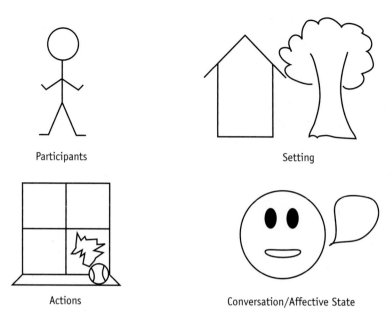

Participants

Setting

Actions

Conversation/Affective State

Figure 6.1 Line Drawings Appearing on Card Categories
Source: Saywitz & Snyder, 1996, p. 1348.

example, "What happened?" Lastly, children are presented with each card and asked, "Does this card remind you to tell something else?"

To test the narrative elaboration procedure, children in Grades 1 and 2 and children in Grades 4, 5, and 6 witnessed a staged event (Saywitz & Snyder, 1996). The children were then interviewed with either the narrative-elaboration procedure (involving training in the use of reminder cue cards), exposure to the cue cards without training, or a "standard" interview without training or cue cards. Children interviewed with the narrative elaboration procedure reported more accurate information but not more inaccurate information for the staged event compared with when just the cue cards were presented without training or the standard interview. Also, children did not fabricate more information with the narrative-elaboration procedure.

Given the positive effects of the narrative-elaboration procedure, Brown and Pipe (2003) considered whether they could further improve the procedure if it was coupled with mental reinstatement. The recall of six- to nine year olds was compared when they received narrative-elaboration training, the narrative-elaboration training with mental reinstatement, or the control condition without training for narrative elaboration. Children trained with the narrative elaboration reported almost twice as much information and were more accurate compared to the control group. Mental reinstatement did not increase accuracy.

As you can see, there are a number of techniques available to those who interview children. These techniques limit the use of direct questions and attempt to have the child provide as much information as possible using a free-recall format. The interview protocols being used by police vary by jurisdiction. For example, the SVA is popular in parts of Europe, while the step-wise procedure is common in parts of Canada.

RECALL FOR PEOPLE

Not only must children report the events that happened, it is likely they will have to describe the culprit, especially if he or she is a stranger. Culprit descriptions—also known as recall for people—by child witnesses have been examined in only a few studies relative to the number of studies that have examined recall for an event.

Describing the Culprit

In one study, Davies, Tarrant, and Flin (1989) asked for descriptions of a stranger from younger (age six to seven) and older (age 10 to 11) children. The younger children recalled fewer items (M = 1 descriptor) than the older children (M = 2.21 descriptors). The researchers also found that older children recalled more interior facial features, such as freckles and nose, than younger children. Hair was the most frequently mentioned feature by both younger and older children.

The exterior feature of hair seems to be a dominant descriptor focused on by both children and adults (Ellis, Shepherd, & Davies, 1980; Sporer, 1996). Pozzulo and Warren (2003) found that exterior facial descriptors such as hair colour and style were predominant and accurately reported by 10- to 14 year olds and adults. Moreover, interior facial features were problematic for *both* youth and adults.

Height, weight, and age are descriptors commonly reported, and if they are not reported, police may ask about them directly. Unfortunately, children and youth may have considerable difficulty with their estimates of such characteristics. Davies, Stevenson-Robb, and Flin (1988) found that children/youth (age 7 to 12 years) were inaccurate when asked to report the height, weight, and age of an unfamiliar visitor. Pozzulo and Warren (2003) found that accuracy for body descriptors such as height and weight were consistently problematic for youth. One possible explanation for this result is that children and youth may not understand the relation between height and weight—that is, taller people are heavier than shorter people of similar girth. Alternatively, children and youth simply may lack experience with height and weight. It is only in later adolescence that people become body conscious and more familiar with weight (and height proportions).

Factors Affecting Children's Person Descriptions

Leichtman and Ceci (1995) examined the effect of stereotypes and suggestions on preschoolers' reports. Children between the ages of three and six years were assigned to one of four groups:

1. Control—no interviews contained suggestive questions.
2. Stereotype—children were given expectations about a stranger who visited the class.
3. Suggestion—children were given misinformation about acts committed by the stranger.
4. Stereotype and suggestion—children were given expectations plus misinformation about the stranger.

Children witnessed a stranger by the name of Sam Stone visit their classroom. Sam was present for a story that was read by the teacher. All children were interviewed repeatedly after the event in one of the four conditions described above. For example, in the stereotype condition children were told that Sam was kind and well meaning but very clumsy and bumbling. In the suggestion condition, children were misled that Sam ripped a book and soiled a teddy bear during his classroom visit. So, which group was most accurate?

Using open-ended interviews, children were most accurate in the control condition and least accurate in the stereotype plus suggestion condition. Children in the stereotype condition produced a fair number of false reports. Children in the suggestion condition produced a great number of false reports. Overall, the older children were more accurate than the younger children.

As this study illustrates, it is important for interviewers not to introduce their own biases or inaccurate information when interviewing children. Once again, the argument can be made that children should be asked to describe the culprit in terms of what he or she did and looked like using a free narrative. Given the few descriptors children provide, it may be important to probe this information for detail. Some of the techniques described above for event recall may be helpful with person recall. More research is needed on how to elicit person descriptions from children, as well as adults.

RECOGNITION

One other task a child victim or witness may be called upon to perform is an identification of the culprit from a lineup. In a meta-analysis comparing children's identification abilities to adults', Pozzulo and Lindsay (1998) found that children over age five produced comparable correct identification rates to adults, provided the culprit was present in the lineup (target-present lineup). However, when the culprit was not in the lineup (target-absent lineup), children as old as 14 produced greater false positives than adults. That is, children were more likely to select an innocent person from a lineup than were adults (see Chapter 5 for a review of general lineup identification issues).

Lineup Procedure and Identification Rates

Pozzulo and Lindsay (1998) examined whether identification rates differed between children and adults as a function of the lineup procedure used. As you may recall from Chapter 5, the sequential lineup has been demonstrated to decrease false-positive responding compared with simultaneous presentation for adults (Lindsay & Wells, 1985), although recently there has been some debate on the sequential superiority effect (McQuiston-Surrett, Malpass, & Tredoux, 2006). Nonetheless, we can examine whether the use of the sequential lineup with children decreases their false-positive responding. Pozzulo and Lindsay (1998) found that with sequential lineup presentation, the gap for false-positive responding between children and adults *increased*. Thus, the sequential lineup increased false-positive responding with child witnesses, whereas for adults the sequential lineup decreased false-positive responding.

An Identification Procedure for Children In an attempt to develop an identification procedure that decreases children's false-positive responding, Pozzulo and Lindsay (1999) proposed a two-judgment theory of identification accuracy. The researchers postulated that to reach an accurate identification decision, witnesses conduct two judgments: relative and absolute. First, witnesses compare across lineup members and choose the most similar-looking lineup member to the culprit, a relative judgment. Second, witnesses compare the most-similar lineup member to their memory of the culprit and decide if it is in fact the culprit, an absolute judgment. Pozzulo and Lindsay (1999) speculated that children often fail to make an absolute judgment and thereby produce greater false positives than adults.

The researchers explain how a failure of making an absolute judgment would result in greater false positives. They argue that with target-present lineups, a relative judgment is *sufficient* to lead to a correct identification because it is likely that the culprit looks most like himself or herself compared with the other lineup members. Thus, the culprit is selected. In contrast, with target-absent lineups, solely relying on a relative judgment may lead to an identification of an innocent person because the most similar-looking lineup member is *not* the culprit—recall that with a target-absent lineup the culprit is not there. An absolute judgment is necessary with target-absent lineups. If children fail to conduct an absolute judgment, a greater false-positive rate may result.

Based on these notions, Pozzulo and Lindsay (1999) developed an identification procedure known as the **elimination lineup** for children that is consistent with the two-judgment theory of identification accuracy. The elimination lineup procedure requests two judgments from the child:

1. All lineup photos are presented to the child and the child is asked to select the lineup member who looks most like the culprit (relative judgment). Once this decision is made, the remaining photos are removed.

2. The child is asked to compare his or her memory of the culprit with the most-similar photo selected in the first stage and decide if the photo is of the culprit (absolute judgment).

Pozzulo and Lindsay (1999) tested variations of this procedure and the "standard" simultaneous procedure with children and adults. The elimination procedure was found to significantly decrease children's false-positive responding with target-absent lineups compared with the simultaneous procedure. In other words, children's correct rejection rate increased using the elimination procedure compared with the simultaneous procedure. Moreover, children's false-positive rate (or correct-rejection rate) with the elimination procedure was similar to that of adults when the simultaneous procedure was used. Figure 6.2 on page 172 illustrates the correct-rejection rates for target-absent lineups for children and adults as a function of lineup procedure.

The elimination procedure continues to be tested with different-aged children and adults while varying the conditions under which an identification needs to be made in order to determine its robustness and viability for use in "real life" (e.g., Pozzulo & Balfour, 2006; Pozzulo, Dempsey, Corey, Girardi, Lawandi, & Aston, in press; Pozzulo & Crescini, 2007). For example, in a study by Pozzulo and Balfour (2006), children aged 8 to 13 were tested along with adults when a culprit underwent a change in appearance following the commission of a theft. Simultaneous and elimination lineup procedures were examined under conditions when the culprit was or was not present in the lineup. The researchers found that correct identification rates decreased following a change in appearance regardless of age of witness and lineup procedure used. In terms of correct-rejection rates, children had an overall lower correct-rejection rate compared to adults. The elimination procedure compared with the simultaneous procedure was more effective at increasing correct rejections when there was no change in appearance from the time the crime was committed and a lineup was viewed. When a change occurred, however, correct-rejection rates were similar across the two identification procedures for both children and adults.

Elimination lineup: Lineup procedure for children that first asks them to pick out the person who looks most like the culprit from the photos displayed. Next, children are asked if the most similar person selected is in fact the culprit.

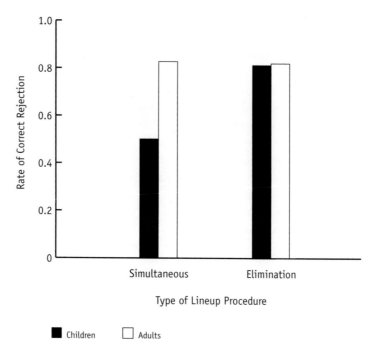

Figure 6.2 Correct-Rejection Rates as a Function of Age Group and Lineup Procedure

Source: Pozzulo & Lindsay, 1999, p. 173.

TESTIFYING IN COURT

Competency inquiry: Questions posed to child witnesses under 14 to determine whether they are able to communicate the evidence and understand the difference between the truth and a lie, and in the circumstances of testifying, feel compelled to tell the truth

Prior to 2006, in Canada (as well as the United States and some European countries), children under 14 had to pass a **competency inquiry** before testifying. The notion behind the competency inquiry was that children must demonstrate that they can communicate what they witnessed or experienced. Also, it was felt that it was critical for children to understand the difference between saying the truth and lying and to feel compelled to tell the truth. It could be argued that the competency inquiry was historically entrenched in the negative views of child witnesses discussed earlier in this chapter.

Bill C-2 came into effect in Canada in the winter of 2006, amending the Canada Evidence Act and the Criminal Code of Canada.

Under the old legislation of the Canada Evidence Act, section 16 stated that witnesses under 14 must (1) be able to communicate the evidence and (2) understand the difference between the truth and a lie, and in the circumstances of testifying feel compelled to tell the truth.

In the first part of the inquiry, children need only demonstrate a general ability to perceive, recall, and communicate rather than demonstrate specific abilities for describing the event/crime in question. Common questions may include

- What grade are you in?
- What is your teacher's name?
- How many siblings do you have?

Children as young as two or three may be able to demonstrate a general ability to communicate.

For the second part of the exam, children are questioned regarding their ability to distinguish between the truth and a lie, and must demonstrate an understanding of the meaning of *oath*. Common themes for questioning in this section include

- defining terms
- religion and church
- consequences of lying

The second part of the inquiry may be particularly difficult for young children (even for some adults). See Box 6.2 for excerpts from Canadian competency inquiries.

Under the new Canada Evidence Act, section 16.1, there is a presumption that children have a capacity to testify. Children (defined as persons under the age of 14) are asked simple questions about past events to determine their ability to understand and respond to questions. Children are requested to promise to tell the truth and testify under such a promise. No questions are asked about their understanding of the notion of *promise* or *truth*.

Preparing Children to Testify

The Centre for Children and Families in the Justice System is a nonprofit agency that is part of the London Family Court Clinic based in London, Ontario. The agency advocates

---

Box 6.2

Questions for a Competency Inquiry

In *R. v. Marquard* (1993), the judge posed the competency inquiry questions to a five-year-old girl. The questions below were posed during the first portion of the competency inquiry that addresses the child's ability to communicate the evidence.

Judge: Do you know what a memory is? Do you remember things that happened?
Child: No.
Judge: You don't? What did you do yesterday?
Child: I went down to the doughnut shop, and I got a drink and bubble gum.
Judge: Okay. That's what I am saying is remembering, okay, so when I ask you do you remember what you did yesterday, that was your answer. You went to the doughnut shop and got a drink and some bubble gum, okay.
Child: I mean gum.
Judge: Plain gum, okay. Well that's good. It's important to be pretty exact. All right, now, Ms. A is going to ask you some questions, and I know you know

the difference between the truth and a lie, and you answer her questions as truthfully and as best as you can remember, okay?

Below are a judge's questions posed during the second portion of a competency inquiry addressing the child's ability to distinguish between *truth* and *lie*. The child is a six-year-old boy.

Q. Okay. Can you tell me whether you know the difference between the truth and a lie?
A. The truth, you tell somebody what the matter and a lie is you don't tell nobody, so it is not a lie.
Q. Yes. If I were to tell you that it was snowing outside right now, would that be a lie?
A. Yeah.
Q. Okay. If I were to tell you that it is raining outside now, would that be a lie.
A. No.
Q. It would be what?
A. Right.

(continued)

(continued)

Q. The truth?
A. Yeah, truth.

. . .

Q. Why is it wrong to tell a lie?
A. Because everybody want to know, or maybe.

. . .

Q. Yeah. What happens if you tell a lie?
A. You tell a lie and then you . . . everybody want . . . to know, because you asked what is the matter and then they say they tell a lie.

Q. Oh, do you think it is wrong to tell a lie?
A. Yeah, it is wrong.
Q. Well if you were allowed to tell something today, would you promise me to tell the truth?
A. Yes.

With Bill C-2, no longer will children be questioned regarding their ability to distinguish between *truth* and *lie*.

Source: Bala, Lindsay, Lee, & Talwar, 2002.

for the special needs of children and families involved in the justice system. A key service provided by the centre is known as the Child Witness Project.

The Child Witness Project consists of a multidisciplinary team that helps children and adolescents who have to give evidence in criminal court. Usually, the children and adolescents are witnesses or victims of alleged physical or sexual abuse. A preparation program exists for the child (and family) to make the process of testifying easier. For example, the child undergoes an individual assessment to determine his or her special needs and to identify the child's salient fears about testifying. There is court preparation for the child during which he or she learns court procedures and etiquette, oath taking, and legal terminology. A mock courtroom, puppets, a judge's gown, and so forth are also used. Children also are taught stress-reduction techniques. Support for parents is available through the project so that they too understand the process. But does such a program work?

A prospective follow-up study of 126 child victims of sexual assault who had been referred to the Child Witness Project for court preparation in 1988 and 1989 was conducted (London Family Court Clinic, 1993). Pre- and post-court data were available for each child, including

- psychological testing
- clinical interview
- court observation
- file data

For the post-court data, 61 children were re-interviewed, in addition to the parents of 73 children. Children were interviewed on average three years following the verdict. A number of key findings emerged:

- Children regretted testifying if the defendant was found not guilty.
- Some children experienced mental health problems.
- Children were better adjusted when a guilty verdict was rendered.
- A mother's support was a critical mediator for children's adjustment.

Children identified a number of fears, including facing the accused, having to describe the details of the abuse, having strangers hear the testimony, and being worried about not understanding the questions posed by lawyers. Children made a variety of suggestions that they felt would improve the criminal justice system for other children testifying. These changes included the following:

1. Not having to see the accused while testifying
2. Receiving preparation for the experience
3. Closing the courtroom to the public
4. Using simpler language
5. Having support people in the courtroom

Courtroom Accommodations

Child witnesses may experience extreme stress and trauma by having to testify in court while facing the defendant (Goodman et al., 1992). The Canadian justice system has responded to child victims and witnesses by providing a set of alternatives to testifying in court in the presence of the defendant. For example, in 1988 legislation was enacted that allowed children to testify from behind a screen or from another room by way of closed-circuit television (Bala, 1999a). These provisions applied to children under the age of 18 who were the complainants in sexual offence cases. Further amendments in 1997 extended these provisions to

A screen used when a child testifies

any child witness for any sexual offence or assault. Bill C-2 further extends these provisions to any offence for which a child (i.e., someone who is under the age of 18) testifies.

Professor Nicholas Bala has conducted extensive work in the area of child witness testimony. Bala (1999a) identifies a number of alternatives to in-court testimony that have been used in the Canadian system and are now available to any witness under the age of 18 and to vulnerable witnesses upon application.

1. A shield/screen to separate the child and defendant so that the child does not see the defendant's face. However, the child is visible to the defendant and the rest of the courtroom and may be able to see the defendant's feet.
2. The child is allowed to provide testimony via a closed-circuit television monitor. The child and lawyers are in a separate room from the courtroom and the child's testimony is televised to the courtroom where the defendant, judge, and jury are present. The defendant can be in touch with his or her lawyer by telephone.
3. The child may have a support person with him or her while providing testimony. The child can decide whom he or she wants, although a person who is a witness in the same case cannot be a support person unless he or she has already provided testimony.

4. A child may be video-recorded while being interviewed about the details of the crime. The video may be admitted into evidence, so that the child does not have to repeat the details in court.

5. Generally, previous statements made by a witness are considered hearsay and not admissible. However, in sexual abuse cases, judges can apply the rules liberally, and statements made by the child during the initial disclosure of the abuse may be allowed as evidence. For example, a mother may testify about what her child said when disclosing the abuse.

6. The judge may close the courtroom to the public and/or media to protect the privacy of the child. A publication ban prohibiting any information that would identify the complainant or any witness also may be granted to protect the child's identity.

These alternatives also are available in the United States. To learn more about Professor Bala and his work, see Box 6.3.

Also, with Bill C-2, children under the age of 18 can no longer be cross-examined personally by the accused (s. 486.2).

Box 6.3

Canadian Researcher Profile: Professor Nicholas Bala

Professor Nicholas Bala has an undergraduate degree in social sciences and received a law degree at Queen's University. His interest in how the law affects children began when he articled for a law firm representing the Children's Aid Society. Following this experience, he completed a graduate degree in law at Harvard. In 1980, he joined the Faculty of Law at Queen's University. His legal scholarship spans many areas that affect children and families.

Professor Bala recalls that when he started his work in the early 1980s, children's reports of being sexually abused were often dismissed by investigators and the justice system. He was writing articles in legal journals, and had a role in bringing about legislative changes in 1988 relating to child witnesses and child sexual abuse in Canada. Even

after these initial reforms, children were still often being disqualified from testifying. One disturbing example involved a five-year-old girl alleging sexual assault perpetrated by an older cousin. After extensive questioning, the trial judge was satisfied that she understood what it meant to "promise to tell the truth" and found the girl competent to testify. The accused was convicted at trial, based primarily on her testimony. However, the defendant appealed the verdict, claiming that the girl should not have been allowed to testify given her poor responses about the meaning of the concept of *promising*. The British Columbia Court of Appeal accepted his argument and ordered a new trial; the parents of the girl (understandably) decided that she would not participate any further in the process, and the charges were dropped.

In the late 1990s, Bala began to collaborate with psychologists on research to establish that children's actual truth-telling behaviour (or lying) was not related to how well they could answer cognitive questions about the meaning of the "promise to tell the truth." Based on laboratory studies conducted at Queen's and on surveys of professionals, including judges, the researchers were able to establish that the law did not promote a search for the truth. As well as writing journal articles in law and psychology, Professor Bala met with officials and politicians to discuss the research findings, and persuaded them to introduce a new law for child witnesses in 2006 (Bill C-2). Canada is now a model for other countries, permitting children to testify if they promise to tell the truth, but precluding questioning them about the abstract concepts of *truth*, *lie*, and *promise*. The only test for competence is the ability to understand and respond to questions about past events.

Professor Bala believes that effective advocacy for law reform needs to be supported with strong empirical research, and would like to see more interdisciplinary education. He continues to engage in collaborative research about child witness issues, and to advocate for better laws and enhanced support services for children.

CHILD MALTREATMENT

So far, we have highlighted sexual abuse against children; however, there are other forms of maltreatment that a child may experience. Other forms of maltreatment require the same considerations as sexual abuse. The Child Maltreatment Section (CMS) of Health Canada distinguishes among four categories of child maltreatment:

1. **Physical abuse** is defined as the deliberate application of force to any part of a child's body that results or may result in a nonaccidental injury. Examples include shaking, choking, biting, kicking, burning, and poisoning. See Box 6.4 for a debate on whether corporal punishment is physical abuse.

   Physical abuse: The deliberate application of force to any part of a child's body that results in or may result in a nonaccidental injury

2. **Sexual abuse** occurs when an adult or youth uses a child for sexual purposes. Examples include fondling, intercourse, incest, sodomy, exhibitionism, and exploitation through prostitution or the production of pornographic materials.

   Sexual abuse: When an adult or youth uses a child for sexual purposes

3. **Neglect/failure to provide** occurs when a child's caregivers do not provide the requisite attention to the child's emotional, psychological, or physical development. Examples include failure to supervise or protect leading to physical harm (such as drunk driving with a child), failure to provide adequate nutrition or clothing, failure to provide medical treatment, and exposing the child to unhygienic or dangerous living conditions. See Box 6.5 on page 178 for a case of a father forgetting his child in a hot car and whether the court found it to be a case of neglect.

   Neglect/failure to provide: When a child's caregivers do not provide the requisite attention to the child's emotional, psychological, or physical development

4. **Emotional maltreatment** is defined as acts or omissions by caregivers that cause or could cause serious behavioural, cognitive, emotional, or mental disorders. Examples include verbal threats, socially isolating a child, intimidation, exploitation, terrorizing, or routinely making unreasonable demands on a child.

   Emotional maltreatment: Acts or omissions by caregivers that cause or could cause serious behavioural, cognitive, emotional, or mental disorders

Box 6.4

Corporal Punishment: Discipline or Physical Abuse?

Seventy-eight-year-old Lucille Poulin was a religious leader in a commune on Prince Edward Island. Poulin was given the responsibility of looking after the children while their parents worked. She believed children needed discipline to prevent them from engaging in evil acts. Poulin used a wooden paddle when disciplining the children, resulting in assault charges in 2002.

At Poulin's trial, several children testified that she often beat them, at times causing them to pass out. Poulin was found guilty of assaulting five children. The court ruled that Poulin went beyond discipline. She was sentenced to eight months in jail and ordered not to live with or care for children younger than age 14 for three years following her release.

(continued)

(continued)

Corporal punishment has been put to the Supreme Court of Canada in a challenge by the Canadian Foundation for Children, Youth, and the Law (*Canadian Foundation for Children, Youth, and the Law v. The Attorney General in Right of Canada*, 2004). The legislation under scrutiny was section 43 of the Canadian Criminal Code that states, "Every schoolteacher, parent, or person standing in the place of a parent is justified in using force by way of correction toward a pupil or child, as the case may be, who is under his or her care, if the force does not exceed what is reasonable under the circumstances."

The Canadian Foundation for Children, Youth, and the Law argued that section 43 of the Criminal Code violates sections 7 (security of the person), 12 (cruel and unusual punishment), and 15 (equality) of the Canadian Charter of Rights and Freedoms and that it conflicts with Canada's obligations under the United Nations' Convention of the Rights of the Child.

In July 2000, the Ontario Superior Court of Justice upheld the constitutionality of section 43. In January 2002, the decision went to the Ontario Court of Appeal, which upheld the lower court's decision and dismissed the appeal. The appeal then went to the Supreme Court of Canada. In January 2004, the Supreme Court held that section 43 was constitutional. The Supreme Court also ruled that

- Corporal punishment is prohibited in schools. Teachers in Canada will still be able to use physical force to remove a student or prevent immediate threats of harm to person or property, but a student can no longer be physically punished.

- Parents are not permitted to spank, slap, or otherwise use any corporal punishment on children younger than 2 or older than 12.

- Parents may use physical force on children between the ages of 3 and 12 but may not use an object to hit them.

- Parents are not permitted to strike children between the ages of 3 and 12 on the head or face, under any circumstances.

Source: *R. v. Poulin*, 2002.

Box 6.5

A Case of Neglect or Forgetfulness?

For Dominic Martin and Sylvie Dubé of Montreal, a weekday's typical morning routine involved dropping off their daughter, Audrey, at daycare, then Martin would drop his wife off at work, and head to work himself. Martin would park his car in the subway parking lot and take the subway to work. On Thursday, July 17, 2003, Martin was running late so he dropped his wife off first. He then headed to the subway parking lot, as he did so many times before, while Audrey lay asleep in the backseat of the car. Martin got on the subway and went to work, forgetting to drop off his 23-month-old daughter.

After approximately eight hours, Martin returned to his car and found Audrey unconscious. It was estimated that the temperature in the car was hotter than 60°C. Audrey later died in the hospital and Martin was charged with manslaughter.

Martin argued that with the change in his morning routine, he had forgotten to drop off his daughter. Audrey was asleep so he did not hear her in the back seat. The initial charges against Martin of manslaughter were dropped (Hanes, 2004).

General Motors commissioned a study in 2001 to determine the number of children who had died of hyperthermia—that is, severe heatstroke or heat exhaustion (as cited in Picard, 2003). One hundred and twenty children were reported to have died from being left in hot, parked cars since 1996. Of course, not all cases are a result of forgetfulness.

Source: Picard, 2003.

It is likely that children experience multiple forms of maltreatment simultaneously. For example, it is hard to imagine that a child who is neglected is not also emotionally abused.

Government agencies have the authority and responsibility to remove children from their caregiver when the child is maltreated or at risk for maltreatment. Also, a child may be removed if a caregiver is unwilling or unable to prevent abuse by a third party. For example, children may be removed from their caregivers' custody because of neglect, physical and sexual abuse, alcohol or other drug use, and mental illness. It is important to recognize that for children to be apprehended, these factors must have negative effects on parenting to the extent that the caregiver cannot adequately parent. The term **in need of protection** is used to describe a child's need to be separated from his or his caregiver due to maltreatment.

With the exception of Yukon Territory, Canadian jurisdictions require the reporting of children suspected to be in need of protection. Legislation across Canada varies the age below which an individual is considered a child. Generally, an individual is no longer considered a child between the ages of 16 and 19. In Ontario, for example, the Child and Family Services Act (i.e., legislation pertaining to children) denotes children as people under 18 years of age. See Box 6.6 on page 180 for a case of physical abuse in which the child was in need of protection but did not receive it.

Beck and Ogloff (1995) surveyed Canadian psychologists and found that more than 98% of the respondents were aware of mandatory reporting laws in their jurisdiction. Although psychologists may be aware of reporting laws, they do not necessarily comply. According to the survey results, psychologists may not report child maltreatment because of insufficient evidence or a belief that child protection agencies cannot help.

When trying to understand how often maltreatment occurs, it is important to clarify the distinction between incidence and prevalence. The CMS defines **incidence** as the "number of new cases in a specific population occurring in a given time period, usually a year." In contrast, the **prevalence** of maltreatment is defined as "the proportion of a population at a specific point in time that was maltreated during childhood."

The second Canadian Incidence Study of Reported Child Abuse and Neglect provides a national estimate of the number of instances of child maltreatment reported to and investigated by child welfare services in 2003. According to the report by Trocme et al. (2005), approximately 217 319 child investigations were conducted across Canada (excluding Quebec due to differences in data collection methodologies in that province)—a rate of 45.68 investigations per 1000 children in Canada. Forty-seven percent of these investigations were substantiated, involving an estimated 103 298 child investigations—an incidence rate of 21.71 substantiated investigations per 1000 children. The rate of substantiated maltreatment in Canada, excluding Quebec, has increased 125%, from 9.64 substantiated cases per 1000 children in 1998 to 21.71 in 2003. This increase in documented maltreatment may be explained by improved and expanded reporting and investigation procedures such as

1. Changes in case-substantiation practices
2. More systematic identification of victimized siblings
3. Greater awareness of emotional maltreatment and exposure to domestic violence

In need of protection: A term used to describe a child's need to be separated from his or her caregiver due to maltreatment

Incidence: Number of new child-maltreatment cases in a specific population occurring in a given time period, usually a year

Prevalence: In the study of child abuse, the proportion of a population at a specific point in time that was maltreated during childhood

One of the Worst Cases of Physical Abuse in Canada's History

Until Randal Dooley was six, he lived in Jamaica with his older brother, Teego, and a number of relatives. Randal's biological father, Tony Dooley, left when Randal was one year old, moving to Canada with his new wife, Marcia. The couple sent for the boys in the fall of 1997.

Shortly after Randal started school in Toronto, Randal's Grade 1 teacher wondered if Randal was maltreated. The first incident that caused her concern was when Randal lost a mitten. He was frantic about finding it. Randal mentioned that he would get a "licking from his mother." By the end of the same month, Randal had a badly broken elbow. The second incident that led his teacher to notify officials occurred when she noticed Randal had welts on his arm. She took Randal to the vice-principal's office, where they looked at his back and saw more than 25 welts. They called the Toronto police. No charges were laid at the time, however.

In April 1998, the Dooley family moved to the east end of Toronto. Mr. Dooley registered Teego at a new school but not Randal. There was no mention of another school-aged child.

Randal was found dead on the lower bunk bed that he shared with Teego on September 25, 1998. Mr. Dooley called 911 to report that his son had committed suicide. Randal's autopsy, however, raised doubts about a suicidal cause. His autopsy described Randal as a gaunt boy, his entire body almost completely covered with welts, bruises, scratches and U-shaped marks, and with extreme internal damage, usually seen when someone has been hit by a car. Randal had four separate brain injuries, 14 fractured ribs,

and a lacerated liver. His elbow had been broken in three places and his own tooth was in his stomach.

Mr. Dooley explained that in late August he had "flogged" Randal with a belt and was concerned that the Children's Aid Society would be called. It also was reported that Marcia Dooley made Randal eat his vomit and would not let him use the bathroom. She was reported to have punched him in the head, kicked him, broken his arm by putting her foot in his back and twisting it, and to have thrown Randal against a door where his eye was struck by the doorknob and swollen shut for three days. Moreover, it was reported that Mr. Dooley beat Randal on various occasions.

Tony and Marcia Dooley were charged with second-degree murder in Randal's death. At the trial, medical experts suggested that Randal's vomiting and incontinence were likely a result of a brain injury. Moreover, a pediatric neurosurgeon who testified at the trial noted that in his opinion Randal's death came from a fatal brain injury that caused a seizure.

After three days of deliberation, on April 18, 2002, Tony and Marcia Dooley were convicted of second-degree murder. Superior Court Justice Eugene Ewaschuk who presided over the case stated that Randal "may very well be the worst victim of child abuse in Canadian penal history." Marcia received a life sentence without eligibility for parole for 18 years. Tony also received a life sentence without eligibility for parole for 13 years.

Source: Blatchford, 2002.

Neglect (30%), exposure to domestic violence (28%), and physical abuse (24%) were the three primary categories of substantiated maltreatment. Emotional maltreatment accounted for another 15% of cases while sexual-abuse cases represented only 3% of all substantiated investigations. See Figure 6.3 for the distribution of child-maltreatment categories.

Risk Factors Associated with Child Maltreatment

A number of risk factors—factors that are associated with an increased likelihood of abuse—have been identified for physical and sexual abuse. These can be categorized as child factors, parental factors, and social factors (see Table 6.3 on page 182).

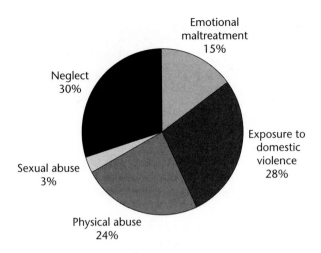

Figure 6.3 Primary Categories of Substantiated Child Maltreatment in Canada (Excluding Quebec)*

*Based on a sample of 5660 substantiated child-maltreatment investigations.

Source: Trocme et al., 2005.

The risk factors for physical and sexual abuse differ. Physical abuse risk factors are varied and include a parent's past childhood physical abuse as well as the parent's attitude toward pregnancy. In contrast, sexual abuse risk factors tend to revolve around family composition.

Short-Term and Long-Term Effects of Physical Abuse

A number of short-term effects of physical abuse have been determined. These include greater perceptual-motor deficits, lower measured intellectual functioning, lower academic achievement, externalizing behaviour such as aggression, and internalizing mental health difficulties such as hopelessness and depression (Ammerman, Cassisi, Hersen, & Van Hasselt, 1986; Conaway & Hansen, 1989; Lamphear, 1985).

In a review of studies examining the long-term effects of physical abuse, Malinosky-Rummell and Hansen (1993) report strong relations between physical abuse and nonfamilial and familial violence. Physically abused persons, especially males, engage in more nonfamilial violence than nonabused persons. In terms of familial violence, about 30% of physically abused or neglected persons abuse their own children (Kaufman & Zigler, 1987; Widom, 1989a). Moreover, being abused as a child predicted inflicting and receiving dating violence in a sample of university students. Also, spouses who were abusive reported higher rates of physical abuse than nonabusive spouses. Thus, experiencing physical abuse appears to increase the likelihood of perpetrating physical abuse.

Table 6.3 Risk Factors for Abuse

	Type of Abuse	
	Physical Abuse	*Sexual Abuse*
Child Factors		
	Male sex	Female sex
Parental Factors		
	Young maternal age	Living in a family without a biological parent
	Single-parent status	Poor relationship between parents
	History of childhood physical abuse	Presence of a stepfather
	Spousal assault	Poor child–parent relations
	Unplanned pregnancy or negative attitude toward pregnancy	
	History of substance abuse	
	Social isolation or lack of social support	
Social Factors		
	Low socioeconomic status	
	Large family size	

Source: MacMillan, 2000, p. 704.

Short-Term and Long-Term Effects of Sexual Abuse

Kendall-Tackett, Williams, and Finkelhor (1993) examined 45 studies that considered the short-term effects of childhood sexual abuse. Common effects across the studies were behaviour problems, lowered self-esteem, inappropriate sexuality, and symptoms consistent with post-traumatic stress disorder. Research has found that within two years of being abused, children report a number of physical difficulties such as sleep disturbance, eating disorders, stomach problems, and headaches (Adams-Tucker, 1982).

Putnam (2003) identified three categories of outcomes in adults with a history of childhood sexual abuse: (1) psychiatric disorders, (2) dysfunctional behaviours, and (3) neurobiological dysregulation.

Under psychiatric disorders, major depression in adulthood has been found to be strongly related to sexual abuse in childhood (Paolucci, Genuis, & Violato, 2001). Sexualized behaviour is one of the most closely related dysfunctional behaviours with those who have a history of childhood sexual abuse (Widom & Ames, 1994). In terms of neurobiological dysregulation, magnetic resonance imaging (MRI) studies have found reduced hippocampal volume in adults who experienced sexual abuse as children, similar to that found in war veterans experiencing post-traumatic stress disorder (Stein et al., 1997). Messman-Moore and Long (2003) reported that adults who were sexually abused as children have an increased risk of being sexually abused as adults. Other long-term risks for sexually abused children include depression, self-injurious behaviours, anxiety, and interpersonal distrust (Browne & Finkelhor, 1986).

In a retrospective study conducted from 1995 to 1997, over 17 000 community members in California were surveyed (Dube et al. 2005). Participants were asked about abuse and dysfunction during childhood and other health-related issues. Childhood sexual abuse was reported by 16% of the male and 25% of the female respondents. If a person suffered childhood sexual abuse, it was found that there would be an increase in the risk of various outcomes. For example, suicide attempts were twice as likely among both men and women who had reported experiencing childhood sexual abuse compared to those who had not reported experiencing it. Also, there was an increased risk of alcohol problems, illicit drug use, and family problems when respondents had experienced childhood sexual abuse.

A recent survey in the United States found that roughly one in five young people is solicited for sex over the internet each year (Mitchell, Finkelhor, & Wolak, 2001; see also Box 6.7). Canadian law is catching up to computer technology with the enactment of Bill C-15A in 2002. Now, it is a criminal offence to use the internet to communicate with a child for the purpose of committing a sexual act (s. 172.1 of the Criminal Code of Canada). This offence carries a maximum five-year prison sentence. This legislation in part satisfies Canada's commitment to a United Nations protocol on the rights of the child that was signed by 105 countries in 2002. An advantage of this protocol is that it sets out consistent law to deal with child issues across countries. Given that the internet does not have borders, this type of consistency is critical.

Behaviours that might predispose a young person to being lured over the internet (Mitchell et al., 2001) include revealing emotional problems, admitting to being in need of help or having low self-esteem, and expressing agreement in chat rooms.

Box 6.7

Luring Children over the Internet

Advances in computer technology provide a host of benefits to its users. Unfortunately, however, this technology can be abused. With the internet, sexual predators have access to countless children while remaining anonymous, until they decide to meet the child. The child may assume he or she is meeting another child, but the internet stranger may be a sexual predator. Some predators do not conceal their true age, however, as was the case with Kenneth Symes.

Mr. Symes was a 36-year-old former church pastor from Ajax, Ontario. Between April 18 and August 10, 2005, Symes began a series of internet chats with two girls that he thought were 12 to 13 years of age. In fact, the girls were undercover investigators. The chat exchange between Symes and the "girls" was sexually explicit and left no doubt that he wanted to have sexual relations with both girls. Symes arranged to meet one of the girls and when he attended the meeting, he was arrested by police. Kenneth Symes pled guilty to 2 counts of internet luring and was sentenced to 12 months in prison, which was reduced to 2 months after double credit was given for time served.

Source: *R. v. Symes*, 2005.

Protective strategies against sexual luring over the internet include

- Avoiding sexually provocative screen names. Sexual predators are more likely to target youth with screen names of a sexual nature (U.S. Department of Justice, 2001).

- Not providing any personal information over the internet.

- Contacting police when sexual solicitation of children and youth has occurred.

CHILD CUSTODY AND ACCESS

Children also may come into contact with the justice system as a result of parents separating or divorcing. The divorce rate in Canada is about 37% and appears to be relatively stable (Statistics Canada, 2006c). Approximately 50% of all divorces involve children under the age of 18 (Amato, 2000). Custody and **access** (the noncustodial parent's right to see the child) issues need to be decided when couples with children dissolve their union. Parents who are splitting usually come to mutually satisfactory agreements about custody and access without the involvement of the legal system. Only about 4% of all custody and access cases are finalized through contested hearings (Department of Justice Canada, 1990). In these instances, courts are faced with the responsibility of determining custody and access. In 1997, mothers received sole custody about 61% of the time. In contrast, fathers received sole custody roughly 11% of the time. Joint custody occurred about 28% of the time (Statistics Canada, 1999).

Legal History of Custody and Access

In the eighteenth century, the rights of children were disregarded when a couple decided to divorce. The courts viewed only the father as having legal status and children were treated as property—their father's property. In 1855, the Custody of Infants Act was enacted in Upper Canada, giving mothers the right to seek custody or access to children under the age of 12 (Bala, 1999b).

In the early twentieth century, mothers were perceived as better caregivers, particularly for young children (Bala, 1999b). Typically, mothers were granted custody, all other factors being equal. One exception to maternal custody was mothers who were judged "morally unfit," such as women who committed adultery.

Another change in legal perspective came in the 1970s when the "best interests of the child" became the guiding principle for custody and access decisions. By 1973, Canadian courts were starting to accept that the "welfare of the child" should be used to decide on custody issues. Although there are wording variations between provincial or territorial and federal legislation, the meaning does not change. Canadian courts made decisions in accordance with the best interests of the child (Bala, 1999b). However, there could be differences in how courts determined the best interest of the child.

The term *joint custody* may be a little deceiving, however, because it does not necessarily mean equal physical custody (Maccoby & Mnookin, 1992). Rather, the child may live with one parent but both parents have legal decision-making power regarding the child's health and welfare (Felner & Terre, 1987). Of course, joint custody may include joint physical custody in which the child alternates living with each parent on a weekly or biweekly basis. An exception to granting joint custody may include situations involving domestic abuse.

Canadian judges recently have started to rule for **parallel parenting** (Tibbetts, 2003), which divides decision-making power between the parents. Courts may choose this option when parents are hostile and cooperative parenting does not seem possible. For example, one parent may make decisions regarding medical care and the other parent makes decisions regarding education.

When the courts are faced with challenging custody and access decisions, psychologists or other mental health professionals may be consulted for assistance.

Parallel parenting: System that divides decision-making power between parents

Factors Related to Divorce

Many studies have examined the relation between parental divorce and children's academic achievement, behaviour, psychological adjustment, self-esteem, social competence, and relationships with parents. Although the results are far from consistent, children from divorced families generally tend to score lower than those from intact families in these areas (Demo & Acock, 1988; Krantz, 1988; Kurdek, 1981).

One long-term follow-up study of adults in their thirties who experienced divorce as children prior to the age of 16 found that females from divorced families had more psychological problems and difficulties in their relationships than those from non-divorced families (Huurre, Junkkari, & Hillevi, 2006). This result was not found to occur in males, however. Overall, both males and females from divorced families (compared to non-divorced families) had a shorter education history, greater unemployment, divorce, negative life events, and more risky health behaviour.

Zill, Morrison, and Coiro (1993) examined longitudinal data from the National Survey of Children, a representative sample of youth in the United States, to determine whether divorce presents long-term difficulties for the children involved. The first part of the survey was conducted in 1976–77 and was based on children aged 7 to 11 years; the second part was conducted in 1981, when the children were aged 12 to 16 years; and the third part was conducted in 1987, when the children, now young adults, were aged 18 to 22 years. The children's ages at the time of their parents' divorce varied. Overall, the average age at disruption was 6 years. For the early-disruption group, the average age was 3 years. For the later-disruption group the average age was 10 years. The analyses showed some negative effects of divorce present 12 to 22 years following the disruption. Such effects included poor relationships with parents, problem behaviours, an increased probability of dropping out of high school, and the receiving of psychological treatment. It should be noted, however, that many of the children who were in the study scored within the "normal range" on many of the well-being indicators examined. The authors stated the fact that "a young person comes from a divorced family does not, in itself, tell us a great deal about how he or she is faring on embarking into adulthood" (p. 100).

A few studies have found a positive outcome for children from divorced families. For example, Arditti (1999) found that children from divorced families, especially females, reported developing a close relationship with their mothers. Children also may be better off if parents in high-conflict relationships divorce rather than remain together (Hanson, 1999).

SUMMARY

1. The accuracy of children's reporting is highly dependent on how they are asked to report. When describing what was witnessed using a free narrative, children are as accurate as adults. As with adults, leading questions are likely to produce erroneous responses in children. Children's suggestibility may be a result of social compliance and/or cognitive factors. Yes/no questions are particularly problematic for very young children. Moreover, children may be unlikely to reply, "I don't know" when they do not have the knowledge or comprehension of what is being asked. The use of anatomically detailed dolls for interviewing children is controversial and should be used with caution. A number of procedures and protocols to increase children's accurate responding have been investigated, including statement validity analysis, the step-wise interview, and narrative elaboration.

2. Children report few person descriptors when asked to describe a stranger or culprit. Interior facial items such as freckles and nose shape are more likely to be reported by older children than younger children. However, accurately reporting these features is difficult. The exterior feature of hair is frequently mentioned by both children and adults. Height, weight, and age are unlikely to be reported accurately by children and youth.

3. Children produce comparable correct identification rates with adults' when presented with a target-present lineup. However, children are more likely than are adults to select an innocent person with a target-absent lineup. A procedure called the elimination lineup asks children first to pick out the person who looks most like the culprit from the pictures displayed. Then the children are asked if that most-similar person is in fact the culprit. This procedure decreases children's false-positive responding compared with a simultaneous lineup procedure.

4. Historically in Canada (and in other countries), children under the age of 14 must pass a competency inquiry before being allowed to testify. Under the new Bill C-2, children are asked simple questions to demonstrate their ability to communicate. Children testify under a promise to tell the truth. Also as a result of Bill C-2, a number of alternatives to in-court testimony are available for persons under 18. These alternatives include screens separating the child from the defendant, providing testimony via closed-circuit television, allowing the child to have a support person, admitting into evidence a video-recorded interview of the child detailing the events, allowing hearsay evidence, and banning the public and media from the courtroom.

5. Maltreatment can be categorized into sexual abuse, physical abuse, neglect/failure to provide, and emotional abuse. Short-term effects of physical abuse include perceptual-motor deficits, lower measured intellectual functioning, lower academic achievement, externalizing behaviour, and internalizing mental health difficulties such as hopelessness and depression. Long-term effects of physical abuse include nonfamilial and familial violence. Short-term effects of sexual abuse include behaviour problems, lowered self-esteem, inappropriate sexuality, and physical symptoms consistent with post-traumatic stress disorder. Long-term effects of sexual abuse

include physical problems, lowered self-esteem, and being abused as an adult. Other long-term risks include depression, self-injurious behaviours, anxiety, and interpersonal distrust.

6. Compared with children from intact homes, children from divorced homes tend to score lower on measures of academic achievement, behaviour, psychological adjustment, self-esteem, social competence, and relationships with parents. Also, children from divorced families tend to show a lower level of well-being than children from intact families.

Key Concepts

access 184

anatomically detailed doll 163

competency inquiry 172

criterion-based content analysis 164

elimination lineup 171

emotional maltreatment 177

fabricating 160

incidence 179

in need of protection 179

narrative elaboration 167

neglect/failure to provide 177

parallel parenting 185

physical abuse 177

prevalence 179

sexual abuse 177

statement validity analysis 164

step-wise interview 166

Discussion Questions

1. In your local community newspaper, you read of a seven-year-old boy who has been physically abused and then left abandoned. You wonder what difficulties this boy may experience in the next couple of years and when he becomes an adult. Describe the short-term and long-term effects of maltreatment.

2. Why is the use of anatomically correct dolls a controversial tool when assessing child sexual abuse?

3. After completing an undergraduate course in forensic psychology, you are interested in telling your colleagues in the police department the best interview techniques to use with child witnesses. You decide to develop a mini-workshop on good and bad interview techniques. Put together a curriculum for your workshop.

4. An eight-year-old girl has witnessed the abduction of her best friend by an adult male. What factors will likely influence this child's ability to describe the kidnapper and what procedures should the police use when conducting a lineup with this child witness?

5. Children are sometimes needed to testify in court. Describe the changes that came into effect with Bill C-2.

6. Your best friend tells you that her parents are getting divorced. She confides in you that she worries her parents' divorce will have negative consequences on her future well-being. Discuss the possible long-term psychological problems of children whose parents get divorced.

7. You have been hired by the Children's Aid Society to help them design a study to identify the risk factors for sexual and physical abuse. Describe the study you would propose, focusing on the methodology and what risk factors you would measure.

Readings

Ceci, S.J., & Hembrooke, H. (1998). *Expert witnesses in child abuse cases: What can and should be said in court*. Washington, DC: American Psychological Association.

Sattler, J.M. (1998). *Clinical and forensic interviewing of children and families: Guidelines for the mental health, education, pediatric, and child maltreatment fields*. La Mesa, CA: Jerome M. Sattler Publishers, Inc.

Websites

Centre for Children and Families in the Justice System
www.lfcc.on.ca/cwp.htm

Canadian Society for the Investigation of Child Abuse
www.csicainfo.com

Chapter 7
Juries: Fact Finders

Learning Objectives

- Describe how jurors are selected in Canada.

- Distinguish between representativeness and impartiality.

- Describe the effects of pretrial publicity and the available options for dealing with it.

- Outline the stages to reaching a jury verdict.

- Describe the categories of variables that have been examined to predict the verdict.

Harry Glickman was excited to be part of the jury to hear a first-degree murder case against an organized crime leader, Jackie "Benny" Benitto. The murder story had made headlines the previous summer when the body of a local steel union chief in Hamilton was found floating in Lake Ontario. News about the case and Benny's lengthy involvement with organized crime was reported on a daily basis for almost the entire summer. Benny's lawyer argued fiercely that it would be impossible for his client to receive a fair trial in Hamilton, given all the pretrial publicity. The judge agreed to move the trial to Toronto, where a larger pool of potential jurors existed and where there had been less media coverage about the case.

Before Harry was accepted to sit on the jury, Benny's lawyer had asked him a few questions. Harry wondered if there was something he said that made him sound sympathetic to the defendant. Maybe it was the way he looked. Or maybe it was because he was an engineer. For the next 4 weeks, Harry sat with 11 others listening to the evidence. Following closing arguments, the jury was required to deliberate and reach a unanimous decision regarding Benny's innocence or guilt. The deliberations took place in a private room with only the jurors present. They reached a verdict in four days, finding Benny not guilty.

As you will see in this chapter, criminal jury trials do not occur often, but when they do, they can be quite involved in terms of jury selection and the trial itself. In this chapter, we will focus on the jury-selection process, how jury research is conducted, and issues related to understanding the rules of law and how well we can predict verdicts. The information we provide in this chapter will focus on criminal trials exclusively unless otherwise stated.

In Canada, the courts deal with both civil and criminal cases. Criminal cases are those in which an act was allegedly committed as found in the Criminal Code of Canada.

In contrast, civil cases are those that involve a breach of contract or other claims of "harm" (known as torts). Civil cases can be heard by jury or judge alone, as can criminal cases. However, the process, jury selection, and decision rules for civil cases are quite different from criminal cases. For example, jury trials for civil cases can have fewer jurors than criminal trials. Six- or eight-member jury trials often occur in civil cases, whereas twelve-member juries are typical in criminal cases. Also, verdicts do not necessarily have to be unanimous in civil trials.

JURY SELECTION IN CANADA

Before a jury trial can begin, a jury needs to be selected or "seated." The process of jury selection differs by province, territory, and country, although there are a number of commonalities across jurisdictions. Before we discuss jury selection, it is important to consider the types of cases juries will hear.

The Cases Heard by Juries

Television has bombarded us with crime shows such as *Law and Order*, *Shark*, and *Boston Legal*. We can even view real-life trials, such as the O.J. Simpson case, from the comfort of our own home. Talk shows, such as *The Verdict with Paula Todd*, *Nancy Grace*, and *Larry King Live*, also highlight the latest developments in various high-profile cases. All this media coverage may distort perceptions of the frequency of trials heard by juries. Only some types of offences can proceed with jury trials. Moreover, in some instances defendants are given an option of a jury trial, but they may opt to be tried by judge alone. Thus, in Canada, relative to the total number of trials that take place, only a few are tried by jury. The remainder of trials are heard and ruled on by judges alone.

There are three types of offences in Canada: (1) summary offences, (2) indictable offences, and (3) hybrid offences.

Summary offences involve a sentence of less than six months in prison and a fine of less than $2000 (section 787 [1] of the Criminal Code). However, for some offences the maximum sentence is 18 months (R.S.C. 1985, C-46, s. 787[1]). These offences are tried by judge alone. Moreover, the defendant charged with a summary offence does not have a right to a trial by jury.

There are three categories of indictable offences:

1. Less serious indictable offences are heard by a judge sitting alone. These are found in section 553 of the Criminal Code and include theft (other than theft of cattle), obtaining money or property by false pretences, and failure to comply with a probation order.

2. Highly serious indictable offences must be tried by judge and jury. These offences include treason, murder, and piracy. However, an exception under section 473 of the Criminal Code indicates that if the attorney general and the accused agree, the trial can proceed without a jury and the judge alone tries the case.

3. For some indictable offences, the accused can choose whether the trial proceeds by judge and jury or judge alone. These are the indictable offences not listed in either section 553 or 469 of the Criminal Code, such as robbery (R.S.C. 1985, C-46, s. 343;

1995, C-34, s. 302), arson (R.S.C. 1985, C-46, s. 433; 1990, C-15, s.1), and sexual assault with a weapon (R.S.C. 1985, C-46, s. 272; 1995, C-39, s. 145). The defendant has the option to choose (1) to be tried by a provincial or territorial court judge without a jury and without having had a preliminary inquiry, (2) to have a preliminary inquiry and to be tried by a judge without a jury, or (3) to have a preliminary inquiry and to be tried by a judge and jury. If a defendant does not make a selection, he or she will have a preliminary inquiry and be tried by a judge and jury.

Hybrid offences are a cross between indictable offences and summary offences. These are offences for which the maximum sentence is five or more years in prison if they proceed by indictment. If the Crown proceeds summarily, the maximum penalty is 6 months, or 18 months in some cases, such as sexual assault. It is up to the Crown attorney to decide whether to proceed with the case as an indictable offence or a summary offence. If the Crown opts for a summary offence, the case is tried by judge alone and the defendant does not have the right to a jury trial.

As you can see, these criteria greatly reduce the number of cases that are tried by jury. Also, it is important to keep in mind that jury trial options vary somewhat across provinces and territories.

Jury Selection

The **Jury Act** is provincial and territorial legislation that outlines the eligibility criteria for jury service and how prospective jurors must be selected. Although legislation varies across jurisdictions, there are a number of commonalities. Box 7.1 on page 192 outlines the criteria for jurors in Ontario and British Columbia. Differences in eligibility criteria across jurisdictions may include the minimum age to be a juror and the professions that keep individuals exempt from jury duty.

Jury Act: Provincial and territorial legislation that outlines the eligibility criteria for jury service and how prospective jurors must be selected

Juror selection is governed by federal law. A set of random names from a community are determined, often by telephone directories or voters' lists. Prospective jurors receive a **jury summons**—that is, a court order that states a time and place for jury duty. Receiving a jury summons does not guarantee that you will be a juror, though. It simply means that you are expected to show up prepared to be a juror. If you ignore a summons and do not show up, you may incur a severe legal penalty such as a fine or jail time.

Jury summons: A court order that states a time and place to go for jury duty

When you arrive at the designated location, typically the courthouse, you are given a number and escorted to a room with other potential jurors. You are not allowed to talk, eat, or drink while in this room. Once everyone has arrived—there can be as many as 100 people—a judge explains the jury selection process and how many will be chosen that day. In Canada, criminal trials have 12-person juries.

If you are selected from the juror pool, you will be a juror unless one of the lawyers presents a challenge. Generally, there are two types of challenges lawyers can use to reject a potential juror: (1) peremptory challenge and (2) challenge for cause.

Both the Crown and defence are allowed a limited number of peremptory challenges. In murder trials, each side has 20 peremptory challenges, whereas for most other crimes each side has 12 peremptory challenges. The Crown or defence can use a peremptory challenge to reject jurors who they believe are unlikely to reach a verdict in their favour. When using a peremptory challenge, the lawyer does not need to provide a reason for rejecting the prospective juror.

Box 7.1

Ontario's and British Columbia's Criteria for Serving on a Jury

Below are Ontario's criteria for serving on a jury. The criteria are fairly similar in most other provinces and territories.

Eligibility Criteria

To serve on a jury in Ontario, a person must

- be a Canadian citizen;
- live in Ontario; and
- be at least 18 years of age.

Ineligibility Criteria

A person may not serve on a jury in Ontario if he or she

- is a member of the Privy Council of Canada or the Executive Council of Ontario, Senate, House of Commons of Canada, or Legislative Assembly;
- is a judge, justice of the peace, barrister, solicitor, or law student;
- is a medical doctor, veterinary surgeon, or coroner;
- works in law enforcement;
- has a physical or mental disability that would prevent him or her from performing the required duties; or
- has been convicted of an indictable offence (unless pardoned).

Every person who has been summoned as a witness or is likely to be called as a witness in a civil or criminal proceeding or has an interest in an action is ineligible to serve as a juror at any sittings at which the proceeding or action might be tried.

Every person who, at any time within three years preceding the year for which the jury roll is prepared, has attended court for jury service in response to a summons after selection from the roll prepared under the Jury Act or any predecessor thereof is ineligible to serve as a juror in that year.

Sources: R.S.O. 1990, J.3; S.O. s. 3,1994, c. 27, s. 48; S.O. 1997, c. 4, s. 82.

Below are British Columbia's criteria for serving on a jury.

Eligibility Criteria

To serve on a jury in British Columbia, a person must

- be a Canadian citizen;
- live in British Columbia; and
- be at least 19 years of age.

Ineligibility Criteria

A person may not serve on a jury in British Columbia if he or she

- is a police officer, lawyer, employee of certain government agencies (or other particular occupations); or
- has been convicted of certain criminal offences within the last five years.

Exemptions

- Individuals over the age of 65 can choose whether they want to serve as a juror in British Columbia.
- Some individuals may be exempted for health reasons.
- Full-time students may be exempted.

Other possible reasons for exemption may include the facts that serving as a juror would cause you extreme hardship (e.g., you are a nursing mother), you have limited ability to speak or understand English, or you have firm travel plans that conflict with the jury selection or trial date.

If you serve as a juror on a trial in B.C., you are exempt from serving again as a juror for two years.

Source: Jury Act for British Columbia,
http://www.qp.gov.bc.ca/statreg/stat/J/96242_01.htm.

In contrast, when using a *challenge for cause*, the lawyer must give a reason for rejecting the prospective juror. We will discuss challenge for cause later in this chapter. Keep in mind that Canadian lawyers have very limited information about prospective jurors. This information includes name, address, occupation, and physical demeanour. Also, in many Canadian cases the lawyers are not allowed to ask prospective jurors questions to gain more information about them. Consequently, lawyers have very little information on which to decide whether a juror will reach a verdict in their favour. If a prospective juror is successfully challenged, he or she will go back to the room with the others who have not yet been selected. Although a prospective juror may be challenged and not able to sit for one trial, he or she may be selected for another trial.

Once the jurors are selected, they are told when the trial will start and where to show up.

Juror Payment

Jurors receive a fee for each day they serve on a jury. Fees increase as the trial continues. The following is an example of a fee schedule for jurors in British Columbia:

- $20 per day for each of the first 10 days
- $60 per day for the 11th to the 49th days
- $100 per day for 50 or more days

Jurors in Ontario receive $40 per day from day 11 to 49 and then $100 per day for 50 days or more.

Jurors are responsible for their own lunches during a trial. When a jury is in deliberation, meals and accommodation typically are provided. For example, if a verdict has not been reached by the end of the day, jurors will be housed in hotel rooms and will remain **sequestered** (i.e., isolated from people except for the other jurors) until a verdict is reached.

Sequestered: When jurors are isolated from others, except other jurors, until a verdict is reached

Are Lawyers Able to Select Favourable Jurors?

In a study examining lawyers' ability to select jurors favourable to their position, Olczak, Kaplan, and Penrod (1991) provided lawyers with the facts of a case and the demographic information for 36 potential jurors. The lawyers were asked to assume the role of the defence attorney in the case and to select 12 jurors that they would want on the jury and 12 jurors that they would want to reject. The results indicated that the lawyers were *not* very good at selecting favourable jurors. The lawyers were more likely to make erroneous decisions than accurate decisions; that is, they discarded jurors who found the defendant not guilty and selected jurors who found the defendant guilty. Thus, demographic information and lawyer judgment may be insufficient for identifying favourable jurors.

Scientific Jury Selection

The idea behind **scientific jury selection** is that prospective jurors are evaluated based on predetermined characteristics to identify those who would be sympathetic or unsympathetic to the case. Many consulting firms in the United States are in the business of identifying these characteristics—which include demographic variables, personality traits, and attitudes—in order to determine whether potential jurors are likely to side with the prosecution or the defence. There are two approaches to scientific jury selection: broad based and case-specific.

Scientific jury selection: Rejecting prospective jurors who would be unsympathetic to one's case and accepting those who would be sympathetic based on predetermined characteristics

Broad-Based Approach The **broad-based approach** to scientific jury selection starts with the presumption that there are certain traits or attitudes that make people more likely to be pro-prosecution than pro-defence. Two traits that are commonly measured using

Broad-based approach: Approach to scientific jury selection that starts with the presumption that there are certain traits or attitudes that people have that make them more likely to be pro-prosecution versus pro-defence a broad-based approach are authoritarianism and dogmatism. Individuals high on authoritarianism or dogmatism may be more likely to side with the prosecution. Thus, without knowing any of the evidence of a particular case, some individuals with these traits will be more inclined to favour the prosecution. Prospective jurors may be given questionnaires assessing these traits/attitudes so that lawyers will know whom they should and should not challenge. Alternatively, lawyers can ask prospective jurors questions to assess these traits directly during the **voir dire**—the question period when selecting people to serve on the jury.

Voir dire: The question period when jurors are selected to serve on the jury

Case-Specific Approach

In contrast to a broad-based approach, the **case-specific approach** to scientific jury selection starts with the issues and facts of the case. A specific questionnaire is developed to assess a number of characteristics that may influence the verdict. Individuals in the community from which the jury pool will be drawn are asked to complete the questionnaire. By analyzing the responses to the questionnaire items, profiles of the ideal juror for the prosecution and the ideal juror for the defence are developed. The trial lawyers can then ask each prospective juror relevant questions to decide whether he or she should be challenged. Some jurisdictions in the United States allow lawyers to distribute questionnaires to the actual jury pool prior to jury selection. The answers to the questionnaires are made available to the lawyers on both sides, who then can "prescreen" the prospective jurors prior to the voir dire.

Case-specific approach: Approach to scientific jury selection that starts with the issues and facts of the case. A specific questionnaire then is developed assessing a number of characteristics that may influence the verdict.

The broad-based and case-specific approaches provide lawyers with information that they may use in an attempt to "stack the jury" in their favour. Recall that in Canada, lawyers do not have the privilege of asking prospective jurors questions in most cases. Consequently, scientific jury selection is not possible in Canada.

In the United States, trial consultants may be retained by lawyers throughout the duration of the trial to monitor and provide feedback on the jury's demeanour. As the trial is being conducted, notes are made about any verbal and nonverbal behaviour exhibited by the jurors. This information can give lawyers an ongoing sense of whether they are "winning" the favour of the jurors. Lawyers can alter their strategy should they feel they are losing the jury. Moreover, trial consultants often can provide help with opening and closing statements, witness preparation, and demonstrative evidence (Strier, 1999).

Some criminal and civil cases in the United States that have used scientific jury selection include those of O.J. Simpson, the Menendez brothers, Martha Stewart, and a case involving the fast-food chain McDonald's (Seltzer, 2006). Currently, many jury consultants *do not* claim they can predict a verdict. Instead, they try to predict attitudes that potential jurors may hold toward a particular case.

Two common methodologies can be seen in use for scientific jury selection: telephone surveys and focus groups/mock trials.

Telephone Surveys

Jury-eligible respondents may be selected at random from the jurisdiction in which the actual trial is being heard. In this type of methodology, questions are often asked about demographics (e.g., age, race, sex, etc.) and religious affiliation. Also, a set of questions probing background attitudes believed to be relevant for the case at hand are asked (e.g., people accused of crimes are usually guilty). Lastly, respondents might be asked questions pertaining to the case (e.g., how much they know about the case and where they got their information).

Focus Groups/Mock Jury Trials Jury-eligible respondents may be called at random and asked if they are willing to participate in a focus group or mock trial that may take a half or full day. The mock jurors may view a video, or the trial may be staged for them live so that opening and closing statements can be "tested." These mock jurors also may be asked to complete a questionnaire and their deliberations may be put on video for analysis.

CHARACTERISTICS AND RESPONSIBILITIES OF JURIES IN CANADA

The Supreme Court of Canada indicated two fundamental characteristics of juries (*R. v. Sherratt*, 1991):

1. A composition that represents the community in which the crime occurred. This is known as **representativeness**.

2. A lack of bias on the part of jurors, known as **impartiality**.

Representativeness: A jury composition that represents the community where the crime occurred

Impartiality: A characteristic of jurors who are unbiased

Representativeness

In order for a jury to be considered "representative," it must allow any possible eligible person from the community the opportunity to be part of the jury. Representativeness is achieved through randomness. For example, a community's telephone directory or voter registration is used as a pool from which to randomly draw 100 or so names for potential jury duty. Of course, one could argue that neither of these "pools" is truly representative of the community because there may be people who can serve on a jury but whose names do not appear on these lists. For example, a homeless person may not have a phone but may be eligible to serve on a jury. Also, the Jury Act lists "exemptions" for those who cannot serve on a jury, thus limiting the true representativeness of the jury pool.

In some cases, the Crown or the defence may challenge the composition of the jury, arguing that it does not represent the community on some characteristic. For example, in *R. v. Nepoose* (1991), the defendant was an Aboriginal woman. The jury composition for her trial was successfully challenged for having too few women. See Box 7.2 on page 196 for a jury-composition challenge of representativeness on the basis of race.

Impartiality

The juror characteristic of impartiality centres on three issues:

1. For a juror to be impartial, he or she must set aside any pre-existing biases, prejudices, or attitudes and judge the case based solely on the admissible evidence. For example, a juror must ignore that the defendant belongs to an ethnic group against which he or she holds a bias. An impartial juror will not let his or her prejudice cloud the evaluation of the evidence.

2. To be impartial also means that the juror must ignore any information that is not part of the admissible evidence. For example, prior to the start of a trial, a case may have received media attention highlighting facts about the defendant that are biased, irrelevant, or inadmissible.

Box 7.2

Balancing a Jury by Race

In 2001, two Caucasian men, Jeffrey Brown and Jeffrey Kindrat, were charged with sexually assaulting a 12-year-old Aboriginal girl. Of approximately 100 potential jurors who showed up for jury duty in Melfort, Saskatchewan, only one was visibly Aboriginal. Not surprisingly, once the jury was composed, all those sitting on the jury were Caucasian.

During the trial, the defendants admitted to picking the girl up, giving her five beers to drink, and then engaging in sexual activity with her outside a truck belonging to a third man, Dean Edmondson. The jury heard the evidence and then deliberated to reach verdicts of not guilty for both Mr. Brown and Mr. Kindrat.

Were these verdicts a product of a racist jury? The case raised concern about the jury-selection process. The Saskatchewan Justice Department stated that it would contact officials across Canada to determine whether changes to the selection process could be made to make juries more racially balanced. The effect of this case on jury selection has yet to be determined.

Interestingly, in the trial of Mr. Edmondson, he was found *guilty*, also with an all-Caucasian jury. One main difference between the cases was the testimony of the victim. The victim testified more fully against Mr. Edmondson; however, she was reluctant to testify against Mr. Brown and Mr. Kindrat, providing far less information.

An appeal from the Crown was allowed in 2005 by the Saskatchewan Court of Appeal, setting aside the acquittals, and a new trial was ordered for Mr. Brown and Mr. Kindrat. The appeal was not based on the racial composition of the jury, however, but rather on the judge's instruction to the jury.

Sources: Warick, 2003; *R. v. Brown*, 2005.

3. It also is important that the juror have no connection to the defendant so that the juror does not view the evidence subjectively and does not unduly influence the other jurors. See Box 7.3 for a Canadian case dealing with juror partiality.

Threats to Impartiality A number of threats to impartiality exist. For example, is it possible to forget the emotionally charged headlines that we read before going to jury duty? Typically, the media attention is negative for the defendant, and that could mean that the defendant does not receive a fair trial. Thus, the concern is that verdicts will be based on emotion and biased media coverage rather than on admissible evidence. Steblay, Besirevic, Fulero, and Jimenez-Lorente (1999) conducted a meta-analysis of 44 studies examining the effects of pretrial publicity. They found a modest, positive relationship between exposure to negative pretrial publicity and judgments of guilt. This relation means that as exposure to negative pretrial publicity increases, so do the number of guilty verdicts.

In one study examining pretrial publicity, Kramer, Kerr, and Carroll (1990) manipulated emotional and factual components of pretrial publicity, as well as the time between the pretrial information and hearing the trial. A number of key results were obtained:

- Juries exposed to pretrial publicity were more likely to render a guilty verdict than were juries without exposure to the publicity.

- Juries exposed to publicity with high factual content were more likely to render a guilty verdict when there was no trial delay.

- Juries exposed to publicity with low factual content were more likely to render a guilty verdict when there was a delay.

Canada's Most Famous Partial Juror

Peter Gill and five others were tried in Vancouver for two gang-style murders in 1995. Gillian Guess was one of the 12 jurors hearing Peter Gill's case. During the trial, Guess and Gill ran into each other outside the courtroom; thereafter, they began to flirt in the courtroom. This flirtation led to a meeting outside the courtroom and escalated into a sexual relationship. Their relationship was ongoing as Guess continued to serve on the jury hearing Gill's case.

The jury, including Guess, found Peter Gill and the other defendants not guilty. When the court became aware of the relationship, both Guess and Gill were charged with obstruction of justice. Guess was found guilty and sentenced to 18 months in jail. She was the first *juror* in North America convicted of attempting to obstruct justice and ended up serving three months in prison. Peter Gill had been convicted of obstruction of justice in the past and was sentenced to five years and ten months in prison. Justice Barry Davies of the Supreme Court of British Columbia noted, "Mr. Gill pursued a deliberate and persistent attack upon one of society's most fundamental democratic institutions" (*R. v. Gill*, 2002, para. 29) by getting involved with Guess.

A new murder trial was ordered for Peter Gill and two other men. The appeal court noted that Guess's impartiality was compromised and that it was hard to imagine a more remarkable violation of a juror's duty.

Sources: *R. v. Budai, Gill, and Kim*, 2001; *R. v. Gill*, 2002; *R. v. Guess*, 1998.

These results imply that people tend to forget the factual details of the information they heard or read, but they remember the emotions that it raised. These emotions can then have a biasing effect when it comes to rendering a verdict. In particular, if the emotion was negative, the jurors are more likely to render guilty verdicts.

Keeping Potential Jurors Impartial Before a case goes to trial, a preliminary hearing occurs in which the Crown presents the evidence against the defendant. The judge then determines whether there is sufficient evidence for the case to proceed to trial. In Canada, at the preliminary hearing the judge typically places a ban on the media's reporting of the evidence before the end of the trial process. If the details of the case can be kept from the public, then the likelihood of potential jurors being exposed to information that may compromise their ability to remain impartial is decreased. Moreover, the likelihood of jurors using only the evidence presented during the trial to reach their verdict is increased.

Unfortunately, details do get leaked, especially in high-profile cases involving child victims or violent offences. For example, details about numerous missing women from Vancouver found buried on Robert Pickton's farm in Port Coquitlam made headlines across Canada before Pickton's case was heard (e.g., Saunders & Thompson, 2002). What are the legal options when the defence or Crown fears a partial or biased jury pool?

Some methods for increasing the likelihood of an impartial jury are as follows:

1. The Crown or defence may argue that the trial should be moved to another community because it would be very difficult to obtain an impartial jury from the local community. This option is called a **change of venue** and is found in section 599(1) of the Criminal Code (R.S.C., 1985, C-46, s.599). The party raising the issue must demonstrate that there is a reasonable likelihood that the local community is biased or prejudiced against the defendant. Factors that may lead to a biased community

Change of venue: Moving a trial to a community other than the one in which the crime occurred include extensive pretrial publicity, a heinous crime, and a small community in which many people know the victim and/or the defendant (Granger, 1996). A change of venue is not granted very often, but when it is, the trial typically stays within the province or territory in which the crime occurred. An example was the trial of Kelly Ellard, a teen charged with the murder of 14-year-old Reena Virk in a suburb of Victoria, British Columbia. Adrian Brooks, the defence lawyer, successfully argued to move the trial from Victoria to Vancouver. Brooks claimed that the media attention the case received would prohibit Ellard from getting a fair trial in Victoria (Meissner, 2000).

2. An alternative to moving a trial to a new community is to allow sufficient time to pass so that the biasing effect of any pretrial prejudicial information has dissipated by the time the trial takes place. Thus, the judge may call for an **adjournment**, delaying the trial until some time in the future. A major limitation to adjourning cases is that not only can prospective jurors' memories fade, so might those of the witnesses. Witnesses may forget critical details that they are to testify about. Also, witnesses may move or die. Consequently, courts infrequently call for an adjournment.

Adjournment: Delaying the trial until some time in the future

3. Another option that may be granted in cases for which bias is suspected among the prospective jury pool is known as a **challenge for cause**. The Crown or defence may argue that, although the prospective jury pool may be partial, if questioned, these prospective jurors could be identified and rejected from serving on the jury. As with the change of venue, the side desiring the judge to allow a challenge for cause must demonstrate that there is reasonable partiality in the community from which the jury pool will be drawn. If the judge grants a challenge for cause, prospective jurors can be probed with a set of predetermined questions approved by the judge. The questions are relatively few (perhaps five or so) and only the prospective jurors' state of mind or thinking can be examined. Lawyers are not allowed to ask prospective jurors about their background or personality. See Box 7.4 for sample questions a lawyer may ask a prospective juror.

Challenge for cause: An option to reject biased jurors

A challenge for cause changes how the jury is selected. This process is unique to Canada (Granger, 1996). First, two individuals are selected from the jury pool and are sworn to act as *triers*. A third person is selected as a prospective juror. The lawyers or judge question the prospective juror, while the two triers listen to the answers provided. The triers then discuss the answers with each other to reach a unanimous decision as to whether the prospective juror is impartial. If the triers decide that the prospective juror is not impartial, another person is selected and the process begins again. If the triers decide that the prospective juror is impartial, then that person becomes the first member of the jury (unless the Crown or defence uses a peremptory challenge) and replaces one of the triers. This first juror acts as a trier for a second juror. Thus, jurors 1 and 2 will act as triers for juror 3, jurors 2 and 3 will act as triers for juror 4, and so on, until 12 jurors are selected.

When trying to evaluate whether a challenge for cause is useful for identifying biased individuals, a number of issues need to be considered:

1. The process may be conducted in open court, where the jury pool can hear the questions the lawyers ask and the responses provided. Moreover, they can hear the answers that lead to a positive or negative decision from the triers. Thus, it is possible for prospective jurors to alter their answers according to whether they want to serve on the jury.

Box 7.4

Cases Allowing a Challenge for Cause

Questions Focused on Racial Bias Ruled Appropriate

In *R. v. McLeod* (2005), two black men of Jamaican origin, Germaine McLeod and Christopher Chung, were charged with murdering a man of Asian descent. The Crown's theory was that all three men were involved in drug trafficking or other illegal activities and that the deceased was killed because he was believed to be a police informant.

The following questions were allowed to be posed to the prospective jurors:

1. Do you believe that black Jamaican men, as a group, are more likely to be violent than other persons generally?

2. Would your ability to judge the evidence in this case without bias, prejudice, or partiality be affected by the fact that the accused persons are black Jamaican men, and the deceased was Asian?

As is the practice in the province of Alberta, where this trial occurred, the trial judge, Judge Slatter, was responsible for posing the questions to the prospective jurors.

Source: *R. v. McLeod*, 2005.

Seating a Jury for the Pig Farmer Trial: A Challenge for Cause Granted

Robert Pickton is a pig farmer from Port Coquitlam, British Columbia, who has been charged with the first-degree murder of 26 women. The charges were divided into two trials to facilitate the hearing of testimony and evidence. Mr. Pickton's first trial focused on six counts of murder. A challenge for cause was declared. The jury selection occurred during December 2006 with Judge Williams questioning potential jurors. Jury selection started with 600 prospective jurors in order to find 12 jurors and 2 alternates. Once a trial begins, alternate jurors cannot replace jurors and the alternates are dismissed. If the jury falls under 10 jurors, a mistrial is declared. The trial began in January 2007, with the Crown completing the presentation of its case in August of the same year. A delay in the trial was granted and the defence was scheduled to commence its case in September 2007. See Box 7.5 on page 200 for more on the Pickton trial.

Sources: Hunter & Baron, 2006; CBC News, August 28, 2007.

2. Prospective jurors may find it difficult to be honest when answering questions about bias that may put them in an unflattering light, especially if the questioning is conducted in open court.

3. Prospective jurors must be aware of their biases and how their biases may influence their behaviour. Some classic work by Nisbett and Wilson (1977) suggests that individuals are unaware of their biases and how their biases affect their behaviour.

Jury Functions

The main legal function of a jury is to apply the law, as provided by the judge, to the admissible evidence in the case and render a verdict of guilt or innocence. As we will discuss, there are cases in which the jury will ignore the law and apply some other criteria to reach a verdict. In addition to the main legal function of juries, four other jury functions have been identified:

1. To use the wisdom of 12 (rather than the wisdom of 1) to reach a verdict

2. To act as the conscience of the community

3. To protect against out-of-date laws

4. To increase knowledge about the justice system

The Pig Farmer Goes to Court

The following are some interesting facts regarding the Robert Pickton case:

- Defendant: Robert William Pickton, 57 years old
- Victims (first trial): Marnie Frey, Brenda Wolfe, Mona Wilson, Andrea Joesbury, Georgina Papin, Sereena Abotsway
- When victims went missing: between August 1997 and November 2001
- When Pickton was first charged: February 22, 2002
- The charges against Pickton: 26 counts of first-degree murder
- Location of trial: New Westminster Supreme Court, B.C.
- Members of the jury: Five women and seven men, ranging in age from their early twenties to their seventies
- The lawyers: The Crown team is led by Mike Petrie, the defence team by Peter Ritchie
- The judge: Justice James W. Williams, 58 years old, was appointed to the Supreme Court of British Columbia in 2002. He was assigned to the Pickton case in 2005.
- Predicted length of trial: one year
- The schedule: Court sat Mondays through Thursdays, 9:30 A.M. to 4:30 P.M., with two 15-minute breaks and one 90-minute lunch break. On Fridays, the judge and lawyers will deal with case-related work outside the presence of the jury.
- Mr. Pickton has pleaded not guilty to all the charges.
- What happens first: The Crown will begin its case with an opening statement. Due to the unusual length of the trial, the defence will also be allowed to make an opening statement at the start of the trial—a departure from the usual procedure.

The following are some interesting numbers regarding the Robert Pickton case:

- **102**: Number of anthropology students hired to collect DNA samples on Mr. Pickton's farm between February 2002 and November 2003
- **21**: Number of months spent collecting 200 000 DNA samples and other physical evidence on Mr. Pickton's 6.8 hectare farm
- **283 000** cubic metres: Amount of soil sifted through on Mr. Pickton's farm in search of evidence
- **750 000**: Number of documents disclosed to date by the Crown
- **2000–2500**: Number of statements taken from witnesses so far
- **1000**: Number of people on the Crown's witness list (not including those who could be called by the defence)
- **$120 million**: Estimated cost of investigating and prosecuting Mr. Pickton
- **500–600**: Number of police officers and civilians who have been employed by the Joint Missing Women Task Force
- **68**: Number of women who disappeared from Vancouver's Downtown Eastside between 1978 and 2001
- **5**: Number of years Mr. Pickton had spent in jail by the time his trial started in January 2007

Sources: Fast Facts about the Pickton Trial, 2007; Sin, 2006.

Jury nullification: Occurs when a jury ignores the law and the evidence, rendering a verdict based on some other criteria

Ignoring the Law The jury has a responsibility to apply the law as defined by the judge to the admissible evidence and to render a verdict. Ignoring that law and the evidence, and rendering a verdict based on some other criteria is known as **jury nullification**. Juries may choose to ignore the law for a number of reasons. For example, they may believe the law is unfair given the circumstances of the case or the punishment accompanying a conviction is too harsh for the crime. In both these instances, jury nullification may result.

Jury nullification typically can occur when the case involves controversial issues such as abortion and euthanasia (see Box 7.6).

Box 7.6

Two Cases of Jury Nullification

Dr. Henry Morgentaler: Baby Killer or Champion of Women's Rights?

Dr. Henry Morgentaler conducted his first abortion, secretly, in 1968. He began performing illegal abortions openly in Montreal in 1969, and in 1970 he was arrested for conducting an abortion. The arrest occurred three years before the U.S. Supreme Court landmark case of *Roe v. Wade* (1973), which made abortion a constitutional right for American women.

A Quebec jury of 11 men and 1 woman found Dr. Morgentaler not guilty. The verdict was appealed and overturned in 1974. Dr. Morgentaler was sentenced to prison. When he was released, he continued conducting illegal abortions. In two more trials, juries returned not guilty verdicts. In 1975, a significant change to Quebec law occurred in which a jury verdict could no longer be overturned on appeal, known as the Morgentaler Amendment. Furthermore, in 1976, the Quebec government announced it would no longer prosecute abortion cases.

In 1983, while conducting abortions in Ontario, Dr. Morgentaler and two colleagues were charged with conducting illegal miscarriages. The jury found them not guilty. The Ontario Court of Appeal then reversed this verdict.

Clearly, the voice of the community, via the jury, was incongruent with the law. Change in legislation occurred in 1988 when the Supreme Court of Canada ruled that Canadian women have the right to a safe abortion. More than 100 000 abortions are conducted in Canada each year.

Robert Latimer: A Loving Father?

Tracy Latimer lived with her family in Wilkie, Saskatchewan. She had severe cerebral palsy, was quadriplegic, and could only communicate by means of facial expression, laughter, and crying. It was estimated that she had the mental capacity of a four-month-old baby. Tracy had five to six seizures a day and it was believed that she was in constant pain. She also underwent several surgeries. Another surgery was scheduled for Tracy when she was 12 years old.

Robert Latimer, Tracy's father, felt that it would be a mutilation and could no longer live with seeing his daughter suffer. He decided that he would end his daughter's life. In 1993, he connected a hose from his pick-up truck's exhaust pipe into the cab and seated Tracy in the cab. Tracy died from carbon monoxide inhalation. At first, Latimer claimed that Tracy had passed away in her sleep, but he later confessed to taking Tracy's life. The jury found Robert Latimer guilty of second-degree murder.

Second-degree murder carries a life sentence without eligibility for parole for a minimum of 10 years and up to 25 years. Juries are allowed to make sentencing recommendations in this situation. The jury sent the judge a note asking if they could recommend less than ten years. The judge explained the mandatory minimum recommendation as outlined in the Criminal Code; however, they could make any recommendation they liked. The jury recommended one year before parole eligibility.

The judge granted a constitutional exemption from the mandatory minimum and sentenced Robert Latimer to one year in prison and one year of probation. In keeping with the law, however, the Court of Appeal upheld the conviction but changed the sentence to life imprisonment with eligibility for parole in ten years. Once again, the law was inconsistent with the community's sentiment, which was expressed by the jury.

Sources: *R. v. Morgentaler*, 1988; O'Malley & Wood, 2003; *R. v. Latimer*, 2001.

If juries are allowed to ignore the law and vote with their conscience, won't we end up with a biased or random system? Won't the result be chaos? Niedermeier, Horowitz, and Kerr (1999) examined whether telling jurors of their option to nullify the law would lead to biased verdicts. In one of their experiments, university students in groups of four were randomly assigned to consider one of four versions of a criminal trial. The trial involved a male victim of an HIV-infected blood transfusion who later died of AIDS. The blood was not screened for HIV prior to the transfusion.

The researchers manipulated the status of the defendant who decided to give the blood transfusion, knowing the blood was not screened: high status (medical director) versus low

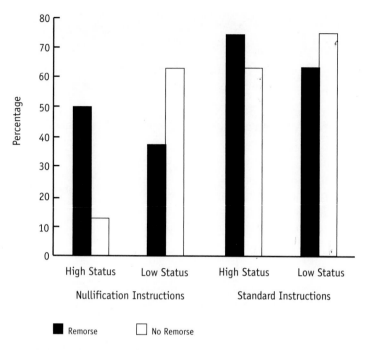

Figure 7.1 Guilty Verdicts Based on Nullification Instructions, Status
of Defendant, and Remorse of Defendant

Source: Adapted from Niedermeier et al., 1999.

status (medical resident). The researchers also manipulated the defendant's remorsefulness
on the outcome of the victim: presence of remorse versus absence of remorse.

These independent variables were examined to determine whether they were affected
by nullification instructions. The four-person juries received either standard or nullification instructions after hearing the trial evidence. The juries were asked to reach a unanimous verdict. See Figure 7.1 for the percentage of guilty verdicts as a function of
nullification instructions, status of the defendant, and remorse of the defendant.

Overall, juries that received nullification instructions were less likely to render guilty
verdicts than juries receiving standard instructions. The high-status defendant who was
not remorseful was given fewer convictions than when he or she did express remorse. In
contrast, the low-status defendant received fewer convictions when he or she expressed
remorse than when not doing so. Thus, in general, informing juries of their power to disregard the law may lead to more *not* guilty verdicts, but there are factors that will interact
with these instructions, including the defendant's status and level of remorse.

HOW DO WE STUDY JUROR AND JURY BEHAVIOUR?

Now that we know how juries are selected, and what their characteristics and responsibilities are, we can start understanding and predicting their behaviour. Many researchers in
the forensic area have focused their careers on trying to predict verdicts and the variables
that affect verdicts. We will now discuss four methodologies that have been used to gain
understanding of juror and jury behaviour.

Post-Trial Interviews

In trying to understand why juries reached particular verdicts, perhaps it seems most logical and simple to ask the jurors themselves why they reached the verdicts they did. In Canada, however, actual jurors are not allowed to discuss what occurred in deliberations. All discourse that occurs during the deliberations is confidential. Breaking this confidentiality is a violation of section 649 of the Criminal Code (R.S.C., 1985, C-46, s. 649). A juror who discusses any part of the deliberation process would be committing a summary offence that carries a fine of up to $2000 and/or imprisonment for up to six months. Although researchers cannot talk to Canadian jurors regarding their deliberations, they can turn to the United States or other countries that do not have this rule.

The main strength of post-trial interviews is high external validity; that is, results come from using real cases and the actual jurors that deliberated. Consequently, results may be more likely to generalize to the real world. This methodology, however, also has a number of weaknesses. For one, jurors' accounts may not be reliable. For example, jurors may recall details inaccurately, they may forget critical aspects of the deliberation, they may embellish or downplay elements to present themselves more favourably, or they may be unaware of the reasons for their decisions and behaviour. Thus, conclusions may be based on data that are unreliable. Moreover, a cause-and-effect relationship cannot be established with this type of methodology. At best, researchers can talk about variables that occur together. Alternative hypotheses cannot be ruled out with this methodology.

Archives

Records of trials, such as transcripts and police interviews of witnesses, can be reviewed to uncover relationships between variables. The strength of this methodology is similar to post-trial interviews in that external validity is high. A similar weakness, however, is the inability to establish cause-and-effect relationships. Also, the researcher is restricted to the data available in that the types of questions that can be posed are limited by the information that can be accessed. The researcher is unable to go back and collect more information. Furthermore, the researcher is unaware of how the information was collected and the reliability of that information. For example, police interviews may have been conducted using biased procedures.

Simulation

One of the most common methodologies used to investigate jury issues is the simulation. Researchers simulate a trial, or aspects of it, using a written, audio, or video format. Participants are presented with the trial information. The information that the participants receive about the trial can be varied and manipulated by the researcher. Examples of possible independent variables of interest include the age of the witness or the race of the defendant. Following the presentation of the trial, participants are asked to respond individually (juror research) or in groups (jury research). Typically, jurors and juries will be asked to render a verdict or make other judgments. Verdicts and other participants' responses can be compared to determine whether the independent variable(s) had an effect.

One of the major strengths of this methodology is its high internal validity; that is, the researcher can reveal cause-and-effect relationships because he or she systematically manipulated the independent variables. However, the control the researcher has over the independent variables limits the external validity of this methodology. For example, in simulations, cases are not real and there are no consequences to the verdicts or decisions the jurors render. Furthermore, the participants typically are university students, who may not be representative of real jury pools. These factors limit the generalizability of the results obtained with simulations.

Field Studies

This methodology involves using actual jurors while they are serving on jury duty, so cooperation from the courts and the jurors is required. Researchers are able to observe variables of interest as they are occurring. For example, they may be interested in how prospective jurors respond to questions posed during the voir dire. Alternatively, researchers may be able to introduce variables that they want to examine. The court may agree to let jurors take notes while the evidence is being presented, for example. Trials in which jurors were allowed to take notes can be compared with trials in which jurors were not allowed to take notes. A comparison of the verdicts can be undertaken across these cases.

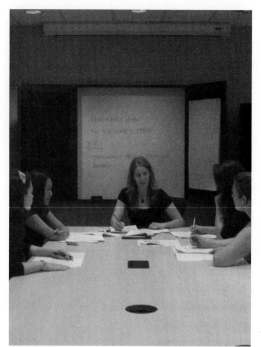
Participants deliberate a mock trial

The strength of field studies is high external validity. A number of limitations, however, are also present. For example, receiving approval from the courts for conducting the research may be difficult. Even when approval is granted, it is likely that only a small sample of participants will be available, and appropriate comparison groups may be difficult to identify. Additionally, there are a host of confounding variables that the researcher may not be able to control, such as the gender of lawyers and witnesses.

As you can see, the researcher interested in juror/jury issues has a variety of methodologies to choose from. Each methodology has some strengths and weaknesses. By using all of these methodologies, we may be able to gain a more accurate understanding of juror and jury behaviour.

REACHING A VERDICT

Deliberation: When jury members discuss the evidence privately among themselves to reach a verdict that is then provided to the court

Once a jury has been selected, their work begins. Jurors must listen to the admissible evidence and disregard any evidence that the judge does not allow. Once the lawyers deliver their closing arguments, the judge provides the jury with the law that they must apply to the evidence in order to reach a verdict. The jury then makes its **deliberation**—that is, they discuss the evidence privately among themselves to reach a verdict, which is then provided to the court. We will discuss each stage involved in reaching a jury verdict and the factors that may affect each stage.

Listening to the Evidence

Two innovations have been proposed as aids for jurors while they listen to the evidence: note taking and asking questions. Advantages and disadvantages have been identified for each aid. We will discuss each aid in turn and the Canadian justice system's position on each.

Note Taking Trials can be lengthy and complex, resulting in missed or forgotten evidence by the time the jury is asked to deliberate. Some have suggested that allowing jurors to take notes may facilitate memory and understanding of the evidence (e.g., Heuer & Penrod, 1994). Moreover, note takers may be more attentive during the trial than those who do not take notes. Not everyone is in agreement, however, that allowing jurors to take notes is advantageous or even preferable. For example, in the Canadian case of *R. v. Andrade* (1985), a number of disadvantages to juror note taking were identified:

- Jurors who take notes may exert influence while in deliberation over those who do not.
- If disagreements occur about the evidence, jurors will rely on those who took notes to clarify the issue.

In one study examining juror note taking, Horowitz and ForsterLee (2001) had community citizens watch a video of a complex civil trial involving multiple plaintiffs. Mock jurors were either allowed to take notes or not allowed to take notes. Also, juries were either allowed to view trial transcripts during deliberations or not. The researchers found that, compared with those who did not take notes, the note takers were better able to differentiate among multiple plaintiffs and were better able to assign monetary awards accordingly. Also, having notes was more helpful for increasing juror knowledge about the evidence than was having access to trial transcripts.

In another study, Rosenhan, Eisner, and Robinson (1994) examined jurors' recall and comprehension of trial evidence from a group who took notes versus a group who did not. Note takers recalled more information than those who did not take notes. Also, the note takers scored higher on comprehension than those who did not take notes.

A review of the research examining juror note taking was conducted by Penrod and Heuer (1997). They reached the following conclusions regarding juror note taking:

- Jurors' notes serve as a memory aid.
- Jurors do not overemphasize the evidence that they have noted at the expense of evidence they have not recorded.
- Notes do not produce a distorted view of the case.
- Note takers can keep up with the evidence as it is being presented.
- Note takers do not distract jurors who do not take notes.
- Note takers do not have an undue influence over those who do not take notes.
- Jurors' notes are an accurate record of the trial.
- Juror note taking does not favour either the prosecution/Crown or the defence.

As you can see, allowing jurors to take notes does not appear to pose major difficulties. At present in Canada, it is up to the trial judge in each case to decide whether jurors will be allowed to take notes (Granger, 1996).

Asking Questions When watching trials on television, or if you have ever had the opportunity to listen to a trial in court, you may have found yourself wondering about a detail that was mentioned. Would it not help if you could stop the trial and ask a question? The courts have considered the issue of jurors being allowed to ask questions. As with note taking, a number of advantages and disadvantages have been identified with regard to this innovation (Heuer & Penrod, 1994).

Some advantages of allowing jurors to ask questions include the following:

- It promotes greater understanding of the evidence.
- It can help reveal the truth.
- It can identify for lawyers issues that are unclear.
- It increases satisfaction with the judicial process.

Some disadvantages include the following:

- Jurors might ask unallowable questions.
- Lawyers might be reluctant to object to jurors' questions.
- Jurors could misunderstand lawyers' objections to their question.
- Jurors could confuse their role in the judicial process and take on an advocate role.

Heurer and Penrod (1994) reported that typically juries have few questions (usually not more than three) and they tend to be concerned with the meaning of key legal terms such as *reasonable doubt*. In a review of the research examining juror questions, Penrod and Heuer (1997) reached the following conclusions:

- Jury questioning promotes juror understanding of the facts and issues.
- Juror questions do not clearly help get to the truth.
- Juror questions do not increase the jurors', judges', or lawyers' satisfaction with the trial and verdict.
- Jurors ask legally appropriate questions.
- If counsel objects, and the objection is sustained, the jury does not draw inappropriate inferences from unanswered questions.
- Jurors do not become advocates.

Thus, the research on allowing jurors to ask questions does not appear to be particularly harmful or helpful. At present in Canada, jurors may submit their questions in writing to the judge after the lawyers have completed their questioning of the witness. The judge then determines whether the question is permissible. Questions that are permissible then are posed by the judge. Ultimately, allowing jurors to ask questions is up to the judge presiding over the trial.

Disregarding Inadmissible Evidence

Are jurors able to "forget" what they heard? This question is not only relevant when we consider pretrial publicity but also when judges request that jurors disregard inadmissible evidence. Often, juries will hear inadmissible evidence when lawyers or witnesses make statements that are not allowable according to legal procedure. Following an inadmissible statement or inadmissible evidence, the judge will instruct the jury to disregard it. The critical component to a fair trial and a just verdict is that only admissible statements and evidence are used by the jury. The question is, are jurors able to disregard evidence they have heard?

In one study by Hans and Doob (1976), participants were given a summary of a hypothetical burglary. Some of the participants were made aware of evidence about the defendant's prior convictions that they were asked to disregard. The remaining participants were not given this inadmissible evidence. Participants who were given the inadmissible evidence were more likely to reach a guilty verdict (40%) than participants who did not receive this evidence (0%). It seems that jurors are not very good at ignoring evidence once they have heard it, even if it is inadmissible.

Factors That Affect Instructions to "Disregard" One factor that seems to influence a jury's ability to disregard inadmissible evidence is the *strength* of the evidence. Sue, Smith, and Caldwell (1973) discovered that when evidence against the defendant was weak, jurors were more likely to consider the inadmissible evidence and render more guilty verdicts than when the inadmissible evidence was not presented at all. In contrast, when evidence against the defendant was strong, jurors were more likely to disregard the inadmissible evidence. Inadmissible evidence also seems to have a greater influence when a crime is of a less serious nature, such as vandalism, compared with a more serious crime such as homicide or arson (Rind, Jaeger, & Strohmetz, 1995).

Kassin and Sommers (1997) argued that whether jurors will follow a judge's instruction to disregard inadmissible evidence is related to the reason for the instruction rather than to the instruction itself. In their study, mock jurors were presented with a murder trial, and a piece of evidence was manipulated. Jurors in the control condition received only circumstantial and ambiguous evidence. In the experimental conditions, an audiotaped telephone conversation in which the defendant confessed to the murder was included. When this audiotape was admitted into evidence, the defence lawyer objected. The judge either overruled the objection, allowing it into evidence, or sustained the objection and asked jurors to disregard it because it was either illegally obtained or difficult to comprehend. When jurors were asked to disregard the evidence because it was illegally collected, their verdicts were similar to the jurors who received the ruling that the tape was admissible. In contrast, when jurors were instructed to disregard the tape because of comprehension difficulty, they rendered verdicts similar to the control jurors who had not heard about the inadmissible evidence. Thus, Kassin and Sommers concluded that jurors will disregard evidence when they are provided with a logical and legitimate reason for the judge's decision to disregard it.

One other interesting result has been found with the instruction to disregard. Some researchers have found that a judge's instruction to disregard evidence simply makes the evidence more memorable than if no instruction were given. This is known as the *backfire effect* (Paglia & Schuller, 1998). Thus, jurors are more likely to pay attention to inadmissible evidence following a disregard instruction than if no instruction was provided.

Overall, the influence of the disregard instruction is not straightforward. There are other factors that come into play and interact with the effect of the instruction.

Judge's Instructions

A number of studies have examined jurors' abilities to understand the legally dense instructions that the judge charges the jury with prior to their deliberation. The results of these studies generally are not positive. Lieberman and Sales (1997) have concluded that jurors do not remember, understand, or accurately apply judges' instructions. Reifman, Gusick, and Ellsworth (1992) surveyed 224 citizens from Michigan who were called for jury duty. The goal was to assess jurors' comprehension of judges' instructions. These prospective jurors understood less than 50% of the instructions they received.

Four reforms for judges' instructions have been proposed: (1) rewriting instructions, (2) providing a written copy of the instructions to jurors, (3) pre- and post-evidence instructions, and (4) having lawyers clarify legal instruction during their presentation to the jury.

Rewriting Instructions Judges' instructions often contain several legal terms and complex sentence structure. These instructions could be simplified by relying on psycholinguistic and cognitive research. However, there is some disagreement as to whether rewriting instructions aids comprehension (Kagehiro, 1990). In a review of the research, Tanford (1992) reported that errors in comprehension remain fairly high, at about 75%, even with rewritten instructions.

Providing Written Instructions The notion behind providing jurors with written instructions is that jurors have the judge's instructions in a supplemental form that they can access as they deliberate. In a review of studies examining this supplement to judges' oral instructions, Lieberman and Sales (1997) found that written instructions can aid juror understanding of the judge's oral instructions. However, some studies have not found a difference in comprehension as a function of supplemental written instructions (e.g., Heuer & Penrod, 1989). It seems that the jury is still out on whether written instructions are a helpful supplement to a judge's oral instructions to the jury.

Pre- and Post-Evidence Instructions Some researchers have argued that providing jurors with instructions both before and after they hear the evidence may help in their comprehension of the instructions. For example, Smith (1991) found that when mock jurors were given instructions both before and after they heard the evidence, they were correct on 70% of the questions probing their comprehension of the instructions. When mock jurors heard the instructions only after the evidence was presented, they were correct on 68% of the questions. This difference between groups is not significant. However, with different dependent measures, it is possible to demonstrate that pre- and post-evidence instructions are more beneficial than just post-evidence instructions (Smith, 1991).

Lawyer Clarification Ellsworth and Reifman (2000) have suggested that lawyers could clarify complex legal terms during their closing arguments to aid juror comprehension of judges' instructions. Little direct research exists on this topic to determine whether this technique would increase juror comprehension. Thus, it is not clear whether lawyer clarification will be beneficial to jurors trying to comprehend judges' instructions.

These four proposed reforms have not been implemented with any consistency within the Canadian justice system.

Jury Decision-Making Models

How do jurors combine the trial evidence to reach a verdict? Moreover, what is the process by which verdicts are reached? Although a number of models of juror/jury decision making have been proposed, they may be categorized as using either a mathematical or explanation-based approach.

A jury listens to evidence.

Mathematical Models The common theme with mathematical models is that they view jurors as conducting a set of mental calculations regarding the importance and strength of each piece of evidence (Hastie, 1993). A guilty or not guilty verdict is determined by the outcome of the calculations for all the relevant evidence. For example, an eyewitness who identified the defendant may be perceived as strong evidence and be weighed heavily toward a guilty verdict; however, learning that the DNA found at the crime scene does not match the defendant's decreases the likelihood of a guilty verdict. The verdict is a function of the calculation of all the relevant evidence.

Ellsworth and Mauro (1998) examined the congruency of mental calculations and how jurors perceive their process of reaching a verdict. They found that a mathematical approach was inconsistent with how jurors report that they reach verdicts. Jurors do not appear to provide a value for each piece of evidence presented. Moreover, it may be difficult to partition evidence into discrete pieces of evidence that can then be assigned a value. Perhaps an explanation-based approach is more consistent with how jurors process the trial evidence.

Explanation Models In contrast to mathematical models, explanation models suggest that evidence is organized into a coherent whole. Pennington and Hastie's (1986) explanation approach is called the *story model*. They proposed that jurors are active at understanding and processing the evidence. Jurors interpret and elaborate on the evidence and make causal connections, and in doing so, they create a story structure. These "stories" are then compared with each verdict option presented by the judge. The verdict option most consistent with the story is the verdict reached.

Of course, jurors listening to the same evidence may construct different stories that are consistent with alternative verdicts. That is to say, individual differences can influence the story-construction process. Jurors bring in their personal experiences, knowledge, beliefs, and attitudes when constructing their story. Thus, jurors may reach different decisions after hearing the same evidence.

To test the story model, Pennington and Hastie (1986) had 26 participants watch a simulated murder trial and then make individual verdicts at the end of the trial. Following their verdicts, participants were interviewed to determine how they thought about the evidence. The researchers found that participants put the evidence into a story format and different stories were related to different verdicts.

In a follow-up study, Pennington and Hastie (1988) varied how easily a particular story could be constructed by altering the order in which the evidence was presented. They found that when the evidence was presented in a chronological order, it was more likely that the verdict reached was consistent with that story order. This information could be useful to lawyers who may choose to present evidence in a story format that is consistent with the verdict they want. The story model seems to be consistent with how jurors process trial evidence and reach a verdict.

Deliberations

As you may recall, a 12-person jury is necessary for criminal cases in Canada. However, cases can continue as long as no more than two members are excused, possibly for illness or other reasons, during the trial (Granger, 1996). For example, in the 2003 murder trial of Matti Baranovski in Toronto, an 11-person jury convicted Lee Cochrane and Meir Mariani of manslaughter.

Once all the evidence has been heard and the judge has delivered instructions to the jurors, the jury retires to a secluded room to deliberate. In Canada, the jury is sequestered until the final verdict is reached—then, the jury is dismissed by the judge (Granger, 1996). This means that the jury is not allowed to talk to anyone outside their 12-person panel, with the exception of the court-appointed officer in the event that they have a request or question.

The expectation from the justice system is that the jury reviews the evidence and determines the most consistent match between the verdict options that were provided by the judge and the admissible evidence. A number of factors can influence a juror's position on the case. A phenomenon known as **polarization** occurs when individuals tend to become more extreme in their initial position following a group discussion (Baron & Bryne, 1991). In contrast, a **leniency bias** also has been found whereby jurors move toward greater leniency following deliberations (MacCoun & Kerr, 1988).

The Final Verdict

A Canadian jury must reach a unanimous verdict. If not, the jury is said to be a **hung jury** or deadlocked and a mistrial is declared. Following a hung-jury outcome, the Crown must decide whether it will retry the case.

In contrast to required unanimous verdicts in Canada, the United States has permitted majority votes of eleven to one, ten to two, and nine to three. Similarly, the United Kingdom has allowed juries to render eleven-to-one or ten-to-two majority votes provided that the jury has deliberated for a minimum of two hours. In a meta-analysis examining the effects of jury size, Saks and Marti (1997) found that six-person juries are less representative of the community, they remember less of the evidence, they return quicker verdicts, and they are more likely to reach a unanimous verdict than 12-person juries. Hastie, Penrod, and

Polarization: When individuals tend to become more extreme in their initial position following a group discussion

Leniency bias: When jurors move toward greater leniency during deliberations

Hung jury: A jury that cannot reach a unanimous verdict

Pennington (1983) found that when a jury could retire with a majority vote, they tended to reach a decision faster and did not fully discuss both the evidence and law, compared with when the jury was required to reach a unanimous verdict.

In general, when a first verdict poll is taken, the final verdict tends to be consistent with the first poll in about 90% of cases (Kalvern & Zeisel, 1966; Sandys & Dillehay, 1995). MacCoun and Kerr (1988) conducted a meta-analysis of 12 studies examining juror preferences at the beginning of deliberation as well as final verdicts. They found that a pro-defence faction was more persuasive than a pro-prosecution faction. More specifically, if seven or fewer jurors vote guilty at the beginning of deliberation, the jury will tend to render a not guilty verdict. If ten or more jurors initially vote guilty, the final verdict will likely be guilty. If eight or nine jurors initially vote guilty, the final verdict is unpredictable.

Hastie, Penrod, and Pennington (1983) identified two broad styles that juries tend to adopt when trying to reach a verdict: verdict driven and evidence driven. Verdict-driven juries tend to start the deliberation process by taking an initial verdict poll. In contrast, evidence-driven juries tend to start the deliberation process by discussing the evidence. A verdict poll is not taken until much later during the deliberation. These two styles can influence the outcome of the initial verdict poll (Sandys & Dillehay, 1995).

PREDICTING VERDICTS

A great deal of research on juror characteristics has been conducted to determine whether verdicts can be predicted based on these characteristics. We will examine the following six types of variables that have been studied and their relation to the verdict: (1) demographic variables, (2) personality traits, (3) attitudes, (4) defendant characteristics, (5) victim characteristics, and (6) expert testimony.

Demographic Variables

Variables such as the gender, race, socioeconomic status, and education of jurors are demographic variables that have been examined, in part because they are readily available to lawyers but also because they can be used to challenge witnesses. For example, are female jurors more lenient? Are Caucasians more likely to render guilty verdicts?

Racial bias as it relates to jury decision making can be defined as disparate treatment of racial out-groups. In a number of U.S. studies, black defendants have been found to be treated more harshly than white defendants, particularly in cases involving murder or sexual assault (for a review, see Sommers & Ellsworth, 2001). It should be noted, however, that not all studies find a racial bias, and some studies find the opposite effect, with white defendants treated more harshly than black defendants (e.g., Poulson, 1990). In a recent meta-analysis examining racial bias on verdict and sentencing decisions, Mitchell, Haw, Pfeifer, and Meissner (2005) found a small significant effect of racial bias on jury decisions. Participants were more likely to render guilty verdicts for "other-race" defendants than for defendants of their own race. Also, participants rendered longer sentences for other-race defendants. These effects are moderated by a number of factors that can lead to a greater effect for racial bias (e.g., when jury instructions were not provided or when participants were black).

Racial bias: The disparate treatment of racial out-groups

Some researchers highlight a more intriguing finding that there is an interaction between juror demographic variables and defendant demographic variables (Devine, Clayton, Dunford, Seying, & Pryce, 2001). For example, the defendant's race has been found to interact with the race of the juror. In a study on race, Perez, Hosch, Ponder, and Trejo (1993) found that juries made up predominantly of white people were more likely to render guilty verdicts for Hispanic defendants versus white defendants. However, the relationship was not straightforward. Results were influenced by the strength of the evidence. When the evidence was weak or ambiguous (not clearly favouring one side), similarity between defendant and jury led to leniency. When evidence was strong, similarity between defendant and jury led to punitiveness. This is known as the **black sheep effect** (Chadee, 1996).

Black sheep effect: When evidence is strong, similarity between defendant and jury leads to punitiveness

Unfortunately, when using juror demographic variables to predict verdicts, results are less than reliable. Overall, only a small and inconsistent relation exists between juror demographic variables and jury verdicts (e.g., Bonazzoli, 1998).

Personality Traits

The two personality traits that have been commonly measured in connection to jurors are authoritarianism and dogmatism. Individuals high in authoritarianism tend to have right-wing political views and are conservative and rigid thinkers who acquiesce to authority. Similarly, individuals high in dogmatism also tend to be rigid and closed-minded but without the political overtones found with the authoritarianism construct. Are personality traits better for predicting verdicts than demographic variables?

Given the underlying traits associated with dogmatism and authoritarianism, anyone would predict that jurors who score high on these constructs would be more likely to align themselves with the prosecution and, thus, render more guilty verdicts than jurors who score low on these constructs. In a meta-analysis that examined authoritarianism and juror verdicts across 20 studies, Narby, Cutler, and Moran (1993) found a moderate, positive relationship between authoritarianism and verdict such that those who score high on these traits tend to be more inclined to render guilty verdicts. That is, they have a pro-prosecution bias.

One also needs to consider that jurors are required to reach a unanimous decision, possibly by persuading other jurors. What type of person or what personality traits tend to be the most persuasive? In a study by Rotenberg, Hewlett, and Siegwart (1998), mock jurors who were extroverted and had higher moral reasoning were found to be more persuasive than other mock jurors. In another study, by Marcus, Lyons, and Guyton (2000), the "big five" personality dimensions were examined for persuasiveness:

- Extroversion: outgoing, sociable, and animated
- Agreeableness: altruistic, interpersonally pleasant, and positive
- Conscientiousness: self-disciplined, determined, and dutiful
- Emotional stability: calm, even-tempered, and able to handle stressful situations
- Openness to experience: imaginative, sensitive, intellectually curious, and unconventional

The researchers found that participants who showed a high level on conscientiousness were most likely to report being persuaded by other participants. In contrast, participants who scored high on openness were least likely to be persuaded by other participants. Those exhibiting high levels of extroversion were most persuasive, and being male wielded more influence than being female. Intriguingly, extroverted, *tall* males were even more persuasive than extroverted, *shorter* males.

Jurors' personality traits seem to be more reliable for predicting verdicts than demographic variables.

Attitudes

Researchers have examined a variety of attitudes linked to specific topics or issues that may be present in cases, such as drunk driving, rape, child sexual abuse, and capital punishment. For example, Spanos, DuBreuil, and Gwynn (1991–1992) examined rape myths (e.g., a woman who wears provocative clothing is interested in having sex) in connection to a date-rape case. University students heard a version of a date-rape case involving expert testimony about rape myths and cross-examination of such, and then deliberated in small groups to reach a verdict. A gender split was observed in which females did not believe the defendant and voted him guilty more often than male mock jurors. However, regardless of the gender of the mock jurors, those with feminist attitudes were more likely not to believe the defendant's testimony.

Devine et al. (2001) reported that no group of attitudes or values has received sufficient investigation to reach a definitive conclusion at this point. The one notable exception is attitudes toward capital punishment. For example, Horowitz and Seguin (1986) reported that juries comprising death-qualified jurors (i.e., jurors who are willing to impose the death sentence) had a 19% higher conviction rate than non-death-qualified jurors. In general, death-qualified jurors are more likely than non-death-qualified jurors to vote for conviction at the end of a trial (Ellsworth & Mauro, 1998).

Overall, attitudes that are case-specific seem to have more predictive power over verdict than more general attitudes do.

Defendant Characteristics

A number of studies have examined defendant characteristics and their influence on verdicts. For example, if jurors hear about a defendant's prior criminal record that contains one or more convictions, they are more likely to find the defendant guilty than if the jurors did not have this knowledge (Hans & Doob, 1976).

There also seems to be a small relationship between the attractiveness of the defendant and jury verdict. Izzett and Leginski (1974) provided mock jurors with either a picture of an unattractive defendant or an attractive defendant and found verdict preferences to be more lenient for the attractive defendant and more severe for the unattractive defendant.

Defendant characteristics often are examined in relation to other characteristics, such as victim characteristics.

Victim Characteristics

Characteristics of the victim may become particularly relevant in cases of sexual assault in which a guilty verdict may hinge on the testimony of the alleged victim. In Canada, before the mid-1980s, a woman's prior sexual history was admissible and could be used to infer her credibility and the likelihood that she consented to sexual relations with the defendant. In 1985, rape-shield provisions were legislated, which prevented lawyers from introducing a woman's prior sexual history (R.S.C. 1985, c. C-46, s. 276).

In the early 1990s, however, some began to challenge these provisions on the grounds that they prevented defendants from receiving a fair trial (*R. v. Seaboyer*, 1991; *R. v. Gayme*, 1991). Defence lawyers argued that it was necessary to admit the accuser's prior sexual history because it would support defendants' claims of an honest but mistaken belief in consent. The rape shield provisions were amended in 1992, allowing inquiry into a woman's sexual history at the judge's discretion (R.S.C. 1985, C-46, s. 276; 1992, c. 38, s.2). Only if a woman's sexual history was deemed relevant would the judge allow it to be heard by the jury. Further, the Supreme Court of Canada (*R. v. Seaboyer*, 1991) recommended that the trial judge provide the jury with cautionary instructions on how this evidence should be used. More specifically, the jurors must be cautioned that a woman's sexual history should be used only in determining a defendant's claim of an "honest but mistaken belief in consent." A woman's sexual history must not be used to demonstrate that the woman is less trustworthy or that she is likely to consent to sexual intercourse. Some have argued that such a distinction is too fine to be made by jurors.

Schuller and Hastings (2002) conducted a study in which the victim's sexual history was varied to include either sexual intercourse, kissing and touching, or no history information in a sexual assault trial. In addition, a judge's instructions limiting the use of the sexual history information was examined. Compared with the participants who heard no sexual history information, those who heard that the victim and defendant had sexual intercourse in the past were less likely to find the alleged victim credible, more likely to find her blameworthy, and more likely to believe she consented to sexual intercourse. Thus, they were more likely to find the defendant innocent. The sexual history information did not influence participants' judgments about the defendant's belief in consent, which is contrary to the goal of judges' instructions as intended by the Supreme Court of Canada. It would appear that a judge's instruction to limit the use of the sexual history information is not effective. If a woman's sexual history is admitted into evidence, it is used to assess her credibility.

Cases have continued to challenge the 1992 rape shield provisions. In *R. v. Darrach* (2000), the defendant, Andrew Darrach was found guilty of sexually assaulting his former girlfriend. Mr. Darrach appealed his conviction arguing that he did not receive a fair trial because he was unable to present information about his prior sexual history with the accuser. Mr. Darrach stated that, given his past relationship with the accused, he thought that the sexual encounter was consensual. During the trial, the judge heard the defence's arguments and ruled that the evidence was inadmissible when Mr. Darrach refused to testify or be cross-examined on the claims he was making. In Mr. Darrach's appeal, he claimed that the law unfairly required him to testify and denied him access to a full defence. In October 2000, the Supreme Court of Canada upheld Mr. Darrach's conviction and upheld the country's rape-shield provisions. The Supreme Court noted that the onus is on the defendant to demonstrate that the accuser's sexual history is relevant before it will be allowed (*R. v. Darrach*, 2000).

Expert Testimony

How well do jurors understand the evidence presented? Sometimes, jurors don't have the background knowledge to understand certain types of evidence, such as DNA. Lawyers may ask that an expert be allowed to testify to explain the evidence. What influence does expert evidence have on jurors' decisions?

A number of findings about expert testimony are available, but no simple conclusion has emerged. For example, the influence of expert testimony may vary depending on the race and gender of the expert. Memon and Shuman (1998) presented participants with one of four experts: a black female, a black male, a white female, or a white male. The experts testified as to whether a doctor was negligent in a civil case regarding a birth defect. The black female expert was rated as most persuasive and she garnered the most support from the white jurors. It was speculated that the content of the testimony might interact with the gender of the expert. For example, if the subject of the testimony is a women's issue, it may be more effective to have a female expert. The race of the expert may interact with the race of the juror and may be complicated by the content of the testimony. It is not clear how these factors work together.

Schuller, Terry, and McKimmie (2005) examined whether the expert's gender is used as a cue to evaluate the testimony provided. Along with the gender of the expert, the complexity of the testimony was varied such that the testimony was either more or less complex (e.g., using technical jargon). In a civil case that involved an alleged price-fixing arrangement between a crushed-rock supplier and a road construction company, the plaintiff was suing the two companies for damages of $490 000 due to the price-fixing agreement. When the testimony was more complex, higher damages were awarded to the plaintiff when the expert was male compared to female. When testimony was less complex, although not significantly so, higher damages were awarded when the expert was female compared to male. Participants may be using gender differently depending on their ability to process the testimony.

Cooper, Bennett, and Sukel (1996) examined the complexity of testimony and the expert's credentials. Participants watched a videotaped civil trial during which two experts provided evidence regarding the cause of a plaintiff's illness. The complexity (easy versus difficult) of the testimony as well as the expert's credentials (strong versus weak) were varied. Participants were more convinced by a strong expert witness than by a weak one, but only when the testimony was complex. When the testimony was easier to follow, expert credentials had little impact on the persuasiveness of the testimony; rather, participants relied on the content of the testimony.

Expert testimony need not produce a positive effect, however, and jurors may disregard it completely. For example, Sundby (1997) examined the transcripts of 152 jurors who participated in 36 first-degree murder cases in California. Jurors were asked about their perceptions and reactions to three types of witnesses: professional experts, lay experts, and families/friends of the defendant. Professional experts were most likely to be viewed negatively and with little credibility along with hurting the side they were testifying for. Overall, expert testimony may be carefully considered by jurors.

A Special Case of Expert Testimony on Battered Women's Syndrome

Dr. Regina Schuller and her colleagues have conducted a number of studies examining battered women who kill their abusers and the influence of expert testimony (Schuller, 1992, 1995; Schuller & Hastings, 1996; Schuller & Rzepa, 2002; Schuller, Smith, & Olson, 1994). See Box 7.7 on page 216 to learn more about Dr. Schuller and her research.

In one study, Schuller, Smith, and Olson (1994) examined the impact of four variables, including jurors' pre-existing beliefs about wife abuse, jurors' beliefs in a "just world"

Box 7.7

Canadian Researcher Profile: Dr. Regina Schuller

Dr. Regina Schuller mentions how she was bitten by the jury bug as a graduate student at the University of Western Ontario. Her supervisor, Neil Vidmar, was just finishing up his now classic book *Judging the Jury* (co-authored with Valerie Hans) and had asked her to read a preliminary copy. Dr. Schuller has never looked back. She immersed herself in the psychology-law area, completing her Ph.D. at Western and also spending two years at Northwestern University in the United States, where she was part of an interdisciplinary program focused on the law and social science.

While in the United States, she also spent a significant amount of time working with Tom Tyler at the American Bar Foundation in Chicago. Dr. Schuller joined the faculty in the department of psychology at York University in Toronto in 1990. She has been there ever since, receiving numerous awards and distinctions for her work. At York, she has also held a number of important administrative positions in the department, such as undergraduate program director (1997–2000) and, more recently, graduate program director (2004–2007).

Dr. Schuller describes her program of research as centring on issues of gender in the legal system. For example, she has investigated violence against women in the form of expert testimony pertaining to battered women in the trials of women who killed their abusers. She also has an interest in investigating the impact of legislative changes that allow for greater information about a claimant's (typically a woman's) sexual history into the court. And more recently, she has turned her attention to the issue of racial bias in the courtroom.

Dr. Schuller notes that one of her favourite pieces of research was a study conducted with Patricia Hastings examining alternative ways to introduce expert testimony on battered women and its influence on juror verdicts and evaluations of the defendant (i.e., the woman who killed her abuser). She states that it was important to consider empirically whether there might be some negative effects associated with battered woman syndrome testimony. For instance, might it pathologize battered women, as some critics were suggesting? This research study was published in the journal *Law and Human Behavior*.

Dr. Schuller primarily uses laboratory simulations to conduct her research. She says that the reason for this methodology is twofold. First, in Canada, researchers are restricted from talking to actual jurors, so fieldwork is virtually impossible. Second, simulation provides a strong methodology when researchers are trying to isolate the impact of numerous variables on the decision process.

When asked what keeps her going in the field of jury research, she emphatically says, "It's fun." The entire process is fun, from creating mock trials to collecting the data and writing it up for others to read. She also states how jury research is an application of the broader area of social psychology and it is fascinating to see how social psychological phenomena occur in the microcosm of the jury, such as how group processes can affect jury verdicts.

Her philosophy for training future leaders in the field includes a strong suggestion for psychologists to immerse themselves in reading case law. Dr. Schuller stresses that we need to keep in mind that if we want lawyers, judges, and the justice system to listen to what we have to say, we need to understand the context in which the research will be applied.

Dr. Schuller uses an apprenticeship model with the students she trains. She works closely with them, from conceptualizing research ideas to designing studies and manuscript writing. It is clear that Dr. Schuller is a great role model and mentor for future researchers in the psychology-law area.

Regina Schuller lives with her partner, Richard, two children, René and Andrée, and their dog, Ootsie, in the Toronto area. In her spare time, she enjoys running marathons and tries to maintain a long-distance running schedule.

(believing that you receive what you deserve), the presence or absence of expert testimony on battered women's syndrome, and sex of the juror (male versus female). Mock jurors listened to a homicide trial involving a woman who killed her abusive husband. They then made various judgments about the case. The mock jurors who heard the expert testimony were more likely to believe the woman's account of what happened than were those who did not hear expert testimony. Those who had a weak belief in a just world were more lenient in their judgments and felt that the expert testimony was more relevant to the battered woman than did those who had a strong belief in a just world. Female mock jurors who had a weak belief in a just world were more likely to find the defendant not guilty.

In another study involving a trial of a homicide in which a battered woman killed her abuser, Schuller and Cripps (1998) varied the gender of the expert providing testimony. They also varied the timing of that testimony. The expert testimony was either heard early, before the defendant's testimony, or it was heard late, after the defendant's testimony. University students acted as jurors and listened to a version of the trial. See Table 7.1 for percentages of guilty verdicts as a function of the gender of the expert and the timing of the testimony.

Once again, these results suggest that the gender of an expert witness may interact with the content of testimony. That is, expert testimony about female issues may be viewed as more credible when the expert is female, and vice versa for males. When the expert witness in this study was female, jurors tended to evaluate the expert evidence more favourably and were more lenient in sentencing the defendant. Moreover, in keeping with the story model of jury decision making, expert testimony that occurs early may be helpful in setting up a particular structure of the evidence that will be heard later on. Indeed, it was found that when the expert testimony was presented before the defendant's testimony, jurors were more likely to believe the defendant and to place more responsibility on the husband.

Table 7.1 Guilty Verdicts as a Function of Expert's Gender and Timing of Testimony

Timing of Testimony	Gender of Expert		
	Male	Female	No Expert
Early			
Murder	22.9%	2.8%	
Manslaughter	54.3%	52.8%	
Self-defence	22.9%	44.4%	
Late			
Murder	13.5%	22.2%	
Manslaughter	54.1%	27.8%	
Self-defence	32.4%	50.0%	
Murder			20.0%
Manslaughter			48.6%
Self-defence			31.4%

Source: Schuller & Cripps, 1998.

SUMMARY

1. In Canada, prospective jurors are selected from a set of random names from the community. These prospective jurors receive a jury summons stating the time and place to go for jury duty. When they arrive to the designated location, typically the courthouse, they are given a number and escorted to a room with others who also are potential jurors. Once everyone has arrived a judge will explain the jury-selection process and how many juries will be chosen that day. If you are selected from the juror pool, you will be a juror unless one of the lawyers presents a challenge.

2. In order for a jury to be considered representative, it must allow any possible eligible juror from the community the opportunity to be part of the jury. Representativeness is achieved through randomness. Juror impartiality centres on three issues: (1) being able to set aside any pre-existing biases, prejudices, or attitudes to solely judge the case based on admissible evidence; (2) ignoring any information that is not part of the admissible evidence; and (3) not being connected to the defendant in any way.

3. Pretrial publicity threatens juror impartiality. Typically, the media attention is negative for the defendant, which could mean that the defendant does not receive a fair trial. Thus, the concern is that verdicts will be based on emotion and biased media coverage rather than on admissible evidence. In order to reduce or limit the negative effects of pretrial publicity, the judge can order a publication ban until the end of the trial. Other options for dealing with pretrial publicity are for the Crown or defence to request a change of venue, an adjournment, or a challenge for cause.

4. Once a jury has been selected, their work begins by listening to the admissible evidence and disregarding any evidence that the judge does not allow. Once the lawyers deliver their closing arguments, the judge provides the jury with the law that they must apply to the evidence to reach a verdict. The jury then deliberates to reach a verdict.

5. Categories that have been examined in terms of predicting verdicts include demographic variables, personality variables, attitudes, defendant characteristics, victim characteristics, and expert testimony.

Key Concepts

adjournment 198

black sheep effect 212

broad-based approach 193

case-specific approach 194

challenge for cause 198

change of venue 197

deliberation 204

hung jury 210

impartiality 195

Jury Act 191

jury nullification 200

jury summons 191

leniency bias 210

polarization 210

racial bias 211

representativeness 195

scientific jury selection 193

sequestered 193

voir dire 194

Discussion Questions

1. You have recently graduated with a degree in psychology. Given your interest in forensic psychology, you decide to move to the United States and become a jury consultant. Describe the approach you would take to scientific jury selection. What variables would you consider critical to evaluate when giving advice to lawyers?

2. You have decided to take a summer job with a criminal defence lawyer. After working there for a few weeks, you realize that the lawyer does not "win" very many cases. What advice would you give to your boss to help with his track record?

3. Design a study to evaluate jury aids (e.g., note taking, asking questions) to ensure that they do not negatively alter the judicial process.

4. Your neighbour drops by for coffee. She has received a summons for jury duty and asks you about the jury-selection process. Describe the jury-selection process and the fundamental qualities of a "good juror."

5. A battered woman who shot and killed her sleeping abusive husband is standing trial for murder. The defence has retained a prominent forensic psychologist to give expert testimony. What impact do you think this expert will have on the jury? Discuss factors that can interact with expert testimony.

6. Should juries be permitted to ignore the law? Discuss the issues surrounding jury nullification.

7. To study juror decision making, researchers have used four different methodologies. Describe the advantages and disadvantages of each method.

Readings

Lieberman, J.D., & Sales, B.D. (2006). *Scientific jury selection.* Washington, D.C.: American Psychological Association.

Tanovich, D.M., Paciocco, D.M., & Skurka, S. (1997). *Jury selection in criminal trials: Skills, science, and the law.* Toronto: Irwin Law.

Wrightsman, L.S. (1999). *Judicial decision making: Is psychology relevant?* New York: Plenum.

Website

The Criminal Code of Canada
http://laws.justice.gc.ca/en/c-46

Chapter 8
The Role of Mental Illness in Court

Learning Objectives

- Outline the fitness standard and the changes made to legislation.

- Contrast unfit and fit offenders.

- Explain Canada's insanity standard.

- Describe automatism and examples of cases in which it was used as a defence.

- State the explanations for high rates of mental illness in offender populations.

- Explain the various treatment goals and options for offenders with mental disorders.

Monica Singh was a 52-year-old single female. She had not been able to keep a job for more than six months. Her employers would often comment on her strange behaviour. For example, Monica would talk to herself and often said that TV cooking shows were directed at her, mocking her cooking skills. Monica had received a diagnosis of schizophrenia when she was in university and was given anti-psychotic medication that she would need to take for the rest of her life. Monica rarely took her medication, though, because she disliked the side effects. When she didn't take her medication, Monica would often shoplift, mostly food items.

Thanksgiving was a week away and Monica decided that she wanted a turkey. She walked to the local grocery store and put a frozen turkey under her coat. The store manager, familiar with Monica's behaviours, called the police and Monica was arrested and charged with shoplifting.

At the police station, Monica was incoherent, and when the officer started asking her questions, she started to talk in a language she had made up as a teenager. The officer called a lawyer from the legal aid office for Monica, given that she was not in a state where she could do it herself. When the lawyer arrived to meet with Monica, he quickly became concerned that Monica would not be able to assist in her own defence. The lawyer requested that the court order an assessment of Monica's fitness to stand trial.

Although a number of people convicted of crime may suffer from mental illness, this chapter will consider mental illness as it relates to the ability to stand trial and to the commission of a crime. In this chapter, we will explore what is meant by the term *fitness to stand trial* within the Canadian criminal justice system. We also will examine the term *mental state at the time of offence* as it pertains to Canadian criminal law and forensic psychology.

PRESUMPTIONS IN CANADA'S LEGAL SYSTEM

The cornerstone of English-Canadian law identifies two elements that must be present for criminal guilt to be established: (1) a wrongful deed, also known as **actus reus**, and (2) criminal intent, also known as **mens rea**. Both of these elements (and the elements of the specific case) must be found beyond a reasonable doubt for a guilty verdict to be reached. Issues of fitness, insanity, automatism, and mental disorders all call into question these two basic elements of criminal law.

Actus reus: A wrongful deed

Mens rea: Criminal intent

FITNESS TO STAND TRIAL

It is reasonable to expect that in order for individuals who are charged with the commission of a crime to be tried fairly, they should have some understanding of the charges and proceedings and be able to help in preparing their defence. A defendant who is deficient in these domains, possibly because of a mental disorder, may be considered unfit to stand trial. Thus, **unfit to stand trial** refers to an inability of a defendant to conduct a defence at any stage of the proceedings on account of a mental disorder. For example, a defendant may be found unfit to stand trial if he or she is experiencing an episode of schizophrenia and lacks the ability to understand the situation and tell the lawyer the facts of the case. Also, in a recent Canadian case, *R. v. Balliram* (2003), it was concluded that an unfit person could not be sentenced. The degree of impairment necessary for an unfit determination has been difficult to pinpoint, however.

Unfit to stand trial: Refers to an inability to conduct a defence at any stage of the proceedings on account of a person's mental disorder

Historically, little direction was provided by means of legislation for a finding of unfitness; rather, case law was used to determine the criteria that should be met. Specifically, the case of *R. v. Prichard* (1836) has been considered the key case for the fitness standard (Lindsay, 1977). Three criteria were delineated in the Prichard case:

- Whether the defendant is mute of malice (i.e., intentionality)
- Whether the defendant can plead to the indictment
- Whether the defendant has sufficient cognitive capacity to understand the trial proceedings

Prior to the enactment of Bill C-30 (1992) and by the mid-1980s, the federal Department of Justice acknowledged a number of problems with the mental disorder provisions of the Criminal Code of Canada (e.g., inconsistencies, omissions, lack of clarity and guidance). Also, there were issues regarding the incompatibility of these provisions with the Canadian Charter of Rights and Freedoms. For example, someone who was declared unfit to stand trial could be confined indefinitely. A number of changes were instituted with the enactment of Bill C-30.

With the enactment of Bill C-30 in 1992, the Criminal Code stated a fitness standard. The fitness standard can be found in section 2 of the Code: A defendant is unfit to stand trial if he or she is unable on account of mental disorder to conduct a defence at any stage of the proceedings before a verdict is rendered or to instruct counsel to do so, and, in particular, unable on account of mental disorder to a) understand the nature or object of the proceedings b) understand the possible consequences of the proceedings, or c) communicate with counsel. (R.S.C., 1985, c. C-46, s. 2; 1992, c. 20, s. 216, c. 51, s. 32)

This last point about communicating with counsel has been further specified in case law in *R. v. Taylor* (1992). In this case, the Ontario Court of Appeal stated that the test to be applied in terms of "communication with counsel" is with regard to limited cognitive capacity. The court ruled that a defendant need only be able to state the facts relating to the offence that would allow an appropriate defence. Moreover, the defendant need not be able to communicate facts that are in his or her best interests. The court decided that applying the "best interest rule" was too strict a criterion.

One other issue that was altered with Bill C-30 was the length of time a defendant could be held in custody for a fitness evaluation. A five-day limit on court-ordered assessments was legislated, with provisions for extensions, if necessary, to complete the evaluation. The extension, however, is not to exceed 30 days, and the entire length of detention should not exceed 60 days (R.S.C., 1985, C-46, s. 672.15). The evaluation can occur while the defendant is in a detention, outpatient, or inpatient facility. Roesch, Ogloff, Hart, Dempster, Zapf, and Whittemore (1997) found that the average length of time for evaluation was approximately three weeks and that 88% occurred in inpatient facilities (also Zapf & Roesch, 1998). It should be noted that mental health law (i.e., commitment and treatment in psychiatric facilities) is under provincial/territorial jurisdiction.

Raising the Issue of Fitness

The issue of a defendant's fitness may be raised at various points from the time of arrest to the defendant's sentence determination. Examples of instances in which the issue of fitness may be raised include when a plea is entered, when a defendant chooses not to be represented by counsel, and during sentencing (Ogloff, Wallace, & Otto, 1991). The Canadian Criminal Code states that a defendant is assumed to be fit to stand trial unless the court is satisfied on the balance of probabilities that he or she is unfit (R.S.C., 1985, C-46, s. 672.22). The defence or Crown may raise the issue of a defendant's fitness. Also noted in the Code is that the burden of proving unfitness is on the party who raises the issue (R.S.C., 1985, C-46, s. 672.23(2)).

How Many Defendants Are Referred for Fitness Evaluations?

Webster, Menzies, Butler, and Turner (1982) estimated that approximately 5000 fitness evaluations were conducted annually in Canada. In a more recent investigation, Roesch et al. (1997) found that 61% of a sample from a remand facility in British Columbia underwent fitness evaluations. Moreover, 24% were held for assessments of both fitness and criminal responsibility (we will discuss criminal responsibility in more detail later in the chapter). In the United States, Bonnie and Grisso (2000) estimated that somewhere between 2% and 8% of all felony defendants are referred for fitness evaluations—that is, about 25 000 to

38 000 defendants (Hoge, Poythress, Bonnie, Monahan, Eisenberg, & Feucht-Haviar, 1997). See Table 8.1 for a distribution of the number of accused ruled unfit in seven Canadian jurisdictions during the period 1992–2004. (See also Table 8.3 on page 234 for the total percentage of cases in which the accused is ruled as unfit or not criminally responsible on account of mental disorder across seven jurisdictions in Canada for the period 1992–2004.)

Who Can Assess Fitness?

Traditionally, only medical practitioners have been allowed to conduct court-ordered assessments of such aspects as fitness to stand trial and criminal responsibility (Viljoen, Roesch, Ogloff, & Zapf, 2003). Unlike in the United States and Australia, the Canadian Criminal Justice system continues to take this position. In fact, the Canadian Criminal Code excludes psychologists from conducting court-ordered assessments. The Code specifies that these assessments must be carried out by medical practitioners (R.S.C., 1985, C- 46, s. 672.1). It is important to note that the medical practitioners need not have any background in psychiatry or experience with forensic populations. In contrast, Farkas, DeLeon, and Newman (1997) reported that 47 U.S. states allow psychologists to conduct fitness and criminal responsibility evaluations.

Canadian psychologists can, however, be involved in court-ordered assessments in a variety of ways. For example, psychologists may be asked to conduct psychological testing and to *assist* with the assessment of defendants who are referred for evaluation. Psychologists submit their results to psychiatrists or other medical practitioners, who then incorporate the results into a report to the court.

Fitness Instruments

A number of screening instruments have been developed to help evaluators quickly screen out defendants who are competent to stand trial. Comprehensive fitness assessments can then be reserved for those defendants who are "screened in." Zapf and Roesch (1998) examined the fitness decisions that were made using a screening instrument versus those decisions made

Table 8.1 Number of Accused Given the Legal Status of Unfit, by Jurisdiction (1992–2004)

Jurisdiction	Number of Accused Ruled Unfit
Prince Edward Island	4
Quebec	399
Ontario	1151
Alberta	94
British Columbia	216
Nunavut	2
Yukon	10

Source: Latimer & Lawrence, 2006.

following a stay in a psychiatric facility. The researchers found that the two sets of decisions were consistent with each other. They concluded that long stays in mental facilities were unnecessary for most of the fitness decisions. Rather, many fitness decisions could be made quickly using a screening instrument and would result in a more cost-effective system.

One screening instrument that has particular relevance for Canadians is the Fitness Interview Test Revised (FIT-R) (Roesch, Zapf, Eaves, & Webster, 1998), which was developed to meet the fitness criteria outlined in the Canadian Criminal Code. The FIT-R is in the form of a semi-structured interview and assesses the three psychological abilities stated in the Code's fitness standard. Each section contains several items that the evaluator probes with the defendant. For example,

- Understand the nature or object of the proceedings
  - Factual knowledge of criminal procedure
    i defendant's understanding of the arrest process
    ii the nature and severity of the current charges
    iii the role of key participants
- Understand the possible consequences of the proceedings
  - Appreciation of personal involvement in and importance of the proceedings
    i appreciation of range and nature of possible penalties and defences
- Communicate with counsel
  - Ability to participate in defence
    i defendant's ability to *communicate* facts
    ii relate to his or her attorney
    iii plan legal strategy

Each response is rated on a three-point scale ranging from 0 (indicates no to little impairment) to 2 (indicates severe impairment). Once the interview is complete, the evaluator must make a decision regarding overall fitness. The final decision involves three stages: (1) determining the existence of a mental disorder, (2) determining the defendant's capacity regarding each of the three psychological abilities stated above, and (3) examining the previous information. Although performance on the items contained in each section is considered in determining the section rating, decisions are not made based on a specific cut-off score. Instead, these section ratings constitute a separate judgment based on the severity of impairment and its perceived importance. See Box 8.1 for a look at some other fitness instruments.

Distinguishing between Fit and Unfit Defendants

Viljoen and Zapf (2002) examined the characteristics of 80 defendants who were referred for fitness evaluations and 80 defendants who were not referred. As shown in Table 8.2 on page 227, a number of characteristics differed significantly between the referred and non-referred defendants.

Using the Fit-R, referred defendants were significantly more likely to show impairment on one or more sections. For example, referred defendants were less likely to understand the nature and object of the proceedings, and possible consequences of the proceedings. No significant difference between the referred and non-referred defendants was found in terms of being able to communicate with counsel.

Box 8.1

Fitness Instruments

Competency Screening Test (CST)

The CST (Lipsitt, Lelos, & McGarry, 1971) has 22 uncompleted sentences that the respondent must finish. For example,

- The lawyer told Bill that . . .
- When I go to court the lawyer will . . .
- Jack felt that the judge . . .

The items measure three constructs: the potential for a constructive relationship between the defendant and his lawyer, the defendant's understanding of the court process, and the ability of the defendant to emotionally cope with the criminal process. Responses are scored using a three-point scale (0, 1, 2) depending on the relation between the defendant's response and example responses provided in the scoring manual. A score of 0 would be assigned if the response demonstrated a low level of legal understanding. For example, "The lawyer told Bill that he is guilty" would receive 0 points (Ackerman, 1999). A score of 2 would be assigned if the response demonstrated a high level of legal understanding. For example, "The lawyer told Bill that he should plead guilty" would receive 2 points (Ackerman, 1999). Scores for each of the items are summed to produce a total CST score. The CST score, in addition to a brief psychiatric interview, is aimed at distinguishing between competent defendants who could proceed to trial and those defendants who should undergo a more complete competency assessment. A score of 20 or below suggests that the defendant should undergo a more comprehensive evaluation.

Competency to Stand Trial Assessment Instrument (CAI)

The CAI (Laboratory of Community Psychiatry, Harvard Medical School, 1973) was designed to accompany the CST in that the CAI is a semi-structured interview and constitutes a comprehensive competency evaluation. The CAI assesses 13 functions corresponding to a defendant's ability to participate in the criminal process on behalf of his or her best interests. Each function is represented in a statement with two or three sample questions that the evaluator may pose to the defendant. For example (Ackerman, 1999),

Function: Appraisal of available legal defences

Statement: The defendant's awareness of possible legal defences and how consistent they are with the reality of his or her particular circumstances

Question: How do you think you can be defended against these charges?

Following a response, the evaluator can ask follow-up questions to further probe the defendant's response if it is unclear or ambiguous. For each function, responses are rated on a scale from 1 (reflecting a total lack of capacity for function) to 5 (reflecting no impairment, defendant can function adequately). A score of 6 can be given when there is insufficient information to rate the function. The evaluator examines the scores for each function and then makes an overall determination.

Interdisciplinary Fitness Interview (IFI)

The IFI (Golding, Roesch, & Schreiber, 1984) was developed following an analysis of the CAI. As with the CAI, the IFI is a semi- structured interview measuring three areas of competency: functional memory, appropriate relationship with lawyer, and understanding of the justice system. There are four main sections to the IFI:

Section A: Legal items

Section B: Psychopathological items

Section C: Overall evaluation

Section D: Consensual judgment

Each section has a number of subsections and areas within each subsection that can be assessed. The revision of the IFI (IFI-R) (Golding, 1993) retains the semi-structured interview protocol; however, there are only two sections: Current Clinical Condition and Psycho-Legal Abilities. Each section has a number of subsections. For example, under the heading "current clinical condition" are the following categories:

- Attention/consciousness
- Delusions
- Hallucinations

(continued)

(continued)

- Impaired reasoning and judgment
- Impaired memory
- Mood and affect

The evaluator assesses these major areas of clinical dysfunction. Responses are rated with a scale ranging from 0 (absent or does not bear on defendant's fitness) to 2 (symptom is likely to significantly impair the defendant's fitness).

Under the "Psycho-Legal Abilities" section there are four subsections:

- Capacity to appreciate charges and to disclose pertinent facts, events, and motives
- Courtroom demeanour and capacity to understand the adversarial nature of proceedings
- Quality of relationship with attorney
- Appreciation of and reasoned choice with respect to legal option and consequences

Responses are rated on a scale ranging from 0 (no or minimal capacity) to 2 (substantial capacity). It also has been recommended that when conducting a competency assessment, the defendant's lawyer, previous mental health contacts, and jail personnel be interviewed. In addition, mental health reports, police reports, and prior arrest history should be reviewed (Golding, as cited in Ackerman, 1999).

MacArthur Competence Assessment Tool— Criminal Adjudication (MacCAT-CA)

The MacCAT-CA (Hoge, Bonnie, Poythress, & Monahan, 1992) is a structured interview containing 22 items that assess competencies in three areas:

- Factual understanding of the legal system and the adjudication process
- Reasoning ability
- Understanding of own legal situation and circumstances

These areas are assessed via hypothetical scenarios. Following the presentation of the scenario, the defendant is asked a series of specific questions. The evaluator assigns a score of 0, 1, or 2 based on the scoring criteria. For each area, score ranges are provided for three levels of impairment: none to minimal, mild, or clinically significant.

Zapf and Roesch (1998) examined the demographic, mental health, and criminal characteristics that differentiate fit from unfit defendants using a sample of 180 males undergoing evaluation in a facility in British Columbia. Using the fit/unfit decision offered to the court by the psychiatrist, the data were divided into these two categories and then compared across criteria.

In examining the demographic variables, only marital status was significant. Fit defendants were significantly more likely to have been married (married, divorced, separated, common law) than were unfit defendants. Previous studies have found defendants who are referred for fitness evaluations to be primarily single, unemployed, and living alone (Roesch et al., 1981; Webster et al., 1982). In a meta-analysis of 30 studies conducted in both Canada and the United States, Nicholson and Kugler (1991) found that fit and unfit defendants differed on age, gender, race, and marital resources. Unfit defendants were more likely to be older females belonging to a minority group and to have fewer marital resources.

Zapf and Roesch (1998) also found that defendants who were unfit were four times more likely to have met criteria for a psychotic disorder, whereas defendants who were fit were about as likely to have been diagnosed with a psychotic disorder as not. It is important to note that not all psychotic defendants are unfit, and the presence of psychosis is not sufficient or equivalent to unfitness (Golding et al., 1984). Substance abuse disorders were significantly less likely to be found in unfit defendants than in the fit defendants.

In examining criminological variables, Zapf and Roesch (1998) found that there were no significant differences between fit and unfit defendants. The two groups were similar in

Table 8.2 Demographic, Criminological, and Mental Health Characteristics for Defendants Referred versus Not Referred for Fitness Evaluations

Characteristic	Referred Defendants (n = 80)	Non-Referred Defendants (n = 80)
Never Married	56.3% (45)	46.3% (37)**
White	81.3% (65)	72.5% (58)
Didn't Complete High School	56.3% (45)	68.8% (55)
Living Alone	32.5% (26)	13.8% (11)**
Unemployed	55.0% (44)	48.8% (39)
Current Violent Offence	71.3% (57)	26.3% (21)**
Previous Arrests	76.3% (61)	92.5% (74)*
Current Primary Diagnosis		
Psychotic	41.3% (33)	3.8% (3)**
Affective Disorder	20.0% (16)	12.5% (10)
Substance Abuse	10.0% (8)	41.3% (33)**
No Diagnosis	28.8% (23)	42.5% (34)
Lifetime Diagnosis		
Psychotic	41.3% (33)	5.0% (4)**
Affective Disorder	53.7% (43)	28.8% (23)**
Substance Abuse	71.3% (57)	85.0% (68)*
No Diagnosis	7.5% (6)	12.5% (10)
Antisocial Personality Disorder	32.5% (26)	47.5% (38)*
Previous Mental Health Services	85.0% (68)	56.3% (45)**
Previous Hospitalizations	66.3% (53)	11.3% (9)**

* $p < .05$
** $p < .01$
Source: Viljoen & Zapf, 2002.

the frequency with which they had committed violent, property, and miscellaneous crimes. Moreover, both groups had a similar criminal history and were just as likely to have previously been in prison.

As you can see, Dr. Ron Roesch has worked extensively in the area of fitness to stand trial. To learn more about Dr. Roesch and his research, see Box 8.2 on page 228.

How Is Fitness Restored?

When a defendant is found unfit to stand trial, the goal of the criminal justice system is to get the defendant fit. The most common form of treatment for fitness is medication. A question facing the justice system concerning this form of treatment is whether a defendant

Box 8.2

Canadian Researcher Profile: Dr. Ron Roesch

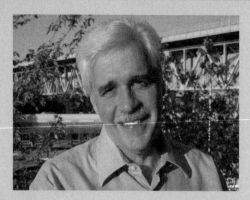

Early in Dr. Ron Roesch's career, his research on fitness to stand trial won awards and gained substantial recognition. His Ph.D. dissertation on fitness was awarded the best psychological dissertation concerned with social issues by the Society for the Psychological Studies of Social Issues. It also won the Consulting Psychology Research Award for being the most fruitful research of the year related to consultation. Dr. Roesch used his dissertation research to produce a book with Dr. Stephen Golding called *Competency to Stand Trial* in 1980. This book won a merit award in the American Bar Association Gavel Awards Competition.

Dr. Roesch followed his graduate studies at the University of Illinois with a faculty position at Simon Fraser University, where he is now a professor of psychology and the director of the Mental Health, Law, and Policy Institute.

Dr. Roesch remains interested in research focusing on fitness issues for both adult and juvenile offenders. His current focus is on competency to waive arrest rights, such as the right to a lawyer. This research considers developmental differences in a juvenile offender's capacity to understand rights as well as make decisions about the conduct of his or her defence. Dr. Roesch also has stated that he is interested in pursuing research focused on interventions to be used with youth: "So much of my research has focused on assessment that I would like to shift to examining the effectiveness of interventions with high-risk juveniles." Dr. Roesch finds that the changing nature of the law makes researching psycholegal issues an exciting endeavour.

Dr. Roesch has worked toward changing laws in Canada that restrict the role of psychologists in forensic areas. For example, he developed the Fitness Interview Test, a structured interview and rating scale to assess fitness to stand trial. However, until recently, as a clinical psychologist he was not allowed to provide expert testimony on this issue, as Canadian legislation noted that only medical physicians can provide court-ordered fitness assessments. Dr. Roesch testified before a parliamentary committee reviewing this law, and he was pleased to see that changes in the law now make it possible for psychologists to conduct fitness assessments.

Dr. Roesch is excited about training future forensic psychologists. He remains dedicated to teaching and graduate training. Dr. Roesch teaches a psychology and law foundation course for graduate students that provides a broad overview of the field. Preparing for this course helps to keep him well informed of the latest developments in the field and provides an excellent foundation for students in this area of research.

In his spare time, Dr. Roesch enjoys travelling with his wife, Kim. He has formed many partnerships and collaborations for research with colleagues throughout the world and makes efforts to meet with them on a regular basis. Dr. Roesch and his wife also enjoy running. They maintain a regular running schedule to keep fit for 10 km races that they enter often.

has the right to refuse medication. Under the Health Care Consent Act and the Mental Health Act, an individual can refuse medication; however, if that person is incapable of making decisions concerning his or her medical treatment, a decision may be imposed by the law (R.S.O., 1996, s. 25). The courts will take into account the individual's capacity to comprehend and appreciate the consequences of his or her actions and public safety. Defendants sometimes may argue for not taking medication because of the serious side

Box 8.3

Mentally Ill but Competent to Make Treatment Decisions?

Scott Starson (also known as Scott Jeffery Schutzman) has a special skill in physics. Without having formal training, he works with the top physics researchers in the world. In 1991, he co-authored an article with a physics professor from Stanford University. In addition to his physics ability, Starson also has a long history of battling a mental disorder. He has been diagnosed as having bipolar affective disorder. Starson has been admitted to several mental health facilities over the years.

In 1998, Starson was charged with uttering two death threats to tenants in his apartment complex. He was found not criminally responsible on account of mental disorder. In January 1999, the Ontario Review Board ordered that he be detained at the Centre for Addiction and Mental Health (CAMH) in Toronto. Dr. Ian Swayze and Dr. Paul Posner, both psychiatrists at CAMH, proposed to treat Starson with mood stabilizers, anti-psychotic, anti-anxiety, and anti-parkinsonian medication. Starson refused pharmaceutical intervention and appealed the Ontario Review Board's decision in provincial court. He argued that "he would not be able to do his work while on the proposed medication, not because of the side effects, but because of the very effects that the drugs are intended to achieve. . . . Starson said that after periods of treatment with such medications, it would always take him some time to 'work his way up the academic ladder'" (*Starson v. Swayze*, 1999, para 55).

In November 1999, the Ontario Superior Court of Justice overturned the Ontario Review Board's decision, stating that it was unreasonable. Justice Molloy stated that the Board's conclusion that Starson was in denial of his mental illness was an error and that it was wrong for the Board to accept unsubstantiated claims that Starson suffered delusions that others were out to harm him. Starson's doctors appealed the decision to the Ontario Court of Appeal. The appeal court ruled that Starson was capable of making treatment decisions and could appreciate the possible consequences of refusing treatment. The doctors appealed to the Supreme Court of Canada. In June 2003, the Supreme Court upheld the lower court's decision that Starson had the capacity to refuse medical treatment.

Sources: *Starson v. Swayze*, 1999; *Starson v. Swayze*, 2003.

effects. A treatment order may be imposed by the court (R.S.C., 1985, C-46, s. 672.58); however, the courts also must grapple with having a heavily medicated defendant and whether this serves justice. See Box 8.3 for a look at a case involving a defendant with a mental illness, who fought against medication.

What Happens after a Finding of Unfitness?

The proceedings against a defendant who is found unfit to stand trial are halted until competency is restored. In the United States, almost all jurisdictions limit the time a defendant may be "held" as unfit. In the landmark case of *Jackson v. Indiana* (1972), the United States Supreme Court stated that a defendant should not be held for more than a reasonable period of time to determine whether there is a likelihood of the person gaining competency fitness. Of course, what constitutes a reasonable period of time is open to interpretation.

For unfit defendants in Canada, the judge may order that the defendant be detained in a hospital or that the defendant be conditionally discharged. The defendant is reassessed for fitness within 45 days. In the event that the defendant becomes fit, he or she returns to court and the proceedings resume (R.S.C., 1985, C-46, s. 672.28). If the defendant remains unfit after 90 days, he or she is referred to a review board for assessment and disposition (R.S.C., 1985, C-46, s. 672.47). Cases of defendants who continue to be unfit are reviewed on an annual basis by the review board. In these cases, the Crown must prove that there is sufficient evidence to bring the case to trial (referred to as making a **prima facie case**) every two years and at any time the defendant requests the proceeding. For youth found unfit, the court must review the case every year instead of every two years, according to section 141(10) of the Youth Criminal Justice Act. If the court determines that sufficient evidence is no longer available to prosecute the case, the case is dropped and the defendant is found not guilty (R.S.C., 1985, C-46, s. 672.33).

Prima facie case: Case in which the Crown prosecutor must prove there is sufficient evidence to bring the case to trial

Even though a defendant may be restored to fitness, it is possible that he or she will become unfit once again during the trial proceedings. If unfitness occurs again, the proceedings stop until the defendant becomes fit. If a defendant becomes fit while in custody (e.g., detained in a mental facility) and there is reason to believe that he or she may become unfit if released, the defendant will be required to remain in the mental facility until the trial is complete (R.S.C., 1985, C-46, s. 672.29).

What if a defendant is unlikely to become fit (e.g., possibly due to permanent brain damage)? Until recently, an absolute discharge could not be issued to defendants unlikely to become fit. However, in *R. v. Demers* (2004), the Supreme Court of Canada ruled that the inability of the courts or review boards to issue an absolute discharge to defendants who are unlikely to become fit and who pose no significant threat to society was in violation of the liberties guaranteed under section 7 of the Charter of Rights and Freedoms. This infringement was addressed by an amendment to the Criminal Code with the passing of Bill C-10, occurring in January 2006. A court now has the authority to stay the proceedings for a defendant who is unlikely to become fit if any the following are true:

- The accused is unlikely ever to become fit.
- The accused does not pose a significant threat to the safety of the public.
- A stay of proceedings is in the interests of the proper administration of justice.

Bill C-10 still does not provide review boards with the ability to absolutely discharge an accused who is found unfit; this power is only given to the courts. A review board, however, can recommend to a court that an inquiry be undertaken to determine if a stay of proceedings is in the proper administration of justice. If a stay is not ordered, the accused remains under the disposition determined by the review board.

See Figure 8.1 for key processes in cases involving fitness.

MENTAL STATE AT TIME OF OFFENCE

Insanity: Impairment of mental or emotional functioning that affects perceptions, beliefs, and motivations at the time of the offence

Insanity has been defined as not being of sound mind, and being mentally deranged and irrational (Sykes, 1982). In a legal context, insanity removes the responsibility for performing a particular act because of uncontrollable impulses or delusions, such as hearing voices. There have been two primary British cases that have shaped the current standard of insanity in Canada (as cited in Moran, 1985). The first was that of James Hadfield who in 1800 attempted to assassinate King George III. Hadfield had suffered a brain injury while fighting against the French. His lawyer successfully argued that he was out of touch with reality and therefore met the insanity standard of the time. Following this case, the Criminal Lunatics Act (1800) was established, and it stated the insanity standard of the day.

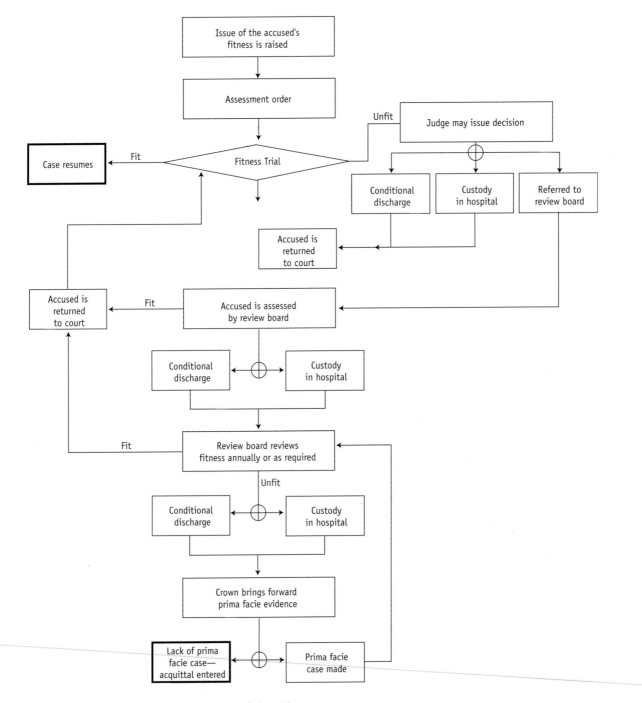

Figure 8.1 Key Processes in Cases Involving Fitness

*Although both the court and review board have the authority to detain a person found NCRMD in hospital, the accused may refuse treatment while detained.

**In accordance with the decision of the Supreme Court of Canada in *R. v. Swain* in 1991, the Crown may not raise the issue of the accused's mental state before the Crown proved that the crime had been committed or where the accused had put their mental capacity into issue.

The second case influencing Canada's current insanity standard was that of Daniel McNaughton in 1843 (*R. v. McNaughton*, 1843). Daniel McNaughton was born and raised in Glasgow, Scotland. Eventually he found his way to London in July 1842. While in London, he purchased two pistols that he carried in his waistcoat. On Friday, January 20, 1843, he walked behind Edward Drummond, one of Prime Minister Robert Peel's secretaries, who was coming back from Drummonds Bank. McNaughton approached Drummond from behind, took a pistol out of his pocket, and shot Drummond in the back. Drummond then turned to see who shot him and saw McNaughton and pointed to him. McNaughton reached for his other pistol and at that point was tackled by James Silver, a constable. McNaughton was handcuffed and his weapons were removed. Drummond died five days later.

There is some debate as to McNaughton's reason for shooting and whether Drummond or Prime Minister Robert Peel was the intended target.

McNaughton was charged with murder, and the judge interpreted his plea as "not guilty." McNaughton was found not guilty because of his mental status—insanity. He would serve out his life in a mental institute (see Dalby, 2006, for the full details of the story).

There were five critical elements that emerged from the McNaughton verdict, with three specific to the insanity defences of today:

1. A defendant must be found to be suffering from a defect of reason/disease of the mind.

2. A defendant must not know the nature and quality of the act he or she is performing.

3. A defendant must not know that what he or she is doing is wrong.

The elements in the McNaughton standard emerged in legislation in parts of the United States, England, and Canada. Little would change for the insanity standard in Canada for many years.

In the mid-1970s, a review of the policies for offenders with mental disorders was undertaken by the Law Reform Commission of Canada. Forty-four recommendations on law and policy were provided (Law Reform Commission of Canada, 1976). In response to this review, the Department of Justice commissioned the Mental Disorder Project in the early 1980s. This review found that the mental disorder legislation in the Criminal Code was in conflict with the Charter of Rights and Freedoms. The ruling from the Supreme Court of Canada in *R. v. Swain* (1991) was consistent with the review and foreshadowed the changes to the Criminal Code. For example, in *R. v. Swain* (1991), the Supreme Court ruled that "the automatic detention of defendants found not guilty by reason of insanity without any hearing to determine the level of dangerousness or the appropriate disposition was in conflict with the Charter." The Court also stated that "the Crown could not raise the issue of the defendant's mental capacity before the Crown proved that the crime had been committed or until the accused put their mental capacity into issue. The accused however had the right to raise the issue at any point during the trial."

In 1992, Bill C-30 was enacted and the following changes were made to the justice system:

■ The term "not guilty by reason of insanity" was changed to "not criminally responsible on account of mental disorder" (NCRMD).

■ The wording of the standard was altered and stated in section 16 of the Criminal Code of Canada: "No person is criminally responsible for an act committed or an omission made while suffering from a mental disorder that rendered the person incapable of appreciating the nature and quality of the act or omission or of knowing that it was wrong."

■ **Review boards** were created. These were legal bodies mandated to oversee the care and disposition of defendants found unfit and/or not criminally responsible on account of a mental disorder. Review boards were required to review each unfit and NCRMD case every year.

Review boards: Legal bodies mandated to oversee the care and disposition of defendants found unfit and/or not criminally responsible on account of a mental disorder

Another change occurred in 1999. In *Winko v. British Columbia*, the Supreme Court of Canada stated that a defendant who is NCRMD should only be detained if he or she poses a criminal threat to the public; otherwise, the defendant should receive an absolute discharge. Another review on justice and human rights was undertaken in 2002 concerning mental disorder provisions in the Criminal Code. A second review for 2007 has been recommended, and it will allow data to be collected on the issues that have emerged. See Box 8.4 for a description of a case in which the defendant was found NCRMD.

Box 8.4

Sportscaster Shot Dead by Patient with a Mental Illness

Brian Smith, a former hockey player, was a sportscaster for CJOH, an Ottawa television station. On August 1, 1995, after his evening sportscast, Smith left the station and walked out to the parking lot, where he was shot in the head. A day later, Smith died in the hospital. In the reports of Smith's death, many questioned the reason for his murder. Why would someone kill him? Jeffrey Arenburg, the confessed killer, said that he was angry with the media and wanted to harm a media personality. Arenburg said he went to the CJOH parking lot and shot the first media personality he recognized, Brian Smith.

Before Arenburg was tried for Smith's murder, he was assessed for fitness to stand trial. The jury found Arenburg fit and he was charged with first-degree murder. The defence raised the issue of Arenburg's sanity and argued for an NCRMD verdict. Indeed, in May 1997 Arenburg was found NCRMD for first-degree murder. He was sent to a maximum-security psychiatric facility, the Ontario Mental Health Centre in Penetanguishene, for an indefinite period of time. Less than ten years after the shooting, Arenburg wanted to be released. He had a mandatory review before the Ontario Review Board in May 2003, at which time his lawyer argued for a conditional discharge. Arenburg was granted a conditional discharge and was required to live with his brother in Barrie, Ontario. In the fall of 2003,

Arenburg was free to attend classes at Georgian College during the day, having to return to live with his brother in the evening. He graduated in June 2005.

In November 2006, the Ontario Review Board granted Arenburg an absolute discharge. The Board heard that Arenburg no longer poses a significant risk to the community and no longer suffers from the symptoms of paranoid schizophrenia.

This case drew a great deal of attention to current legislation regarding the Mental Health Act. Arenburg had a history of mental illness. For example, in 1990, he went to a Nova Scotia courthouse demanding to be seen by a judge. When taken to the local hospital, he said that he heard his thoughts being broadcast by television and radio. He was diagnosed with paranoid psychosis and released. In 1991, he was brought to the Royal Ottawa Hospital because he had threatened a radio station. Once again, Arenburg stated that he was hearing voices. Arenburg was committed to the hospital. However, he appealed his commitment to the psychiatric review board. The board did not find Arenburg mentally ill or at risk to hurt others. However, it did find that Arenburg was not competent to refuse treatment. Arenburg discharged himself against doctors' advice. Arenburg was able to refuse treatment for two years following Smith's shooting. In

(continued)

(continued)

response to an inquest into Smith's death, it was recommended that there should be more public protection against people with mental illnesses. Both the Mental Health Act and the Health Care Consent Act in Ontario were reviewed, and in 2000, Bill 68, also known as Brian's Law, was passed.

Brian's Law led to the implementation of community treatment orders, which are requirements for people with mental illnesses who are living in the community to report to a mental health caregiver on a regular basis. Also, as a condition of being released from a mental health facility to the community, those who have a mental illness may be forced to take prescribed medication. If they refuse medication, they can be re-institutionalized. Also under the new legislation, the word *imminent* was removed from the Mental Health Act. This change means that there no longer must be an immediate danger for someone to be confined to a psychiatric facility (R.S.O., 1990, s. 33.1). Other provinces, including British Columbia, Manitoba, and Saskatchewan, have similar legislation.

Sources: Campbell, 2004; http://en.wikipedia.org/wiki/Jeffrey_Arenburg.

Raising the Issue of Insanity

Studies find that few defendants use the insanity defence. For example, in the United States, one study found that less than 1% of all felony cases will argue an insanity defence (Steadman, McGreevy, Morrissey, Callahan, Robbins, & Cirincione, 1993). Moreover, the success rate of such a defence is variable. It has been reported that approximately 25% of defendants who argue an insanity defence succeed (Steadman et al., 1993). See Table 8.3 for a distribution of NCRMD and unfit cases in Canada.

Insanity defences typically occur when opposing sides (prosecution and defence) agree to such a verdict (Melton, Petrila, Poythress, & Slobogin, 1997). It is not common to have opposing experts testify on this issue in jury trials. Ogloff, Schweighofer, Turnbull, and Whittemore (1992) reported that defendants found NCRMD are likely to have major psychiatric disorders, such as schizophrenia, and many past mental health problems that resulted in hospitalization or prior rulings of unfitness.

Table 8.3 Number of Accused Given the Legal Status of NCRMD and Unfit, by Jurisdiction (1992–2004)

Jurisdiction	Number of NCRMD	% of Total Cases That Are NCRMD and Unfit
Prince Edward Island	8	0.1%
Quebec	3378	43.5%
Ontario	2059	37.0%
Alberta	306	4.6%
British Columbia	1036	14.4%
Nunavut	6	0.1%
Yukon	10	0.2%

Source: Latimer & Lawrence, 2006.

Within the Canadian criminal justice system, a defendant is considered not to suffer from a mental disorder. Of course, the defendant may raise the issue of insanity for his or her defence. In Canada, there are only two situations in which the Crown may raise the issue of insanity:

1. Following a guilty verdict, the Crown could argue that the defendant was NCRMD. This situation may occur if the Crown believes that the defendant requires psychiatric treatment and a mental facility is best suited for the defendant's needs.

2. If the defence states that the defendant has a mental illness, the Crown can then argue it.

The party that raises the issue must prove it beyond a balance of the probabilities (R.S.C., 1985, c. C-46, s. 16).

Assessing Insanity

Just as with fitness to stand trial, an insanity defence requires a psychiatric assessment. Richard Rogers developed the first standardized assessment scales for criminal responsibility: the Rogers Criminal Responsibility Assessment Scales (R-CRAS) (Rogers, 1984).

The R-CRAS is the only instrument of its kind. It has five scales:

- patient reliability
- organicity
- psychopathology
- cognitive control
- behavioural control

Each scale has 30 items, which are given a score from 0 to 6, with higher values representing greater severity (Rogers & Sewell, 1999). It is important to note that the R-CRAS was developed to standardize evaluations and ensure particular areas are evaluated, rather than produce a cut-off score to indicate criminal responsibility (Rogers & Ewing, 1992). The clinician is to take all the information into account and use it as the basis for a decision regarding the defendant's mental status and criminal responsibility.

What Happens to a Defendant Found NCRMD?

There are three dispositions that can be made following a finding of NCRMD. If the defendant is not a threat to society or poses low risk for reoffending, the court or review board can order an **absolute discharge**. That is, the defendant is released into the community without restrictions on his or her behaviour. A second disposition option is to order a discharge with conditions, known as a **conditional discharge**. In this case, the defendant is released but must meet certain conditions, such as not possessing firearms. Failure to meet the conditions imposed with a conditional discharge may result in the defendant being incarcerated or sent to a psychiatric facility. Lastly, the court or review board may order that the defendant be sent to a psychiatric facility (R.S.C., 1985, C-46, s. 672.54).

Absolute discharge: The defendant is released into the community without restrictions to his or her behaviour

Conditional discharge: A defendant is released; however, release carries certain conditions (e.g., not to possess firearms) that the defendant must meet. Failure to meet the conditions imposed with a conditional discharge may result in the defendant being incarcerated or sent to a psychiatric facility

It is important to note that a defendant who is sent to a psychiatric facility need not comply with treatment. It is only when the defendant's mental health has deteriorated to a point that he or she is no longer competent to make treatment decisions that steps may be taken to force treatment on the defendant (R.S.C., 1985, C-46, s. 672.54). In such instances, the provincial and territorial mental health policies would be followed.

In Canada, dispositions may be made by the court or referred to a provincial or territorial review board. Dispositions that are made by the court also are reviewed by a review board within 90 days and can be changed at any point. An exception to this rule occurs if the court makes an absolute discharge (R.S.C., 1985, C-46, s. 672.81). This decision does not go before a review board. In addition, review boards review the defendant's disposition every year. There is a great deal of information that review boards will take into account, including

- charge information
- trial transcript
- criminal history
- risk assessment
- clinical history, such as previous admissions to hospital
- psychological testing
- hospital's recommendation

As you read earlier, historically, defendants who were found insane would spend the remainder of their lives in an insane asylum. More recently, it was not uncommon for "insane" defendants to be given indeterminate sentences, only to be released when they were deemed sane. Moreover, insane defendants often would serve more time in a mental institute than their prison sentence would have been following a standard guilty verdict. Bill C-30 introduced **capping**, which refers to the maximum period of time a person with a mental illness can be affected by his or her disposition. For example, the disposition period for a defendant with a mental illness who committed a violent offence is ten years, the same length of time as the prison term. Once the cap is reached, the defendant may be released without restrictions. However, if the defendant is still perceived to be dangerous, he or she could be involuntarily committed to a secure hospital. Moreover, if the defendant was declared a mentally disordered dangerous/violent offender, this designation could increase the cap.

When deciding on a disposition, the court and review board must choose the option that is least limiting to the defendant. There are four main criteria that are considered when deciding a disposition:

- public safety
- mental state of the defendant
- reintegration of the defendant into society
- other needs of the defendant

See Figure 8.2 for key process in cases involving NCRMD defences.

Capping: Notion introduced through Bill C-30 where there is a maximum period of time a person with a mental illness could be affected by their disposition

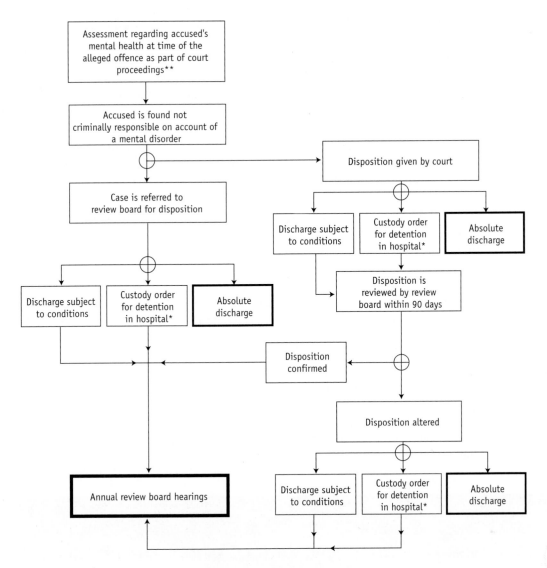

Figure 8.2 Key Processes in Cases Involving NCRMD Defences

*Although both the court and review board have the authority to detain a person found NCRMD in hospital, the accused may refuse treatment while detained.

**In accordance with the decision of the Supreme Court of Canada in *R. v. Swain* in 1991, the Crown may not raise the issue of the accused's mental state before the Crown proved that the crime had been committed or where the accused had put their mental capacity into issue.

AUTOMATISM

If you don't have control over your behaviour, should you be held responsible for your actions? Consider the case of Kenneth Parks (*R. v. Parks*, 1992). He got up in the middle of the night, got dressed, got into his car, and drove to where his parents-in-law lived. He went into their home, got a kitchen knife, stabbed his mother-in-law to death and almost

Automatism: Unconscious, involuntary behaviour such that the person committing the act is not aware of what he or she is doing

killed his father-in-law. He then drove to the police station and turned himself in. He was charged and tried for murder and attempted murder. Parks's defence was that he was sleepwalking, a form of automatism. **Automatism** refers to unconscious, involuntary behaviour; that is, the person committing the act is not aware of what he or she is doing. Parks was acquitted on both charges. See Box 8.5 for an example of automatism involving a Canadian socialite.

The Criminal Code of Canada does not specifically address automatism as a defence; rather, judges have had to rely on their own judgment and case law when such defences are raised. Recently, in *R. v. Stone* (1999) (see Box 8.6), the Supreme Court of Canada stated that there were two forms of automatism: noninsane and insane. Noninsane automatism refers to involuntary behaviour that occurs because of an external factor. The verdict in such cases is "not guilty." Insane automatism refers to an involuntary action that occurs because of a mental disorder. In these cases, a finding of NCRMD would be entered and the legislation for NCRMD would be applied.

In *R. v. Stone* (1999) the Supreme Court outlined a two-stage process for addressing defences of automatism. First, the trial judge must decide whether there is sufficient evidence that a jury could find that the defendant's behaviour was involuntary. The following factors are considered:

- psychiatric assessments
- severity of triggering event
- history of automatic behaviour

Second, the trial judge determines if the condition is a mental disorder (insane) or non-mental-disorder (noninsane) automatism.

Box 8.5

A Gas Company, a Tire Company, and a Case of Automatism

Dorothy and Earl Joudrie were teen sweethearts. They married in 1957 and although they had only $25 at the time, they managed to amass quite a fortune. They had a 650-square-metre home, a vacation home in Hawaii, and were millionaires. Earl had become the chair of both Gulf Canada Resources Limited and the Canadian Tire Corporation, to name just two of his many accomplishments. In 1989, the couple separated. In 1994, Earl petitioned for a divorce but Dorothy contested the petition.

It was January 21, 1995, when Dorothy Joudrie took a handgun and shot Earl Joudrie six times. The motivation for the shooting was unclear. Abuse early in the marriage? Loss of marital status? Or some other reason? Dorothy had no memory of the shooting. Three psychiatrists told the court

that Dorothy was in a dissociative state at the time of the shooting. One psychiatrist for the Crown, Dr. Arboleda-Florez, stated that Dorothy was in an automatistic state at the time of the shooting. There are two types of automatism; sane and insane. Dorothy's state was determined to be insane automatism (more about this distinction in the main text). The jury of 11 women and 1 man reached the same conclusion, returning a "not criminally responsible on account of mental disorder" decision. Dorothy Joudrie was ordered to undergo a psychiatric assessment. Dorothy spent five months in a psychiatric facility after the verdict and then was given an absolute discharge. The Joudries were divorced in 1995.

Source: Adapted from Nemeth, 1996.

Box 8.6

Can Insults Lead to Automatism?

There was no question that Bert Stone stabbed his wife 47 times (*R. v. Stone*, 1999). He was holding a hunting knife and his wife was dead in her seat. His defence was that his behaviour was not under his control. Stone argued that when he stabbed her, he was in an automatistic state that was triggered by his wife's insults. After Stone stabbed his wife, he got rid of the body, cleaned up, left a note for his stepdaughter, and then checked into a hotel. Later, he sold his car and flew to Mexico. It was here that he woke up one morning to a feeling of having his throat cut. While trying to remember this bad dream, he remembered stabbing his wife two times. After about six weeks, Stone returned to Canada and gave himself up to police. He was charged with murder. Stone was found guilty and sentenced to seven years in prison.

If the judge decides that the condition is the result of an external factor, the defence can argue noninsane automatism. The judge and/or jury will need to decide whether the defendant acted involuntarily. If so, the defendant will be found not guilty. If the judge decides that the condition is the result of a mental disorder, the defence can argue insane automatism, and the case proceeds as an NCRMD case. The NCRMD standard as outlined in section 16 of the Canadian Criminal Code must be met. A successful defence in this situation would result in an NCRMD verdict.

Canadian courts have recognized defences of noninsane automatism in the following circumstances:

- a physical blow (e.g., a blow to the head)
- physical ailments such as stroke
- hypoglycemia (e.g., low blood sugar)
- carbon monoxide poisoning
- sleepwalking
- involuntary intoxication
- psychological blow from an extraordinary external event that might reasonably be expected to cause a dissociative state in an average, normal person

It is important to note that everyday life stresses that may lead to a dissociative state would not be sufficient for a defence of automatism. Dissociative states from psychological factors, such as grief and mourning or anxiety, are more consistent with diseases of the mind and may be applicable for the insanity defence.

How Do NCRMD and Automatism Differ?

The main difference between defences of NCRMD and automatism lies in their verdict outcomes. An NCRMD verdict may result in the defendant being sent to a mental health facility. In contrast, a successful (noninsane) automatism verdict means that the defendant is not guilty and is then released without conditions. Insane automatism verdicts result in an NCRMD ruling. The defendants in these cases are subject to the same dispositions as those with a successful NCRMD defence.

Intoxication as a Defence

One evening, Mr. Daviault brought a 40-ounce bottle of brandy over to Ms. X's home at her request (*R. v. Daviault*, 1994). Ms. X was 65 years old and partially paralyzed. She was confined to a wheelchair. Ms. X had a half glass of brandy and fell asleep in her wheelchair. During the middle of the night, she awoke to go to the bathroom, at which point Mr. Daviault sexually assaulted her and left the apartment. Ms. X noticed that the bottle of brandy was empty. Mr. Daviault had drunk the remainder of the bottle; he was an alcoholic. During the trial proceedings, Mr. Daviault stated that he had had seven or eight bottles of beer earlier that day. Although he remembered having a glass of brandy when he arrived at Ms. X's, he did not remember what happened afterward and that he awoke naked in Ms. X's bed. He denied sexually assaulting her.

A pharmacologist testified for the defence and stated that "an individual with this level of alcohol in his blood might suffer an episode of 'L'amnesie-automatisme,' also known as a blackout. In such a state the individual loses contact with reality and the brain is temporarily dissociated from normal functioning. The individual has no awareness of his actions when he is in such a state and will likely have no memory of them the next day" (*R. v. Daviault*, 1994, para. 73).

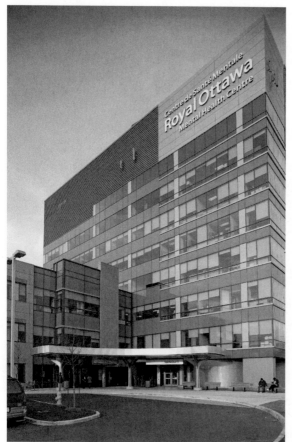

Royal Ottawa Mental
Health Centre

The judge found that the defendant committed the offence but, because of the level of intoxication, found that he did not have the intent to commit the act. Mr. Daviault was found not guilty. On appeal, the court reversed the judge's decision, entering a guilty verdict for Mr. Daviault. The appeal court stated that self-induced intoxication resulting in a state similar to automatism is not available as a defence for a general intent offence—that is, an offence that requires only an intention to commit the act. Moreover, in 1995 Bill C-72 was passed, which stated that intoxication was not recognized as a defence for violent crimes.

As you can see, automatism is not a straightforward defence. It is a challenge to prove and may result in variable verdicts. Until legislation can clarify this defence, there will remain ambiguity in the use and success of this defence.

DEFENDANTS WITH MENTAL DISORDERS

If a defendant does not receive an unfit finding or an NCRMD verdict, this does not necessarily mean that he or she does not have mental health difficulties. In a Canadian study examining males from the Edmonton Remand Centre, Bland, Newman, Dyck, and Orn (1990) found that 92% of the sample had a lifetime prevalence of psychiatric disorders (see Table 8.4).

Table 8.4 Prevalence Rates of Psychiatric Disorders in an Edmonton Sample of Defendants

Type of Mental Disorder	Rate
Substance abuse	87%
Antisocial personality disorder	57%
Affective disorder	23%
Anxiety/somatoform disorders	16%
Schizophrenia	2%

Source: Bland et al., 1990.

Why Are There Such High Rates of Mental Illness in Offender Populations?

A variety of explanations have been postulated to understand the high rates of mental illness in offender populations in Canada (Bland et al., 1990):

1. Individuals with a mental illness are likely to be arrested at a disproportionately high rate compared with those who do not have a mental illness.

2. Individuals with a mental illness are less adept at committing crime and therefore more likely to get caught.

3. Individuals with a mental illness are more likely to plead guilty, possibly because of an inability to access good representation or to understand the consequences of their plea.

It is possible that all these explanations are appropriate. Moreover, there may be alternative explanations to the high rates of mental illness in offender populations that have yet to be articulated. Further research is needed to explain this phenomenon.

Dealing with Offenders Who Are Mentally Ill

Police have great latitude in how they deal with offenders who are mentally ill in the community. Provincial and territorial mental health legislation grants police two options for handling these offenders. If an individual has a mental disorder and poses a threat to him- or herself or to others, the police may bring the individual to a hospital or mental health facility for assessment and possible treatment. As an alternative, the police may charge and arrest the individual. In this scenario, mental health services may be obtained through the criminal justice system. Thus, the mental health system and the criminal justice system are both available to police, providing two alternative routes for dealing with people with a mental illness. Some have argued that people with a mental illness are more likely to be processed through the justice system because of the difficulty of obtaining services for them through the mental health system (Teplin, 1984).

Bias against Mentally Ill Offenders

As part of a Canadian national study examining mental health problems in federally incarcerated offenders, Porporino and Motiuk (1995) compared 36 male offenders meeting criteria for a mental disorder (e.g., mania or schizophrenia) with 36 male offenders not meeting these criteria. The two groups were similar on a number of variables including age, type of crime committed, and history of criminal activity. The researchers were interested in the conditional release patterns for both groups. Specifically, they wanted to know whether offenders with a mental illness were treated differently.

There are two ways in which offenders can receive a conditional release from a federal facility in Canada: parole or mandatory supervision. Parole is determined by a parole board and is dependent on eligibility criteria. Ultimately, the National Parole Board has discretionary power in whether parole is granted. In contrast, mandatory supervision occurs after serving two-thirds of a sentence.

Porporino and Mortiuk found that a similar proportion of offenders from both groups (67% of those with a mental disorder versus 75% of those without one) received conditional releases. However, the reason for granting a conditional release differed across the two groups. Offenders with mental disorders were more likely to be conditionally released as a result of mandatory supervision, whereas offenders who did not have a mental disorder were more likely to be conditionally released because of parole.

Moreover, the researchers found that the offenders with mental disorders were more likely to have their release suspended (e.g., for not abiding by their supervision order) compared with other offenders. The offenders without mental disorders were likely to be re-admitted for committing a new offence. Thus, offenders with mental disorders may be treated cautiously by the criminal justice system because of a presumption that they are a greater risk for committing more crime. Is this presumption correct?

In a six-year follow-up study, Teplin, Abram, and McClelland (1994) examined the relationship between post-release arrest rate for violent crime and mental disorders. Offenders with either schizophrenia or a major affective disorder had a 43% likelihood of re-arrest. Those with substance abuse had a similar re-arrest rate of 46%. Moreover, offenders with a prior history of violent crime were twice as likely to be re-arrested as those with no prior history. Offenders with a history of hallucinations and delusions (i.e., schizophrenia symptoms) were not more likely to be subsequently arrested. As you can see, a number of factors can be related to rates of re-arrest, not just mental illness.

Are People with Mental Illnesses Violent?

A commonly held belief is that those who have a mental illness are violent predators. Does the research support this view? Two epidemiological surveys were conducted to examine the relationship between violence and mental disorders. In a Canadian study conducted in Edmonton, violence referred to physical acts such as fist fighting and using weapons (Bland & Orn, 1986). Mental disorders included antisocial personality disorder, major depression, and alcohol/drug dependence. Approximately 55% of respondents who met criteria for a psychiatric diagnosis committed violent acts. In contrast, only about 16% of respondents who did not meet criteria for a psychiatric diagnosis engaged in violent behaviour. When respondents met criteria for two diagnoses—for example, alcoholism and antisocial personality disorder and/or depression—80% to 93% of these respondents committed violent acts. Similar results were found in a sample from the United States (Swanson, Holzer, Ganju, & Jono, 1990). Over 50% of the U.S. respondents who met criteria for a psychiatric disorder committed violent acts. In both studies, substance abuse increased the risk of engaging in violence.

Examining a European sample, Hodgins (1992, 1993) reviewed the criminal and mental health records of approximately fifteen thousand 30 year olds born in Stockholm, Sweden, in 1953. Persons who had been admitted to mental health facilities were classified according to their most serious diagnosis. For example, participants were grouped according to whether they had a major mental disorder such as schizophrenia, alcohol and/or drug abuse or dependency, or another mental disorder. Hodgins found that individuals with a major mental disorder, especially those individuals with substance abuse or dependency, were significantly more likely to have committed a crime than those without a mental disorder. However, most persons with a major mental disorder who committed offences committed them before the age of 18, before the symptoms of the major mental disorder would have been present. Thus, these results cast doubt on the notion that major mental illness precipitates violence.

Cirincione, Steadman, Clark-Robbins, and Monahan (1992) examined the degree to which a diagnosis of schizophrenia was predictive of violence, after controlling for arrest history. Two cohorts, one from 1968 and one from 1978, in a New York State psychiatric facility were reviewed. Results differed across cohorts. Prior arrest was a significant predictor of violence in both cohorts. A schizophrenia diagnosis was predictive of violence in the 1968 cohort but not in the 1978 cohort. For those without a history of prior arrest, a diagnosis of schizophrenia did not predict engaging in later violence. This research indicates that prior violence and substance abuse seem to have much greater effects on the likelihood of future violence than psychiatric diagnoses such as schizophrenia.

A meta-analysis examining the recidivism of over 15 000 mentally disordered offenders was conducted by Bonta, Law, and Hanson (1998). The disordered offenders were followed for an average of 4.8 years in the community after having been released from prisons and hospitals. Mentally disordered offenders were found less likely to recidivate violently than offenders who did not have major psychological or psychiatric disorders. The researchers suggest that some data finds a greater likelihood of violence when an individual is experiencing a psychotic phase with symptoms of a paranoid nature. Overall, the notion that people with mental illness are more violent may not be a completely accurate view.

Types of Offences Committed by People with Mental Illnesses

Rice and Harris (1990) compared three groups of offenders: a group of males found NCRMD, a random group of convicted offenders who were sent for pretrial psychiatric evaluations, and a group of convicted offenders who were matched on the offence committed. The researchers found that NCRMD defendants were more likely to have committed murder or attempted murder than the other groups. Overall, however, offenders with mental disorders committed a variety of crimes, such as fraud, shoplifting, and murder. In other words, mentally disordered offenders were similar to other offenders and not distinguishable based solely on offence type (Rice & Harris, 1997b).

Recidivism Rates and People with Mental Illnesses

In order to determine whether offenders with mental disorders are more likely to reoffend, Rice and Harris (1992) examined 96 NCRMD defendants who were diagnosed with schizophrenia and 96 nonschizophrenic offenders. The two groups were matched on age, offence, and criminal history. The schizophrenics were less likely, although not significantly so, to violently reoffend than were the nonschizophrenics. In another study using some of the same participants as in the Rice and Harris (1992) examination, 210 NCRMD defendants were compared on post-release recidivism to a matched convicted group (Rice & Harris, 1990). The NCRMD defendants had lower rates of both general and violent recidivism than the convicted offenders. It appears that, compared with other offenders, those with a major mental illness are not more likely to commit future crimes, especially violent crimes.

Treatment of Offenders with Mental Disorders

The goals for treatment for offenders with mental disorders vary greatly and are somewhat dependent on whether the offender is dealt with through the mental health system or the criminal justice system. Some of the treatment goals identified for those with mental disorders include symptom reduction, decreased length of stay in the facility, and no need to be re-admitted to hospital (Test, 1992). Of course, reducing the risk of recidivism has garnered much attention as a treatment goal among those in the criminal justice system (Lipsey, 1992).

There are a number of types of facilities at which mentally disordered offenders can receive treatment: psychiatric institutions, general hospitals, and assisted housing units. There appears to be little agreement on which type of treatment is appropriate for offenders with mental disorders (Quinsey & Maguire, 1983). However, for those who experience active psychotic symptoms such as delusions, hallucinations, suspicion, and noncompliance with medication, there are two key treatment options: anti-psychotic drugs and behaviour therapy (Breslin, 1992). Medication can help control psychotic symptoms, while behaviour therapy can help to ensure that patients take the medication consistently. The critical aspects of behaviour therapy appear to be in providing positive social and material reward for appropriate behaviour, while decreasing or eliminating attention for symptomatic behaviour (Beck, Menditto, Baldwin, Angelone, & Maddox, 1991; Paul & Lentz, 1977).

Penetanguishene Mental Health Centre

The availability of facilities and the treatment programs offered vary across the country. Moreover, the willingness of an offender to engage in a particular program will vary. Even if an offender is motivated to receive treatment, an appropriate program may not be available at a particular facility. Thus, there are difficulties in matching programs to offenders' needs and willingness to participate.

One overarching treatment goal of many offender programs is to reintegrate the offender into society. The mental health and criminal justice system has developed options with this goal in mind. For example, a **community treatment order** allows the offender who has a mental illness to live in the community, with the stipulation that he or

Community treatment order: Sentence that allows the mentally ill offender to live in the community, with the stipulation that the person will agree to treatment or detention in the event his or her condition deteriorates she will agree to treatment or detention in the event that his or her condition deteriorates. Another option for the courts dealing with offenders with mental illnesses who are facing minor charges is **diversion**—that is, diverting them directly into a treatment program rather than having them go through the court process. Generally, only defendants who are willing to participate in treatment will be diverted.

Treatment can be critical for offenders who have certain mental disorders such as schizophrenia.

Diversion: A decision not to prosecute a young offender, but rather have him or her undergo an educational or community-service program. Also an option for the courts dealing with offenders with mental illnesses who are facing minor charges. The court can divert the offender directly into a treatment program rather than have him or her go through the court process.

A NEW COURT FOR THE MENTALLY ILL: THE MENTAL HEALTH COURTS

A new court is in town, designed for those in need of fitness examinations and criminal responsibility assessments, guilty pleas, and sentencing hearings. These courts, known as mental health courts, have been emerging across Canada since the mid 1990s (Bloom & Schneider, 2007). These courts attempt to redirect those with mental health needs back into the mental health care system (rather than the criminal justice system). Mental health courts have four main objectives (Schneider, Bloom, & Heerema, 2007):

1. To divert accused who have been charged with minor to moderately serious criminal offences and offer them an alternative
2. To facilitate a defendant's fitness to stand trial evaluation
3. To ensure treatment for a defendant's mental disorders
4. To decrease the cycle that mentally disordered offenders experience by becoming repeat offenders

In general, mental health courts offer a rehabilitative reaction to behaviour that would otherwise have been dealt with through the criminal justice system. Alternatives to serving a sentence in prison for less serious offences such as theft, shoplifting, property damage, and minor assaults are available. One goal for these courts is to ensure that defendants and offenders receive the proper assessments and treatments. The courts make referrals to medical experts, as well as case workers who help develop a "release plan" (e.g., provide clothes, find housing, and treatment options) once the accused is in the community. Mental health courts can be found in a number of communities across Canada, including those in Saskatchewan, Ontario, and Newfoundland and Labrador.

Are Mental Health Courts Effective?

At the outset, it must be noted that little research has been conducted evaluating mental health courts. What we do know is that there is a lot of variability across different courts. For example, courts may differ on how defendants are referred, the criteria for a defendant's eligibility, and the quality and quantity of services available. It also appears to be the case that defendants going through mental health courts are more likely to be connected to services than those not going through such a court (Schneider, Bloom, & Heerema, 2007). Those having gone through the mental health system also report being more satisfied with the process and perceiving higher levels of fairness, lower levels of coercion, and increased confidence with the administration of justice. As for whether recidivism rates are lower for those going through these courts, the data are not yet in. We will have to wait to see what the research says.

SUMMARY

1. A defendant is found to be unfit if he or she is unable, due to a mental disorder, to understand the nature of the proceedings, understand the consequences of the proceedings, or communicate with counsel. The Ontario Court of Appeal in *R. v. Taylor* (1992) ruled that a defendant need only be able to tell counsel the facts. The defendant need not be able to communicate facts that are in his or her best interests. One other change to legislation that was introduced in Bill C-30 in 1992 was with regard to the length of time a defendant could be held in custody for a fitness evaluation. A five-day limit with provisions if necessary was legislated.

2. Compared with fit defendants, unfit defendants are more likely to be unemployed and living alone, and to never have been married. Moreover, unfit defendants tend to be older females belonging to a minority group who have fewer marital resources. In terms of mental disorders, unfit defendants have been found to be four times more likely to have met criteria for a psychotic disorder, whereas defendants who were found fit were about as likely to have been diagnosed with a psychotic disorder as not. Also, unfit defendants are less likely to have problems with substance abuse than fit defendants.

3. The term used for Canada's insanity standard is "not criminally responsible on account of mental disorder" (NCRMD). The defendant is not criminally responsible for an act that was committed (or omitted) while he or she was suffering from a mental disorder to the extent that he or she could not appreciate the nature or quality of the act or of knowing that it was wrong.

4. Automatism is defined as unconscious, involuntary behaviour. Canadian courts have recognized factors such as a physical blow, carbon monoxide poisoning, and sleep-walking as defences for automatism.

5. A number of explanations have been suggested for the high rates of mental illness in offender populations. For example, individuals with a mental illness may be more likely to be arrested at a disproportionately higher rate compared with those who do not have a mental illness. Alternatively, individuals with a mental illness may be less adept at committing crime and, therefore, more likely to get caught. Lastly, people with mental illnesses may be more likely to plead guilty, possibly because they do not have access to good counsel or because they do not understand the ramifications of their plea.

6. Treatment goals for offenders with mental disorders vary greatly. Some goals are symptom reduction, decreased length of stay in the facility, no need to be re-admitted to hospital, and reduced recidivism. Medication and behaviour therapy are two common types of treatment for offenders with mental disorders. Mental health courts allow for nonviolent mentally disordered offenders to be processed separately from nondisordered offenders.

Key Concepts

absolute discharge 235

actus reus 221

automatism 238

capping 236

community treatment order 244

conditional discharge 235

diversion 245

insanity 230

mens rea 221

prima facie case 230

review boards 233

unfit to stand trial 221

Discussion Questions

1. As part of your summer internship program at the courthouse, the judge has asked you to review the cases heard over the past year and identify the ones in which noninsane automatism was used as a defence. Describe some factors that may lead to automatism and that may come up in the cases you will review.

2. While having dinner with your parents, your father mentions an article that he read in the newspaper highlighting the dangerousness of offenders with mental disorders. He makes the inference that mental illness leads to violent offending. Describe the data that calls your father's conclusion into question.

3. When you show up for your social psychology class, you are informed that the professor has been arrested for voyeurism. When she was arrested, she was confused and incoherent. She is scheduled to undergo a fitness to stand trial evaluation. Your friends mention that they heard a rumour about the professor having some sort of mental illness. Describe the characteristics associated with unfit defendants and the process your professor will undergo following an unfit determination.

4. You have been hired by the police department to help police quickly identify those who may need psychiatric services rather than need to be processed through the criminal justice system. Develop a brief checklist for police to use when they come in contact with disorderly individuals so that they can take the most appropriate action.

5. Legislation changes with regard to offenders with mental disorders and their dispositions. Design a study to evaluate the various dispositions and their influence on recidivism—the likelihood of reoffending.

6. The evening news reported that offenders with mental disorders are likely to engage in more violent crime. Having taken a forensic psychology course, you feel this report is inaccurate. Describe how a researcher might go about testing the relationship between mental status and types of offences likely to be committed.

Readings

Bloom, H., & Schneider, R.D. (2006). *Mental disorder and law: A primer for legal and mental health professionals.* Toronto: Irwin Law.

Howells, K., & Hollin, C. (1993). *Clinical approaches to the mentally disordered offender.* New York: John Wiley & Sons.

Websites

The Schizophrenia Society of Canada
www.schizophrenia.ca

Schizophrenia: A Handbook for Families
www.mentalhealth.com/book/p40-sc01.html

Chapter 9

Sentencing and Parole in Canada: Practices and Public Opinions

Learning Objectives

- Describe the structure of the Canadian court system.

- List the primary purposes and principles of sentencing.

- Describe the various sentencing options available in Canada.

- Define the term *sentencing disparity* and explain how it can be studied.

- List the principles that form the basis for effective correctional interventions.

- Describe some of the myths associated with parole decision making.

Judge Harrison is sitting in his office in a Toronto courthouse reviewing a case he has recently presided over. Jeremy Patterson, a young man of 22, has pleaded guilty to the crime of breaking and entering. Late one night, Jeremy broke into his neighbour's house and stole thousands of dollars worth of stereo equipment. This is the first time Jeremy has ever been charged with a crime and, despite the fact he has a full-time job, Jeremy told the court he stole the equipment in order to buy food for his wife and newborn child.

Given the circumstances, Judge Harrison feels it might be counterproductive to sentence Jeremy to prison, even though Canada's Criminal Code prescribes a maximum penalty for break and enter that does involve prison time. In Judge Harrison's view, a prison term would probably cost Jeremy his job and his family would suffer greatly as a result. Not only that, but Jeremy would be placed in an environment in which he would be forced to interact with more serious criminals, and this might result in Jeremy becoming involved in more serious crime upon his release. Instead, Judge Harrison sentences Jeremy to one year of community service, hoping he will learn a good lesson from his experience in court.

In a Vancouver courthouse at about the same time, Judge Fidell is considering a similar case. In fact, this case is just one in a long list of similar cases Judge Fidell has presided over. The defendant, 24-year-old Paul Lorenzo, broke into a neighbourhood house and was charged for the first time. Like Jeremy, Paul has a full-time job and a young family, and the stolen items from the house are worth about $2000. However, unlike Judge Harrison, Judge Fidell has developed the view that the only way to teach young men they cannot get away with breaking the law is to send them to prison. As a result, Paul receives a sentence of one year in prison.

Thus, two judges from Canada, who were both fully aware of Canada's Criminal Code, handed down very different sentences to very similar offenders who committed very similar crimes. How could this happen in a country that is supposed to have a fair criminal justice system?

Throughout this chapter, we will discuss sentencing and parole of adult offenders in Canada by focusing on issues similar to those raised in the opening vignette. We will first describe the structure of the Canadian court system and discuss the sentencing process, focusing specifically on the purposes and principles of sentencing and the various sentencing options available to Canadian judges. Our attention will then turn to one of the major problems that can result from this process and various solutions that have been proposed to solve this problem. More specifically, we will focus on the sentencing disparity that can often result from the high degree of discretion Canadian judges have when deciding on appropriate sentences. We will finish our discussion of sentencing by reviewing research that examines whether the goals of sentencing are actually achieved and what we can do if they are not. We will then move on to describe in some detail the parole process as it is commonly practised by Canada's National Parole Board. We will focus on parole decision making and on research that looks at the effectiveness of these decisions. To conclude the chapter, we will present research findings that deal with Canadians' perceptions toward sentencing and parole and discuss where these perceptions come from.

THE STRUCTURE OF THE CANADIAN COURT SYSTEM

The Canadian court system is one component of the larger Canadian criminal justice system that includes policing agencies and correctional institutions. Some of the major roles of courts in Canada include hearing evidence presented at trial, determining guilt and innocence, and rendering sentencing decisions across a wide range of criminal and civil cases. In this chapter, we will focus on the sentencing aspect of the Canadian court system. However, before we do that, we will first briefly discuss the structure of our court system in Canada.

As illustrated in Figure 9.1, the court system in Canada is relatively complex in that it is made up of numerous types of courts that are separated by jurisdiction and levels of legal superiority (Horner, 2007). In terms of jurisdiction, courts in Canada can be split into provincial/territorial courts and federal courts. Canadian courts can be conceptualized as forming a four-tier hierarchy of legal superiority; the ones at higher levels of the hierarchy possess more legal authority than courts at lower levels. By this we mean that Canadian courts are essentially bound by the rulings of the courts above them in the hierarchy (Horner, 2007).

The bottom layer of Figure 9.1 represents administrative tribunals. These tribunals resemble courts in a variety of ways, but they are not officially part of the Canadian court system (DOJ, 2007b; Horner, 2007). These tribunals are responsible for resolving disputes over a wide range of administrative issues in both provincial/territorial and federal jurisdictions (e.g., disability benefits, refugee claims, employment insurance, etc.). One example of a provincial administrative tribunal is the Liquor Licensing Board. An example at the federal level is the National Parole Board, which will be discussed at the end of this chapter.

Outline of Canada's Court System

Figure 9.1 The Canadian Court System

Source: Department of Justice Canada (DOJ), 2007b.

Thus, the lowest level of the actual court hierarchy in Canada consists of provincial/territorial courts, sometimes referred to as "inferior" courts, which can be found in all provinces and territories with the exception of Nunavut (Horner, 2007). The range of cases heard in these courts is broad and can include criminal offences (e.g., traffic violations) and civil issues (e.g., small claims) (DOJ, 2007b). In addition, a number of courts at this level of the hierarchy specialize in particular areas. These can include youth courts, drug treatment courts, and domestic violence courts (Horner, 2007). Furthermore, provincial/territorial courts can hear appeals from administrative tribunals. Military courts, which will not be discussed in detail here, deal with offences committed by members of the Canadian Armed Forces (including civilians) under the National Defence Act.

The next level up in the court system hierarchy in provincial/territorial jurisdictions includes provincial/territorial superior courts. One of the primary roles of these courts is to act as the court of first appeal for courts at the lowest level of the hierarchy (DOJ, 2007b). In addition, these courts try the most serious criminal and civil cases—cases that often involve juries (Horner, 2007). As with provincial/territorial courts, provincial/territorial superior courts often specialize in a particular area. For example, a separate division of the superior courts deals with matters related to family law (Horner, 2007). At the federal level, the court at this position in the hierarchy is referred to simply as the Federal Court of Canada, which is akin to provincial/territorial superior courts. This court primarily serves to review administrative decisions made by federal administrative tribunals that are related to matters such as immigration, intellectual property, and maritime law. A specialized court in the federal system, the Tax Court of Canada, deals with tax disputes between the federal government and Canadian taxpayers (DOJ, 2007b).

Above these courts in the hierarchy can be found the provincial courts of appeal and the Federal Court of Appeal (the Court Martial Appeal Court hears appeals from military courts). The function of these courts is to review decisions rendered by the superior-level courts. Unlike superior-level courts, however, appellate courts do not normally conduct trials or hear evidence from witnesses. When allowed, a court of appeal may reaffirm the decision of the trial court, may render an acquittal judgment, or may order a new trial (Horner, 2007).

Finally, at the top of the court hierarchy in Canada is the **Supreme Court of Canada** (SCC), which was created in 1875 (SCC, 2007). The SCC is the final court of appeal in Canada. However, before the SCC will hear an appeal, the case must typically have been appealed in the relevant courts lower in the hierarchy—and even then, people still have limited rights to appeal to the SCC (Horner, 2007). The SCC also provides guidance to the federal government on law-related matters (e.g., interpretation of the Canadian Constitution). The SCC consists of eight judges plus the chief justice (currently Beverley McLachlin). These judges are all appointed by the federal government.

Supreme Court of Canada: Created in 1875, the Supreme Court of Canada consists of eight judges plus the chief justice, who are all appointed by the federal government. The Supreme Court is the final court of appeal in Canada, and lower Canadian courts are bound by its rulings. The Supreme Court also provides guidance to the federal government on law-related matters, such as the interpretation of the Canadian Constitution.

SENTENCING IN CANADA

Probably the most visible and controversial component of the court system in Canada is the sentencing process, which is defined as "the judicial determination of a legal sanction upon a person convicted of an offence" (Canadian Centre for Justice

The Supreme Court of Canada in Ottawa

Statistics, 1997). According to Roberts (1991), the sentencing process is highly visible because, unlike the majority of decisions made in the criminal justice system, sentencing decisions are made in the open and presented before the court. The sentencing process is highly controversial because of the great number of problems that can potentially result from the sentencing process, such as issues with sentencing effectiveness (Roberts, 1991). As a result, the sentencing process in Canada has been the subject of extensive research.

The Purposes of Sentencing

In order to understand the sentencing process in Canada, we must begin by discussing the reasons that we sentence offenders. Perhaps the most obvious goal of sentencing is to change the behaviour of convicted offenders and the behaviour of potential offenders who reside in the community. More specifically, offenders are sentenced to reduce the probability that they, and the rest of the community, will violate the law (referred to as **specific deterrence** and **general deterrence**, respectively). One of the reasons that sentencing attracts so much attention from forensic psychologists is that psychologists as a group are interested in understanding human behaviour and how that behaviour can be changed (Roberts, 1991). The area of sentencing provides fertile ground for psychologists to explore many issues in this area.

Specific deterrence: Sentencing in order to reduce the probability that an offender will reoffend in the future

General deterrence: Sentencing in order to reduce the probability that members of the general public will offend in the future

As made clear in the Criminal Code of Canada, there are also many other reasons that we sentence offenders. In fact, the Criminal Code lays out explicitly the various purposes of sentencing in an attempt to provide direction to judges in making sentencing decisions. For example, as stated in section 718 of the Criminal Code, the fundamental purpose of sentencing is to contribute to respect for the law and the maintenance of a just, peaceful, and safe society by imposing sanctions on individuals who commit crimes. Other objectives include the following:

■ To denounce unlawful conduct
■ To separate offenders from society
■ To assist in rehabilitating offenders
■ To provide **reparations** for harm done to victims or the community
■ To promote a sense of responsibility in offenders

Reparations: A sentence where the offender has to make a monetary payment to the victim or the community

At present, it is not clear if one of these sentencing goals is any more dominant than another. The following facts, however, are clear:

1. Judges often consider more than one goal when handing down a sentence. For example, an offender may be sentenced to prison in order to reduce the probability that he or she will commit another crime and to separate that offender from society.

2. These goals can, at times, be incompatible with one another. For example, handing down a sentence of 25 years in prison will separate an offender from society but it may not be an effective way of rehabilitating an offender.

3. Different judges across Canada often hand down sentences for different reasons, even when dealing with offenders and offences that are similar. For example, under similar circumstances, one judge may hand down a sentence that he or she feels promotes a sense of responsibility in the offender, while another judge may hand down a sentence primarily intended to deter the general public from violating the law.

The Principles of Sentencing

Just as there are numerous reasons for imposing sanctions on offenders, there are also numerous sentencing principles in Canada, which are meant to guide sentencing decisions. Again, these are laid out explicitly in the Criminal Code. The **fundamental principle of sentencing**, as defined in section 718.1 of the Criminal Code, is that a sentence must be proportionate to the gravity of the offence and the degree of responsibility of the offender. Thus, when handing down a sentence in Canada, judges should consider the seriousness of the specific offence in addition to any other factor that might relate to the offender's degree of responsibility, such as the offender's age at the time of the offence.

However, beyond this fundamental principle, the Criminal Code also consists of other sentencing principles. For example, section 718.2 indicates that, when handing down sentences, judges should take into account the following principles:

- A sentence should be adjusted to account for any relevant aggravating or mitigating circumstances relating to the offence or the offender. For example, if the offender abused a position of authority when committing his or her offence, this should be considered.

- A sentence should be similar for similar offenders committing similar offences under similar circumstances.

- Where consecutive sentences are imposed, the combined sentence should not be unduly harsh.

- An offender should not be deprived of liberty (e.g., imprisoned) if less restrictive sanctions are appropriate under the circumstances.

- If reasonable, sanctions other than imprisonment should be considered for all offenders.

Sentencing Options in Canada

In addition to the purposes and principles of sentencing, Canada's Criminal Code also describes the various sentencing options available for particular offences and the maximum penalties that can be handed down. However, although the Criminal Code provides a general framework for making sentencing decisions, judges still have a great deal of discretion. For example, while it is possible to sentence a petty criminal to prison for a substantial amount of time, it is highly likely that some other sentencing option will be used instead, such as a fine. Indeed, Roberts and Birkenmayer (1997) found that judges in Canada rarely provide the maximum penalty that is prescribed in the Criminal Code for any offence. For example, the maximum penalty for breaking and entering in Canada is life in prison, but the median sentence length reported by Roberts and Birkenmayer for Canadian judges was just three months imprisonment. Box 9.1 provides a detailed description of some of the sentencing options available to judges in Canada.

Fundamental principle of sentencing: The belief that sentences should be proportionate to the gravity of the offence and the degree of responsibility of the offender

Absolute discharge: The defendant is released into the community without restrictions to his or her behaviour

Conditional discharge: A defendant is released; however, release carries certain conditions (e.g., not to possess firearms) that the defendant must meet. Failure to meet the conditions imposed with a conditional discharge may result in the defendant being incarcerated or sent to a psychiatric facility

Probation: The defendant is released into the community with certain restrictions on his or her behaviour

Restitution: See **reparations**, on p. 253.

Fine: A sentence where the offender has to make a monetary payment to the courts

Community service: A sentence that involves the offender performing a duty in the community, often as a way of paying off a fine

Conditional sentence: A sentence served in the community

Imprisonment: A sentence served in prison

Box 9.1

Sentencing Options in Canada

Depending on the offence being considered, judges in Canada have many sentencing options available to them, including the following:

■ *Absolute or conditional discharge.* Canadian judges have the option to impose an **absolute discharge** or **conditional discharge**. When making this decision, judges will consider whether a discharge would be in the best interest of the offender and the community. If an offender is given an absolute discharge, that person is released and is free to do as he or she wishes in the community. An offender who is given a conditional discharge will have to follow certain rules in the community for a specified period of time in order for the discharge to become absolute. If the offender breaks these rules, he or she can serve time in prison. The important point about a discharge, which makes it different from, say, a conditional sentence (see below) is that the accused is not convicted of an offence, despite being found guilty of the offence, and therefore he or she is spared the stigmatising consequences of a criminal record.

■ *Probation.* Offenders placed on **probation** are released into the community and must follow certain conditions. For example, while on probation, offenders will have to (1) be of good behaviour, (2) appear before the court when required to do so, (3) have regular contact with their probation officer, and (4) notify their probation officer of any change of name, address, or employment status. Other conditions may also be put in place, such as abstaining from alcohol and drug use. Offenders who break the conditions of their probation order may be imprisoned for up to two years.

■ *Restitution.* **Restitution** is a payment made by an offender to the victim to cover expenses resulting from a crime, such as monetary loss resulting from property damage. When someone is injured, restitution can be used to cover medical bills and lost income.

■ *Fines and community service.* The most common sentencing option in Canada is the **fine**. A court that fines an offender will set the amount of the fine, the way the fine is to be paid, and the time by which the fine must be paid. In many cases, the offender will be able to pay off the fine by performing **community service**. If an offender, without a reasonable excuse, does not pay the fine, he or she can serve a term of imprisonment.

■ *Conditional sentence.* A **conditional sentence** is a prison sentence served in the community. This sentencing option was introduced to Canada only in 1996 as part of Bill C-41. An offender serving a conditional sentence is released into the community and must follow a set of rules for a specific period of time. The prison sentence is suspended as long as the offender abides by these rules. If an offender breaks these rules, he or she may be required to serve the remainder of the sentence in prison.

■ *Imprisonment.* **Imprisonment** is a last resort reserved for situations in which less restrictive sanctions are inappropriate. For summary (i.e., less serious) offences, the maximum term of incarceration is six months. For indictable (i.e., more serious) offences, the term of incarceration varies by offence and can include life imprisonment. Offenders sentenced to prison terms of less than two years serve their sentences in provincial or territorial prisons. Sentences of two or more years are served in federal prisons.

Source: John Howard Society, 1999.

In addition to the options discussed in Box 9.1, Canadian judges have a number of additional options open to them when handing down sentences of imprisonment, especially for high-risk offenders. One of these options is to declare the offender a **dangerous offender**. The prosecution can submit a dangerous offender application to the court for any offender convicted of a serious personal injury offence who constitutes a danger to others (John Howard Society, 1999). According to the Criminal

Dangerous offender: A label attached to offenders who are proven to constitute a significant danger to others

Code, the determination of dangerousness in these cases is based on evidence that one of the following conditions is met:

1. The offender exhibits a pattern of unrestrained behaviour that is likely to cause danger.

2. The offender exhibits a pattern of aggressive behaviour with indifference as to the consequences of this behaviour.

3. The offender exhibits behaviour that is of such a brutal nature that ordinary standards of restraint will not control it.

4. The offender shows a failure to control sexual impulses that are likely to harm others.

If someone receives the dangerous offender designation, that person can be imprisoned for an indefinite period of time. This is a very extreme measure and, therefore, it is important that the appropriate offenders are targeted. Fortunately, this does appear to be happening in Canada. For example, Bonta, Zinger, Harris, and Carriere (1998) compared a group of dangerous offenders from Canadian prisons with a group of offenders who had been released from prison only to go on to commit a violent crime. The assumption was that "similarities between the two groups would imply that [dangerous offenders] would also be at high risk to offend violently if released" (Bonta, Zinger, et al., 1998, p. 383). In accordance with what should happen if the appropriate offenders are being targeted for the dangerous offender designation, Bonta, Zinger, et al. found that the two groups in their study were quite similar. Offenders in both groups had similar criminal histories and had committed offences against similar victims. The groups also had similar backgrounds with respect to education, employment, marital status, and upbringing. Objective risk-assessment scales did not distinguish between the two groups of offenders either.

Alternatively, prosecutors can submit an application to the court to have an offender designated as a **long-term offender**. This is a relatively new sentencing option in Canada. Based on the description provided in section 753.1 of the Criminal Code, any offender who meets the following criteria can be designated a long-term offender:

Long-term offender: A label attached to offenders who are proven to be a high risk for reoffending

1. It would be appropriate to impose a sentence of two years or more for the offence.

2. There is a substantial risk that the offender will reoffend.

3. There is a reasonable possibility of eventual control of risk in the community.

A long-term offender will be given a sentence of imprisonment of at least two years, followed by a period of supervision in the community (John Howard Society, 1999).

Factors That Affect Sentencing Decisions

We will now briefly discuss factors affecting sentencing decisions. As indicated above, the Criminal Code highlights various factors that should be taken into account when judges decide on sentences in Canada. These include the seriousness of the offence, the offender's degree of responsibility, various aggravating and mitigating factors, the harshness of the sentence, and so forth. According to Roberts (1991), some researchers suggest that these legally relevant factors can explain most of the variation that occurs in sentencing decisions across judges (e.g., Andrews, Robblee, & Saunders, 1984). This clearly is as it should be. However, other researchers argue that many judges appear to rely on extra-legal factors (i.e., factors that have little to do with either the offender or the crime) when making their sentencing decisions, and this is cause for concern.

For example, in an important study by Hogarth (1971), he found that "only about 9% of the variation in sentencing could be explained by objectively defined facts, while more than 50% of such variation could be accounted for simply by knowing certain pieces of information about the judge himself" (p. 382). Likewise, in a more recent study, Ulmer (1997) found that a variety of extra-legal factors influence sentencing even when relevant factors such as crime seriousness and prior criminal history are held constant. Some of these factors included the gender and race of the defendant (e.g., in Pennsylvania, males and blacks were approximately 50% more likely than women and whites to be incarcerated for their crimes). Canadian studies of sentencing decisions report similar findings. For example, as you will see in Chapter 13, a number of researchers have suggested that certain groups of offenders in Canada, especially Aboriginal offenders, are more likely to be incarcerated for their crimes (e.g., LaPrairie, 1989).

Sentencing Disparity

One of the reasons that it is important to appreciate the various factors that affect sentencing decisions is so that we can understand **sentencing disparity**. Sentencing disparity is defined as "any difference in severity between the sentence that an offender receives from one judge on a particular occasion and what an identical offender with the identical crime would receive from either the same judge on a different occasion or a different judge on the same or a different occasion" (McFatter, 1986, pp. 151–152). Because sentencing disparity can lead to serious injustices, it is commonly viewed as a major problem within our criminal justice system. Indeed, a number of leading Canadian researchers have proposed that sentencing disparity is one of the most important problems with sentencing (e.g., Roberts, 1991). And in fact, sentencing disparity has been viewed as a serious problem for a long time. For example, Roberts (1991) cites a study by Gaudet (1938) that dealt with this very issue.

Sentencing disparity: Variations in sentencing severity for similar crimes committed under similar circumstances

A prison cell in one of Canada's maximum-security prisons

Sources of Unwarranted Sentencing Disparity The real problem occurs when disparities in sentencing happen because of a reliance on extra-legal factors. In this case, we can refer to the disparity as **unwarranted sentencing disparity** (Roberts, 1991). Unwarranted sentencing disparity can result from many factors and researchers have attempted to classify these factors into groups. For example, McFatter (1986) discusses two major sources of unwarranted sentencing disparity: **systematic disparity** and **unsystematic disparity**. Systematic disparity represents *consistent* disagreement among judges about sentencing, such as how lenient they feel sentences should be. As you saw in this chapter's opening vignette, sources of systematic disparity can include differences between judges in terms of their personality, philosophy, experience, and so on.

Unsystematic disparity, conversely, results from a given judge's *inconsistency* over occasions in judging the same type of offender or crime. This type of disparity can also arise from a number of sources, including fluctuations in mood, focusing on irrelevant stimuli, or the way in which the facts of the case are interpreted by the judge on any particular day (McFatter, 1986). Why is it important to understand these different sources of sentencing disparity? As McFatter (1986) suggests, only by understanding the various sources of sentencing disparity can we come up with effective strategies to combat its existence.

Studying Sentencing Disparity Researchers in this area typically use one of two procedures to study sentencing disparity—laboratory-based simulation studies or the use of official sentencing statistics. Of the two procedures, simulation studies are more common. Here, researchers present mock judges, or real judges, with the details of a trial, and the researcher manipulates particular variables of interest, such as the defendant's age, ethnicity, or gender. The goal is to manipulate these variables while attempting to control for as many other variables as possible, so that if evidence for sentencing disparity is found, the researcher can be fairly confident as to what caused it.

Simulation Studies The experiment conducted by McFatter (1986) provides an excellent example of a simulation study. He provided six judges with 13 crime and offender descriptions, which included brief details of the crime and the offender's age, prior record, drug use, and employment status. The descriptions were chosen to represent a wide range of typical crime and offender descriptions. For example, the crimes ranged from a fight that broke out after a minor traffic accident to a rape and murder of an 11-year-old girl. In the first phase of the study, judges were asked to rate various aspects of the crime, such as its seriousness, and to recommend a sentence. Approximately two months later, the judges were given the same crime and offender descriptions and were asked to make ratings and recommend sentences once again. In both phases, the severity of sentences handed down by judges was transformed into numbers using the scale developed by Diamond and Zeisel (1975), which is provided in Table 9.1.

The raw severity scores for the sentences handed down by the judges in each phase of McFatter's (1986) experiment are presented in Table 9.2 on page 260. A number of interesting things emerge from these data:

1. The results indicate that there is a good deal of agreement among judges about the severity of sentences appropriate for each crime. For example, all six judges consistently handed down very lenient sentences for crime 1 (the fight that resulted from a minor traffic accident), while five of the six judges consistently handed down very serious sentences for crime 13 (the rape and murder of the 11-year-old girl).

Table 9.1 Sentencing Severity Scores

Sentence	Severity Score
Fine or suspended sentence	1
Probation (months)	
1–12	1
13–36	2
Over 36	3
Split sentence (jail + probation)	4
Prison	
1–6 months	3
7–12 months	5
13–24 months	7
25–36 months	9
(Add 2 points for every year up to 50 years)	
50 years	103
Life imprisonment or death	103

Source: Adapted from McFatter, 1986.

2. However, despite these similarities, there are also many instances of unwarranted sentencing disparity. For example, the sentences handed down for crime 9 (an armed robbery that took place on the street) varied drastically across judges, with severity scores ranging from 2 to 53.

3. Most of this disparity appears to come from unsystematic sources. In a large number of cases, the same judge handed down different sentences when presented with the same crime and offender after a two-month delay. Indeed, in some cases the degree of disparity was extremely high, as in the case of crime 12 and 13, where judge 4 handed down much more lenient sentences in phase 1 compared with phase 2.

Similar findings have also been reported in simulation studies conducted in Canada (e.g., Palys & Divorski, 1986).

Studies Based on Official Statistics Studies using official sentencing statistics have come to the same conclusion—a relatively high degree of disparity does exist in judicial sentencing decisions. For example, Birkenmayer and Roberts (1997) have found high levels of sentencing disparity in incarceration rates from courts across Canada. Based on their analyses, certain provincial courts appear to be much harsher in terms of the number of prison terms they hand out. For example, in Ontario, 72% of break and enter offences resulted in incarceration, whereas only 33% of such offences in Quebec resulted in incarceration.

Reducing Sentencing Disparity Regardless of how sentencing disparity is studied, the conclusion is typically that a high degree of disparity exists across sentences handed down by different judges considering similar crimes and across sentences handed down by the

Table 9.2 Sentencing Severity Scores for the Judges

Crime	1(1)	1(2)	2(1)	2(2)	3(1)	3(2)	4(1)	4(2)	5(1)	5(2)	6(1)	6(2)
					Judge (Phase)							
1	1	1	2	4	2	2	2	3	1	4	1	4
2	3	2	4	4	1	2	2	2	1	4	3	2
3	2	1	5	4	4	2	3	4	2	2	2	3
4	5	5	9	9	3	3	3	3	3	3	2	3
5	3	3	4	9	4	4	3	4	7	4	7	3
6	5	2	7	7	4	4	3	3	3	3	3	13
7	2	4	5	4	3	3	4	5	13	3	4	13
8	4	3	5	9	23	5	13	4	1	4	4	3
9	53	39	53	43	2	5	13	5	3	4	13	23
10	103	103	103	103	5	103	23	23	12	23	103	53
11	63	103	103	103	103	43	13	13	103	103	13	23
12	103	103	103	103	103	103	53	103	103	103	103	103
13	103	103	103	103	103	103	53	103	103	103	103	103

Source: McFatter, 1986.

same judge when considering similar crimes on different occasions. As discussed above, there are a number of sources that can account for this disparity but, ultimately, sentencing disparity exists because the law in Canada allows judges a great deal of discretion when making sentencing decisions. Although sentencing guidelines exist in Canada's Criminal Code, these guidelines are often so broad that they do little to decrease sentencing disparity. For example, as Roberts (1991) points out, "there are over 70 offences contained in the Criminal Code that can be punished by dispositions ranging from a discharge to a sentence of imprisonment of 14 years or life" (p. 471).

Although certain forms of sentencing disparity are probably inevitable (some would argue essential), there has been a move within Canada in recent years toward reducing unwarranted disparity. Just as people debate the extent to which sentencing disparity exists, debates are also ongoing as to how this disparity can best be minimized. The most common approach for reducing sentencing disparity, especially in Canada, is to implement **sentencing guidelines**. In this section, we will briefly discuss what sentencing guidelines are, what they are meant to achieve, and whether existing research suggests they work.

Sentencing guidelines: Guidelines that are intended to reduce the degree of discretion that judges have when handing down sentences

Sentencing Guidelines in Canada

Many different types of sentencing guidelines have been proposed, but they all have one thing in common: they all attempt to provide a more consistent, structured way of arriving at sentencing decisions. The following is a partial list, provided by Roberts (1991), of various guidelines that could be used to reduce sentencing disparity:

1. *Advisory guidelines*. These guidelines are purely suggestive in nature when it comes to sentencing decisions and have no force in the law.

Table 9.3 Mandatory Minimum Sentences for Selected Offences

Offence	Minimum	Maximum
High treason	Life	Life
First-degree murder	Life	Life
Kidnapping—firearm	4 years	Life
Robbery—firearm	4 years	Life
Sexual assault—firearm	4 years	14 years
Aggravated sexual assault—firearm	4 years	14 years
Driving while impaired	14 days	5 years
Refusing to provide breath sample	14 days	5 years

Source: Adapted from Gabor & Crutcher, 2002.

2. *Presumptive sentencing guidelines.* These guidelines force a judge to make specific sentencing decisions unless there are important reasons for departing from the recommendation.

3. *Mandatory sentencing laws.* Such laws require the judge to make specific sentencing decisions when confronted with particular crimes, regardless of case-specific circumstances.

By 1999, sentencing guidelines in the Criminal Code specified mandatory minimum sentences (MMS) for a total of 29 offences (Gabor & Crutcher, 2002). Table 9.3 provides the guidelines for some of these offences. One reason that these MMS were introduced was to reduce unwarranted sentencing disparity by decreasing the amount of discretion that judges have when making sentencing decisions. Unfortunately, there is little in the way of empirical research to suggest whether current sentencing guidelines in this country are effective in this regard. However, there is research from the United States that has examined the issue. This research frequently suggests that, although judicial discretion seems to be reduced by MMS, sentencing disparity often is not. The likely reason is that the discretion of judges is simply shifted to other criminal justice professionals—namely prosecutors and police officers (Wallace, 1993).

Despite some negative findings, there are examples in which guidelines have resulted in decreased levels of sentencing disparity. For example, Roberts (1991) discusses Minnesota's sentencing guidelines, which have been in place since the early 1980s. Citing from the original report, Roberts (1991) states that "disparity in sentencing decreased under the sentencing guidelines. The reduction in disparity is indicated by increased sentence uniformity and proportionality. Sentences were more uniform in terms of who goes to prison and in how long imprisoned offenders serve" (p. 473). Thus, there are examples in which sentencing guidelines have been successful, just as there are examples in which they have not. What this indicates is that more research is clearly needed to understand the discrepancy in these results. Only in this way will the Canadian criminal justice system learn from these experiences.

Are the Goals of Sentencing Achieved?

Recall from the beginning of this chapter that there are many different goals of sentencing. As a result, the question of whether the goals of sentencing are achieved is a difficult one to answer because, to a large extent, the answer depends on what goal we are most concerned with. For some goals, the answer to this question is often yes. For example, if we sentence an offender to a term in prison, we can be reasonably confident that the offender will be separated from society for a certain period of time. However, with respect to some other goals, the answer is less clear-cut. In particular, there is an ongoing debate as to whether current sentencing practices in Canada achieve the goals of deterring people from committing crimes and whether they assist in the rehabilitation of offenders. Canadian forensic psychologists have played, and continue to play, a crucial role in this debate. See Motiuk and Serin (2001) for an excellent overview of the contributions made by these psychologists.

A lot of recent research has focused specifically on the effectiveness of "get tough" strategies (Cullen & Gendreau, 2000), including a range of punishment-based sentencing options, some consisting of incarceration. Other strategies fall under the heading of intermediate strategies, which are less severe than incarceration but more severe than probation (Gendreau, Goggin, Cullen, & Andrews, 2001). These include "confining offenders to their homes, enforcing curfews, submitting offenders to random drug testing, requiring offenders to pay restitution to victims, electronically monitoring offenders, and requiring offenders to pay for the privilege of being supervised" (Gendreau et al., 2001, pp. 18–19). It has long been assumed that experiencing one of these sanctions would change the antisocial behaviour of offenders and reduce the likelihood that they will reoffend. However, as is the case with the most serious of sanctions, the death penalty, recent research does not support this hypothesis (Gendreau et al., 2001). See Box 9.2 for a discussion of this issue as it relates to the death penalty.

Recent research suggests that "get-tough" strategies for offenders, such as incarceration, may not reduce the chance of reoffending.

The Death Penalty in Canada: Were We Right to Abolish It?

At 12:02 A.M. on December 11, 1962, in Toronto, Ontario, Arthur Lucas and Robert Turpin were the last people to be executed in Canada. Although the death penalty in Canada was formally abolished in 1976 for offences under the Criminal Code, and in 1999 for military offences under the National Defence Act, there are three very good reasons that it is still important to discuss this issue. The first reason is that, since the time when the death penalty was abolished in Canada, there have been attempts to reinstate capital punishment. Indeed, as recently as 1987, Canadian MPs voted on the issue in the House of Commons, with a close vote (148 versus 127) in favour of not reinstating the death penalty. The second reason is that these attempts to reinstate the death penalty seem to reflect public opinion on the issue. Although public support for the death penalty has varied over time, recent Canadian polls indicate that the majority of Canadians are in favour of reinstating the death penalty (notably, the 1998 Gallup poll indicates that 61% of Canadians are in favour of the death penalty for murder) (Edwards & Mazzuca, 1998). The third reason, and one that we will explore here, is that most of the research examining the death penalty suggests that it should not be reinstated in Canada. Although many members of the public believe that the death penalty acts as an effective crime deterrent, research does not support this view.

Existing research suggests there are a number of problems with the crime deterrent argument. First, this argument assumes that offenders think about the punishment before acting. This simply does not appear to be the case for the majority of offenders (Benaquisto, 2000). In fact, a very large number of murders are committed in the heat of passion, or under the influence of alcohol or other drugs, with the offenders paying very little attention to the consequences of their crimes. Second, if the death penalty did act as a crime deterrent, we would expect to see an increase in the Canadian murder rate since abolition. However, the murder rate in Canada has continually declined since 1975. Third, the argument that the death penalty ensures that offenders will never murder again is based on the belief that a high proportion of those released will murder again. In fact, as you will see when we get to the section on parole later in this chapter, it is relatively rare for convicted murderers to commit another murder upon their release from prison.

Source: John Howard Society, 2007.

In a review, Gendreau et al. (2001) examined the rehabilitative and deterrent effect of various community-based sanctions and prison sentences. These researchers used the technique of meta-analysis to summarize findings from research studies that examined the impact of specific sanctions. For our purposes here, the most important measures to focus on from the study are the rate of recidivism for offenders who experienced the sanction, the rate of recidivism for offenders who experienced regular probation (used as a control group), and the average effect size that resulted from a comparison of these two rates. The consideration of effect size is particularly important since this measure summarizes the impact that a particular sanction was found to have across a range of studies. In this case, effect sizes can range from +1.00 to −1.00, with positive effect sizes indicating that the sanction increased recidivism (i.e., compared with probation, those offenders who received the sanction reoffended at a higher rate) and negative effect sizes indicating that the sanction decreased recidivism (i.e., compared with probation, those offenders who received the sanction reoffended at a lower rate).

Based on the results from this study, it must be concluded that there is very little evidence that community sanctions lead to substantial decreases in recidivism rates

Table 9.4 Effects of Community-Based Sanctions and Incarceration on Recidivism

Type of Sanction	Sample Size	Average Effect Size
Supervision program	19 403	0.00
Arrest	7 779	0.01
Fine	7 162	−0.04
Restitution	8 715	−0.02
Boot camp	6 831	0.00
Scared straight	1 891	0.07
Drug testing	419	0.05
Electronic monitoring	1 414	0.05
More versus less prison	68 248	0.03
Prison versus community	267 804	0.07

Source: Adapted from Gendreau et al., 2001.

(compared to regular probation). Indeed, most of the average effect sizes listed in Table 9.4 are positive, indicating that, on average, the particular sanctions listed in this table resulted in moderate increases in recidivism. There were only two sanctions (fines and restitution) that resulted in average effect sizes that were negative, and in these cases the observed decrease in recidivism rates was very small (−0.04 and −0.02, respectively). In addition, this study found that sanctions consisting of incarceration also had little impact on recidivism. In fact, longer periods of incarceration led to slightly higher rates of recidivism across the studies that were examined (+0.03). In addition, those offenders who were sent to prison for brief periods of time also exhibited higher rates of recidivism compared with offenders who received a community-based sanction (+0.07).

What Works in Offender Treatment?

So, given these results, does this mean that nothing can be done to deter or rehabilitate offenders? Historically, some researchers have taken the view that nothing will work with offenders (most notably Martinson, 1974), but new research suggests that this is not the case. In fact, Canadian researchers have led the way in establishing principles of effective correctional intervention, and a growing body of research is beginning to show the value of these principles (Andrews & Bonta, 2006). Although quite a large number of principles are emerging as potentially important (Andrews, 2001), we will focus on three that appear to be particularly valuable in determining which correctional interventions will be effective.

The first of these principles is known as the **need principle**. It states that effective intervention will target known criminogenic needs (factors that are known to contribute to reoffending), including (1) antisocial attitudes, beliefs, and values, (2) antisocial associates, (3) antisocial personality factors (such as impulsivity, risk taking, and low self-control), and (4) antisocial behaviours (Cullen & Gendreau, 2000).

The second principle is known as the **risk principle**. It states that effective interventions will focus on those offenders who are at high risk of reoffending (Cullen & Gendreau,

Need principle: Principle that correctional interventions should target known criminogenic needs (i.e., factors that relate to reoffending)

Risk principle: Principle that correctional interventions should target offenders who are at high risk to reoffend

2000). Not only are low-risk offenders unlikely to reoffend, their chances of reoffending may actually increase if exposed to an intervention, due to the fact they will be brought into contact with people who hold antisocial attitudes (Andrews, 2001).

The third principle is known as the **responsivity principle**. It states that effective interventions will match the general learning styles, motivations, and abilities of the offender being targeted as well as more specific factors such as the offender's personality, gender, ethnicity, and so on (Cullen & Gendreau, 2000).

Responsivity principle: Principle that correctional interventions should match the general learning style of offenders

The often-cited meta-analytic study conducted by Andrews, Zinger, Hoge, Bonta, Gendreau, and Cullen (1990) was one of the first attempts to determine whether interventions with a wide range of juvenile and adult offenders, which consist of these core principles, do in fact lead to reductions in recidivism. These researchers examined 80 program evaluation studies and coded the interventions in each study as appropriate, inappropriate, or unspecified. Interventions were defined as appropriate if they included the three principles of effective intervention described above (most of these programs involved the use of behavioural and social learning principles, which included techniques such as behavioural modelling, rehearsal, role playing, reinforcement, etc.). Interventions were coded as inappropriate if they were inconsistent with these principles (many of these programs were based on get-tough or psychodynamic strategies). Interventions were coded as unspecified if they could not be categorized as appropriate or inappropriate due to a lack of information. The hypothesis in this study was that offenders exposed to appropriate interventions would exhibit lower rates of recidivism compared with offenders exposed to inappropriate interventions. This is exactly what was found. Offenders taking part in appropriate programs exhibited a decrease in recidivism, whereas offenders taking part in inappropriate programs exhibited an increase in recidivism. Offenders taking part in unspecified programs exhibited a decrease in recidivism, though less of a decrease compared to offenders in appropriate programs. Since this study, this same general pattern of results has been found on numerous occasions, for various offending groups (e.g., Andrews, Dowden, & Gendreau, 1999; Antonowicz & Ross, 1994; Pearson, Lipton, & Cleland, 1996).

In conclusion, then, it does appear that something can be done to deter and rehabilitate offenders. By focusing on current research in the area of forensic psychology, interventions can be developed that significantly reduce the chance that offenders will go on to commit further crimes. Certainly, this does not suggest that all new sentencing options will be effective, since many of these new options will not be consistent with the principles of effective correctional programming. However, a number of options have been developed—many in Canada—that do correspond with these principles. Early indications suggest that they hold promise for achieving some of the goals of sentencing that we discussed at the beginning of this chapter (Motiuk & Serin, 2001).

PAROLE IN CANADA

Ever since August 11, 1899, when Parliament enacted the Ticket of Leave Act, **parole** has played an important part in the history of criminal justice in Canada. Sir Wilfrid Laurier, the prime minister at the time, recognized the value of actively reintegrating certain offenders into society as soon as possible in order to enhance their chances of

Parole: The release of offenders from prison into the community before their sentence term is complete rehabilitation (NPB, 2007a). Indeed, he even went so far as to describe the sort of offender that the Act was meant for:

> . . . a young man of good character, who may have committed a crime in a moment of passion, or perhaps, have fallen victim to bad example, or the influence of unworthy friends. There is a good report on him while in confinement and it is supposed that if he were given another chance, he would be a good citizen. (NPB, 2007a)

Since the time of Laurier, many things about parole have changed, but the essence of parole remains the same. Notably, parole still involves (1) the conditional release of offenders into a community so they can serve the remainder of their sentence outside an institution, (2) an attempt to rehabilitate offenders so they can become productive contributors to society, (3) a high degree of community supervision to ensure the parolee is abiding by certain rules, and (4) a clause that, if the conditions of parole are not complied with, an offender's parole can be revoked and he or she can be sent back to prison.

Parole Decision Making

Although the essence of parole may be similar to what it was a century ago, parole decision making has changed drastically. Compared with how parole decisions were once made, the decision-making process is now far more complex and objective. The process that currently exists is more complex because of the range of information that is considered when making parole decisions and because of the way in which that information is evaluated. The process is more objective because, unlike parole decisions made in the past, where an elected member of government was responsible for the decision, parole decisions are now made by a group of individuals forming Canada's **National Parole Board** (NPB). The process that the NPB goes through when making its decisions is open to scrutiny by the public because members of the public are allowed to attend and observe parole hearings and to request copies of written parole board decisions (NPB, 2007b). See Box 9.3 for more information about the NPB.

So, how are parole decisions made? In Canada, an offender must usually serve the first third of the sentence or the first seven years, whichever is less, before being eligible for full parole (NPB, 2007b). Most parole decisions are made after a formal hearing with the offender. When making their decisions, NPB members carefully review the risk that an offender might present to society if he or she is released. According to the NPB (2007b), this involves an initial risk assessment where the following issues are considered:

1. Information about the offender's current offence
2. The offender's criminal history
3. Social problems experienced by the offender, such as drug use and family violence
4. The offender's mental status
5. Performance on earlier releases
6. Information about the offender's relationships and employment history
7. Psychological or psychiatric reports

National Parole Board: The organization in Canada responsible for making parole decisions

Box 9.3

Myths and Realities Concerning Parole Decision Making

The general public has many misconceptions when it comes to issues of parole, and the NPB continually strives to correct them. The following list provides some of the myths people adhere to, along with the correct information provided by the NPB.

Myth #1: Parole reduces the sentence imposed by the courts.

Parole does not reduce the sentence imposed by the courts; it affects only the way in which a sentence will be served. Parole allows offenders to serve their sentences in the community under strict conditions and the supervision of a parole officer. If offenders abide by these conditions, they will remain in the community until their sentence is completed in full, or for life in the case of offenders serving life or indeterminate sentences.

Myth #2: Parole is automatically granted when an inmate becomes eligible for parole consideration.

Parole is not automatically granted when inmates become eligible. In fact, the NPB denies full parole to approximately six out of ten offenders at their first parole review date.

Myth #3: The NPB grants parole to offenders who express remorse for the offences they have committed.

Whether offenders express remorse is only one of the factors the NPB considers. Of greater importance is

whether offenders understand the factors that contributed to their criminal behaviour, the progress they made while incarcerated, and the feasibility of their plans upon release.

Myth #4: Most of the offenders released on parole are convicted of new crimes.

Most offenders released on parole successfully complete their sentences without committing new offences or breaching the conditions of their parole.

Myth #5: Victims do not have a role in the parole process and their views are not taken into account.

Victims and their families have a significant role in the parole process. They have the opportunity to present a statement directly to the NPB about any concerns they have for their safety or the safety of the community. In addition, victims may remain in contact with the NPB while the offender is under sentence. Moreover, the NPB allows victims, as well as other members of the public, to observe parole hearings and to request copies of written decisions.

Source: NPB, 2007c.

8. Opinions from other professionals, such as police officers
9. Information from victims
10. Any other information indicating whether release would pose a risk to society

After this initial assessment, the NPB examines specific risk factors, such as

1. The offender's institutional behaviour

2. Information that indicates evidence of change and insight into the offender's own behaviour

3. Benefits derived from treatment that may reduce the risk posed by the offender

4. The feasibility of the offender's release plans

The NPB members then decide whether to grant parole.

Types of Parole

The NPB can grant various types of parole to offenders. These include temporary absence, day parole, full parole, and statutory release.

Temporary Absence A **temporary absence** is usually the first type of release an offender will be granted (NPB, 2007b). Offenders may be granted unescorted or escorted temporary absence (unescorted absences would typically follow successful escorted absences) so that they can take part in activities such as substance abuse programs, family violence counselling, technical training courses, and so on.

Day Parole Day parole allows offenders to participate in community-based activities. Offenders on day parole must typically return to their institution or halfway house at the end of the day (NPB, 2007b). Performance on day parole is considered when the NPB reviews an offender's application for full parole.

Full Parole Full parole allows the offender to serve the remainder of the sentence under supervision in the community. Before an offender is granted full parole, a thorough assessment is done to predict the likelihood of reoffending (NPB, 2007b). Consideration is also given to what conditions should be implemented to address the chance of risk. In order to be granted full parole, offenders must usually have been granted (and successfully completed) unescorted temporary absences and day parole.

Statutory Release By law, most federal inmates must be released with supervision after serving two-thirds of their sentence, which is known as **statutory release** (NPB, 2007b). (Offenders serving life, however, are not eligible for statutory release.) As with full parole, an assessment is done to predict the likelihood of reoffending and consideration is given as to what conditions should be implemented to address the chance of risk.

In each of the above cases, Correctional Service Canada is responsible for supervising offenders on parole, usually with the assistance of community agencies such as the John Howard Society. If an offender does not abide by the parole conditions, he or she may be returned to prison. The following is a partial list of general parole conditions provided by the NPB (2007b):

1. Offenders must report to their residence immediately upon release.
2. Offenders must report to their parole office on dates set by their parole officer.
3. Offenders must remain in Canada.
4. Offenders must obey the law and keep the peace.
5. Offenders must inform their parole officer if they come into contact with the police.
6. Offenders must advise their parole officer of any changes in address or employment.
7. Offenders must not own or possess any weapon.

Other parole conditions may be specific to the crime that the offender was convicted for (e.g., convicted child molesters may be required to avoid contact with children).

Research on the Effectiveness of Parole

As we noted earlier with regard to sentencing, there has been a great deal of research examining the effectiveness of parole decision making. In fact, the NPB provides updates on the success of their parolees on an annual basis. Many of the statistics published by the NPB compare the success rates of offenders granted day and full parole to those offenders granted statutory release. Recall that, by law, most federal inmates must be released with supervision after serving two-thirds of their sentence. If the NPB is making effective decisions, we would expect to see higher rates of success for offenders on day and full parole, compared with those who have been granted statutory release. This is exactly what the statistics suggest.

For example, as indicated in the most recent *Performance Monitoring Report* published by the NPB (2007), offenders who are granted parole based on an assessment of their risk of re-offending, are more likely to complete their supervision period in the community compared to offenders released as a result of statute-based systems. Of course, this is not to say that offenders granted day or full parole never breach the conditions of their parole or commit further crimes—just that this tends to be the exception rather than the rule.

In support of these claims by the NPB, Figure 9.2 provides data relating to the rate of parole revocation for breach of conditions across different types of parole. This graph clearly indicates that, during the period 2002 to 2007, offenders who were granted statutory release were far more likely to have their parole revoked due to a breach of conditions; however, even in the case of statutory release, a large majority of offenders do not breach their conditions (NPB, 2007).

A similar picture emerges when we examine the rate of revocation due to nonviolent or violent offences. As indicated in Figure 9.3, offenders granted statutory release

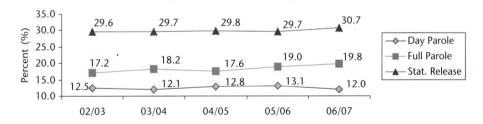

Figure 9.2 Parole Revocation for Breach of Conditions

Source: NPB, 2007.

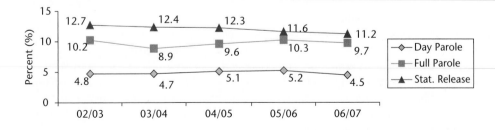

Figure 9.3 Parole Revocation for Nonviolent or Violent Offences

Source: NPB, 2007.

are again the most likely to have their parole revoked due to the commission of a nonviolent or violent offence; however, even these offenders are unlikely to commit further crimes.

PUBLIC ATTITUDES TOWARD SENTENCING AND PAROLE

Having examined in some detail the sentencing and parole process in Canada, let us now focus our attention on the attitudes that Canadians have about these processes. In fact, there is a great deal of research that examines public opinion of the criminal justice system in Canada. Much of this research has been conducted by Dr. Julian Roberts, who is profiled in Box 9.4. This research typically involves the use of one of the following research methods: public opinion surveys, simulation studies, or focus groups (in which a small number of people are brought together for an in-depth discussion of their views on a particular topic). Mostly, the results that emerge from these three different approaches are similar, so we will focus our discussion on the results from public opinion surveys because they are the most commonly used.

Box 9.4

Canadian Researcher Profile: Professor Julian V. Roberts

Since being a graduate student at the University of Toronto, Julian Roberts has been interested in what the public thinks about criminal justice issues. In fact, this is what led him to the area of sentencing research in the first place. He realized this was the criminal justice topic of greatest concern to members of the public. Over the past 30 years, Roberts has built up a research program around this general issue and has conducted research that is both academically important and practically important in terms of its impact on criminal justice policy.

For example, Dr. Roberts recalls a favourite study he conducted with one of his graduate students. The study examined peoples' attitudes toward community-based punishments, specifically conditional sentences. Respondents to a national survey were asked to read a scenario and sentence the offender. When respondents were simply given the choice between a prison sentence and a conditional sentence, they favoured the prison sentence. However, when they were given specific details of what a conditional sentence entails, the large majority favoured

that option, indicating clearly that public opposition to the conditional sentence reflects a lack of knowledge. Since this study was published in the *Canadian Journal of Behavioural Science* in 2000, it has been cited in numerous legal judgments.

After working in various government agencies, such as the Department of Justice Canada and the Canadian Sentencing Commission, Julian Roberts is now a professor of criminology at the University of Oxford. He is very well known for his research in the area of public attitudes toward criminal justice, especially as those attitudes relate to sentencing. Much of this research is available in the books he has written or co-written, including *Understanding Public Attitudes to Criminal Justice*; *Public Opinion, Crime, and Criminal Justice*; *Making Sense of Sentencing*; and *Criminal Justice in Canada: A Reader*. In addition, Professor Roberts was the editor of the *Canadian Journal of Criminology* for several years and is currently the editor of the *European Journal of Criminology*.

A number of general trends can be observed from the results of public opinion surveys. We will provide details of some of the more interesting and important ones before briefly exploring where these attitudes may come from.

1. *Canadians believe that offenders are treated too leniently.* In general, the results from public opinion polls indicate that Canadians perceive that offenders are treated too leniently (Stein, 2001). For example, when respondents are asked about how particular criminal justice institutions deal with offenders, their view is that the courts and the federal government do not treat criminals harshly enough (see Table 9.5). Interestingly, as seen in Table 9.5, Canadians do not necessarily hold the same view of police agencies. This may indicate, as Stein (2001) argues, that these views are specific to agencies involved in the sentencing process.

2. *Canadians do not have a lot of confidence in our criminal justice system.* A similarly negative picture emerges when the general public is asked about the level of confidence they have in the Canadian criminal justice system. For example, relatively few respondents to public opinion polls have a lot of confidence in the criminal justice system, but the degree of confidence varies widely depending on the institution considered (Ipsos-Reid, 2002; Stein, 2001). The institution the public has the most confidence in is the police. The institutions responsible for sentencing and releasing offenders—courts, judges, prosecutors, and parole boards—are viewed with much less confidence. Of course, these findings of low confidence may relate to perceptions that these agencies treat offenders too leniently, as seen in Table 9.5.

3. *Canadians support alternatives to sentencing, but only under certain conditions.* Responses to pubic opinion surveys indicate that a large majority of the public is supportive, in principle, of alternative sentences, such as conditional sentences (Stein, 2001). However, this finding varies depending on the type of penalty and the type of crime considered. For example, the highest level of public support is found for penalties consisting of community service (85%), while the lowest level of support is for parole (37%), but these results hold only for certain offences. For example, conditional sentences are viewed as a viable option for minor assaults (76% in favour of a conditional sentence versus 24% in favour of imprisonment). They are not considered viable for offenders charged with sexual assault (3% in favour of a conditional sentence versus 97% in favour of imprisonment) (Stein, 2001).

Table 9.5 Perceptions of How Criminal Justice Institutions Deal with Offenders

	Not Harshly Enough	Correct Manner	Too Harshly	No Opinion
Courts	72%	19%	2%	7%
Federal government	63%	24%	2%	10%
Police agencies	27%	59%	9%	6%

Source: Adapted from Stein, 2001.

Factors That Influence Public Opinion

Many researchers have claimed that public opinion on issues of sentencing and parole does not fairly reflect the state of affairs in Canada (e.g., Sprott & Doob, 1997). It has been suggested that this discrepancy between public opinion and reality occurs because of an inadequate understanding on the part of the public of crime and our criminal justice system (Sprott & Doob, 1997). Certainly, the results of public opinion surveys support the idea that the public lacks the knowledge required to develop accurate perceptions of the criminal justice system, as do experimental studies that have looked at this issue more directly (e.g., Doob & Roberts, 1988). For example, a very common finding in public opinion surveys is that the public believe that violent crime in general is increasing in Canada (Stein, 2001). This perception, however, does not correspond to actual crime trends in Canada, which indicate a steady decrease in violent crime. Likewise, as indicated above, the public clearly has views on the appropriateness of conditional sentences. Yet, responses to public opinion polls indicate that most people (57%) cannot select the correct definition of a conditional sentence from a list that includes definitions of a conditional sentence, parole, and bail (Stein, 2001).

So, if public opinion is not based on the facts, where does public opinion come from? Sprott and Doob (1997) discuss the view that one important contributing factor is the media or, more specifically, the way the media portray criminal justice issues in Canada. Many studies have shown that the media provide a biased view of our criminal justice system (Doob, 1985), and many researchers hold the view that "members of the public do not adequately correct for the unrepresentative range of cases they hear about in the news media. As a result, the negative feelings and perceptions of leniency that the news media create are perpetuated" (Sprott & Doob, 1997, p. 276). The few experiments that have been done to examine media effects on public opinion in the area of sentencing and parole confirm these views (e.g., Doob & Roberts, 1988).

Another factor that may contribute to this discrepancy, particularly the discrepancy between public opinion of sentencing severity and actual sentencing severity, is the fear people have about being victimized. For example, Sprott and Doob (1997) hypothesized that, the higher the fear of victimization, the more likely a person will be to view the criminal justice system in a negative light. Their reasoning is that fear of crime may motivate an individual to do something about the source of their fear. These individuals may look to the judicial system for safety. Since the judicial system has been unable to adequately deal with the crime problem, those with the most fear might be more likely to view the courts as being too lenient. Because many Canadians are afraid of being victims of crime (Hung & Bowles, 1995), Sprott and Doob's reasoning leads to an expectation that a large portion of the Canadian public will view the criminal justice as lenient, which is exactly what public opinion surveys indicate. By using pre-existing data, Sprott and Doob (1997) were able to examine the relationship between fear of crime and attitudes toward the criminal justice system. Their results confirm their hypotheses. Generally, they found that as "level of fear increased, so did perceptions of leniency in sentencing, dissatisfaction with the courts generally, and dissatisfaction with the police" (Sprott & Doob, 1997, pp. 285–286).

SUMMARY

1. The Canadian court system is one component of the larger Canadian criminal justice system that includes policing agencies and correctional institutions. The court system in Canada is made up of numerous types of courts that are separated by jurisdiction and levels of legal superiority.

2. Sentences are supposed to serve a number of different purposes in Canada. Deterring people from committing crimes and offender rehabilitation are two of the primary purposes. Sentencing in Canada is also guided by numerous principles, such as the fundamental sentencing principle, which states that a sentence must be proportionate to the gravity of the offence and the degree of responsibility of the offender. Such principles are meant to provide judges with guidance when handing down sentences.

3. Judges have many sentencing options at their disposal. The most common sentencing option in Canada is the monetary fine, and the most serious option is imprisonment. New sentencing options have also been recently proposed, such as the conditional sentence, in which an offender can serve his or her prison time in the community.

4. One of the major problems with sentencing in Canada is unwarranted sentencing disparity, which refers to differences in the severity of sentences handed down by different judges (or the same judge on different occasions) due to a reliance on extra-legal factors. These factors can include the judge's personality, philosophy, experience, and so on. One of the primary strategies for reducing sentencing disparity is to implement sentencing guidelines.

5. Research examining the impact of punishment-based sentences suggests they are not effective for reducing recidivism. In contrast, correctional interventions based on core correctional principles show more promise. These principles include the need principle (effective interventions target criminogenic needs), the risk principle (effective interventions target high-risk offenders), and the responsivity principle (effective interventions match the general learning style, and the particular characteristics, of the offender).

6. The NPB makes parole decisions in Canada. Contrary to popular belief, parole is not automatically granted to offenders as soon as they become eligible. Offender remorse plays only a very small part in parole decisions. Most offenders let out on parole do not go on to commit more crimes, and victims do have a significant say in the parole process.

Key Concepts

absolute discharge 254

community service 254

conditional discharge 254

conditional sentence 254

dangerous offender 255

day parole 268

fine 256

full parole 268

fundamental principle of sentencing 254

general deterrence 253

imprisonment 254

long-term offender 256

National Parole Board 266

need principle 264

parole 265

probation 254

reparations 253

responsivity principle 265

restitution 254

risk principle 264

sentencing disparity 257

sentencing guidelines 260

specific deterrence 253

statutory release 268

Supreme Court of Canada 252

systematic disparity 258

temporary absence 268

unsystematic disparity 258

unwarranted sentencing disparity 258

Discussion Questions

1. You are a provincial court judge and have to hand down a sentence to an offender who has committed armed robbery. From the list of sentencing goals presented in this chapter, what is the most important goal that you would try to accomplish with the sentence you hand down? What factors influence your answer and why?

2. In your opinion, should offenders who are convicted of serious crimes such as sexual assault ever become eligible for parole? Why or why not?

3. Imagine that you are a judge giving a guest lecture in an undergraduate forensic psychology class like the one that you are enrolled in now. One of the bright students attending your lecture asks what it really means when an offender is sentenced to life in prison. Does a life sentence really mean life? How would you answer that student?

4. You have just been hired as a research assistant by one of your professors. She is working on a government project looking at ways to deal with sentencing disparity. Together, you and your professor must propose strategies, beyond the sentencing guidelines that currently exist, that could be used to reduce unwarranted sentencing disparity in Canada. What types of strategies would you propose?

5. Your neighbour thinks Canada is getting soft on crime by providing community "rehabilitation" programs. He thinks the only way to really rehabilitate offenders is to lock them up in cells with nothing to do but ruminate on the crimes they've committed. Do you think your neighbour is right? Explain.

6. Recent results from public opinion polls suggest that, even when the public is told that the death penalty has little impact as a crime deterrent, the majority still support the death penalty. Why do you think this happens?

7. Beyond the factors we have discussed in this chapter, what might account for the inaccurate perceptions of the public when it comes to sentencing and parole practices in Canada? What can be done to decrease these inaccurate perceptions?

Readings

Andrews, D., & Bonta, J. (2006). *The psychology of criminal conduct* (4th edition). Cincinnati: Anderson Publishing Company.

Palys, T.S., & Divorski, S. (1986). Explaining sentencing disparity. *Canadian Journal of Criminology, 28,* 347–362.

Roberts, J.V., & Cole, D. (Eds.). (1999). *Making sense of sentencing.* Toronto: University of Toronto Press.

Websites

Correctional Service Canada
www.csc-scc.gc.ca

The John Howard Society
www.johnhoward.ca

Canada's National Parole Board
www.npb-cnlc.gc.ca/about/about_e.htm

Chapter 10
Domestic Violence and Sexual Offenders

Learning Objectives

- Explain why some women remain in, or return to, an abusive relationship.

- Describe the various types of male batterers.

- Outline how social learning theory has been used to explain domestic violence.

- List the different typologies of child molesters and rapists.

- Outline the treatment targets for sexual offenders.

- Describe the effectiveness of sexual offender treatment.

Mohadaseh Farias is serving a federal sentence for two counts of sexual assault. He has been attending a cognitive-behavioural treatment program for sexual offenders for two months. The program consists of individual and group therapy. One therapist thinks Mohadaseh is making considerable progress in treatment, whereas the other therapist is less optimistic. In group therapy, Mohadaseh is evasive when challenged, has been vindictive toward other group members, and is continually testing boundaries. The therapist that has been concerned with Mohadaseh's attitudes and behaviour thinks that Mohadaseh is not genuinely interested in changing.

Violence has a major impact on victims and society. Media such as television and newspapers focus on violent crime and, as a consequence, violence is often on the minds of the public. Violence and its aftermath is also a major focus of forensic psychology, with psychologists involved in developing assessment and intervention programs for violent offenders. This chapter is divided into two parts. In the first part, we cover violence in domestic settings; in the second part, we examine sexual violence. Major themes in each section are the prevalence of violence, its causes, and interventions.

DOMESTIC VIOLENCE

Domestic violence: Any violence occurring between family members

The term **domestic violence** refers to any violence occurring between family members. Domestic violence typically occurs in private settings. Although not necessarily condoned, historically it was tolerated and was not subject to effective legal sanctions. Reasons for this were varied, but religious and cultural attitudes generally positioned women and children in deferential roles within families. In Canada, little attention was paid to domestic violence prior to the 1980s. It was the women's liberation movement and the growth of feminism that gave women the courage to speak out against such violence. Since that time, however, domestic violence has become a major focus of research and legal action. The Jane (Stafford) Hurshman-Corkum case in Nova Scotia brought to the forefront the plight of abused women (see Chapter 13).

In this section, we will focus on violence occurring between intimate partners who are living together or separated (called spousal violence or **intimate partner violence**). Abuse and aggression within intimate relationships has a long history and is, unfortunately, still common. Violence against partners is varied in terms of types and severity and includes physical (e.g., hitting, punching, stabbing, burning), sexual, financial (e.g., restricting access to personal funds, forcing complete financial responsibility, theft of paycheques), and emotional abuse (e.g., verbal attacks, degradation, threats to hurt family members or pets, isolation from family members, unwarranted accusations about infidelity).

Intimate partner violence: Any violence occurring between intimate partners who are living together or separated. Also known as spousal violence

THE CONFLICT TACTICS SCALE

The scale most commonly used to measure domestic assault has been the Conflict Tactics Scale (CTS) (Straus, 1979). This scale consists of 18 items intended to measure how the person and his or her partner resolve conflict. The items range from constructive problem solving (e.g., discuss the item calmly) to verbal or indirect aggression (e.g., swearing or threatening to hit) to physical aggression (e.g., slapping or using a gun). Respondents are asked how frequently they have engaged in the behaviour and how often they have experienced these acts. Researchers using the CTS have found that male and female respondents report the same frequency and severity of violent behaviour (Magdol, Moffitt, & Caspi, 1997). Box 10.1 on page 278 provides more details about the prevalence and severity of mutual violence, as well as gender-specific differences.

A victim of domestic violence

Box 10.1

Husband Battering Does Exist

Domestic violence is certainly not exclusively initiated by men. In a recent review of the literature on women as perpetrators of intimate violence, Carney, Buttell, and Dutton (2007) address the following questions.

■ Is domestic violence invariably male-initiated?

The answer is no. It appears that women engage in the same amount of violence as men, and some studies found that women engaged in more minor violence than men (Archer, 2002). Williams and Frieze (2005) analyzed the different violence patterns of 3519 couples and found that the most common type of violence was mutual mild violence, followed by mutual severe violence. Thus, the long-assumed gender gap does not exist. As Carney et al. (2007) conclude, "female violence is common, [and] occurs at the same rate as male violence" (p. 113).

■ Do males suffer any serious consequences of female-initiated violence?

The answer is yes. Felson and Cares (2005) reported that in intimate partner violence, men were more likely than women to suffer serious injuries. In a recent reanalysis of the Canadian General Social Survey data, Laroche (2005) found that 83% of men "feared for their life," as compared to 77% of women, when being unilaterally terrorized by their partner. Rates of domestic terrorism were similar for men and women across several measures. Men and women who were victims of intimate partner violence received medical care (84% for both men and women), sought psychological counselling (62% of men and 63% of women), and reported everyday routines being disrupted (80% of men and 74% of women). Based on their review of the literature, Carney et al. (2007) conclude, "(1) women are injured more than men but (2) men are injured as well and are not immune to being seriously injured." (p. 110).

■ Is there a gender bias in police responses to domestic violence?

The limited research indicates the answer is yes. Brown (2004) studied differences in arrest rates in cases of injury and no-injury assaults. When the female partner was injured, the male was charged in 91% of the cases; however, when the male was injured, the female was charged 60% of the time. When no injury occurred, the female was charged in 13% of cases as compared to 52% of the time for males.

■ Do the courts treat men and women charged with domestic violence the same way?

The answer is no. Women are more likely to have the charges against them dropped by prosecutors and are less likely to be found guilty. For example, Brown (2004) reported that in severe injury cases, 71% of men and 22% of women defendants were found guilty. A major factor for why such a low percentage of women were found guilty was that the male victim was not willing to testify.

Archer (2002) conducted a meta-analysis of 48 studies using the CTS and found that females are more likely to engage in minor physical aggression, such as slapping, kicking, or hitting with an object, whereas men are more likely to beat up or to choke their partner. Large differences were found when comparing community, university student, and treatment samples (couples in treatment for the husband's violence). Within treatment samples, men engage in much higher rates of minor and severe physical violence compared with students and community samples. Within community and university student samples, males and females commit equal amounts of violence. Comparing self- and partner reports, respondents report fewer violent acts than their partners, and men are more likely to under-report than women.

Although commonly used, the CTS is often criticized for a number of reasons (Dobash & Dobash, 1979; Ratner, 1998):

1. The way it is introduced to respondents has been criticized. Respondents read the following: "No matter how well a couple get along, there are times when they disagree, get annoyed with the other person or just have spats or fights because

they're in a bad mood or for some other reason. They also use many different ways of trying to settle their differences" (Straus, 1990, p. 33). The introduction to a questionnaire is crucial since it provides respondents with information on what to focus on. In the case of the CTS, it is on how they settle disputes. However, some acts of violence are not precipitated by an argument and therefore the respondent may not report these.

2. The CTS does not include the full range of potential violent acts. For example, sexual aggression is not included.

3. It is likely that different results would be found if acts like kicking, biting, and punching were not combined into one item.

4. The CTS does not take into account the different consequences of the same act for men and women. For example, treating a punch by a woman and man as equivalent ignores the difference in the injury that might be inflicted (Nazroo, 1995). Surveys have consistently shown that women are more likely than men are to suffer both physical and psychological consequences from domestic violence (Saunders, 2002). Tjaden and Thoennes (2001) reported an injury rate of 42% for women versus 19% for men in the most recent violent episode. Canadian women reported that they had been physically injured in 44% of all cases of intimate violence, and in 13% of cases they sought and received medical care.

5. The CTS does not assess motive for violence and therefore offensive violence is treated as equal to a defensive response. For example, consider the case of a couple arguing. If he threatens to punch her, and she pushes him away from her, both acts would be included on the CTS.

6. Items on the CTS may be interpreted differently depending on the gender of the respondent.

In response to these and other criticisms, Straus, Hamby, Boney-McCoy, and Sugarman (1996) revised the CTS (CTS2), deleting some items and adding new items. For example, physically aggressive acts, such as slamming a person against a wall, burning them on purpose, and sexual aggression, have been included. Moreover, the consequence (physical injury) has also been added. Researchers are beginning to use the CTS2 in studies of domestic violence.

Intimate Partners: A Risky Relationship

In the 1993 Statistics Canada Violence Against Women Survey, 51% of women reported at least one incident of physical or sexual violence since the age of 16 (Johnson, 1996). Violence within dating relationships is also common in university students. DeKeseredy and Kelly (1993) surveyed 3142 university students across Canada and reported that 35% of female students and 17% of male students had been physically abused at least once in a dating relationship.

The most recent Canadian survey on intimate partner assault was conducted by Statistics Canada in 2004 (Statistics Canada, 2006a). This survey used a modified CTS to measure psychological, physical, and sexual violence in intimate relationships. Large samples of men (10 604) and women (13 162) from all provinces and territories were asked questions about their experiences with various forms of intimate partner violence, ranging from threats to sexual assault, in the last 12 months and the past five years. In the year preceding the survey, 2% of men and women experienced physical and/or sexual assault. Seven percent of female and 6% of male respondents reported having experienced physical and/or sexual assault between 1999 and 2004. Table 10.1 presents the percentage of men and women experiencing different types of violence in the past five years. The results indicate that both men and women experience violence, although women report experiencing more severe forms of violence (i.e., being choked, sexually assaulted, threatened by a partner with a knife or gun). Respondents were asked about whether the violence was reported to police. Violence against women was more likely to be reported to the police (36%) than was violence against men (17%).

Theories of Intimate Violence

Some researchers believe that a patriarchal society contributes to the domestic assault of women by men (e.g., Dobash & Dobash, 1979; Ellis, 1989; Straus, 1977). The theory of patriarchy was first described in the 1970s and is often associated with sociology and feminism. **Patriarchy** refers to a broad set of cultural beliefs and values that support the male dominance of women. As stated by Dobash and Dobash (1979), "the seeds of wife beating lie in the subordination of females and in their subjection to male authority and control" (p. 33). Smith (1990) has proposed a distinction between "social" patriarchy (male domination at the social level) and "familial" patriarchy (male domination within the family). To study the association between patriarchy and spousal abuse, Yllo and Straus (1990) compared the rates of spousal abuse across American states with the degree to which each state was characterized by patriarchal structure. States with male-dominant norms had much higher rates of spousal assault than those with more egalitarian norms.

Patriarchy: Broad set of cultural beliefs and values that support the male dominance of women

Table 10.1 Types of Relationship Violence Experienced over the Past Five Years

Type of Violence	Men (%)	Women (%)
Threw something	49	44
Pushed, shoved	48	81
Threatened to hit	53	61
Slapped	57	36
Hit with object	23	23
Kicked, bit, hit	40	27
Beat up	8	19
Forced sex	—	16
Choked	5	19
Threatened to use/used gun or knife	9	11

Note: — = data not available
Source: Statistics Canada, 2006a.

Patriarchy likely influences the development of individual expectations about the appropriate level of authority within intimate relationships. One difficulty for patriarchal accounts of domestic violence is that it does not predict which individuals within a system will engage in intimate violence. Other factors operating in the community (e.g., work, peers), family (e.g., communication level between couple), and individual (e.g., coping skills, empathy) are needed to provide an explanation (Dutton, 1995). For example, consider two men who are raised to value the same cultural beliefs, who have similar social supports and identical levels of conflict in the home; one man may react with violence whereas the other does not.

Social learning theory was developed by Bandura (1973) to explain aggression and has been applied by Dutton (1995) to explain spousal assault. There are three main components to social learning theory: origins of aggression, instigators of aggression, and regulators of aggression. One way people acquire new behaviours is via **observational learning**. Bandura (1973) describes three major sources for observational learning: family of origin, the subculture the person lives in, and televised violence. Studies of the family background of male batterers have found they are much more likely to have witnessed parental violence than are nonviolent men (Kalmuss, 1984; Straus, Gelles, & Steinmetz, 1980). Not all behaviour that is observed, however, will be practised. Social learning theory posits that in order for a person to acquire a behaviour, it must have functional value for him or her. Behaviour that is rewarded increases in likelihood of occurrence and behaviour that is punished decreases in likelihood of occurrence.

> **Social learning theory:** A theory of human behaviour based on learning from watching others in the social environment and reinforcement contingencies

> **Observational learning:** Learning behaviours by watching others perform these behaviours

The next requirement is that even acquired behaviours are only manifested if there is an appropriate event in the environment to act as a stimulus for the behaviour. These are called **instigators**. Dutton (1995) describes two types of instigators in domestic assault: aversive instigators and incentive instigators. Aversive instigators produce emotional arousal and how a person labels that emotional arousal will influence how he or she responds. Studies with male batterers have found that they tend to label many different emotional states as anger (Gondolf, 1985, labels this the *male-emotional funnel system*). Incentive instigators are perceived rewards for engaging in aggression. When people believe they can satisfy their needs by using aggression, they may decide to be violent.

> **Instigators:** In social learning theory, these are events in the environment that act as a stimulus for acquired behaviours

Social learning theory assumes that behaviour is regulated by its consequences. Two types of **regulators** include external punishment and self-punishment. An example of external punishment would be if the person was arrested for engaging in violence. An example of self-punishment would be if the person felt remorse for engaging in violence. If the consequences outweigh the rewards for engaging in the behaviour and if alternatives are provided to cope with instigators, the likelihood of violence should diminish.

> **Regulators:** In social learning theory, these are consequences of behaviours

Why Do Battered Women Stay?

One of the more perplexing questions is, "If a woman is in an abusive relationship, why doesn't she just leave?" Although intimate violence is no longer sanctioned by society, negative myths and stereotypes concerning battered woman still prevail. These myths include that a battered woman has a masochistic desire to be beaten, that she is emotionally disturbed, that the violence cannot be as bad as she claims, and that the woman is partially to blame for her victimization (Ewing & Aubrey, 1987; Harrison & Esqueda, 1999; Walker, 1979).

The extent to which people believe such myths varies (Ewing & Aubrey, 1987; Greene, Raitz, & Lindblad, 1989). To examine myths about battered women, Ewing and Aubrey (1987) gave community samples a hypothetical scenario about a couple having ongoing marital problems, including a description of an incident in which the husband assaulted his wife (the husband accused his wife of cheating on him and grabbed her and threw her to the floor). The percentage of males and females agreeing with each statement are shown in parentheses:

- The female victim "bears at least some responsibility." (Males = 47%; Females = 30%)
- The battered woman could simply leave her battering husband. (Males = 57%; Females = 71%)
- The battered woman who stays is "somewhat masochistic." (Males = 24%; Females = 50%)
- The woman can prevent battering by seeking counselling. (Males = 86%; Females 81%)
- Battering is an isolated event. (Males = 40%; Females = 27%)
- The woman can rely on the police to protect her. (Males = 18%; Females = 15%)

Researchers have asked victims of domestic violence why they stay in the relationship, and for those who returned after separating, why they did so. The decision to stay with, to leave, or to return to an abusive partner is complex. According to the Violence Against Women Survey (Johnson, 1996), 42% of women left their abusive partners for a short while or permanently. The primary reasons given for leaving were related to the increases in the severity of the violence (e.g., if they feared for their lives or were physically injured), having children witness the violence, and reporting the abuse to the police. Seventy percent of women who left their abusive partners returned home at least once. The most common reasons for returning were

- for the sake of the children (31%)
- to give the relationship another chance (24%)
- the partner promised to change (17%)
- lack of money or a place to go (9%)

Similar findings have been reported by Anderson, Gillig, Sitaker, McCloskey, Malloy, and Grigsby (2003) in a study of victims of intimate violence. In this study, 400 women who sought help from a domestic violence advocacy centre were asked, "If you never left your mate or returned to your mate after separating, check those factors that affected your decision" (p. 152). Thirty-two potential factors were listed and most women endorsed several different reasons. The reasons included

- mate promised to change (71%)
- lack of money (46%)
- mate needed me (36%)
- nowhere to go or stay (29%)
- threats of mate to find me and kill me (22%)
- children [with me] wanted to go back (19%)
- shelter was full (5%)

This study and others point to the environmental, socialization, and psychological barriers that exist for victims. In order for a woman to leave, she needs resources such as money, a place to go, and support from the criminal justice system (examples of environmental barriers). Women are socialized to be the primary caretaker in relationships and appear to place a high value on the promises of the abuser to change. In addition, they return because they do not want their children to suffer (35%). Psychological barriers also exist. Some victims reported that they felt safer remaining in the relationship than leaving, because they knew what the abuser was doing (22%).

Recently, researchers have begun to study the link between family violence and animal maltreatment. Growing evidence suggests that batterers often threaten or harm their partners' pets and that one reason women delay leaving is out of concern for the welfare of their pets (Ascione, 1998; Faver & Strand, 2003; Flynn, 2000). Box 10.2 describes one such study. Although a link between maltreatment of animals and domestic violence may appear insignificant in relation to other factors, it underscores the complexity of the variables associated with remaining in a violent relationship.

Box 10.2

Woman's Best Friend: Pet Abuse and Intimate Violence

Only recently have researchers started to investigate the link between animal maltreatment and violence against women (Ascione, 1998; Ascione, Weber, Thompson, Heath, Maruyama, & Hayashi, 2007; Faver & Strand, 2003). In a study of women in domestic violence shelters, Ascione (1998) reported that 72% said their partners had either threatened to harm or actually had harmed their pets. Moreover, 54% reported that their pets had actually been injured or killed by their abusive partners. Compared to women who said they had not experienced intimate *violence*, Ascione et al. (2007) found that women in domestic violence shelters were 11 times more likely to indicate that their partner had hurt or killed pets. Faver and Strand (2003) questioned 50 abused women who owned pets and found that 49% reported their partners had threatened their pets and 46% indicated that their partner had actually harmed their pets.

Flynn (2000) asked a series of questions about the women's experiences with their pets:

1. In dealing with the abuse, how important has your pet been as a source of emotional support?

2. Has your partner ever threatened to harm your pet, actually harmed your pet, or killed your pet?

3. Where is your pet now?

4. Did concern about your pet's safety keep you from seeking shelter sooner?

Flynn divided the sample of 42 battered women into a pet-abuse group ($n = 20$) and the no-pet-abuse group ($n = 22$). Ninety percent of the women in the pet-abuse group considered their pet a source of emotional support, compared with 47% of the no-pet-abuse group. About half of the pets in both groups were left with the abusive partner. In light of the partner's history of pet abuse, it is not surprising that 65% of the women in the pet-abuse group worried about the safety of their pets, whereas only 15% of the women in the no-pet-abuse group were concerned. Eight women actually delayed leaving their abusive partner out of concern for their pets' safety, with five of these women reporting that they delayed leaving for more than two months. Flynn concluded that "efforts to prevent and end such violence must not only recognize the interconnections, but grant legitimacy to all victims, human and animal" (p. 176).

A Heterogeneous Population: Typologies of Male Batterers

There is an increasing body of empirical research demonstrating that not all batterers are alike. Categories of male batterers have been developed in order to help understand the causes of intimate violence. Holtzworth-Munroe and Stuart (1994) divided male batterers into three types based on severity of violence, generality of violence, and personality disorder characteristics: family only, dysphoric/borderline, and generally violent/antisocial.

Family-only batterer: A male spousal batterer who is typically not violent outside the home, does not show much psychopathology, and does not possess negative attitudes supportive of violence

The **family-only batterer**

- of all types of batterers, engages in the least amount of violence
- typically neither is violent outside the home nor engages in other criminal behaviours
- does not show much psychopathology, and if a personality disorder is present, it would most likely be passive-dependent personality
- does not report negative attitudes supportive of violence and has moderate impulse-control problems
- typically displays no disturbance in attachment to his partner

Dysphoric/borderline batterer: A male spousal batterer who exhibits some violence outside the family, is depressed and has borderline personality traits, and has problems with jealousy

The **dysphoric/borderline batterer**

- engages in moderate to severe violence
- exhibits some extra-familial violence and criminal behaviour
- of all types of batterers, displays the most depression and borderline personality traits, and has problems with jealousy
- has moderate problems with impulsivity and alcohol and drug use
- has an attachment style that would be best described as preoccupied

Generally violent/antisocial batterer: A male spousal batterer who is violent outside the home, engages in other criminal acts, has drug and alcohol problems, has impulse-control problems, and possesses violence-supportive beliefs

The **generally violent/antisocial batterer**

- engages in moderate to severe violence
- of all types of batterers, engages in the most violence outside of the home and in criminal behaviour
- has antisocial and narcissistic personality features
- likely has drug and alcohol problems
- has high levels of impulse-control problems and many violence-supportive beliefs
- shows a dismissive attachment style

Several studies have provided support for this typology both in offender and in community samples of male batterers (Tweed & Dutton, 1998; Waltz, Babcock, Jacobson, & Gottman, 2000). Other typologies have also been proposed. For example, Gondolf (1988), using data from battered women admitted to shelters in Texas, proposed three typologies. The Type I batterer, identified as the *sociopathic* (accounting for about 5% to 8% of batterers), engaged in the most severe abuse against both women and children and was most likely to have a criminal record. The Type II batterer, labelled *antisocial* (accounting for about 30% to 40% of batterers), was similar to the sociopathic batterer but was less likely to have a criminal record. The Type III batterer, referred to as the *typical* batterer (most common type), perpetrated less severe violence, was more likely to be apologetic after abusive behaviour, and was least likely to have a criminal record. Based on a review of the existing batterer typologies, Cavanaugh and Gelles (2005) suggested that batterer subtypes can be classified along four descriptive dimensions: (1) severity of violence, (2) frequency of violence, (3) male batterer's psychopathology, and (4) criminal history. Using these dimensions, they propose three major subtypes: low-, medium-, and high-risk batterers. Low-risk batterers engage in low severity and frequency of violence, exhibit little or no psychopathology, and usually have no criminal history. Medium-risk batterers engage in moderate frequency and severity and have moderate to high psychopathology. Finally, high-risk batterers engage in the most frequent and severe violence, have a high level of psychopathology, and usually have a criminal history.

Criminal Justice Response

For centuries, wife battering was seen as a private family matter and police were reluctant to become involved (Dobash & Dobash, 1979). When called to a domestic violence scene, police would attempt to calm the people involved and, once order was restored, they would leave (Jaffe, Hastings, Reitzel, & Austin, 1993). Since the 1980s, however, mandatory charging policies have been in effect in Canada and in most jurisdictions in the United States. **Mandatory charging policies** give police the authority to lay charges against a suspect when there are reasonable and probable grounds to believe that an assault has occurred. Prior to mandatory charging, women were required to bring charges against their husbands. Women were often too intimidated and feared further violence—as a result, charges were usually not laid.

Mandatory charging policies: Policies that give police the authority to lay charges against a suspect where there is reasonable and probable grounds to believe a domestic assault has occurred

The first experimental study to examine the specific deterrence effect of arrest on spousal violence was conducted by Sherman and Berk (1984) in Minneapolis. This study involved the random assignment of 314 domestic assault calls to three police responses: separation (order for suspect to leave premises for at least eight hours), mediation (provide advice to victim), or arrest. A six-month follow-up of the men was conducted using both police reports and victim reports. Figure 10.1 on page 286 presents the recidivism rates across the groups for both police and victim reports. The recidivism rates for the arrested men were much lower than those of men in the separation or mediation groups. Attempts to replicate this finding have met with mixed results. Tolman and Weisz (1995) also found a deterrent effect for arrest, whereas Hirschell, Hutchinson, and Dean (1990) did not. In an attempt to replicate their findings, Sherman, Schmidt, and Rogan (1992) randomly assigned police calls of domestic violence to nonarrest or arrest. Using police and victim reports, lower rates of recidivism were reported in the short term (30 days after police contact) for both arrest and nonarrest groups. However, in the long-term follow-up (seven to nine months after police contact) the arrest group had slightly higher rates of recidivism than did the nonarrest group. The authors found that arrest does not work for those offenders who were unemployed. In other words, arrest worked as a deterrent only for those men who had something to lose.

Do mandatory arrest policies increase the probability of domestic abusers being arrested? Arrest rates for intimate partner violence have increased dramatically since mandatory arrest policies were implemented. For example, in the 1970s and 1980s, arrest rates in Canada and the United States ranged from 7% to 15%, whereas more recent rates

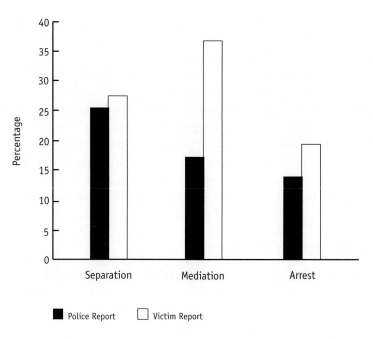

Figure 10.1 Rates of Recidivism for Different Police Responses

Source: Sherman and Berk, 1984.

of 30% to 75% have been reported. However, one unanticipated outcome of these policies has been an increase in dual arrests (Hirschel & Buzawa, 2002). If the police are unable to determine the identity of the primary aggressor, and if there are minor injuries to both parties, the police will charge both the man and woman.

Another consequence of the increase in the number of arrests for domestic assault has been the dramatic increase in the number of men who are court-mandated to attend treatment. Since most batterers are not motivated to attend treatment programs, having judges impose a treatment order forces men to obtain treatment. If the man fails to attend treatment, a prison term can be imposed. The use of court-mandated treatment is based on the belief that it is possible to treat male batterers. However, the effectiveness of treatment for batterers is still very much in question.

Does Treatment of Male Batterers Work?

A number of different procedures have been developed to treat male batterers. The two most common forms of intervention are feminist psychoeducational group therapy (also referred to as the Duluth model, since the treatment was designed at the Duluth Domestic Abuse Intervention Project in Minnesota) and cognitive-behavioural group therapy. According to the Duluth model (Pence & Paymar, 1993), the primary cause of domestic violence is patriarchal ideology. Group therapy in this model focuses on challenging the man's perceived right to control his partner.

In contrast, cognitive-behavioural therapy subscribes to the belief that violence is a learned behaviour and that use of violence is reinforcing for the offender by obtaining victim compliance and by reducing feelings of tension (Sonkin, Martin, & Walker, 1985).

Cognitive-behavioural therapy focuses on the costs of engaging in violence. Alternatives to violence are taught, such as anger-management and communication-skills training. Some cognitive-behavioural treatment programs also address perpetrators' attitudes about control and dominance. The rationale for using group therapy is to help break through the barriers of denial and minimization.

Babcock, Green, and Robie (2004) conducted a meta-analysis of 22 studies to evaluate the efficacy of treatment for male batterers. Studies were included only if the outcome was measured by either police reports or partner reports of violence (i.e., studies using only batterer self-report were not included). Studies were also divided into three types of treatment:

Group therapy for male batterers

the Duluth model, cognitive-behavioural, and other (e.g., couples therapy). There were no differences in efficacy among the three treatment types in terms of recidivism rates. Based on partner reports, the effect size for quasi-experimental studies was $d = 0.34$ and for experimental studies it was $d = 0.09$. The authors conclude that "regardless of reporting method, study design, and type of treatment, the effect on recidivism rates remains in the small range" (p. 1044). Based on experimental studies and using partner reports, these results mean there is a 5% increase in success rate due to treatment. This small effect does not mean we should abandon attempts to treat batterers. As stated by the authors, "a 5% decrease in violence . . . in [the] United States . . . would equate to approximately 42,000 women per year no longer being battered" (p. 1044). Although the effects appear to be small, they are similar to treatment effects for alcohol abuse if abstinence from alcohol is the outcome (Agosti, 1995).

Recent research, however, is more optimistic about the promise of domestic violence treatment. Bennett, Stoops, Call, and Flett (2007) found that even when controlling for differences in the history of violence, personality, demographic variables, and motivation, men who completed treatment were less than half as likely to be re-arrested for domestic violence than those who did not finish the intervention program. Bowen and Gilchrist (2006) identified participant characteristics that predict program attrition, including youthful age, having served a previous prison sentence, and self-reporting a low level of partner violence. The researchers recommended using these static factors to tailor domestic violence treatment and prevent program attrition so that participants can benefit from treatment. In another study, Lee, Uken and Sebold (2007) recommended the inclusion of more self-determined goals for offenders in treatment, based on their study of 88 male perpetrators of domestic violence participating in court-mandated treatment. They found that goal specificity and the facilitator's agreement with the participant's goals positively predicted offenders' confidence to achieve their goals, which in turn had a negative relationship with recidivism.

Future research should examine the treatment response of specific subsamples, such as types of batterers (e.g., family-only, borderline/dysphoric, and generally violent/antisocial), batterers with substance abuse problems, and batterers at different levels of motivation. As Saunders (2001) has asserted, "The best intervention outcomes for men who batter may be obtained when the type of offender is matched to the type of treatment" (p. 237). Failure to match a batterer to treatment services may lead to a batterer completing a program that does not meet his specific treatment needs. Cavanagh and Gelles (2005) point out that a victim could thus be led to having a "false sense of security, with the belief that she is now safer when, in fact, she is not." (p. 162). According to Gondolf and Fisher (1988), the variable most predictive of whether or not a woman will return to a violent partner after a shelter stay is if the batterer has sought treatment. In addition, future research needs to focus on women's use of violence and to develop interventions for domestically violent women.

SEXUAL OFFENDERS
Nature and Extent of Sexual Violence

Sexual violence is on par with homicide in terms of how perpetrators are vilified by society. In 2005, just over 23 000 sexual assaults were reported to the police in Canada (Statistics Canada, 2006a). The rate per 100 000 population was 72 and has remained stable over the past 5 years. However, official statistics do not provide an accurate measure of the true incidence of this type of crime, since the majority of victims do not report the crime to the police (Yurchesyn, Keith, & Renner, 1992). Approximately 8% of sexual assault victims reported the crime to the police in 2003 (Statistics Canada, 2006a).

Sexual assault affects a large percentage of the population. High victimization rates are reported among children and youth (roughly 1 in 12 in the United States) (Finkelhor, Ormrod, Turner, & Hamby, 2005) and adult women (10% to 20% report being raped; Johnson & Sacco, 1995; Koss, 1993). In a review of community samples, Gorey and Leslie (1997) calculated the prevalence of childhood sexual abuse as 17% for females and 8% for males. Given the large number of victims, it is not surprising that sexual offenders admit to having many victims. For example, Abel, Becker, Mittelman, and Cunningham-Rathner (1987) investigated the number of victims reported by 127 rapists, 224 female-victim child molesters, and 153 male-victim child molesters. High victim rates were reported, with rapists having on average 7 victims, female-victim child molesters having 20 victims, and male-victim child molesters averaging 150 victims. In studies of community samples (e.g., university students, hospital staff) in which the respondent was assured there would be no negative consequences of reporting, 10% to 20% of men admit to sexually assaulting women or children (Hanson & Scott, 1995; Lisak & Roth, 1988). Society's recognition of the seriousness and widespread occurrence of sexual assault has been in part responsible for the substantial increase in the number of Canadian federal sexual offenders. Since the late 1970s, the number of sexual offenders incarcerated has grown rapidly. For example, in 1984 there were 870 federal sex offenders (Robinson, 1989), but that number climbed to 2300 in 2004 (Motiuk & Vuong, 2005).

Sexual aggression has serious negative psychological and physical consequences. Victims of rape report high levels of stress and fear that disrupt social, sexual, and occupational functioning, while also generating high levels of anxiety and depression (Hanson,

1990). Physically, Koss (1993) reports that up to 30% of rape victims contract sexually transmitted diseases, and pregnancy results in about 5% of cases.

Child victims of sexual abuse develop a wide range of short- and long-term problems. In the year following disclosure of the abuse, up to 70% of children experience significant psychological symptoms. Longer-term problems include substance abuse, depression, eating disorders, and prostitution (Hanson, 1990).

Definition of Sexual Assault

In Canada, the definition of sexual assault has undergone substantial change over the past 25 years. Prior to 1983, a number of different offences were lumped together under the label of *rape*, which was defined as "a male person commits rape when he has sexual intercourse with a female person who is not his wife... without her consent" (section 143, Criminal Code of Canada). In response to criticism, and to make the definition more inclusive of diverse sexual relationships and more representative of the nature of sexual assault, rape was reclassified. Sexual assault became defined as any nonconsensual sexual act by either a male or female person to either male or female persons, regardless of the relationship between the people involved. Sexual assault, like physical assault, was divided into three levels based on severity issues and with different maximum penalties: simple sexual assault (maximum sentence: 10 years), sexual assault with a weapon or causing bodily harm (maximum sentence: 14 years), and aggravated sexual assault (maximum sentence: life imprisonment).

Rape Myths

Rape myths are stereotypic ideas people have about rape, such as the following: women falsely accuse men of rape, women want or enjoy rape, rape is not harmful, or women cause or deserve rape by the way they dress or act (Burt, 1980). According to Lonsway and Fitzgerald (1994), rape myths "are generally false but are widely and persistently held, and serve to deny and justify male aggression against women" (p. 217). Rape myths appear to be accepted across many levels of society, including high school students (Kershner, 1996), university students (Szymanski, Devlin, Chrisler, & Vyse, 1993), and prosecuting lawyers (Gylys & McNamara, 1996). One of the most consistent findings is that men are more accepting of rape myths than women are (Bohner et al., 1998). Ethnicity also appears to play a role in the acceptance of rape myths. In a study by Kennedy and Gorzalka (2002) conducted at the University of British Columbia, it was found that Asian students were more likely to accept rape myths than non-Asian students, particularly if their exposure to Western culture was limited (i.e., recent immigrants).

Box 10.3 on page 290 lists some of the common rape myths.

Effects of Rape

The term **rape trauma syndrome** was first used by Burgess and Holmstrom (1974) to describe the after-effects of rape. Burgess and Holmstrom interviewed 92 women who had been raped; the interviews took place within 30 minutes of the women's arriving at the hospital and

Rape trauma syndrome:
A group of symptoms or behaviours that are frequent after-effects of having been raped

Box 10.3

Sexual Assault: Discounting Rape Myths

There are many myths associated with sexual assault. Below is a list of myths followed by facts that challenge these false beliefs.

Myth 1: Sexual assault is not a common problem.

One in every four women and one in every six men have experienced some type of sexual assault. You likely know someone who has been sexually assaulted.

Myth 2: Sexual assault is most often committed by strangers.

Women face the greatest risk of sexual assault from men they know, not from strangers. About half of all rapes occur in dating relationships. In about 80% of cases, victims of sexual assault knew the attacker.

Myth 3: Women who are sexually assaulted "ask for it" by the way they dress or act.

Victims of sexual assault range across the age span (from infants to elderly) and sexual assaults can occur in almost any situation. No woman "deserves" to be sexually assaulted regardless of what she wears, where she goes, or how she acts. Blaming sexual assault on how a victim behaves would be like blaming a mugging on a person for carrying a wallet.

Myth 4: Avoid being alone in dark, deserted places, such as parks or parking lots, and this will protect you from being sexually assaulted.

Most sexual assaults occur in a private home and many in the victim's home.

Myth 5: Women derive pleasure from being a victim.

Sexual assault is associated with both short- and long-term serious problems. High rates of anxiety, fear, depression, and post-traumatic stress disorder are seen in survivors of sexual assault. Some women are physically injured during an assault.

Myth 6: Women lie about sexual assault.

False accusations are very rare. Sexual assault is a vastly under-reported crime, and most sexual assaults are not reported to the police.

---

1 month later. The effects of rape were divided into two phases: an acute crisis phase and a long-term reactions phase. The acute crisis phase lasts for a few days to several weeks and the symptoms are often quite severe. Those who have been raped often report very high levels of fear, anxiety, and depression. They often ask questions about why the rape happened to them and commonly engage in self-blame (Janoff-Bulman, 1979). For example, they might say, "I shouldn't have taken that shortcut home" or "I shouldn't have gone back to his apartment." Heightened levels of distrust and self-doubt are also common reactions.

The second phase is more protracted, lasting anywhere from a few months to several years. One-quarter of women who have been raped do not significantly recover, even after several years (Resick, 1993). Long-term reactions include the development of phobias, such as the fear of being left alone or the fear of leaving the house. Another long-term reaction is the development of sexual problems and depression. Often, victims make dramatic changes in their lifestyles.

Post-traumatic stress disorder: Anxiety disorder that can develop in response to exposure to an extremely traumatic event. Symptoms include frequent, distressing, and intrusive memories of the event, avoiding stimuli associated with the traumatic event, and persistent anxiety or increased arousal symptoms.

The psychological consequences of rape victimization also include **post-traumatic stress disorder** (PTSD). The *DSM-IV* (American Psychiatric Association, 1994) defines PTSD as an anxiety disorder that can develop in response to exposure to an extremely traumatic event. PTSD symptoms include frequent, distressing, and intrusive memories of the event, avoiding stimuli associated with the traumatic event, and persistent anxiety or increased arousal symptoms. Rothbaum, Foa, Riggs, Murdock, and Walsh (1992) assessed the PTSD symptoms in 95 female rape victims over a 9-month follow-up period. One month after the rape, 65% of victims were diagnosed with PTSD and at nine months 47% were classified as having PTSD. Some victims continue to experience PTSD symptoms years after the rape. An average of 15 years after the rape, 16.5% of rape victims had PTSD (Kilpatrick, Saunders, Veronen, Best, & Von, 1987). Cortina and Kubiak (2006) examined data from 591 victims of partner violence collected in the National Violence Against Women Survey and concluded that higher rates of PTSD and greater symptom severity in women were the result of higher rates of sexual victimization among women. Effective treatment programs have been developed to help rape victims overcome the emotional suffering caused by this trauma (Foa & Rothbaum, 1998).

Classification of Sexual Offenders

Sexual offenders are usually divided into categories based on the type of sexually deviant behaviour, the relationship between victim and offender, and the age of the victim. **Voyeurs** obtain sexual gratification by observing unsuspecting people, usually strangers, who are either naked, in the process of undressing, or engaging in sexual activity. **Exhibitionists** obtain sexual gratification by exposing their genitals to strangers. These two types of sexual offenders are sometimes referred to as hands-off or no-contact sexual offenders. **Rapists** are offenders who sexually assault victims aged 16 years or older. The term *pedophilia* means "love of children." Thus, **pedophile** is often used to refer to an adult whose primary sexual orientation is toward children. Other researchers use the term **child molester** to refer to individuals who have actually sexually molested a child. Child molesters are also divided into two types: intra-familial and extra-familial. **Intra-familial child molesters** (also called incest offenders) are those who sexually abuse their own biological children or children for whom they assume a parental role, such as a stepfather or live-in boyfriend. **Extra-familial child molesters** sexually abuse children outside the family. Child molesters have also been classified into groups based on whether they target male or female victims.

Perceptions of sexual offenders are uniformly negative. Studies examining perceptions of sex offenders have found that nonsexual offenders, correctional staff, treatment providers, psychologists, and students all judge them very negatively (Hogue & Peebles, 1997; Lea, Auburn, & Kibblewhite, 1999; Valliant, Furac, & Antonowicz, 1994). Sex offenders who commit sex offences against children are judged more harshly than sex offenders who commit offences against adult women.

Rapist Typologies

Rapists are not a homogeneous group and do not all engage in sexual assault for the same reasons. Several different rapist typologies have been proposed. During the 1990s, an ambitious project was undertaken at the Massachusetts Treatment Center to develop and empirically validate a typology for rapists. The resulting classification system, *The Revised Rapist Typology, Version 3* (MTC:R3) (Knight & Prentky, 1990), consists of five primary subtypes of rapists based on motivational differences:

1. The opportunistic type commits sexual assault that is generally impulsive, void of sexual fantasies, controlled primarily by situational or contextual factors, and void of gratuitous violence. These offenders often engage in other criminal behaviours. For example, a rapist who breaks into a home with the intention of stealing but who rapes the female occupant could be classified as opportunistic.

Voyeurs: People who obtain sexual gratification by observing unsuspecting people, usually strangers, who are either naked, in the process of undressing, or engaging in sexual activity

Exhibitionist: Someone who obtains sexual gratification by exposing genitals to strangers

Rapist: Person who sexually assaults victims over 16 years of age

Pedophile: Person whose primary sexual orientation is toward children

Child molester: Someone who has actually sexually molested a child

Intra-familial child molesters: People who sexually abuse their own biological children or children for whom they assume a parental role, such as a stepfather or live-in boyfriend. Also known as incest offenders.

Extra-familial child molester: Someone who sexually abuses children not related to the abuser

2. The pervasively angry type has a high level of anger that is directed toward both men and women. These offenders tend to be impulsive, use unnecessary force, cause serious victim injury, and are void of sexual fantasies.

3. The sexual type is distinguished from the other types in that these offenders' crimes are primarily motivated by sexual preoccupation or sexual fantasies.

4. The sadistic type is differentiated from sexual type in that there must be a sadistic element to the offence.

5. The fifth type is labelled vindictive. In contrast to the pervasively angry type, the vindictive rapist's anger is focused solely on women. These offenders are not impulsive, nor are they preoccupied by sexual fantasies. The goal of this type of rapist is to demean and degrade the victim.

The opportunistic, sexual, and vindictive subtypes are further subdivided based on their level of social competence. The sadistic type is also further subdivided into overt or muted sadists based on the presence or absence of gratuitous violence (Knight & Prentky, 1990). Research using the MTC:R3 has found that these types differ on prevalence of psychopathy (Barbaree, Seto, Serin, Amos, & Preston, 1994; Brown & Forth, 1997), rates of sexual recidivism (Knight, Prentky, & Cerce, 1994), and treatment needs (Knight, 1999). Knight and Guay (2006) describe a restructuring of the MTC:R3 in which the muted sadistic type of sexual offender has been dropped since the existence of this type of sexual offender has not been supported by the research.

Another typology that uses motivations to classify rapists was proposed by Groth (1979). Groth proposed that rapists can be divided into three main types: anger rapists, power rapists, and sadistic rapists.

Anger rapist: A rapist, as defined by Groth, who uses more force than necessary to obtain compliance from the victim and who engages in a variety of sexual acts to degrade the victim

The features of the **anger rapist** include

■ the use of more force than necessary to obtain compliance and engagement in a variety of sexual acts to degrade the victim

■ high levels of anger directed solely toward women

■ not being motivated primarily by sexual gratification

Most of these rapes are precipitated by conflict or perceived humiliation by some significant woman, such as the offender's wife, mother, or boss. Approximately 50% of rapists fit this type.

Power rapist: A rapist, as defined by Groth, who seeks to establish dominance and control over the victim

The features of the **power rapist** include

■ the intention to assert dominance and control over the victim

■ variation in the amount of force used depending on the degree of submission shown by the victim

■ not being motivated primarily by sexual gratification

■ frequent rape fantasies

About 40% of rapists fit into this category.

Sadistic rapist: A rapist, as defined by Groth, who obtains sexual gratification by hurting the victim

The features of the **sadistic rapist** include

■ obtaining sexual gratification by hurting the victim

■ high levels of victim injury, including torture and sometimes death

■ frequent violent sexual fantasies

Approximately 5% of rapists fit this type.

There is considerable overlap between the MTC:R3 and Groth typologies. Both typologies describe a sadistic rapist. The vindictive rapist is similar to the anger rapist and the pervasively angry rapist shares some of the features of the power rapist.

Is Resisting a Sexual Attack a Good Idea?

One question often posed by women is, "If attacked, should I fight back or not?" Based on the typologies described above, the answer will likely depend on the type of rapist attacking them. Research with incarcerated rapists indicates that they search for vulnerable victims in certain areas and attack women they believe cannot or will not resist the attack (Stevens, 1994). Studies of women who were raped or who avoided being raped have found that forceful verbal resistance, physical resistance, and fleeing are all associated with rape avoidance (Ullman & Knight, 1993; Zoucha-Jensen & Coyne, 1993), whereas nonresistance strategies (e.g., pleading with rapists, crying, reasoning) are not.

The association between victim injury and resistance is inconclusive. Zoucha-Jensen and Coyne (1993) found no association between resistance and injury. In contrast, Ullman and Knight (1993) found that if the offender had a weapon, women who resisted the rape suffered more physical injury than those who did not resist. In a review of universities' sexual assault prevention programs, Söchting, Fairbrother, and Koch (2004) conclude that the most promising prevention program is teaching self-defence skills.

Child Molester Typologies

The most widely used typology is Groth's typology of the fixated and regressed child molester (Groth, Hobson, & Gary, 1982). Groth developed his typology based on research with incarcerated child molesters.

Fixated child molesters tend to have the following features:

- Their primary sexual orientation is toward children, and they have little or no sexual contact with adults.
- Their sexual interest in children begins in adolescence and is persistent.
- Male children are their primary targets.
- Precipitating stress is not evident.
- Their offences are planned.
- They are emotionally immature, have poor social skills, and are usually single.
- They usually have no history of alcohol or drug abuse.
- They often feel no remorse or distress over their behaviour.

Regressed child molesters usually have the following characteristics:

- Their primary sexual orientation is toward adults.
- Their sexual interest in children begins in adulthood and is episodic.
- Female children are their primary targets.

Fixated child molester: A child molester, as defined by Groth, who has a long-standing, exclusive sexual orientation preference for children

Regressed child molester: A child molester, as defined by Groth, whose primary sexual orientation is toward adults, but whose sexual interests revert to children after a stressful event or due to feelings of inadequacy

- Precipitating stress and feelings of inadequacy are usually present.

- Their offences are more impulsive.

- They are often married and are having marital problems.

- Many of their offences are related to alcohol use.

- They are more likely to report feeling remorse for their behaviour.

Groth also subdivided child molesters into two types based on the type of coercion they used. The *sex-pressure* child molester uses persuasion or entrapment to make the child feel obligated to participate in sexual acts. For example, this type of child molester may buy the child gifts or take the child on fun outings. The *sex-force* child molester threatens or uses physical force to overcome any resistance by the child. This latter group has been divided into the exploitative type who uses the threat of force to obtain compliance and the sadistic type who obtains gratification from hurting a child. The sadistic type of child molester is, fortunately, rare.

Theories of Sexual Aggression

It is important that we understand why child molestation and rape occurs, and a number of theories have been proposed to account for child molestation and rape. One of the most popular and widely cited theories is Finkelhor's precondition model (1984). Finkelhor's theory of child molesting proposes that in order for the sexual abuse to occur there are four preconditions:

1. The offender must be motivated to sexually abuse. Motivation is due to three factors: (1) emotional congruence, which is the offender's desire for the child to satisfy an emotional need; (2) sexual attraction to the child; and (3) blockage of emotional outlets for the offender to meet his sexual and emotional needs.

2. The next precondition relates to the offender's lack of internal inhibitions. For example, alcohol and impulse-control problems can weaken the offender's ability to restrain the behaviours that lead to abuse.

3. The offender must overcome external inhibitors for the abuse to occur. For example, the offender might need to create opportunities to be alone with the child.

4. The offender must overcome the child's resistance. Offenders will reward the child with attention or bribes in order to encourage the child to cooperate. Alternatively, some offenders will use the threat of harm to intimidate the child.

Marshall and Barbaree (1990) have proposed an integrated model of sexual aggression that includes biological factors, childhood experiences, sociocultural influences, and situational events. They argue that males normally learn to inhibit sexually aggressive behaviour via a socialization process that promotes the development of strong, positive attachments. The authors suggest that sexual offenders fail to acquire effective inhibitory control because they experienced childhood abuse (emotional, physical, or sexual abuse) or because they were raised in extremely dysfunctional families (e.g., harsh and inconsistent punishment, lack of supervision, hostility). They also acknowledged the importance of the structure of society that reinforces the use of aggression and the acceptance of negative attitudes toward women.

More recently, Ward and Siegert (2002) have proposed a pathway model of child sexual abuse that integrates Finkelhor's precondition model, Marshall and Barbaree's integrated model, and Hall and Hirschman's quadripartite model (Hall & Hirschman's model is not discussed here; for more information on their model, see Hall & Hirschman, 1992). The pathway model proposes that there are different causal pathways, each having its own set of dysfunctional mechanisms, including inappropriate emotions, deviant sexual arousal, cognitive distortions, and intimacy deficits. For example, one pathway, labelled *emotional dysregulation*, focuses on individuals who have problems controlling their emotions and who use sex as an emotional coping strategy. For these offenders, the association between sex and negative emotions increases the probability they will sexually molest a child.

A number of theorists have applied evolutionary theory to sexual offending (Quinsey & Lalumière, 1995; Thornhill & Palmer, 2000). Evolutionary theories focus on how behaviour is the product of our ancestral history and how features that are related to reproductive success become more frequent. Vernon Quinsey (2002) provides a clear example of a mating strategy that would not be very successful. "Consider a man in an ancestral environment who preferred trees as sexual partners. We can surmise that this man is very unlikely to be among our ancestors if his tree preference was caused by genes, because these genes would decrease in frequency over generations" (p. 2). Quinsey and others view rape as a consequence of a mating strategy that was selected for because it resulted in a reproductive advantage for males. For a more detailed description of how evolution can explain the causes of rape, see Lalumière, Harris, Quinsey, and Rice (2005). More information about Quinsey's research is found in Box 10.4. on page 296. Evolutionary theories of sexual aggression have been criticized both for having a limited scope and lacking explanatory depth (see Ward & Siegert, 2002, for a detailed criticism).

Adolescent Sexual Offenders

Prior to the 1980s, sexually aggressive behaviour by adolescents was not deemed serious and was discounted by some as normal experimentation. However, crime reports and victimization surveys indicate that about 20% of rapes and between 30% and 50% of child sexual abuse is committed by adolescents (Davis & Leitenberg, 1987). In Canada, 1630 adolescents were tried in youth court for sexual assault in 2004 (Public Safety and Emergency Preparedness Canada, 2006).

Like their adult counterparts, adolescent sexual offenders consistently report having been victims of sexual abuse themselves. The prevalence rate for sexual abuse committed against adolescent sexual offenders ranges from about 40% to 80% (Friedrich & Luecke, 1988; Ryan, Miyoshi, Metzner, Krugman, & Fryer, 1996). Although early sexual victimization and later sexual offending are related, the majority of sexually abused children do not go on to become adolescent or adult sexual offenders. Clearly, being the victim of sexual abuse is only one factor that affects later sexual offending. Rasmussen, Burton, and Christopherson (1992) suggest that in addition to sexual abuse, other factors such as social inadequacy, lack of intimacy, and impulsiveness also play a role.

Prior history of childhood sexual victimization is not related to sexual recidivism in samples of adult sexual offenders (Hanson & Bussière, 1998) or samples of adolescent sexual offenders (Worling & Curwen, 2000).

In a national sample of adolescent sex offenders undergoing treatment, Ryan et al. (1996) investigated victim characteristics and found that adolescent sexual offenders tend to sexually abuse young female victims. Notably, the researchers found that 63% of the adolescent sexual offenders' victims were younger than age nine.

Box 10.4

Canadian Researcher Profile: Dr. Vernon Quinsey

Dr. Vernon Quinsey completed his Ph.D. in biopsychology in 1970 at the University of Massachusetts at Amherst, studying behavioural contingencies in rats. In the early 1970s, he started working as a psychologist at the Oak Ridge Division of the Penetanguishene Mental Health Centre in Ontario. He decided he wanted to study aggression and to "do good" by applying scientific knowledge to important but understudied applied problems. The maximum-security forensic hospital at Penetanguishene seemed ideal for this purpose because institutional violence was a significant problem there and involved observable, relatively frequent, and serious aggressive behaviours.

Dr. Quinsey established and became the first director of the Department of Research at the Penetanguishene Mental Health Centre and began a collaboration with departmental staff and the two subsequent directors of the department, Marnie Rice and Grant Harris—a collaboration that has lasted until the present. In 1988, he returned to academe by accepting a professorship at Queen's University in Kingston, Ontario.

Dr. Quinsey describes himself as doing research on the dark side of psychology, focusing on violent and sexual offenders. Although he acknowledges the difficulties of doing this research, he believes research on the dark side is a worthwhile and sometimes rewarding endeavour that is a source of endless intellectual fascination. He uses different methodologies depending on what question he is trying to answer, but he primarily uses the experimental method to understand sexual offending and aggression.

Dr. Quinsey has conducted an impressive amount of research in the following applied areas: appraisal of risk for violence, sex offending, institutional violence, and program evaluation. His favourite studies are phallometric studies of sexual preference. He states that these studies were small enough to be very manageable, stimuli could easily be created, and the data were extremely lawful. The unambiguous manifestation of the sexual preferences of individual participants in these assessments often seemed like magic to him.

Although he was trained as a behaviourist, Dr. Quinsey has become convinced of the limitations of behavioural and psychological explanations for sexual aggression. Over the past ten years, he has turned to concepts and methods from genetics, neuroscience, and Darwinian theories to help to explain sexual and aggressive behaviour.

Dr. Quinsey is currently departmental head and a professor of psychology at Queen's University. In this position, he is dedicated to conducting research and training future researchers. He believes that future forensic psychology researchers should have a strong foundation in such areas as neuroscience, evolutionary and developmental biology, and genetics. The courses he most enjoys teaching are "The Psychology of Crime" and "Human Behaviour and Evolution." Dr. Quinsey acknowledges his numerous highly capable graduate students, many of whom have gone on to establish successful research careers.

Dr. Quinsey has received numerous distinctions for his work, including the Canadian Psychological Association's Career Contribution Award in 2005. His plans for the future include continuing to investigate conflict associated with sex differences in reproductive strategy.

Dr. Quinsey was also a keen cyclist and a karate instructor in his pre-arthritic phase. When not studying violent offenders, he reads about history and enjoys true-crime novels.

Female Sexual Offenders

Research on female sexual offenders is limited. This relative lack of attention is probably because only 2% to 5% of incarcerated sex offenders are female. However, some researchers have suggested that sexual abuse of children by women is more prevalent than previously believed.

The rates of sexual abuse by females vary dramatically depending on the definition used. For example, should a female be classified as a sexual abuser if she knew that her husband was sexually abusing their child and did nothing to stop the abuse? Does a mother sleeping with her child constitute sexual abuse in the absence of sexual touching? What if the child is a teenager who becomes sexually aroused by sleeping with his mother? Most people would agree that it is sexual abuse for a 20 year old to have sexual contact with an 8-year-old boy, but not if the boy is 16. However, what about if the boy is 14? If the 14-year-old boy initiates the sexual act and views it positively, should this be classified as sexual abuse?

Retrospective surveys of university students have found that a large percentage of perpetrators were females. For example, Fritz, Stoll, and Wagner (1981) reported that of the 5% of college men who were molested as children, 60% were molested by females, most being older female adolescents. In a large survey of 2972 university students that used broad criteria for sexual abuse, Risin and Koss (1987) reported that 7.3% were abused. They found that almost half of the perpetrators were female (43%), and of these almost half were female adolescent babysitters. Similar to other studies, about half of the male respondents reported that they participated in the sexual acts voluntarily and did not feel victimized. Fewer female perpetrators have been reported by other researchers (Finkelhor, 1984; Reinhart, 1987). For example, Finkelhor (1984) found that only 6% of university women and 16% of university men who reported childhood sexual abuse indicated that the offender was a woman.

Some researchers have speculated that the rate of sexual abuse by females is underestimated. Some reasons include the following (Banning, 1989; Groth, 1979):

- Women are able to mask their sexually abusive behaviours through caregiving activities and thus are more difficult to recognize.

- Women sexual offenders are more likely to target their own children, who are less likely to disclose the abuse.

- Boys are more frequent targets than girls, and boys are less likely to disclose abuse.

Research designed to determine the characteristics of female sexual offenders has generally been plagued with very small sample sizes. Whether the findings will generalize to larger samples of female sexual offenders remains to be investigated. Keeping this limitation in mind, Atkinson (1996) suggests there are four types of female sexual offenders:

1. *Teacher/lover*. These offenders initiate sexual abuse of a male adolescent that they relate to as a peer. The offender is often in a position of authority or power. It is unknown how common this type of female sex offender is because the victim rarely reports the abuse to authorities. This type has not likely experienced childhood sexual abuse, although substance-use problems are common. These offenders often are not aware that their behaviour is inappropriate. Teacher/lovers often describe themselves as being "in love" with the victim. Victims often report they participated voluntarily and do not feel victimized.

2. *Male-coerced*. These offenders are coerced or forced into sexual abuse by an abusive male. Often the victim is the female offender's own daughter. These offenders are unassertive, dependent on men, and are relatively passive partners in the abuse.

3. *Male-accompanied*. These offenders also engage in sexual abuse with a male partner. However, they are more willing participants than are the male-coerced type. Victims are both inside and outside the family.

4. *Predisposed.* This offender initiates the sexual abuse alone. She has often experienced severe and persistent childhood sexual abuse and has been a victim of intimate violence. This type often reports having deviant sexual fantasies, the offences are more violent and bizarre, and they typically involve younger children. Victims are often their own children, and they also frequently physically abuse and neglect the victim.

In a study of 40 female sexual offenders, Faller (1987) reported that most had significant psychological and social functioning problems. Most of the offenders (29 out of the 40, or 73%) were classified as engaging in poly-incestuous abuse, which involved two perpetrators and generally two or more victims. The male offender usually instigated the sexual abuse, while the women played a secondary role.

Vandiver and Teske (2006) compared 61 juvenile female sex offenders to 122 juvenile male sex offenders using sex offender registration data and criminal records. The female offenders were found to be younger than their male counterparts at the time of their arrest. The female offenders also had younger victims and chose both male and female victims equally while male offenders chose female victims more often.

In summary, female sexual offenders, although relatively rare, do exist. Gender differences have been found among sex offenders and in the nature of sex offences, including victim characteristics. In a recent study, Cortoni and Hanson (2005) reported that female sexual offenders have much lower sexual recidivism rates (about 1%) as compared to male sexual offenders (about 13%). Most retrospective surveys of university men who reported sexual abuse by women have found that most of the men engaged in the sexual incidents voluntarily and did not feel victimized. Finally, most of the incarcerated female sexual offenders have engaged in abuse in conjunction with a dominant male.

Assessment and Treatment of Sexual Offenders

Much of the assessment of sexual offenders is to help determine future risk for reoffending, to identify treatment needs, and to evaluate whether or not the treatment has had the desired effect. Risk factors for sexual reoffending will be discussed in Chapter 12. The focus of this section will be on the assessment of treatment needs and the effectiveness of treatment programs.

Most treatment programs are designed to address the following: denial, minimizations and cognitive distortions, victim empathy, modification of deviant sexual interest, enhanced social skills, substance-abuse problems, and the development of relapse-prevention plans (Marshall, 1999).

Denial, Minimizations, and Cognitive Distortions Sex offenders often deny (i.e., they claim they didn't do what they are accused of or that the victim consented) or fail to take full responsibility for their sexual offending (Barbaree, 1991). Often, blame is shifted to someone else, including the victim or some external factor. For example, "The victim wanted to have sex with me" or "I was drunk and didn't know what I was doing." Assessments of denial and acceptance of responsibility are most often done through self-report questionnaires such as the Clarke Sex History

Questionnaire (Langevin, Handy, Paitich, & Russon, 1985) or by a comparison of police and victim reports with what the offenders admit in interviews. Most research has not found a link between denial and sexual recidivism. Recently, however, Nunes, Hanson, Firestone, Moulden, Greenberg, and Bradford (2007) have found that only in low-risk sexual offenders and incest offenders is denial related to increased sexual recidivism.

Cognitive distortions are deviant cognitions, values, and beliefs that are used by the sexual offender to justify deviant behaviours. For example, a child molester might state, "Having sex with a child in a loving relationship is a good way to teach a child about sex"; or an incest offender might claim, "It was better for her to have her first sexual experience with me since I love her, rather than with some teenager who would just want to use her." Both these child molesters are reporting cognitive distortions that are self-serving and inhibit them from taking full responsibility for their offences.

Some treatment programs refuse to accept deniers. The reason is that if the person refuses to admit to having committed a sexual offence, it is difficult for that person to fully participate in the treatment, since the focus is on sexual offending. In treatment, offenders are asked to disclose in detail what happened before, during, and after the sexual abuse. The therapist has access to the police and victim reports in order to challenge an offender who is denying or minimizing aspects of the event. Other group members are encouraged to also challenge what the offender discloses.

Empathy Although some sex offenders have a general deficit in empathy (e.g., psychopathic sex offenders), most have a specific deficit in empathy toward their victims (Marshall, Barbaree, & Fernandez, 1995). Empathy is the ability to perceive others' perspectives and to recognize and respond in a compassionate way to the feelings of others. Empathy problems in sexual offenders arise in part due to cognitive distortions. Because they minimize the amount of harm they have done, they do not think the victim has suffered, and therefore they do not empathize with the victim. Measures of empathy have focused on self-report scales such as the Rape Empathy Scale (Deitz, Blackwell, Daley, & Bentley, 1982) and interviews.

Empathy training typically focuses on getting the offender to understand the impact of the abuse on the victim and the pain caused, and to develop feelings such as remorse. Offenders read survivor accounts of rape and child abuse and compare these accounts with how their victim likely felt. Videos of victims describing the emotional damage they have suffered and the long-term problems they experience are often used. Some therapy programs use role-playing, with the offender taking the part of the victim. Finally, although controversial, some programs may have sexual offenders meet with adult survivors of rape or child sexual abuse. Only those sexual offenders who are demonstrating empathy are permitted to take part in these meetings.

Social Skills Sexual offenders have been found lacking in a variety of social skills, including self-confidence in interpersonal relations, capacity for intimacy, assertiveness, and dealing with anger (Bumby & Hansen, 1997; Marshall, Anderson, & Champagne, 1997; Marshall et al., 1995). Self-report questionnaires, interviews, and responses to scenarios have all been developed to assess social-skill deficits (see Marshall, 1999, for review). Treatment programs for sexual offenders vary in terms of which social-skill deficits are targeted. Some programs focus on anger and communication skills (Pithers, Martin, & Cumming, 1989), whereas others target relationship skills, anger control, and self-esteem (Marshall et al., 1997).

Substance Abuse Substance abuse problems are common in nonsexual offenders and sexual offenders (Lightfoot & Barbaree, 1993). It is likely that some sexual offenders use alcohol to facilitate offending by reducing their inhibitions. Self-report measures are often used to assess problems with alcohol and drugs.

Sexual offenders with substance-abuse problems are often referred to substance-abuse programs. These programs are usually based on the relapse-prevention model developed by Marlatt and his colleagues (Marlatt & Gordon, 1985).

Deviant Sexual Interests Deviant sexual interests motivate some sexual offenders. However, many other salient motives also play a role, including power and control over others, anger toward others, and desire for emotional intimacy. One of the most popular methods to assess deviant sexual interests is the use of **penile phallometry**. Penile phallometry involves placing a measurement device around the penis to measure changes in sexual arousal. To measure deviant sexual interests in child molesters, photos of naked male and female children and adults are presented, as well as rapists' recorded descriptions of nondeviant and deviant sexual behaviour. Phallometric assessments have been used to differentiate extra-familial child molesters from nonoffenders. However, most intra-familial child molesters do not differ in their phallometric responses from nonoffenders (see Marshall, 1999, for review). Research with rapists is mixed. Some studies have found differences between rapists and nonrapists (Quinsey, Chaplin, & Upfold, 1984), whereas others have not (Marshall & Fernandez, 2003). Another problem has been the relatively high rate of nonresponders. About 20% of all sexual offenders fail to show any arousal during phallometric testing.

There are also ethical concerns with showing images of naked children or having rapists listen to graphic, violent sexual assaults. Unfortunately, simply asking offenders to indicate their sexual interests is not an option due to the tendency of all individuals, including offenders, to portray themselves in the best possible light.

Many different techniques have been developed to train offenders to eliminate deviant thoughts and interests and to increase the frequency of appropriate sexual thoughts and interests. For example, in aversion therapy, the offender is given an aversive substance to smell (e.g., ammonia) whenever he has a deviant sexual fantasy. The underlying goal is to reduce the attractiveness of these deviant fantasies by pairing them with a negative event. The 1971 Stanley Kubrick film *A Clockwork Orange* (based on Anthony Burgess's novel) provides a graphic illustration of aversion therapy.

Another approach is called masturbatory satiation. In this treatment, the offender is told to masturbate to ejaculation to a nondeviant fantasy. After ejaculation, he is told to switch to a deviant fantasy, thus pairing the inability to become aroused to this deviant fantasy. The effectiveness of these techniques to change deviant sexual interests has been questioned by several researchers (Quinsey & Earls, 1990).

Penile phallometry:
A measurement device placed around the penis to measure changes in sexual arousal

Pharmacological interventions appear to be effective at suppressing deviant sexual desires (Bradford & Pawlak, 1993). Drugs used in the past acted to suppress all sexual interests and compliance was a serious problem (Langevin, 1979). The use of serotonin-reuptake inhibitors (SSRIs) has shown to be effective at controlling deviant sexual fantasies and not eliminating all sexual functioning (Federoff & Federoff, 1992).

Relapse Prevention Sexual offenders need to identify their offence cycle (e.g., emotional states and stress factors that put them at risk; grooming strategies) and develop ways to avoid these problems or to deal with them.

Programs with a **relapse prevention** (RP) component usually consist of two main parts. First, offenders are asked to list emotional and situational risk factors that lead to either fantasizing about sexual abuse or actually committing the abuse. For example, for a rapist, perhaps feelings of anger toward women would be a risk factor; for a child molester, perhaps feeling lonely and sitting on a bench, watching children in a playground would be a risk factor. Second, offenders need to develop plans to deal more effectively with their problems (e.g., meeting their emotional needs in a prosocial way) and ways to avoid or cope with high-risk situations. Box 10.5 on page 302 describes in more detail how the relapse prevention model has been applied with sexual offenders.

Relapse prevention: A method of treatment designed to prevent the occurrence of an undesired behaviour (e.g., sexual assault)

Effectiveness of Psychological Treatment of Sexual Offenders

If we are going to treat sexual offenders, it is important to know whether the treatment works. There is a lack of consensus about whether sex offender treatment is effective. Some researchers argue that treatment does not work (Quinsey, Harris, Rice, & Lalumière, 1993), whereas others are more optimistic (Marshall, Eccles, & Barbaree, 1991).

What we do know is that incarceration does not appear to be a deterrent for sexual or other offenders. Nunes, Firestone, Wexler, Jensen, and Bradford (2007) reported that there was no association between incarceration and sexual recidivism rates in a sample of 627 Canadian adult male sexual offenders. Certainly, incarceration may be the only effective method for handling high-risk sexual offenders. However, for the majority of sexual offenders, community alternatives may be a more effective and less expensive option.

There are numerous problems facing researchers wanting to evaluate the effectiveness of treatment programs. The main problem is that it is unethical to carry out the ideal controlled study. The optimal design would randomly assign motivated sexual offenders (i.e., offenders all wanting treatment) to either treatment or no treatment. Then, both treated and untreated sexual offenders would be released at the same time and followed up for several years and rates of reoffending would be measured. Most treatment outcome studies have not used this design (see Marques, 1999, for one of the few studies to use random assignment). It is unlikely that many sexual offenders would agree to participate in this ideal study since untreated sexual offenders are held in

Box 10.5

Relapse Prevention with Sexual Offenders

Relapse prevention (RP) is a self-control program designed to teach sexual offenders to recognize risky situations that could lead to reoffending and to learn coping and avoidance strategies to deal with those situations. The RP model was initially developed for the treatment of addictive behaviours such as smoking, alcohol abuse, and overeating (Marlatt & Gordon, 1985). Sexual offenders are asked to develop a personalized sexual offence cycle that identifies their pre-offence thoughts, feelings, and behaviours. At each step of the cycle, the offender generates options or alternative behaviours that interrupt the offence cycle. RP is not considered a cure but it helps the sexual offender to manage the urge to offend sexually. RP is a way of teaching sexual offenders to think and look ahead in order to prevent committing another sexual offence. In order for RP to be successful, the sexual offender must be motivated to stop offending.

The following are some relevant terms (used in Figure 10.2) associated with relapse prevention:

■ *Lapse:* Any occurrence of fantasizing about sexual offending or engaging in behaviours in the offence cycle

■ *Relapse:* Occurrence of a sexual offence

■ *High-risk situation:* Any situation that increases the likelihood of a lapse or relapse

■ *Apparently irrelevant decisions:* Conscious or unconscious decisions made by offenders that put them in high-risk situations

■ *Coping response:* Development of avoidance strategies to sidestep high-risk situations and escape plans if the high-risk situation cannot be avoided

■ *Abstinence violation effect:* Refers to how the offender reacts to a lapse. Both cognitive reactions (e.g., lack of willpower) and emotional states (e.g., feeling guilty) are considered. If the offender views the lapse as an irreversible failure, this can promote a relapse. Alternatively, if the lapse is seen as a reasonable mistake in a learning process, the offender can become more confident in his ability to avoid or handle future lapses.

Figure 10.2 presents the sequences of events that may lead to a relapse in a child molester.

Figure 10.2 Sequence of Events Leading to Relapse in a Child Molester custody longer than treated offenders. Another challenge for researchers has been the relatively low base rates of sexual recidivism, even in untreated offenders (Barbaree, 1997). On average, only 15% of sex offenders are detected committing a new sexual offence after five years and 20% after ten years (Hanson & Bussière, 1998; Hanson & Thornton, 2000). Thus, in order for researchers to detect any differences between treatment groups, they need to wait many years. Some researchers have begun to use unofficial data, such as child protection agency files, or self-reports to detect reoffending (see Marshall & Barbaree, 1988).

Five meta-analyses of sexual offender treatment programs have been published (Alexander, 1999; Gallagher, Wilson, Hirschfield, Coggeshall, & MacKenzie, 1999; Hall, 1995; Hanson et al., 2002; Lösel & Schmucker, 2005). Hanson et al. (2002) examined 42 studies with a total of 5078 treated sex offenders and 4376 untreated sex offenders. Averaged across the different types of treatment, the sexual recidivism rate was 12.3% for the treated sex offenders and 16.8% for the untreated sexual offenders. The following results were found:

- Sexual offenders who refused treatment or who dropped out of treatment had higher sexual recidivism rates compared to those who completed the treatment.
- Treatment effects are equally effective for adolescent and adult sex offenders.
- Both institutional treatment and community treatment are associated with reductions in sexual recidivism.
- Current treatments (cognitive-behavioural or systematic) were associated with stronger treatment effects than older treatment programs (behavioural or psychotherapy).

"The treatments that appeared most effective," Hanson et al. (2002) conclude, "were recent programs providing some form of cognitive-behavioral treatment, and, for adolescent sex offenders, systemic treatment aimed at a range of current life problems (e.g., family, school, peers)" (p. 187). The treatment type that Lösel and Schmucker (2005) reported to be the most effective was surgical castration. However, this form of treatment has been considered by some to be unethical. In addition, the sexual offenders willing to participate in this form of intervention are a very select group and highly motivated. Not all studies have reported positive effects of sexual offender treatment. For example, Hanson, Broom, and Stephenson (2004) compared the sexual recidivism rates of 403 treated sexual offenders with 321 untreated sexual offenders. In a 12-year follow-up, the rates of sexual reoffending were almost identical—21.1% for the treated group and 21.8% for the untreated group.

Bilby, Brooks-Gordon, and Wells (2006) reviewed 9 randomized control trials carried out between 1998 and 2003 involving over 500 men in cognitive-behavioural sex offender treatment in groups. They found that treatment reduced reoffence at one year as compared to nontreatment groups, but increased re-arrest after ten years. In another review of quasi-experimental studies involving sex offender treatment, seven studies showed significant results while ten showed non-significant effects of treatment (Brooks-Gordon, Bilby, & Wells, 2006). There remains a great deal of uncertainty surrounding sex offender treatment and its effects. Sex offender treatment remains a controversial subject for researchers and the general public alike.

SUMMARY

1. Abused women remain in, or return to, an abusive relationship for a number of reasons. Environmental, socialization, and psychological barriers exist that make it difficult for abused women to leave an abusive relationship.

2. Holtzworth-Munroe and Stuart (1994) divided male batterers into three types based on severity of violence, generality of violence, and personality disorder characteristics: family only, dysphoric/borderline, and generally violent/antisocial. The family-only is violent solely within his home, engages in the least amount of violence, and has little psychopathology or attachment problems. The dysphoric/borderline exhibits some extra-familial violence, engages in moderate to severe violence, is often depressed with borderline personality traits, has some substance-use problems, and has a preoccupied attachment style. The generally violent/antisocial partakes in the most violence outside the home, engages in moderate to severe violence, has antisocial and narcissistic personality traits, has substance-use and impulse-control problems, and has a dismissive attachment style. Cavanaugh and Gelles (2005) proposed that male batterers be classified into three main types: low, moderate, and high risk.

3. Social learning theory has been used to explain domestic violence. There are three main components to social learning theory: origins of aggression, instigators of aggression, and regulators of aggression. One way people acquire new behaviours is via observational learning. Instigators are events in the environment that act as stimuli for the behaviour, and behaviour is regulated by the prospect of its consequences. Behaviours that are rewarded increase in frequency, and behaviours that are punished decrease in frequency.

4. Rapists are offenders who sexually assault adults, and child molesters are offenders who sexually assault children. Typologies of both rapists and child molesters have been proposed that focus on the motives for sexual abuse. Rapists have been classified into the following five primary types based on research by Knight and Prentky: opportunistic, pervasively angry, sexual, sadistic, and vindictive. Groth proposes a different rapist typology consisting of the following three types: angry, power, and sadistic. Groth proposes that child molesters be classified into two main types: regressed and fixated.

5. Treatment for sexual offenders involves recognizing denial, minimizations, and cognitive distortions; gaining victim empathy; modifying deviant sexual interest; enhancing social skills; dealing with substance-abuse problems; and developing relapse-prevention plans.

6. Meta-analyses of sexual offender treatment programs have found the following: (a) sexual offenders who complete treatment have lower rates of sexual recidivism than do dropouts or treatment refusers, (b) treatment is effective for both adolescent and adult sexual offenders, (c) both institutional and community treatment programs are associated with reductions in sexual recidivism, and (d) cognitive-behavioural treatments are more effective than other forms of treatment.

Key Concepts

anger rapist 292

child molester 291

domestic violence 276

dysphoric/borderline batterer 284

exhibitionists 291

extra-familial child molesters 291

family-only batterer 284

fixated child molester 293

generally violent/antisocial batterer 284

instigators 281

intimate partner violence 277

intra-familial child molesters 291

mandatory charging policies 285

observational learning 281

patriarchy 280

pedophile 291

penile phallometry 300

post-traumatic stress disorder 290

power rapist 292

rape trauma syndrome 289

rapist 291

regressed child molester 293

regulators 281

relapse prevention 301

sadistic rapist 292

social learning theory 281

voyeurs 291

Discussion Questions

1. What are the barriers to some battered women leaving an abusive relationship? What could be done at both an individual and a societal level to help battered women?

2. You have been hired by the Ministry of Public Safety and Emergency Preparedness to write a report on the costs and benefits associated with mandatory charging policies for domestic assault cases. What do you include in your report? What conclusions would you draw concerning mandatory charging policies?

3. You are having a discussion with your friends about date-related violence and one of them states that women engage solely in self-defence violence. Describe the data that calls your friend's statement into question.

4. Correctional Service Canada has proposed a new treatment program for sexual offenders. You have been hired to develop an evaluation of the program to determine whether it would be effective. Describe how you plan to evaluate this program.

5. Several typologies have been proposed for child molesters and rapists. What are the similarities and differences?

6. You are interested in doing a study on the association between childhood sexual abuse and sexual offending later in life. Describe the methodology you would use and what variables you would measure.

Readings

Dutton, D. (1995). *The domestic assault of women.* Vancouver: UBC Press.

Laliumière, M., Harris, G., Quinsey, V., & Rice, M. (2005). *The causes of rape. Understanding individual differences in male propensity for sexual aggression.* Washington, DC: American Psychological Association.

Quinn, J.F., Forsyth, C.J., & Mullen-Quinn, C. (2004). Societal reaction to sex offenders: A review of the origins and results of the myths surrounding their crimes and treatment amenability. *Deviant Behavior, 25,* 215–232.

Websites

The National Clearinghouse on Family Violence (NCFV)
www.phac-aspc.gc.ca/ncfv-cnvif/familyviolence

Correctional Service of Canada
www.csc-scc.gc.ca

Chapter 11

Homicidal and Psychopathic Offenders

Learning Objectives

■ Describe the common characteristics of homicide in Canada.

■ Differentiate between instrumental and reactive violence.

■ Describe the different types of multiple murderers.

■ Define the construct of psychopathy and describe the association between psychopathy and violence.

■ Identify the concerns associated with labelling a youth as a psychopath.

■ Explain the two main theories of psychopathy.

Jason Roach is a 19 year old working in a convenience store. He dropped out of college and spends most of his time partying getting drunk and stoned. He decides that he does not want to spend the rest of his life working in a convenience store—a job he describes as "menial." One of his 16-year-old friends, Shawn, has been complaining about his parents and has started talking about wanting to "get rid of them." Jason offers to help, stating that if he helps he wants half of the insurance money. Jason convinces another 17-year-old friend with a car to help them with their murderous plan. Jason knows that they will need to have an alibi, so on the night of the murder they go to the nearby town to a strip bar. Jason gets into an altercation with the bouncer to ensure the bouncer will remember them. Around midnight, armed with a baseball bat and a tire iron, they enter Shawn's house and beat his parents and his 14-year-old sister. While the beatings are taking place, Jason pours gasoline downstairs. As the offenders leave, Jason sets the house on fire. Two people die, and one is severely injured. Jason and his two friends are all charged and convicted of first-degree murder. At his trial, Jason describes himself as the "puppet master," appears proud of his ability to manipulate his younger friends, and shows no remorse for his actions.

The ultimate violent act is homicide. Although the homicide rate in Canada, the United States, and the United Kingdom has been dropping over the past decade, there is a substantial fear and fascination about homicide in the community. Newspapers and television focus on homicides, particularly those that are bizarre or those in which several victims are killed. As a consequence, the public believes homicide is much more common than it is. In this chapter, we describe several types of homicidal offenders, including mass and serial murderers. We end the chapter with a description of the psychopath—an individual who is particularly prone to violence.

HOMICIDAL OFFENDERS

Canadian criminal law recognizes four different types of homicide: first-degree murder, second-degree murder, manslaughter, and infanticide. Different penalties are imposed for each type, with a maximum of five years for infanticide and life in prison for the other three. In considering the different kinds of homicide, it should be noted that some killing is exempt from penalties, such as killing during war or killing in self-defence.

Homicide scene: The ultimate violent crime

First-degree murder includes all murder that is planned and deliberate. It also includes the murder of a law enforcement officer or correctional staff member, or a murder occurring during the commission of another violent offence (e.g., sexual assault, kidnapping), regardless of whether the murder was unplanned or deliberate.

All murder that is not considered first-degree murder is classified as second-degree murder. Manslaughter is unintentional murder that occurs during the "heat of passion" or due to criminal negligence. For example, if a man returned home unexpectedly from a business trip and found his wife in bed with her lover, and during the ensuing altercation he grabbed a rifle and shot and killed the lover, the man would be charged with manslaughter.

Infanticide: Although the term literally means "the killing of an infant," it has been used more specifically to refer to a woman killing her newly born child due to a mental disorder arising from the effects of childbirth

Infanticide occurs when a woman kills her newly born child due to a mental disorder arising from the effects of childbirth. Infanticide is a controversial legal category (Dobson & Sales, 2000). Are women in the year following childbirth at such an increased risk of a mental illness that they would not be held fully responsible if they murdered their baby? In 1984, the Law Reform Commission of Canada recommended that infanticide as a distinct legal entity be abolished. Despite this recommendation, infanticide remains in the Criminal Code of Canada.

Canada's homicide rate peaked in the 1970s and gradually declined from 1975 to 2003, when it reached a 30-year low. The homicide rate increased in 2004 and 2005, reaching its highest point in nearly a decade (Statistics Canada, 2006b). Figure 11.1 presents the homicide rate in Canada between 1961 and 2005. In 2005, the homicide rate was 2.04 per 100 000 population, reflecting 658 homicides committed. This was a slight increase in the homicide rate from 2004. Although the rate of homicide is substantially higher in the United States (5.6 per 100 000 in 2001 and 2002), the U.S. homicide rate has also been declining, and the rates of 2001 and 2002 resemble low rates seen in the 1960s in that country (Department of Justice, 2004).

Homicide rate. 1961 to 2005
Rate per 100 000 population

Average rate = 2.17

Figure 11.1 Homicide Rate in Canada, 1961–2005

Source: Statistics Canada, 2006b.

Characteristics of homicide in Canada include the following (Statistics Canada, 2006b):

- You are most likely to be killed by someone you know. In 2005, only 18% of solved homicides were committed by a stranger. Thirty-five percent of solved homicides were committed by family and current or former partners.

- Females are more likely to be killed by an intimate partner than are males. The spousal homicide rate against women was five times higher than that of men in 2005.

- There were 107 gang-related homicides in 2005, 35 more than in 2004. This may be the result of a change in data collection, however, as the 2005 rate officially includes cases of "suspected" gang-related activity, as well as activity that was "determined" to be gang-related, while prior rates may or may not have included suspected activity.

- There are regional differences in homicide rates across Canada. Homicide rates have been consistently higher in the Western provinces than in the Eastern provinces, with a 2005 homicide rate in Saskatchewan of 4.33 homicides per 100 000 population marking the highest rate in almost 30 years in that province.

Filicide: When Parents Kill

The killing of a child by a parent is difficult to understand. Fortunately, it is a rare event. The term **filicide** refers to the killing of children by their biological parents or step-parents and includes neonaticide (killing a baby within 24 hours of birth) and infanticide (killing a baby within first year of life). Attitudes toward parents killing their children vary across cultures and time. For example, in ancient Rome, a father had a right to kill his children (Finkel, Burke, & Chavez, 2000). A few cultures have sanctioned the gender-based killing of children. Notably, in China and India, female children are more likely to be killed due

Filicide: The killing of children by their biological parents or step-parents; includes neonaticide (killing a baby within 24 hours of birth) and infanticide (killing a baby within first year of life)

to the greater value these societies place on male children. In the past, certain Inuit and African societies killed infants that had birth defects or killed one infant when twins were born (Garber, 1947; Stewart, 2000).

Child murder in Canada is uncommon. In 2004, 55 children and youth under the age of 18 were killed (including 30 male victims and 25 female victims). This is the lowest rate since the first recording of these rates in 1974, but the murder of children and youth still accounted for about 9% of national homicides in 2004. The majority (62%) of these homicides were perpetrated by family members, and 85% of these homicides were committed by a parent. The father was the perpetrator in 59% of homicides against children by a family member between 1995 and 2004, while 32% involved the mother. Overall, it is more common for a father to be accused of killing his child than for a mother to be so accused, but the difference is not apparent for infants (Statistics Canada, 2006b). Some studies have found that stepfathers are more likely to kill a child than are biological fathers (Daly & Wilson, 1996). However, a recent study in Sweden failed to replicate this finding (Temrin, Buchmayer, & Enquist, 2000). In Canada, the proportion of step-parents accused of killing a stepchild in their family has increased in the last decade, with 14% of all parents accused of killing their child between 1995 and 2004 being a stepfather or stepmother of the child. Infants have consistently been at higher risk of homicide by a family member, and baby boys are at higher risk than baby girls, although as children age and their overall risk decreases, the gender difference also disappears (Statistics Canada, 2006b).

Mothers Who Kill

Why would a mother kill her child? Several studies have classified maternal filicides (Cheung, 1986; Resnick, 1970). Stanton and Simpson (2002) reviewed these and other studies of child murder and concluded there are three broad types of maternal filicides: (1) neonaticides, (2) those committed by battering mothers, and (3) those committed by mothers with mental illnesses.

The neonaticide group, those who kill their children within 24 hours of birth, are typically young, unmarried women with no prior history of mental illness, who are not suicidal, and who have concealed their pregnancy, fearing rejection or disapproval from their family. Battering mothers have killed their children impulsively in response to the behaviour of the child. These mothers have the highest rates of social and family stress, including marital stress and financial problems. The group with mental disorders tend to be older and married. They are likely to have killed older children, to have multiple victims, and to be diagnosed with a psychosis or depression, and they are the group most likely to attempt suicide after the murder. Some researchers have used the term "altruistic filicide" (Resnick, 1969) to describe mothers who kill out of love. In these cases, the murder is in response to the mother's delusional beliefs that the child's death will somehow protect the child.

Infanticide and Mental Illness

Does childbirth trigger mental illness? The assumption underlying the offence of infanticide is that women who kill their infants are suffering from a mental illness related to childbirth. Three types of mental illness have been identified during the postpartum period (period after childbirth): postpartum blues, postpartum depression, and postpartum psychosis. The most common type of mental illness is postpartum blues (experienced by up to 85% of women), which includes crying, irritability, and anxiety beginning within a few days of childbirth and lasting from a few hours to days but rarely continuing past day 12 (Affonso & Domino, 1984; O'Hara, 1995). Given the onset and short time span of postpartum blues, it has not been considered a causal factor in either neonaticide or filicide.

Postpartum depression (experienced by 7% to 19% of women) occurs within the first few weeks or months after birth and usually lasts for several months (O'Hara, 1995). The symptoms are identical to clinical depression and include depressed mood, loss of appetite, concentration and sleep problems, and suicidal thoughts. Recent studies have found that postpartum depression is not a mental illness that occurs as a consequence of childbirth (O'Hara, 1995).

The most severe and rare type of mental illness that has been associated with childbirth is postpartum psychosis (occurring in 1 or 2 of every 1000 births). Postpartum psychosis usually involves delusions, hallucinations, and suicidal or homicidal thoughts within the first three months after childbirth (Millis & Kornblith, 1992). Research does support a link between childbirth and postpartum psychosis. For example, in a study done in Scotland, Kendell, Chalmers, and Platz (1987) tracked the number of admissions for psychosis prior to and after childbirth. In the three months following childbirth, the number of women admitted to hospital with a diagnosis of psychosis was 25 times higher than the number admitted prior to childbirth. Box 11.1 describes the case of Andrea Yates, the Houston mother who killed her five children, and the case of Suzanne Killinger Johnson, who jumped in front of a Toronto subway train holding her infant son. These cases illustrate the potential lethality of postpartum psychosis.

Box 11.1

From Devotion to Depression: Mothers Who Kill

Postpartum depression affects about 10% of new mothers; this rate increases to about 20% to 30% for those who have had previous depressive episodes. If a mother has experienced postpartum depression with one child, she has about a 50% chance of developing postpartum depression if she has another baby.

Postpartum psychosis is the rarest but also the most severe postpartum mental illness. It afflicts about 1 in 1000 mothers within 6 months of birth. Symptoms include hearing voices, seeing things, and feeling an irrational guilt that they have somehow done something wrong. Without treatment, women may try to harm themselves or their infants. The following two cases illustrate the potential lethality of postpartum depression and psychosis.

Suzanne Killinger Johnson

Suzanne Killinger Johnson was a physician with a psychotherapy practice in Toronto. She had a history of depression while in medical school at the University of Western Ontario. She had a successful marriage, flourishing career, and supportive family and friends. In February 2000, she gave birth to a son named Cuyler. Sometime after the birth, Killinger Johnson started to become more and more obsessive about caring for Cuyler. By the spring, she started to see a therapist and was taking medication for depression. In July, she stopped taking her antidepressants, worried about the effects of the medicine in her breast milk, avoided her friends, and missed her therapy appointments. Her husband, family, and friends attempted to help her.

(continued)

However, at 6:30 A.M. on August 11, while her father had left her alone for a few minutes, she took her son, drove to a nearby subway station, and with Cuyler in her arms, jumped in front of a train. Cuyler died instantly and his mother died eight days later on August 19, 2000.

Andrea Yates

Andrea Yates had been diagnosed with postpartum depression after the birth of her fourth son, Paul. She had attempted suicide twice, was hospitalized, and was given antidepressant medication. After the birth of her daughter, Mary, Yates also experienced severe postpartum depression, was hospitalized twice, and was given antidepressants. According to her defence lawyers and mental health experts, Andrea Yates was not only experiencing postpartum depression but also postpartum psychosis.

On June 20, 2001, after her husband had left to go to work and prior to her mother arriving to help her, Andrea Yates drowned each of her five children—Noah (age seven), John (five), Luke (three), Paul (two), and Mary (six months)—in a bathtub at their family home. According to

the defence lawyers, Yates was delusional when she murdered her children, believing that she had to murder them in order to save them from Satan. The prosecution agreed that Andrea Yates had a mental illness but that she knew what she was doing and knew that killing them was wrong.

In March 2002, it took a jury four hours to reject Andrea Yates's insanity plea and find her guilty of capital murder. A week later, the same jury took 40 minutes to reject the death penalty but to sentence her to life in prison. In 2005, the Texas Court of Appeals reversed Yates's convictions because of false testimony given by a psychiatrist witness for the prosecution. A new trial ended on July 26, 2006, when Yates was found not guilty by reason of insanity and committed to a state mental hospital.

Treatment of postpartum depression and postpartum psychosis is possible. However, in both of these cases, the women had sought medical intervention but the treatment had limited success. Continuing research holds the promise of improved treatment and, ultimately, the prevention of these devastating illnesses.

Fathers Who Kill

Fathers rarely commit neonaticide. In contrast to maternal filicides, paternal filicides are often described as fatal child abuse (Brewster, Nelson, & Hymel, 1998). Fathers have lower rates of psychotic disorder but higher rates of alcohol abuse and previous criminality. Within the past decade, a history of family violence was twice as likely to be present in cases in which a father has killed a child (36%) than in cases in which a mother is accused (18%) (Statistics Canada, 2006b).

Familicide: The killing of a spouse and children

Familicide occurs when a spouse and children are killed. It is almost always committed by a man, and is often accompanied by a history of spousal and child abuse prior to the offence. Wilson, Daly, and Daniele (1995) examined 109 Canadian and British cases and found that in about half of the cases the killer committed suicide. They also found that those who killed their spouse and their own children (i.e., genetic offspring) had a greater likelihood of committing suicide than those who killed their spouse and their stepchildren. Wilson et al. (1995) also described two types of familicide murderers: the despondent nonhostile killer and the hostile accusatory killer. The despondent nonhostile killer is depressed and worried about an impending disaster for himself or his family. He kills his family and then commits suicide. Past acts of violence toward children and spouse are not characteristic of this type of killer. The hostile accusatory killer, however, expresses hostility toward his wife, often related to alleged infidelities or her intentions to terminate the relationship. A past history of violent acts is common for this type of killer.

Youth Who Kill

Sixty-five youths aged 12 to 17 were accused of homicide in Canada in 2005 (Statistics Canada, 2006b). The juvenile homicide rate in Canada has remained relatively stable over the past decade. Researchers have searched for distinguishing characteristics among youth who commit murder. Although the number of homicides by youth is approximately one-tenth that of the total number of homicides in Canada, homicide by youth holds a particular fascination in the mind of the public. What motivates youth to kill? What factors underlie homicide by youth? Corder, Ball, Haizlip, Rollins, and Beaumont (1976) compared ten youths charged with killing parents with ten youths charged with killing relatives or acquaintances with ten youths charged with killing strangers. Youth charged with parricide (killing parents) were more likely to have been physically abused, to have witnessed spousal abuse, and to report amnesia for the murders, compared with the other youth who committed murder. More recently, Darby, Allan, Kashani, Hartke, and Reid (1998) examined the association between family abuse and suicide attempts in a sample of 112 adolescents convicted of homicide. Abused youth were younger, more often Caucasian, and more likely to have attempted suicide prior to the homicide than nonabused youth.

Cornell, Benedek, and Benedek (1987) developed a typology of juvenile homicide offenders based on the circumstances of the offence: psychotic (youth who had symptoms of severe mental illness at time of murder); conflict (youth who were engaged in an argument or conflict with the victim when the killing occurred); and crime (youth who killed during the commission of another crime, such as robbery or sexual assault). When the classification system was applied to 72 juveniles charged with murder, 7% were assigned to the psychotic subgroup, 42% to the conflict subgroup, and 51% to the crime subgroup. Differences across these homicide subgroups in family background, criminal history, and psychopathology have been reported (Greco & Cornell, 1992).

Myers, Scott, Burgess, and Burgess (1995) classified 25 juvenile homicide offenders using the *FBI Crime Classification Manual*. Offenders were classified as either as "criminal enterprise" or "personal crime." Youth in the criminal enterprise group were more likely to have been abused and to have killed an adult or elderly stranger. Personal crime group murderers tended to select child or adolescent victims whom they knew.

What is the appropriate sentence for a youth who kills? Some people feel that if a youth commits "an adult crime" they should do "adult time." In nearly every state in the United States, juveniles who commit murder are automatically transferred to adult court where they can face adult penalties, which until recently included the death penalty. In Canada, the maximum sentence a youth can receive for murder is ten years. Should a juvenile who murders be treated the same as an adult who murders? Many psychologists would argue, no, they should not. Adolescents differ from adults in psychosocial functioning, including being more susceptible to peer influence, having more immature decision-making capabilities, focusing more on short-term as opposed to long-term consequences of behaviour, and being more risk-taking and impulsive (Cauffman & Steinberg, 2000).

Spousal Killers

During the period 1974–1983 in Canada, 812 wives and 248 husbands were killed by their spouses (Daly & Wilson, 1988). As this statistic makes clear, husbands are much more likely to kill their wives than wives are to kill their husbands. **Femicide** is the general term

Femicide: The killing of women

applied to the killing of women, *uxoricide* is the more specific term denoting the killing of a wife by her husband, and *mariticide* is the term denoting the killing of a husband by his wife. In 2005, 74 spousal homicides occurred in Canada, with women's victimization rates five times higher than men's (Statistics Canada, 2006b). A married woman in Canada is about nine times more likely to be killed by her partner than by a stranger (Wilson & Daly, 1993). In a study of 896 femicides in Ontario between 1974 and 1990, Crawford and Gartner (1992) found that 551 (62%) of the femicides were uxoricides. A consistent finding concerning uxoricide is the high incidence of perpetrator suicide following the murder (Crawford & Gartner, 1992). Offenders rarely commit suicide after killing acquaintances or strangers (Stack, 1997). For example, Crawford and Gartner (1992) found that after the homicide, 32% of the men committed suicide and 7% attempted suicide. Shackelford and Mouzos (2005) examined data on over 4400 homicides in Australia between 1989 and 2002 and found that women in cohabiting relationships were at a 9.5 times higher risk of homicide by their partner than were married women. Women's risk was also found to decrease with age, and risk became greater with increases in age difference between partners. Perpetrators of partner homicide were also more likely to be younger men.

Why do men kill their spouses? Crawford and Gartner (1992) found that the most common motive for uxoricide (in 43% of cases) was the perpetrators' anger over either estrangement from their partners or sexual jealously about perceived infidelity. Comparing police records in Canada, Australia, and the United States, Wilson and Daly (1993) found that recent or imminent departure by the eventual victim was associated only with a husband killing his wife and not with a wife killing her husband. A study of risk factors for femicide in abusive relationships by Campbell, Webster, and Koziol-McLain (2003) found the following factors increased the risk for homicide: offender access to a gun, previous threats with a weapon, estrangement, and the victim having left for another partner.

In a study of 90 Canadian offenders convicted of spousal homicide, Dutton and Kerry (1999) reported the following: 87% of murders were reactive and unplanned, 33% of the time the offender attempted suicide, in 67% of cases there was a history of domestic assault, and in 67% there was evidence of estrangement. This study also compared Millon Clinical Multiaxial Inventory scores (Millon, 1987) from a subsample of 50 of the spousal killers with 50 men who were attending a court-mandated treatment program for domestic violence. The most prevalent types of personality disorder in the spousal killers were passive-aggressive, avoidant, self-defeating, and dependent. In the domestic assault group, the most common personality disorders were passive-aggressive, sadistic, and antisocial.

Aldridge and Browne (2003) reviewed 22 studies and identified 9 major risk factors for spousal homicide of female victims by a male partner. These risk factors included the male partner witnessing or being a victim of violence in childhood, being in a common-law or non-marital relationship, having a larger age difference between partners, substance abuse by the male partner, sexual jealousy by the male partner, separation or the threat of separation by the female partner, length of separation (with risk decreasing over time after separation), previous stalking behaviour shown by the male partner, and the male partner having a personality disorder such as borderline, antisocial, or dependent personality disorder. In their review, the authors found that male perpetrators of spousal homicide seemed qualitatively similar to male perpetrators of nonlethal partner violence.

Bimodal Classification of Homicide

Over the past few decades, a number of researchers have attempted to characterize aggression in animals and humans in a bimodal manner (Weinshenker & Siegel, 2002). In animals, a distinction has been made between affective defence and predatory attack behaviours. In the former, an aggressive response occurs in the presence or perceived presence of fear or threat. For example, a mother animal attacks an animal that approaches her young. Predatory attack is aggression that occurs in response to prey. When you see your domestic cat stalk and try to catch a bird, it is an example of this type of aggression. Animal research has found that you can elicit affective defence or predatory attack behaviours by electrical stimulation of different parts of an animal's brain (Luo, Cheu, & Siegel, 1998).

Similarly, Kingsbury, Lambert, and Hendrickse (1997) proposed a bimodal classification scheme for the study of aggression and homicide in humans, in which homicides are classified as **reactive (or affective) aggression** and **instrumental (or predatory) aggression**. Reactive homicide is defined as impulsive, unplanned, immediate, driven by negative emotions, and occurring in response to some perceived provocation. Instrumental homicide is defined as proactive rather than reactive, and is a premeditated, calculated behaviour, motivated by some goal. This goal could be to obtain money, power, control, or even the gratification of sadistic fantasies (Meloy, 1997).

Reactive aggression: Violence that is impulsive, unplanned, immediate, driven by negative emotions, and occurring in response to some perceived provocation. Also known as *affective violence.*

Instrumental aggression: Violence that is premeditated, calculated behaviour, motivated by some goal. Also known as *predatory violence.*

Reactive homicide occurs more often among relatives, and instrumental homicide among strangers (Daly & Wilson, 1982). The majority of homicides are reactive in nature. In a large-scale study, Miethe and Drass (1999) coded 34 329 single-victim, single-offender homicides in the United States between 1990 and 1994. Eighty percent were classified as reactive, and 20% as instrumental. In this study, the victim–offender relationship was divided into three categories: strangers, acquaintances, and family members/intimates. Most of the homicides involved acquaintances (55%), with most of these being classified as reactive (80%). Family members and intimate partners accounted for 28% of the cases, with nearly all of these homicides being classified as reactive (93%). Finally, in 17% of the cases, the victim was a stranger, with 52% being classified as reactive. This study indicates that instrumental homicides do not occur exclusively among strangers, nor are reactive homicides confined to those who are well known to each other.

In a Canadian study, Woodworth and Porter (2002) used a continuum of violence—from purely reactive, reactive-instrumental, instrumental-reactive, to purely instrumental—to code homicides committed by 125 adult male offenders. In this sample, 12.8% were coded as purely reactive, 23.2% as reactive-instrumental, 20% as instrumental-reactive, and 36% as purely instrumental (8% of the sample could not be coded).

Some homicide offenders report psychological problems as a consequence of killing. One of the necessary diagnostic criteria for post-traumatic stress disorder (PTSD) is exposure to a traumatic event. Pollock (1999) speculated that offenders who engage in reactive homicide are more likely than those committing instrumental homicide to develop PTSD symptoms. Eighty British male adult homicide offenders were classified as committing an instrumental (38%) or reactive (62%) homicide. Of these, 52% were diagnosed with PTSD and nearly all (95%) had committed a reactive homicide. Thus, reactive homicide is associated with a diagnosis of PTSD following the homicide.

Multiple Murder: What Is Known

What motivates a person to kill repeatedly or to kill a group of people at once? The systematic killing of 14 university women by Marc Lépine at Montreal's École Polytechnique, the Columbine High School killing of 13, or the actions of alleged serial murderer Robert "Willie" Pickton all pose a real challenge for forensic psychologists. Both mass murder and serial murder are relatively rare events, yet they produce a morbid fascination in the public mind out of all proportion to their incidence. Their rarity is also a major factor that limits the development of a theoretical basis for understanding them. The scope of this section is limited to mass murder and serial murder that occurs outside of wartime or terrorism circumstances in which combinations of ideological, political, or racial factors provide the motivation for the murders.

Mass murder is not a new phenomenon. In 1927, Andrew Kehoe detonated 300 kg of explosives in a school located in Bath, Michigan, killing 42 and injuring 61. In 1949, Howard Unruh killed 13 people and wounded another 13 in East Camden New Jersey. In addition to the École Polytechnique murders, recent mass murders in Canada include the murder of eight biker gang members in April 2006 in London, Ontario, and the murder of four RCMP officers by James Roszko in Mayerthorpe, Alberta, in March 2005.

Serial murder is also not a new phenomenon. The first documented serial murderer in the United States was Herman Webster Mudgett, who in the late 1880s killed 27 women in Chicago. Perhaps the best-known serial murderer who has never been identified is Jack the Ripper, who killed at least five prostitutes in London in the late 1800s.

Serial murderers' motives, methods, and type of victims vary. Theodore (Ted) Bundy is believed to have killed 28 young university students; he was executed in 1989 in Florida. Jeffrey Dahmer killed 17 young men in Milwaukee and was killed in 1994 in prison by another inmate. Green River Killer David Ridgeway killed 48 young women in Washington State and remains incarcerated. In Canada, our most notorious and prolific serial killer is Clifford Olson (Robert Pickton will earn this nefarious title if convicted). (Olson is described in Box 11.4 on page 327).

Serial murder: The killing of a minimum of three people over time. The time interval between the murders varies and has been called a cooling-off period. Subsequent murders occur at different times, have no apparent connection to the initial murder, and are usually committed in different locations

Multiple murders can be classified into three types. The term **serial murder** was first coined in the early 1980s, and there is a considerable amount of disagreement regarding the definition of this term. For example, how many victims are needed?; should the motive for killing matter? (e.g., should a Mafia hit man who kills five people be labelled a serial murderer?); and should the relationship between murderer and victim be considered? Most definitions of serial murder include the criterion of the killing of a minimum of three people over time. The time interval between the murders varies and has been called a "cooling-off period." Subsequent murders occur at different times, have no apparent connection to the initial murder, and are usually committed in different locations. Most serial murderers are men who target specific types of victims (e.g., sex trade workers, homeless persons, migrant workers, runaways, hospital patients) and who engage in some planning.

Mass murder: The killing of three or more victims at a single location during one event with no cooling-off period

Mass murder is defined as the killing of three or more victims at a single location during one event with no cooling-off period. School shootings such as those at Columbine and, more recently, Virginia Tech are examples of mass murder. In the classic mass murder, an individual goes to a public place and kills strangers at that location. In contrast, in a family mass murder, three or more family members are killed, usually by another family member. Mass murderers are much more likely to commit suicide or get killed by police during the killing rampage than are serial murderers. Mass murders can also occur when the murderer intends to kill a specific person but, in doing so, kills others, as illustrated by the case of Joseph-Albert Guay. Guay placed a bomb on a Canadian Pacific Airlines flight between Quebec City and Baie-Comeau on September 9, 1949, in order to kill his wife Rita. In the ensuing explosion over Sault-au-Cochon, not only was his wife killed but 22 others were killed also.

Spree murder occurs when an individual kills three or more victims in two or more locations without a cooling-off period. The initial murder occurs while the person is in the process of committing another crime. Andrew Cunanan's killing spree in 1997 has been described as a spree murder. Cunanan killed five men across four states, finally killing Italian designer Gianni Versace in Miami. Cunanan committed suicide when the police located him on a houseboat.

Most research has focused on understanding serial murderers as compared to spree or mass murderers.

Serial Murderers: The Ultimate Predator

How many serial murderers are there? Is serial murder on the increase? Based on media reports and U.S. statistics, it appears that there has been an increase in the number of serial murderers. However, it is difficult to know the true prevalence rate of serial murderers. The apparent increase in the number of serial murderers may be due to better police investigation and communication among law enforcement agencies, which has led to better detection. What is clear from the official statistics is that the percentage of murder victims killed by strangers or unknown persons has increased dramatically in the United States. For example, in 1965, only 5% of murders were committed by strangers or by unknown persons, whereas in 1999, 51% of murders were committed by strangers or persons unknown. Egger (1999) has suggested that some of this increase is due to an increase in the number of drug-related murders but that at least part of it is the result of an increase in serial murder.

There appear to be regional differences in the rate of male serial killers. For example, DeFronzo, Ditta, Hannon, and Pruchrow (2007) measured the rate of serial killers per 10 million in various U.S. locations, and found 18.6 in California, 10.3 in Florida, 7.0 in Texas, 6.3 in New York, and 3.0 in Pennsylvania. The researchers propose that sociocultural factors may help explain these differential rates. For example, cultures that are supportive of violence appear to have higher rates of serial homicide.

Common characteristics of serial murderers include the following:

- Most serial murderers are male. In a review of 399 serial murderers in the United States between 1825 and 1995, Hickey (2006) reported that 83% were male and 17% were female.

- Most serial murderers operate on their own. However, there are team murders that are committed by two or more offenders working together. Between 1875 and 1995, there were 47 serial killer teams in the United States (Hickey, 2006). For example, the Hillside Stranglers were Kenneth Bianchi and his cousin Angelo Buono. In Canada, the most notorious team killers are Paul Bernardo and Karla Homolka, who together killed three young women, including Homolka's younger sister.

- Most serial murderers in the United States are Caucasian. Hickey (2006) in his review reported that 73% of serial murderers were Caucasian and 22% African American.

- Victims of serial murderers are usually young females who are not related to the murderer. However, the age and sex of the victim can vary. For example, Dr. Harold Shipman, England's most prolific known serial murderer, is suspected of having killed 215 people, mostly elderly women who were his patients. In addition, some serial murderers target men. John Wayne Gacy killed 33 young men in Chicago.

Female Serial Murderers Like female offenders in general, female serial murderers have not been a focus of research. One reason is that serial killing by females is extremely rare. Most female serial killers are either "black widows," those who kill husbands or family members for financial gain, or "angels of death," nurses who kill their patients. For example, Dorothea Puente was charged with nine murders of her tenants and, in 1993, convicted of three of the murders. The murders were supposedly done in order for Puente to collect the tenants' social security cheques. Puente claims that the seven people whose bodies were found in her yard had all died of natural causes and that she is innocent.

Aileen Wuornos is one of the few female serial murderers who did not kill family members or for financial gain (although she stole cash, belongings, and some of the victims' cars). In 1989 and 1990, she killed seven men she had agreed to have sex with. Initially, Wuornos claimed she had killed each of them in self-defence because they had become violent with her. Wuornos was executed in Florida in 2002.

Table 11.1 summarizes the differences between male and female serial murders. As compared to male serial murderers, female serial murders are more likely to have no prior

Table 11.1 Differences between Male and Female Serial Murderers

Point of Comparison	Male Serial Murderers	Female Serial Murderers
Prior criminal history	Males tend to have a prior criminal history.	Females tend not to have a prior criminal history.
Accomplice	Only about 25% of males have an accomplice.	About 50% of females have an accomplice.
Murder method[a]	Males are more likely to use a firearm or to strangle or stab their victims.	Females are much more likely to use poison.
Murder motive[b]	Males are more likely to kill for sexual gratification or for control.	Females are more likely to kill for money.
Victim type[c]	Males are more likely to kill strangers.	Females are much more likely to kill family members.
Geographic type	Males tend to be more geographically mobile.	Females are more likely to be place specific (i.e., to carry out all killings in one location).

[a] Hickey (2006) reported that 35% of female serial murderers killed using poison, as compared to only 5% of male serial murderers.
[b] Hickey (2006) reported that in 74% of female serial murders, money played a role, as compared to only 26% of male serial murders. In contrast, he reported that sexual gratification played a role in 55% of male serial murders, as compared to only 10% of female serial murders.
[c] Hickey (2006) found that 50% of female serial murderers had killed at least one family member, as compared to 1% of males.

Source: Hickey, 2006.

criminal record, have an accomplice, use poison, kill for money, and kill a family member or someone they know.

Serial Murderers: Why Do They Do It?

Serial murderers kill for a variety of reasons. However, research in this area is difficult to carry out because of the relatively low incidence of serial murder. This low incidence makes it challenging for researchers to come up with the kinds of generalizations that would facilitate the development of a theory to account for serial murder. As a consequence, there have been very few theories proposed to explain serial killing. The most popular model is the **trauma-control model of serial murder**, proposed by Hickey (2006), which is presented in Figure 11.2. According to this model, a multitude of factors are involved in predicting who may be predisposed to commit serial murder. Predispositional factors (e.g., biological or temperament) may be present that can impact on how individuals respond to traumatic events. Childhood traumas include a range of negative events (e.g., physical or sexual abuse, death of parent, severe parental rejection). Hickey acknowledges that the majority of people who experience traumas do not become serial killers or even become violent. He proposes that it is the combined effects of repeated traumas and how the individual copes with his or her feelings about the traumas that can lead to feelings of inadequacy, self-doubt, and worthlessness in some people. In response to these feelings, some people will start to fantasize about being in control and will develop a "veneer of self-confidence" (p. 116). As seen in Figure 11.2, some children will dissociate from the traumatic experience. This is a control mechanism for people to attempt to cope with the fear, hurt, and anger they feel about the event. However, in some people the effects of the trauma will re-emerge and they will develop low self-esteem and cope by fantasizing about having control of both themselves and others. A critical component in this model is violent fantasy. The offender fantasizes that he is in total control of the victim. He imagines committing violent acts against the victim that are often sexual in nature. The trauma-control model describes facilitators that function to decrease inhibitions or to enhance the violent fantasies. For example,

Trauma-control model of serial murder: The model suggesting that a multitude of factors are involved in predicting who may be predisposed to commit serial murder

Figure 11.2 Trauma-Control Model of Serial Murder

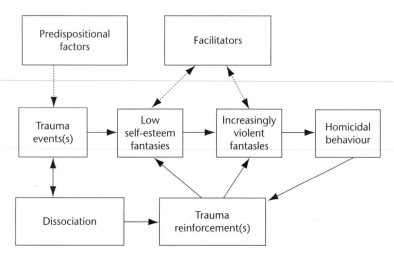

Source: Hickey, 2006.

"fantasies may be fuelled by pornography and facilitated by alcohol" (Hickey, 2006, p. 123). The broken-line arrows in Figure 11.2 indicate that there are a limited number of empirical studies to support the connection. A few people in this group will begin to act out their fantasies often by stalking others or engaging in behavioural try-outs (engaging in parts of their fantasies but not killing). Some individuals in this group will escalate to homicide.

Little research has been done to test the validity of the trauma-control model. Many, but not all, serial murderers have experienced childhood traumas. What types of fantasies do serial murderers have and what leads some people who have violent sexual fantasies to act on these fantasies whereas most do not? A study by Prentky et al. (1989) examined the role of fantasy in 17 single sexual homicide murderers and 25 serial sexual murderers. Fantasies of rape and murder were present in 86% of the serial murderers as compared to 23% of the single murderers. The trauma-control model provides a host of intriguing avenues for empirical research.

Typologies of Serial Murderers

A number of classification systems have been developed to classify serial murderers, although most have yet to be subjected to empirical verification. One typology that focuses on crime scenes and offenders is the organized-disorganized model proposed by the FBI in the 1980s. This typology is described in Chapter 3.

In 1998, Holmes and Holmes used 110 case files of serial murderers to develop a classification system based on victim characteristics and on the method and location of the murder. They proposed four major types of serial murders: (1) visionary, (2) mission-oriented, (3) hedonistic, and (4) power/control oriented. The **visionary serial murderer** kills in response to voices or visions telling him or her to kill. This type of serial murderer would most likely be diagnosed as delusional or psychotic.

The **mission-oriented serial murderer** believes there is a group of undesirable people who should be eliminated, such as homeless people, sex-trade workers, or a specific minority group.

Hedonistic serial murderers are motivated by self-gratification. These killers have been divided into three subtypes, based on the motivation for killing: lust, thrill, or comfort. The **lust serial murderer** is motivated by sexual gratification. The lust killer enjoys killing and becomes stimulated and excited by the process of killing. The **thrill murderer** derives excitement from seeing his or her victims experience terror or pain. The response of the victim stimulates and provides a sense of exhilaration for the murderer. The **comfort serial murderer** is motivated by material or financial gain. This is the only type of killer who is primarily female and who targets people known to the killer.

The **power/control serial murderer** is not motivated by sexual gratification but by wanting to have absolute dominance over the victim. These murderers may or may not engage in sexual acts, but if they do it is in order to degrade the victim.

The above typology is compelling but has been criticized for the following reasons. First, there is considerable overlap among categories. For example, lust, thrill, and power/control murders are all characterized by a controlled crime scene, a focus on process (i.e., an enjoyment of the act of killing), and a selection of specific victims. Second, the typology's developers have failed to test it empirically. Recently, Canter and Wentink (2004) tested whether or not the characteristics within each type would tend to co-occur in 100 U.S. serial murderers. The researchers failed to find support for the proposed

---

Visionary serial murderer: A murderer who kills in response to voices or visions telling him or her to kill

Mission-oriented serial murderer: A murderer who targets individuals from a group that he or she considers to be "undesirable"

Lust serial murderer: A murderer who is motivated by sexual gratification

Thrill murderer: A murderer who is motivated by the excitement associated with the act of killing

Comfort serial murderer: A murderer who is motivated by material or financial gain

Power/control serial murderer: A murderer who is motivated not by sexual gratification but by wanting to have absolute dominance over the victim typologies. One reason for the lack of support for this typology is that murderers' motives may change over the course of their killings.

Keppel and Walter (1999) applied the motivational rapist typology proposed by Groth, Burgess, and Holmstrom (1977) to classify sexual murder. They proposed two types of sexual murders that reflect the theme of power (power-assertive and power-reassurance) and two types reflecting the theme of anger (anger-retaliation and anger-excitation). The authors describe how these types differ with regard to crime scene characteristics. For example, the power-reassurance type commits a planned rape that escalates to an unplanned overkill of the victim. In contrast, the anger-excitation type commits a planned rape and murder of the victim. Using prison files from the Michigan Department of Corrections, Keppel and Walter (1999) classified 2475 sexual homicide offenders as follows: 38% power-assertive, 34% anger-retaliation, 21% power-reassurance, and 7% anger-excitation.

How well this typology will apply to serial sexual murders and whether or not it will help with the identification of serial sexual homicides remains to be tested.

Mass Murderers

Mass murderers are not all motivated by the same reasons but the outcome is always the same: the deaths of many innocent people. Mass murderers are often depressed, angry, frustrated individuals who believe they have not succeeded in life. They are often described as socially isolated and lacking in interpersonal skills. In some cases, the murder is triggered by what they perceive as a serious loss. In most cases, these offenders select targets that represent who they hate or blame for their problems. They often feel rejected by others and come to regard suicide and homicide as justified acts of revenge. A good example of a mass murderer is Marc Lépine, who is described in Box 11.2 on page 322. Most mass murderers plan their crimes and obtain semi-automatic guns in order to maximize the number of deaths. In other words, they do not "just snap" but in fact display warning signs that if recognized by others may help to prevent a tragedy (more information about threat assessment is provided in Chapter 12). In addition, mass murderers often plan to commit suicide or get killed by law enforcement officers. To date, the most deadly mass murder in North America occurred on April 16, 2007, when Seung-Hui Cho killed 32 people (27 students and 5 faculty members) on the campus of Virginia Tech before committing suicide. Thirty-two-year-old Cho was a student majoring in English at Virginia Tech and was described as being a

Memorial for victims of violent crime

Box 11.2

Canada's Deadliest Mass Murder

On December 6, 1989, 25-year-old Marc Lépine walked into a classroom at the Montreal engineering school École Polytechnique, fired a shot into the ceiling and said, "Separate. The girls on the left and the guys on the right." He told the men to leave. He then stated, "I am fighting feminism." One of the nine women left behind responded, "I am not a feminist." All nine of the women were shot (six died and three were injured). Lépine then proceeded to other parts of the school, where he shot and killed others. In total, 14 women were killed, and 10 women and 4 men were injured that day at École Polytechnique. The killing ended when Lépine committed suicide.

What prompted Marc Lépine to commit this massacre, and why did he target women? According to media reports, Lépine's father had little respect for women and was verbally and physically abusive toward both his wife and their two children (Marc and his sister). Lépine's parents separated when he was 7 years old and divorced when he was 12. He graduated from high school and attended CEGEP but dropped out during his last term. In 1986, he applied to study engineering at École Polytechnique and was offered admission conditional on completing two courses at CEGEP. Lépine has been described as quiet and shy, as showing little emotion, and as having problems with accepting authority. He had no history of alcohol or drug problems or prior criminal behaviour. Lépine was apparently uncomfortable around women and expressed his dislike of career women and women who held jobs in traditionally male occupations, such as the police force and military. He applied to the military but was not accepted.

Lépine applied for a firearms acquisition in September and received his permit in October 1989. On November 21, 1989, he purchased a Ruger Mini-14 semi-automatic rifle, which he used in the shootings. A suicide note found on Lépine's body stated "The feminists have always enraged me. They want to keep the advantages of women (e.g., cheaper insurance, extended maternity leave preceded by a preventative leave, etc.) while seizing for themselves those of men."

It is unlikely that we will ever be able to predict a tragedy such as the one that occurred on December 6, 1989. Lépine was similar to other mass murderers: socially isolated, equipped with poor interpersonal skills, frustrated and angry, and targeting a group that he blamed for the lack of success in his personal life.

A memorial plaque outside École Polytechnique lists the names of the 14 women whose lives were lost:

Geneviève Bergeron (21 years) – civil engineering student

Hélène Colgan (23 years) – mechanical engineering student

Nathalie Croteau (23 years) – mechanical engineering student

Barbara Daigneault (22 years) – mechanical engineering student

Anne-Marie Edward (21 years) – chemical engineering student

Maud Haviernick (29 years) – materials engineering student

Maryse Laganière (25 years) – budget clerk

Maryse Leclair (23 years) – materials engineering student

Anne-Marie Lemay (22 years) – mechanical engineering student

Sonia Pelletier (28 years) – mechanical engineering student

Michèle Richard (21 years) – materials engineering student

Annie St-Arneault (23 years) – mechanical engineering student

Annie Turcotte (20 years) – materials engineering student

Barbara Klucznik-Widajewicz (31 years) – nursing student

Each year on December 6, Canadians mark the day with a National Day of Remembrance and Action on Violence Against Women.

loner. Professors had encouraged him to seek counselling due to the violent themes in his writing, and he had been investigated for stalking two female students. In the suicide note he left, Cho expressed his hatred of wealthy students. In the United States, the Virginia Tech shooting has raised a fierce debate over the importance of civil liberty on the one hand and public safety on the other in domains including media coverage (i.e., whether or not to show the videos made by Cho), mental health treatment, and firearms regulations.

THE PSYCHOPATH

Psychopaths have been called intra-species predators (Hare, 1993). They seek vulnerable victims to use for their own benefit. Sometimes they get what they want by charming their victims, while at other times they use violence and intimidation to achieve their goals. Lacking in conscience and feelings for others, they satisfy their own selfish needs by preying on others. Psychopathy is defined as a personality disorder that has a collection of interpersonal, affective, and behavioural characteristics. Psychopaths are dominant, selfish, manipulative individuals who engage in impulsive and antisocial acts and who feel no remorse or shame for behaviour that often has a negative impact on others.

Descriptions of psychopathy exist in most cultures. Murphy (1976) found that the Inuit in Alaska use the term *kulangeta* to described an individual who "repeatedly lies and cheats and steals things and does not go hunting and, when the other men are out of the village, takes sexual advantage of many women—someone who does not pay attention to reprimands and who is always being brought to the elders for punishment" (p. 1026).

> **Psychopath:** An individual who is defined by a collection of interpersonal, affective, and behavioural characteristics including manipulation, lack of remorse or empathy, impulsivity, and antisocial behaviours

Assessment of Psychopathy

Hervey Cleckley (1976), a psychiatrist in Georgia, provided one of the most comprehensive clinical descriptions of the psychopath in his book *The Mask of Sanity*. The characteristics considered by Cleckley to be typical of the psychopath included superficial charm and good intelligence, unreliability and untruthfulness, lack of remorse or shame, inadequately motivated antisocial behaviour, failure to learn from experience, pathologic egocentricity, general poverty in affective relations, and a failure to follow any life plan.

Currently, the most popular method of assessing psychopathy in adults is the **Hare Psychopathy Checklist–Revised** (PCL-R) (Hare, 1991, 2003). This assessment instrument was developed by Robert Hare at the University of British Columbia and is now being used around the world. The development of PCL-R was strongly influenced by the work of Hervey Cleckley. The PCL-R is a 20-item rating scale that uses a semi-structured interview and a review of file information to assess interpersonal (e.g., grandiosity, manipulativeness), affective (e.g., lack of remorse, shallow emotions), and behavioural (e.g., impulsivity, antisocial acts) features of psychopathy. Each item is scored on a three-point scale: 2 indicates that the item definitely applies to the individual; 1 that it applies to some extent; and 0 indicates that the symptom definitely does not apply. The items are summed to obtain a total score ranging from 0 to 40. Researchers have often subdivided those administered the PCL-R into three groups: a high-PCL-R group (often called psychopaths) defined by a score of 30 or greater; a middle-scoring group (mixed group), with scores between about 20 and 30; and a low-scoring group (often called nonpsychopaths), with scores of below 20.

Initial factor analyses of the PCL-R indicated that it consisted of two correlated factors (Hare, Harpur, Hakstian, Forth, Hart, & Newman, 1990). Factor 1 reflects the combination of interpersonal and affective traits, whereas factor 2 is a combination of unstable and socially deviant traits. Researchers examined the differential correlates of these two factors and have found that factor 1 is more strongly related to predatory violence, emotional processing deficits, and poor treatment response (Hare, Clark, Grant, & Thornton, 2000; Patrick, Bradley, & Lang, 1993; Seto & Barbaree, 1999; Woodworth & Porter, 2002), whereas factor 2 is strongly related to reoffending, substance abuse, lack of education, and poor family background (Hare, 2003; Hemphill, Hare, & Wong, 1998;

> **Hare Psychopathy Checklist–Revised:** The most popular method of assessing psychopathy in adults

Porter, Birt, & Boer, 2001; Rutherford, Alterman, Cacciola, & McKay, 1997). Some researchers have argued for a three-factor model of psychopathy (Cooke & Michie, 2001). These three factors are (1) arrogant and deceitful interpersonal style, (2) deficient affective experience, and (3) impulsive and irresponsible behavioural style. This factor structure splits the original factor 1 into two factors and removes some of the antisocial items from factor 2. The most recent factor structure of the PCL-R includes these three factors plus a fourth factor entitled "Antisocial" that includes the antisocial items (Hare, 2003).

There has been a considerable amount of research supporting the use of the PCL-R in a range of samples, including male and female offenders, forensic psychiatric patients, sexual offenders, and substance abusers (Hare, 2003). Dr. Hare has been studying psychopaths for more than 35 years and is profiled in Box 11.3.

Box 11.3

Canadian Researcher Profile: Dr. Robert Hare

Dr. Robert Hare is one of the world's leading authorities on psychopathy. Currently, he is a professor (emeritus) in the Department of Psychology at the University of British Columbia and honorary professor of psychology at Cardiff University in Wales. Dr. Hare has a B.A. and M.A. from the University of Alberta and a Ph.D. from the University of Western Ontario.

Dr. Hare's more-than-35-year career studying psychopathy began when he encountered a manipulative inmate while working as a prison psychologist between his M.A. and Ph.D. studies. Hervey Cleckley's book, *The Mask of Sanity*, played a pivotal role in his thinking about the clinical nature of psychopathy. Dr. Hare's early research focused on the use of theories, concepts, and procedures from learning, motivation, and psychophysiology in the laboratory study of psychopathy, with emphasis on information-processing and emotional correlates. However, a recurrent issue was the lack of a reliable, valid, and generally acceptable method for assessing the disorder. In the late 1970s, he and his students and colleagues began development of what was to become the Hare Psychopathy Checklist-Revised (PCL-R). The PCL-R is recognized worldwide as the leading instrument for the assessment of the disorder, both for scientific research and for practical applications in mental health and criminal justice.

Dr. Hare consistently acknowledges and praises the important contributions of his students to the theory and research on psychopathy, and he is pleased that many of his students have established themselves as major figures in the field. He describes the collaborative efforts with his former students as invigorating and fruitful, with major advances being made in the assessment of psychopathy, its neurobiological nature, and its implications for the mental health and criminal justice systems. Currently, he is involved in a number of international research projects on assessment and treatment issues, risk for recidivism and violence, and functional neuroimaging. Although Dr. Hare has most often studied psychopaths in prison, he has recently begun to study them in a very different sphere—the corporate world.

He lectures widely about psychopathy, and consults with law enforcement, including the FBI, the RCMP, and

(continued)

324   Chapter 11

Her Majesty's Prison Service. He has been recognized worldwide for his research on psychopathy, receiving the Silver Medal of the Queen Sophia Center in Spain, the Canadian Psychological Association Award for Distinguished Applications to the field of Psychology, the Isaac Ray Award from the American Psychiatric Association, the American Academy of Psychiatry and Law Award for Outstanding Contributions to Forensic Psychiatry and Psychiatric Jurisprudence, and the B. Jaye Anno Award for Excellence in Communication from the National Commission on Correctional Health Care. He was the first recipient of the R.D. Hare Lifetime Achievement Award by the Society for the Scientific Study of Psychopathy.

Dr. Hare believes future forensic psychology researchers and clinicians should ensure that they are familiar with the important advances being made in cognitive/affective neuroscience and their implications for forensic psychology. The courses he most enjoyed teaching at the undergraduate level were "Brain and Behaviour" (third year) and "Forensic Psychology" (fourth year).

Dr. Hare enjoys listening to jazz and blues and is an avid sailor. He credits his wife, Averil, whom he met in the back row of a course in abnormal psychology at the University of Alberta, with much of his success. In spite of a demanding professional career of her own, she found the time and energy to actively support and encourage his work. To this day, she remains his best friend and closest confidant. Their only child, Cheryl, died in 2005 after a long battle with multiple sclerosis and leukemia. Her courage and dignity in the face of adversity had a profound influence on their appreciation of the power of the human spirit.

Psychopathy and Antisocial Personality Disorder

Antisocial personality disorder (APD) (American Psychiatric Association, 1994) refers to a personality disorder in which there is evidence for conduct disorder before age 15 and a chronic pattern of disregarding the rights of others since age 15. After age 15, a person diagnosed with APD would need to display three or more of the following symptoms:

Antisocial personality disorder: A personality disorder characterized by a history of behaviour in which the rights of others are violated

- repeatedly engaging in criminal acts
- deceitfulness
- impulsivity
- irritability
- reckless behaviours
- irresponsibility
- lack of remorse

Although psychopathy and APD share some features, APD places more emphasis on antisocial behaviours than does the PCL-R. The prevalence of APD is very high in prisons, with up to 80% of adult offenders being diagnosed with this disorder (Hare, Forth, & Strachan, 1992; Motiuk & Porporino, 1991). Using a cut-off of 30 on the PCL-R, 10% to 25% of adult offenders can be classified as psychopaths (Hare, 2003). An asymmetrical relation exists between these two disorders: nearly all psychopathic offenders meet the diagnostic criteria for APD, but most offenders diagnosed with APD are not psychopaths. APD symptoms are most strongly related to the behavioural features of psychopathy and not to the interpersonal or affective features. Figure 11.3 on page 326 illustrates the overlap between psychopathy and APD.

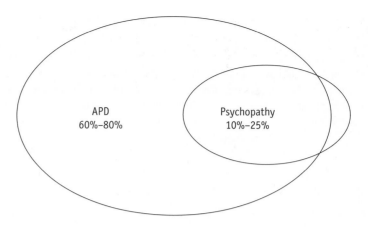

Figure 11.3 DSM-IV Antisocial Personality Disorder and PCL-R Psychopathy: Construct Overlap

Psychopathy and Violence

The characteristics that define psychopathy are compatible with a criminal lifestyle and a lack of concern for societal norms. Characteristics that ordinarily help to inhibit aggression and violence, such as empathy, close emotional bonds, and internal inhibitions, are lacking or relatively ineffective in psychopaths. Psychopathy is significant because of its association with criminal behaviour in general and violence in particular. Although psychopaths make up a relatively small proportion of the population, their involvement in serious repetitive crime and violence is out of proportion to their numbers. As stated by Hart (1998), "The two are so intimately connected that a full understanding of violence is impossible without consideration of the role played by psychopathy" (p. 367). See Box 11.4 for a description of a psychopath.

Psychopaths are high-density (prolific), versatile offenders. The crimes of psychopaths run the gamut from minor theft and fraud to cold-blooded murder. Compared to nonpsychopathic offenders, they start their criminal career at a younger age and persist longer, engage in more violent offences, commit a greater variety of violent offences, engage in more violence within institutions, and, as we will see in Chapter 12, they are more likely to be violent after release (Hare, 2003). For example, Hemphill, Templeton, Wong, and Hare (1998) reported that in a sample of 274 Canadian offenders, the mean age of first conviction for psychopaths was 18.6 years and for nonpsychopaths it was 24.3 years.

The nature of psychopaths' violence also differs from other types: "Psychopathic violence is more likely to be predatory in nature, motivated by readily identifiable goals, and carried out in a callous, calculated manner without the emotional context that usually characterizes the violence of other offenders" (Hare, 2003, p. 136). Several studies have found that offenders who engage in instrumental violence score significantly higher on measures of psychopathy than do offenders engaging in reactive violence (Cornell, Warren, Hawk, Stafford, Oram, & Pine, 1996; Serin, 1991). One study by Williamson, Hare, and Wong (1987) found that when nonpsychopaths commit violence, they are likely to target people they know and their violent behaviour is likely to occur in the context of strong emotional arousal. In contrast, psychopaths are more likely to target strangers and to be motivated by revenge or material

Box 11.4

Clifford Olson: A Predatory Psychopath

On August 22, 1997, a jury in Surrey, B.C., took just 15 minutes to reject Clifford Olson's bid for early parole. Olson is serving a life sentence for the murders of 11 children in 1980 and 1981. Clifford Olson is notorious, not only for being one of Canada's most prolific serial killers, but also for what he calls his "cash for corpses" deal he made with the police. Olson negotiated a payment of $10 000 for each body he uncovered for the RCMP. The money did not go to Olson but was put into trust for Olson's wife. In total, $100 000 was paid to this trust fund.

According to section 745 of the Criminal Code of Canada, first-degree and second-degree murderers can apply for a judicial hearing to request an earlier parole eligibility date after serving 15 years. This provision has been called the "faint hope clause" and was introduced in 1976, when the death penalty was abolished and replaced by mandatory life sentences for first-degree and second-degree murder. The parole ineligibility period for first-degree murder was 25 years; for second-degree murder it was 10 years, although the judge has the power to increase this period to up to 25 years. The underlying motivation for this clause was to provide murderers with an incentive to behave in prison, making prisons safer for correctional officers, and to motivate murderers to participate in rehabilitation.

Dr. Stanley Semrau, a forensic psychiatrist, was hired by the Crown prosecution to evaluate Clifford Olson for this judicial review hearing. Dr. Semrau assessed Clifford Olson on the Hare Psychopathy Checklist–Revised and gave him a score of 38 out of 40. At the judicial review hearing he stated, "It's certainly the highest score I have ever given anyone." Dr. Semrau also concluded that Olson was "completely untreatable" and was more dangerous now than he was when arrested in 1981, since he currently sees himself as "the ultimate serial killer."

In Dr. Semrau and Judy Gale's book, *Murderous Minds on Trial*, they devote a chapter to describing the evaluation Dr. Semrau conducted on Clifford Olson. In this chapter, he states, "I saw almost nothing that wasn't a perfect fit with the psychopath's cold, guilt-free use of others for his own ends, and chronically antisocial and deviant lifestyle."

Partly in response to Clifford Olson's use of the "faint hope clause," changes were made to section 745 of the Criminal Code. On January 1, 1997, these changes came into force. Multiple (including serial) murderers are now ineligible for a section 745 review. Clifford Olson currently remains incarcerated in the maximum-security Saskatchewan Federal Institution. He is in protective custody in order to protect him from other offenders. Clifford Olson is allowed out of his cell for one hour a day to participate in solitary exercise, to work alone as a cleaner, or for meetings.

gain. A recent study of adolescent offenders found that youth who engaged in instrumental violence were more psychopathic than other youth (Flight & Forth, 2007).

Psychopaths' use of instrumental motives extends to homicide. Woodworth and Porter (2002) investigated the association between psychopathy and the nature of homicides committed by 135 Canadian offenders. Using PCL-R scores to divide the offenders into the three groups described above—nonpsychopaths (PCL-R scores of less than 20), medium scorers (PCL-R scores between 20 and 30), and psychopaths (PCL-R scores of 30 or greater)—the percentage of homicides that were primarily instrumental (planned and motivated by an external goal) were 28%, 67%, and 93%, respectively. The researchers concluded that psychopaths engage in "cold-blooded" homicides much more often than nonpsychopaths.

Not all psychopaths are violent, nor do they all end up in prison. Hare (1998) has estimated that about 1% of the general population are psychopaths. As Hare (1993) notes, "[We] are far more likely to lose our life savings to an oily tongued swindler than our lives to a steely-eyed killer" (p. 6). Paul Babiak (2000), an organizational psychologist, consulted with six companies undergoing dramatic organizational change, such as merging and downsizing.

In each of these companies, Babiak found employees with many psychopathic features to be at the root of some of the company problems. These employees were skilled at getting information on other employees, spreading unwarranted vicious rumours about others, and causing dissension among employees. What they were not doing was pulling their own weight on the job. They were particularly good at manipulating the key players in the organization (employees who can provide them with information or upper management) and blaming others for their failures (see Babiak [1995] for a case study of the industrial psychopath).

Psychopathy and Sexual Violence

Psychopathy and sexual violence have been the focus of much research. As described above, psychopathy is associated with violent offences but is only weakly associated with sexual offences. For example, Brown and Forth (1997) reported that in a sample of 60 rapists, their PCL-R score was associated with their number of prior offences but not the number of prior sexual offences. In a larger sample of offenders, Porter, Fairweather, Drugge, Hervé, Birt, and Boer (2000) found that psychopaths engaged in significantly more violent offences than nonpsychopaths (7.3 versus 3.0, respectively) but engaged in *fewer* sexual offences (2.9 versus 5.9, respectively). One potential explanation for this finding is the high rate of sexual offending found in child molesters, who tend not to be psychopaths.

In general, offenders who commit sexual homicides are the most psychopathic, followed by mixed sexual offenders (those who sexually assault both children and adults), followed by rapists, with the lowest psychopathy scores found among child molesters (Brown & Forth, 1997; Firestone, Bradford, Greenberg, & Larose, 1998; Porter, Fairweather, et al., 2000; Quinsey, Rice, & Harris, 1995).

Other studies have evaluated the motivations of psychopaths when committing sexual crimes. Brown and Forth (1997) examined specific motivations for psychopathic and nonpsychopathic rapists. The Massachusetts Treatment Center Rapist Typology (MTC: R3) (Knight & Prentky, 1990) identifies different types of rapists based on motivation and level of social competence. Brown and Forth reported that 81% of psychopathic rapists were opportunistic or vindictive, as compared to 56% of the nonpsychopathic rapists. Nonpsychopaths were more likely to report feelings of anxiety or alienation in the 24-hour period leading up to the rape, whereas psychopaths reported positive emotions. Porter, Woodworth, Earle, Drugge, and Boer (2003) investigated the relation between psychopathy and severity of violence in a sample of 38 sexual homicide offenders. Level of sadistic violence (evidence for overkill and that the offender obtained enjoyment from hurting the victim) was related to the PCL-R total scores and with the interpersonal and affective features of psychopathy.

Psychopathy and Treatment

Are psychopathic adults responsive to treatment? Most clinicians and researchers are pessimistic, although some (e.g., Salekin, 2002) are more optimistic. As Hare (1998) states, "Unlike most other offenders, they suffer little personal distress, see little wrong with their attitudes and behavior, and seek treatment only when it is in their best interests to do so (such as when seeking probation or parole)" (p. 202).

The best-known study of treatment outcome in psychopaths was a retrospective study by Rice, Harris, and Cormier (1992). These researchers investigated the effects of an intensive therapeutic treatment program on violent psychopathic and nonpsychopathic forensic psychiatric patients. Using a matched group design, forensic patients who spent two years in the treatment program (treated group) were paired with forensic patients who were assessed but not admitted to the program (untreated group). Using file information, all patients were scored on the PCL-R using file information and were divided into psychopaths (scores of 25 or greater) and nonpsychopaths (scores of less than 25). Patients were followed for an average of 10 years after release. The violent recidivism rate was 39% for untreated nonpsychopaths, 22% for treated nonpsychopaths, 55% for untreated psychopaths, and 77% for treated psychopaths. Treatment was associated with a *reduction* in violent recidivism among nonpsychopaths, but an *increase* in violent recidivism among psychopaths. Some clinicians have concluded from the above study that we should not bother to treat psychopaths, since treatment will only make them worse: "This was the wrong program for serious psychopathic offenders" (Quinsey, Harris, Rice, & Cormier, 1998, p. 88).

Caution is required in interpreting the results of studies such as that carried out by Rice et al. (1992). Although at first glance such research implies that psychopaths are untreatable, an alternative but perhaps equally plausible account is that the treatments for psychopaths that have been tried so far have not worked (Hare et al., 2000; Richards, Casey, & Lucente, 2003; Seto & Barbaree, 1999). Reasons why a treatment may not work include the use of an inappropriate treatment and problems in implementing the treatment, such as inadequate training of those administering the treatment or lack of support from management.

Psychopathy in Youth

Research is increasingly focused on identifying the emergence of psychopathic traits in youth. The assumption is that psychopathy does not suddenly appear in adulthood but instead gradually develops from various environmental and biological antecedents. In line with this viewpoint, several measures have been recently developed to identify psychopathic traits early in development. Two assessment instruments have been adapted from the PCL-R: one for use with children and the other for adolescents. The Antisocial Process Screening Device (APSD) (Frick & Hare, 2001) is designed for assessing the precursors of psychopathic traits in children. The child is assigned a rating on various questions by parents or teachers. A self-report version of this scale also has been developed for use with adolescents. Frick, Bodin, and Barry (2000) found that the APSD has a three-dimensional structure consisting of a callous-unemotional factor, an impulsivity factor, and a narcissism factor. The Psychopathy Checklist: Youth Version (PCL:YV) (Forth, Kosson, & Hare, 2003) is a rating scale designed to measure psychopathic traits and behaviours in male and female adolescents aged 12 to 18 years.

Reservations have been raised concerning the appropriateness of applying the construct of psychopathy to children and adolescents (Edens, Skeem, Cruise, & Cauffman, 2001; Seagrave & Grisso, 2002; Zinger & Forth, 1998). One concern has been the use of the label "psychopath," a label that has many negative connotations for the public and for mental health and criminal justice professionals. As stated by Murrie, Cornell, Kaplan, McConville, & Levy-Elkon (2004), "The use of the label 'psychopath' has ominous connotations that may adversely influence treatment decisions, social service

Box 11.5

Psychopathy Label: The Potential for Stigma

If an individual is called a psychopath in court, are judges and juries likely to be more punitive toward him or her? The results from mock juror decision-making trials have been mixed. Two studies examined the effect of the psychopath label in a death penalty trial: one in which the defendant was an adult (Edens, Colwell, Deforges, & Fernandez, 2005) and one in which the defendant was a juvenile (Edens, Guy, & Fernandez, 2003). The methodology used in both studies was to present to undergraduates a written description of a defendant in a murder case. All aspects about the case are the same when presented to the various students except that the authors manipulate the diagnosis or personality traits of the defendant. In the Edens et al. (2005) study, the defendant was described as a psychopath, a psychotic, or having no mental disorder. As can be seen in Figure 11.4, mock jurors were more likely to support the death penalty for the psychopathic defendant than for the psychotic or nondisordered defendant.

Edens et al. (2003), a study that examined the influence of psychopathic traits, presented undergraduates with one of two versions of a modified newspaper clipping about a 16-year-old facing the death penalty. In one version, the juvenile defendant was described as having psychopathic traits; he was "the kind of teenager who did not feel remorse for his

behavior or guilt when he got into trouble . . . a pathological liar who manipulated people . . . arrogant" (p. 22). In contrast, the nonpsychopathic traits version described the youth as "the kind of teenager who felt remorseful and guilty when he got into trouble . . . a trustworthy adolescent who never conned people . . . modest and humble (p. 22). In this study, the mock jurors presented with the psychopathic traits version were more likely to support the death penalty and to be less supportive of the defendant receiving intervention in prison. As can be seen in Figure 11.4, mock jurors also were less likely to support the death penalty for juveniles than for adults.

Murrie, Cornell, and McCoy (2005) investigated the potential influence of a diagnosis of psychopathy, conduct disorder, or no diagnosis with juvenile probation officers. In contrast to the above studies, the diagnostic label was not strongly related to probation officers' recommendations of type of sanction, risk level, or treatment amenability. Murrie et al. (2005) state, "there was little evidence that a specific diagnosis of psychopathy affected JPO [juvenile probation officer] judgments" (p. 338). Murrie and his colleagues have also studied the impact of the psychopathy label on juvenile court judges and clinicians (Murrie, Boccaccini, McCoy, & Cornell, 2007; Rockett, Murrie, & Boccaccini, 2007).

Figure 11.4 Death Penalty Verdicts Based on Mental Disorder of Offender and Age of Offender

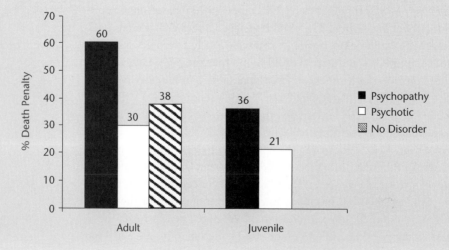

plans, and juvenile justice determinations" (p. 64). Studies examining the effects of the psychopathy label in adults and juveniles are described in Box 11.5.

Psychopathy in adults is associated with violence, is assumed to be a stable trait, and is resistant to intervention attempts. Whether psychopathic traits in youth are stable has recently been studied. For example, a study using the APSD has indicated fairly high stability across a four-year period (Frick, Kimonis, Dandreaux, & Farell, 2003). The only longitudinal study to assess psychopathic traits in youth and to reassess for psychopathy in adulthood was recently completed by Lynam, Caspi, Moffitt, Loeber, and Southamer-Loeber (2007). The results indicated that there was a moderate degree of stability in psychopathic traits from age 13 to age 24. Another concern that has been raised is whether "scores on measures of psychopathy arguably may be inflated by general characteristics of adolescence" (Edens et al. 2001, p. 59). Arguing against this last point are the few studies measuring psychopathic traits in community youth that have found the scores on psychopathy measures to be very low (Forth et al., 2003; Skilling, Quinsey, & Craig, 2001).

Research has provided some support for extending the construct of psychopathy to youth. For example, boys who score high on the callous/unemotional dimension of the APSD have more police contacts, more conduct problems, and are more likely to have a parent with APD than are children who score low on this dimension. Research using the PCL:YV has found that adolescents with many psychopathic traits become involved in criminal behaviours at an earlier age, engage in more violence in institutions and in the community, and are at a higher risk of reoffending once released as compared to other adolescents (Corrado, Vincent, Hart, & Cohen, 2004; Forth et al., 2003; Kosson, Cyterski, Steuerwald, Neumann, & Walker-Matthews, 2002; Murrie et al., 2004). In contrast, however, more recent research has questioned the utility of the PCL:YV to predict violence in adolescent female offenders (Odgers, Reppucci, & Moretti, 2005; Schmidt, McKinnon, Chattha, & Brownlee, 2006). Research has also looked at the association between psychopathic traits and other symptoms in youth. For example, Campbell, Porter, and Santor (2004) found that psychopathic traits were related to delinquency and aggression but not to anxiety or depression symptoms in a sample of male and female adolescent offenders.

One aspect of psychopathy in youth that may differ from its adult counterpart is that youth with psychopathic traits may be more responsive to interventions (Salekin, Rogers, & Machin, 2001). In contrast, however, O'Neill, Lidz, and Heilbrun (2003) examined treatment outcome in a sample of 64 adolescent substance abusers and found that youth scoring high on the PCL:YV showed poor program attendance, poor quality of participation, and less clinical improvement, and were more likely to reoffend after completing the program. Caldwell, Skeem, Salekin, and Van Rybroek (2006) compared the treatment outcome of two groups of incarcerated youth, both with very high PCL:YV scores. Youth who were given intensive treatment at a juvenile treatment centre were compared to youth who were given treatment at a juvenile correctional centre. Youth who were released from the correctional centre violently reoffended at twice the rate in a two-year follow-up as compared to the youth receiving the intensive treatment at the treatment centre. These results suggest that with the appropriate intensive treatment, youth with many psychopathic traits are amenable to treatment (Caldwell, McCormick, Umstead, & Van Rybroek, 2007).

Psychopathy: Nature versus Nurture?

The nature versus nurture debate focuses on the relative importance of a person's innate characteristics (nature) as compared to his or her personal experiences (nurture). There is growing evidence that suggests a strong genetic contribution to psychopathy.

In all research designed to tease apart the role of genes (nature) and environment (nurture) in the development of psychological traits, investigators try to hold constant the effect of either genes or environment. Typically, this involves comparing individuals who have similar genes but who are raised in different environments. Variations on this basic idea can take several forms. Identical twins (who have identical genes) can be compared when raised apart from each other. This holds genetic influences constant while allowing the environment to vary. In this kind of study, the twins are usually compared to randomly paired individuals. Also, fraternal twins (who share half their genes) raised together can be compared to identical twins (who share all their genes) raised together. Finally, biological siblings (who share half their genes) raised together can be compared to adoptive siblings (who share no genes but who are raised in the same environment).

To date, the only type of studies that have been done to measure the heritability of psychopathic traits are studies comparing identical and fraternal twins. Several twin studies have been done and all have yielded similar findings. In a study of adult male twins, Blonigen, Carlson, Krueger, and Patrick (2003) had each pair of identical and fraternal twins complete the Psychopathic Personality Inventory (PPI) (Lilienfeld & Andrews, 1996). Identical twins were much more similar in their PPI scores than were fraternal twins. Genetic influences accounted for between 29% and 59% of the variance for each of the different PPI subscales. In a recent adolescent twin study in Sweden, Larsson, Andershed, and Lichtenstein (2006) also found a strong genetic influence using the Youth Psychopathic Inventory (Andershed, Gustafson, Kerr, & Håkan, 2002). Finally, in a sample of seven-year-old twin pairs in the United Kingdom, Viding, Blair, Moffitt, and Plomin (2005) found that callous-unemotional traits were moderately to highly heritable. These studies point to the importance of genetic factors, but environmental factors such as adverse family background may influence how these innate traits are expressed.

Does Family Matter?

The best research method to determine whether family experiences are related to the development of psychopathy is to do a prospective longitudinal study. Such research would study a group of young children and follow them through childhood, adolescence, and into adulthood, measuring family background variables and psychopathic traits. The strength of this type of study is that it allows researchers to avoid retrospective bias (the tendency to reconstruct past events so that they are consistent with an individual's current beliefs) and to establish causal order. Unfortunately, there are very few prospective longitudinal studies that specifically investigate the development of psychopathy.

The Cambridge Study in Delinquent Development is a 40-year prospective study of antisocial behaviour of 411 London boys who have been followed up from age 8 to age 48. At age 48, the men were assessed using the Hare Psychopathy Checklist: Screening Version (PCL:SV) (Hart, Cox, & Hare, 1995). Farrington (2006) reported that of those men scoring 10 or more on the PCL:SV, 97% had been convicted of an offence and 48.5% of these men were chronic offenders (convicted more than ten times). Measuring family background variables at ages eight to ten, the best predictors of adult psychopathy were having a criminal father or mother, a son having a father who was uninvolved with him, having a low family income, coming from a disrupted family, and experiencing physical neglect.

In another longitudinal study, Weiler and Widom (1996) used court records to identify over 900 children who had been abused or neglected prior to age eleven and compared them to a control group matched on age, race, gender, elementary school class, and place of residence. Children were followed-up after 20 years and assessed on a modified PCL-R. Children who had been abused had slightly higher modified PCL-R scores as compared to the control sample.

Likely no single variable or combination of family background variables is responsible for the development of psychopathy. Current research is consistent with the view that there are multiple developmental pathways to the development of psychopathy, some of which involve family background and others in which psychopathy emerges irrespective of family background.

Psychopathy and Law Enforcement

According to O'Toole (2007), "psychopathy can be described as one of law enforcement's greatest challenges" (p. 305). Psychopaths engage in high rates of crime, including violent offences. Thus, law enforcement personnel will often come into contact with psychopaths. In some cases, the contact can lead to lethal consequences. For example, Pinizzotto and Davis (1992) conducted a study of the characteristics of killers of police officers. Almost half of these killers had personality and behaviour features consistent with psychopathy. O'Toole (2007) describes the potential crime scene characteristics manifested by a psychopathic violent offender. For example, impulsivity (a feature of psychopathy) can be manifested at a crime scene by injury pattern to the victim, choice of weapon, and time and location of crime. Some psychopaths are charming and manipulative and will be more likely to use a con to minimize the threat they pose when approaching a victim. For example, a prolific serial killer convinced sex trade workers that he was not a threat by having children's toys visible in his car and a photograph of his young son on the dashboard. Another challenge for law enforcement personnel is to develop effective methods for interrogating psychopathic suspects with. For example, when interrogating a suspected psychopathic serial killer, trying to get the suspect to confess by saying such things as, "Think about the family of the victims" or "You will feel better if you tell us about it" will likely be counterproductive. Instead, appealing to the psychopath's sense of grandiosity and need for status might be more productive.

What Makes Them Tick?: Cognitive and Affective Models of Psychopathy

A number of theories have been proposed to help forensic psychologists to understand the development of psychopathy. Two of the most prominent theories of psychopathy place emphasis on either cognitive or affective processes. Newman, Brinkley, Lorenz, Hiatt, and MacCoon (2007) have proposed that psychopaths have a response modulation deficit. According to this theory, psychopaths fail to use contextual cues that are peripheral to a dominant response set to modulate their behaviour. In other words, if a psychopath is engaging in a specific rewarded behaviour, they will not pay attention to other information that might inhibit their behaviour. This theory has been used to explain why psychopaths fail to learn to avoid punishment (i.e., have poor passive avoidance).

The other theory proposes that psychopaths have a deficit in the experience of certain critical emotions that guide prosocial behaviour and inhibit deviance (Blair, 2006; Hare, 2007; Patrick, 2007). Hervey Cleckley (1976) was the first person to theorize that psychopaths had a deep-rooted emotional deficit that involved the disconnection between cognitive-linguistic processing and emotional experience. In one of the first experimental studies to measure this deficit, Williamson, Harpur, and Hare (1991) showed that psychopaths fail to show the normal, faster reaction times to emotional words on a lexical-decision task ("Is the word you see on the screen a real word or a nonword?)". In addition, the study found that psychopaths' brain wave activity does not differentiate between emotional and neutral words.

Researchers are now testing these two theories in youth to determine which of these deficits may be present early in life and which may develop later.

SUMMARY

1. Although homicide receives extensive media coverage, it occurs relatively infrequently in Canada. Certain trends are present in homicide statistics: individuals are most likely to be killed by someone they know, and females are more likely to be killed by an intimate partner than are males. While the overall incidence of homicides has been declining since the mid-1970s, one area in which it has been increasing is in gang-related murders. Homicide rates vary across regions in Canada, with higher rates in the Western provinces than in the Eastern provinces.

2. Reactive homicide is defined as impulsive, unplanned, immediate, driven by negative emotions, and occurring in response to some perceived provocation. Instrumental homicide is defined as proactive rather than reactive and is a premeditated, calculated behaviour, motivated by some goal.

3. Three types of multiple murders have been distinguished. Serial murder is the killing of a minimum of three people over time. The time interval between the murders varies and has been called a cooling-off period. Mass murder is the killing of three or more victims at a single location during one event, with no cooling off period. Spree murder occurs when an individual kills three or more victims in two or more locations without a cooling off period. The initial murder occurs while the person is in the process of committing another crime.

4. Psychopathy is a personality disorder defined by a cluster of interpersonal, affective, and behavioural features. Psychopaths begin their criminal career earlier, persist longer, and are more violent and versatile than other offenders. Most of the murders committed by psychopaths are instrumental.

5. Research is increasingly focused on identifying the emergence of psychopathic traits in youth, and assessment instruments have been developed to measure psychopathic

traits in children and adolescents with some success. Concerns have been raised about the potential problems with labelling youth as psychopaths. These concerns have focused on (1) the issue of labelling a youth as a psychopath, (2) the stability of psychopathic traits from late childhood to early adulthood, and (3) the possibility that characteristics of psychopathy are common features of normally developing youth.

6. Two of the most prominent theories of psychopathy place emphasis on either cognitive or affective processes. Newman and his colleagues have proposed that psychopaths have a response modulation deficit. According to this theory, psychopaths fail to use contextual cues that are peripheral to a dominant response set to modulate their behaviour. The other theory proposes that psychopaths have a deficit in the experience of certain critical emotions that guide prosocial behaviour and inhibit deviance.

Key Concepts

antisocial personality disorder 325

comfort serial murder 320

familicide 312

femicide 313

filicide 309

Hare Psychopathy Checklist–Revised 323

infanticide 308

instrumental (predatory) aggression 315

lust serial murderer 320

mass murder 316

mission-oriented serial murderer 320

power/control serial murder 320

psychopaths 323

reactive (affective) aggression 315

serial murder 316

spree murder 317

thrill murderer 320

trauma-control model of serial murder 319

visionary serial murderer 320

Discussion Questions

1. Your friend has been following the Robert Pickton serial murder case in the newspaper and realizes that she has heard of hardly any female serial killers. She knows you have been studying forensic psychology and asks you about female serial killers. Describe the characteristics associated with male and female serial killers.

2. Homicide offenders have been classified into instrumental and reactive types. What are the treatment implications for these two types of murderers?

3. You are going to conduct a study on the differences between youth and adult murderers. Describe the methodology you would use and the variables you would measure.

4. You have been hired by the police department to consult on a serial killing case. You suspect the serial killer might be a psychopath. Describe to the homicide investigators the key features of psychopathy and the potential crime scene characteristics of psychopathic serial killers.

5. Psychopaths have been called intra-species predators. How strong is the link between psychopathy and violence?

6. The term psychopathy has many negative connotations. What are the potential problems with using this label to identify youth?

Readings

Babiak, P., & Hare, R.D. (2006). *Snakes in suits: When psychopaths go to work.* New York: Harper Collins.

Hare, R.D. (1993). *Without conscience: The disturbing world of psychopaths among us.* New York: Guilford Press.

Hickey, E.W. (2006). *Serial murderers and their victims.* Belmont, CA: Thomson.

Websites

Dr. Robert Hare's Homepage
www.hare.org

Society for the Scientific Study of Psychopathy
www.psychopathysociety.org

Statistics Canada
www.statcan.ca

Chapter 12
Risk Assessment

Learning Objectives

- Define the components of risk assessment.

- List what role risk assessments play in Canada.

- Describe the types of correct and incorrect risk predictions.

- Differentiate among static, stable, and acute dynamic risk factors.

- Describe unstructured clinical judgment, actuarial prediction, and structured professional judgment.

- List the four major types of risk factors.

Joanne Marshall has served one year of a three-year sentence for the offence of assault causing bodily harm. The assault occurred late one evening after Joanne had returned home from drinking with her friends. She got into a heated argument with her boyfriend, grabbed a knife from the kitchen, and stabbed him in the shoulder. A prison psychologist has completed a risk assessment and her case management officer is supporting her application for parole. Joanne is going to appear tomorrow in front of three members from the National Parole Board (NPB) to discuss the offence she committed, her plans if released, and what intervention programs she has participated in. The NPB members will need to consider what level of risk Joanne poses for reoffending, including whether or not she will engage in another violent act. They will also attempt to determine whether she has developed more appropriate ways of dealing with interpersonal conflict.

Every day, individuals make judgments about the likelihood of events. Predictions are made about midterm exam grades, being admitted into law school, recovering from an episode of depression, or committing a criminal act after release from prison. Our legal system frequently requires decisions about the likelihood of future criminal acts that can significantly influence the lives of individuals. With the possibility that offenders could spend years or even the remainder of their lives in confinement, decisions by psychologists can have a significant impact. Predicting future violence has been described as "one of the most complex and controversial issues in behavioral science and law" (Borum, 1996, p. 945).

Although it is clear that significant advances have taken place since the 1990s, risk assessment and prediction remains imperfect. Bonta (2002) concludes that "risk assessment is a double-edged sword. It can be used to justify the application of severe sanctions or to moderate extreme penalties. . . . However, the identification of the violent recidivist is not infallible. We are not at the point where we can achieve a level of prediction free of error" (p. 375). Nonetheless, the systematic assessment of risk provides judicial decision makers, such as judges and the National Parole Board, with much needed information to help them make challenging decisions.

The goal of this chapter is explore the major issues associated with risk prediction in a forensic context. In particular, the focus will be on understanding the task of assessing risk and predicting violence.

WHAT IS RISK ASSESSMENT?

In the past two decades, we have seen a change in the way risk is viewed. Prior to the 1990s, risk was seen as a dichotomy—the individual was either dangerous or not dangerous. Nowadays, risk is regarded as a range—the individual can vary in the degree to which he or she is considered dangerous (Steadman, 2000). In other words, the shift has added a dimension of probability to the assessment of whether a person will commit violence. The focus on probability reflects two considerations. First, it highlights the idea that probabilities may change across time. Second, it recognizes that risk level reflects an interaction among a person's characteristics, background, and possible future situations that will affect whether or not the person engages in violent behaviour.

The process of risk assessment includes both a "prediction" and "management" component (Hart, 1998). The prediction component describes the probability that an individual will commit future criminal or violent acts. The focus of this component is on

Risk assessment: The necessary components

identifying the risk factors that are related to this likelihood of future violence. The management component describes the development of interventions to manage or reduce the likelihood of future violence. The focus of this component is on identifying what treatment(s) might reduce the individual's level of risk or what conditions need to be implemented to manage the individual's risk. As described by Hart (1998), "the critical function of risk assessments is violence *prevention*, not violence *prediction*" (emphasis in the original; p. 123).

RISK ASSESSMENTS: WHEN ARE THEY CONDUCTED?

Risk assessments are routinely conducted in the civil and criminal contexts. Civil contexts refer to the private rights of individuals and the legal proceedings connected with such rights. Criminal contexts refer to situations in which an individual has been charged with a crime. Common to both contexts is a need for information that would enable legal judgments to be made concerning the probability of individuals committing some kind of act that would disrupt the peace and order of the state or individuals within the state.

Civil Setting

A number of civil contexts require risk assessment:

- *Civil commitment* requires a individual to be hospitalized involuntarily if he or she has a mental illness and poses a danger to himself or herself or others. A mental health worker, usually a psychiatrist or psychologist, would need to know the probability of violence associated with various mental disorders and be able to identify whether the circumstances associated with individual patients would affect the likelihood that they would harm others or themselves.

- Assessment of risk in *child protection* contexts involves the laws that are in place to protect children from abuse. The risk of physical or sexual abuse or neglect is considered when a government protection agency, such as the Children's Aid Society, decides whether to temporarily remove a child or to terminate parental rights. In order to provide assistance to protection agencies, professionals need to be familiar with the risk factors that predict childhood maltreatment.

- *Immigration* laws prohibit the admission of individuals into Canada if there are reasonable grounds to believe they will engage in acts of violence.

- *School* and *labour regulations* also provide provisions to prevent any kind of act that would endanger others.

- Other civil contexts include *duty to warn* and *limits of confidentiality*.

Mental health professionals are expected to consider the likelihood that their patients will act in a violent manner and to intervene to prevent such behaviour. According to Birch (1992), litigation surrounding duty to protect is only just beginning in Canada. In her review of Canadian cases, she found none in which a mental health professional had been sued by a third party for injuries their clients had committed against a third party. The Canadian Psychological Association's Code of Ethics for Psychologists includes a guide to help psychologists decide the most ethical action for any potential dilemma; this guide is closely connected to ethical theory, but lacks empirical support (Hadjistavropoulos & Malloy, 2000).

Patients may decide not to disclose their deviant thoughts and fantasies to professionals for fear that their doctors will contact the police. In the United Kingdom, the precedent-setting case that balances the duty of confidentiality and the duty to disclose is *W. v. Egdell* (1990). In this case, W. was a patient confined to a psychiatric facility after committing a series of murders. Dr. Egdell, a psychiatrist, was hired by W.'s lawyers to conduct mental health assessment. The psychiatrist's report concluded that W. expressed a lack of remorse and maintained an interest in making homemade bombs. Dr. Egdell asked the lawyers for their permission to send his report to the medical director of the hospital where W. was institutionalized. Dr. Edgell's request was refused, but he went ahead anyway and forwarded his report to the hospital. W. launched an injunction to stop the hospital from using the report and for damages for breaching confidentiality. W.'s suit was dismissed, showing that public safety overrides the duties of confidentiality.

Criminal Settings

The assessment of risk occurs at nearly every major decision point in the criminal justice and forensic psychiatric systems, including pretrial, sentencing, and release. A person can be denied bail if there is a substantial likelihood that he or she will commit another criminal offence. In the case of adolescent offenders, the judge can decide to apply adult criminal sanctions depending on the age, type of offence, and risk level posed by the youth. Risk also plays a role in decisions about whether a youth should be sent to secure custody or not. For example, adolescent offenders should only be committed to secure custody if they are considered at high risk if placed in open custody, or if they were to serve a probation term in the community.

As in civil settings, an important issue in risk assessment in criminal settings is the disclosure of information about potential risk. However, in criminal settings, this must be considered in light of the solicitor–client privilege that is fundamental to criminal proceedings. In order for lawyers to adequately represent their clients, they must be able to freely discuss the case with the clients.

This privilege is also extended to experts retained by lawyers. A case in Canada has clarified when solicitor–client privilege and doctor–patient confidentiality must be set aside for the protection of members of the public. *Smith v. Jones* (1999) involved a psychiatrist who was hired to aid a defence lawyer in preparing a case. The client was a man accused of aggravated sexual assault on a prostitute. The accused told the psychiatrist of his plans to kidnap, sexually assault, and kill prostitutes. The psychiatrist told the defence lawyer about his concerns that the accused was likely to commit future violent offences unless he received treatment. When the psychiatrist found out that the defence lawyer was not going to address his concerns at the sentencing hearing (the accused pled guilty to the charge of aggravated assault), he filed an affidavit providing his opinion about the level of risk posed by the accused. The trial judge ruled that due to concerns about public safety, the psychiatrist was duty-bound to disclose to the police and the Crown counsel the information he obtained. The case was appealed to the Supreme Court, which ruled that in cases where there is "clear, serious, and imminent danger," public safety outweighs solicitor–client privilege.

Although risk assessment is a routine component of many sentencing decisions, it is a critical component of certain kinds of sentencing decisions. For example, after 1947, when habitual criminal legislation was introduced, offenders could be sentenced to an indefinite period of incarceration. In 1977, dangerous offender legislation was enacted that requires mental health professionals to provide an assessment of risk for violence. Changes to the legislation in 1997 made indefinite incarceration the only option if an offender is found to be a dangerous offender (see Chapter 9 for more information about dangerous offenders). At the same time, a new category of dangerous persons was created, referred to as long-term offenders. To be declared a long-term offender, a person must pose a substantial risk for violently reoffending. Thus, risk assessment is also a core component of this legislation.

Risk assessment is also required for decisions concerning release from correctional and forensic psychiatric institutions, such as parole. If a person is sentenced to prison in Canada, he or she can apply to the National Parole Board to get early release. Parole Board members use a variety of sources of information (including risk assessments provided by institutional psychologists) to decide the likelihood that the offender will commit another violent offence if released. Although most offenders get released on statutory release (after serving two-thirds of their sentence), statutory release can be denied if the offender is likely to commit further violent offences. Finally, a patient who has been found not criminally responsible on account of a mental disorder (see Chapter 8) can be released from a secure forensic psychiatric facility only if a risk assessment is completed.

Clearly, risk assessment plays an integral role in legal decision making, both in civil and criminal settings, allowing informed decisions that weigh the likelihood that an individual will engage in a dangerous or criminal act in the future. In the sections that follow, we will look at the predictive accuracy of these assessments, as well as the factors that actually predict violence.

TYPES OF PREDICTION OUTCOMES

Predicting future events will result in one of four possible outcomes. Two of these outcomes are correct, and two are incorrect. The definitions provided below are stated in terms of predicting violent acts but could be used for any specific outcome (see also Table 12.1 on page 342):

- A **true positive** represents a correct prediction and occurs when a person who is predicted to be violent engages in violence.

- A **true negative** is also a correct prediction and occurs when a person who is predicted not to be violent does not act violently.

- A **false positive** represents an incorrect prediction and occurs when a person is predicted to be violent but is not.

- A **false negative** is also an incorrect prediction and occurs when a person is predicted to be nonviolent but acts violently.

[handwritten margin note: corred →will]

True positive: A correct prediction that occurs when a person who is predicted to engage in some type of behaviour (e.g., violent act) does so

True negative: A correct prediction that occurs when a person who is predicted not to engage in some type of behaviour (e.g., violent act) does not

False positive: An incorrect prediction that occurs when a person is predicted to engage in some type of behaviour (e.g., violent acts) but does not

False negative: An incorrect prediction that occurs when a person is predicted not to engage in some type of behaviour (e.g., violent acts) but does

Table 12.1 Predictions: Decisions versus Outcomes

	Outcome	
Decision	*Reoffends*	*Does Not Reoffend*
Predicted to reoffend	True positive (correct prediction)	False positive (incorrect prediction)
Predicted to not reoffend	False negative (incorrect prediction)	True negative (correct prediction)

The two types of errors are dependent on each other. Minimizing the number of false positive errors results in an increase in the number of false negative errors. The implication of these errors varies depending on the decisions associated with them, and in many cases the stakes are high. A false positive error has implications for the individual being assessed (such as denial of freedom), whereas a false negative error has implications for society and the potential victim (such as another child victimized by a sexual offender). In some cases, it is perhaps tolerable to have a high rate of false positives if the consequences of such an error are not severe. For example, if the consequence of being falsely labelled as potentially violent is being supervised more closely while released on parole, the consequence may be acceptable. However, if the consequence of being falsely labelled as potentially violent contributes to a juror's decision to decide in favour of the death penalty, then this is too high a price to pay. As in many legal settings, the consequences for the individual must be weighed in relation to the consequences for society at large.

The Base Rate Problem

A problem with attempting to predict violence is determining base rates. The **base rate** represents the percentage of people within a given population who commit a criminal or

Deadly violence: Students escaping from a school shooter

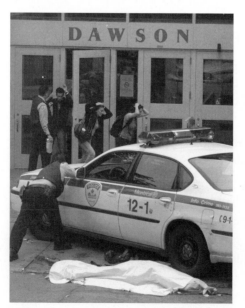

violent act. It is difficult to make accurate predictions when the base rates are too high or too low. A problem that emerges when attempting to predict events that have a low base rate is that many false positives will occur. For example, the past decade has seen several high-profile school shootings. However, although these events generate much media coverage, they occur infrequently. Any attempt to predict which individual youths might engage in a school shooting would result in many youths being wrongly classified as potential shooters.

The base rate can vary dramatically depending on the group being studied, what is being predicted, and the length of follow-up period over which the individual is monitored. For example, the base rate of sexual violence tends to be relatively low, even over extended follow-up periods, whereas the base rate for violating the conditions of a conditional release is very high. The base rate problem is not such a concern if predictions of violence are limited to groups with a high base rate of violence, such as incarcerated offenders. The general rule is that it is easier to predict frequent events than infrequent events.

A History of Risk Assessment

Before 1966, relatively little attention was paid to how well professionals could assess risk of violence. In the 1960s, civil rights concerns provided the rare opportunity to study the accuracy of mental health professionals to predict violence. In the case of *Baxstrom v. Herald* (1966), the U.S. Supreme Court ruled that the plaintiff Johnnie Baxstrom had been detained beyond his sentence expiry and was ordered released into the community. As a result of this case, more than 300 mentally ill offenders from the Dannemora State Hospital for the Criminally Insane and another state hospital were released into the community or transferred to less secure institutions. Steadman and Cocozza (1974) followed 98 of these patients who were released into the community but had been considered by mental health professionals as too dangerous to be released. Only 20 of these patients were arrested over a four-year period, and of these, only seven committed a violent offence.

In a larger study, Thornberry and Jacoby (1979) followed 400 forensic patients released into the community due to a similar civil rights case in Pennsylvania (*Dixon v. Attorney General of the Commonwealth of Pennsylvania*, 1971). During an average three-year follow-up period, 60 patients were either arrested or rehospitalized for a violent incident.

The two studies we have just described are known as the Baxstrom and Dixon studies. These cases and similar ones call into question the ability of mental health professionals to make accurate predictions of violence. Two key findings emerged from the research. First, the base rate for violence was relatively low. For example, in the Baxstrom study, 7 out of 98 (roughly 7%) violently reoffended, as did 60 out of 400 (15%) in the Dixon study. Second, the false positive rate was very high. In the Baxstrom and Dixon studies, the false positive rates were 86% and 85%, respectively. These findings indicate that in the past many mentally disordered forensic patients were needlessly kept in restrictive institutions based on erroneous judgments of violence risk.

Ennis and Litwack (1974) characterized clinical expertise in violence risk assessment as similar to "flipping coins in the courtroom" and argued that clinical testimony be barred from the courtroom. Other researchers have gone even further, concluding that "no expertise to predict dangerous behavior exists and . . . the attempt to apply this supposed knowledge to predict who will be dangerous results in a complete failure" (Cocozza & Steadman, 1978, p. 274).

This pessimism continued into the 1980s. John Monahan, a leading U.S. researcher, summarized the literature in 1981 and concluded that "psychiatrists and psychologists are accurate in no more than one out of three predictions of violent behavior over a several-year period among institutionalized populations that had both committed violence in the past (and thus had a high base rate for it) and who were diagnosed as mentally ill" (Monahan, 1981, p. 47).

Notwithstanding the above conclusion, both Canadian and U.S. courts have ruled that predictions of violence risk do not violate the basic tenets of fundamental justice, nor are they unconstitutional. In *Barefoot v. Estelle* (1983), the U.S. Supreme Court determined the constitutionality of a Texas death penalty appeal decision. Thomas Barefoot burned down a bar and shot and killed a police officer. Barefoot was convicted of capital murder and, at the sentencing phase of the trial, testimony was presented from two psychiatrists (one being Dr. James Grigson, whom we will discuss later in the chapter) about the threat of future dangerousness posed by Thomas Barefoot. Both psychiatrists testified, based on a hypothetical fact situation, that the individual described would be a threat to society. The judge sentenced Barefoot to death. The U.S. Supreme Court rejected the defendant's challenge that psychiatrists were unable to make sufficient accurate predictions of violence and ruled that the use of hypothetical questions to establish future dangerousness was admissible. The court concluded that mental health professionals' predictions were "not always wrong . . . only most of the time" (p. 901).

Canadian courts have also supported the role of mental health professionals in the prediction of violent behaviour (*Re Moore and the Queen*, 1984). For example, in a dangerous offender case, the issue of whether psychiatric testimony should be admitted as evidence was evaluated. The court concluded, "The test for admissibility is relevance, not infallibility . . . psychiatric evidence is clearly relevant to the issue whether a person is likely to behave in a certain way" (*R. v. Lyons*, 1987).

METHODOLOGICAL ISSUES

Risk assessment assumes that risk can be measured. Measurement, in turn, assumes that an instrument exists for the measurement of risk. What would be the ideal way to evaluate an instrument designed to measure risk? The way to proceed would be to assess a large number of offenders and then, regardless of their risk level, release them into the community. The offenders would then be tracked to see if they commit another criminal act. This way, the risk instrument could be evaluated to determine if it could accurately predict future criminal acts. However, although this is an ideal scenario from a research perspective, it is not ethically feasible to release high-risk individuals into the community. In reality, the sample available for evaluating a risk-assessment instrument is limited to those with a relatively low risk of reoffending. This constrains the kinds of conclusions that can be drawn when risk assessment is evaluated in the real world.

Monahan and Steadman (1994) have identified three main weaknesses of research on the prediction of violence. The first issue concerns the limited number of risk factors being studied. Violent behaviour is due to a complex interaction between individual dispositions and situational factors. In other words, there are many different reasons that someone engages in violence. Thus, many risk factors are likely involved, including the person's background, social situation, and biological and psychological features. Many studies have focused on only a limited number of risk factors. Assessment of risk may be improved by measuring more of the reasons people engage in violence.

The second issue concerns how the criterion variable (the variable you are trying to measure) is measured. Researchers have often used official criminal records as their criterion measure. However, many crimes may never be reported to police. Thus, many false positives may be undiscovered true positives. Even violent crimes may go undiscovered and many violent sexual crimes are recorded as simply violent in nature. Some research shows that the number of recorded *violent* crimes of sexual offenders is a better estimate of the number of *sexual* crimes they may have committed (Rice, Harris, Lang, & Cormier, 2006). In short, use of official records underestimates violence. When official records are combined with interviews with patients or offenders and with collateral reports (information from people or agencies who know the patient or offender), the rate of violence increases. The MacArthur Violence Risk Assessment Study (Steadman et al., 1998) illustrates the effect of using different measures. Using official agency records, the base rate for violence was 4.5%, but, when patient and collateral reports were added, the base rate increased to 27.5%, a rate of violence six times higher than the original base rate.

Finally, how the criterion variable is defined is a concern. In some studies researchers will classify their participants as having either engaged in violence or not. Monahan and Steadman (1994) recommend that researchers expand this coding to include the severity of violence (threatened violence versus severe violence), types of violence (spousal violence versus sexual violence), targets of violence (family versus stranger-directed violence), location (institutions versus community), and motivation (reactive [violence as the outcome of or reaction to an event] versus instrumental [violence used as an instrument in the pursuit of some goal]). It is likely that some risk factors will be associated with certain forms of violence; for example, a history of sexual offences may predict future sexual offences but not future bank robberies.

JUDGMENT ERROR AND BIASES

How do psychologists make decisions when conducting risk assessments? Researchers have identified the typical errors and biases in clinical decision making (Elbogen, 2002). The shortcuts people use to help make decisions are called heuristics (Tversky & Kahneman, 1981). Some of these heuristics lead to inaccurate decisions. Clinicians may make several types of decision errors. Clinicians include traits they intuitively believe to be important or assume to be associated with the risk but that actually are not (Odeh, Zeiss, & Huss, 2006). Chapman and Chapman (1967) define an **illusory correlation** as the belief that a correlation exists between two events that in reality are either not correlated or correlated to a much lesser degree. For example, a clinician might assume a strong correlation between a diagnosis of mental disorder and high risk for violent behaviour. Although some forms of mental disorder are related to an increased risk, a relationship has not been consistently found (Monahan & Steadman, 1994). Clinicians also tend to ignore base rates of violence (Monahan, 1981). Clinicians working in prisons or forensic psychiatric facilities may not be aware of how often individuals with specific characteristics act violently. For example, the base rate for recidivism in homicide offenders is extremely low. Other investigators (Borum, Otto, & Golding, 1993) have noted the tendency to rely on highly salient or unique cues, such as bizarre delusions.

Illusory correlation: Belief that a correlation exists between two events that in reality are either not correlated or correlated to a much lesser degree

In general, people tend to be overconfident in their judgments (see Kahneman & Tversky, 1982). In one of the few studies that have investigated the link between confidence and violence prediction, McNiel, Sandberg, and Binder (1998) measured the association between clinicians' ratings of the probability of inpatient violence and their confidence level in their ratings. Clinicians working in an acute psychiatric unit were asked to rate the likelihood a patient would physically attack other people within one week of arrival and to indicate their degree of confidence (i.e., low, moderate, or high). The prediction of violence accuracy depended on the confidence of the clinician. The more confidence expressed by a clinician in his or her risk judgment, the more accurate that person was. Conversely, clinicians who were less confident were less accurate in their risk judgments. For example, clinicians rated eight patients with a high likelihood of committing a physical attack and expressed a high level of confidence in their ratings for these patients. Of these patients, six (75%) were later physically assaultive. In contrast, clinicians rated 11 patients as very likely to commit a physical attack but expressed a low level of confidence in their estimate. Of these patients, only four (36%) were later physically assaultive. However, clinicians may be most confident in their decision when they recognize that the information they used to make their decision was of the best quality (Douglas & Ogloff, 2003). Low confidence may be related to low accuracy simply because clinicians cannot be confident that they had enough information to make a good decision.

There is some evidence that the gender of the decision maker may be influential. Elbogen, Williams, Kim, Tomkins, and Scalora (2001) asked 81 male and female clinicians (including nurses, psychiatrists, psychologists, and social workers) to rate the dangerousness of male and female patients. Male clinicians perceived the level of dangerousness to be similar for male and female patients. However, female clinicians judged male patients to be significantly more dangerous than female patients. Other researchers have also found that both male and female clinicians tend to underpredict female violence (Lidz, Mulvey, & Gardner, 1993). Although clinicians underestimate females' risk to commit violence, research shows that clinicians accurately characterize females as committing more violent acts in the home rather than in more public places (Skeem et al., 2005).

APPROACHES TO THE ASSESSMENT OF RISK

Unstructured clinical judgment: Decisions characterized by a substantial amount of professional discretion and lack of guidelines

What are the existing methods of risk assessment? There are three methods of risk assessment most commonly described. **Unstructured clinical judgment** is characterized by a substantial amount of professional discretion and lack of guidelines. There are no predefined rules about what risk factors should be considered, what sources of information should be used, or how the risk factors should be combined to make a decision about risk. Thus, risk factors considered vary across clinicians and vary across cases (Grove & Meehl, 1996; Grove, Zald, Lebow, Snitz, & Nelson, 2000). Grove and Meehl (1996) have described this type of risk assessment as relying on an "informal, 'in the head,' subjective, impressionistic, subjective conclusion, reached (somehow) by a human clinical judge" (p. 294). See Box 12.1 for an example of a professional using this type of risk assessment.

Actuarial prediction: Decisions are based on risk factors that are selected and combined based on their empirical or statistical association with a specific outcome

In contrast, mechanical prediction involves predefined rules about what risk factors to consider, how information should be collected, and how information should be combined to make a risk decision. Thus, risk factors do not vary as a function of the clinician and the same risk factors are considered for each case. A common type of mechanical prediction is called **actuarial prediction**. With actuarial prediction, the risk factors used have been selected and combined based on their empirical or statistical association with a specific outcome (Grove & Meehl, 1996; Grove et al., 2000). In other words, a study has been done in which a number of risk factors have been measured, a sample of offenders have been followed for a specific time period, and only those risk factors that were actually related to reoffending in this sample are selected (for an example of an actuarial scale, see the Violence Risk Appraisal Guide described later in this chapter).

Dr. Death: A Legendary (Notorious) Forensic Psychiatrist

Dr. James Grigson was a Dallas psychiatrist who earned the nicknames "Dr. Death" and "the hanging shrink" because of his effectiveness at testifying for the prosecution in death-penalty cases. For nearly three decades, Dr. Grigson testified in death-penalty cases in Texas.

Death-penalty trials are divided into two phases. First, whether or not the defendant is guilty is decided. Next, the same judge and jury decide whether to impose life in prison or to sentence the defendant to die. One of the issues the jurors must decide on is "whether there is a probability that the defendant would commit criminal acts of violence that would constitute a continuing threat to society." Psychiatrists and psychologists are often hired to testify about the likelihood of future violence.

Dr. Grigson's testimony was very effective. He often diagnosed defendants as being sociopaths and stated with 100% certainty they will kill again. For example, in *Estelle v. Smith* (1981), Dr. Grigson testified on the basis of a brief examination that the defendant Smith was a "very severe sociopath," who, if given the opportunity, would commit another criminal act. The diagnosis of sociopath appears to have been based on the sole fact that Mr. Smith "lacked remorse."

Dr. Grigson has been proven wrong. In the case of Randall Dale Adams (documentarian Errol Morris made a movie about Adams's story in 1988, called *The Thin Blue Line*, which helped to get the case reopened), Dr. Grigson testified that Randall Adams was a "very extreme" sociopath and would continue to be a threat to society even if kept locked in prison. Randall Adams was sentenced to death.

However, after spending 12 years on death row, his conviction was overturned and he was released (another inmate confessed to the murder). It has been 13 years since Randall Adams has been released. He is now married, employed, and living a nonviolent life. Dr. Grigson was wrong in this case—and potentially in how many others?

In 1995, Dr. Grigson was expelled from the American Psychiatric Association (APA) for ethical violations. He was expelled for claiming he could predict with 100% certainty that a defendant will commit another violent act (and, on at least one occasion, testifying that the defendant had a "1000%" chance of committing another violent act). The APA was also concerned that Dr. Grigson often testified in court based on hypothetical situations and diagnosed an individual without even examining the defendant. Dr. Grigson often diagnosed defendants as sociopaths on the basis of his own clinical opinion and not on any structured assessment procedures.

Dr. Grigson was also involved in the death-penalty case of Canadian Joseph Stanley Faulder, who was convicted and sentenced to death for the robbery and murder of Inez Phillips. Dr. Grigson testified that Stanley Faulder was an "extremely severe sociopath," that there was no cure, and that he would certainly kill again. We will never assess the accuracy of Dr. Grigson's predictions, since on June 17, 1999, after spending 22 years on death row, Stanley Faulder was executed. When Dr. Grigson died in 2004 at the age of 72, he had testified in 167 trials. How many of these defendants fell victim to Dr. Grigson and his misguided attempt to protect society is unknown.

A debate in the literature exists concerning the comparative accuracy of unstructured clinical versus actuarial prediction. The first study to compare actuarial and unstructured clinical judgment was conducted by sociologist Ann Burgess in 1928. Burgess compared the accuracy of 21 objective risk factors (such as age, number of past offences, and length of sentence) to clinical judgments of three psychiatrists in predicting parole failure in a sample of 3000 criminal offenders. The actuarial scale was markedly superior to the psychiatrists in identifying which offenders would fail on parole. In a review of 20 studies, Paul Meehl (1954) concluded that actuarial prediction was equal to or better than unstructured clinical judgment in all cases. A similar conclusion was reached almost 50 years later, when Meehl and his colleagues (Grove et al., 2000) conducted a meta-analysis of prediction studies for human health and behaviour (including criminal behaviour). In sum, the weight of the evidence clearly favours actuarial assessments of risk (Ægisdóttir et al., 2006; Mossman, 1994), even with samples of offenders with mental disorders (Bonta, Law, & Hanson, 1998; Phillips et al., 2005) and sex offenders (Hanson & Bussière, 1998; Hanson & Morton-Bourgon, 2005).

Arising from the limitations associated with unstructured clinical judgment and concern that the actuarial method did not allow for individualized risk appraisal or for consideration of the impact of situational factors to modify risk level, a new approach to risk assessment has emerged—**structured professional judgment** (SPJ) (Borum, 1996; Webster, Douglas, Eaves, & Hart, 1997). According to this method, the professional (the term "professional" is used to acknowledge that it is not only clinicians who make evaluations of risk but a diverse group, including law enforcement officers, probation officers, and social workers) is guided by a predetermined list of risk factors that have been selected from the research and professional literature. The professional considers the presence and severity of each risk factor, but the final judgment of risk level is based on the evaluator's professional judgment. The reliability and predictive utility of these risk summary judgments are only beginning to be assessed. Dr. Christopher Webster, the Canadian researcher profiled in Box 12.2, has done extensive research in the use of SPJ.

Types of Predictors

There are hundreds of potential risk factors that clinicians and researchers might use to predict antisocial and violent behaviour. A **risk factor** is a measurable feature of an individual that predicts the behaviour of interest, such as violence. Traditionally, risk factors were divided into two main types: static and dynamic.

Static risk factors are factors that do not fluctuate over time and are not changed by treatment. Age at first arrest is an example of a static risk factor, since no amount of time or treatment will change this risk factor. **Dynamic risk factors** fluctuate over time and are amenable to changing. An antisocial attitude is an example of a dynamic risk factor, since it is possible that treatment could modify this variable.

More recently, correctional researchers have begun to conceptualize risk factors as a continuous construct (Douglas & Skeem, 2005; Grann, Belfrage, & Tengström, 2000; Zamble & Quinsey, 1997). At one end of the continuum are the static risk factors described above. At the other end are acute dynamic risk factors. These risk factors change rapidly within days, hours, or minutes and often occur just prior to an offence. Factors at this end of the continuum include variables such as negative mood and level of intoxication. In the middle of the continuum are stable dynamic risk factors. These are risk factors that change but only over long periods of time such as months or years and are variables that should be targeted for treatment. These factors include criminal attitudes, coping ability, and impulse control. Some researchers also include enduring personality traits such as psychopathy as a stable dynamic risk factor (Zamble & Quinsey, 1997), although whether or not the psychopathic traits observed in some adults can be modified through appropriate treatment remains to be determined.

Structured professional judgment: Decisions are guided by a predetermined list of risk factors that have been selected from the research and professional literature. Judgment of risk level is based on the evaluator's professional judgment

Risk factor: A measurable feature of an individual that predicts the behaviour of interest (e.g. violence or psychopathology)

Static risk factor: Risk factor that does not fluctuate over time and is not changed by treatment (e.g., age at first arrest). Also known as historical risk factor

Dynamic risk factor: Risk factors that fluctuate over time and are amenable to changing

Box 12.2

Canadian Researcher Profile: Dr. Christopher Webster

Dr. Christopher Webster completed his undergraduate degree at the University of British Columbia, his master's at Queen's University, and his Ph.D. at Dalhousie University. His doctoral thesis focused on avoidance conditioning in guinea pigs. Currently, Dr. Webster is a consultant to various forensic and mental health agencies in Ontario and is professor emeritus with the Department of Psychiatry at the University of Toronto and the Department of Psychology at Simon Fraser University.

Dr. Webster's first position after graduating was as a research scientist at the Addiction Research Foundation in Toronto. Later he transferred to the Clarke Institute of Psychiatry (now the Centre for Addiction and Mental Health [CAMH]), where he established clinical and research programs for autistic children and their families. Later, at CAMH, he conducted fitness and criminal responsibility evaluations of defendants in court.

In the late 1970s, he accepted a position as senior research scientist with a new forensic program

established by the Clarke Institute. He also began collaborating with practitioners and researchers from different disciplines and started conducting research on risk assessment and risk management. Over the past three decades, Dr. Webster has made substantial contributions to the risk-assessment field, and his work has provided clinicians with essential ways to structure their risk assessments.

Dr. Webster notes that one of his favourite pieces of research was a study conducted with Robert Menzies (at that time a graduate student in sociology at the University of Toronto, now a professor at Simon Fraser University), identifying risk factors for violence in a large sample of offenders with mental disorders. In 1993, Dr. Webster joined and became chair of the Department of Psychology at Simon Fraser University. One of the many projects he worked on while there was the development of a structured professional judgment manual called the HCR-20 (this was done in collaboration with Stephen Hart, Kevin Douglas, and Derek Eaves). Research that Dr. Webster finds particularly rewarding entails working with an interdisciplinary team and collaborating with researchers and clinicians from different countries. "Manualization" of violence risk is the essential theme of his work.

Of the many courses he has taught, his two favourites are "Psychology and the Law" and "Clinical Criminology." He thinks one important aspect of training future forensic researchers is having undergraduates involved in conducting research in forensic settings.

Dr. Webster owns a 1957 Triumph TRW motorcycle (military model). It came complete with an original manual, which should be helpful, as so far he has spent about as much time pushing it as riding it.

IMPORTANT RISK FACTORS

Since the late 1980s, a great deal of research has investigated what factors are associated with future violence. These can be classified into historical, dispositional, clinical, and contextual risk factors. **Historical risk factors** (sometimes called *static risk factors*) are events experienced in the past and include general social history and specific criminal history variables, such as employment problems and a history of violence. **Dispositional risk factors** are those that reflect the person's traits, tendencies, or style and include

Historical risk factor: Risk factor that refers to events that have been experienced in the past (e.g., age at first arrest). Also known as static risk factor

Dispositional risk factor: Risk factors that reflect the individual's traits, tendencies, or styles (e.g., negative attitudes)

demographic, attitudinal, and personality variables, such as gender, age, negative attitudes, and psychopathy. **Clinical risk factors** are the symptoms of mental disorders that can contribute to violence, such as substance abuse or major psychoses. **Contextual risk factors** (sometimes referred to as *situational risk factors*) are aspects of the individual's current environment that can elevate the risk, such as access to victims or weapons, lack of social supports, and perceived stress.

Some of these factors are likely relevant to risk assessment only, while others are relevant to both risk assessment and risk management. These factors vary in terms of how much they are subject to change. For example, some are fixed (e.g., gender), some cannot be undone (e.g., age of onset of criminal behaviour), and some may be resistant to change (e.g., psychopathy), whereas others (e.g., social support or negative attitudes) may be subject to intervention or may vary across time.

There have been several meta-analytic reviews examining the predictors of general and violent recidivism in adult offenders, sexual offenders, and patients with mental disorders (Bonta, Law, et al., 1998; Gendreau, Little, & Goggin, 1996; Hanson & Morton-Bourgon, 2005). Two key findings have emerged. First, factors that predict general recidivism also predict violent or sexual recidivism. Second, predictors of recidivism in offenders with mental disorders overlap considerably with predictors found among offenders who do not have a mental disorder. A recent meta-analytic study examined the predictors of general recidivism in 23 studies of adolescent offenders (Cottle, Lee, & Heilbrun, 2001). The strongest predictors were age of first police contact, nonsevere pathology (e.g., stress or anxiety), family problems, conduct problems (e.g., presence of conduct disordered symptoms), ineffective use of leisure time, and delinquent peers.

Dispositional Factors

Demographics Researchers in the 1970s identified young age as a risk factor for violence (Steadman & Cocozza, 1974): the younger the person is at the time of his or her first offence, the greater the likelihood that person will engage in criminal behaviour and violence. Dozens of studies have firmly established age of first offence as a risk factor for both general and violent recidivism in both offenders with mental disorders (Bonta, Law, et al., 1998) and offenders without mental disorders (Gendreau et al., 1996). Offenders who are arrested prior to age 14 tend to have more serious and more extensive criminal careers than those who are first arrested after age 14 (DeLisi, 2006; Piquero & Chung, 2001). Males are at higher risk than are females for general offending (Cottle et al., 2001; Gendreau et al., 1996). Notably, males engage in more serious violent acts, such as sexual assaults, homicides, and assaults causing bodily harm (Odgers & Moretti, 2002). Some studies using self-report measures have found that females engage in similar or even higher rates of less serious violence (Nichols, Graber, Brooks-Gunn, & Botvin, 2006; Steadman et al., 1994). Newhill, Mulvey, and Lidz (1995) conducted a six-month follow-up of 495 male and 317 female civil psychiatric patients who returned to the community. Men and women did not differ in terms of subsequent violence but had different targets of their violence (family members: males 38%, females 53%) and committed the violence at different locations (home: males 57%, females 75%).

Personality Characteristics Two personality characteristics have been extensively examined: impulsiveness and psychopathy. Not being able to regulate behaviour in response to impulses or thoughts increases the likelihood of engaging in crime and violence (Webster & Jackson, 1997). Lifestyle impulsivity (being impulsive in most areas of life) distinguishes recidivistic rapists from non-recidivistic rapists (Prentky, Knight, Lee, & Cerce, 1995).

Psychopathy is a personality disorder defined as a callous and unemotional interpersonal style characterized by grandiosity, manipulation, lack of remorse, impulsivity, and irresponsibility (see Chapter 11 for more information on psychopaths). Given these features, it is not surprising that psychopathic individuals engage in diverse and chronic criminal behaviours. Five meta-analytic reviews have found that psychopathy is moderately (Gendreau, Goggin, & Smith, 2002; Hemphill, Hare, & Wong,

Psychologist conducting a risk-assessment interview

1998; Walters, 2003) to strongly (Salekin, Rogers, & Sewell, 1996) related to general and violent recidivism and moderately related to violence in a prison setting (Guy, Edens, Anthony, & Douglas, 2005). For example, Serin and Amos (1995) measured general and violent recidivism rates of 300 federal male offenders followed for an average of 5.5 years. The general failure rate for psychopathic offenders was about 80%, compared with 32% for nonpsychopathic offenders. The violent failure rate was about 35% for the psychopathic offenders and only 5% for the nonpsychopathic offenders. Psychopathic offenders also reoffend sooner after release compared with other offenders (Hart, Kropp, & Hare, 1988; Porter, Birt, & Boer, 2001). For example, Porter and colleagues (2001) found that psychopaths spent an average of 473 days, and nonpsychopaths 797 days, on conditional release before returning to prison. Psychopathy predicts reoffending across different countries (e.g., Canada, the United States, the United Kingdom, Belgium, the Netherlands, New Zealand, Sweden) (Hare, 2003), in both male and female offenders (Richards, Casey, & Lucente, 2003), offenders with mental disorders (Nicholls, Ogloff, & Douglas, 2004; Steadman et al., 2000; Strand, Belfrage, Fransson, & Levander, 1999), male adolescent offenders (Corrado, Vincent, Hart, & Cohen, 2004; Forth, Hart, & Hare, 1990; Gretton, Hare, & Catchpole, 2004; Murrie et al., 2004), and sexual offenders (Barbaree, Seto, Langton, & Peacock, 2001; Rice & Harris, 1997a). However, psychopathy may be weakly related or unrelated to violent reoffending in adolescent females (Odgers, Repucci, & Moretti, 2005; Schmidt, McKinnon, Chattha, & Brownlee, 2006).

Several studies have found that the combination of psychopathy and deviant sexual arousal predicts sexual recidivism (Hildebrand, de Rutter, & de Vogel, 2004; Olver & Wong, 2006; Rice & Harris, 1997a). Deviant sexual arousal is defined as evidence that the sexual offender shows a relative preference for inappropriate stimuli, such as children or violent nonconsensual sex. For example, Rice and Harris (1997a) found that about 70% of sexual offenders with psychopathic features and evidence of deviant sexual arousal committed a new sexual offence, compared with about 40% of the other offender groups.

Historical Factors

Past Behaviour The most accurate predictor of future behaviour is past behaviour. Past violent behaviour was first identified as a predictor in the 1960s and 1970s (see Cocozza, Melick, & Steadman, 1978) and has consistently been associated with future violence in diverse samples, including adolescents and adults, correctional offenders, mentally disordered offenders, and civil psychiatric patients (Farrington, 1991; McNiel et al., 1988; Phillips et al., 2005). Interestingly, it is not only past violent behaviour that predicts violence but also past nonviolent behaviour (Harris, Rice., & Quinsey, 1993; Lipsey & Derzon, 1998). For example, offenders who have a history of break and enter offences are at an increased risk for future violence.

Age of Onset As noted earlier, individuals who start their antisocial behaviour at an earlier age are more chronic and serious offenders (Farrington, 1991; Tolan & Thomas, 1995). For example, Farrington (1991) found that 50% of the boys who committed a violent offence prior to age 16 were convicted of a violent offence in early adulthood. In another longitudinal study, Elliott (1994) reported that 50% of male youth who committed their first violent acts prior to age 11 continued their violent behaviour into adulthood, compared with 30% whose first violence was between the ages of 11 and 13, and only 10% of those whose first violent act occurred during adolescence. Age of onset is not as strong a predictor for female offending (Piquero & Chung, 2001).

Childhood History of Maltreatment Having a history of childhood physical abuse or neglect is associated with increased risk for violence (Smith & Thornberry, 1995; Zingraff, Leiter, Johnsen, & Myers, 1994). In a large-scale study of childhood abuse, Widom (1989b) reported that victims of sexual abuse were no more likely than those who were not sexually abused to commit delinquent or violent offences. Those who were victims of physical abuse or who were victims of neglect were much more likely to commit criminal acts as compared to those who were not abused. Being abused in childhood predicts initiation into delinquency, but continued abuse predicts chronic offending (Lemmon, 2006). Physical abuse in adolescence is also directly related to adolescent offending and may be related to some types of offending in adulthood as well (Fagan, 2005; Smith, Ireland, & Thornberry, 2005).

Past Supervision Failure, Escape, or Institution Maladjustment Offenders and patients who have failed to comply with release conditions in the past are at an increased risk for engaging in general and violent recidivism (Bonta, Law, et al., 1998; Harris et al., 1993; Swanson, Borum, Swartz, Hiday, Wagner, & Burns, 2001). Ball, Young, Dotson, and Brothers (1994) found that forensic inpatients who were judged to be an escape risk were more likely to behave violently in the institution than those who were not a risk. Poor institutional adjustment has also been linked to higher rates of general and violent recidivism in offenders with mental disorders (Bonta, Law, et al., 1998).

Clinical Factors

Substance Use Drug and alcohol use has been associated with criminal behaviour and violence. The obvious link between drugs and crime is that the use, possession, and sale of illegal drugs are crimes. In some cases, the individual commits offences in order to support a drug habit (Klassen & O'Connor, 1994). For example, Chaiken and Chaiken (1983) found that severe drug users commit 15 times as many robberies and 20 times as many burglaries as compared with non-drug-using offenders. The drug that has been most associated with crime is heroin (Inciardi, 1986). A large study of 653 opiate users in Edmonton, Montreal, Quebec City, Toronto, and Vancouver concluded that individuals with greater heroin and crack use are at the greatest risk to commit property crimes (Manzoni, Brochu, Fischer, & Rehm, 2006).

Dowden and Brown (2002) conducted a meta-analysis of 45 studies to examine the association between substance abuse and recidivism. Alcohol and drug use problems were moderately related to general recidivism. Zanis, Mulvaney, Coviello, Alterman, Savitz, and Thompson (2003) followed a sample of 569 offenders with a prior history of substance abuse or dependence for two years after release from prison on parole. Factors relating to a new conviction included the number of prior convictions, younger age, parole without treatment, and cocaine dependence.

Drug abusers also come in contact with antisocial people, thus leading to violent confrontations. Laboratory research (Taylor & Sears, 1988) has found that aggression displayed by intoxicated individuals is a joint function of the pharmacological effects of alcohol intoxication (disinhibition effects), expectancies, and the situation (what is happening in the environment). Neuropsychological deficits (i.e., executive functioning) also play a role in the effects of alcohol on aggression (Giancola, Parrott, & Roth, 2006).

In one of the largest surveys done, Swanson (1994) interviewed 7000 individuals in two U.S. cities (Durham and Los Angeles), asking about the presence of substance abuse, psychiatric disorders, and violent behaviour. Based on data from the previous year, less than 3% of men and women with no psychiatric diagnosis committed violence. However, for those with a diagnosis of substance abuse, the rates of violence for men and women were 22% and 17% respectively.

Mental Disorder Much controversy exists over the connection between major mental disorder and violence. Although most people with mental disorders are not violent, a diagnosis of affective disorders and schizophrenia has been linked to higher rates of violence (Swanson, 1994). Hillbrand (1995) reported that in a sample of forensic psychiatric patients, those with a history of suicide attempts and engaging in self-harm behaviours were more likely to engage in verbal and physical aggression than were other patients.

Considerable research has investigated the link between psychotic symptoms (experiencing hallucinations and delusions) and violence (McNiel & Binder, 1994). Link and Steuve (1994) investigated the link between violence and specific types of psychotic symptoms. They proposed that symptoms overriding a person's self-control (i.e., feeling as if your mind is being dominated by forces beyond your control) or threatening a person's safety (i.e., thinking that someone is planning to hurt him or her) increase the likelihood of violence. They have labelled these types of symptoms "threat/control override" (TCO) symptoms. They compared these psychotic symptoms with other symptoms, such as having thoughts taken away, seeing visions, or hearing voices. TCO symptoms were strongly related to violence (hitting, fighting, and use of weapons) in both patients and community controls. TCO symptoms were a significant predictor of violence even when the other psychotic symptoms were held constant. Individuals with TCO symptoms have been shown to be almost 3 times more likely to engage in violence in a large study of more than 10 000 people (Swanson, Borum, Swartz, & Monahan, 1996). More recently, Mojtabai (2006) found that the presence of *any* psychotic symptoms (not just TCO symptoms) was related to violence in a study of more than 35 000 people. Swanson et al. (1996) found that a combination of TCO symptoms and other mental disorder diagnoses are related to violence. The highest prevalence of violence was the combination of major mental disorder, substance abuse, and TCO symptoms, with an amazing 86% of such individuals reporting violence; for individuals with major mental disorders and TCO symptoms, the rate was 63%; for individuals with major mental disorders and no TCO symptoms, the rate dropped to 39%; and for individuals with no disorder and no TCO symptoms, the rate was 17%. These results demonstrate the importance of major mental disorders, substance abuse, and TCO symptoms in explaining violence. Whether TCO symptoms are related to violence does depend on the sex of the individual, however. Men are *more* likely to commit violence, but women are *less* likely to commit violence when suffering from TCO symptoms (Teasdale, Silver, & Monahan, 2006).

Research has also examined the link between command hallucinations (hearing a voice telling you to harm yourself or others) and violence. Junginger (1990) reported a weak link between command hallucinations and dangerous behaviour. In a sample of 51 patients who reported experiencing command hallucinations, 20 (39%) complied with them but only 8 (17%) complied by committing acts that were a danger to themselves or others. A recent review has concluded that there are mixed, inconclusive results as to whether there is truly a link between command hallucinations and violence (Barrowcliff & Haddock, 2006). Other psychological processes appear to influence whether someone complies with the voice hallucinations such as beliefs about what consequences will occur if they do not comply as well as whether the individual recognizes the voice as a force of evil or good (Barrowcliff & Haddock, 2006).

Contextual Factors

Lack of Social Support This risk factor refers to the absence of strong support systems to help the individual in his or her day-to-day life. Henggeler, Schoenwald, Borduin, Rowland, and Cunningham (1998) describe four kinds of support: (1) *instrumental*, "to provide the necessities of life"; (2) *emotional*, "to give strength to; (3) *appraisal*, "to give aid or courage to"; and (4) *information*, "by providing new facts." Assessing the kinds and levels of support a person has and what types of support must be created will help to evaluate that person's level of risk. Klassen and O'Connor (1989) found that the current relationship an offender with a mental disorder has with his or her parents and siblings is related to violence.

Risk Factors Relating to Stalking

Interest in stalking has increased dramatically over the past decade. Often, it has been the cases of celebrity stalking that have caught the attention of the media. However, celebrities aren't the only ones who get stalked. A national survey done in the United States found that around 1 million women are stalked annually, and 8% of women and 2% of men will be stalked at some point in their lifetime (Tjaden & Thoennes, 1998). Stalking refers to the repeated and unwanted communicating with, following, or approaching of other people. It has also been referred to as harassment or obsessional following. Most stalkers are men and most victims are women. Most victims know their stalkers. In fact, the stalker is usually a current or ex-romantic partner of the victim.

If you are a victim of harassment, one of the most important questions to ask is, "What is the likelihood of being a victim of a violent act?" A meta-analysis has attempted to discriminate between stalkers who represent a significant risk of violence and those who pose less of a risk (Rosenfeld, 2004). Rosenfeld analyzed 10 studies that included 1055 stalking offenders. Violence occurred in 38.6% of the cases. The following variables were significantly related to violence:

- *Clinical variables.* Substance-abuse disorder, personality disorder, and the absence of a psychotic disorder predicted violence.

- *Case-related variables.* A former intimate relationship between offender and victim and threats toward the victim predicted violence.

Stalking offenders who are at the greatest risk for continuing stalking behaviour after release from prison are those who have both a personality disorder and a history of substance abuse (Rosenfeld, 2003).

Access to Weapons or Victims If the offender is released into an environment that permits easy access to weapons or victims, the potential for another violent act increases. An offender who moves into a skid-row rooming house in which there are many other antisocial individuals living and there is easy access to drugs may start associating with antisocial people or using drugs (Monahan & Steadman, 1994). If the offender has engaged in violence with other associates or under the influence of substances, then releasing the offender to live in the same circumstances that led to past violence may induce future violence. In addition, if offenders who have assaulted their spouse and refused treatment for domestic violence return to live with their spouse, they have a much higher likelihood of violence than those who do not have easy access to a past victim. See Box 12.3 for a look at the risk factors associated with stalking.

RISK-ASSESSMENT INSTRUMENTS AND PREDICTIVE ACCURACY

Many of the factors affecting risk assessment that we've discussed above serve as the basis for various kinds of risk-assessment instruments. Some instruments have been developed to predict specific kinds of risk, while others utilize particular strategies outlined above, such as actuarial or structured clinical assessments. The instruments that we describe below do not exhaust those that are available but illustrate the range of options open for the systematic evaluation of risk.

Actuarial Instruments

General Statistical Information on Recidivism

The one instrument that is routinely used by Correctional Service Canada and the National Parole Board is the General Statistical Information on Recidivism (GSIR) (Nuffield, 1982). All of the 15 items in the scale are static risk factors that were statistically selected because they predicted general reoffending in a sample of federal male offenders during a three-year follow-up period. Twelve of the items measure the nature and extent of past criminal involvement, while the remaining three consider whether the offender was married, employed, or had dependants at the time of their most recent criminal offence. Scores are differentially weighted (based on their statistical association with recidivism) to create five risk categories ranging from very good risk (80% chance of not reoffending) to poor risk (33% chance of not reoffending).

The GSIR scale has proven to be a good predictor of criminal behaviour. In a validation study by Bonta, Harman, Hann, and Cormier (1996) involving 3267 male offenders, the GSIR was found to be a strong predictor of general recidivism. A weaker association has been reported between the GSIR and violent recidivism (Bonta et al., 1996), and the GSIR has been found to be less predictive when used with female federal offenders (Bonta, Pang, & Wallace-Capretta, 1995). More recently the GSIR has been revised to include information about female offenders (Motiuk & Nafekh, 2001), and does a better job at predicting recidivism in female offenders (Nafekh, 2003).

Violence Risk Appraisal Guide

An actuarial risk-for-violence instrument developed in Ontario is the Violence Risk Appraisal Guide (VRAG) (Harris, Rice, & Quinsey, 1993). The VRAG is an empirically derived 12-item measure designed to assess the long-term risk for violent recidivism in offenders with mental disorders. Researchers coded about 50 risk factors from institutional files in a sample of 618 male adult patients with mental disorders who had been transferred to less secure institutions or released into the community. Statistical analyses were used to select the 12 best predictors of violence from childhood history, adult adjustment, offence history, and assessment results. The 12 predictors varied in terms of how strongly they were related to violent recidivism and included the following (ordered from most to least predictive):

- Hare Psychopathy Checklist–Revised score
- elementary school maladjustment
- diagnosis of any personality disorder
- age at index offence (young age, higher risk)
- separation from biological parents prior to age 16
- failure on prior conditional release
- prior nonviolent offences
- single marital status at time of offence
- diagnosis of schizophrenia (lower risk)
- victim injury (less injury, higher risk)
- history of alcohol problems
- victim gender (female victim, lower risk)

Using scores on each of these risk factors, nine risk categories—or "bins"—were created. Each risk bin has a probably of violent recidivism within ten years ranging from 9% (bin 1) to 35% (bin 5) to 100% (bin 9). However, some research has shown that the violent reoffending probabilities associated with these risk bins do not replicate in samples of correctional offenders (Mills, Jones, & Kroner, 2005).

Subsequent research has found the VRAG predicts violence with other samples of offenders with mental disorders (Harris, Rice, & Cormier, 2002), civil psychiatric patients (Harris, Rice, & Camilleri, 2004), and sexual offenders (Barbaree et al., 2001; Rice & Harris, 1997a). The VRAG also predicts violent recidivism well in Switzerland (Urbaniok et al., 2006) and Belgium (Pham, Ducro, Marghem, & Réveillère, 2005). There is some evidence that the relationship between the VRAG and violent recidivism is not as strong in correctional samples (Glover, Nicholson, & Hemmati, 2002; Kroner & Mills, 2001) or with Swedish schizophrenic forensic patients (Grann et al., 2000). In addition, some evidence shows that the only component of the VRAG that predicts violence in civil psychiatric patients is the Psychopathy Checklist: Screening Version score (Edens, Skeem, & Douglas, 2006).

Iterative Classification Tree The Iterative Classification Tree (ICT) (Steadman et al., 2000) was designed as a tool to assess the risk for violence in samples of psychiatric patients. This approach to risk assessment allows for many different combinations of risk factors to be used to classify a person into low- and high-risk categories. A clinician scores the patient on one risk factor and, contingent on how the patient is scored, assesses the patient on another risk factor. This sequence continues until the patient is classified into a risk category.

The ICT has been validated using a large-scale study of risk factors for violence in civil psychiatric patients (MacArthur Violence Risk Assessment Study) (Steadman et al., 2000). Researchers coded 134 risk factors in 939 male and female civil psychiatric patients admitted to psychiatric in-patient hospitals in the United States. Most of these patients were diagnosed with depression (42%), followed by alcohol/drug abuse (22%), schizophrenia (17%), and bipolar disorder (14%). Patients were followed up for 20 weeks following discharge from the hospital. Using arrest and rehospitalization records and patient and collateral interviews, patients were assessed for engaging in any violent behaviour toward others (physical violence resulting in injury, sexual assaults, assaults with a weapon, or threats with a weapon). The base rate for violence was 18.7% (i.e., the percentage committing one violent act during the 20-week follow-up period). Low-risk groups were those whose rate of violence was half the base rate (i.e., 9% or less) and high-risk groups were defined as those whose rate of violence was greater than twice the base rate (i.e., 37% or greater).

The ICT contains 12 risk factors that form six risk groups (four low-risk groups and two high-risk groups). The first risk factor that differentiates the risk groups is the score on the Hare Psychopathy Checklist: Screening Version (Hart, Cox, & Hare, 1995). If the patient scored high on the measure of psychopathy, the clinician would inquire about whether the patient had experienced serious childhood abuse. If the patient responded yes, the clinician would indicate whether the patient had a diagnosis of alcohol or drug abuse. If the patient did have such a diagnosis, the clinician would indicate whether the patient had been admitted to the hospital for a suicide attempt. If the patient had not been admitted for a suicide attempt, the patient would be placed in risk group C, a group of 53 patients of whom 58.5% committed a violent act. If, however, the patient scored low on the psychopathy measure, a different series of risk factors would be assessed. For example, none of the 66 patients in Risk Group A committed a violent act. Monahan et al. (2000) have developed another ICT based on 15 risk factors that are easiest to obtain and that can be administered quickly. The predictive validity of the ICT has been tested with other civil psychiatric samples, and has been found to moderately predict violence (Monahan et al., 2005). Recently, a software program based on the ICT, called the Classification of Violence Risk, has been developed to help clinicians make decisions about whether or not a patient will be violent toward others after discharge from the hospital (Monahan et al., 2006).

Most of the items in the actuarial scales described above comprise static risk factors. Scales that rely primarily on static factors have a number of limitations. First, they provide little practical information about what risk factors need to be targeted for intervention. Second, they do not allow for the incorporation of treatment gain into the prediction, nor can they indicate when an offender might fail, or when the level of supervision should be changed (Zamble & Quinsey, 1997). Third, they have been criticized for not being theoretically derived (Krauss, Sales, Becker, & Figueredo, 2000). From a practical standpoint, whether or not the risk factors are derived from a specific theory may not be very important as long as they accurately predict the outcome.

In response to the limitations associated with actuarial measures, risk-assessment methods that include dynamic risk factors have been developed.

Structured Professional Judgment Schemes

Level of Service Inventory–Revised   The Level of Service Inventory–Revised (LSI-R) (Andrews & Bonta, 1995) consists of static and dynamic risk items that tap into the theoretical model of criminal behaviour outlined by Andrews and Bonta (1995). The 52 items are divided into 10 main subscales:

- criminal history
- education/employment
- financial
- family/marital
- accommodation
- leisure recreation
- companions
- alcohol/drug problems
- emotional/personal
- attitudes/orientation

These subscales highlight the areas that should be targeted for intervention. The LSI-R total score has also been used for assigning offenders to different levels of supervision based on their likelihood for recidivism. The LSI-R has been used with a variety of offenders, including male sex offenders (Simourd & Malcolm, 1998) and female and male nonsexual offenders (Lowenkamp, Holsinger, & Latessa, 2001), and a modified version with adolescent offenders (Ilacqua, Coulson, Lombardo, & Nutbrown, 1999). The LSI-R predicted recidivism in

British (Hollin & Palmer, 2006) and German (Dahle, 2006) samples, but may not be valid for Native American populations, especially Native American female offenders (Holsinger, Lowenkamp, & Latessa, 2006). The LSI-R under predicts risk for recidivism in longer term offenders (Simourd, 2004) and is more suitable for predicting general recidivism than sexual recidivism in sexual offenders (Gentry, Dulmus, & Theriot, 2005). A meta-analysis reported by Gendreau et al. (2002) found that the LSI-R functioned effectively as a predictor of general recidivism and, to a lesser extent, of violent recidivism.

HCR-20 The HCR-20 (Webster et al., 1997) was designed to predict violent behaviour in correctional and forensic psychiatric samples. The HCR-20 uses the structured professional judgment approach to risk assessment developed by a group of researchers in British Columbia. In this approach, the evaluator conducts a systematic risk assessment and refers to a list of risk factors, each having specific coding criteria and a demonstrated relationship with violent recidivism based on the existing professional and empirical literature. The HCR-20 stands for the list of 20 items organized into three main scales that align risk factors into past (historical), present (clinical), and future (risk management):

Historical (primarily static in nature):

- past violence
- age at first violent offence
- relationship instability
- employment instability
- relationship problems
- substance use problems
- major mental disorder
- psychopathy
- early maladjustment
- personality disorder
- prior supervision failure

Clinical (reflect current, dynamic risk factors):

- lack of insight
- negative attitudes
- active mental disorder symptoms
- impulsivity
- treatability

Risk Management (future community or institutional adjustment of the individual):

- feasibility of plans
- exposure to destabilizers
- level of personal support
- stress
- likelihood of treatment compliance

The validity of the HCR-20 has been investigated in forensic psychiatric and correctional samples. Research with Swedish forensic patients reported that the Historical scale of the HCR-20 was related to violent recidivism in patients with personality disorders and schizophrenia (Grann et al., 2000). The HCR-20 was strongly related to violent recidivism in forensic patients in Sweden (Strand, Belfrage, Frannson, & Levander, 1999) and the Netherlands (de Vogel & de Ruiter, 2006). The HCR-20 has also shown moderate predictive ability in forensic samples in England (Dolan & Khawaja, 2004; Gray, Snowden, MacCulloch, Phillips, Taylor, & MacCulloch, 2004), Germany (Dahle, 2006), and Belgium (Pham et al., 2005).

Strand et al. (1999) reported that the Clinical and Risk Management scales were better than the Historical scale at differentiating the violent and nonviolent recidivists. The Historical and Clinical scales of the HCR-20 were correlated with past violence in a sample of Canadian male offenders (Douglas & Webster, 1999), but the total HCR-20 scores were only related to past nonviolent crime in female offenders (Warren et al., 2005). However, in another sample, the HCR-20 was a better predictor of females' future violence than males' (Nicholls et al., 2004). Kroner and Mills (2001) found that the Historical and Clinical scales were only weakly related to future violence in a sample of Canadian male offenders, although other researchers have reported that HCR-20 is a strong predictor of future violence in this sample (Douglas, Yeomans, & Boer, 2005).

The Violence Risk Scale The VRS (Wong & Gordon, 2006) represents the most recent assessment tool designed to provide information on offenders' risk to reoffend while at the same time establishing what treatment goals need to be set to reduce an offender's risk. The VRS aims to integrate four goals into one risk-assessment tool: (1) assess risk to reoffend, (2) identify which aspects of an offender need to be targeted in treatment to reduce that risk, (3) determine whether the offender is in denial about or receptive to changing the aspects that lead him into crime, and (4) measure whether these changes have occurred once treatment is completed. The individual items used in the VRS were based on theories of the psychology of crime, the principles of effective offender treatment, and a psychological model of behaviour change. Of the 26 VRS items, 6 items are static variables, and the remaining 20 are dynamic variables that can be changed with appropriate treatment.

Static (variables that cannot be changed though treatment):

■ age of first violent conviction

■ number of juvenile convictions

■ violence throughout life span

■ stability of family upbringing

■ prior release failures/escapes (this variable can increase over time)

■ current age (this variable does increase over time)

Dynamic (7 examples of the total 20 variables that can be changed through treatment)

■ work ethic (Does the individual want to work for a living or does the individual use violence or other socially inappropriate ways—e.g., pimping, drug dealing—of supporting him- or herself?)

■ emotional regulation/control (Is the individual able to control his or her emotions, or is there a persistent relationship between inability to control emotions and violence?)

- insight into violence (Does the individual understand what factors are related to why they have committed violence or does the individual lack insight by denying responsibility, blaming others, or refusing recommended intervention?)

- community support (Does the individual have access to and a willingness to use positive community support—e.g., vocational training, counselling—or does the individual lack access to or refuse to utilize positive community support if released?)

- released to high-risk situations (Has the individual developed realistic plans to avoid being released to high-risk situations—e.g., criminal peers—or does the individual plan to return to high-risk situations when released?)

- impulsivity (Does the individual consider the consequences of his or her behaviour, or is the individual still reacting impulsively?)

- cognitive distortion (Has the individual modified his or her distorted thinking patterns—e.g., minimization, denial, blaming others—or is the individual still engaging in cognitive distortions?)

The VRS was developed by Canadian psychologists using a sample of 918 male offenders in Alberta, Saskatchewan, and Manitoba. The tool was shown to have a moderate ability to predict violent and nonviolent reconvictions. Both the static and dynamic scales were equally capable of predicting further convictions in this sample. Offenders who scored highest on the VRS were also the offenders who reoffended earliest once released from prison. How the VRS will work with other samples of offenders remains to be tested.

CAN WE PREDICT SPECIFIC TYPES OF VIOLENCE?

The instruments described above were designed to predict criminal behaviour or any form of violence. Instruments also have been developed for specific populations and more narrowly defined types of violence. Two types of violence that have been a focus of much research are sexual violence and spousal assault (see also Chapter 10).

Spousal Assault

The Spousal Assault Risk Assessment (SARA) (Kropp, Hart, Webster, & Eaves, 1999) consists of 20 risk factors designed to assess the risk for spousal violence. The risk factors were identified on the basis of a review of the empirical literature. The SARA consists of ten general violence risk factors (Part 1) and ten spousal violence risk factors (Part 2). Part 1 items code for past history of violence and substance use, as well as employment and relationship problems. Part 2 items code the nature and severity of violence in the most recent spousal assault incident, attitudes concerning spousal assault, and violations of "no contact" orders. Users code each of the 20 items using a 3-point scale, indicate the presence of any additional case-specific risk factors, designate any "critical" risk factors (those that are particularly salient to the degree of risk), and make a summary risk judgment (low, moderate, or high) for future spousal violence.

Research by Kropp and Hart (2000) has found that offenders with a spousal assault history score higher on the SARA than do offenders with no history of spousal assault. Recidivistic spousal assaulters scored higher on Part 2 (spousal violence) of the SARA as compared with nonrecidivistic spousal assaulters. When examining the summary risk judgments, 60% of the high-risk ratings were recidivists, as compared with 33% of the moderate-risk ratings, and 8% of the low-risk ratings. Two other studies have evaluated the predictive validity of the SARA. In Sweden, Grann and Wedin (2002) used files to code SARA items on a sample of 88 male spousal assaulters. During the seven-year follow-up period, 28% of the individuals in the sample were reconvicted of spousal assault. The SARA total score was moderately related to spousal assault recidivism. Three SARA items were most strongly related: past violation of conditional release, personality disorder, and extreme minimization or denial of spousal assault history. In the United States, Williams and Houghton (2004) followed up 434 spousal assault offenders for 18 months. The SARA total score was moderately related to both general and spousal assault recidivism.

Sexual Violence

In a meta-analysis of 82 studies, Hanson and Morton-Bourgon (2005) investigated the predictors of sexual recidivism. Of the 29 450 sex offenders followed for an average of four to five years, the rate of sexual recidivism was 13.7%, 14.3% for nonsexual violent recidivism, and 36.2% for any offence. The strongest predictors of sexual recidivism were sexual deviance variables (including phallometric assessment of sexual deviance and emotional identification with children) and antisocial orientation variables (antisocial personality, psychopathy, substance abuse, and a history of crime and rule violation). Other significant predictors, although less strongly related to sexual recidivism, were adverse childhood environment and general psychological problems. Factors unrelated to sexual recidivism included experiencing childhood sexual abuse, loneliness, and psychological problems such as depression or poor self-esteem. It is widely accepted that there are enough important differences between sex offender subtypes (i.e., child molesters, rapists) that risk assessment should take these subgroups into account (Craig, Browne, & Stringer, 2004).

Rapid Risk Assessment for Sex Offence Recidivism The simplest scale developed to predict sexual recidivism is the Rapid Risk Assessment for Sex Offence Recidivism (RRASOR) (Hanson, 1997). Using the risk factors identified in the Hanson and Bussière (1998) meta-analysis, the four best predictors were selected using data from seven different follow-up studies from several countries: prior sexual offences, younger age, male victim of a sexual offence, and unrelated victim of sexual offence. Despite consisting of only four items, the RRASOR predicts sexual recidivism (Barbaree et al., 2001; Sjöstedt & Langström, 2002). The RRASOR primarily assesses the sexual deviance component of risk to commit sexual offences (Barbaree, Langton, & Peacock, 2006). However, the RRASOR does not provide (nor was it intended to provide) a comprehensive measure of all the factors relevant to the prediction of sexual recidivism. Hanson (1997) recommends that it be used only to screen offenders for more intensive assessment. There is some evidence that the RRASOR may not be appropriate for use with non-white, Aboriginal, or non-European populations (Allan, Dawson, & Allan, 2006; Langström, 2004). The RRASOR may also only be appropriate for use with pedophile sex offenders (Bartosh, Garby, Lewis, & Gray, 2003).

Static-99 In 1999, David Thornton and Karl Hanson decided to combine two measures to create a new ten-item scale they called the Static-99 (Hanson & Thornton, 1999). This scale includes the four items from the RRASOR plus six items focusing on prior nonsexual violent history, current nonsexual violence, prior non-contact sexual offences, marital status, number of sentences received, and stranger victim. Explicit scoring is provided and individuals are assigned to one of four risk categories: low, medium-low, medium-high, and high risk. On a combined sample of 1208 sexual offenders, the Static-99 correlated 0.33 with sexual recidivism and 0.32 with violent recidivism (Hanson & Thornton, 2000). Other researchers have also found that the Static-99 predicts sexual recidivism in Canada (Barbaree et al., 2001), Sweden (Sjöstedt & Langström, 2001), Belgium (Ducro & Pham, 2006), Australia (Allan et al., 2006), Germany (Stadtland, Hollweg, Kleindienst, Dietl, Reich, & Nedopil, 2005), and the Netherlands (de Vogel, de Ruiter, van Beek, & Mead, 2004). There is some evidence that the Static-99 predicts future offences even among those suspected of molestation, but not convicted (Soothill, Harman, Francis, & Kirby, 2005). The Static-99, however, is less accurate for rapists (Bartosh et al., 2003) and non-white ethnicities (Langström, 2004). In addition, the Static-99 overestimates risk to reoffend in some samples, especially those who have received treatment (Doren, 2004; Looman, 2006). The accuracy of Static-99 scores may be improved if history of childhood abuse (Craissati & Beech, 2005) and phallometric-assessment scores indicating a sexual preference for children (Nunes et al., 2002) are also taken into account.

The above two scales are actuarial and consist only of static risk factors. Recent research has attempted to identify dynamic predictors of sexual offence recidivism. Hanson and Harris (2000) explored dynamic risk factors in a sample of 200 sexual recidivists and 201 nonrecidivists using file information and interviews with community supervision officers. Dynamic factors were coded twice: one month and six months prior to the sexual offence for the recidivists and at one month and six months for the nonrecidivists (i.e., at intervals that corresponded to the periods measured for the recidivists). The following factors changed for the worse and were related to sexual recidivism: poor social supports, antisocial lifestyles, poor supervision compliance, attitudes supportive of sexual aggression, and negative mood (anger and distress).

CURRENT ISSUES

Where Is the Theory?

Much of the focus in risk-assessment research has been on perfecting the prediction of violence. This is especially true for actuarial methods of risk assessment in which risk factors are selected based on their statistical relation to a specific outcome. There is less attention as to *why* these risk factors are linked to violence. Understanding the causes of violence will aid in the development of prevention and intervention programs. Box 12.4 on page 364 presents one model to explain criminal recidivism. Recently, Silver (2006) has recommended that researchers use criminological theories to help guide "the next generation of empirical research in the area of mental disorder and violence" (p. 686).

Box 12.4

Coping-Relapse Model of Criminal Recidivism

Zamble and Quinsey (1997) have attempted to explain why an individual will commit another offence after release. Figure 12.1 illustrates the recidivism process and how each level interacts. According to the model, the first event is some type of environmental trigger. What will be considered a trigger varies across individuals and can range from stressful life events, such as losing a job, having relationship problems, and financial difficulties, to more mundane daily events, such as being stuck in a traffic jam. Once the event has occurred, the individual will invoke both an emotional and cognitive appraisal of the event. If this appraisal process results in the experience of negative emotions (e.g., anger, hostility, fear) or elevated levels of stress, the individual will attempt to deal with these unpleasant feelings. If the individual does not possess adequate coping mechanisms, a worsening cycle of negative emotions and maladaptive cognitions occurs, eventually resulting in criminal behaviour. The model also posits that how an individual perceives and responds to an environmental trigger is dependent on two factors: individual and response mechanisms.

Individual influences include factors such as criminal history and enduring personality traits (e.g., psychopathy, emotional reactivity). These factors influence how an individual will perceive an event and the likelihood they will engage in criminal conduct, both of which are relatively stable. For example, research has found that psychopathic individuals are more likely to interpret ambiguous events as hostile (Serin, 1991) and are impulsive. These factors increase the likelihood of engaging in criminal behaviour.

Available response mechanisms also influence how an individual will perceive a situation, in turn mediating that person's response. These factors are considered to be more dynamic in nature and thus important targets for intervention. Examples of these factors include coping ability, substance use, criminal attitudes and associates, and social supports. Imagine an individual who loses his job. He becomes angry and upset, and reverts to drinking to deal with these negative feelings. His drinking angers his intimate partner who becomes less and less supportive of him. These factors increase the likelihood that he will resume his criminal behaviour.

Figure 12.1 The Recidivism Process

What about Protective Factors?

Various historical, dispositional, clinical, and contextual risk factors have been shown to have predictive utility. **Protective factors** are factors that mitigate or reduce the likelihood of antisocial acts or violence in high-risk offenders (Borum, 1996). Understanding the positive attributes could help explain why some individuals with many risk factors do not become violent. For example, a youth may have antisocial parents at home (a risk factor) but also be strongly attached to school (a protective factor). Like risk factors, protective factors vary across time, and the impact they have depends on the situation. Most of the research on protective factors has been conducted with children and youth. The following factors have been identified as protective factors: prosocial involvement, strong social supports, positive social orientation (school, work), strong attachments (as long as attachment is not to an antisocial other), and intelligence (Caldwell, Silverman, Lefforge, & Silver, 2004; Caprara, Barbaranelli, & Pastorelli, 2001; Hoge, Andrews, & Leschied, 1996; Lipsey & Derzon, 1998). More research on protective factors in adult offenders is beginning. A variable identified as a potential protective factor for high-risk offenders is employment stability, whereas strong family connections appears to be a protective factor for lower-risk male offenders (DeMatteo, Heilbrun, & Marczyk, 2005).

The importance of protective or strength factors has recently been incorporated in a new structured professional judgment instrument developed by Webster et al. (Webster, Nicholls, Martin, Desmarais, & Brink, 2006). The Short-Term Assessment of Risk and Treatability (START) (Webster, Martin, Brink, Nicholls, & Middleton, 2004) is designed to help guide decision making for a number of risk domains, including violence, self-harm, suicide, substance use, victimization, self-neglect, and unauthorized leave in forensic psychiatric patients. According to this approach the 20 factors are rated on two separate scales: both a risk and a strength scale. For example, a factor such as coping could be seen as a strength (having adaptive coping skills) or a risk (having maladaptive coping skills). Preliminary research with the START in a sample of forensic psychiatric patients in British Columbia has obtained promising results (Nicholls, Brink, Desmarais, Webster, & Martin, 2006).

Are Decision Makers Using the Scientific Research?

Despite the considerable strides that have been made in refining methods of violence prediction, many practitioners are not using these instruments. This gap in integrating science and clinical practice represents a significant challenge to this area. A survey by Boothby and Clements (2000) asked 820 correctional psychologists what tests they used in their assessments. The most commonly used test was the Minnesota Multiphasic Personality Inventory, used by 87% of the psychologists. Only 11% of the respondents mentioned using the Hare PCL-R, and less than 1% mentioned using the VRAG or the LSI-R. It is not clear why so few correctional psychologists are using these instruments. Research is needed to understand the obstacles to the adoption of new risk-assessment measures. One potential reason is that these newer instruments have not been part of the training programs for psychologists. Borum (1996) has recommended that clinical practice guidelines for risk assessment be developed. Development of such guidelines by professional organizations such as the American Psychological Association and the Canadian Psychological Association would result in more standardized use.

What is the impact of psychologists' recommendations on forensic decision making? Past research has found that judicial decision making relies heavily on recommendations made by mental health professionals (Konecni & Ebbesen, 1984). In Canada, decisions to release forensic patients are strongly related to recommendations by clinicians (Quinsey & Ambtman, 1979), and reports by clinicians about treatment gains made by sex offenders strongly influence decisions about granting parole (Quinsey, Khanna, & Malcolm, 1998). Another related question is whether decision makers are relying on results of the newly developed actuarial risk instruments. Hilton and Simmons (2001) studied the influence of VRAG scores and clinical judgments on decisions made to transfer offenders with mental disorders in a maximum-security facility to less secure institutions. Review board decisions were not related to scores on the VRAG but to senior clinicians' testimony at the review board hearing. Patients who caused few institutional problems, who were compliant with medication, who were more physically attractive, and who had less serious criminal histories were more likely to be recommended by the clinician for transfer. Clinicians make more accurate decisions when they are given a statement that summarizes an individual's risk along with case information (i.e., "64% of people in Mr. Smith's risk category reoffended violently within 10 years after release") (Hilton, Harris, Rawson, & Beach, 2005). Clinicians also are able to make accurate decisions when they are provided with the information that relates to risk.

Why Do Some Individuals Stop Committing Crimes?

Much of the research discussed in this chapter focuses on the risk factors related to engaging in crime and violence. However, if we want to prevent or reduce crime, knowledge about the factors relating to desistance from crime is probably equally important. Research even shows that a majority of offenders show large declines in their criminal activity in early adulthood (Blumstein & Cohen, 1987; Piquero, Blumstein, Brame, Haapanen, Mulvey, & Nagin, 2001). As many as 70% of offenders show significant declines in crime (and only a small percentage of offenders maintain criminal activity well into adulthood) (Piquero et al., 2001). Yet, the reasons why offenders give up crime is poorly understood. Some research shows that the factors that relate to the onset of a criminal career do not necessarily explain desistance from crime (Stouthamer-Loeber, Wei, Loeber, & Masten, 2004). The desistance process occurs at the same time and may be caused by such factors as "good" work or "good" marriages (Laub, Nagin, & Sampson, 1998; Maume, Ousey, & Beaver, 2005; Uggen, 1999). Age is strongly related to criminal behaviour, and the age-related decline in criminal offending is connected to the maturation process (Menard & Huizinga, 1989). LeBlanc (1993) defines maturation as the "development of self- and social control" (p. 65). Shover and Thompson (1992) have suggested that as people age, they become less interested in a criminal lifestyle and are more able to understand and fear the consequences of engaging in crime. See Box 12.5 for excerpts from a study that examines why high-risk offenders stop offending.

Box 12.5

Why Do High-Risk Violent Offenders Stop Offending?

In a study entitled "Against All Odds: A Qualitative Follow-up of High-Risk Violent Offenders Who Were Not Reconvicted," Haggard, Gumpert, and Grann (2001) explored what factors were related to why repeat violent offenders stopped reoffending. To be eligible to participate in the study, the offender had to score high on the historical subscale of the HCR-20, to have been convicted of at least two violent crimes, and not to have been convicted for any crime for at least ten years. From a sample of 401 violent offenders, only 6 individuals were eligible to participate. Of these 6, only 4 consented to be interviewed. The following factors were reported by the participants to be related to desistance. For each factor, a quotation from one of the participants is provided.

■ *Insight triggered by negative events connected to their criminal lifestyle.* "It grows within during a long time,

the insight, but you have to reach a point where it feels wrong. . . . To me, it was mostly due to the last time, when I was admitted to the forensic psychiatric hospital. The whole thing was crazy, and then I realized how off track I was—when you strike down a person with an axe because of a trivial thing . . . then you start wondering. I did anyway." (p. 1055)

■ *Social avoidance.* "I have a terrible temper and I can become violent, very violent. . . . You have to avoid different situations, you have to think about it all the time so that you don't put yourself in situations you can't handle." (p. 1057)

■ *Orientation to the family.* "After I served my sentence, I became more committed to my children. To help them not to make the same mistake I did." (p. 1057)

SUMMARY

1. An assessment of risk requires two components: an analysis of the likelihood of future criminal or violent acts and the development of strategies to manage or reduce the risk level.

2. Risk assessments are routinely conducted in the civil and criminal contexts. Risk assessments in civil contexts include civil commitments, child protection, immigration, and duty to warn. In criminal settings, the assessment of risk occurs at pretrial, sentencing, and release stages.

3. There are different types of errors when attempting to make predictions. Each of these errors has different consequences. False-positive errors affect the offender, whereas false-negative errors affect society and the victim.

4. Risk factors vary in terms of how fixed or changeable they are. Static factors either do not change or are highly resistant to change. Dynamic factors are changeable and are often targeted for intervention.

5. Various approaches have been developed to assess violent prediction. These include unstructured clinical judgment, actuarial prediction, and structured professional judgment. There are advantages and disadvantages to each approach.

6. Major risk factors can be classified into historical, dispositional, clinical, and contextual factors. Historical risk factors include general social history and specific criminal history variables, such as employment problems and past history of violence. Dispositional

factors include demographic, attitudinal, and personality variables such as gender, age, negative attitudes, and psychopathy. Clinical factors refer to those that contribute to violence, such as substance abuse or major psychoses. Contextual factors refer to aspects of the individual's situation that can elevate the risk, such as access to victims or weapons, lack of social supports, or perceived stress.

Key Concepts

actuarial prediction 346

base rate 342

clinical risk factors 350

contextual risk factors 350

dispositional risk factors 349

dynamic risk factor 348

false negative 341

false positive 341

historical risk factors 349

illusory correlation 345

protective factors 365

risk factor 348

static risk factor 348

structured professional judgment 348

true negative 341

true positive 341

unstructured clinical judgment 346

Discussion Questions

1. Do you think Canadian courts should allow expert testimony about the risk for violence? What level of predictive accuracy do you think should be required before allowing a clinician to use a newly developed risk-assessment instrument?

2. You have decided to take a summer job working at Correctional Service Canada. You are asked to help devise a study to evaluate the accuracy of a new instrument designed to predict hostage taking by federal offenders. How would you approach this task?

3. What factors do you think the National Parole Board should rely on when making decisions about whether to release offenders?

4. Distinguish among the different types of risk assessment: unstructured clinical judgment, actuarial prediction, and structured professional judgment. Develop a study to evaluate which of these types of risk assessment is most accurate.

5. You think there should be more research on why offenders decide to stop offending. Describe a study you would conduct, focusing on the methodology and what factors you would measure that might relate to the desistance process.

6. Researchers have developed several risk-assessment instruments, but not all psychologists conducting risk assessments are using these scales. Why is this? What could be done to encourage forensic psychologists to start using these instruments?

7. A school board has contacted you wanting to know how to identify the next potential school shooter. Describe what you know about threat assessment and problems with trying to identify low-base-rate violent acts.

Readings

Bonta, J. (2002). Offender risk assessment: Guidelines for selection and use. *Criminal Justice and Behavior, 29*, 355–379.

Maruna, S. (2001). *Making good: How ex-convicts reform and rebuild their lives.* Washington, DC: American Psychological Association.

Zamble, E., & Quinsey, V.L. (1997). *The criminal recidivism process.* Cambridge: Cambridge University Press.

Websites

Correctional Service Canada
www.csc-scc.gc.ca

Public Safety Canada
www.ps-sp.gc.ca/index-en.asp

Chapter 13

Assessment and Treatment of Young, Female, and Aboriginal Offenders

Learning Objectives

- Describe the history of young offender legislation.

- Identify the psychiatric diagnoses and their trajectories relevant to young offenders.

- List the risk and protective factors associated with externalizing disorders in youth.

- List the factors that differentiate male and female adult offenders.

- Describe the components associated with battered women syndrome.

- Describe why Aboriginals are overrepresented in the criminal justice system.

- Describe what an Aboriginal healing lodge is and explain why such lodges are used.

As a child, Allison Kelly was no angel. She got into fights at school and in her neighbourhood on a daily basis. She would pick fights not only with children her own age and older, but even with adults. Her teacher also reported that on several occasions, Allison sneaked into the school during recess and rummaged through the other children's backpacks, taking toys or other belongings she wanted. It was not uncommon for Allison to throw a temper tantrum when she did not get her way. She often refused to follow rules and would argue until the adults gave in to her demands.

When both the school and Allison's mother failed to get Allison to change her behaviour, her mother brought her to a psychologist for an assessment. Allison refused to cooperate with the psychologist, throwing a stuffed bear at her and telling her that she could assess it instead. Based on the psychologist's observations, parent interviews, and teacher ratings, Allison was diagnosed with oppositional defiant disorder (ODD), a diagnosis that puts Allison at an increased risk for interaction with the criminal justice system.

In this chapter, we will focus on three types of "special forensic populations"; young, female, and Aboriginal offenders. We will consider the assessment and treatment of these three groups along with their various crime rates. Lastly, we will provide a discussion regarding the legal sanctions available to each group.

YOUNG OFFENDERS

Adolescents (i.e., older than 12 years and younger than 18 years, generally) who come into contact with the criminal justice system pose several challenges to the adult-based system. Legislation has changed over the years in an attempt to address the special needs of adolescents. Moreover, it is critical to consider the developmental paths to youthful offending in order to prevent and rehabilitate. A number of treatment options have been developed for young offenders. It should be noted that anyone younger than 12 years engaging in criminal acts is processed through family and social service agencies usually under provincial or territorial legislation.

Historical Overview

Youth who committed criminal acts in Canada during the seventeenth and eighteenth centuries were treated as adult offenders. The criminal justice system made no accommodations or considerations for how youth were charged, sentenced, or incarcerated. They were kept in the same facilities as adults while awaiting their trials, received the same penalties as adults, and served their sentences with adults. Even in cases involving the death penalty, youth were dealt with in a similar manner as adults.

Canada enacted the Juvenile Delinquents Act (JDA) in 1908, partly in response to the justice system's past disregard for the special population of youthful offenders. The JDA applied to children and youth between the ages of 7 and 16 years (18 years in some jurisdictions). Terminology was used to reflect a difference between youth and adults. For example, youth were called "delinquents" rather than "offenders" and were considered to commit acts of delinquency such as truancy rather than criminal offences. A separate court system for youth was established, and it was suggested that court proceedings be as informal as possible in that delinquents were seen as misguided children in need of guidance and support. When possible, parents were encouraged to be part of the judicial process. In serious cases, the JDA made it possible for delinquents to be transferred to adult court. Punishments for delinquents were to be consistent with how a parent would discipline a child. For example, delinquents could be sentenced to an industrial school where they learned skills or a trade for future employment. Other dispositions for delinquents included adjournment without penalty, fines, probation, and foster care. Table 13.1 highlights the key changes to the Canadian criminal justice system under the JDA.

Table 13.1 The Juvenile Delinquents Act's Key Changes to Canadian Criminal Justice

1. A separate court system for youth was established.
2. A minimum age (seven years old) was set for which a child could be charged with a criminal offence.
3. Judges had sentencing discretion and options increased (e.g., foster care, fines, and institutionalization).
4. Parents were encouraged to be part of the judicial process.

Many saw the JDA as a positive step toward youth justice. However, the JDA was not without criticism. For example, the services to be provided to delinquents as outlined in the JDA were not always available. Also, given the informality of youth court, some youth were denied their rights, such as the right to counsel and the right to appeal, and judges could impose open-ended sentences. Furthermore, the broad definition of delinquency included acts that were not illegal for adults.

The JDA was in effect until 1984, when it was replaced with the Young Offenders Act (YOA). The YOA represented a shift in how youth who broke the law were perceived. Youth were to be held responsible for their actions. However, the YOA acknowledged that youth were different from adults, having a different level of cognitive development, for example. The differences between youths and adults were to be recognized through the level of accountability and the consequences of the behaviour committed. The YOA also recognized the need to protect the public from young offenders. Lastly, the YOA recognized that youths should be afforded all of the rights stated in the Canadian Charter of Rights and Freedoms (R.S.C., 1985, c. Y-1, s. 3).

Changes in the YOA included the age of criminal responsibility. Under the YOA, youth had to be at least 12 years old (and up to 18 years) to be processed through the justice system. Children under 12 would be dealt with through child and family services. Some of the changes brought forward with the JDA remained with the YOA. For example, youth courts continued under the YOA. As with the JDA, for serious indictable offences such as murder, youth could be transferred to adult courts, provided they were at least 14 years of age (R.S.C., 1985, c. Y-1, s. 16).

The YOA allowed for youth cases to be diverted. **Diversion** is a decision not to prosecute the young offender but rather have him or her undergo an educational or community service program. However, for diversion to be possible, the young offender would have to plead guilty (R.S.C., 1985, c. Y-1, s. 4). Other dispositions available for young offenders included absolute discharge (i.e., the young offender received no sentence other than a guilty verdict), fine, compensation for loss or damaged property, restitution to the victim, prohibition order (i.e., no weapons), community service, probation, and custody. Two types of custody are available: open (placing the youth in a community residential facility, group home, childcare facility, or wilderness camp) or secure (incarcerating the youth in a prison facility; R.S.C., 1985, c. Y-1, s. 20).

There were a number of amendments made to the YOA. For example, Bill C-106 section 16 (1986) required the youth court to consider whether the Crown or defence would like to make an application to transfer the case to adult court. This amendment was introduced to address the problem of defendants making guilty pleas to avoid transfers. Bill C-37 changed section 16 once again in 1995. With this amendment, 16 and 17 year olds charged with murder, manslaughter, or aggravated sexual assault would go to adult court. On application, these cases could stay in youth court, if the youth court felt the objectives of rehabilitation and public protection could be reconciled. Also under Bill C-37, sentences for youth changed. For first-degree murder, a ten-year maximum, with a six-year maximum to be served incarcerated, was available. For second-degree murder, a seven-year maximum, with a four-year maximum to be served incarcerated, was available. Table 13.2 highlights the key changes to the Canadian criminal justice system under the YOA.

Overall, the YOA attempted to make youth more accountable for their behaviour while supporting rehabilitation through treatment programs and providing alternatives to incarceration for less serious crimes. One of the major criticisms of the YOA was that serious, violent offences carried relatively short ("light") sentences. Other criticisms

Diversion: A decision not to prosecute a young offender but rather have him or her undergo an educational or community-service program. Also an option for the courts dealing with offenders with mental illnesses who are facing minor charges. The court can divert the offender directly into a treatment program rather than have him or her go through the court process.

Table 13.2 The Young Offenders Act's Key Changes to Canadian Criminal Justice

1. Youth are to be held accountable for their actions, however, not to the full extent that adults are.
2. The public has the right to be protected from young offenders.
3. Young offenders have legal rights and freedoms including those described in the Canadian Charter of Rights and Freedoms.
4. Children have to be at least 12 years of age to be charged with a criminal offence.

included disagreement over raising the minimum age of responsibility from age seven to twelve. Also, the YOA allowed for discrepancies in the factors leading to transfer to adult court that suggested an arbitrariness in how cases were handled.

On April 1, 2003, the Youth Criminal Justice Act (YCJA) replaced the YOA. The three main objectives of the YCJA are to

1. Prevent youth crime
2. Provide meaningful consequences and encourage responsibility of behaviour
3. Improve rehabilitation and reintegration of youth into the community

With the YCJA, there is a movement to keep young offenders out of the court and out of custody. There is an onus on police to consider community outlets and less serious alternatives for youth before bringing them to the attention of youth court (Youth Criminal Justice Act, 2002, s. 7). These alternatives are called **extrajudicial** measures and include giving a warning or making a referral for treatment (with the consent of the youth; Youth Criminal Justice Act, 2002, s. 10).

> **Extrajudicial:** Term applied to measures taken to keep young offenders out of court and out of custody (e.g., giving a warning or making a referral for treatment)

Sentencing options have also increased under the YCJA. Judges are able to provide a reprimand (i.e., lecture or warning to the youth), an intensive support and supervision order, an attendance order (i.e., youth must attend a specific program), a deferred custody and supervision order (i.e., youth can serve sentence in community as long as imposed conditions are met), and an intensive rehabilitative custody and supervision order (i.e., youth in custody receive intensive services and supervision) (Youth Criminal Justice Act, 2002, s. 42).

In terms of transferring youth to adult court, the YCJA has made a number of changes from the process outlined in the YOA. Under the YCJA, the transfer process is eliminated. Rather, youth court determines whether the youthful defendant is guilty, and if so, the judge can impose an adult sentence with youth as young as 14 years old (can be set at 15 or 16 years). An adult sentence cannot be applied unless the Crown notifies the youth court that it will be seeking an adult sentence (Youth Criminal Justice Act, 2002, s. 61). A key issue in determining sentencing is that the sentence must be proportionate to the seriousness of the offence (Youth Criminal Justice Act, 2002, s. 38(2)(c)).

The YCJA has made a serious attempt at improving the interests of victims. Under the YCJA, victims are to be informed of the court proceedings and given an opportunity to participate. Victims also have the right to access youth court records. Moreover, victims can participate in community-based dispositions (Youth Criminal Justice Act, 2002, s. 3). Table 13.3 on page 374 highlights the key changes to the Canadian criminal justice system under the YCJA.

Table 13.3 The Youth Criminal Justice Act's Key Changes to the Canadian Criminal Justice System

1. Less serious and less violent offences should be kept out of the formal court process.
2. The number of extrajudicial measures are increased.
3. There is greater focus on prevention and reintegration into the community.
4. Transfers to adult court are removed; instead, youth court judges can impose adult sentences.
5. The interests and needs of victims are recognized.

A youth vandalizes a wall in the community.

Youth Crime Rates

Generally, the total number of crimes committed by youth has been decreasing for the past few years. This pattern also can be seen for violent and property offences. See Table 13.4 for a distribution of youthful cases by major crime category. See Box 13.1 for a case illustration of a serious youthful offence.

Regarding sentencing in youth court, probation is the most frequent sentence imposed. Roughly 63% of youth under supervision by the criminal justice system in 2003 were on probation. Sentences of secure custody occurred in about 23% of the cases in 2003. However, Canada's youth incarceration reached its lowest point in eight years in 2002–03. Overall, since the implementation of the YCJA, the number of youth in sentenced custody has decreased by half (Statistics Canada, 2003a, 2004b, 2005b).

Table 13.4 Canadian Youthful Cases by Major Crime Category

Crime Category	2000	2001	2002	2003
Total cases	87 617	85 640	84 592	70 465
Violent crimes	22 674	22 510	22 462	20 416
Property crimes	34 694	33 086	32 465	25 663
Administration of justice offences	7 917	7 698	7 790	6 784
Other Criminal Code offences	4 506	4 525	4 267	3 896
Drug-related offences	5 767	6 058	5 907	3 931
Young Offender Act offences	10 766	10 414	10 325	7 692
Other federal statute offences	127	138	151	962

Source: Adapted from Statistics Canada, 2005a.

Box 13.1

Do Youthful Offenders Get Away with Murder?

One evening while lying in bed in a cottage in Gatineau, Quebec, Bob Dagenais heard someone drive up, so he got out of bed to check. He realized there were two males coming into his house, so he called 911. Before he could speak to the operator, he was shot. By now, his wife Bonnie was up and saw her husband fall to the ground. She was then shot dead also. Police arrived within an hour and found 27-year-old René Michaud and a 15 year old sleeping, along with two shotguns, in a truck nearby. The pair were charged with the first- and second-degree murder of Bonnie and Bob Dagenais.

During Michaud's trial, he testified that he killed Bob Dagenais, but that it was an accident. The youth admitted to killing Bonnie Dagenais but said Michaud had told him to do it. The youth stated that Michaud talked about the possibility of killing someone as they started a break-in spree at cottages. The youth admitted that he wanted to live that experience. A jury verdict found Michaud guilty on the charges. Such a verdict receives an automatic 25 years to life in prison.

Although an argument was made for the youth to be transferred to adult court, it was not successful. In a surprise move, the youth, whose name is protected by law, pleaded guilty to first-degree murder in Bonnie's death and second-degree murder in Bob's death. He received a nine-year sentence. The young offender will spend the first five years of his sentence in a juvenile detention centre and the remainder of the sentence under surveillance in the community.

Sources: CBC News, 2003 (October 23); CBC News, 2003 (November 13); CBC News Ottawa, 2002; CBC News Ottawa, 2003.

Assessment of Young Offenders

Often there are two levels of consent a clinician will obtain before commencing the assessment of a child or adolescent. Because children and adolescents are not legally capable of providing consent, consent will be sought from parents or guardians. Following parental consent, assent or agreement to conduct the assessment will be sought from the child or adolescent. Although court-ordered assessments do not necessarily require consent or assent, clinicians often will seek consent/assent before commencing the assessment.

Broadly, children's and youths' emotional and behavioural difficulties can be categorized as **internalizing** or **externalizing problems** (Rutter, 1990). Internalizing problems are emotional difficulties such as anxiety, depression, and obsessions. Externalizing problems are behavioural difficulties such as delinquency, fighting, bullying, lying, and destructive behaviour. Externalizing problems have been considered more difficult to treat and more likely to have long-term persistence (Ebata, Peterson, & Conger, 1990; Robins, 1986). Externalizing disorders have been known to be quite stable, though symptoms often peak in teenage years and decrease in the late twenties (Rutter, 1995). Males are more likely to have externalizing difficulties than females, with a ratio of about 10:1 (Barkley, 1997; Rutter, 1990). It should be noted that internalizing problems might co-occur with externalizing difficulties that should also be assessed and treated.

To assess externalizing problems, multiple informants are necessary to obtain an accurate assessment because the child or youth may not be aware of his or her behaviour or the influence it has on others (McMahon, 1994). Parents, teachers, and peers may be interviewed or asked to rate the child or adolescent. Also, it is important that behaviour be viewed within a developmental context. For example, rebelling against rules set by parents may be normative for adolescents but worrisome if younger children are oppositional

Internalizing problems:
Emotional difficulties such as anxiety, depression, and obsessions experienced by a youth

Externalizing problems:
Behavioural difficulties such as delinquency, fighting, bullying, lying, or destructive behaviour experienced by a youth

and continually refuse to comply with parents' requests. The duration, severity, and frequency of troublesome behaviours should be measured.

There are three childhood psychiatric diagnoses that occur with some frequency in young offenders—**attention deficit hyperactivity disorder** (ADHD), **oppositional defiant disorder** (ODD), and **conduct disorder** (CD). ADHD is described in the *DSM-IV* as an inattention and restlessness (APA, 1994). Some examples of features associated with ADHD include the following: does not appear to listen when spoken to, has difficulty in organization, loses items, fidgets, and talks excessively. To qualify for an ADHD diagnosis, a number of symptoms must be present, occur in two or more settings, and persist for at least six months. When making an ADHD diagnosis, it is important to consider the age of the child. In young children, many of the symptoms of ADHD are part of normal development and behaviour and may not lead to criminal activity later on. However, there may be some hyperactive-impulsive or inattentive symptoms before the age of 7 years that caused impairment. Many children with ADHD also receive diagnoses of ODD or CD (Barkley, 1991).

ODD is described as a "pattern of negativistic, hostile, and defiant behaviour" (APA, 1994, p. 93). Some examples of features associated with ODD include loses temper, deliberately annoys others, and is vindictive. Approximately 40% of children with ODD develop CD (Loeber et al., 1993). If a child with ODD qualifies for a CD diagnosis, an ODD diagnosis is not used. Some examples of features associated with CD include initiates physical fights, is physically cruel to animals, sets fires, lies for gain, and is truant before 13 years of age. Approximately 50% of children meeting criteria for CD go on to receive diagnoses of antisocial personality disorder in adulthood (APA, 1994; Loeber & Farrington, 2000). Thus, CD often is the precursor to antisocial personality disorder. ODD and CD are not diagnosed if the individual is 18 years or older (the individual may meet criteria for Antisocial Personality Disorder).

Attention deficit hyperactivity disorder: A disorder in a youth characterized by a persistent pattern of inattention and hyperactivity or impulsivity

Oppositional defiant disorder: A disorder in a youth characterized by a persistent pattern of negativistic, hostile, and defiant behaviours

Conduct disorder: A disorder characterized by a persistent pattern of behaviour in which a youth violates the rights of others or age-appropriate societal norms or rules

Rates of Behaviour Disorders in Youth

It has been estimated that approximately 5% to 15% of children display severe behavioural problems (Rutter, 1990). This estimate may, however, be too low. Notably, in the Ontario Child Health Study in 1987, approximately 18% of children between the ages of 4 and 16 years were found to experience conduct disorder, hyperactivity, emotional disturbance, or a combination of these (Offord et al., 1987). Researchers have found that behavioural disorders commonly co-occur. For example, 20% to 50% of children with ADHD also have symptoms consistent with CD or ODD (Offord, Lipman, & Duku, 2001).

Trajectories of Youthful Offenders

When examining the aggressive histories of young offenders, two categories emerge. Young offenders may be categorized as those who started with social transgressions and behavioural problems in very early childhood (child-onset, life-course persistent) or those whose problem behaviours emerged in the teen years (adolescent-onset, adolescent limited; Moffitt, 1993). Thus, two developmental pathways to youthful antisocial behaviour have been suggested—childhood onset versus adolescent onset.

Age of onset is a critical factor in the trajectory to adult offending. A number of researchers have found that early onset of antisocial behaviour is related to more serious and persistent antisocial behaviour later in life (Fergusson & Woodward, 2000; Loeber & Farrington, 2000). Those with a childhood onset also may have a number of other difficulties, such as ADHD, learning disabilities, and academic difficulties (Hinshaw, Lahey, & Hart, 1993). The childhood-onset trajectory is a less frequent occurrence than adolescent onset, with about 3% to 5% of the general population showing a childhood-onset trajectory (Moffitt, 1993). It is important to remember, however, that most young children with behavioural difficulties do not go on to become adult offenders (or even young offenders for that matter).

The adolescent-onset pattern occurs in about 70% of the general population (Moffitt, 1993). Many young people engage in social transgressions during their adolescence, but adolescents who only engage in a few antisocial acts do not qualify for a CD diagnosis. Although it is more common for adolescent-onset youth to desist their antisocial behaviour in their early adulthood than for those with a childhood onset, some of these adolescent-onset youth continue to engage in antisocial acts in adulthood (Moffitt et al., 2002).

Dr. Richard Tremblay has conducted numerous studies examining the developmental paths of conduct-disordered youth (see Box 13.2 on page 378 to learn more about Dr. Tremblay and his research). In a study by Brame, Nagin, and Tremblay (2001), a group of boys from Montreal were followed from the time they entered kindergarten through to their late teen years. The researchers found that participants' overall level of aggression decreased at they got older regardless of how high it was when the participants were youngsters. It was notable, however, that for a small proportion of youngsters with high levels of aggression, these high levels continued into their teen years. A much larger proportion of youngsters with high levels of aggression reported little to no aggression in their teen years. Thus, for a small group of youngsters with high levels of aggression, these levels will continue into later years.

Theories to Explain Antisocial Behaviour

Biological Theories To explain why some youth engage in antisocial acts, researchers have examined the relation between frontal lobe functioning and antisocial behaviour. The frontal lobe is responsible for the planning and inhibiting of behaviour. Moffit and Henry (1989) have found that conduct-disordered youth have less frontal lobe inhibition of behaviour. Thus, the likelihood that these youth will act impulsively is increased, making it more likely that they will make poor behavioural choices.

Physiologically, conduct-disordered youth have been found to have slower heart rates than youth who do not engage in antisocial behaviour (Wadsworth, 1976). Genetic studies have found a relation between paternal antisocial behaviour and child offspring antisocial behaviour (Frick et al., 1992). Moreover, adoption and twin studies also find a biological link to youthful offending. That is, children who have an antisocial biological father are more likely to engage in antisocial behaviour, even when raised apart from the biological father (Cadoret & Cain, 1980; Jarey & Stewart, 1985). Overall, the research explaining the relation among biology, physiology, genetics, and behaviour is preliminary at this point.

Cognitive Theories Kenneth Dodge and his colleagues proposed a model of conduct-disordered behaviour that focuses on the thought processes that occur in social interactions (Crick & Dodge, 1994; Dodge, 2000). Thought processes start when individuals pay attention

Box 13.2

Canadian Researcher Profile: Dr. Richard Tremblay

After Dr. Richard Tremblay completed his master's degree at the University of Montreal, he started working with offenders who had mental illnesses. It was at this time that he first started wondering what causes people to have such incredible problems.

Dr. Tremblay describes wanting to know "how nice kindergarten children become juvenile delinquents and violent offenders." While at the University of London, England, doing his Ph.D., Dr. Tremblay decided to start answering some of the developmental questions he had wondered about. For his doctoral dissertation, he examined how juvenile delinquents changed over the course of the treatment they were receiving for their problems. Dr. Tremblay has stayed on this research path for more than 30 years now.

Dr. Tremblay uses longitudinal-experimental methodology (collecting data on participants at different points in time over their lifespan) to understand developmental paths and the factors that affect them. He has noted that it is important to study participants over long periods so that

their changes can be identified, along with the factors that lead to the changes. An interesting trend in Dr. Tremblay's research is that the age of his participants is getting younger. When Dr. Tremblay first embarked on his research, his participants were adolescents. Over the years, he has realized the need to look at younger and younger children, especially if the ultimate goal is to prevent deviant outcomes from ever occurring.

Over the next ten years, Dr. Tremblay plans to examine different preventative interventions with pregnant women at high risk of having chronically aggressive children. He will be taking into account genetic factors and changing parents' behaviour. With the use of scans, he will examine how these factors affect the brain development of the fetuses and the long-term development of their behaviour. Dr. Tremblay believes the future of the field will be to study gene–environment interactions to understand deviant development.

Dr. Tremblay holds a prestigious position as a Canada Research Chair in Child Development at the University of Montreal. In this position, he is dedicated to conducting research and training future researchers in the area. He believes that graduate students should have the experience of working on concrete problems and should become involved in research projects that are going on internationally. Dr. Tremblay's view on undergraduate training is to have students come in contact with leaders in the field via books, video, conferences, and invited speakers to their universities. He believes that in order for the field to advance, it is important that future researchers—students—identify what we do not yet know.

Dr. Tremblay's research is funded by numerous government agencies. His advances in the field of child development have been recognized with many awards and honours. Most recently, Dr. Tremblay was identified as one of Canada's top five medical scientists by *Time* magazine in 2003.

to and interpret social and emotional cues in their environment. The following step in the model is to consider alternative responses to the cues. Finally, a response is chosen and performed. Conduct-disordered youth demonstrate cognitive deficits and distortions (Fontaine, Burks, & Dodge, 2002). These youth often attend to fewer cues and misattribute hostile intent to ambiguous situations. Moreover, conduct-disordered youth demonstrate limited problem-solving skills, producing few solutions to problems, and these solutions are usually aggressive in nature. Cognitive deficits are likely to be present in early childhood and may contribute to child-onset conduct disorder (Coy, Speltz, DeKlyen, & Jones, 2001).

Dodge and his colleagues also have distinguished between two types of aggressive behaviour—reactive aggression and proactive aggression (Dodge, 1991; Schwartz et al., 1998). Reactive aggression is described as an emotionally aggressive response to a perceived threat or frustration. In contrast, proactive aggression is aggression directed at achieving a goal or receiving positive reinforcers. Referring to Dodge's model, deficiencies in the process occur at different points for reactive and proactive aggression. Reactively aggressive youth are likely to demonstrate deficiencies early in the cognitive process, such as focusing on only a few social cues and misattributing hostile intent to ambiguous situations. In contrast, proactive aggressive youth are likely to have deficiencies in generating alternative responses and often choose an aggressive response. Furthermore, reactive and proactive aggressors tend to have different trajectories. Reactive aggressors tend to have an earlier onset of problems than proactive aggressors (Dodge, Lochman, Harnish, Bate, & Pettit, 1997).

Social Theories Bandura's (1965) **social learning theory** suggests that children learn their behaviour from observing others. Children are more likely to imitate behaviour that receives positive reinforcement than behaviour that receives negative reinforcement or punishment. As children are developing, numerous models are available to imitate, including parents, siblings, peers, and media figures. Studies have found that children who are highly aggressive and engage in antisocial behaviour often have witnessed parents, siblings, or grandparents engage in aggression and antisocial behaviour (Farrington, 1995; Waschbusch, 2002). This is a pattern of intergenerational aggression, in which one aggressive generation produces the next generation that also is aggressive (Glueck & Glueck, 1968; Huesmann, Eron, Lefkowitz, & Walder, 1984).

Watching extremely violent television and movies in which actors are rewarded for their aggression also increases children's likelihood of acting aggressively (Bushman & Anderson, 2001). In addition, playing aggressive video games presents a forum for youth to be reinforced for their aggression and, in turn, may increase the likelihood of children acting aggressively in real life (Anderson & Dill, 2000). Moreover, some data find a link between violent video exposure and aggressive behaviour to brain processes believed to by associated with desensitization to real-world violence (Barthlow, Bushman, & Sestir, 2006).

Social learning theory: A theory of human behaviour based on learning from watching others in the social environment and reinforcement contingencies

Risk Factors

There are a number of individual and social factors, known as **risk factors**, that place children at increased risk for developmental psychopathology, such as emotional and behavioural problems (Coie et al., 1992; Fitzpatrick, 1997; Jessor, Turbin, & Costa, 1998; Rutter, 1988, 1990; Wasserman & Saracini, 2001; Werner & Smith, 1992). It is important to remember that it is not just one risk factor but rather multiple risk factors that can lead to negative child outcomes (Rutter, 1979).

Risk factor: A factor that increases the likelihood for emotional and/or behavioural problems

Individual Risk Factors A variety of genetic or biological factors have been linked to behavioural problems. Even before a child is born, there are factors that can operate to increase the likelihood for later behavioural difficulties. For example, a parent's own history of ADHD or behavioural difficulties are known risk factors for their offspring, especially sons (Cohen, Adler, Kaplan, Pelcovitz, & Mandel, 2002; National Crime Prevention Council, 1995, 1997).

A pregnant woman's use of drugs and alcohol can place the fetus at risk for later behavioural problems (Cohen et al., 2002). Once the child is born, diet and exposure to high levels of lead are risk factors for externalizing disorders (Cohen et al., 2002; National Crime Prevention Council, 1995, 1997).

A child's temperament also can be a risk factor. For example, children who are difficult to soothe or have a negative disposition can be at risk for later behavioural difficulties (Farrington, 1995). It also has been found that children who are impulsive are at risk for behavioural problems (Farrington, 1995).

Familial Risk Factors Parents play a critical role in the development of their children. Children of parents who are neglectful (Shaw, Keenan, & Vondra, 1994) or children who do not attach securely to their parents are at risk for later behavioural problems (Fagot & Kavanagh, 1990). Divorce and familial conflict are risk factors for children (Amato & Keith, 1991; Cummings, Davies, & Campbell, 2000). Parenting style also can be problematic. For example, parents who are inconsistent, overly strict, and apply harsh discipline pose risk to the child (Dekovic, 1999). In addition, not properly supervising a child presents a risk factor to the child for later behavioural problems (Dekovic, 1999; Farrington, 1995; Hoge, Andrews, & Leschied, 1996; National Crime Prevention Council, 1995, 1997; Patterson, Reid, & Dishion, 1998; Rutter, 1990).

It has been suggested that parents who drink heavily are less likely to respond appropriately to their children's behaviour, thus increasing the likelihood of future negative behaviour (Lahey, Waldman, & McBurnett, 1999). Also, heavy drinking has been implicated in inept monitoring of children and less parental involvement, both being familial risk factors (Lahey et al., 1999).

Consequences of child abuse may be psychological, physical, behavioural, academic, sexual, interpersonal, self-perceptual, or spiritual (Health Canada, 2003). Boys, in particular, may respond to abuse by acting aggressively and later engaging in spousal abuse (Fergusson & Lynskey, 1997; Health Canada, 2003; Loos & Alexander, 1997). Cohen et al. (2002) found that physical abuse experienced during adolescence increases the risk for developing lifetime mental health difficulties and behaviour problems.

Numerous other family variables have been reported as risk factors, including low socioeconomic status, large family size, and parental mental health problems (Frick, 1994; Patterson, Reid, & Dishion, 1998; Waschbusch, 2002).

School and Social Risk Factors Having trouble reading and having a lower intelligence are both risk factors for antisocial behaviour (Elkins, Iacono, Doyle, & McGue, 1997; Rutter, 1990). The school environment also provides an opportunity for peer influences on behaviour. Young children who play with aggressive peers at an early age are at risk for externalizing behaviour (Fergusson & Horwood, 1998; Laird, Jordan, Dodge, Petit, & Bates, 2001). Children with early CD symptoms who do not end up with CD tend to associate with less delinquent peers compared with children who later qualify for a CD diagnosis (Fergusson & Horwood, 1996).

Social disapproval and being rejected are likely to occur with aggressive children and adolescents (Coie, Belding, & Underwood, 1988; Ebata et al., 1990; Rutter, 1990), and these rejected, aggressive children are at risk for behavioural problems (Parker & Asher, 1987; Rudolph & Asher, 2000).

Protective Factors

Although children may experience a similar environment and adversity, children's responses and outcomes vary, with some children prevailing and prospering, and others having a number of difficulties and negative outcomes. The child who has multiple risk factors but who can overcome them and prevail has been termed **resilient**. Resilience has been described as the ability to overcome stress and adversity (Winfield, 1994).

It has been suggested that resilient children may have **protective factors** that allow them to persevere in the face of adversity. The notion of protection and protective factors was introduced in the early 1980s (Garmezy, 1985). Garmezy (1991) identified a number of areas in which protectiveness can be present: genetic variables, personality dispositions, supportive family environments, and community supports. There is some debate over the definition of protective factors and how protective factors work. Many agree, however, that protective factors help improve or sustain some part of an individual's life (Leadbeater, Kuperminc, Blatt, & Hertzog, 1999). Rutter (1990) identifies four ways that protective factors are effective:

1. Protective factors reduce negative outcomes by changing the risk level of the child's exposure to a risk factor.
2. They change the negative chain reaction following exposure to risk.
3. They help develop and maintain self-esteem and self-efficacy.
4. They avail opportunities to children they would not otherwise have.

Protective factors can be grouped intro three categories: individual, familial, and social/external factors (Grossman et al., 1992).

Individual Protective Factors Protective factors that reside within the individual, known as resilient temperaments (Hoge, 1999), include exceptional social skills, child competencies, confident perceptions, values, attitudes, and beliefs within the child (Vance, 2001).

Work from twin studies has suggested that social support may have a heritable component, which is influenced by personality. For example, likeable children may respond to good role models in a positive manner, thus promoting a positive and continuing relationship.

Familial Factors Protective familial factors are those positive aspects of the child's parents/guardians and home environment. For example, a child who has a positive and supportive relationship with an adult may display less negative behaviour. Thus, a good parent/adult–child relationship is a protective factor for the child who is growing up in an underprivileged community.

Social/External Protective Factors Peer groups can have a strong effect on child outcomes (Vance, 2001). Associating with deviant peers is a risk factor for antisocial behaviour. The converse is a protective factor. That is, associating with prosocial children is a protective factor against antisocial behaviour (Fergusson & Horwood, 1996).

Just as there are risk factors leading to increased negative outcomes, so too are there protective factors that may reduce negative outcomes in the presence of risk factors (Grossman, Beinashowitz, Anderson, Sakurai, Finnin, & Flaherty, 1992; Masten, Best, & Garmezy, 1990). Protective factors may counteract risk (Loeber & Farrington, 1998; Rutter, 1988). Further research is necessary to understand the role protective factors play in positive outcomes.

Resilient: Characteristic of a child who has multiple risk factors but who does not develop problem behaviours or negative symptoms

Protective factors: Factors that mitigate or reduce the likelihood of a negative outcome (e.g., aggression, psychopathology)

Treatment

Conduct-disordered youth are a very challenging population to treat. Often treatment studies show negligible effects at reducing future antisocial behaviour. Below are descriptions of common approaches to the treatment of CD.

Parent Training Given parenting style may pose a risk to children, it should not be surprising to find that often parents of conduct-disordered youth are provided with parent training. Parents are taught how to change their parent–child interactions such that the child's prosocial behaviour is emphasized and antisocial behaviour is de-emphasized (Kazdin, 1997). Parents are given strategies on how to reinforce positive behaviour. For example, parents may be told to put children on a reinforcement schedule. For every prosocial behaviour the child displays, a point is awarded. Once the child accumulates a certain number of points, the child can trade the points for a privilege or monetary reward. Parents are instructed on alternatives to corporal punishment such as imposing a "time out," in which the child cannot interact with anyone for a set time period. Overall, parent-training programs are more effective at reducing conduct-disordered behaviour in younger children than with conduct-disordered adolescents (Kazdin, 1993).

Cognitive and Social-Skills Training Cognitive and social-skills training focuses on the child's thought processes and interpersonal skills. Deficiencies and distortions in how children perceive and think about interpersonal interactions are challenged (Lochman, Whidby, & FitzGerald, 2000). Children are given concrete strategies to resolve interpersonal difficulties. Children practise these strategies in the treatment session. Often they will be taught to "self-talk"—that is, to make statements to themselves that help focus on nonaggressive solutions to problems. Role-playing and modelling of prosocial behaviour and positive interactions also occur in the treatment sessions. Children are requested to keep a log of their behaviour at home and school to monitor their progress (Kazdin, 1997). Cognitive and social-skills training programs often demonstrate a change in behaviour but for short periods.

Multisystemic Therapy Multisystemic therapy (MST) is a treatment approach that considers the child in the various contexts or systems where he or she exists—family, peers, school, neighbourhood, and community (Henggeler & Borduin, 1990; Henggeler, Melton, & Smith, 1992; Henggeler, Rodick, Borduin, Hanson, Watson, & Urey, 1986; Henggeler, Schoenwald, & Pickrel, 1995; Henggeler, Schoenwald, Borduin, Rowland, & Cunningham, 1998). At the start of MST, conduct-disordered youth are assessed to determine their specific needs. Assessments include considering youth within their family context and their external influences of peers, school, neighbourhood, and community. Based on this assessment, adolescents and their families are provided service. Areas that may be targeted in treatment include family communication, parent management, and cognitive-behavioural issues. Each youth is given a case manager who is accessible 24 hours a day, 7 days a week, to deal with crises and coordinate services and treatment.

MST has been implemented in various parts of Canada and the United States. To evaluate MST's effectiveness, a four-year randomized study was conducted across four Ontario communities: London, Mississauga, Simcoe County, and Ottawa (Cunningham, 2002; Leschied & Cunningham, 2002). Approximately 200 families received MST from 1997 to 2001. During the same time period, another 200 families were asked to access the

Multisystemic therapy: A treatment approach that considers the youth in the various contexts or systems where he or she exists—family, peers, school, neighbourhood, and community services that were available through their local youth justice and social service organizations. These services included probation and specialized programs.

All families participating in this study underwent psychological testing at the start of the study and then once again at the end. The psychological testing included measures to assess family functioning, caregiver depression, youths' social skills, pro-criminal attitudes, and behaviour problems. In addition, the youth were followed for three years after the end of treatment (until 2004). Overall, MST has not been found to be more effective than the usual services available in Ontario. For example, after the three-year follow-up, 68% of the participants in the MST group had at least one conviction compared to 67% of those in the "control" group. The average number of days to reconviction for the MST group was about 283 and 310 days for the control group (note that this difference was not statistically significant). It is important to note, however, that MST may have benefited youths and their families on factors that were not measured. Moreover, some studies evaluating MST in the United States have found it more effective than incarceration, individual counselling, and probation (Henggeler et al., 1986, 1992, 1995). Targeted treatment that meets the needs of young people and their families may be critical to effective treatment.

FEMALE OFFENDERS

Female offenders might be described as the "forgotten minority." As you have seen in other chapters, a substantial amount of research has focused on male offenders. Why has there been so little research on female offenders? One reason is that few females commit crime. This gender bias in offending has been true across time periods, across different cultures, and across the age span (Wilson & Herrnstein, 1985). Also, there was an implicit assumption that research conducted with men could be applied to women. If the causes and explanations of female and male criminality were similar, then assessment procedures and treatment programs developed on male offenders could be applied directly to females. However, if there are important differences between female and male criminality, then it may be inappropriate to apply assessments and treatment developed on male offenders to females. Only recently have separate classification and assessment instruments been developed for female offenders. This section will focus on what we know and need to know about female offenders.

Historical Overview

Historically, much of the controversy in Canada surrounding female offenders has revolved around the issue of placement. The first federal prison for women in Canada was opened in 1934 in Kingston, Ontario. Federal women offenders were previously housed in separate wings of male institutions. With the opening of the Prison for Women, federal female offenders from across Canada were sent to Kingston to serve their sentences. This resulted in many women being separated not only by walls and bars from their family, friends, and communities, but also being geographically isolated from them. Within four years of opening, the Archambault Commission recommended the Prison for Women be closed. Numerous subsequent Royal Commissions and a 1981 Canadian Human Rights Commission all identified weaknesses in the variety and quality of vocational, educational, and intervention programs available to women.

Federal prison for women in Kingston. Now closed.

In 1990, upon the recommendation of the report *Creating Choices: Report of the Task Force on Federally Sentenced Women*, the Solicitor General of Canada announced that the Prison for Women would be closed and be replaced by five regional facilities, including an Aboriginal healing lodge. Between 1995 and 1997, these new community-style regional facilities were opened; on May 8, 2000, the last inmate left the Prison for Women; and on July 6, 2000, the Prison for Women was officially closed.

The opening of these regional facilities was a mixed success. Although they provided more appropriate venues for dealing with female offenders, they were initially subject to several problems, chiefly the management of the more violent women offenders. Since the new regional facilities did not have the capability to manage maximum-security women, in 1996 Correctional Service of Canada transferred them to units in more secure men's institutions. In 2003 and 2004, additional secure units were built at each of the regional facilities to permit the return of women requiring maximum-security management.

Rates

In 2005–2006, women represented 5.8% of admissions to federal custody (Public Safety and Emergency Preparedness Canada, 2006). In April 2006, there were 408 women serving sentences in Canadian federal prisons. Prison sentences for men tend to be longer than for women. For example, in 2003–2004, 55% of men and 73% of women were given a sentence of one month or less and 88% of men received sentences of six months or less compared to 94% of women (Public Safety and Emergency Preparedness Canada, 2006). As Table 13.5 shows, more men are serving federal sentences for violent offences, whereas women are more likely to be incarcerated for serious drug offences.

There are also dramatic differences in the costs of keeping male and female federal offenders in penitentiaries. In 2004–2005, the average annual cost of keeping a female offender incarcerated in a federal institution was $166 642, compared with an average of $85 927 for male offenders (Public Safety and Emergency Preparedness Canada, 2006). The higher costs associated with keeping females incarcerated are due to their low numbers.

There is an overrepresentation of Aboriginals in the criminal justice system, particularly among women offenders. About 3% of the Canadian population is Aboriginal, but Aboriginal women represent 31% of all federally incarcerated women, and 18% of federally incarcerated men are Aboriginal (Public Safety and Emergency Preparedness Canada,

Table 13.5 Types of Offences Committed by Federal Offenders

Type of Offence	Women	Men	Total
First- and second-degree murder	16%	19%	19%
Schedule I* offences	40%	52%	51%
Schedule II** offences	30%	14%	15%
Nonviolent offences	16%	16%	16%

*Schedule I offences: manslaughter, assault, armed robbery, and sexual offences.
**Schedule II offences: importing and trafficking narcotics.
Source: Adapted from Public Safety and Emergency Preparedness Canada, 2006.

2006). The number of Aboriginal women in federal prisons has also increased at a higher rate than the number of men—from 62 in 1996–1997 to 128 in 2005–2006, compared to 2014 to 2245 for men (increases of 107% and 12% in ten years, for women and men, respectively). In addition, Aboriginal women offenders (76%) are more likely to be serving a federal sentence for a violent offence (murder and schedule I offences) than non-Aboriginal women offenders (48%). The high number of Aboriginal women offenders was the motivation behind the development of the Okimaw Ohci Healing Lodge for women offenders.

Theories of Female Criminality

Early theories focused on a biological or physiological basis for female criminality. For example, Cesare Lombroso, an Italian physician, believed that the biological constitution of women was incompatible (being more maternal in nature) with crime, and that in order for a woman to commit a crime, she was assumed to have a biological abnormality (Lombroso & Ferrero, 1895).

In the 1970s, crime rates increased in both the United States and Canada (Wilson & Herrnstein, 1985). For men, this increase was partly attributed to an increased population of men in the age group of highest criminal activity. However, for women an alternative explanation was proposed. Adler (1975) attributed the increase in female crime to the women's liberation movement. Adler proposed that as women began to emerge from the narrow role of housewife into previously male-dominated areas, they also emulated male criminal behaviours. Adler called this new crime wave by women the "shady aspect of liberation" (p. 16). Research has failed to support Adler's theory (Campbell, Mackenzie, & Robinson, 1987; Trice & Lamb, 1996). In contrast to Adler's predictions, most female offenders actually endorse more sex-role stereotypes than nonoffenders do.

More recently, sociological theories of criminal behaviour, such as differential association, strain, and social control theories, have been tested to see if they can adequately explain female criminality (see Chapter 1 for a discussion of these theories). Alarid, Burton, and Cullen (2000) found support for both differential association and social control theories to account for the self-reported criminal behaviour in incarcerated female offenders. Katz (2000) used strain theory to illustrate how stressful events in the family and in the neighbourhood (e.g., early childhood victimization, adult racial discrimination, sexual discrimination, and having been a victim of domestic violence) all contributed to explaining women's involvement in criminal behaviour.

Contemporary theories of female criminality that approach gender as a central issue in women's offending and do not attempt to explain criminal behaviour in women through simply tailoring traditionally male-based theories to suit women are becoming more prolific. One example of this is **relational theory**, which emphasizes the role of relationships in women's overall lives and functioning and claims this role is more central for women than for men. Although this theory is more often used to inform treatment than explain crime, some have interpreted the theory as indicating that women may be less likely to jeopardize their relationships by engaging in criminal activity, thereby lowering the rates of female offending (Blanchette & Brown, 2006). Benda (2005) found that variables related to positive relationships with partners, friends, and other family were greater predictors of success for female offenders than male offenders in a five-year follow-up of boot-camp graduates.

Another popular theory is **feminist pathways research**, which asserts that childhood victimization/abuse is the main reason behind criminal behaviour in girls and women. This theory posits that abuse or neglect leads to coping behaviours, including substance abuse and running away from home, which in turn lead to criminal behaviour through feelings of worthlessness or distress and unhealthy attitudes towards others or through simple survival strategies while living on the streets. Another pathway to female crime, according to this theory, is through coercion by an abusive partner (Blanchette & Brown, 2006). In her five-year follow-up of boot-camp graduates, Benda (2005) also found that childhood victimization predicted recidivism in women more strongly than in men.

What Do We Know about Female Offenders?

Available research on female offenders is sparse, with much focused on examining a limited range of variables (e.g., sex-role stereotypes) or unrepresentative subgroups of offenders (e.g., battered women who kill or prostitutes). Women in prison come from similar backgrounds to those of men in prison. Like male offenders, female offenders tend to be, on average, in their early 30s, with Grade 9 education or lower, and on social assistance or in low-paying jobs at admission. Nonetheless, male and female offenders differ in several ways. About two-thirds of women offenders are mothers, with most being the sole supporters of their children. Compared with male offenders, female offenders are more likely to be victims of physical and sexual abuse, to engage in suicidal and self-injurious behaviours, to have less extensive criminal histories, and to have elevated rates of mental disorders.

In 1989, Correctional Service Canada conducted a mental health survey of 77 federal female offenders at the Prison for Women. A mere 5% of the sample showed no evidence of a disorder, whereas almost 50% showed evidence of multiple disorders. Table 13.6 presents lifetime prevalence rates of *DSM-III* disorders in a sample of 1928 adult females in the community (Bland, Orn, & Newman, 1988), a sample of 77 federal female offenders (Correctional Service Canada, 1989), and a sample of 2185 federal male offenders (Motiuk & Porporino, 1991). All studies used the Diagnostic Interview Schedule to assess the mental disorder (exclusion criteria ignored). Female offenders had substantially higher rates of mental disorder than women in the general population and slightly higher

Relational theory: A theory that emphasizes the role of relationships in women's overall lives and functioning and claims this role is more central for women than for men

Feminist pathways research: A theory asserting that childhood victimization/abuse is the main reason behind criminal behaviour in girls and women

Table 13.6 Lifetime Prevalence of Mental Disorders in Canadian General and Offender Populations

Disorder	Bland et al. (1988) Community Women (%)	CSC (1989) Women Offenders (%)	Motiuk and Porporino (1991) Male Offenders (%)
Schizophrenia	0.6	13.0	4.9
Post-traumatic stress disorder	—	29.9	—
Obsessive compulsive disorder	3.1	14.3	—
Bipolar disorder	—	7.8	3.6
Depression	11.4	49.4	21.4
Alcohol abuse	6.7	62.3	70.1
Drug abuse	3.2	57.1	53.7
Phobia	11.7	62.3	28.3
Generalized anxiety disorder	—	55.8	46.7
Panic disorder	1.7	13.0	3.7
Antisocial personality disorder	0.8	59.7	75.4

rates as compared to federal male offenders. In both male and female offenders, common disorders included antisocial personality disorder, alcohol abuse, and drug abuse. The high rates of mental disorder in female offenders have also been reported in more recent research (Teplin, Abram, & McClelland, 1996; Warren, Burnette, South, Chauhan, Bale, & Friend, 2002). In 2005–2006, twice as many female offenders as male offenders had a mental health diagnosis or were prescribed medication for mental health issues upon admission, and 31% of female offenders had previous hospital admissions for mental health concerns, compared to 15% of male offenders (Public Safety and Emergency Preparedness Canada, 2006). The most common mental disorders in women offenders include substance abuse, post-traumatic stress disorder, and major depression. There are also high levels of personality disorders in women offenders, notably antisocial personality and borderline personality disorder (Hurley & Dunne, 1991; Jordan et al., 1996).

Victimization Rates

The past decade has brought growing awareness of the high rates of sexual and physical victimization reported by women offenders. The prevalence of child abuse is difficult to obtain due to the different methodologies used. An Ontario survey of 3648 women from the community found that 12% of women report childhood sexual abuse and 21% report being physically abused (MacMillan et al., 2001). Substantially higher rates have been found with incarcerated samples. For example, about 50% of incarcerated federal women offenders report childhood sexual abuse and about 70% experienced childhood physical abuse (Shaw, 1994). Even higher rates have been reported for Aboriginal women offenders (60% report sexual abuse and 90% report physical abuse).

Browne, Miller, and Maguin (1999) examined the relation between earlier and later victimization in 150 incarcerated women. The authors found that 70% of the women reported experiencing severe physical abuse as a child or adolescent, and 59% were sexually abused. Eighty percent of women who reported experiencing severe physical abuse prior to age 18 also reported experiencing severe domestic violence; 40% of women who reported being sexually abused before age 18 reported being sexually assaulted by someone other than a spouse or dating partner in adulthood. This study illustrates the high degree of continuity between childhood victimization and adult victimization.

Haney and Kristianson (1997) describe how this high rate of childhood abuse among incarcerated offenders has implications for the mental health of women during incarceration. These authors have linked Finkelhor and Browne's (1985) traumatizing processes underlying child abuse, such as traumatic sexualization and powerlessness, to experiences of women in prison. The high rates of self-inflicted injuries, suicide, substance use, and violence of incarcerated women may be how these women cope with being exposed to situations that parallel their childhood abusive experiences. As stated by Haney and Kristianson (1997), "women might be less likely to re-offend if society also freed them of their revictimization during their incarceration" (p. 42).

Risk Factors

Although gender-specific risk factors may exist, the research to date has found more similarities than differences in both adolescents and adults (Blanchette, 2001; Simourd & Andrews, 1994). Blanchette (2001) provides a review of static and dynamic risk factors in female offenders. She concludes that many of the static risk factors associated with recidivism in men, such as criminal history and age, are also predictors with women. Similar dynamic risk factors for women and men include substance abuse, antisocial attitudes, and antisocial associates. Evidence also suggests that women have further risk factors, such as a history of self-injury or attempted suicide and self-esteem problems. Female offenders reoffend at a lower rate than do male offenders. In 2005–2006, the percentage of successful full paroles and statutory releases for women was higher than for men (78% versus 70% full parole, and 63% versus 59% for statutory release) (Public Safety and Emergency Preparedness Canada, 2006). Overall, additional research is needed to understand the static and dynamic risk factors for recidivism in women offenders. Further research is also needed to fully understand protective factors that may improve women's success in the community upon release from prison. As previously discussed, Benda (2005) found positive relationships to be particularly predictive of success in women offenders, as compared to male offenders.

How well do the risk assessment instruments described in Chapter 12 predict reoffending in female offenders? The results have varied depending on the measures. The General Statistical Information on Recidivism (GSIR) scale provides an estimate of the probability that an offender will reoffend within a three-year follow-up period. Bonta, Pang, and Wallace-Capretta (1995) investigated the predictive validity of the GSIR in a sample of 81 female offenders. When compared with male offenders, female offenders tend to score lower on the GSIR, reflecting lower levels of risk. Although the GSIR was correlated with reoffending, there was no linear increase in recidivism rates found across the different levels of risk categories. When Nafekh and Motiuk (2002) applied a modified version of the GSIR to the case files of 342 female offenders, they found that scores were correlated with recidivism in a three-year follow-up, and that a linear relationship existed between risk categories and recidivism rates. Although the GSIR is used routinely with male offenders, Correctional Service Canada does not use the GSIR with female offenders.

Another scale used to assess the risk of recidivism is the Level of Service Inventory–Revised (LSI-R). Similar to the GSIR, the LSI-R also tends to assess provincial female offenders at a lower risk than male provincial offenders (Coulson et al., 1996). Coulson and colleagues (1996) followed 526 provincial female offenders for three years. LSI-R total scores were positively related to general recidivism, parole failure, and halfway-house failure, indicating that the LSI-R is useful for predicting female reoffending. Holtfreter, Reisig, and Morash (2004) applied the LSI-R to a sample of female offenders in the United States and found scores to predict self-reported re-arrest and probation or parole violation. However, when adjusting for poverty, the effect of LSI-R score was no longer significant.

The Hare Psychopathy Checklist–Revised (PCL-R) (Hare, 2003) is a scale for the assessment of psychopathy. Although not originally designed as a risk-assessment measure, the PCL-R is a robust predictor of violent recidivism in diverse samples, including correctional offenders, young offenders, sexual offenders, and offenders with mental disorders. Several studies have examined psychopathy in female offenders, all reporting a lower prevalence in women than in men (Salekin, Rogers, & Sewell, 1997; Vitale, Smith, Brinkely, & Newman, 2002; Warren et al., 2003). There is some evidence that the predictive validity of the PCL-R may extend to female offenders. Salekin, Rogers, Ustad, and Sewell (1998) followed 78 female inmates in a state jail in Texas for 14 months. PCL-R total scores were only weakly associated with general recidivism during this period. Stronger findings have been reported by Loucks and Zamble (2000), who followed 81 federal female offenders for about three years. The PCL-R was moderately correlated with new charges or major violations while on release ($r = 0.45$). In a large sample of 239 female offenders released from a maximum-security treatment institution, Richards, Casey, and Lucente (2003) reported that 60% of the offenders with high PCL-R scores were re-incarcerated, compared with 30% of those with low scores.

Finally, HCR-20 scores for male and female mentally disordered patients in Sweden were compared by Strand and Belfrage (2001). There were no gender differences in the HCR-20 total or on the Historical, Clinical and Risk Management subscales. Warren et al. (2005) applied the HCR-20 to a sample of 132 female offenders and found that scores were most closely associated with past minor charges but failed to predict past violent offences; no analyses involving future crime were performed. Whether or not the HCR-20 has predictive validity with females has yet to be established.

The above research indicates that some risk-assessment instruments developed and validated with male offenders may also be used with women. However, it is not appropriate to assume that this will always be the case, and a considerable amount of research still needs to be conducted.

Battered Women Who Kill

Each year in Canada, about 15 men are killed by their partner. Most of these homicides are committed by women who kill their abusive partner. If a battered woman picks up a gun, shoots, and kills her husband while he lies sleeping on the couch, her defence lawyer will likely argue that his client's actions should be considered as **self-defence**. According

Self-defence: The principle that if you are attacked, you should be able to take reasonable actions to defend yourself to section 34(1) and (2) of the Canadian Criminal Code, self-defence requires that at the time of the murder the person should have a reasonable apprehension of death or serious bodily injury and that equal force or the least amount of force be used to repel the threat. Gellespie (1989) has described the problems when battered women who kill attempt to advance a self-defence plea. First, triers of fact (e.g., judges and juries) hold misconceptions about battered women, and second, triers of fact must be convinced of the "reasonableness" of these lethal actions. Box 13.3 describes the case of Jane (Stafford) Hurshman-Corkum, a woman who killed her abusive husband.

The term **battered woman syndrome** (BWS) was coined by Lenore Walker (1984) to describe a woman's reactions to prolonged physical and psychological abuse inflicted by her spouse. BWS is now being used in trials that involve battered women who kill their abusers. The two key components of BWS that are often presented by court experts include **learned helplessness** and the **cycle-of-violence theory**.

Walker applied Martin Seligman's (1975) theory and research on animals to battered women. Seligman subjected dogs to electric shocks in one condition where the dogs learned to respond to a tone that sounded and ran to safety and in another condition where the dogs had no escape and eventually stopped responding and lay "helpless" in their cages. Walker linked these dogs' behaviours to battered woman who are exposed to repeated and often unpredictable attacks. These women often report feeling helpless, having no options, and focusing on survival rather than leaving (Walker, 1993).

Battered woman syndrome: A collection of symptoms and behaviours believed to be common to women who have experienced chronic and severe intimate abuse

Learned helplessness: A learned passive and withdrawing response to events in which the person perceives he or she has little control

Cycle-of-violence theory: The theory that within intimate violence, there is a tension-building phase, an acute battering act phase, and a contrition phase

---

Box 13.3

The Breaking Point: When Battered Women Kill

On March 11, 1982, Jane Hurshman-Corkum shot and killed her husband, Billy Stafford, while he was unconscious. Billy was killed by a single shot to his head. For five years, Jane had experienced regular beatings by her husband. Billy had shot at her, held a knife to her throat, raped her, and forced her to engage in bizarre sexual acts. Billy also directed his violence toward his son, Darren.

Billy Stafford was known and feared in the Bangs Falls area of Nova Scotia. He had a violent temper, was unpredictable, and would physically attack others.

Why didn't Jane leave Billy Stafford? Billy's two previous partners left after being abused by him. Jane described feeling totally trapped with nowhere and no one to turn to. Billy had threatened to track her down and kill her, her sons, and her family if she ever tried to leave him.

On that fateful day, Billy had said that he planned to set fire to his neighbour's trailer and that he would "deal" with Jane's 16-year-old son Allen who was temporarily living with them. Jane finally decided that she had had enough and killed Billy.

Jane was charged with first-degree murder. At her first trial, her lawyer argued that she had acted in self-defence. The jury agreed and she was found not guilty. The courtroom applauded when the verdict was announced. The Crown appealed and 15 months later, on the advice of her lawyer, Jane pleaded guilty to the charge of manslaughter. She was sentenced to six months in jail and two years probation.

After her release from jail, Jane became a vocal advocate for battered women. She lobbied for the establishment of transition houses for battered women, and she became a symbol of hope and resistance in the fight against domestic violence.

Jane Hurshman-Corkum never got over the trauma of the abuse. She was often depressed and was embarrassed by her kleptomania (uncontrollable urges to steal that led to several shoplifting convictions). On February 22, 1992, she was found dead in her car in Halifax. The autopsy report ruled that Jane died from a point-blank bullet wound to her chest that was consistent with suicide.

Source: Vallée, 1998.

According to the cycle-of-violence theory, there are three phases of abuse. During the tension-building phase, there is minor verbal or physical abuse. The woman often attempts to appease the batterer by changing her behaviour. The acute battering act phase involves physical or sexual assault, followed by apologies and promises to change in the contrition phase. This cycle repeats itself often, with the violence becoming more severe and the contrition phase becoming shorter and sometimes disappearing. These components were developed by conducting extensive interviews with 435 battered women (Walker, 1984).

Almost as soon as BWS was described by Walker (1984), concerns were raised that it framed battered women's behaviour as mental illness (Browne, 1987; Faigman & Wright, 1997; Schneider, 1986). There were also concerns about the components of BWS. Not all batterers display the phases described by the cycle of violence, and many battered women are not passive, submissive, or helpless (Blackman, 1990; Bowker, 1993; Fisher, Vidmar, & Ellis, 1993; McMahon, 1999). If a battered woman who kills her violent tormentor does not fit the BWS profile, triers of fact might question her claim of self-defence (Terrance & Matheson, 2003). We discussed jury decision-making research in Chapter 7.

Jury simulation studies have found that expert testimony about BWS is associated with more lenient verdicts regardless of whether the woman is described as passive or active (Schuller & Hastings, 1996; Schuller & Rzepa, 2002). However, Schuller and Rzepa (2002) found that participants simulating jury members considered women portrayed as active (i.e., who verbally and physically defended herself) as less sympathetic, were less likely to believe the woman's report of threat, and thought that she had more options, compared with women portrayed as passive (i.e., who attempted to appease her abusive husband).

Court Decisions Although battered women who kill have attempted to use the self-defence plea, usually they are not successful. For example, Ewing (1987) reported on the court decisions for 100 battered women who committed murder. Of the 85 who attempted to use the self-defence plea, 63 were convicted of some form of criminal homicide and 22 were acquitted (a conviction rate of 74%). There was enormous variability in the sentences given, ranging from four years' probation to life in prison. In 44 of the 85 cases, an attempt was made to introduce expert testimony by the defence, and in 26 cases it was deemed admissible (in 17 of these 26 cases the woman was convicted). It is likely that the use and admissibility of expert testimony relating to battered women has increased since this study. Whether or not an increasing reliance on expert testimony results in a greater number of acquittals is unknown.

Characteristics of Women Who Kill Their Abusers Browne (1987) interviewed 42 women who were charged with murder or attempted murder of their abusive spouse. A nonhomicide comparison sample of 205 abused women who had been physically abused at least twice and who were either still with their abusive partner or had left the relationship within one year were also interviewed. Much of the data was based on self-report, although all available police and hospital records, and any collateral information (family member reports), were reviewed.

Few differences were found between the women in the homicide group and the comparison group. The homicide group was slightly older than the comparison group (36 years versus 31 years) but there were no group differences in education level or employment history. Women in both the homicide and the nonhomicide comparison group had either witnessed parental violence or had been physically abused as a child (71% versus 65%) and about half had been sexually abused (57% versus 54%). Group differences were primarily in the behaviours of the men. Men in the homicide group were more likely to abuse drugs and alcohol, more likely to engage in frequent injurious behaviour, more likely to commit sexual assault, more likely to threaten to kill someone, and more likely to abuse their children. Women in the homicide group were more likely to think of committing suicide than were women in the nonhomicide comparison group. Many of the women in the homicide group had experienced many years of abuse prior to the homicide. What was the turning point for these women? Most of them reported that there was a change in the pattern or severity of violence. For example, "He had never threatened the baby before" or "It was one thing when he was beating me, but when he hurt my daughter . . . " (Browne, 1987, pp. 129–130).

Campbell (1986) reported that females convicted of spousal homicide were more likely than males convicted for spousal homicide to be responding to violence than to be initiating violence. Roberts (1996) compared 105 battered women who killed their abusive partners with a group of 105 battered women who did not kill their abusive partner. The battered women who killed were more likely (1) to have dropped out of high school, (2) to have a history of childhood sexual abuse, (3) to have a poor employment history, (4) to have cohabited with the partner, (5) to have attempted suicide, (6) to have a history of drug problems, and (7) to have access to a gun.

Hamilton and Sutterfield (1997) examined help-seeking behaviours (contacting family, friends, mental health professionals, and police) in 20 women incarcerated for killing their abusive partner and 29 women who had received services from a shelter for battered women. Help-seeking behaviours did not differ between the two groups, but police response did. Police had been called by 60% of the incarcerated women and 65% of the women in shelters. Arrest of their partners was the most common police intervention for the shelter group (31%), whereas only 5% of the incarcerated women reported their partners were arrested. If a battered woman calls the police for help and none is forthcoming, this will likely reinforce her belief that there is no escape from the violence. As Hamilton and Sutterfeld (1997) explain, "Failure of the community to respond to domestic violence can and does result in homicides, of victim and of abuser" (p. 54).

It is important to remember that in a lethal altercation between partners, it is more typically the woman who loses her life. Each year in Canada and the United States, about two-thirds of homicides between partners were of husbands killing wives, while one-third were wives killing husbands. For example, in Canada in 2005, 74 spouses were killed. As in previous years, the spousal homicide rate against women in 2005 was five times higher than the corresponding rate for men (Statistics Canada, 2006b).

Treatment

A considerable amount of research has examined the effectiveness of intervention programs with male adolescent and adult offenders (e.g., Andrews, Zinger, Hoge, Bonta, Gendreau, & Cullen, 1990; Izzo & Ross, 1990). However, much less is known about what works with female offenders. Koons, Burrow, Morash, and Bynum (1997) conducted a survey of U.S. correctional and program administrators, asking them to identify promising treatment programs for female offenders. The programs that targeted substance-abuse education (55%), substance-abuse treatment (47%), parenting (44%) and life skills (42%), relationships (37%), and basic education (24%) were mentioned most often. Koons et al. (1997) conducted focus groups with 104 program participants from promising programs (i.e., program addressed specific need and there was empirical evidence of effectiveness). Program participants felt that the most important factor relating to success was having qualified, dedicated, and caring staff, and a program that focused on skills acquisition.

In a study of 773 Canadian federal women offenders, Delveaux, Blanchette, and Wickett (2005) found that the two most prevalent criminogenic needs were substance abuse (identified by 60% of women) and emotional problems (identified by 81% of women). Any treatment program designed to treat women needs to ensure that these two criminogenic needs are targeted. Belknap (2001) reviewed studies on differences between men and women in the area of using and dealing drugs. She found that women tended to have lower-level positions in drug dealing operations than did men, that they learned about drug use from an intimate partner more than did men, and they used drugs primarily as a coping mechanism (in contrast to men who used drugs primarily as a result of peer pressure and for the sensation of pleasure provided by drugs).

Meta-analytic studies with male offenders (e.g., Andrews & Bonta, 1998; Andrews et al., 1990) have found that effective treatment programs are those that follow the principles of effective correctional treatment (i.e., risk, need, and responsivity principles; see Chapter 10 for a description of these principles). Dowden and Andrews (1999) conducted a meta-analysis of 26 studies to examine if these principles would also be associated with effective treatment for female adolescent and adult offenders. Stronger treatment effects were found for programs that targeted high-risk as compared to low-risk offenders (risk principle), that provided treatment of criminogenic needs as compared with noncriminogenic needs (need principle), and that used cognitive-behavioural interventions as compared to nonbehavioural interventions (responsivity principle). Promising targets include family (supervision and affection), antisocial associates, and antisocial cognitions. Less promising targets were substance abuse and school/work interventions. In a more recent meta-analysis, Andrews and Dowden (2006) found there is stronger evidence supporting the risk principle for female offenders than for male offenders, particularly within programs following need and responsivity principles.

New Directions in Treatment: Dialectical Behaviour Therapy High rates of borderline personality disorder are observed in female offenders (Jordan, Schlenger, Fairbank, & Caddell, 1996). **Dialectical behaviour therapy** (DBT) was originally developed by Linehan (1993) to treat patients with borderline personality disorder in the community. DBT is designed to obtain a balance between acceptance of one's current capabilities and the development of new coping skills. Personal and situational factors that reinforce maladaptive behaviours are identified and skills are developed to address problems with self-regulation (including emotions, cognitions, and relationships).

Dialectical behaviour therapy: Therapy designed to treat borderline personality disordered patients

Promising outcome results have been obtained for inpatients, suicidal patients, and drug-dependent patients (Bohus, Haaf, Stiglmayr, Pohl, Boehme, & Linehan, 2000; Linehan, Schmidt, Dimeff, Craft, Kanter, & Comtois, 1999). Correctional Service Canada has adapted DBT (see McDonagh, Taylor, & Blanchette, 2002) to address correctional-specific targets, to use in different environments (prison versus inpatient or outpatient hospital), and to meet the needs of different samples of offenders (maximum-security offenders versus general offenders). In 2001, Correctional Service Canada implemented the adapted version of DBT in four of the regional women's institutions. Although a comprehensive evaluation of the program will be conducted as part of the implementation, no information is yet available about its success. Trupin, Stewart, Beach, and Boesky (2002) tested the use of DBT in a sample of incarcerated female juvenile offenders in the U.S. Their overall findings were mixed, but a significant decrease in behaviour problems was found over the course of the study for girls in a mental health unit. The authors concluded that their mixed results might be due to the quality of staff training as well as the specific behaviour problems of the sample and whether they match DBT therapeutic targets.

ABORIGINAL OFFENDERS
Historical Overview

The disproportionate involvement of Aboriginals in the criminal justice system has been recognized in Canada for a long time (LaPrairie, 1996; Rugge, 2006). Indeed, since at least the early 1970s, Aboriginal people have been a concern to various Canadian criminal justice agencies (Aboriginal Task Force, 1989). Slowly, researchers, practitioners, and policymakers have begun to recognize the unique circumstances surrounding Aboriginal offenders, resulting in numerous initiatives to reduce the number of Aboriginal people who come into contact with the law. In 1985, for example, Correctional Service Canada (CSC) started to introduce policies stressing the importance of Aboriginal culture. CSC began examining the process Aboriginal offenders went through once they entered the criminal justice system and started to work toward developing correctional programs that would better meet their needs. By 1993, the Corrections and Conditional Release Act (CCRA) stated explicitly that CSC must provide a range of Aboriginal-specific correctional programs (CCRA, 1992, s. 80). In addition, provisions were put in place to transfer Aboriginal offenders to the Aboriginal community, where they could have access to services and programs that reflect their culture (CCRA, 1992, s. 81).

The federal government has also made attempts to deal with the overrepresentation of Aboriginal offenders in the criminal justice system. For example, in 1996, Parliament passed Bill C-41, which discussed the principles and purposes of sentencing and introduced new sentencing options, such as the conditional sentence (see Chapter 9). In section 718.2 of Bill C-41, which deals with the use of incarceration, the government included the qualification "all available sanctions other than imprisonment should be considered for all offenders, *with particular attention to the circumstances of Aboriginal offenders*" (italics added, R.S.C., 1985, s. 718.2(e)). As discussed by Roberts and Melchers (2003), that section of Bill C-41 has been interpreted by the Supreme Court of Canada in R. v. *Gladue* (1999) as an attempt to "ameliorate the serious problem of overrepresentation of aboriginal people in prisons" (para. 93). Furthermore, the Supreme Court concluded that "the jail term for an Aboriginal offender may in some circumstances be less than the term imposed on a non-Aboriginal offender for the same offence" (para. 93). One significant result of this ruling has been the development of courts in Canada that focus on processing Aboriginal offenders. One of these courts is known as the Gladue Court (see Box 13.4). Other Aboriginal courts can be found in Saskatchewan and Alberta.

The Gladue Court

On April 23, 1999, the Supreme Court of Canada released its decision in *R. v. Gladue*, stating that section 718.2 of the Criminal Code should change the way judges approach the sentencing process. The Court stressed that prison terms were being relied on too often in Canada as a way of dealing with criminal behaviour, especially when it came to Aboriginal offenders. Following this ruling, Canadian judges expressed concern over how the Gladue decision should be applied. Judges had concerns about whether the courts had the time or expertise to deal with the special circumstances of Aboriginal offenders. In response to these concerns, it was proposed that a special court be developed, the Gladue

Court, as a way of addressing the special circumstances of Aboriginal offenders.

The Gladue Court, located in Toronto, is now available to all Aboriginal people whose cases would normally have gone through the Old City Hall Courts located in Toronto. Currently, the Gladue Court performs the same activities as the Old City Hall Court: it accepts guilty pleas, sentences offenders, and does bail hearings. The difference is that the people working in the Gladue Court have an in-depth understanding of the range of programs and services available to Aboriginal offenders in Toronto.

Source: Aboriginal Legal Services of Toronto, 2001.

Rates

Despite attempts to reduce Aboriginal involvement with the law, Aboriginal offenders are still greatly overrepresented in the Canadian criminal justice system. According to the most recent statistics, although Aboriginal people make up about 3% of the general population in Canada, Aboriginal offenders make up approximately 16% of federal prison inmates and 20% of the provincial/territorial inmate population (Rugge, 2006). Furthermore, Aboriginal offenders represent approximately 12% of all offenders who are serving their sentence in the community (Trevethan, Moore, & Rastin, 2002). As illustrated in Figure 13.1 on page 396, this overrepresentation occurs across all regions of Canada, though it is more pronounced in certain regions. For example, in the Atlantic region, Aboriginals make up about 1% of the general population, 7% of the federal prison population, and 4% of the population of offenders serving time in the community. In contrast, Aboriginals make up about 6% of the general population in the Prairie provinces, but represent a staggering 40% of the federal prison population in that region, and about 31% of the population of offenders on conditional release. It is not yet totally clear why these significant differences in overrepresentation exist between regions.

Aboriginal and non-Aboriginal offenders are also known to differ in terms of the crimes for which they are incarcerated. For example, research has consistently shown that Aboriginal offenders are more likely to be incarcerated for crimes against the person than non-Aboriginal offenders are (Trevethan, Moore, & Rastin, 2002). As illustrated in Table 13.7 on page 396, larger proportions of Aboriginal offenders than non-Aboriginal offenders are currently incarcerated for homicide, attempted murder, assault, and sexual assault. Non-Aboriginal offenders, however, are more often incarcerated for drug-related offences, robbery, and property-related offences.

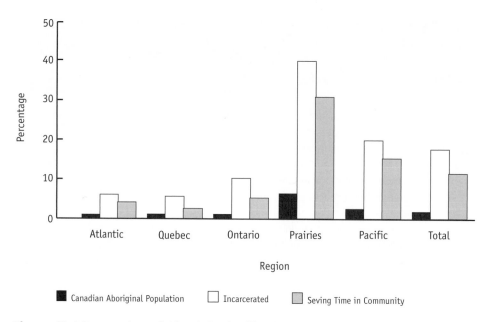

Figure 13.1 Proportion of Aboriginal Offenders Serving Time in Federal Prisons and in the Community

Source: Trevethan, Moore, & Rastin, 2002.

Other Aspects of Overrepresentation

It is important to stress—so as to not minimize the problem—that Aboriginal overrepresentation goes far beyond just overrepresentation in prison and community-offender populations. The problem is much more pervasive than that. For example, compared with non-Aboriginal offenders, Aboriginal offenders are also known to have more extensive contact with the criminal justice system prior to their current incarceration period, their chances of reoffending are consistently rated as much higher, and the perceived likelihood of their successful reintegration into society is much lower (Rugge, 2006; Trevethan, Moore, & Rastin, 2002).

Table 13.7 Offences Leading to Federal Incarceration: Aboriginal and Non-Aboriginal Offenders

Offence	Aboriginal	Non-Aboriginal
Homicide or attempted murder	29%	27%
Robbery	22%	25%
Sexual assault	17%	14%
Assault	15%	9%
Property offence	8%	10%
Drug offence	3%	8%
Impaired driving	1%	<1%

Source: Trevethan, Moore, & Rastin, 2002.

Possible Explanations for Aboriginal Overrepresentation How do we explain this overrepresentation of Aboriginal offenders in the Canadian criminal justice system? According to LaPrairie (1996), four possible, overlapping explanations have been provided:

1. Higher Aboriginal offending rates
2. The commission, by Aboriginal offenders, of offences that are more likely to result in prison sentences
3. Criminal justice policies and practices that have a differential impact on Aboriginal offenders due to their socioeconomic conditions
4. Differential processing through the criminal justice system as a result of culture conflict and racial discrimination

Little research has examined any of these potential causes. Currently, the primary contributing factors appear to be a higher Aboriginal offending rate and the fact that Aboriginal offenders tend to commit crimes that are more likely to result in prison sentences (i.e., crimes against the person) (LaPrairie, 1996). This is not to say, however, that the other two factors play no role at all. For example, as LaPrairie (1996) suggests, criminal justice policies and practices can have a differential impact on socially and economically disadvantaged Aboriginal offenders. Consider an Aboriginal offender who has committed a crime and receives a hefty fine. Due to his economic situation he cannot pay the fine and, as a result, gets sent to prison. This situation no doubt contributes to Aboriginal overrepresentation, since more Aboriginal than non-Aboriginal offenders are known to be serving time for fine defaults (Hallett, 2000), but the first two factors listed above appear to be more important.

Risk Factors

As forensic psychologists, our goal must be to understand "why Aboriginal offenders are so disproportionately involved in and vulnerable to the policies and practices of the criminal justice system" (LaPrairie, 1996, p. 64). A significant part of this endeavour will likely involve an understanding of the various risk factors that Aboriginal offenders possess. Based on existing research, it is clear that Aboriginal offenders generally represent a particularly high-risk group with respect to both their childhood and adult backgrounds.

Childhood Risk Factors When surveyed, a large number of Aboriginal offenders report serious traumas in their childhood that could have potentially contributed to their later involvement with the criminal justice system. For example, Johnston (2000) reports the results from two studies he conducted with Aboriginal offenders in Canadian federal institutions. Both studies indicate similar traumatic experiences, including poverty, parental absence, behavioural problems, learning problems, physical abuse, alcohol abuse, and drug abuse occurring in a significant portion of each sample, and in higher proportions than what is found in the non-Aboriginal offending population. Another recent study has confirmed that early childhood instability is prevalent among Aboriginal offenders, and more so than in non-Aboriginal offenders. Specifically, Trevethan, Moore, Auger, MacDonald, and Sinclair (2002) interviewed 175 Aboriginal and 148 non-Aboriginal offenders in Canadian federal institutions and found that a significantly higher proportion of Aboriginal offenders rated their childhood as unstable (36% versus 26%) and were involved in the child welfare system (63% versus 36%). Compared with non-Aboriginal offenders, Aboriginal offenders also reported significantly higher rates of family violence in their household, higher rates of substance use by family members, poorer economic conditions while growing up, and more family members involved in criminal activity.

Adult Risk Factors In adulthood, Aboriginal offenders also appear to exhibit a range of risk factors. Many of these risk factors appear to be the same ones that non-Aboriginal offenders exhibit (Rugge, 2006). For example, Bonta, LaPrairie, and Wallace-Capretta (1997) set out to determine whether a risk assessment tool developed on non-Aboriginal offenders, the Manitoba Risk-Needs Scale, could be used successfully with Aboriginal offender populations. They collected data from 390 Aboriginal and 513 non-Aboriginal offenders and found that scores on the assessment scale were significantly related to recidivism for both their non-Aboriginal and Aboriginal sample. In addition, they found that almost all of the scale items that predicted risk in the non-Aboriginal sample also predicted risk in the Aboriginal sample. Included among these factors were a history of substance abuse, prior criminal convictions, antisocial attitudes, and association with antisocial peers.

These findings suggest that predictors of recidivism may, to some extent at least, be independent of culture, as some researchers have argued (e.g., Andrews & Bonta, 2006). This is not to say that Aboriginal-specific factors are unimportant, however. Recent research suggests that there are a number of factors specific to Aboriginal offenders that may assist in predicting whether an offender will reoffend. For example, in a study by Sioui and Thibault (2002), participation in cultural and spiritual activities while incarcerated, and involvement in Aboriginal-specific education and employment programs, were both related to decreases in recidivism for Aboriginal offenders.

Recidivism Regardless of whether Aboriginal and non-Aboriginal offenders exhibit the same risk factors, it now seems to be generally accepted that Aboriginal offenders reoffend at a significantly higher rate than non-Aboriginal offenders, at least at the federal level. For example, Sioui and Thibault (2002) examined the recidivism rates (i.e., technical violations or new offences) of 30 041 male offenders who were released on day parole, full parole, or statutory release from federal penitentiaries in Canada. Eighty-four percent of these offenders were non-Aboriginal and the remaining 16% were Aboriginal. Consistent with other studies, Sioui and Thibault found that a larger proportion of Aboriginal than non-Aboriginal offenders were re-admitted to a federal institution, regardless of the type of release. More specifically, 18% of Aboriginal offenders were re-admitted in the first six months after release, compared with 11% of non-Aboriginal offenders. What is not yet clear is whether these findings hold for offenders serving time in provincial prisons. For example, Bonta (1989) found only nonsignificant differences in the re-incarceration rates for Aboriginal and non-Aboriginal offenders when he examined offenders released from provincial institutions (incarceration rates of 43.8% and 42.3%, respectively, one year after release). The reasons for these differences between federal and provincial offenders are not yet understood and require further research.

TREATMENT

Although Aboriginal and non-Aboriginal offenders often exhibit similar sorts of treatment needs while incarcerated, the level of need is not the same (LaPrairie, 1996). Studies have consistently shown that larger proportions of Aboriginal offenders are rated as being high need. For example, Trevethan, Moore, and Rastin (2002) recently conducted a study in which they compared the treatment needs of Aboriginal and non-Aboriginal offenders in federal custody. They found that Aboriginal offenders were rated as having higher treatment needs in the following areas: personal/emotional issues, substance abuse, employment, marital/family issues, and social interactions/peer associations (see Figure 13.2). In contrast, the only domain in which non-Aboriginal offenders were rated as having higher treatment needs was with their attitudes.

Aboriginal Correctional Programs It is often assumed that loss of culture is at the heart of the Aboriginal overrepresentation problem. This has led to the belief that re-establishing culture is at least part of the solution, thus prompting correctional agencies to develop and implement a range of programs tailored to Aboriginal offenders in provincial and federal custody, as well as in the community. The correctional programs that are now being offered to Aboriginal offenders through CSC include traditional spiritual practices, substance abuse treatment, Aboriginal literacy classes, Aboriginal cultural skills, sweat lodge ceremonies, and family violence programs (LaPrairie, 1996). Many of these

Figure 13.2 Need Ratings for Aboriginal and Non-Aboriginal Offenders in Federal Custody

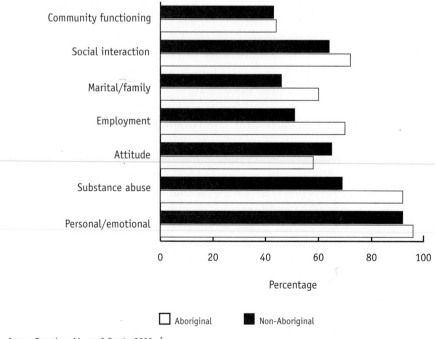

Source: Trevethan, Moore, & Rastin, 2002.

programs are offered to Aboriginal offenders in **Aboriginal healing lodges**, which we will focus on in the next section.

Healing Lodges for Aboriginal Offenders

Section 81 of the Corrections and Conditional Release Act allows for the Aboriginal community to take responsibility for overseeing Aboriginal offenders under certain conditions (e.g., the offender must agree to the arrangement). This enables the Aboriginal community to provide correctional services to Aboriginal offenders in a manner that respects the culture of Aboriginal people. These services are often provided in Aboriginal healing lodges, which were initially introduced by CSC about 15 years ago. According to CSC (2004), healing lodges

> offer services and programs that reflect Aboriginal culture in a space that incorporates Aboriginal peoples' tradition and beliefs. In the healing lodge, the needs of Aboriginal offenders serving federal sentences are addressed through Aboriginal teachings and ceremonies, contact with Elders and children, and interaction with nature. A holistic philosophy governs the approach, whereby individualized programming is delivered within a context of community interaction, with a focus on preparing for release. In the healing lodges, an emphasis is placed on spiritual leadership and on the value of the life experience of staff members, who act as role models. (p. 1)

Currently, there are ten Aboriginal healing lodges across Canada. These healing lodges differ in many ways, but they all focus on providing correctional services that respect the Aboriginal culture (Crutcher & Trevethan, 2002). Some of the lodges are managed directly by CSC, whereas Aboriginal agencies or communities manage others. Only one of the lodges is for female offenders (see Box 13.5). Some healing lodges offer correctional programs in structures that resemble correctional facilities, while others offer their programs in structures that are more traditional in nature (Crutcher & Trevethan, 2002) (see the photograph of the Okimaw Ohci spiritual lodge in Box 13.5).

Little research is available on the effectiveness of Aboriginal healing lodges. The research that does exist can be divided into three categories: research that has examined recidivism in Aboriginal offenders once they leave the healing lodge, indirect research that has examined the impact of culture-specific interventions more generally, and survey research that has focused on the views of offenders who have served time in healing lodges. To some extent, the research findings that emerge from these studies are contradictory.

For example, direct research indicates that, of the 426 healing lodge residents that have so far been released, 166 of them have been re-admitted to a federal facility (Trevethan, Crutcher, et al., 2002). Half of these re-admissions were for technical violations (e.g., failing to appear at the probation office at a scheduled time) and half were for the commission of a new offence. The recidivism rate for new offences was approximately 19%, which is significantly higher than the 13% recidivism rate for new offences for Aboriginal offenders released from minimum-security facilities. It must be noted, however, that significant differences exist in the recidivism rates across healing lodges (with some rates being about 13%) and that, at intake, residents of healing lodges are assessed as higher risk to reoffend than Aboriginal offenders in minimum-security facilities.

These findings are unexpected given the results of research from the other two categories. For example, a number of studies have found that culturally appropriate

Box 13.5

The Okimaw Ohci Healing Lodge

The spiritual lodge at the Okimaw Ohci Healing Lodge for women offenders

Opened in November 1995, the CSC-run Okimaw Ohci Healing Lodge is the only North American correctional facility designed specifically for female Aboriginal offenders. Okimaw Ohci is Cree for Thunder Hills, the location in Maple Creek, Saskatchewan, where the healing lodge is located. The healing lodge consists of 28 shared accommodation beds, two segregation cells, and a spiritual lodge built in the form of a teepee. Okimaw Ohci provides a range of programs for its residents. Like other correctional facilities in Canada, some of these programs consist of conventional anger-management classes and substance-abuse programs. Other programs focus more directly on promoting healing through cultural means, such as sweetgrass ceremonies.

One particularly important aspect of the healing lodge is its mother–child program, which consists of several toddlers living full-time with their mothers at the lodge. This reflects the belief within the Aboriginal community that children can play a central role in the healing process of adults. Nature also plays a role in the rehabilitation process at Okimaw Ohci and a variety of wildlife, including beavers, moose, and deer, are regularly seen by the residents. Okimaw Ohci accommodates federally sentenced female Aboriginal and non-Aboriginal offenders for all or part of their sentence (though the large majority of offenders have been Aboriginal). By December 2003, the Lodge had accepted more than 170 offender transfers. The number of residents who have been re-admitted (for committing a new offence) after release from Okimaw Ohci is relatively low (approximately 12%).

Sources: Warick, 1997; Trevethan, Crutcher, & Rastin, 2002.

programs for Aboriginal offenders contribute to program completion and decreases in recidivism. For instance, Ellerby and MacPherson (2001) found that traditional Aboriginal healing methods are more effective than non-Aboriginal approaches for treating Aboriginal sex offenders, as did Trevethan, Moore, and Allegri (2005) for Aboriginal offenders with a history of violent offending. Furthermore, Sioui and Thibault (2001) found that elder involvement and participation in cultural and spiritual activities was associated with a decrease in recidivism in Aboriginal offenders. Moreover, some research has suggested that program delivery by Aboriginal staff is also important. Johnston (1997), for example, found that Aboriginal offenders were more comfortable dealing with Aboriginal staff and viewed them as more trustworthy than non-Aboriginal staff.

Surveys of offenders serving their time in healing lodges also indicate that healing lodges are viewed in a positive light and should result in lower recidivism rates compared with conventional correctional programs. For example, Pfeifer and Hart-Mitchell (2001), who examined provincial offenders at Wahpeton Healing Lodge in Saskatchewan, found that many offenders were viewed by the offenders as more comfortable participating in cultural activities at the lodge because the staff were viewed by the offenders as more attentive and nonjudgmental than institutional staff. In addition, the offenders generally felt that the culture-specific programming would enable them to trust people, stay out of trouble, and deal more positively with their problems. Likewise, in their interviews with healing lodge residents, Crutcher and Trevethan (2002) found that 80% of offenders were very satisfied with their experience at the healing lodge. They felt that the healing lodge helped them better understand themselves, and they felt less angry and more in control of their behaviour.

Is an End to Aboriginal Overrepresentation in Sight?

No simple answer exists to this question, just as no simple answer exists as to why Aboriginal overrepresentation occurs in the first place. To be sure, various objectives are being pursued to bring the problem of Aboriginal overrepresentation to an end. For example, relevant policies and procedures have been put in place by both government and criminal justice agencies. Unfortunately, while some (e.g., Roberts & Melchers, 2003) have argued that these policies and procedures are having an effect on the rate of overrepresentation in recent years, albeit a limited effect, others have argued that Aboriginal overrepresentation in the criminal justice system continues to get worse (e.g., Boe, 2002; Royal Commission on Aboriginal Peoples, 1996; Trevethan, Tremblay, & Carter, 2000). The problem is that several factors are working against attempts to reduce Aboriginal overrepresentation. The two factors discussed most often are the increase in the Aboriginal youth population and the growing concentration of Aboriginal people in urban areas, especially in the Western provinces (Boe, 2000).

Compared with the general Canadian population, the Aboriginal population in Canada today is much younger and, as a consequence, "there are proportionally many more Aboriginal people in the *high-risk* youth age groups" (italics added, Boe, 2002, p. 13). For example, according to Boe (2000), the average age of the Aboriginal population was 25.5 years in 1996, compared with an approximate average age in the general Canadian population of 35 years. Furthermore, children under 15 years of age accounted for about 35% of the Aboriginal population in 1996, compared with 20% of the general population. Given the higher birth rate that exists in the Canadian Aboriginal community, this problem is bound to increase. Indeed, as Boe (2000) reports, in 1996 there were approximately 144 000 Aboriginal people in Canada between the ages of 15 and 24. Based on Statistics Canada data, this number went up to roughly 170 000 by 2006 (Statistics Canada, 2007).

If current trends continue, chances are that these young individuals will also primarily reside in urban areas. For example, in 1951, approximately 27% of Aboriginal people lived in urban areas. By 1996, this percentage rose to a staggering 63% (LaPrairie, 2002). The relocation of Aboriginal people into large urban areas is expected to increase the chances of Aboriginal overrepresentation in the criminal justice system because Aboriginal groups living in urban areas are more likely to become involved with the criminal justice system (LaPrairie, 1992, 2002). The reason for this appears to be that many of the Aboriginal people leaving reserves lack the education and skills needed to make it in large urban areas, and some suffer from substance abuse problems that contribute to their involvement in crime (LaPrairie, 1996).

What these findings indicate is that criminal justice interventions may help manage Aboriginal overrepresentation in the short term, but large-scale social issues need to be addressed if we ever hope to eliminate the problem totally.

SUMMARY

1. The Juvenile Delinquents Act (JDA) in 1908 was the first piece of legislation in Canada to address youthful offenders. In 1984, the Young Offender's Act (YOA) replaced the JDA with several notable changes to youth justice. Although the YOA underwent several amendments, it was eventually replaced in 2003 with the Youth Criminal Justice Act.

2. There are three common disorders diagnosed in youthful offenders: attention-deficit hyperactivity disorder (ADHD), oppositional defiant disorder (ODD), and conduct disorder (CD). Young children diagnosed with conduct disorder are at greatest risk for youthful and adult criminal offending.

3. Risk factors increase the likelihood of behavioural (and emotional) disorders in children and youth. These include individual factors such as difficult temperament, familial factors such as poor parental supervision, school factors such as reading difficulties, and social factors such as delinquent peers. Protective factors provide a buffer against the risk factors a child may experience. Protective factors include individual factors such as adaptive coping mechanisms, familial factors such as a warm and caring parent–child relationship, and social factors such as positive role models.

4. Women engage in much lower rates of offending than do men. Although gender-specific risk factors may exist, the research to date has found more similarities than differences in both adolescents and adults. Compared with male offenders, female offenders are more likely to be victims of physical and sexual abuse, to engage in suicidal and self-injurious behaviours, to have less extensive criminal histories, and to have elevated rates of mental disorders.

5. Battered woman syndrome (BWS) is now being used in trials that involve battered women who kill their batterers. The two key components of BWS often presented by court experts are learned helplessness and the cycle-of-violence theory.

6. There are four common explanations for Aboriginal overrepresentation. These include (1) a higher Aboriginal offending rate, (2) the commission by Aboriginal offenders of crimes that are more likely to result in prison sentences, (3) criminal justice practices that have a differential impact on Aboriginal offenders due to their socioeconomic situation, and (4) differential processing through the criminal justice system as a result of discrimination. Although all factors probably contribute to Aboriginal overrepresentation, the two primary factors appear to be higher offending rates and the commission of offences that are more likely to result in prison sentences.

7. To deal with the issue of Aboriginal overrepresentation in the criminal justice system, Aboriginal-specific correctional programs have been developed. One of these programs involves transferring offenders out of prisons and into Aboriginal healing lodges. These lodges provide conventional correctional programs, such as substance abuse counselling, but they also have an Aboriginal focus, stressing Aboriginal teachings and ceremonies, contact with elders and children, and interaction with nature. The results of research that has examined the effectiveness of these healing lodges, in terms of offender rehabilitation, is mixed.

Key Concepts

Aboriginal healing lodge 400

attention deficit hyperactivity disorder 376

battered woman syndrome 390

conduct disorder 376.

cycle-of-violence theory 390

dialectical behaviour therapy 393

diversion 372

extrajudicial 373

externalizing problems 375

feminist pathways research 386

internalizing problems 375

learned helplessness 390

multisystemic therapy 382

oppositional defiant disorder 376

protective factors 381

relational theory 386

resilient 381

risk factors 379

self-defence 389

social learning theory 379

Discussion Questions

1. Fifteen-year-old Andrew Smith is appearing before Judge Brown in youth court for the third time in two years. Andrew's most current offences are robbery and possession of a handgun. Given the objectives of the Youth Criminal Justice Act, discuss the sentencing options available to Judge Brown. Consider what option is most appropriate in this case. Why?

2. In your opinion, what factors should the courts consider when determining whether a young offender should be given an adult sentence?

3. Various unconventional treatment approaches have been proposed as a way of dealing with young offenders. For example, taking young offenders to prison to witness first-hand the prison environment or taking young offenders to the morgue. Do you think these sorts of approaches will successfully rehabilitate young offenders? Why or why not?

4. Under what circumstances should expert testimony concerning battered woman syndrome be admissible in court? Do you think changes are needed to the self-defence plea?

5. There is controversy over whether gender-specific risk factors exist. Develop a study to address this issue.

6. Imagine that you are an offender who is being sentenced for a crime. Do you think that you should be given the same sentencing options as an Aboriginal offender (e.g., the opportunity to serve your sentence in an Aboriginal healing lodge)? If so, how would you argue your case to the judge?

7. The federal government has just proposed a new policy it believes will reduce the problem of Aboriginal overrepresentation in the Canadian criminal justice system by the year 2015. As a forensic psychologist who is interested in this area, attempt to develop a study that will allow the government to determine whether the policy is working.

Readings

Blanchette, K., & Brown, S.L. (2006). *The assessment and treatment of women offenders: An integrative perspective.* Wiley Series in Forensic Clinical Psychology. Chichester, UK: John Wiley & Sons.

Hoge, R.D., & Andrews, D.A. (1996). *Assessing the youthful offender: Issues and techniques.* New York: Plenum.

LaPrairie, C. (1996). *Examining Aboriginal corrections.* Ottawa: Solicitor General of Canada, Corrections Branch.

Vallée, B. (1998). *Life and death with Billy.* Toronto: Random House.

Websites

The Institute for the Study of Antisocial Behaviour in Youth
www.iay.org

The Canadian Association of Elizabeth Fry Societies
www.elizabethfry.ca

The Aboriginal Initiatives Directorate at Correctional Service Canada
www.csc-scc.gc.ca/text/prgrm/correctional/abissues/who_e.shtml

Glossary

Aboriginal healing lodge A facility in which Aboriginal offenders can be exposed to correctional services in an environment that incorporates Aboriginal traditions and beliefs

Absolute discharge The defendant is released into the community without restrictions to his or her behaviour

Absolute judgment Witness compares each lineup member to his or her memory of the culprit to decide whether the lineup member is the culprit

Access Noncustodial parents' right to see their children

Actuarial prediction Decisions are based on risk factors that are selected and combined based on their empirical or statistical association with a specific outcome

Actus reus A wrongful deed

Adaptive coping skills Skills that allow people to deal more effectively with stressful events

Adjournment Delaying the trial to some time in the future

Alternate forms reliability Coefficient of association between two forms of the same measure

Anatomically detailed doll A doll, sometimes like a rag doll, that is consistent with the male or female anatomy

Anger rapist A rapist, as defined by Groth, who uses more force than necessary to obtain compliance from the victim and who engages in a variety of sexual acts to degrade the victim

Anterograde amnesia Memory deficits consisting of an impaired ability to establish new memories

Antisocial personality disorder A personality disorder characterized by a history of behaviour in which the rights of others are violated

Assent Agreeableness to participate

Assessment centre A facility in which the behaviour of police applicants can be observed in a number of situations by multiple observers

Attention deficit hyperactivity disorder A disorder in a youth characterized by a persistent pattern of inattention and hyperactivity or impulsivity

Automatism Unconscious, involuntary behaviour such that the person committing the act is not aware of what he or she is doing

Base rate Represents the percentage of people within a given population who engage in a specific behaviour or have a mental disorder

Baseline Normal pattern of responding

Battered woman syndrome A collection of symptoms and behaviours believed to be common to women who have experienced chronic and severe intimate abuse

Biased lineup A lineup that "suggests" who the police suspect and thereby who the witness should identify

Black sheep effect When evidence is strong, similarity between defendant and jury leads to punitiveness

Broad-based approach Approach to scientific jury selection that starts with the presumption that there are certain traits or attitudes that people have that make them more likely to be pro-prosecution versus pro-defence

Capping Notion introduced through Bill C-30 where there is a maximum period of time a person with a mental illness could be affected by their disposition

Case-specific approach Approach to scientific jury selection that starts with the issues and facts of the case. A specific questionnaire then is developed assessing a number of characteristics that may influence the verdict

Challenge for cause An option to reject biased jurors

Change of venue Moving a trial to a community other than the one in which the crime occurred

Child molester Someone who has actually sexually molested a child. See also pedophile

Classic trait model A model of personality that assumes the primary determinants of behaviour are stable, internal traits

Clinical forensic psychologists Psychologists who are broadly concerned with the assessment and treatment of mental health issues as they pertain to the law or legal system

Clinical risk factors Types and symptoms of mental disorders (e.g., substance abuse)

Coerced-compliant false confession A confession that results from a desire to escape a coercive interrogation environment or gain a benefit promised by the police

Coerced-internalized false confession A confession that results from suggestive interrogation techniques, whereby the confessor actually comes to believe he or she committed the crime

Cognitive ability tests Procedure for measuring verbal, mathematical, memory, and reasoning abilities

Cognitive interview Interview procedure for use with eyewitnesses based on principles of memory storage and retrieval

Cohort effects The effect of belonging to a given generation that may be responsible for differences on the dependent variable

Comfort serial murderer A murderer who is motivated by material or financial gain

Community service A sentence that involves the offender performing a duty in the community, often as a way of paying off a fine

Community treatment order Sentence that allows the mentally ill offender to live in the community, with the stipulation that the person will agree to treatment or detention in the event his or her condition deteriorates

Competency inquiry Questions posed to child witnesses under the age of 14 to determine whether they are able to communicate the evidence and understand the difference between the truth and a lie, and in the circumstances of testifying, feel compelled to tell the truth

Compliance A tendency to go along with demands made by people perceived to be in authority, even though the person may not agree with them

Conditional discharge A defendant is released; however, release carries certain conditions (e.g., not to possess firearms) that the defendant must meet. Failure to meet the conditions imposed with a conditional discharge may result in the defendant being incarcerated or sent to a psychiatric facility

Conditional sentence A sentence served in the community

Conduct disorder A disorder characterized by a persistent pattern of behaviour in which a youth violates the rights of others or age-appropriate societal norms or rules

Confabulation Making things up

Confederate Someone who is hired by the researcher and is informed to act in a certain way to produce an experimental condition

Confound When a variable co-varies with the independent variable that the researcher is unaware of

Contextual risk factors Risk factors that refer to aspects of the current environment (e.g., access to victims or weapons). Sometimes called situational risk factors

Control Question Test Type of polygraph test that includes irrelevant questions that are unrelated to the crime, relevant questions concerning the crime being investigated, and control questions concerning the person's honesty and past history prior to the event being investigated

Convergent validity The degree that different measures that are intended to measure the same construct produce similar results

Correlation coefficient The statistic used to describe the relationship between variables and is a number that can vary from −1.00 to +1.00

Countermeasures As applied to polygraph research, techniques used to try to conceal guilt

Criminal profiling An investigative technique for identifying the major personality and behavioural characteristics of an individual based upon an analysis of the crimes he or she has committed

Criterion-based content analysis Analysis using criteria to distinguish truthful from false statements made by children

Cronbach's alpha Coefficient that results by correlating the response for each item with each other item from a measure

Cross-race effect The phenomenon of witnesses remembering own-race faces with greater accuracy than faces from other races. Also known as the other-race effect

Cue-utilization hypothesis Proposed by Easterbrook (1959) to explain why a witness may focus on the weapon rather than other details. The hypothesis suggests that when emotional arousal increases, attentional capacity decreases

Culprit The guilty person who committed the crime

Cycle-of-violence theory The theory that within intimate violence there is a tension-building phase, an acute battering act phase, and a contrition phase

Dangerous offender A label attached to offenders who are proven to constitute a significant danger to others

Daubert criteria A standard for accepting expert testimony, which states that scientific evidence is valid if the research upon which it is based has been peer reviewed, is testable, has a recognized rate of error, and adheres to professional standards

Day parole A form of parole that allows the offender to enter the community for up to one day (e.g., for the purpose of holding down a job)

Deception detection Detecting when someone is being deceptive

Deductive criminal profiling Profiling the background characteristics of an unknown offender based on evidence left at the crime scenes by that particular offender

Defensiveness Conscious denial or extreme minimization of physical or psychological symptoms

Deliberation When jury members discuss the evidence privately among themselves to reach a verdict that is then provided to the court

Demand characteristics Any factors (including experimenter bias) present in the study, other than the independent variables, that suggest to the participant how to respond

Dependent variables Variables that are measured

Dialectical behaviour therapy Therapy designed to treat borderline personality disordered patients

Direct question recall Witnesses are asked a series of specific questions about the crime or the culprit

Dispositional risk factor Risk factors that reflect the individual's traits, tendencies, or styles (e.g., negative attitudes)

Disputed confession A confession that is later disputed at trial

Distractors Lineup members who are known to be innocent for the crime in question. Also known as foils

Divergent validity The degree to which measures purported to assess different constructs do not agree with each other

Diversion A decision not to prosecute a young offender but rather have him or her undergo an educational or community-service program. Also an option for the courts dealing with offenders with mental illnesses who are facing minor charges. The court can divert the offender directly into a treatment program rather than have him or her go through the court process

Domestic violence Any violence occurring between family members

Dynamic risk factor Risk factors that fluctuate over time and are amenable to changing

Dysphoric/borderline batterer A male spousal batterer who exhibits some violence outside the family, is depressed and has borderline personality traits, and has problems with jealousy

Effect size A measure of the strength of the relationship between the independent and dependent variable

Elimination lineup Lineup procedure for children that first asks them to pick out the person who looks most like the culprit from the photos displayed. Next, children are asked if the most similar person selected is in fact the culprit

Emotional maltreatment Acts or omissions by caregivers that cause or could cause serious behavioural, cognitive, emotional, or mental disorders

Enhanced cognitive interview Interview procedure that includes various principles of social dynamics in addition to the memory retrieval principles used in the original cognitive interview

Estimator variables Variables that are present at the time of the crime and that cannot be changed

Event-related brain potentials Brain activity measured by placing electrodes on the scalp and electrical patterns related to presentation of a stimulus are recorded

Exhibitionist Someone who obtains sexual gratification by exposing genitals to strangers

Experimental forensic psychologists Psychologists who are broadly concerned with the study of human behaviour as it relates to the law or legal system

Experimenter bias The subtle cues that are displayed by the researcher suggesting how a participant should respond

Expert witness A witness who provides the court with information (often an opinion on a particular matter) that assists the court in understanding an issue of relevance to a case

External validity The degree to which we can generalize our results to different populations, settings, and conditions

Externalizing problems Behavioural difficulties such as delinquency, fighting, bullying, lying, or destructive behaviour experienced by a youth

Extra-familial child molester Someone who sexually abuses children not related to the abuser

Extrajudicial Term applied to measures taken to keep young offenders out of court and out of custody (e.g., giving a warning or making a referral for treatment)

Extroversion A personality trait that some researchers believe is the result of cortical underarousal

Fabricating Making false claims

Factitious disorder A disorder in which the person's physical and psychological symptoms are intentionally produced and are adopted to assume the role of a sick person

Fair lineup A lineup where the suspect does not stand out from the other lineup members

False confession A confession that is either intentionally fabricated or is not based on actual knowledge of the facts that form its content

False memory syndrome Term to describe clients' false beliefs that they were sexually abused as children, having no memories of this abuse until they enter therapy to deal with some other psychological problem such as depression or substance abuse

False negative An incorrect prediction that occurs when a person is predicted not to engage in some type of behaviour (e.g., violent acts) but does

False positive An incorrect prediction that occurs when a person is predicted to engage in some type of behaviour (e.g., violent acts) but does not

Familicide Refers to the killing of a spouse and children

Family-only batterer A male spousal batterer who is typically not violent outside the home, does not show much psychopathology, and does not posses negative attitudes supportive of violence

Femicide The killing of women

Feminist pathways research A theory asserting that childhood victimization/abuse is the main reason behind criminal behaviour in girls and women

Filicide Refers to the killing of children by their biological parents or stepparents and includes neonaticide (killing a baby within 24 hours of birth) and infanticide (killing a baby within first year of life)

Fine A sentence where the offender has to make a monetary payment to the courts

Fixated child molester A child molester, as defined by Groth, who has a long-standing, exclusive sexual orientation preference for children

Foils Lineup members who are known to be innocent for the crime in question. Also known as distractors

Forensic psychiatry A field of medicine that deals with all aspects of human behaviour as it relates to the law or legal system

Forensic psychology A field of psychology that deals with all aspects of human behaviour as it relates to the law or legal system

Free narrative Witnesses are asked to either write or orally state all they remember about the event without the officer (or experimenter) asking questions. Also known as open-ended recall

Full parole A form of parole that allows the offender to serve the remainder of his or her sentence under supervision in the community

Fundamental principle of sentencing Belief that sentences should be proportionate to the gravity of the offence and the degree of responsibility of the offender

General acceptance test A standard for accepting expert testimony, which states that expert testimony will be admissible in court if the basis of the testimony is generally accepted within the relevant scientific community

General deterrence Sentencing in order to reduce the probability that members of the general public will offend in the future

Generally violent/antisocial batterer A male spousal batterer who is violent outside the home, engages in other criminal acts, has drug and alcohol problems, has impulse-control problems, and possesses violence-supportive beliefs

Geographic profiling An investigative technique that uses crime scene locations to predict the most likely area where an offender resides

Geographic profiling systems Computer systems that use mathematical models of offender spatial behaviour to make predictions about where unknown serial offenders are likely to reside

Ground truth As applied to polygraph research, the knowledge of whether the person is actually guilty or innocent

Gudjonsson Compliance Scale A scale developed by Gisli Gudjonsson that is used to measure a person's level of compliance

Gudjonsson Suggestibility Scale A scale developed by Gisli Gudjonsson that is used to measure a person's level of suggestibility

Guilty Knowledge Test Type of polygraph test designed to determine if the person knows details about a crime

Hare Psychopathy Checklist-Revised The most popular method of assessing psychopathy in adults

Heuristics Simple rules of thumb that can be used to make decisions and solve problems. In some instances, a reliance on heuristics can result in biased decisions. In other cases, heuristics can result in reasonably accurate decisions.

Historic child sexual abuse (HCSA) Allegations of child abuse having occurred several years, often decades from when they are being prosecuted

Historical risk factor Risk factor that refers to events that have been experienced in the past (e.g., age at first arrest). Also known as static risk factor

Hung jury A jury that cannot reach a unanimous verdict

Hypnotically refreshed memory Where a hypnotized person is able to produce a greater number of details than a person who has not been hypnotized

Hypothesis A testable explanation for a phenomenon

Idiographic An attempt to understand something by examining the specific details of individual cases

Illusory correlation Belief that a correlation exists between two events that in reality are either not correlated or correlated to a much lesser degree

Impartiality A characteristic of jurors who are unbiased

Imprisonment A sentence served in prison

In need of protection A term used to describe a child's need to be separated from his or his caregiver due to maltreatment

Incidence Number of new cases in a specific population occurring in a given time period, usually a year

Independent variables Variables that are manipulated or selected to be examined

Inductive criminal profiling Profiling the background characteristics of an unknown offender based on what we know about other solved cases

Infanticide Although the term literally means "killing of an infant," it has been used more specifically to refer to a woman killing her newly born child due to a mental disorder arising from the effects of childbirth

Informed consent An explicitly expressed willingness to participate in a research project based on clear understanding of the nature of the research, of the consequences of participating (or not participating), and of all factors that might be expected to influence willingness to participate

Insanity Impairment of mental or emotional functioning that affects perceptions, beliefs, and motivations at the time of the offence

Instigators In social learning theory, these are events in the environment that act as a stimulus for acquired behaviours

Instrumental aggression Violence that is premeditated, calculated behaviour, motivated by some goal. Also known as predatory violence

Internal validity The degree to which differences in the dependent variable can be attributed to the effect of the independent variable rather than some other ambiguous variable

Internalization Accepting that something suggested to you is true

Internalizing problems Emotional difficulties such as anxiety, depression, and obsessions experienced by a youth

Inter-rater reliability The degree to which different raters give similar ratings to each report

Intimate partner violence Any violence occurring between intimate partners who are living together or separated. Also known as spousal violence

Intra-familial child molesters People who sexually abuse their own biological children or children for whom they assume a parental role, such as a stepfather or live-in boyfriend. Also known as incest offenders

Investigator bias Bias that can result when police officers enter an interrogation setting already believing that the suspect is guilty

Inwald Personality Inventory An assessment instrument used to identify police applicants who are suitable for police work by measuring their personality attributes and behaviour patterns

Job analysis A procedure for identifying the knowledge, skills, and abilities that make up a good police officer

Jury Act Provincial and territorial legislation that outlines the eligibility criteria for jury service and how prospective jurors must be selected

Jury nullification Occurs when a jury ignores the law and the evidence, rendering a verdict based on some other criteria

Jury summons A court order that states a time and place to go for jury duty

Known-groups design As applied to malingering research, involves comparing genuine patients and malingers attempting to fake the disorder the patients have

Learned helplessness A learned passive and withdrawing response to events in which the person perceives he or she has little control

Learning theories Theories that attempt to explain criminal conduct by focusing on principles of conditioning (e.g., being rewarded for criminal behaviour)

Leniency bias When jurors move toward greater leniency during deliberations

Levels Variations of a particular independent variable

Lineup A set of people presented to the witness who must state whether the culprit is present and, if so, which one

Linkage blindness An inability on the part of the police to link geographically dispersed serial crimes committed by the same offender because of a lack of information sharing among police agencies

Long-term offender A label attached to offenders who are proven to be a high risk for reoffending

Lust serial murderer A murderer who is motivated by sexual gratification

Malingering Intentionally faking psychological or physical symptoms for some type of external gain

Mandatory charging policies Policies that give police the authority to lay charges against a suspect where there is reasonable and probable grounds to believe a domestic assault has occurred

Mass murder The killing of three or more victims at a single location during one event with no cooling off period

Maximization techniques Scare tactics used by police interrogators that are designed to intimidate a suspect believed to be guilty

Memory impairment hypothesis Explanation for the misinformation effect where the original memory is replaced with the new, incorrect, information

Mens rea Criminal intent

Minimization techniques Soft sell tactics used by police interrogators that are designed to lull the suspect into a false sense of security

Minnesota Multiphasic Personality Inventory An assessment instrument for identifying people with psychopathological problems

Misinformation acceptance hypothesis Explanation for the misinformation effect where the incorrect information is provided because the witness guesses what the officer or experimenter wants the response to be

Misinformation effect Phenomenon where a witness who is presented with inaccurate information after an event will incorporate that "misinformation" in a subsequent recall task. Also known as post-event information effect

Mission-oriented serial murderer A murderer who targets individuals from a group that he or she considers to be "undesirable"

Mohan **criteria** A standard for accepting expert testimony, which states that expert testimony will be admissible in court if the testimony is relevant, necessary for assisting the trier of fact, does not violate any exclusionary rules, and is provided by a qualified expert

Multisystemic therapy A treatment approach that considers the youth in the various contexts or systems he or she exists— family, peers, school, neighbourhood, and community

Munchausen syndrome A rare factitious disorder in which a person intentionally produces a physical complaint and constantly seeks physician consultations, hospitalizations, and even surgery to treat the nonexistent illness

Narrative elaboration An interview procedure whereby children learn to organize their story into relevant categories—participants, settings, actions, conversation/affective states, and consequences

National Parole Board The organization in Canada responsible for making parole decisions

Need principle Principle that correctional interventions should target known criminogenic needs (i.e., factors that relate to reoffending)

Neglect/failure to provide When a child's caregivers do not provide the requisite attention to the child's emotional, psychological, or physical development

Neuroticism A personality trait that some researchers believe is the result of an overreactive autonomic nervous system

Nomothetic An attempt to understand something by uncovering broad patterns and general trends

Norm Average performance

Observational learning Learning behaviours by watching others perform these behaviours

Observer drift Occurs when an observer changes how he or she is coding behaviours over time due to fatigue or boredom

Occupational stressors In policing, stressors relating to the job itself

Open-ended recall Witnesses are asked to either write or orally state all they remember about the event without the officer (or experimenter) asking questions. Also known as a free narrative

Operational definition Definition of a concept in terms of the operations used to produce and measure it

Oppositional defiant disorder A disorder in a youth characterized by a persistent pattern of negativistic, hostile, and defiant behaviours

Organizational stressors In policing, stressors relating to organizational issues

Organized-disorganized model A profiling model used by the FBI that assumes that the crime scenes and backgrounds of serial offenders can be categorized as organized or disorganized

Other-race effect Phenomenon of witnesses remembering own-race faces with greater accuracy than faces from other races. Also known as the cross-race effect

Parallel parenting System that divides decision-making power between parents

Parole The release of offenders from prison into the community before their sentence term is complete

Patriarchy Broad set of cultural beliefs and values that support the male dominance of women

Pedophile Person whose primary sexual orientation is towards children. See also child molester

Penile phallometry A measurement device placed around the penis to measure changes in sexual arousal

Person characteristics Characteristics that are part of the individual

Personality theories Theories that attempt to explain criminal conduct by focusing on the personality makeup of offenders

Physical abuse The deliberate application of force to any part of a child's body that results in or may result in a nonaccidental injury

Polarization When individuals tend to become more extreme in their initial position following a group discussion

Police discretion A policing task that involves discriminating between circumstances that require absolute adherence to the law and circumstances where a degree of latitude is justified

Police interrogation A process whereby the police interview a suspect for the purpose of gathering evidence and obtaining a confession

Police selection procedures A set of procedures used by the police to either screen out undesirable candidates or select in desirable candidates

Polygraph disclosure tests Polygraph tests that are used to uncover information about an offender's past behaviour

Polygraph A device for recording an individual's autonomic nervous system responses

Post-event information effect Phenomenon where a witness who is presented with inaccurate information after an event will incorporate that "misinformation" in a subsequent recall task. Also known as the misinformation effect

Post-traumatic stress disorder Anxiety disorder that can develop in response to exposure to an extremely traumatic event. Symptoms include frequent, distressing, and intrusive memories of the event, avoiding stimuli associated with the traumatic event, and persistent anxiety or increased arousal symptoms

Power/control serial murder A murderer who is motivated not by sexual gratification but by wanting to have absolute dominance over the victim

Power rapist A rapist, as defined by Groth, who seeks to establish dominance and control over the victim

Prevalence In the study of child abuse, the proportion of a population at a specific point in time that was maltreated during childhood

Prima facie case Case in which the Crown prosecutor must prove there is sufficient evidence to bring the case to trial

Privacy The notion of an individual's right to decide how information about him or her is communicated to others, if at all

Probation The defendant is released into the community with certain restrictions on his or her behaviour

Protective factors Factors that mitigate or reduce the likelihood of a negative outcome (e.g., aggression, psychopathology)

Psychoanalytic theories Theories that attempt to explain criminal conduct by focusing on dynamic internal forces within people and the importance of early childhood events and experiences

Psychology and the law The use of psychology to examine the operation of the legal system

Psychology in the law The use of psychology in the legal system as that system operates

Psychology of the law The use of psychology to examine the law itself

Psychopath An individual who is defined by a collection of interpersonal, affective, and behavioural characteristics including manipulation, lack of remorse or empathy, impulsivity, and antisocial behaviours

Racial bias The disparate treatment of racial out-groups

Racial profiling Police-initiated action that relies on the race or ethnicity of an individual, rather than that individual's criminal behaviour

Random assignment Experimental condition in which each participant starts off with an equal chance of being assigned to any one of the groups or conditions. Also known as randomization

Random error Temporary chance fluctuations

Rape trauma syndrome A group of symptoms or behaviours that are frequent aftereffects of having been raped

Rapist People who sexually assault victims more than 16 years of age

Reactive (affective) aggression Violence that is impulsive, unplanned, immediate, driven by negative emotions, and occurring in response to some perceived provocation. Also known as affective violence

Reactivity The notion where an individual changes his or her behaviour when he or she is aware of being observed

Recall memory Reporting details of a previously witnessed event or person

Recognition memory Determining whether a previously seen item or person is the same as what is currently being viewed

Regressed child molester A child molester, as defined by Groth, whose primary sexual orientation is for adults, but whose sexual interests revert to children after a stressful event or due to feelings of inadequacy

Regulators In social learning theory, these are consequences of behaviours

Reid model A nine-step model of interrogation used frequently in North America to extract confessions from suspects

Relapse prevention A method of treatment designed to prevent the occurrence of an undesired behaviour (e.g., sexual assault)

Relational theory A theory that emphasizes the role of relationships in women's overall lives and functioning and claims this role is more central for women than for men

Relative judgment Witness compares lineup members to each other and the person that looks most like the culprit is identified

Relevant/Irrelevant Test Type of polygraph test that includes relevant questions concerning the crime being investigated and irrelevant questions that are unrelated to the crime

Reliable A measure that provides a consistent or similar result each time you use the measure

Reparations A sentence where the offender has to make a monetary payment to the victim or the community

Representativeness A jury composition that represents the community where the crime occurred

Resilient Characteristic of a child who has multiple risk factors but who does not develop problem behaviours or negative symptoms

Resolution conference Involves an offender and his or her family coming together with the victim and the police in an attempt to solve a problem

Responsivity principle Principle that correctional interventions should match the general learning style of offenders

Restitution See **reparations**

Retracted confessions A confession that the confessor later declares to be false

Retracted confession A confession that the confessor later declares to be false

Retrograde amnesia Memory deficits consisting of an inability to recall specific, highly salient incidents from the past

Review boards Legal bodies mandated to oversee the care and disposition of defendants found unfit and/or not criminally responsible on account of a mental disorder

Risk factor A factor that increases the likelihood for emotional and/or behavioural problems

Risk principle Principle that correctional interventions should target offenders who are at high risk to reoffend

Sadistic rapist A rapist, as defined by Groth, who obtains sexual gratification by hurting the victim

Scientific jury selection Rejecting prospective jurors who would be unsympathetic to one's case and accepting those who would be sympathetic based on predetermined characteristics

Selection interview In recruiting police officers, an interview used by the police to determine the extent to which an applicant possesses the knowledge, skills, and abilities deemed important for the job

Self-defence The principle that if you are attacked you should be able to take reasonable actions to defend yourself

Sentencing disparity Variations in sentencing severity for similar crimes committed under similar circumstances

Sentencing guidelines Guidelines that are intended to reduce the degree of discretion that judges have when handing down sentences

Sequential lineup Alternative lineup procedure where the lineup members are presented serially to the witness and the witness must make a decision as to whether the lineup member is the culprit before seeing another member. Also a witness cannot ask to see previously seen photos and the witness is unaware of the number of photos to be shown

Sequestered When jurors are isolated from others, apart from other jurors, until a verdict is reached

Serial murder The killing of a minimum of three people over time. The time interval between the murders varies and has been called a cooling off period. Subsequent murders occur at different times, have no apparent connection to the initial murder, and are usually committed in a different location

Sexual abuse When an adult or youth uses a child for sexual purposes

Shift The extent to which people who are completing the Gudjonsson Suggestibility Scale alter their answers when put under pressure by the interviewer

Showup Identification procedure that shows one person to the witness: the suspect

Simulation design As applied to malingering research, people are told to pretend they have specific symptoms or disorder

Simultaneous lineup A common lineup procedure that presents all lineup members at one time to the witness

Situational test A simulation of a real-world policing task

Social learning theory A theory of human behaviour based on learning from watching others in the social environment and reinforcement contingencies

Socially desirable responding When a participant provides responses that make him or her look good rather than providing truthful responses

Somatoform disorders A disorder in which physical symptoms suggest a physical illness but have no known underlying physiological cause and the symptoms are not intentionally produced

Source misattribution hypothesis Explanation for the misinformation effect—where the witness has two memories, the original and the misinformation; however, the witness cannot remember where each memory originated or the source of each

Specific deterrence Sentencing in order to reduce the probability that an offender will reoffend in the future

Split-half reliability Coefficient between two halves of the same measure

Spree murder The killing of three or more victims in two or more locations without a cooling off period

Standardization Ensuring that the measure is administered the same way every time

Statement validity analysis A comprehensive protocol to distinguish truthful or false statements made by children containing three parts—a structured interview of the child witness, a systematic analysis of the verbal content of the child's statements (criteria-based content analysis), and the application of the statement validity checklist

Static risk factor Risk factor that does not fluctuate over time and is not changed by treatment (e.g., age at first arrest). Also known as historical risk factor

Statutory release The release of offenders from prison after they have served two-thirds of their sentence

Step-wise interview Interview protocol with a series of "steps" designed to start the interview with the least leading and directive type of questioning then proceeding to more specific forms of questioning, as necessary

Structured professional judgment Decisions are guided by a predetermined list of risk factors that have been selected from the research and professional literature. Judgment of risk level is based on the evaluator's professional judgment

Suggestibility A tendency to accept information communicated during questioning

Supreme Court of Canada Created in 1875, the Supreme Court of Canada consists of eight judges plus the chief justice, who are all appointed by the federal government. The Supreme Court is the final court of appeal in Canada, and lower Canadian courts are bound by its rulings. The Supreme Court also provides guidance to the federal government on law-related matters, such as the interpretation of the Canadian constitution.

Suspect A person the police "suspect" committed the crime, who may be guilty or innocent for the crime in question

System variables Variables that can be manipulated to increase (or decrease) eyewitness accuracy

Systematic disparity Consistent disagreement among judges about sentencing decisions due to factors such as how lenient judges think sentences should be

Target-absent lineup A lineup that does not contain the culprit but contains innocent suspects

Target-present lineup A lineup that contains the culprit

Temporary absence A form of parole that allows the offender to enter the community on a temporary basis (e.g., for the purpose of attending correctional programs)

Test-retest coefficient The coefficient that results between two test administrations of the same measure

Theory of maternal deprivation Theory that early separation from one's mother plays a role in the development of anti-social behaviour

Thrill murderer A murderer who is motivated by the excitement associated with the act of killing

Trauma-control model of serial murder The model suggesting that a multitude of factors are involved in predicting who may be predisposed to commit serial murder

True negative A correct prediction that occurs when a person who is predicted not to engage in some type of behaviour (e.g., violent act) does not

True positive A correct prediction that occurs when a person who is predicted to engage in some type of behaviour (e.g., violent act) does so

Truth-bias The tendency of people to judge more messages as truthful than deceptive

Unfit to stand trial Refers to an inability to conduct a defence at any stage of the proceedings on account of a person's mental disorder

Unsystematic disparity Inconsistent disagreement among judges about sentencing decisions due to factors such as the judge's mood

Unstructured clinical judgment Decisions characterized by a substantial amount of professional discretion and lack of guidelines

Unwarranted sentencing disparity Variations in sentencing severity for similar crimes committed under similar circumstances that result from reliance by the judge on legally irrelevant factors

Use-of-force continuum A model that is supposed to guide police officer decision making in use-of-force situations by providing the officer with some guidance as to what level of force is appropriate given the suspect's behaviour and other environmental conditions

Valid A measure that measures what it was set out to measure

VICLAS The Violent Crime Linkage Analysis System, which was developed by the RCMP to collect and analyze information on serious crimes from across Canada

Visionary serial murderer A murderer who kills in response to voices or visions telling him or her to kill

Voir dire The question period when jurors are selected to serve on the jury

Voluntary false confession A false confession that is provided without any elicitation from the police

Voyeurs People who obtain sexual gratification by observing unsuspecting people, usually strangers, who are either naked, in the process of undressing, or engaging in sexual activity

Walk-by Identification procedure that occurs in a naturalistic environment. The police take the witness to a public location where the suspect is likely to be. Once the suspect is in view, the witness is asked whether he or she sees the culprit

Weapon focus Term used to describe the phenomenon of a witness's attention being focused on the culprit's weapon rather than on the culprit

White lies Untruthful statements told with no malicious intent

Yield The extent to which people who are completing the Gudjonsson Suggestibility Scale give in to leading questions

References

Abdollahi, M.K. (2002). Understanding police stress research. *Journal of Forensic Psychology Practice, 2,* 1–24.

Abel, G.G., Becker, J.V., Mittelman, M., & Cunningham-Rathner, J. (1987). Self-reported sex crimes of nonincarcerated paraphiliacs. *Journal of Interpersonal Violence, 2,* 3–25.

Abootalebi, V., Moradi, M.H., & Khalilzadeh, M.A. (2006). A comparison of methods for ERP assessment in a P300-based GKT. *International Journal of Psychophysiology, 62,* 309–320.

Aboriginal Legal Services of Toronto. (2001). *Gladue* (Aboriginal persons) court. Ontario Court of Justice—Old City Hall. Fact sheet. Retrieved June 10, 2004, from http://www.aboriginallegal.ca/docs/apc_factsheet.htm.

Aboriginal Task Force. (1989). *Task Force on Aboriginal Peoples in Federal Corrections: Final Report.* Ottawa: Solicitor General of Canada.

Ackerman, M.J. (1999). *Forensic psychological assessment.* New York: John Wiley & Sons.

Adams, K. (1999). *What we know about police use of force.* Washington, DC: U.S. Department of Justice.

Adams-Tucker, C. (1982). Proximate effects of sexual abuse in childhood: A report on 28 children. *American Journal of Psychiatry, 139,* 1252–1256.

Adler, F. (1975). *Sisters in crime: The rise of the new female criminal.* New York: McGraw-Hill.

Ægisdóttir, S., White, M.J., Spengler, P.M., Maugherman, A.S., Anderson, L.A., Cook, R.S., Nichols, C.N., Lampropoulos, G.K., Walker, B.S., Cohen, G., & Rush, J.D. (2006). The meta-analysis of clinical judgment project: Fifty-six years of accumulated research on clinical versus statistical prediction. *The Counseling Psychologist, 34,* 341–382.

Affonso, D.D., & Domino, G. (1984). Postpartum depression: A review. *Birth: Issues in Perinatal Care and Education, 11,* 231–235.

Agosti, V. (1995). The efficacy of treatments in reducing alcohol consumption: A meta-analysis. *International Journal of the Addictions, 30,* 1067–1077.

Ainsworth, P.B. (1993). *Psychological testing and police applicant selection: Difficulties and dilemmas.* Paper presented to the European Conference on Law and Psychology, Oxford, UK.

Aitken, C.C.G., Connolly, T., Gammerman, A., Zhang, G., Bailey, D., Gordon, R., & Oldfield, R. (1996). Statistical modelling in specific case analysis. *Science & Justice, 36,* 245–256.

Akers, R.L., & Sellers, C.S. (2003). *Criminological theories: Introduction, evaluation, and application.* Los Angeles, CA: Roxbury Publishing Company.

Alarid, L.F., Burton, V.S. Jr., & Cullen, F.T. (2000). Gender and crime among felony offenders: Assessing the generality of social control and differential association theories. *Journal of Research in Crime and Delinquency, 37,* 171–199.

Aldridge, M.L., & Browne, K.D. (2003). Perpetrators of spousal homicide: A review. *Trauma, Violence, and Abuse, 4*(3), 265–276.

Alexander, D.A., Innes, G., Irving, B.L., Sinclair, S.D., & Walker, L.G. (1991). *Health, stress and policing: A study in Grampian policing.* London, UK: The Police Foundation.

Alexander, M.A. (1999). Sexual offender treatment efficacy revisited. *Sexual Abuse: Journal of Research and Treatment, 11,* 101–116.

Alison, L.J., Bennell, C., Mokros, A., & Ormerod, D. (2002). The personality paradox in offender profiling: A theoretical review of the processes involved in deriving background characteristics from crime scene actions. *Psychology, Public Policy, and Law, 8,* 115–135.

Alison, L.J., Smith, M., Eastman, O., & Rainbow, L. (2003). Toulmin's philosophy of argument and its relevance to offender profiling. *Psychology, Crime and Law, 9,* 173–183.

Alison, L.J., Smith, M., & Morgan, K. (2003). Interpreting the accuracy of offender profiles. *Psychology, Crime and Law, 9,* 185–195.

Allan, A., Dawson, D., & Allan, M.M. (2006). Prediction of the risk of male sexual reoffending in Australia. *Australian Psychologist, 41,* 60–68.

Allen, J.J., & Iacono, W.G. (1997). A comparison of methods for the analysis of event-related potentials in deception detection. *Psychophysiology, 34,* 234–240.

Allen, J.J., Iacono, W.G., & Danielson, K.D. (1992). The identification of concealed memories using the event-related potential and implicit behavioral measures: A methodology for prediction in the face of individual differences. *Psychophysiology, 29,* 504–522.

Allen, J.J.B. (2002). The role of psychophysiology in clinical assessment: ERPs in the evaluation of memory. *Psychophysiology, 39,* 261–280.

Alpert, G.P., & Dunham, R. (1999). *The force factor: Measuring and assessing police use of force and suspect resistance.* Washington, DC: U.S. Department of Justice.

Amato, P.R. (2000). The consequences of divorce for adults and children. *Journal of Marriage and the Family, 62,* 1269–1287.

Amato, P.R., & Keith, B. (1991). Parental divorce and the well being of children: A meta-analysis. *Psychological Bulletin, 110,* 26–46.

American Board of Forensic Psychology & American Psychology-Law Society. (1995). Petition for the recognition of a specialty in professional psychology [Online]. Retrieved June 1, 2004, from http://www.unl.edu/apls/petition.PDF.

American Psychiatric Association. (1994). *Diagnostic and statistical manual of mental disorders* (4th ed.). Washington, DC: American Psychiatric Association.

American Psychological Association. (2007). Psychology and the law: *Jenkins v. United States*. Retrieved June 23, 2007, from http://www.apa.org/psyclaw/jenkins.html.

Ammerman, R.T., Cassisi, J.E., Hersen M., & Van Hasselt, V.B. (1986). Consequences of physical abuse and neglect in children. *Clinical Psychology Review, 6,* 291–310.

Andershed, H.A., Gustafson, S.B., Kerr, M., & Hakån, S. (2002). The usefulness of self-reported *psychopathy*-like traits in the study of antisocial behaviour among non-referred adolescents. *European Journal of Personality, 16,* 383–402.

Anderson, C.A., & Dill, F.E. (2000). Video games and aggressive thoughts, feelings, and behavior in the laboratory and in life. *Journal of Personality and Social Psychology, 78,* 772–790.

Anderson, D.E., Ansfield, M., & DePaulo, B.M. (1999). Love's best habit: Deception in the context of relationships. In P. Philippot, R. S. Feldman & E. J. Coats (Eds.), *The social context of nonverbal behavior* (pp. 372–409). New York: Cambridge University Press.

Anderson, M., Gillig, P.M., Sitaker, M., McCloskey, K., Malloy, K., & Grigsby, N. (2003). "Why doesn't she just leave?": A descriptive study of victim reported impediments to her safety. *Journal of Family Violence, 18,* 151–155.

Andrews, D. (2001). Principles of effective correctional programs. In L. Motiuk and R. Serin (Eds.), *Compendium 2000 on effective correctional programming* (pp. 9–17). Ottawa: Correctional Service Canada.

Andrews, D., Dowden, C., & Gendreau, P. (1999). *Clinically relevant and psychologically informed approaches to reduced re-offending: A meta-analytic study of human service, risk, need, responsivity, and other concerns in justice contexts.* Unpublished manuscript, Carleton University.

Andrews, D., Robblee, M., & Saunders, R. (1984). *The sentencing factors inventory.* Toronto: Ontario Ministry of Correctional Services.

Andrews, D.A., & Bonta, J. (1998). *The psychology of criminal conduct* (2nd ed.). Cincinnati, OH: Anderson Publishing Co.

Andrews, D.A., & Bonta, J. (2006). *The psychology of criminal conduct* (4th ed.). Cincinnati, OH: Anderson Publishing.

Andrews, D.A., & Bonta, J.L. (1995). *The Level of Service Inventory-Revised.* Toronto: Multi-Health Systems.

Andrews, D.A., & Dowden, C. (2006). Risk principle of case classification in correctional treatment: A meta-analytic investigation. *International Journal of Offender Therapy and Comparative Criminology, 50,* 88–100.

Andrews, D.A., Zinger, I., Hoge, R.D., Bonta, J., Gendreau, P., & Cullen, F.T. (1990). Does correctional treatment work? A clinically relevant and psychologically informed meta-analysis. *Criminology, 28,* 369–404.

Anshel, M.H. (2000). A conceptual model and implications for coping with stressful events in police work. *Criminal Justice and Behavior, 27,* 375–400.

Anson, R.H., & Bloom, M.E. (1988). Police stress in an occupational context. *Journal of Police Science and Administration, 16,* 229–235.

Antonowicz, D., & Ross, R. (1994). Essential components of successful rehabilitation programs for offenders. *International Journal of Offender Therapy and Comparative Criminology, 38,* 97–104.

Archer, J. (2002). Sex differences in physically aggressive acts between heterosexual partners: A meta-analytic review. *Aggression and Violent Behavior, 7,* 313–351.

Arditti, J.A. (1999). Rethinking relationships between divorced mothers and their children: Capitalizing on family strengths. *Family Relations, 48,* 109–119.

Artwohl, A. (2002). Perceptual and memory distortion during officer-involved shootings. *FBI Law Enforcement Bulletin, October,* 18–24.

Ascione, F.R. (1998). Battered women's reports of their partners' and their children's cruelty to animals. *Journal of Emotional Abuse, 1,* 119–133.

Ascione, F.R., Weber, C.V., Thompson, T.M., Heath, J. Maruyama, M., & Hayashi, K. (2007) Battered pets and domestic violence: Animal abuse reported by women experiencing intimate violence and by nonabused women. *Violence Against Women, 13,* 354–373.

Ash, P., Slora, K.B., & Britton, C.F. (1990). Police agency officer selection practices. *Journal of Police Science and Administration, 17,* 258–269.

Atkinson, J.L. (1996). Female sex offenders: A literature review. *Forum on Corrections Research, 8,* 39–43.

Babcock, J.C., Green, C.E., & Robie, C. (2004). Does batterers' treatment work? A meta-analytic review of domestic violence treatment. *Clinical Psychology Review, 23,* 1023–1053.

Babiak, P. (1995). When psychopaths go to work: A case study of an industrial psychopath. *Applied Psychology: An International Review, 44,* 171–188.

Babiak, P. (2000). Psychopathic manipulation at work. In C.B. Gacono (Ed.), *Clinical and forensic assessment of psychopathy: A practitioner's guide* (pp. 287–311). Mahwah, NJ: Lawrence Erlbaum Associates, Publishers.

Baeber, R.J., Marston, A., Michelli, J., & Mills, M.J. (1985). A brief test for measuring malingering in schizophrenic individuals. *American Journal of Psychiatry, 142,* 1478–1481.

Baer, R.A., Wetter, M.W., & Berry, D.T.T. (1995). Sensitivity of MMP-2 validity scales to underreporting of symptoms. *Psychological Assessment, 7,* 419–423.

Bagby, R.M., Nicholson, R.A., Bacchiochi, J.R., Ryder, A.B., & Bury, A.S. (2002). The predictive capacity of MMPI-2 and PAI validity scales and indexes of coached and uncoached feigning. *Journal of Personality Assessment, 78,* 69–86.

Bala, N. (1999a). Child witnesses in the Canadian criminal courts. *Psychology, Public Policy, and Law, 5,* 323–354.

Bala, N. (1999b). *The best interests of the child in the post-modern era: A central but paradoxical concept.* Paper presented at the Law Society of Upper Canada Special lectures 2000: Family Law. Toronto, Ontario.

Bala, N., Lindsay, R.C.L., Lee, K., & Talwar, V. (September, 2002). The legal competence of child witnesses: Assessing present practices and the need for law reform. Presentation at the Faculty of Law, Queen's University, Kingston, Ontario, Canada. Retrieved June 24, 2004, from http://qsilver.queensu.ca/law/witness/childcompsept20001_files.

Ball, E.M., Young, D., Dotson, L.A., & Brothers, L.T. (1994). Factors associated with dangerous behavior in forensic inpatients: Results from a pilot study. *Bulletin of the American Academy of Psychiatry and the Law, 22,* 605–620.

Bandura, A. (1965). Influence of models' reinforcement contingencies on the acquisition of imitative responses. *Journal of Personality and Social Psychology, 1,* 589–595.

Bandura, A. (1973). *Aggression: A social learning analysis.* Englewood Cliffs, NJ: Prentice-Hall.

Bandura, A. (1977). *Social learning theory.* New York: Prentice-Hall.

Banning, A. (1989). Mother–son incest: Confronting a prejudice. *Child Abuse and Neglect, 13,* 563–570.

Barbaree, H. (1997). Evaluating treatment efficacy with sexual offenders: The insensitivity of recidivism studies to treatment effects. *Journal of Research and Treatment, 9,* 111–128.

Barbaree, H.E. (1991). Denial and minimization among sex offenders: Assessment and treatment outcome. *Forum on Corrections Research, 3,* 300–333.

Barbaree, H.E., Langton, C.M., & Peacock, E.J. (2006). The factor structure of static actuarial items: Its relation to prediction. *Sexual Abuse: A Journal of Research and Treatment, 18,* 207–226.

Barbaree, H.E., Seto, M.C., Langton, C.M., & Peacock, E.J. (2001). Evaluating the predictive accuracy of six risk assessment instruments for adult sex offenders. *Criminal Justice and Behavior, 28,* 490–521.

Barbaree, H.E., Seto, M.C., Serin, R., Amos, N., & Preston, D. (1994). Comparisons between sexual and nonsexual rapist subtypes: Sexual arousal to rape, offense precursors, and offense characteristics. *Criminal Justice and Behavior, 21,* 95–114.

Barkley, R.A. (1991). Attention deficit hyperactivity disorder. *Psychiatric Annals, 21,* 725–733.

Barkley, R.A. (1997). Attention-deficit/hyperactivity disorder. In E.J. Mash & L.G. Terdal (Eds.), *Assessment of childhood disorders* (pp. 71–129). New York: Guilford Press.

Bartholow, B.D., Bushman, B.J., & Sestir, M. A. (2006). Chronic violent video game exposure and desensitization to violence: Behavioral and event-related brain potential data. *Journal of Experimental Social Psychology, 42,* 532–539.

Baron, R.A., & Bryne, D. (1991). *Social psychology: Understanding human interaction* (6th ed.). Toronto: Allyn & Bacon.

Barthlow, B.D., Bushman, B.J., & Sestir, M. A. (2006). Chronic violent video game exposure and desensitization to violence: Behavioral and event-related brain potential data. *Journal of Experimental Social Psychology, 42,* 532–539.

Bartosh, D.L., Garby, T., Lewis, D., & Gray, S. (2003). Differences in the predictive validity of actuarial risk assessments in relation to sex offender type. *International Journal of Offender Therapy and Comparative Criminology, 47,* 422–438.

Barrowcliff, A.L., & Haddock, G. (2006). The relationship between command hallucinations and factors of compliance: A critical review of the literature. *The Journal of Forensic Psychiatry & Psychology, 17,* 266–298.

Bartol, C.R., & Bartol, A.M. (1994). *Psychology and law* (2nd ed.). Pacific Grove, CA: Brooks/Cole Publishing Company.

Bartol, C.R., & Bartol, A.M. (2004). *Introduction to forensic psychology.* London: Sage Publications.

Bartol, C.R., & Bartol, A.M. (2006). History of forensic psychology. In I.B. Weiner & A. Hess (Eds.), *Handbook of forensic psychology,* 3rd ed. (pp. 3–27). New York: John Wiley & Sons.

Beck, K.A., & Ogloff, J.R.P. (1995). Child abuse reporting in British Columbia: Psychologists' knowledge of and compliance with the reporting law. *Professional Psychology: Research and Practice, 26,* 245–251.

Beck, N.C., Menditto, A.A., Baldwin, L., Angelone, E., & Maddox, M. (1991). Reduced frequency of aggressive behavior in forensic patients in a social learning program. *Hospital and Community Psychiatry, 42,* 750–752.

Behrman, B.W., & Davey, S.L. (2001). Eyewitness identification in actual criminal cases: An archival analysis. *Law and Human Behavior, 25,* 475–491.

Bekerian, D.A., & Dennett, J.L. (1993). The cognitive interview technique: Reviving the issues. *Applied Cognitive Psychology, 7,* 275–298.

Belknap, J. (2001). *The invisible woman: Gender, crime, and justice* (2nd ed.). Cincinnati, OH: Wadsworth.

Benaquisto, L. (2000). Inattention to sanctions in criminal conduct. In R. Silverman, T. Teevan, & V. Sacco (Eds.), *Crime in Canadian society* (pp. 203–215). Toronto: Harcourt Brace and Co.

Benda, B.B. (2005). Gender differences in life-course theory of recidivism: A survival analysis. *International Journal of Offender Therapy and Comparative Criminology, 49,* 325–342.

Benjamin, L.T., & Crouse, E.M. (2002). The American Psychological Association's response to *Brown v. Board of Education:* The case of Kenneth B. Clark. *American Psychologist, 57,* 38–50.

Bennell, C., & Canter, D.V. (2002). Linking commercial burglaries by modus operandi: Tests using regression and ROC analysis. *Science & Justice, 42,* 153–164.

Bennell, C., & Jones, N.J. (2005). Between a ROC and a hard place: A method for linking serial burglaries using an offender's modus operandi. *Journal of Investigative Psychology and Offender Profiling, 2,* 23–41.

Bennell, C., Jones, N.J., Taylor, P.J., & Snook, B. (2006). Validities and abilities in criminal profiling: A critique of the studies conducted by Richard Kocsis and his colleagues. *International Journal of Offender Therapy and Comparative Criminology, 50,* 344–360.

Bennell, C., Taylor, P.J., & Snook, B. (2007). Clinical versus actuarial geographic profiling strategies: A review of the research. *Police Practice and Research, 8,* 335–345.

Bennett, L.W., Stoops, C., Call, C., & Flett, H. (2007). Program completion and re-arrest in a batterer intervention system. *Research on Social Work Practice, 17*(1), 42–54.

Ben-Porath, Y.S. (1994). The ethical dilemma of coached malingering research. *Psychological Assessment, 6,* 14–15.

Ben-Shakhar, G., & Elaad, E. (2003). The validity of psychophysiological detection of information with the guilty knowledge test: A meta-analytic review. *Journal of Applied Psychology, 88,* 131–151.

Ben-Shakhar, G., & Furedy, J. J. (1990). *Theories and applications in the detection of deception: Psychophysiological and cultural perspectives.* New York: Springer-Verlag.

Bilby, C., Brooks-Gordon, B., & Wells, H. (2006). A systematic review of psychological interventions for sexual offenders II: Quasi-experimental and qualitative data. *Journal of Forensic Psychiatry and Psychology, 17,* 467–484.

Binet, A. (1900). *La suggestibilité.* Paris: Schleicher Freres.

Birch, D.E. (1992). Duty to protect: Update and Canadian perspective. *Canadian Psychology, 33,* 94–101.

Birkenmayer, A., & Roberts, J.V. (1997). Sentencing in adult provincial courts. *Juristat, 17,* 1–15.

Bittner, E. (1967). Police discretion in emergency apprehension of mentally ill persons. *Social Problems, 14,* 278–292.

Blackman, J. (1990). Emerging images of severely battered women and the criminal justice system. *Behavioral Sciences and the Law, 8,* 121–130.

Blair, R.J.R. (2006). Subcortical brain systems in psychopathy: The amygdala and associated structures. In C.J. Patrick (Ed.), *Handbook of psychopathy* (pp. 296–312). New York: Guilford Press.

Blanchette, K. (2001). *Classifying female offenders for effective intervention: Application of the case-based principles of risk and need.* Unpublished Comprehensive Paper, Carleton University, Ottawa.

Blanchette, K., & Brown, S.L. (2006). *The assessment and treatment of women offenders: An integrative perspective.* Wiley Series in Forensic Clinical Psychology. Chichester: John Wiley & Sons.

Bland, R., Newman, S., Dyck, R., & Orn, H. (1990). Prevalence of psychiatric disorders and suicide attempts in a prison population. *The Canadian Journal of Psychiatry, 35,* 407–413.

Bland, R., Orn, H., & Newman, S. (1988). Lifetime prevalence of psychiatric disorders in Edmonton. *Acta Psychiatrica Scandinavica, 77,* 24–32.

Bland, R.C., & Orn, H. (1986). Family violence and psychiatric disorder. *Canadian Journal of Psychiatry, 31,* 129–137.

Blatchford, C. (2002, April 19). Dooley parents convicted of murder. *National Post.* Retrieved May 14, 2004, from http://ww.canada.com/national/features/dooleytrial/index.html.

Blatchford, C. (2003, February 21). Fantino report says allegations of racial profiling are "junk science"—Study finds races treated equally. *National Post,* p. A1.

Blonigen, D.M., Carlson, S.R., Krueger, R.F., & Patrick, C.J. (2003). A twin study of self-reported psychopathic personality traits. *Personality and Individual Differences, 35,* 179–197.

Blonigen, D.M., Hicks, B.M., Krueger, R.F., Patrick, C.J. & Iacono, W.G. (2005). Psychopathic personality traits: Heritability and genetic overlap with internalizing and externalizing psychopathology. *Psychological Medicine, 35,* 637–648.

Bloom, H., & Schneider, R.D. (2007). *Mental health courts: Decriminalizing the mentally ill.* Toronto: Irwin Law.

Blumstein, A., & Cohen, J. (1987). Characterizing criminal careers. *Science, 237,* 985–991.

Boaz, T.L., Perry, N.W., Raney, G., Fieschler, I.S., & Shuman, D. (1991). Detection of guilty knowledge with event related potentials. *Journal of Applied Psychology, 76,* 788–795.

Boe, R. (2000). Aboriginal inmates: Demographic trends and projections. *Forum on Corrections Research, 12,* 7–9.

Boe, R. (2002). Future demographic trends may help Canada's Aboriginal youth. *Forum on Corrections, 14,* 13–16.

Bohner, G., Siebler, F., Sturm, S., Effler, D., Litters, M., Reinhard, M., & Rutz, S. (1998). Rape myth acceptance and accessibility of the gender category. *Group Processes and Intergroup Relations, 1,* 67–79.

Bohus, M., Haaf, B., Stiglmayr, C., Pohl, U., Boehme, R., & Linehan, M.M. (2000). Evaluation of behavioral therapy for borderline personality disorder: A prospective study. *Behavior Research & Therapy, 38,* 875–887.

Bok, S. (1978). *Lying: Moral choice in public and private life*. London: Quartet Books.

Bonazzoli, M.J. (1998). Jury selection and bias: Debunking invidious stereotypes through science. *Quinnipiac Law Review, 18*, 247–305.

Bonnie, R.J., & Grisso, T. (2000). Adjudicative competence and youthful offenders. In T. Grisso & R.G. Schwartz (Eds.), *Youth on trial: A developmental perspective on juvenile justice* (pp. 73–103). Chicago: University of Chicago Press.

Bonta, J. (1989). Native inmates: Institutional response, risk, and needs. *Canadian Journal of Criminology, 31*, 49–62.

Bonta, J. (2002). Offender risk assessment: Guidelines for selection and use. *Criminal Justice and Behavior, 29*, 355–379.

Bonta, J., LaPrairie, C., & Wallace-Capretta, S. (1997). Risk prediction and re-offending: Aboriginal and non-aboriginal offenders. *Canadian Journal of Criminology, 39*, 127–144.

Bonta, J., Pang, B., & Wallace-Capretta, S. (1995). Predictors of recidivism among incarcerated female offenders. *Prison Journal, 75*, 277–294.

Bonta, J., Zinger, I., Harris, A., & Carriere, D. (1998). The dangerous offender provisions: Are they targeting the right offenders? *Canadian Journal of Criminology, 40*, 377–400.

Bonta, J.L., Harman, W.G., Hann, R.G., & Cormier, R.B. (1996). The prediction of recidivism among federally sentenced offenders: A re-validation of the SIR scale. *Canadian Journal of Criminology, 38*, 61–79.

Bonta, J.L., Law, M., & Hanson, R.K. (1998). The prediction of criminal and violent recidivism among mentally disordered offenders: A meta-analysis. *Psychological Bulletin, 123*, 123–142.

Boothby, J. & Clements, C.B. (2000). A national survey of correctional psychologists. *Criminal Justice and Behavior, 27*, 715–731.

Borum, R. (1996). Improving the clinical practice of violence risk assessment: Technology, guidelines and training. *American Psychologist, 51*, 945–956.

Borum, R., Otto, R., & Golding, S. (1993). Improving clinical judgment and decision making in forensic evaluation. *Journal of Psychiatry and Law, 21*, 35–76.

Bowen, E., & Gilchrist, E. (2006). Predicting dropout of court-mandated treatment in a British sample of domestic violence offenders. *Psychology, Crime and Law, 12*, 573–587.

Bowker, L. (1993). A battered woman's problems are social, not psychological. In R. Gelles & D. Loseke (Eds.), *Current controversies on family violence* (pp. 154–165). Newbury Park, CA: Sage.

Bowlby, J. (1944). Forty-four juvenile thieves. *International Journal of Psychoanalysis, 25*, 1–57.

Boyd, C. (2003, July 17). Girl's abduction exposes extent of internet luring. *The Globe and Mail*. Retrieved April 30, 2004, from http://www.globeandmail.com.

Bradfield, A.L., Wells, G.L., & Olson, E.A. (2002). The damaging effect of confirming feedback on the relation between eyewitness certainty and identification accuracy. *Journal of Applied Psychology, 87*, 112–120.

Bradford, J.M., & Pawlak, A. (1993). Effects of cyproterone acetate on sexual arousal patterns of pedophiles. *Archives of Sexual Behavior, 22*, 629–641.

Brainerd C.J., & Reyna, V.F. (2004). Fuzzy-trace theory and memory development. *Developmental Review, 24*, 396–439.

Brame, B., Nagin, D.S., & Tremblay, R.E. (2001). Developmental trajectories of physical aggression from school entry to late adolescence. *Journal of Child Psychology and Psychiatry, 42*, 503–512.

Breslin, N.A. (1992). Treatment of schizophrenia: Current practice and future promise. *Hospital and Community Psychiatry, 43*, 877–885.

Brewer, N., Potter, R., Fisher, R.P., Bond, N., & Luszcz (1999). Beliefs and data on the relationship between consistency and accuracy of eyewitness testimony. *Applied Cognitive Psychology, 13*, 297–313.

Brewster, A.L., Nelson, J.P., & Hymel, K.P. (1998). Victim, perpetrator, family, and incident characteristics of 32 infant maltreatment deaths in the United States Air Force. *Child Abuse and Neglect, 22*, 91–101.

Brigham, J.C. (1999). What is forensic psychology, anyway? *Law and Human Behavior, 23*, 273–298.

British Columbia Ministry of Attorney General. (2004). *Policy on the criminal justice system response to violence against women and children: Violence against women in relationships policy*. Victoria, BC: British Columbia Ministry of Attorney General.

Brodsky, S. (1991). *Testifying in court: Guidelines and maxims for the expert witness*. Washington, DC: American Psychological Association.

Brodsky, S. (1999). *The expert witness: More maxims and guidelines for testifying in court*. Washington, DC: American Psychological Association.

Brooks-Gordon, B., Bilby, C., & Wells, H. (2006). A systematic review of psychological interventions for sexual offenders I: Randomised control trials. *Journal of Forensic Psychiatry and Psychology, 17*, 442–466.

Brooks, N. (1983). *Police guidelines: Pretrial identification procedures*. Ottawa: Law Reform Commission.

Brown, D., & Pipe, M-E. (2003). Variations on a technique: Enhancing children's recall using narrative elaboration training. *Applied Cognitive Psychology, 17*, 377–399.

Brown, D., Scheflin, A.W., & Hammond, D.C. (1998). *Memory, trauma treatment, and the law*. New York: Norton.

Brown, G.R. (2004). Gender as a factor in the response of the law-enforcement systems to violence against partners. *Sexuality and Culture, 9*, 1–87.

Brown, J.M., & Campbell, E.A. (1994). *Stress and policing: Sources and strategies*. New York. John Wiley & Sons.

Brown, S.L., & Forth, A.E. (1997). Psychopathy and sexual assault: Static risk factors, emotional precursors, and rapist subtypes. *Journal of Consulting and Clinical Psychology, 65,* 848–857.

Browne, A. (1987). *When battered women kill.* New York: Free Press.

Browne, A., & Finkelhor, D. (1986). Impact of child sexual abuse: A review of the research. *Psychological Bulletin, 99,* 66–77.

Browne, A., Miller, B., & Maguin, E. (1999). Prevalence and severity of lifetime physical and sexual victimization among incarcerated women. *International Journal and Psychiatry, 22,* 301–322.

Bruck, M., & Ceci, S.J. (1999). The suggestibility of children's memory. *Annual Review of Psychology, 50,* 419–439.

Bruck, M., Ceci, S.J., & Hembrooke, H. (1998). Reliability and credibility of young children's reports. From research to policy and practice. *American Psychologist, 53,* 136–51.

Buck, S.M., Warren, A.R., Betman, S., & Brigham, J.C. (2002). Age differences in Criteria-Based Content Analysis scores in typical child sexual abuse interviews. *Journal of Applied Developmental Psychology, 23,* 267–283.

Bull, R., & Clifford, B.R. (1984). Earwitness voice recognition accuracy. In G. Wells, & E. Loftus (Eds.), *Eyewitness testimony, psychological perspectives* (pp. 92–123). Cambridge: Cambridge University Press.

Bumby, K.M., & Hansen, D.J. (1997). Intimacy deficits, fear of intimacy, and loneliness among sexual offenders. *Criminal Justice and Behavior, 24,* 315–331.

Burgess, A.W., & Holmstrom, L.L. (1974). Rape trauma syndrome. *American Journal of Psychiatry, 131,* 981–986.

Burke, R.J. (1993). Work-family stress, conflict, coping, and burnout in police officers. *Stress Medicine, 9,* 171–180.

Burt, M.R. (1980). Cultural myths and supports for rape. *Journal of Personality and Social Psychology, 38,* 217–230.

Bushman, B.J., & Anderson, C.A. (2001). Media violence and the American public: Scientific facts versus media misinformation. *American Psychologist, 56,* 477–489.

Bushman, B.J., Huesmann, L.R. (2006). Short-term and long-term effects of violent media on aggression in children and adults. *Archives of Pediatrics and Adolescent Medicine, 160,* 348–352.

Butcher, J.N., Dahlstrom, W.G., Graham, J.R., Tellegen, A., & Kaemmer, B. (1989). *MMPI-2: Manual for administration and scoring.* Minneapolis: University of Minnesota Press.

Cadoret, R.J., & Cain, C. (1980). Sex differences in predictors of antisocial behavior in adoptees. *Archives of General Psychiatry, 37,* 1171–1175.

Caldwell, M.F., McCormick, D.J., Umstead, D., & Van Rybroek, G.J. (2007). Evidence of treatment progress and therapeutic outcomes among adolescents with psychopathic features. *Criminal Justice and Behavior, 34,* 573–587.

Caldwell, M.F., Skeem, J., Salekin, R. & Van Rybroek, G. (2006). Treatment response of adolescent offenders with psychopathy-like features. *Criminal Justice and Behavior, 33, 5,* 571–596.

Caldwell, R.M., Silverman, J., Lefforge, N., & Silver, N.C. (2004). Adjudicated Mexican American adolescents: The effects of familial emotional support on self-esteem, emotional well-being, and delinquency. *The American Journal of Family Therapy, 32,* 55–69.

Campbell, C. (1976). Portrait of a mass killer. *Psychology Today, 9,* 110–119.

Campbell, C., Mackenzie, D., & Robinson, J. (1987). Female offenders: Criminal behaviour and gender-role identity. *Psychological Reports, 60,* 867–873.

Campbell, D. (2004, April 24). Sportscaster's killer wants release from custody. *Ottawa Citizen,* Section E, p.1, and 2.

Campbell, J.C. (1986). Nursing assessment for risk of homicide with battering women. *Advances in Nursing Science, 8,* 36–51.

Campbell, J.C., Webster, D., & Koziol-McLain, J. (2003). Risk factors for femicide in abusive relationships: Results from a multisite case control study. *American Journal of Public Health, 93,* 1089–1097.

Campbell, M.A., Porter, S., & Santor, D. (2004). Psychopathic traits in adolescent offenders: An evaluation of criminal history, clinical, and psychosocial correlates. *Behavioral Sciences and the Law, 22,* 23–47.

Canadian Association of Chiefs of Police. (2007). The national use of force framework. Retrieved May 25, 2007, from http://www.cacp.ca/english/committees/download.asp?id=169.

Canadian Centre for Justice Statistics. (1997, February). Sentencing in adult provincial courts—A study of nine Canadian jurisdictions. *Juristat, 17.*

Canter, D.V. (1994). *Criminal shadows.* London, UK: Harper Collins.

Canter, D.V. (2000). Offender profiling and criminal differentiation. *Legal and Criminological Psychology, 5,* 23–46.

Canter, D.V., & Alison, L.J. (Eds.) (1999). *Interviewing and deception.* Aldershot, UK: Ashgate Publishing.

Canter, D.V., & Wentink, N. (2004). An empirical test of Holmes and Holmes's serial murder typology. *Criminal Justice and Behavior, 31,* 489–515.

Canter, D.V., Alison, L.J., Alison, E. & Wentink, N., (2004). The organized/ disorganized typology of serial murder: Myth or model? *Psychology, Public Policy, and Law, 10,* 293–320.

Canter, D.V., Coffey, T., Huntley, M., & Missen, C. (2000). Predicting serial killers' home base using a decision support system. *Journal of Quantitative Criminology, 16,* 457–478.

Caprara, G.V., Barbaranelli, C., & Pastorelli, C. (2001). Facing guilt: Role of negative affectivity, need for reparation, and fear of punishment in leading to prosocial behaviour and aggression. *European Journal of Personality, 15*, 219–237.

Carney, M., Buttell, F., & Dutton, D. (2007). Women who perpetrate intimate partner violence: A review of the literature with recommendations for treatment. *Aggression and Violent Behavior, 12*, 108–115.

Cassell, P.G. (1998). Protecting the innocent from false confessions and lost confessions—and from Miranda. *Journal of Criminal Law and Criminology, 88*, 497–556.

Cattell, J.M. (1895). Measurements of the accuracy of recollection. *Science, 2*, 761–766.

Cauffman, E., & Steinberg, L. (2000). (Im)maturity of judgment of adolescence: Why adolescents may be less culpable than adults. *Behavioral Sciences & the Law, 18*, 741–760.

Cavanaugh, M.M. & Gelles, R.J. (2005). The utility of male domestic violence offender typologies: New directions for research, policy, and practice. *Journal of Interpersonal Violence, 20*, 155–166.

CBC News. (2003, November 13). Michaud guilty on both counts. *CBC Online News.* Retrieved June 1, 2004, from http://ottawa.cbc.ca/features/2003/nov13_2.html.

CBC News. (2003, October 23). Shoot her again, teen says co-accused ordered. *CBC News.* Retrieved June 1, 2004, from http://www.cbc.ca/stories.2003/10/23/dagenais_trial 031023.

CBC News, (2007, August 28), Defence arguments in Pickton trial delayed until Sept. 4. Retrieved September 5, 2007, from http://www.cbc.ca/canada/british-columbia/story/ 2007/08/28/bc-pickton.html.

CBC News Ottawa. (2002, November 26). First-degree murder charges laid in Dagenais case. *CBC News Ottawa.* Retrieved June 1, 2004, from http://ottawa.cbc.ca/newsinreview/ nov/nov26.html.

CBC News Ottawa. (2003, December 9). Teenager gets nine years in Dagenais muders. *CBC News Ottawa.* Retrieved June 1, 2004, from http://www.cbc.ca/canada/ottawa/story/ 2003/12/09/ot_dagenais20031209.html.

Ceci, S.J., & Bruck, M. (1993). The suggestibility of the child witness: A historical review and synthesis. *Psychological Bulletin, 113*, 403–439.

Cervone, D., & Shoda, Y. (Eds.) (1999). *The coherence of personality: Social-cognitive bases of consistency, variability and organization.* New York: Guilford Press.

Chadee, D. (1996). Race, trial evidence and jury decision making. *Caribbean Journal of Criminology and Social Psychology, 1*, 59–86.

Chaiken, J. M, & Chaiken, M.R. (1983). Crime rates and the active offender. In J.Q. Wilson (Ed.). *Crime and public policy* (pp. 203–229). New Brunswick, OH: Transaction Books.

Chapman, L.J., & Chapman, J.P. (1967). Genesis of popular but erroneous psychodiagnostic observations. *Journal of Abnormal Psychology, 74*, 193–204.

Cheung, P.T.K. (1986). Maternal filicide in Hong Kong. *Medicine, Science, and Law, 26*, 185–192.

Chiroro, P., & Valentine, T. (1995). An investigation of the contact hypothesis of the own-race bias in face recognition. *Quarterly Journal of Experimental Psychology, 48*, 879–894.

Cirincione, C., Steadman, H.J., Clark-Robbins, P.C., & Monahan, J. (1992). Schizophrenia as a contingent risk factor for criminal violence. *International Journal of Law and Psychiatry, 15*, 347–358.

City of Vancouver Police Department. (2007). Behind the badge. Retrieved May 25, 2007, from http://www.city. vancouver.bc.ca/police/recruiting/badge.htm.

Cleckley, H.R. (1976). *The mask of sanity* (5th ed.). St. Louis, MO: Mosby.

Clifford, B.R. (1980). Voice identification by human listeners: On earwitness reliability. *Law and Human Behavior, 4*, 373–394.

Cochrane, R.E., Tett, R.P., & Vandecreek, L. (2003). Psychological testing and the selection of police officers: A national survey. *Criminal Justice and Behavior, 30*, 511–537.

Cocozza, J.J., Melick, M.E., & Steadman, H.J. (1978). Trends in violent crime among ex-mental patients. *Criminology: An Interdisciplinary Journal, 16*, 317–334.

Cocozza, J.J., & Steadman, H.J. (1978). Prediction in psychiatry: An example of misplaced confidence in experts. *Social Problems, 25*, 265–276.

Cohen, A.J., Adler, N., Kaplan, S.J., Pelcovitz, D., & Mandel, F.G. (2002). Interactional effects of marital status and physical abuse on adolescent psychopathology. *Child Abuse and Neglect, 26*, 277–288.

Coie, J.D., Belding, M., & Underwood, M. (1988). Aggression and peer rejection in childhood. In B.B. Lahey & A.E. Kazdin (Eds.), *Advances in clinical child psychology*, Vol. II (pp. 125–158). New York: Plenum.

Coie, J.D., Lochman, J.E., Terry, R., & Hyman, C. (1992). Predicting early adolescent disorder from childhood aggression and peer rejection. *Journal of Consulting and Clinical Psychology, 60*, 783–792.

Cole, W.G., & Loftus, E.F. (1979). Incorporating new information into memory. *American Journal of Psychology, 92*, 413–425.

Collins, P.I., Johnson, G.F., Choy, A., Davidson, K.T., & Mackay, R.E. (1998). Advances in violent crime analysis and law enforcement: The Canadian violent crime linkage analysis system. *Journal of Government Information, 25*, 277–284.

Conaway, L.P., & Hansen, D.J. (1989). Social behavior of physically abused and neglected children: A critical review. *Clinical Psychology Review, 9*, 627–652.

Connolly, D.A., & Read, J.D. (2006). Delayed prosecutions of historic child sexual abuse: Analyses of 2064 Canadian criminal complaints. *Law and Human Behavior, 30*, 409–434.

Cook, S., & Wilding, J. (1997). Earwitness testimony 2: Voices, faces, and context. *Applied Cognitive Psychology, 11,* 527–541.

Cooke, D.J., & Michie, C. (2001). Refining the construct of psychopathy: Towards a hierarchical model. *Psychological Assessment, 13,* 171–188.

Cooper, J., Bennett, E.A., & Sukel, H.L. (1996). Complex scientific testimony: How do jurors make decisions? *Law and Human Behavior, 20,* 379–394.

Copson, G. (1995). *Coals to Newcastle? Part 1: A study of offender profiling.* London, UK: Home Office.

Corder, B.F., Ball, B.C., Haizlip, T.M., Rollins, R., & Beaumont, R. (1976). Adolescent parricide: A comparison with other adolescent murder. *American Journal of Psychiatry, 133,* 957–961.

Cornell, D.G., & Hawk, G.L. (1989). Clinical presentation of malingerers diagnosed by experienced forensic psychologists. *Law and Human Behavior, 13,* 374–383.

Cornell, D.G., Benedek, E.P., & Benedek, D.M. (1987). Characteristics of adolescents charged with homicide: Review of 72 cases. *Behavioral Sciences and the Law, 5,* 11–23.

Cornell, D.G., Warren, J., Hawk, G., Stafford, E., Oram, G., & Pine, D. (1996). Psychopathy in instrumental and reactive violent offenders. *Journal of Consulting and Clinical Psychology, 64,* 783–790.

Corrado, R.R., Vincent, G.M., Hart, S.D., & Cohen, I.M. (2004). Predictive validity of the Psychopathy Checklist: Youth Version for general and violent recidivism. *Behavioral Sciences and the Law, 22,* 5–22.

Correctional Service Canada. (1989). *Mental health survey of federally sentenced female offenders at Prison for Women.* Unpublished raw data.

Correctional Service Canada. (2004). *Healing lodges for Aboriginal federal offenders.* Ottawa: Correctional Service Canada.

Cortina, L.M., & Kubiak, S.P. (2006). Gender and posttraumatic stress: Sexual violence as an explanation for women's increased risk. *Journal of Abnormal Psychology, 115,* 753–759.

Cortoni, F., & Hanson, R.K. (2005). *A review of recidivism rates of adult female sexual offenders.* User Report-R169. Ottawa: Correctional Services of Canada.

Cottle, C.C., Lee, R.J., & Heilbrun, K. (2001). The prediction of criminal recidivism in juveniles: A meta-analysis. *Criminal Justice and Behavior, 28,* 367–394.

Coulson, G., Ilacqua, G., Nutbrown, V., Giulekas, D., & Cudjoe, F. (1996). Predictive utility of the LSI for incarcerated female offenders. *Criminal Justice and Behavior, 23,* 427–439.

Coy, E., Speltz, M.L., DeKlyen, M., & Jones, K. (2001). Social-cognitive processes in preschool boys with and without oppositional defiant disorder. *Journal of Abnormal Child Psychology, 29,* 107–119.

Craig, L.A., Browne, K.D., & Stringer, I. (2004). Comparing sex offender risk assessment measures on a UK sample. *International Journal of Offender Therapy and Comparative Criminology, 48,* 7–27.

Craissati, J., & Beech, A. (2005). Risk prediction and failure in a complete urban sample of sex offenders. *The Journal of Forensic Psychiatry & Psychology, 16,* 24–40.

Crawford, M., & Gartner, R. (1992). *Women killing: Intimate femicide in Ontario, 1974–1990.* Women's Directorate, Ministry of Social Services, Toronto, Ontario.

Crick, N.R., & Dodge, K.A. (1994). A review and reformulation of social information-processing mechanisms in children's social adjustment. *Psychological Bulletin, 115,* 74–101.

Cross, J.F., Cross, J., & Daly, J. (1971). Sex, race, age, and beauty as factors in recognition of faces. *Perception and Psychophysics, 10,* 393–396.

Cross, T.P., & Saxe, L. (2001). Polygraph testing and sexual abuse: The lure of the magic lasso. *Child Maltreatment: Journal of the American Professional Society of the Abuse of Children, 6,* 195–206.

Crutcher, N., & Trevethan, S. (2002). An examination of healing lodges for federal offenders in Canada. *Forum on Corrections Research, 14,* 52–54.

Cullen, F., & Gendreau, P. (2000). Assessing correctional rehabilitation: Policy, practice, and prospects. In J. Horney (Ed.), *NIJ Criminal justice 2000: Changes in decision-making and discretion in the criminal justice system* (pp. 109–175). Washington, DC: U.S. National Institute of Justice.

Cummings, E.M., Davies, P.T., & Campbell, S.B. (2000). *Developmental psychopathology and family process: Theory, research, and clinical implications.* New York: The Guilford Press.

Cutler, B.L., & Penrod, S.D. (1989a). Forensically relevant moderators of the relationship between eyewitness identification accuracy and confidence. *Journal of Applied Psychology, 74,* 650–652.

Cutler, B.L., & Penrod, S.D. (1989b). Moderators of the confidence-accuracy relation in face recognition: The role of information processing and base rates. *Applied Cognitive Psychology, 3,* 95–107.

Cutler, B.L., Fisher, R.P., & Chicvara, C.L. (1989). Eyewitness identification from live versus videotaped lineups. *Forensic Reports, 2,* 93–106.

Dahle, K.P. (2006). Strengths and limitations of actuarial prediction of criminal reoffence in a German prison sample: A comparative study of LSI-R, HCR-20 and PCL-R. *International Journal of Law and Psychiatry, 29,* 431–442.

Dalby, J.T. (2006). The case of Daniel McNaughton: Let's get the story straight. *American Journal of Forensic Psychiatry, 27,* 17–32.

Daly, M., & Wilson, M. (1988). Evolutionary social psychology and family homicide. *Science, 242,* 519–524.

Daly, M., & Wilson, M.I. (1982). Homicide and kinship. *American Anthropologist, 84,* 372–378.

Daly, M., & Wilson, M.I. (1996). Violence against stepchildren. *Current Directions in Psychological Science, 5,* 77–81.

Darby, P.J., Allan, W.D., Kashani, J.H., Hartke, K.L., & Reid, J.C. (1998). Analysis of 112 juveniles who committed homicide: Characteristics and a closer look at family abuse. *Journal of Family Violence, 13,* 365–375.

Davies, G., Tarrant, A., & Flin, R. (1989). Close encounters of the witness kind: Children's memory for a simulated health inspection. *British Journal of Psychology, 80,* 415–429.

Davies, G.M., Stevenson-Robb, Y., & Flin, R. (1988). Telling tales out of school: Children's memory for an unexpected event. In M. Gruneberg, P. Morris, & R. Sykes (Eds.), *Practical aspects of memory* (pp. 122–127). Chichester: John Wiley & Sons.

Davis, G.E., & Leitenberg, H. (1987). Adolescent sex offenders. *Psychological Bulletin, 101,* 417–427.

Decaire, M.W. (2004). Differences between forensic disciplines. Retrieved June 1, 2004, from http://flash.lakeheadu.ca/~pals/forensics/special.htm.

DeFronzo, J., Ditta, A., Hannon, L., & Prochnow, J. (2007). Male serial homicide: The influence of cultural and structural variables. *Homicide Studies: An Interdisciplinary & International Journal, 11,* 3–14.

Deitz, S.R., Blackwell, K.T., Daley, P.C., & Bentley, B.J. (1982). Measurement of empathy toward rape victims and rapists. *Journal of Personality and Social Psychology, 43,* 372–384.

DeKeseredy, W.S., & Kelly, K. (1993). The incidence and prevalence of woman abuse in Canadian university and college dating relationships. *The Canadian Journal of Sociology, 18,* 57–159.

Dekovic, M. (1999). Risk and protective factors in the development of problem behavior during adolescence. *Journal of Youth and Adolescence, 28,* 667–685.

DeLisi, M. (2006). Zeroing in on early arrest onset: Results from a population of extreme career criminals. *Journal of Criminal Justice, 34,* 17–26.

DeLoache, J.S., & Marzolf, D.P. (1995). The use of dolls to interview young children: Issues of symbolic representation. *Journal of Experimental Child Psychology, 60,* 155–173.

Delveaux, K., Blanchette, K., & Wickett, J. (2005). *Employment, needs, interests, and programming for women offenders.* Research Report No. R-166. Ottawa, ON. Correctional Services of Canada.

DeMatteo, D., Heilbrun, K., & Marczyk, G. (2005). Psychopathy, risk of violence, and protective factors in a noninstitutionalized and noncriminal sample. *International Journal of Forensic Mental Health, 4,* 147–157.

Demo, D.H., & Acock, A.C. (1988). The impact of divorce on children. *Journal of Marriage and the Family, 50,* 619–648.

Department of Justice (May, 1990). Evaluation of the Divorce Act. Phase II: Monitoring and Evaluation. Retrieved June 1, 2004 from http://dsp-psd.pwgsc.gc.ca/Collection-R/LoPBdP/CIR/963-e.htm.

Department of Justice. (2004). Homicide trends in the United States: 2002 update. Retrieved May 10, 2007, from http://www.ojp.usdoj.gov/bjs/pub/pdf/htus02.pdf.

Department of Justice Canada. (2007a). A strategy for the renewal of youth justice. Retrieved May 25, 2007, from http://www.justice.gc.ca/en/ps/yj/aboutus/yoas1.html.

Department of Justice Canada. (2007b). Canada's court system. Retrieved May 1, 2007, from http://www.justice.gc.ca/en/dept/pub/trib/page3.html#provincial.

DePaulo, B.M., Charlton, L., Cooper, H., Lindsay, J.J., & Muhlenbruck, L. (1997). The accuracy-confidence correlation in the detection of deception. *Personality and Social Psychology Review, 1,* 346–357.

DePaulo, B.M., Kashy, D.A., Kirkendol, S.E., Wyer, M.M., & Epstein, J.A. (1996). Lying in everyday life. *Journal of Personality and Social Psychology, 70,* 979–995.

DePaulo, B.M., & Kirkendol, S.E. (1989). The motivational impairment effect in the communication of deception. In Y.C. Yuille (Ed.), *Credibility assessment* (pp. 51–70). Dordrecht: Kluwer.

DePaulo, B.M., Lassiter, G.D., & Stone, J.I. (1982). Attentional determinants of success at detecting deception and truth. *Personality and Social Psychology Bulletin, 8,* 273–279.

DePaulo, B.M., LeMay, C.S., & Epstein, J.A. (1991). Effects of importance of success and expectations for success on effectiveness at deceiving. *Personality and Social Psychology Bulletin, 17,* 14–24.

DePaulo, B.M., Lindsay, J.J., Malone, B.E., Muhlenbruck, L., Charlton, K., & Cooper, H. (2003). Cues to deception. *Psychological Bulletin, 129,* 74–118.

DePaulo, B.M., & Pfeifer, R.L. (1996). On-the-job experience and skill at detecting deception. *Journal of Applied Social Psychology, 16,* 249–267.

Deregowski, J.B., Ellis, HD., & Shepherd, J.W. (1975). Descriptions of White and Black faces by White and Black subjects. *International Journal of Psychology, 10,* 119–123.

Devine, D.J., Clayton, L.D., Dunford, B.B., Seying, R., & Pryce, J. (2001). Jury decision making: 45 years of empirical research on deliberating groups. *Psychology, Public Policy, and Law, 7,* 622–727.

Devlin, Honourable Lord Patrick (chair). (1976). *Report to the secretary of state for the Home Department of the departmental committee on evidence of identification in criminal cases.* London: Her Majesty's Stationery Office.

de Vogel, V., & de Ruiter, C. (2006). Structured professional judgment of violence risk in forensic clinical practice:

A prospective study into the predictive validity of the Dutch HCR-20. *Psychology, Crime & Law, 12,* 321–336.

de Vogel, V., de Ruiter, C., van Beek, D., & Mead, G. (2004). Predictive validity of the SVR-20 and Static-99 in a Dutch sample of treated sex offenders. *Law and Human Behavior, 28,* 235–251.

Diamond, S.S., & Zeisel, H. (1975). Sentencing councils: A study of sentencing disparity and its reduction. *University of Chicago Law Review, 43,* 109–149.

Dobash, R., & Dobash, R.E. (1979). Violence against women. New York: Free Press.

Dobson, V., & Sales, B.D. (2000). The science of infanticide and mental illness. *Psychology, Public Policy, and Law, 6,* 1098–1112.

Dodge, K.A. (1991). The structure and function of reactive and proactive aggression. In D. Pepler & K. Rubin (Eds.), *The development and treatment of childhood aggression* (pp. 201–218). Hillsdale, NJ: Earlbaum.

Dodge, K.A. (2000). Conduct disorder. In A.J. Sameroff, M. Lewis, & S.M. Miller (Eds.), *Handbook of developmental psychopathology* (2nd ed., pp. 447–463). New York: Kluwer Academic/Plenum Publishers.

Dodge, K.A., Lochman, J.E., Harnish, J.D., Bates, J.E., & Pettit, G.S. (1997). Reactive and proactive aggression in school children and psychiatrically impaired chronically assaultive youth. *Journal of Abnormal Psychology, 106,* 37–51.

Doehring, D.G., & Ross, R.W. (1972). Voice recognition by matching the sample. *Journal of Psycholinguistic Research, 1,* 233–242.

Doerner, W.G. (1997). The utility of the oral interview board in selecting police academy admissions. *Policing: An International Journal of Police Strategies & Management, 20,* 777–785.

Dolan, M., & Khawaja, A. (2004). The HCR-20 and post-discharge outcome in male patients discharged from medium security in the UK. *Aggressive Behavior, 30,* 469–483.

Doob, A.N. (1985). The many realities of crime. In A.N. Doob & E.L. Greenspan (Eds.), *Perspectives in criminal law* (pp. 103–122). Aurora: Canada Law Book.

Doob, A.N., & Roberts, J.A. (1988). Public punitiveness and knowledge of the facts: Some Canadian surveys. In N. Walker and M. Hough (Eds.), *Public attitudes to sentencing: Surveys from five countries* (pp. 111–133). Aldershot: Gower.

Doren, D.M. (2004). Stability of the interpretative risk percentages for the RRASOR and Static-99. *Sexual Abuse: A Journal of Research and Treatment, 16,* 25–36.

Douglas, J.E., Burgess, A.W., Burgess, A.G., & Ressler, R.K. (1992). *Crime classification Manual.* New York: Lexington Books.

Douglas, J.E., & Burgess, A.W. (1986). Criminal profiling: A viable investigative tool against violent crime. *FBI Law Enforcement Bulletin, 12,* 9–13.

Douglas, J.E., & Olshaker, M. (1995). *Mindhunter: Inside the FBI's elite serial crime unit.* New York: Charles Scribner's.

Douglas, J.E., Ressler, R.K., Burgess, A.W., & Hartman, C.R. (1986). Criminal profiling from crime scene analysis. *Behavioral Sciences and the Law, 4,* 401–421.

Douglas, K.S., & Ogloff, J.R.P. (2003). The impact of confidence on the accuracy of structured professional and actuarial violence risk judgments in a sample of forensic psychiatric patients. *Law and Human Behavior, 27,* 573–587.

Douglas, K.S., & Skeem, J.L. (2005). Violence risk assessment: Getting specific about being dynamic. *Psychology, Public Policy, and Law, 11,* 347–383.

Douglas, K.S., & Webster, C.D. (1999). Predicting violence in mentally and personality disordered individuals. In R. Roesch, S.D. Hart, & J.P. Ogloff (Eds.), *Psychology and the law: The state of the discipline* (pp. 175–239). New York: Kluwer Academic/Plenum.

Douglas, K.S., Yeomans, M., & Boer, D.P. (2005). Comparative validity analysis of multiple measures of violence risk in a sample of criminal offenders. *Criminal Justice and Behavior, 32,* 479–510.

Dowden, C., & Andrews, D.A. (1999). What works for female offenders: A meta- analytic review. *Crime & Delinquency, 45,* 438–452.

Dowden, C., & Brown, S.L. (2002). The role of substance abuse factors in predicting recidivism: A meta-analysis. *Psychology, Crime, and Law, 8,* 243–264.

Dube, S.R., Anda, R.F., Whitfield, C.L., Brown, D.W., Felitti, V.J., Dong, M., & Giles, W. (2005). Long-term consequences of childhood sexual abuse by gender of victim. *American Journal of Preventive Medicine, 28,* 430–438.

Ducro, C., & Pham, T. (2006). Evaluation of the SORAG and the Static-99 on Belgian sex offenders committed to a forensic facility. *Sexual Abuse: A Journal of Research and Treatment, 18,* 15–26.

Dutton, D.G. (1995). *The domestic assault of women: Psychological and criminal justice perspectives.* Vancouver, BC: University of British Columbia Press.

Dutton, D.G., & Kerry, G. (1999). Modus operandi and personality disorder in incarcerated spousal killers. *International Journal of Law and Psychiatry, 22,* 287–299.

Dysart, J.E., Lindsay, R.C.L., & Dupuis, P. (2006). Showups: The critical issue of clothing bias. *Applied Cognitive Psychology, 20,* 1009–1023.

Easterbrook, J.A. (1959). The effect of emotion on cue utilization and the organization of behavior. *Psychological Review, 66,* 183–201.

Ebata, A.T., Peterson, A.C., & Conger, J.J. (1990). The development of psychopathology in adolescence. In J. Rolf, A.S. Masten, D. Cicchetti, K. Nuechterlein, & S. Weintraub

(Eds.), *Risk and protective factors in the development of psychopathology* (pp. 308–333). Cambridge, MA: Cambridge University Press.

Ebbesen, E.G., & Konecni, V.J. (1997). Eyewitness memory research: Probative versus prejudicial value. *Expert Evidence, 5*, 2–28.

Edens, J.F., Colwell, L.H., Desforges, D.M. & Fernandez, K. (2005). The impact of mental health evidence on support for capital punishment: Are defendants labeled psychopathic considered more deserving of death. *Behavioral Sciences and the Law, 23*, 603–625.

Edens, J.F., Guy, L.S. & Fernandez, K. (2003). Psychopathic traits predict attitudes toward a juvenile capital murderer. *Behavioral Sciences & the Law, 21*, 807–828.

Edens, J.F., Skeem, J.L., Cruise, K.R., & Cauffman, E. (2001). Assessment of "Juvenile Psychopathy" and its association with violence: A critical review. *Behavioral Sciences and the Law, 19*, 53–80.

Edens, J.F., Skeem, J.L., & Douglas, K.S. (2006). Incremental validity analyses of the violence risk appraisal guide and the Psychopathy Checklist: Screening Version in a civil psychiatric sample. *Assessment, 13*, 368–374.

Edwards, G., & Mazzuca, J. (1998). Sixty-one percent support death penalty for murder. *The Gallup Poll, 58*, 68.

Egeth, H.E. (1993). What do we not know about eyewitness identification. *American Psychologist, 48*, 577–580.

Egger, S.A. (1999). Psychological profiling: Past, present and future. *Journal of Contemporary Criminal Justice, 15*, 242–261.

Egger, S.A. (2002). *The serial killers among us: An examination of serial murder and its investigation* (2nd ed.). New Jersey: Prentice Hall.

Eisendrath, S.J. (1996). Current overview of physical factitious disorders. In M.D. Feldman & S.J. Eisendrath (Eds.), *The spectrum of factitious disorders* (pp. 21–36). Washington DC: American Psychiatric Association.

Ekman, P. (1992). *Telling lies: Clues to deceit in the marketplace, politics, and marriage.* New York: W. W. Norton.

Ekman, P., & Friesen, W.V. (1974). Detecting deception from the body or face. *Journal of Personality and Social Psychology, 29*, 288–298.

Ekman, P., & O'Sullivan, M. (1991). Who can catch a liar? *American Psychologist, 46*, 913–920.

Ekman, P., & O'Sullivan, M., & Frank, M.G. (1999). A few can catch a liar. *Psychological Science, 10*, 263–266.

Elaad, E. (1990). Detection of guilty knowledge in real-life criminal applications. *Journal of Applied Psychology, 75*, 521–529.

Elaad, E., Ginton, A., & Jungman, N. (1992). Detection measures in real-life criminal guilty knowledge tests. *Journal of Applied Psychology, 77*, 757–767.

Elbogen, E.B. (2002). The process of violence risk assessment: A review of descriptive research. *Aggression and Violent Behavior, 7*, 591–604.

Elbogen, E.B., Williams, A.L., Kim, D., Tomkins, A.J., & Scalora, M.J. (2001). Gender and perceptions of dangerousness in civil psychiatric patients. *Legal and Criminological Psychology, 6*, 215–228.

Elkins, I.J., Iacono, W.G., Doyle, A.E., & McGue, M. (1997). Characteristics associated with the persistence of antisocial behavior: Results from recent longitudinal research. *Aggression and Violent Behavior, 2*, 102–124.

Ellerby, L.A., & MacPherson, M. (2001). *Exploring the profile of Aboriginal sex offenders: Contrasting Aboriginal and non-Aboriginal sexual offenders to determine unique client characteristics and potential implications for sex offender assessment and treatment strategies.* Research Report No. R-122. Ottawa: Correctional Service Canada.

Elliott, D. (1994). Serious violent offenders: Onset, development course, and termination. The American Society of Criminology 1993 presidential address. *Criminology, 32*, 1–21.

Ellis, D. (1989). Male abuse of a married or cohabiting female partner: The application of sociological theory to research findings. *Violence and Victims, 4*, 235–255.

Ellis, H.D., Shepherd, J.W., & Davies, G.M. (1980). The deterioration of verbal descriptions of faces over different delay intervals. *Journal of Police Science and Administration, 8*, 101–106.

Ellsworth, P.C., & Mauro, R. (1998). Psychology and law. In D.T. Gilbert, S.T. Fiske, & G. Lindzey. *The handbook of social psychology* (pp. 684–732). New York: Aronson.

Ellsworth, P.C., & Reifman, A. (2000). Juror comprehension and public policy: Perceived problems and proposed solutions. *Psychology, Public Policy, and Law, 6*, 788–821.

Ennis, B. J., & Litwack, T.R. (1974). Psychiatry and the presumption of expertise: Flipping coins in the courtroom. *California Law Review, 62*, 693–752.

Ewing, C. (1987). *Battered women who kill: Psychological self-defence as legal justification.* Lexington, MA: Lexington Books.

Ewing, C.P., & Aubrey, M. (1987). Battered woman and public opinion: Some realities about the myths. *Journal of Family Violence, 2*, 257–264.

Ex-marine jailed for abduction. (2004, April 2). *This Is London.* Retrieved April 30, 2004, from http://www.thisislondon.com.

Ex-marine: No sex with girl. (2003, July 17). *CBS News.* Retrieved April 30, 2004, from http://www.cbsnews.com.

Eysenck, H. J. (1977). *Crime and personality.* London: Routledge & Kegan Paul.

Fabricatore, J.M. (1979). Pre-entry assessment and training: Performance evaluation of police officers. In C.D. Speilberger (Ed.), *Police selection and evaluation: Issues and techniques* (pp. 77–86). New York: Praeger Publishers.

Fagan, A.A. (2005). The relationship between adolescent physical abuse and criminal offending: Support for an enduring and generalized cycle of violence. *Journal of Family Violence, 20,* 279–290.

Fagot, B.I., & Kavanagh, K. (1990). The prediction of antisocial behavior from avoidant attachment classifications. *Child Development, 61,* 864–873.

Faigman, D.L., & Wright, A.J. (1997). The battered woman syndrome in the age of science. *Arizona Law Review, 39,* 67–115.

Falkenberg, S., Gaines, L.K,. & Cordner, G. (1991). An examination of the constructs underlying police performance appraisals. *Journal of Criminal Justice, 19,* 151–160.

Faller, K.C. (1987). Women who sexually abuse children. *Violence and Victims, 2,* 263–276.

Fang, F., Liu, Y., & Shen, Z. (2003). Lie detection with contingent negative variation. *International Journal of Psychophysiology, 50,* 247–255.

Farkas, G.M., DeLeon, P.H., & Newman, R. (1997). Sanity examiner certification: An evolving national agenda. *Professional Psychology: Research and Practice, 28,* 73–76.

Farrington, D. (2006). Family background and psychopathy. In C.J. Patrick (Ed.), *Handbook of psychopathy* (pp. 229–250). New York: Guilford Press.

Farrington, D.P. (1989). Early predictors of adolescent aggression and adult violence. *Violence and Victims, 4,* 79–100.

Farrington, D.P. (1991). Psychological contributions to the explanation of offending. *Issues in Criminological and Legal Psychology, 1,* 7–19.

Farrington, D.P. (1995). The development of offending and antisocial behavior from childhood: Key findings from the Cambridge Study in Delinquent Development. *Journal of Child Psychology and Psychiatry, 36,* 929–964.

Farwell, L.A., & Donchin, E. (1991). The truth will out: Interrogative polygraphy ("lie detection") with event-related brain potentials. *Psychophysiology, 28,* 531–547.

Fast facts about the Pickton trial. (2007, January 22). *Ottawa Citizen,* p. A3.

Faver, C.A., & Strand, E.B. (2003). To leave or to stay? Battered women's concern for vulnerable pets. *Journal of interpersonal violence, 18,* 1367–1377.

Federoff, J.P., & Federoff, I.C. (1992). Buspirone and paraphilic sexual behavior. *Journal of Offender Rehabilitation, 18,* 89–108.

Feinman, S., & Entwisle, D.R. (1976). Children's ability to recognize other children's faces. *Child Development, 47,* 506–510.

Feldman, M.P. (1977). *Criminal behaviour: A psychological analysis.* Chichester, UK: John Wiley & Sons.

Felner, R.D., & Terre, L. (1987). Child custody dispositions and children's adaptation following divorce. In L.A. Weithorn (Ed.), *Psychology and child custody determinations: Knowledge, roles, and expertise* (pp. 106–153). Lincoln: University of Nebraska Press.

Felson, R.B. & Cares, A.C. (2005). Gender and the seriousness of assaults on intimate partners and other victims. *Journal of Marriage and Family, 67*(5), 182–195.

Fergusson, D.M., & Horwood, L.J. (1996). The role of adolescent peer affiliations in the continuity between childhood behavioral adjustment and juvenile offending. *Journal of Abnormal Child Psychology, 24,* 205–221.

Fergusson, D.M., & Horwood, L.J. (1998). Early conduct problems and later life opportunities. *Journal of Child Psychology and Psychiatry, 39,* 1097–1108.

Fergusson, D.M., & Lynskey, M.T. (1997). Early reading difficulties and later conduct problems. *Journal of Child Psychology and Psychiatry, 38,* 899–907.

Fergusson, D.M., & Woodward, L.J. (2000). Educational, psychological, and sexual outcomes of girls with conduct problems in early adolescence. *Journal of Child Psychology and Psychiatry, 41,* 779–792.

Fiedler, K., & Walka, I. (1993). Training lie detectors to use nonverbal cues instead of global heuristics. *Human Communication Research, 20,* 199–223.

Finkel, N.J., Burke, J.E., & Chavez, L.J. (2000). Commonsense judgments of infanticide: Murder, manslaughter, madness, or miscellaneous? *Psychology, Public Policy, and Law, 6,* 1113–1137.

Finkelhor, D. (1984). *Child sexual abuse: New theory and research.* New York: Free Press.

Finkelhor, D., & Browne, A. (1985). The traumatic impact of child sexual abuse: A conceptualization. *American Journal of Orthopsychiatry, 55,* 530–541.

Finkelhor, D., Hotaling, G., Lewis, I.A., & Smith, C. (1990). Sexual abuse in a national survey of adult men and women: Prevalence, characteristics, and risk factors. *Child Abuse and Neglect, 14,* 19–28.

Finkelhor, D., Ormrod, R., Turner, H., & Hamby, S. (2005). The victimization of children and youth: A comprehensive, national survey. *Child Maltreatreatment, 10,* 5–25.

Finn, P., & Tomz, J.E. (1996). *Developing a law enforcement stress program for officers and their families.* Washington, DC: U.S. Department of Justice.

Firestone, P., Bradford, J.M., Greenberg, D.M., & Larose, M.R. (1998). Homicidal sex offenders: Psychological, phallometric, and diagnostic features. *Journal of the American Academy of Psychiatry and the Law, 26,* 537–552.

Fisher, K., Vidmar, N., & Ellis, R. (1993). The culture of battering and role of mediation in domestic violence cases. *SMU Law Review, 46,* 2117–2173.

Fisher, R.P. (1995) Interviewing victims and witnesses of crime. *Psychology, Public Police, and Law, 1,* 732–764.

Fisher, R.P., & Geiselman, R.E. (1992). *Memory-enhancing techniques for investigative interviewing.* Springfield: Charles C. Thomas.

Fisher, R.P., Geiselman, R.E., & Raymond, D.S. (1987). Critical analysis of police interviewing techniques. *Journal of Police Science and Administration*, 15, 177–185.

Fitzgerald, M. (1999). *Searches in London*. London, UK: Home Office.

Fitzpatrick, K.M. (1997). Fighting among America's youth: A risk and protective factors approach. *Journal of Health and Social Behavior*, 38, 131–148.

Flight, J., & Forth, A.E. (2007). Instrumentally violent youth: The roles of psychopathic traits, empathy, and attachment. *Criminal Justice and Behavior*, 34, 721–738.

Flynn, C.P. (2000). Woman's best friend: Pet abuse and the role of companion animals in the lives of battered women. *Violence against women*, 6, 162–177.

Foa, E.B., & Rothbaum, B.O. (1998). *Treating the trauma of rape: Cognitive-behavioral therapy for PTSD*. New York: Guilford.

Fontaine, R.G., Burks, V.S., & Dodge, K.A. (2002). Response decision processes and externalizing behavior problems in adolescents. *Development and Psychopathology*, 14, 107–122.

Forcese, D. (1999). *Policing Canadian society*. Scarborough, ON: Prentice Hall.

Forrest, J.A., & Feldman, R.S. (2000). Detecting deception and judge's involvement: Lower task involvement leads to better lie detection. *Personality and Social Psychology Bulletin*, 26, 118–125.

Forth, A.E., Hart, S.D., & Hare, R.D. (1990). Assessment of psychopathy in male young offenders. *Psychological Assessment: A Journal of Consulting and Clinical Psychology*, 2, 342–344.

Forth, A.E., Kosson, D.S., & Hare, R.D. (2003). *The Psychopathy Checklist: Youth Version manual*. Toronto: Multi-Health Systems.

Fowlie, J. (2004, January 7). Toronto crime figures reveal racial disparity. *The Globe and Mail*, p. A8.

Frank, M.G., & Ekman, P. (1997). The ability to detect deceit generalizes across different types of high-stake lies. *Journal of Personality and Social Psychology*, 72, 1429–1439.

Franke, W.D., Collins, S.A., & Hinz, P.N. (1998). Cardiovascular disease morbidity in an Iowa law enforcement cohort, compared with the general population. *Journal of Occupational and Environmental Medicine*, 40, 441–444.

Frederick, R.I., Crosby, R.D., & Wynkoop, T.F. (2000). Performance curve classification of invalid responding on the Validity Indicator Profile. *Archives of Clinical Neuropsychology*, 15, 281–300.

Freud, S. (1906/1959). Psycho-analysis and the establishment of the facts in legal proceedings. In J. Stachey (Ed.), *The standard edition of the complete psychological works of Sigmund Freud* (Volume 9) (pp. 103–114). London: Hogarth.

Frick, P.J. (1994). Family dysfunction and the disruptive disorders: A review of recent empirical findings. In T.H. Ollendick & Prinz, R.J. (Eds.), *Advances in clinical child psychology*. (Vol. 16) New York: Plenum Press.

Frick, P.J., Bodin, S.D., & Barry, C.T. (2000). Psychopathic traits and conduct problems in community and clinic-referred samples of children: Further development of the Psychopathy Screening Device. *Psychological Assessment*, 12, 382–393.

Frick, P.J., & Hare, R.D. (2001). *Antisocial Process Screening Device*. Toronto: Multi-Health Systems.

Frick, P.J., Kimonis, E.R., Dandreaux, D.M., & Farell, J.M. (2003). The 4 year stability of psychopathic traits in non-referred youth. *Behavioral Sciences and the Law*, 21, 713–736.

Frick, P.J., Lahey, B.B., Loeber, R., Stouthamer, M., Christ, M.A.G., & Hanson, K. (1992). Familial risk factors to oppositional defiant disorder and conduct disorder: parental psychopathology and maternal parenting. *Journal of Consulting and Clinical Psychology*, 60, 49–55.

Friedrich, W.N., & Luecke, W.J. (1988). Young school-age sexually aggressive children. *Professional Psychology: Research and Practice*, 19, 155–164.

Fritz, G., Stoll, K., & Wagner, N. (1981). A comparison of males and females who were sexually molested as children. *Journal of Sex and Marital Therapy*, 7, 54–58.

Fukuda, K. (2001). Eye blinks: New indices for the detection of deception. *International Journal of Psychophysiology*, 40, 239–245.

Fulero, S.M., & Everington, C. (2004). Mental retardation, competency to waive Miranda rights, and false confessions. In G.D. Lassiter (Ed.), *Interrogations, confessions, and entrapment* (pp. 163–179). New York: Kluwer Academic.

Furedy, J.J. (1996). The North American Polygraph and psychophysiology: Disinterested, uninterested, and interested perspectives. *International Journal of Psychophysiology*, 21, 97–105.

Fyfe, J.J. (1979). Administrative interventions on police shooting discretion: An empirical examination. *Journal of Criminal Justice*, 7, 309–324.

Fyfe, J.J. (1981). Who shoots? A look at officer race and police shooting. *Journal of Police Science and Administration*, 9, 367–382.

Gabor, T. (2004). Inflammatory rhetoric on racial profiling can undermine police services. *Canadian Journal of Criminology and Criminal Justice*, 46, 457–466.

Gabor, T., & Crutcher, N. (2002). *Mandatory minimum penalties: Their effect on crime, sentencing disparities, and justice system expenditures*. Ottawa: Department of Justice Canada.

Gallagher, C.A., Wilson, D.B., Hirschfield, P., Coggeshall, M.B., & MacKenzie, D.L. (1999). A quantitative review of the effects of sex offender treatment of sexual reoffending. *Corrections Management Quarterly*, 3, 19–29.

Gallup Poll. (1999). *Racial profiling is seen as wide-spread, particularly among young black men*. Princeton, NJ: Gallup Poll Organization.

Gamer, M., Rill, H.-G., Vossel, G., & Gödert, H.W. (2005). Psychophysiological and vocal measures in the detection of guilty knowledge. *International Journal of Psychophysiology, 60,* 76–87.

Ganis, G., Kosslyn, S.M., Stose, S., Thompson, W.L., & Yurgelun-Todd, D.A. (2003). Neural correlates of different types of deception: An fMRI investigation. *Cerebral Cortex, 13,* 830–836.

Garber, C.M. (1947). Eskimo infanticide. *Scientific Monthly, 64,* 98–102.

Gardner, J., Scogin, F., Vipperman, R., & Varela, J.G. (1998). The predictive validity of peer assessment in law enforcement: A 6-year follow-up. *Behavioral Sciences and the Law, 16,* 473–478.

Garmezy, N. (1985). Stress-resistant children: The search for protective factors. In J.E. Stevenson (Ed.), *Recent research in developmental psychopathology* (pp. 213–233). New York: Pergamon.

Garmezy, N. (1991). Resilience in children's adaptation to negative life events and stressed environments. *Pediatric Annals, 20,* 460–466.

Gaudet, F.J. (1938). Individual differences in the sentencing tendencies of judges. *Archives of Psychology, 230,* 1–57.

Geberth, V.J. (1990). *Practical homicide investigation: Tactics, procedures, and forensic techniques* (2nd ed.). New York: Elsevier.

Geiselman, R.E., Fisher, R.P., Firstenberg, I., Hutton, L.A., Sullivan, S., Avetissian, I., & Prosk, A. (1984). Enhancement of eyewitness memory: An empirical evaluation of the cognitive interview. *Journal of Police Science and Administration, 12,* 74–80.

Geiselman, R.E., Fisher, R.P., MacKinnon, D.P., & Holland, H.L. (1985). Eyewitness memory enhancement in the police interview: Cognitive retrieval mnemonics versus hypnosis. *Journal of Applied Psychology, 70,* 401–412.

Geiselman, R.E., Fisher, R.P., MacKinnon, D.P., & Holland, H.L. (1986). Enhancement of eyewitness memory with the cognitive interview. *American Journal of Psychology, 99,* 385–401.

Geller, W., & Scott, M.S. (1992). *Deadly force: What we know.* Washington, DC: Police Executive Forum.

Gellespie, C. (1989). *Justifiable homicide.* Columbus, OH: Ohio State University Press.

Gendreau, P., Goggin, C., & Smith, P. (2002). Is the PCL-R really the "unparalleled" measure of offender risk? A lesson in knowledge cumulation. *Criminal Justice and Behavior, 29,* 397–426.

Gendreau, P., Goggin, C., Cullen, F., & Andrews, D. (2001). The effects of community sanctions and incarceration of recidivism. In L. Motiuk and R. Serin (Eds.), *Compendium 2000 on effective correctional programming* (pp. 18–21). Ottawa: Correctional Service Canada.

Gendreau, P., Little, T., & Goggin, C. (1996). A meta-analysis of the predictors of adult offender recidivism: What works! *Criminology, 34,* 575–607.

Gentry, A.L., Dulmus, C.N., & Theriot, M.T. (2005). Comparing sex offender risk classification using the Static-99 and LSI-R assessment instruments. *Research on Social Work Practice, 15,* 557–563.

Giancola, P.R., Parrott, D.J., & Roth, R.M. (2006). The influence of difficult temperament on alcohol-related aggression: Better accounted for by executive functioning? *Addictive Behaviors, 31,* 2169–2187.

Ginton, A., Daie, N., Elaad, E., & Ben-Shakhar, G. (1982). A method for evaluating the use of the polygraph in a real-life situation. *Journal of Applied Psychology, 67,* 131–137.

Glover, A.J.J., Nicholson, D.E., & Hemmati, T. (2002). A comparison of predictors of general and violent recidivism among high-risk federal offenders. *Criminal Justice and Behavior, 29,* 235–249.

Glueck, S., & Glueck, E.T. (1968). *Delinquents and nondelinquents in perspective.* Cambridge, MA: Harvard University Press.

Golding, S.L. (1993). *Training manual: Interdisciplinary fitness interview revised.* Department of Psychology, University of Utah.

Golding, S.L., Roesch, R., & Schreiber, J. (1984). Assessment and conceptualization of competency to stand trial. Preliminary data on the interdisciplinary fitness interview. *Law and Human Behavior, 8,* 321–334.

Goldstein, A.G. (1979). Race-related variation of facial features: Anthropometric data I. *Bulletin of the Psychonomic Society, 13,* 187–190.

Gondolf, E.W. (1985). *Men who batter: An integrated approach for stopping wife abuse.* Holmes Beach, CA: Learning Publications.

Gondolf, E.W. (1988). Who are these guys? Towards a behavioral typology of batterers. *Violence and Victims, 3,* 187–202.

Gondolf, E., & Fisher, E. (1988). *Battered women as survivors: An alternative to treating learned helplessness.* Lexington, MA: Lexington Books.

Gonzalez, R., Ellsworth, P., & Pembroke, M. (1993). Response biases in lineups and showups. *Journal of Personality and Social Psychology, 64,* 525–537.

Goodman, G.S., Pyle-Taub, E.P., Jones, D.P.H., England, P., Port, L.K., Rudy, L., & Prado, L. (1992). Testifying in court: The effects on child sexual assault victims. *Monographs of the Society for Research in Child Development, 57 (Serial No. 229),* 1–163.

Goodman, G.S., Quas, J.A., Batterman-Faunce, J.M., Riddlesberger, M., & Kuhn, J. (1997). Children's reactions to and memory for a stressful event: Influences of age, anatomical dolls, knowledge, and parental attachment. *Applied Developmental Science, 1,* 54–75.

Gordon, N.J., Mohamed, F.B., Faro, S.H., Platek, S.M., Ahmad, H., & Williams, J.M. (2006). Integrated zone comparison polygraph technique accuracy with scoring algorithms. *Physiology & Behavior, 87,* 251–254.

Gorey, K., & Leslie, D. (1997). The prevalence of child sexual abuse: Integrative review adjustment for potential response and measurement bias. *Child Abuse and Neglect, 21,* 391–398.

Gough, H.G. (1950). The F minus K dissimulation index for the MMPI. *Journal of Consulting Psychology, 14,* 408–413.

Gowan, M.A., & Gatewood, R.D. (1995). Personnel selection. In N. Brewer & C. Wilson (Eds.), *Psychology and policing* (pp. 177–204). Hillsdale, NJ: Lawrence Erlbaum Associates.

Graham, J.R. (1999). *MMPI-2: Assessing personality and psychopathology* (3rd ed.). New York: Oxford University Press.

Granger, C. (1996). *The criminal jury trial in Canada.* Toronto: Carswell.

Grann, M., Belfrage, H., & Tengström, A. (2000). Actuarial assessment of risk for violence: Predictive validity of the VRAG and the historical part of the HCR-20. *Criminal Justice and Behavior, 27,* 97–114.

Grann, M., & Wedin, I. (2002). Risk factors for recidivism among spousal assault and spousal homicide offenders. *Psychology, Crime and Law, 8,* 5–23.

Gray, N.S., Snowden, R.J., MacCulloch, S., Phillips, H., Taylor, J., & MacCulloch, M.J. (2004). Relative efficacy of criminological, clinical, and personality measures of future risk of offending in mentally disordered offenders: A comparative study of HCR-20, PCL:SV, and OGRS. *Journal of Consulting and Clinical Psychology, 72,* 523–530.

Greco, C.M., & Cornell, D.G. (1992). Rorschach object relations of adolescents who committed homicide. *Journal of Personality Assessment, 59,* 574–583.

Greene, E., Raitz, A., & Lindblad, H. (1989). Jurors' knowledge of battered women. *Journal of Family Violence, 4,* 105–125.

Gretton, H.M., Hare, R.D., & Catchpole, R.E.H. (2004). Psychopathy and offending from adolescence to adulthood: A 10-year follow-up. *Journal of Consulting and Clinical Psychology, 72,* 636–645.

Greve, K.W., & Bianchini, K.J. (2006). Should the retention trial of the test of memory malingering be optional? *Archives of Clinical Neuropsychology, 21,* 117–119.

Grossman, F.K., Beinashowitz, J., Anderson, L., Sakurai, M., Finnin, L., & Flaherty, M. (1992). Risk and resilience in young adolescents. *Journal of Youth and Adolescence, 21,* 529–550.

Groth, A.N. (1979). *Men who rape: The psychology of the offender.* New York: Plenum.

Groth, A.N., Burgess, A.W. & Holmstrom, L.L. (1977). Rape: Power, anger, and sexuality. *American Journal of Psychiatry, 134,* 1239–1243.

Groth, A.N., Hobson, W.F., & Gary, T.S. (1982). The child molester: Clinical observations. *Journal of Social Work and Human Sexuality, 1,* 129–144.

Grove, W., & Meehl, P (1996). Comparative efficiency of informal (subjective, impressionistic) and formal (mechanical, algorithmic) prediction procedures: The clinical-statistical controversy. *Psychology, Public Policy and Law, 2,* 293–323.

Grove, W.M., Zald, D.H., Lebow, B.S., Snitz, B.E., & Nelson, C. (2000). Clinical versus mechanical prediction: A meta-analysis. *Psychological Assessment, 12,* 19–30.

Gudjonsson, G.H. (1984). A new scale of interrogative suggestibility. *Personality and Individual Differences, 5,* 303–314.

Gudjonsson, G.H. (1989). Compliance in an interrogation context: A new scale. *Personality and Individual Differences, 10,* 535–540.

Gudjonsson, G.H. (1992). Interrogation and false confessions: Vulnerability factors. *British Journal of Hospital Medicine, 47,* 597–599.

Gudjonsson, G.H. (2003). *The psychology of interrogations, confessions, and testimony.* Chichester, UK: John Wiley & Sons.

Gudjonsson, G.H., & MacKeith, J.A.C. (1988). Retracted confessions: Legal, psychological and psychiatric aspects. *Medicine, Science, and the Law, 28,* 187–194.

Gudjonsson, G.H., & Sigurdsson, J.F. (1994). How frequently do false confessions occur? An empirical study among prison inmates. *Psychology, Crime and Law, 1,* 21–26.

Gureje, O., Simon, G.E., Ustun, T. B., & Goldberg, D.P. (1997). Somatization in cross-cultural perspective: A world health organization study in primary care. *American Journal of Psychiatry, 154,* 989–995.

Guy, L.S., Edens, J.F., Anthony, C., & Douglas, K.S. (2005). Does psychopathy predict institutional misconduct among adults? A meta-analytic investigation. *Journal of Consulting and Clinical Psychology, 73,* 1056–1064.

Guy, L.S., Kwartner, P.P., & Miller, H.A. (2006). Investigating the M-FAST: Psychometric properties and utility to detect diagnostic specific malingering. *Behavioral Sciences & the Law, 24,* 687–702.

Guy, L.S., & Miller, H.A. (2004). Screening for malingered psychopathology in a correctional setting: Utility of the Miller-Forensic Assessment of Symptoms Test (M-FAST). *Criminal Justice and Behavior, 31,* 695–716.

Gylys, J.A., & McNamara, J.R. (1996). Acceptance of rape myths among prosecuting attorneys. *Psychological Reports, 79,* 15–18.

Hadjistavropoulos, T., & Malloy, D.C. (2000). Making ethical choices: A comprehensive decision-making model for Canadian psychologists. *Canadian Psychology, 41,* 104–115.

Haggard, U., Gumpert, C.H., & Grann, M. (2001). Against all odds: A qualitative follow-up study of high-risk violent offenders who were not reconvicted. *Journal of Interpersonal Violence, 16,* 1048–1065.

Hall, G.C. (1995). Sexual offender recidivism revisited: A meta-analysis of recent treatment studies. *Journal of Consulting and Clinical Psychology, 63,* 802–809.

Hall, G. C. N., & Hirschman, R. (1992). Sexual aggression against children: A conceptual perspective of etiology. *Criminal Justice and Behavior, 19,* 8–23.

Hallett, B. (2000). *Aboriginal people in Manitoba 2000.* Winnipeg, Manitoba: Human Resources Development Canada.

Hamilton, G. & Sutterfield, T. (1997). Comparison of women who have and have not murdered their abusive partners. *Women & Therapy, 20,* 45–55.

Hanes, A. (2004, April 28). Charge dropped for father who forgot child in car for 8 hours. *National Post.* Retrieved May 5, 2004, from http://www.canada.com.

Haney, C. (1980). Psychology and legal change: On the limits of a factual jurisprudence. *Law and Human Behavior, 17,* 371–398.

Haney, J., & Kristianson, C. M. (1997). An analysis of the impact of prison on women survivors of childhood sexual abuse. *Women & Therapy, 20,* 29–44.

Hankins, G.C., Barnard, G.W., & Robbins, L. (1993). The validity of the M Test in residential forensic facility. *Bulletin of the American Academy of Psychiatry and Law, 21,* 111–121.

Hans, V.P., & Doob, A.N. (1976). Section 12 of the Canada Evidence Act and the deliberation of simulated juries. *Criminal Law Quarterly, 18,* 235–253.

Hanson, R.K. (1990). The psychological impact of sexual assault on women and children: A review. *Annals of Sex Research, 3,* 187–232.

Hanson, R.K. (1997). Invoking sympathy-assessment and treatment of empathy deficits among sexual offenders. In B.K. Schwartz & H.R. Cellini (Eds.), *The sex offender: New insights, treatment innovations and legal developments* (pp. 1.1–1.12). Kingston, NJ: Civic Research Institute.

Hanson, R.K., Broom, I., & Stephenson, M. (2004). Evaluating community sex offender treatment programs: A 12-year follow-up of 724 offenders. *Canadian Journal of Behavioural Sciences, 36,* 85–94.

Hanson, R.K., & Bussière, M.T. (1998). Predicting relapse: A meta-analysis of sexual offender recidivism studies. *Journal of Consulting and Clinical Psychology, 66,* 348–362.

Hanson, R. K., Gordon, A., Harris, A.J.R., Marques, J.K., Murphy, W., Quinsey, V.L., & Seto, M.C. (2002). First report of the Collaborative Outcome Data Project on the effectiveness of psychological treatment of sex offenders. *Sexual Abuse: A Journal of Research and Treatment, 14,* 169–194.

Hanson, R.K., & Harris, A.J. (2000). Where should we intervene? Dynamic predictors of sexual offense recidivism. *Criminal Justice and Behavior, 27,* 6–35.

Hanson, R.K., & Morton-Bourgon, K.E. (2005). The characteristics of persistent sexual offenders: A meta-analysis of recidivism studies. *Journal of Consulting and Clinical Psychology, 73,* 1154–1163.

Hanson, R.K., & Scott, H. (1995). Assessing perspective-taking among sexual offenders, nonsexual criminals, and offenders. *Sexual Abuse: Journal of Research and Treatment, 7,* 259–277.

Hanson, R.K., & Thornton, D. (1999). *Static-99: Improving actuarial risk assessment for sexual offenders.* Ottawa: Department of Solicitor General.

Hanson, R.K., & Thornton, D. (2000). Improving risk assessments for sex offenders: A comparison of three actuarial scales. *Law and Human Behavior, 24,* 119–136.

Hanson, T.L. (1999). Does parental conflict explain why divorce is negatively associated with child welfare. *Social Forces, 77,* 1283–1316.

Hare, R.D. (1991). *The Hare Psychopathy Checklist–Revised.* Toronto: Multi-Health Systems.

Hare, R.D. (1993). *Without conscience: The disturbing world of the psychopaths among us.* New York: Pocket Books.

Hare, R.D. (1998). The Hare PCL-R: Some issues concerning its use and misuse. *Legal and Criminological Psychology, 3,* 99–119.

Hare, R.D. (2003). *The Hare Psychopathy Checklist–Revised.* (2nd ed.). Toronto: Multi-Health Systems.

Hare, R.D. (2007). Forty years aren't enough: Recollections, prognostications, and random musings. In H. Hervé & J.C. Yuille (Eds.). *The psychopath: Theory, research and practice* (pp. 3–28). Mahway, NJ: Erlbaum.

Hare, R.D., Clark, D., Grant, M., & Thornton, D. (2000). Psychopathy and the predictive validity of the PCL-R: An international perspective. *Behavioral Sciences and the Law, 18,* 623–645.

Hare, R.D., Forth, A.E., & Strachan, K.E. (1992). Psychopathy and crime across the life span. In R.D. Peters & R.J. McMahon (Eds.), *Aggression and violence throughout the life span* (pp. 285–300). Thousand Oaks, CA: Sage Publications Inc.

Hare, R.D., Harpur, T.J., Hakstian, A.R., Forth, A.E., Hart, S.D., & Newman, J.P. (1990). The Revised Psychopathy Checklist: Reliability and factor structure. *Psychological Assessment: A Journal of Consulting and Clinical Psychology, 2,* 338–341.

Hargrave, G.E., & Hiatt, D. (1987). Law enforcement selection with the interview, MMPI, and CPI: A study of reliability and validity. *Journal of Police Science and Administration, 15,* 110–117.

Harris, D. (1999a). *Driving while black: Racial profiling on our nation's highways.* Washington, DC: American Civil Liberties Union.

Harris, D. (1999b). The stories, the statistics, and the law: Why "driving while black" matters. *Minnesota Law Review, 84,* 265–326.

Harris, G.T., Rice, M.E., & Camilleri, J.A. (2004). Applying a forensic actuarial assessment (the Violence Risk Appraisal Guide) to nonforensic patients. *Journal of Interpersonal Violence, 19,* 1063–1074.

Harris, R.D., Rice, M.E., & Cormier, C.A. (2002). Prospective replication of the Violence Risk Appraisal Guide in predicting violent recidivism among forensic patients. *Law and Human Behavior, 26*, 377–394.

Harris, G.T., Rice, M.E., & Quinsey, V.L. (1993). Violent recidivism of mentally disordered offenders: The development of a statistical prediction instrument. *Criminal Justice and Behavior, 20*, 315–335.

Harrison, L.A., & Esqueda, C.W. (1999). Myths and stereotypes of actors involved in domestic violence: Implications for domestic violence culpability attributions. *Aggression and Violent Behavior, 4*, 129–138.

Harrison, S. (1993). *Diary of Jack the Ripper: The discovery, the investigation, the debate.* New York: Hyperion.

Hart, S.D. (1998). The role of psychopathy in assessing risk for violence: Conceptual and methodological issues. *Legal and Criminological Psychology, 3*, 121–137.

Hart, S.D., Cox, D.N., & Hare, R.D. (1995). *Manual for the Psychopathy Checklist: Screening Version (PCL: SV).* Toronto: Multi-Health Systems.

Hart, S.D., Kropp, P.R., & Hare, R.D. (1988). Performance of male psychopaths following conditional release from prison. *Journal of Consulting and Clinical Psychology, 56*, 227–232.

Hastie, R. (Ed.). (1993). *Inside the juror: The psychology of juror decision making.* New York: Cambridge University Press.

Hastie, R., Penrod, S.D., & Pennington, N. (1983). *Inside the jury.* Cambridge, MA: Harvard University Press.

Hathaway, S.R., & McKinley, J.C. (1942). *The Minnesota Multiphasic Personality Inventory Manual.* New York: Psychological Corporation.

Hazelwood, R.R., & Douglas, J.E. (1980). The lust murderer. *FBI Law Enforcement Bulletin, 50*, 18–22.

Health Canada. (2003). *The consequences of child maltreatment: A reference guide for health practitioners.* Report prepared by Jeff Latimer. Ottawa: Health Canada.

Hemphill, J. F., Hare, R.D., & Wong, S. (1998). Psychopathy and recidivism: A review. *Legal and Criminological Psychology, 3*, 139–170.

Hemphill, J. F., Templeman, R., Wong, S., & Hare, R.D. (1998). Psychopathy and crime: Recidivism and criminal careers. In D.J. Cooke, A.E. Forth, & R.D. Hare (Eds.) *Psychopathy: Theory, Research and implications for society* (pp. 375–398). Boston: Kluwer.

Henggeler, S.W., & Borduin, C.M. (1990). *Family therapy and beyond: A multisystemic approach to treating the behavior problems of children and adolescents.* Pacific Grove, CA: Brooks/Cole.

Henggeler, S.W., Melton, G.B., & Smith, L.A. (1992). Family preservation using multisystemic therapy: An effective alternative to incarcerating serious juvenile offenders. *Journal of Consulting and Clinical Psychology, 60*, 953–961.

Henggeler, S.W., Rodick, J.D., Borduin, C.M., Hanson, C.L., Watson, S.M., & Urey, J.R. (1986). Multisystemic treatment of juvenile offenders: Effects on adolescent behavior and family interaction. *Developmental Psychology, 22*, 132–141.

Henggeler, S.W., Schoenwald, S.K. Borduin, C.M., Rowland, M.D., & Cunningham, P.B. (1998). *Multisystemic treatment of antisocial behavior in children and adolescents.* New York: Guilford Press.

Henggeler, S.W., Schoenwald, S.K., & Pickrel, S.A.G. (1995). Multisystemic therapy: Bridging the gap between university and community-based treatment. *Journal of Consulting and Clinical Psychology, 63*, 709–717.

Hess, A.K. (1987). Dimensions of forensic psychology. In I.B. Weiner & A.K. Hess (Eds.), *The handbook of forensic psychology* (1st ed.) (pp. 22–49). New York: John Wiley & Sons.

Hess, A.K. (1999). Defining forensic psychology. In A.K. Hess & I.B. Weiner (Eds.), *The handbook of forensic psychology* (2nd ed.) (pp. 24–47). New York: John Wiley & Sons.

Heuer, L., & Penrod, S. (1989). Instructing jurors: A field experiment with written and preliminary instructions. *Law and Human Behavior, 13*, 409–430.

Heuer, L., & Penrod, S. (1994). Juror note taking and question asking during trials: A national field experiment. *Law and Human Behavior, 18*, 121–150.

Hickey, E. W. (2006). *Serial murderers and their victims.* Belmont, CA: Wadsworth.

Hicks, S.J., & Sales, B.D. (2006). *Criminal profiling: Developing an effective science and practice.* Washington, DC: American Psychological Association.

Hildebrand, M., de Ruiter, C., & de Vogel, V. (2004). Psychopathy and sexual deviance in treated rapists: Association with sexual and nonsexual recidivism. *Sexual Abuse: A Journal of Research and Treatment, 16*, 1–24.

Hilgard, E.R. (1965). *Hypnotic susceptibility.* New York: Harcourt Brace Javanovich.

Hillbrand, M. (1995). Aggression against self and aggression against others in violent psychiatric patients. *Journal of Consulting and Clinical Psychology, 63*, 668–671.

Hilton, N.Z., Harris, G.T., Rawson, K., & Beach, C.A. (2005). Communicating violence risk information to forensic decision makers. *Criminal Justice and Behavior, 32*, 97–116.

Hilton, N.Z., & Simmons, J.L. (2001). The influence of actuarial risk assessment in clinical judgments and tribunal decisions about mentally disordered offenders in maximum security. *Law and Human Behavior, 25*, 393–408.

Hinshaw, S.P., Lahey, B.B., & Hart, E.L. (1993). Issues of taxonomy and comorbidity in the development of conduct disorder. *Development and Psychopathology, 5*, 31–49.

Hirschel, D., & Buzawa, E. (2002). Understanding the context of dual arrest with directions for future research. *Violence Against Women, 8*, 1449–1473.

Hirschell, J.D., Hutchison, I.W., & Dean, C.W. (1990). The failure of arrest to deter spouse abuse. *Journal of Research in Crime and Delinquency, 29*, 7–33.

Hirschi, T. (1969). *Causes of delinquency*. Los Angeles, CA: University of California Press.

Hirsh, H.R., Northrop, L.C., & Schmidt, F.L. (1986). Validity generalization for law enforcement occupations. *Personnel Psychology, 39*, 399–420.

Ho, T. (1999). Assessment of police officer applicants and testing instruments. *Journal of Offender Rehabilitation, 29*, 1–23.

Hodgins, S. (1992). Mental disorder, intellectual deficiency and crime: Evidence from a birth cohort. *Archives of General Psychiatry, 49*, 476–483.

Hodgins, S. (Ed.) (1993). The criminality of mentally disordered person. In S. Hodgins (Ed.), *Mental disorder and crime* (pp. 3–21). Newbury Park, CA: Sage

Hogarth, J. (1971). *Sentencing as a human process*. Toronto: University of Toronto Press.

Hoge, R.D. (1999). *Assessing adolescents in educational, counselling, and other settings*. Mahwah, New Jersey: Lawrence Erlbaum Associates.

Hoge, R.D., Andrews, D.A., & Lescheid, A.W. (1996). An investigation of risk and protective factors in a sample of youthful offenders. *Journal of Child Psychology and Psychiatry and Allied Disciplines, 37*, 419–424.

Hoge, S., Poythress, N., Bonnie, R., Monahan, J., Eisenberg, M., & Feucht-Haviar, T. (1997). The MacArthur Adjudication Competence Study: Diagnosis, psychopathology, and adjudicative competence-related abilities. *Behavioral Sciences and the Law, 15*, 329–345.

Hoge, S.K., Bonnie, R.J., Poythress, N., & Monahan, J. (1992). Attorney–client decision-making in criminal cases: Client competence and participation as perceived by their attorneys. *Behavioral Sciences and the Law, 10*, 385–394.

Hogue, T.E., & Peebles, J. (1997). The influence of remorse, intent, and attitudes toward sex offenders on judgments of a rapist. *Psychology, Crime, and Law, 3*, 249–259.

Hollin, C. (1989). *Psychology and crime: An introduction to criminological psychology*. New York: Routledge.

Hollin, C.R., & Palmer, E.J. (2006). The Level of Service Inventory-Revised profile of English prisoners: Risk and reconviction analysis. *Criminal Justice and Behavior, 33*, 347–366.

Holmes, R.M., & Holmes, S.T. (1998). *Serial murder* (2nd ed.). Thousand Oaks, CA: Sage.

Holmes, R.M., & Holmes, S.T. (2002). *Profiling violent crimes: An investigative tool* (3rd ed.). Thousand Oaks, CA: Sage.

Holsinger, A.M., Lowenkamp, C.T., & Latessa, E.J. (2006). Exploring the validity of the Level of Service Inventory-Revised with Native American offenders. *Journal of Criminal Justice, 34*, 331–337.

Holtfreter, K., Reisig, M. D., & Morash, M. (2004). Poverty, state capital, and recidivism among women offenders. *Criminology and Public Policy, 3*, 185–208.

Holtzworth-Munroe, A., & Stuart, G.L. (1994). Typologies of male batterers: Three subtypes and the differences among them. *Psychological Bulletin, 116*, 476–497.

Homant, R.J., & Kennedy, D.B. (1998). Psychological aspects of crime scene profiling: Validity research. *Criminal Justice and Behavior, 25*, 319–343.

Home Office. (1998). *Statistics on race and the criminal justice system*. London: Home Office.

Honts, C.R., & Raskin, D.C. (1988). A field study of the validity of the directed lie control question. *Journal of Police Science and Administration, 16*, 56–61.

Honts, C.R., Raskin, D.C., & Kircher, J.C. (1994). Mental and physical countermeasures reduce the accuracy of polygraph tests. *Journal of Applied Social Psychology, 79*, 252–259.

Horner, J.J. (2007). *Canadian law and the Canadian legal system*. Toronto: Pearson Canada.

Horowitz, I.A., & ForsterLee, L. (2001). The effects of note-taking and trial transcript access on mock jury decisions in a complex civil trial. *Law and Human Behavior, 25*, 373–391.

Horowitz, I.A., & Seguin, D.G. (1986). The effects of bifurcation and death qualification on assignment of penalty in capital crimes. *Journal of Applied Social Psychology, 16*, 165–185.

Horselenberg, R., Merckelbach, H., & Josephs, S. (2003). Individual differences and false confessions: A conceptual replication of Kassin and Kiechel (1996). *Psychology, Crime & Law, 9*, 1–8.

Howitt, D. (2002). *Forensic and criminal psychology*. London, UK: Pearson Education.

Huesmann, L.R., Eron, L.D., Lefkowitz, M.M., & Walder, L.O. (1984). Stability of aggression over time and generations. *Developmental Psychology, 20*, 1120–1134.

Huff, C.R., Rattner, A., & Sagarin, E. (1996). *Convicted but innocent: Wrongful conviction and public policy*. Thousand Oaks, CA: Sage.

Hughes, M., & Grieve, R. (1980). On asking children bizarre questions. *First Language, 1*, 149–160.

Humm, D.G., & Humm, K.A. (1950). Humm-Wadsworth temperament scale appraisals compared with criteria of job success in the Los Angeles Police Department. *The Journal of Psychology, 30*, 63–57.

Hung, K., & Bowles, S. (1995). Public perceptions of crime. *Juristat, 15*.

Hunter, S., & Baron, E. (2006, December). A daunting task for Pickton jury. *Ottawa Citizen*, p. A3.

Hurley, W., & Dunne, M. (1991). Psychological distress and psychiatric morbidity in women prisoners. *Australia and New Zealand Journal of Psychiatry, 25*, 461–470.

Huurre, T., Junkkari, H., & Hillevi, A. (2006). Long-term psychosocial effects of parental divorce. *European Archives of Psychiatry and Clinical Neuroscience, 256*, 256–263.

Iacono, W.G., Cerri, A.M., Patrick, C.J., & Fleming, J.A.E. (1992). Use of antianxiety drugs as countermeasures in the detection of guilty knowledge. *Journal of Applied Psychology, 77,* 60–64.

Iacono, W.G., & Lykken, D.T. (1997). The validity of the lie detector: Two surveys of scientific opinion. *Journal of Applied Psychology, 82,* 426–433.

Iacono, W.G., & Patrick, C. J. (1988). Polygraphy techniques. In R. Rogers (Ed.), *Clinical assessment of malingering and deception,* 2nd ed. (pp. 252–281). New York: Guilford Press.

Iacono, W.G., & Patrick, C.J. (1999). Polygraph ("lie detector") testing: The state of the art. In A.K. Hess & I.B. Weiner (Eds.), *The handbook of forensic psychology* (2nd ed., pp. 440–473). New York: John Wiley & Sons.

Iacono, W.G., & Patrick, C.J. (2006). Polygraph ("lie detector") testing: Current status and emerging trends. In I.B. Weiner & A. Hess (Eds.), *Handbook of forensic psychology,* 3rd ed. (pp. 552–588). New York: John Wiley & Sons.

Ilacqua, G.E., Coulson, G.E., Lombardo, D., & Nutbrown, V. (1999). Predictive validity of the Young Offender Level of Service Inventory for criminal recidivism of male and female young offenders. *Psychological Reports, 84,* 1214–1218.

Inbau, F.E., Reid, J.E., Buckley, J.P., & Jayne, B.C. (2001). *Criminal interrogation and confessions* (4th ed.). Gaithersberg, MD: Aspen.

Inciardi, J.A. (1986). Getting busted for drugs. In G. Beschner & A.S. Friedman (Eds.). *Teen drug use* (pp. 63–83). Lexington, MA: Lexington Books.

Ipsos-Reid. (2002). Public views on information sharing in the criminal justice system. *Final Report.* Ottawa: Solicitor General Canada.

Inwald, R.E. (1992). *Inwald personality inventory technical manual* (revised ed.). Kew Gardens, NY: Hilson Research.

Izzett, R.R., & Leginski, W. (1974). Group discussion and the influence of defendant characteristics in a simulated jury setting. *The Journal of Social Psychology, 93,* 271–279.

Izzo, R.L., & Ross, R.R. (1990). Meta-analysis of rehabilitation programs for juvenile delinquents. *Criminal Justice and Behavior, 17,* 134–142.

Jackson, J.L., Sijlbing, R., & Thiecke, M.G. (1996). The role of human memory processes in witness reporting. *Expert Evidence, 5,* 98–105.

Jackson, R.L., Rogers, R., & Sewell, K.W. (2005). Forensic application of the *Miller Forensic Assessment of Symptoms Test* (MFAST): Screening for feigned disorders in competency to stand trial evaluations. *Law and Human Behavior, 29,* 199–210.

Jacobs, P.A., Brunton, M., Melville, M.M., Brittain, M.M., & McClemonts, W.F. (1965). Aggressive behaviour, mental subnormality, and the XYY male. *Nature, 208,* 351–352.

Jaffe, P., Hastings, E., Reitzel, D., & Austin, G. (1993). The impact of police laying charges. In Z. Hilton (Ed.) *Legal responses to wife assault: Current trends and evaluation* (pp. 62–95). Newbury Park, CA: Sage.

Janoff-Bulman, R. (1979). Characterological versus behavioral self-blame: Inquiries into depression and rape. *Journal of Personality and Social Psychology, 37,* 1798–1809.

Jarey, M.L., & Stewart, M.A. (1985). Psychiatric disorder in the parents of adopted children with aggressive conduct disorder. *Neuropsychobiology, 13,* 7–11.

Jayne, B.C. (1986). The psychological principles of criminal interrogation: An appendix. In F.E. Inbau, J.E. Reid, & J.P. Buckley (Eds.), *Criminal interrogation and confessions,* 3rd ed. (pp. 327–347). Baltimore: Williams and Williams.

Jenkins, P. (1988). Myth and murder: The serial killer panic of 1983–1985. *Criminal Justice Research Bulletin, 3,* 1–7.

Jessor, R., Turbin, M.S., & Costa, F. (1998). Risk and protection in successful outcomes among disadvantaged adolescents. *Applied Developmental Science, 2,* 194–208.

John Howard Society. (1999). *Sentencing in Canada.* Toronto: John Howard Society.

John Howard Society. (2007). The death penalty: Any nation's shame. Retrieved April 19, 2007, from http://www.johnhoward.on.ca/Library/death/1mar01.htm.

Johnson, H. (1996). *Dangerous domains: Violence against women in Canada.* Scarborough, ON: Nelson.

Johnson, H., & Sacco, V.F. (1995). Researching violence against women: Statistics Canada's national survey. *Canadian Journal of Criminology, 37,* 281–304.

Johnson, R., Jr., Barnhardt, J., & Zhu, J. (2004). The contribution of executive processes to deceptive responding. *Neuropsychologia, 42,* 878–901.

Johnston, J.C. (1997). *Aboriginal offender survey: Case files and interview sample.* Research Report No. R-61. Ottawa: Correctional Service Canada.

Johnston, J.C. (2000). Aboriginal federal offender surveys: A synopsis. *Forum on Corrections Research, 12,* 25–27.

Jokinen, A., Santilla, P., Ravaja, N., & Puttonen, S. (2006). Salience of guilty knowledge test items affects accuracy in realistic mock crimes. *International Journal of Psychophysiology, 62,* 175–184.

Jones, A.B., & Llewellyn, J. (1917). *Malingering.* London: Heinemann.

Jones, W.D. (1997). *Murder of justice: New Jersey's greatest shame.* New York: Vantage Press.

Jordan, B.K., Schlenger, W.E., Fairbank, J.A., & Caddell, J.M. (1996). Prevalence of psychiatric disorders among incarcerated women II. Convicted felons entering prison. *Archives of General Psychiatry, 53,* 513–519.

Junginger, J. (1990). Predicting compliance with command hallucinations. *American Journal of Psychiatry, 147,* 245–247.

Kagehiro, D.K. (1990). Defining the standard of proof injury instructions. *Psychological Science, 1*, 194–200.

Kahneman, D., & Tversky, A. (1982). Variants of uncertainty. *Cognition, 11*, 143–157.

Kalmuss, D.S. (1984). The intergenerational transmission of marital aggression. *Journal of Marriage and the Family, 46*, 11–19.

Kalvern, H., & Zeisel, H. (1966). *The American jury.* Boston: Little, Brown.

Kanas, N. & Barr, M.A. (1984). Self-control of psychotic productions in schizophrenics [Letter to the editor]. *Archives of General Psychiatry, 41*, 919–920.

Kask, K., Bull, R., & Davies, G. (2006). Trying to improve young adults' person descriptions. *Psychiatry, Psychology, and Law, 13*, 174–181.

Kassin, S.M. (1997). The psychology of confession evidence. *American Psychologist, 52*, 221–233.

Kassin, S.M. (1998). Eyewitness identification procedures: The fifth rule. *Law and Human Behavior, 22*, 649–653.

Kassin, S.M., Ellsworth, P., & Smith, V.L. (1989). The "general acceptance" of psychological research on eyewitness testimony. *American Psychologist, 49*, 878–893.

Kassin, S.M., Goldstein, C.C., & Savitsky, K. (2003). Behavioral confirmation in the interrogation room: On the dangers of presuming guilt. *Law and Human Behavior, 27*, 187–203.

Kassin, S.M., & Gudjonsson, G.H. (2004). The psychology of confessions: A review of the literature and issues. *Psychological Science in the Public Interest, 5*, 33–67.

Kassin, S.M., & Kiechel, K.L. (1996). The social psychology of false confessions: Compliance, internalization, and confabulation. *Psychological Science, 7*, 125–128.

Kassin, S.M., & Sommers, S.R. (1997). Inadmissible testimony, instructions to disregard, and the jury: Substantive versus procedural considerations. *Personality and Social Psychology Bulletin, 23*, 1046–1054.

Kassin, S.M., & Sukel, H. (1997). Coerced confessions and the jury: An experimental test of the "harmless error" rule. *Law and Human Behavior, 21*, 27–46.

Kassin, S.M., Tubb, V., Hosch, H.M., & Memon, A. (2001). On the "general acceptance" of eyewitness testimony research. *American Psychologist, 56*, 405–416.

Kassin, S.M., & Wrightsman, L.S. (1985). Confession evidence. In S.M. Kassin & L.S. Wrightsman (Eds.), *The psychology of evidence and trial procedures* (pp. 67–94). London, UK, Sage.

Katz, R.S. (2000). Explaining girls' and women's crime and desistance in the context of their victimization experiences: A developmental test of revised strain theory and the life course perspective. *Violence Against Women, 6*, 633–660.

Kaufman, J., & Zigler, E. (1987). Do abused children become abusive parents? *American Journal of Orthopsychiatry, 57*, 186–192.

Kazdin, A.E. (1993). Treatment of conduct disorder: Progress and directions in psychotherapy research. *Development and Psychopathology, 5*, 277–310.

Kazdin, A.E. (1997). Practitioner review: Psychosocial treatments for conduct disorder in children. *Journal of Child Psychology and Psychiatry and Allied Disciplines, 38*, 161–178.

Kebbell, M.R., & Wagstaff, G.F. (1998). Hypnotic interviewing: The best way to interview eyewitnesses. *Behavioural Sciences and the Law, 16*, 115–129.

Kemp, R., Towell, N., & Pike, G. (1997). When seeing should not be believing: Photographs, credit cards, and fraud. *Applied Cognitive Psychology, 11*, 211–222.

Kendall-Tackett, K.A., Williams, L.M., & Finkelhor, D. (1993). Impact of sexual abuse in children: A review and synthesis of recent empirical studies. *Psychological Bulletin, 113*, 164–180.

Kendell, R.E., Chalmers, J.C., & Platz, C.L. (1987). Epidemiology of puerperal psychoses. *British Journal of Psychiatry, 150*, 662–673.

Kennedy, M.A. & Gorzalka, B.B. (2002). Asian and non-Asian attitudes toward rape, sexual harassment, and sexuality. *Sex Roles, 467*, 227–238.

Keppel, R.D., & Walter, R. (1999). Profiling killers: A revised classification model for understanding sexual murder. *International Journal of Offender Therapy and Comparative Criminology, 43*, 417–437.

Kershner, R. (1996). Adolescent attitudes about rape. *Adolescence, 31*, 29–33.

Kerstholt, J.H., Jansen, N.J.M., Van Amelsvoort, A.G., & Broeders, A.P.A. (2006). Earwitnesses: Effects of accent, retention, and telephone. *Applied Cognitive Psychology, 20*, 187–197.

Kilpatrick, D.G., Saunders, B.E., Veronen, L.J., Best, C.L., & Von, J.M. (1987). Criminal victimization: Lifetime prevalence, reporting to police, and psychological impact. *Crime and Delinquency, 33*, 479–489.

Kind, S.S. (1987). Navigational ideas and the Yorkshire ripper investigation. *Journal of Navigation, 40*, 385–393.

Kingsbury, S.J., Lambert, M.T., & Hendrickse, W. (1997). A two-factor model of aggression. *Psychiatry: Interpersonal and Biological Processes, 60*, 224–232.

Kircher, J.C., & Raskin, D.C. (1988). Human vs. computerized lie detection. *Journal of Applied Psychology, 73*, 291–302

Klassen, D., & O'Connor, W.A. (1989). Assessing the risk of violence in released mental patients: A cross-validation study. *Psychological Assessment, 1*, 75–81.

Klassen, D., & O'Connor, W.A. (1994). Demographic and case history variables in risk assessment. In J. Monahan & H.J. Steadman (Eds.). *Violence and mental disorder: Developments in risk assessment* (pp. 229–257). Chicago, IL: University of Chicago Press.

Kleinman, L., & Gordon, M. (1986). An examination of the relationship between police training and academy performance. *Journal of Police Science and Administration, 14,* 293–299.

Kleinmuntz, B., & Szucko, J.J. (1984). Lie detection in ancient and modern times: A call for contemporary scientific study. *American Psychologist, 39,* 766–776.

Knight, R.A. (1999). Validation of a typology for rapists. *Journal of Interpersonal Violence, 14,* 303–330.

Knight, R.A, & Guay, J.P. (2006). The role of psychopathy in sexual coercion against women. In C.J. Patrick (Ed.), *Handbook of psychopathy* (pp. 512–532). New York: Guilford.

Knight, R.A., & Prentky, R.A. (1990). Classifying sexual offenders: The development and corroboration of taxonomic models. In W.L. Marshall & D.R. Laws (Eds.). *Handbook of sexual assault: Issues, theories, and treatment of the offender* (pp. 23–52). New York: Plenum Press.

Knight, R.A., Prentky, R.A., & Cerce, D.D. (1994). The development, reliability, and validity of an inventory for the multidimensional assessment of sex and aggression. *Criminal Justice and Behavior, 21,* 72–94.

Kocsis, R.N. (2003). Criminal psychological profiling: Validities and abilities. *International Journal of Offender Therapy and Comparative Criminology, 47,* 126–144.

Kocsis, R.N. Irwin, H.J., Hayes, A.F., & Nunn, R. (2000). Expertise in psychological profiling: A comparative assessment. *Journal of Interpersonal Violence, 15,* 311–331.

Köehnken, G. (1987). Training police officers to detect deceptive eyewitness statements. Does it work? *Social Behavior, 2,* 1–17.

Köehnken, G. (1995). Interviewing adults. In R. Bull and D. Carson (Eds.), *Handbook of psychology in legal contexts* (pp. 215–233). Toronto: John Wiley & Sons.

Konecni, V.J., & Ebbesen, E.B. (1984). The mythology of legal decision making. *International Journal of Law and Psychiatry, 7,* 5–18.

Koocher, G.P., Goodman, G.S., White, C.S., Friedrich, W.N., Sivan, A.B., & Reynolds, C.R. (1995). Psychological science and the use of anatomically detailed dolls in child sexual-abuse assessments. *Psychological Bulletin, 118,* 199–222.

Koons, B.A., Burrow, J.D., Morash, M., & Bynum, T. (1997). Expert and offender perceptions of program elements linked to successful outcomes for incarcerated women. *Crime & Delinquency, 43,* 512–532.

Koss, M.P. (1993). Detecting the scope of rape: A review of the prevalence research methods. *Journal of Interpersonal Violence, 8,* 198–222.

Kosson, D.S., Cyterski, T.D., Steuerwald, B.L., Neumann, C.S., & Walker-Matthews, S. (2002). Reliability and validity of the Psychopathy Checklist: Youth Version (PCL:YV) in nonincarcerated adolescents males. *Psychological Assessment, 14,* 97–109.

Kozel, F.A., Johnson, K.A., Mu, Q., Grenesko, E.L., Laken, S.J., & George, M.S. (2005). Detecting deception using functional magnetic resonance imaging. *Biological Psychiatry, 58,* 605–613.

Kramer, G.P., Kerr, N.L., & Carroll, J.S. (1990). Pretrial publicity, judicial remedies, and jury bias. *Law and Human Behavior, 14,* 409–438.

Krantz, S.E. (1988). The impact of divorce on children. In S.M. Dornbusch & M.H. Strober (Eds.), *Feminism, children, and the new families* (pp. 249–273). New York: Guilford Press.

Krauss, D.A., Sales, B.D., Becker, J.V., & Figueredo, A.J. (2000). Beyond prediction to explanation in risk assessment research: A comparison of two explanatory theories of criminality and recidivism. *International Journal of Law and Psychiatry, 23,* 91–112.

Kraut, R.E. (1980). Humans as lie detectors: Some second thoughts. *Journal of Communication, 30,* 209–216.

Kroes, W.H., Margolis, B.L., & Hurrell, J.J. (1974). Job stress in policemen. *Journal of Police Science and Administration, 2,* 145–155.

Kroner, D.G., & Mills, J.F. (2001). The accuracy of five risk appraisal instruments in predicting institutional misconduct and new convictions. *Criminal Justice and Behavior, 28,* 471–489.

Kropp, P.R., & Hart, S.D. (2000). The Spousal Assault Risk Assessment (SARA) Guide: Reliability and validity in adult male offenders. *Law and Human Behavior, 24,* 101–118.

Kropp, P.R., Hart, S., Webster, C., & Eaves, D. (1999). *Manual for the Spousal Assault Risk Assessment Guide* (3rd ed). Toronto: Multi-Health Systems.

Kurdek, L.A. (1981). An integrative perspective on children's divorce adjustment. *American Psychologist, 26,* 856–866.

Laboratory of Community Psychiatry, Harvard Medical School. (1973). *Competency to stand trial and mental fitness* (DHEW Pub. No. ADM-77-103). Rockville, MD: Department of Health, Education, and Welfare.

Lahey, B.B., Waldman, I.D., & McBurnett, K. (1999). The development of antisocial behavior: An integrative causal model. *Journal of Child Psychology and Psychiatry, 40,* 669–682.

Laird, R.D., Jordan, K.Y., Dodge, K.A., Petit, G.S., & Bates, J.E. (2001). Peer rejection in childhood, involvement with antisocial peers in early adolescence and the development of externalizing behavior problems. *Development and Psychopathology, 13,* 337–354.

Laliumière, M., Harris, G., Quinsey, V., & Rice, M. (2005). *The causes of rape. Understanding individual differences in male propensity for sexual aggression.* Washington, DC: American Psychological Association.

Lamberth, J. (August 16, 1999). Driving while black: A statistician proves that prejudice still rules the road. *Washington Post.*

Lamphear, V.S. (1985). The impact of maltreatment on children's psychosocial adjustment: A review of the research. *Child Abuse and Neglect, 9,* 251–263.

Langevin, R. (1979). The effect of assertiveness training, Provera and sex of therapist in the treatment of genital exhibitionism. *Journal of Behavior Therapy and Experimental Psychiatry, 10,* 275–282.

Langevin, R., Handy, L., Paitich, D., & Russon, A. (1985). A new version of the Clarke Sex History Questionnaire for Males. In R. Langevin (Ed.), *Erotic preference, gender identity, and aggression in men: New research studies* (pp. 287–306). Hillsdale, NJ: Erlbaum.

Langleben, D.D., Loughead, J.W., Bilker, W.B., Ruparel, K., Childress, A.R., Busch, S.I., et al. (2005). Telling truth from lie in individual subjects with fast event-related fMRI. *Human Brain Mapping, 26,* 262–272.

Langleben, D.D., Schroeder, L., Maldjian, J.A., Gur, R.C., McDonald, S., Ragland, J.D., O'Brien, C.P., & Childress, A.R. (2002). Brain activity during simulated deception: An event-related functional magnetic resonance study. *Neuroimage, 15,* 727–732.

Langström, N. (2004). Accuracy of actuarial procedures for assessment of sexual offender recidivism risk may vary across ethnicity. *Sexual Abuse: A Journal of Research and Treatment, 16,* 107–120.

LaPrairie, C. (1989). *The role of sentencing in the over-representation of aboriginal people in correctional institutions.* Ottawa: Department of Justice Canada.

LaPrairie, C. (1992). Aboriginal crime and justice: Explaining the present, exploring the future. *Canadian Journal of Criminology, 34,* 281–298.

LaPrairie, C. (1996). *Examining Aboriginal corrections.* Ottawa: Solicitor General of Canada, Corrections Branch.

LaPrairie, C. (2002). Aboriginal over-representation in the criminal justice system: A tale of nine cities. *Canadian Journal of Criminology, 44,* 181–208.

Laroche, D. (2005). *Aspects of the context and consequences of domestic violence: Situational couple violence and intimate terrorism in Canada in 1999.* Quebec City: Government of Quebec.

Larsson, H., Andershed, H. & Lichtenstein, P. (2006). A genetic factor explains most of the variation in the psychopathic personality. *Journal of Abnormal Psychology, 115,* 221–230.

Larson, J.A. (1921). Modification of the Marston deception test. *Journal of the American Institute of Criminal Law and Criminology, 12,* 391–399.

Lassiter, G.D., Geers, A.L., Handley, I.M., Weiland, P.E., & Munhall, P.J. (2002). Videotaped interrogations and confessions: A simple change in camera perspective alters verdicts in simulated trials. *Journal of Applied Psychology, 87,* 867–874.

Latimer, J., & Lawrence, A. (2006). The Review Board systems in Canada: An overview of results from the mentally disordered accused data collection study. Research and Statistics Division, Department of Justice Canada.

Laub, J.H., Nagin, D.S., & Sampson, R.J. (1998). Trajectories of change in criminal offending: Good marriages and the desistance process. *American Sociological Review, 63,* 225–238.

Lea, S., Auburn, T., & Kibblewhite, K. (1999). Working with sex offenders: The perceptions and experiences of professionals and paraprofessionals. *International Journal of Offender Therapy and Comparative Criminology, 43,* 103–119.

Leach, A.-M.,Talwar, V., Lee, K., Bala, N., & Lindsay, R.C.L. (2004). "Intuitive" lie detection of children's deception by law enforcement officials and university students. *Law and Human Behavior, 28,* 661–685.

Leadbeater, B.J., Kuperminc, G.P., Blatt, S.J., & Hertzog, C. (1999). A multivariate model of gender differences in adolescents' internalizing and externalizing problems. *Developmental Psychology, 35,* 1268–1282.

LeBlanc, M. (1993). Late adolescent deceleration of criminal activity and development of self- and social control. *Studies on Crime and Crime Prevention, 2,* 51–68.

Lee, M.Y., Uken, A., & Sebold, J. (2007). Role of self-determined goals in predicting recidivism in domestic violence offenders. *Research on Social Work Practice, 17,* 30–41.

Lees-Haley, P.R. (1997). MMPI-2 base rates for 492 personal injury plaintiffs: Implications and challenges for forensic assessment. *Journal of Clinical Psychology, 53,* 745–755.

Leippe, M.R. (1995). The case for expert testimony about eyewitness memory. *Psychology, Public Policy, and Law, 1,* 909–959.

Leichtman, M.D., & Ceci, S.J. (1995). The effects of stereotypes and suggestions on preschoolers' reports. *Developmental Psychology, 31,* 568–578.

Lemmon, J.H. (2006). The effects of maltreatment recurrence and child welfare services on dimensions of delinquency. *Criminal Justice Review, 31,* 5–32.

Leo, R.A. (1992). From coercion to deception: The changing nature of police interrogation in America. *Crime, Law and Social Change, 18,* 35–39.

Leo, R.A. (1996a). Miranda's revenge: Police interrogation as a confidence game. *Law and Society Review, 30,* 259–288.

Leo, R.A. (1996b). Inside the interrogation room. *The Journal of Criminal Law and Criminology, 86,* 266–303.

Leo, R.A., & Ofshe, R.J. (1998). The consequences of false confessions: Deprivations of liberty and miscarriages of justice in the age of psychological interrogation. *The Journal of Criminal Law and Criminology, 88,* 429–496.

Leschied, A., & Cunningham, A. (February, 2002). *Seeking effective interventions for serious young offenders: Interim results of a four-year randomized study of multisystemic therapy in Ontario, Canada.* Centre for Children & Families in the Justice System, London.

Lidz, C.W., Mulvey, E.P., & Gardner, W. (1993). The accuracy of predictions of violence to others. *Journal of the American Medical Association, 269,* 1007–1011.

Lieberman, J.D., & Sales, B.D. (1997). What social science teaches us about the jury instruction process. *Psychology, Public Policy, and Law, 3*, 589–644.

Lightfoot, L.O., & Barbaree, H.E. (1993). The relationship between substance use and abuse and sexual offending in adolescents. In H.E. Barbaree & W.L. Marshall (Eds.), *Juvenile sex offender* (pp. 203–224). New York: Guilford Press.

Lilienfeld, S.O. & Andrews, B.P. (1996). Development and preliminary validation of a self-report measure of psychopathic personality traits in noncriminal populations. *Journal of Personality Assessment, 66*, 488–524.

Lindberg, M., Chapman, M.T., Samsock, D., Thomas, S.W., & Lindberg, A. (2003). Comparisons of three different investigative interview techniques with young children. *The Journal of Genetic Psychology, 164*, 5–28.

Lindsay, D.S. (1994). Memory source monitoring and eyewitness testimony. In D.F. Ross, J.D. Read, & M.P. Toglia (Eds.), *Adult eyewitness testimony: Current trends and development* (pp. 27–55). New York: Cambridge University Press.

Lindsay, D.S., & Read, J.D. (1995). "Memory work" and recovered memories of childhood sexual abuse: Scientific evidence and public, professional, and personal issues. *Psychology, Public Policy, and Law, 1*, 846–909.

Lindsay, P.S. (1977). Fitness to stand trial in Canada: An overview in light of the recommendations of the law reform commission of Canada. *Criminal Law Quarterly, 19*, 303–348.

Lindsay, R.C.L., Lea, J.A., & Fulford, J.A. (1991). Sequential lineup presentation: Technique matters. *Journal of Applied Psychology, 76*, 741–745.

Lindsay, R.C.L., Martin, R., & Webber, L. (1994). Default values in eyewitness descriptions: A problem for the match-to-description lineup foil selection strategy. *Law and Human Behavior, 18*, 527–541.

Lindsay, R.C.L., Wallbridge, H., & Drennan, D. (1987). Do clothes make the man? An exploration of the effect of lineup attire on eyewitness identification accuracy. *Canadian Journal of Behavioural Science, 19*, 463–478.

Lindsay, R.C.L., & Wells, G.L. (1985). Improving eyewitness identification from lineups: Simultaneous versus sequential lineup presentations. *Journal of Applied Psychology, 70*, 556–564.

Linehan, M.M., Schmidt, H., Dimeff, L.A., Craft, J.C., Kanter, J., & Comtois, K.A. (1999). Dialectical behavior therapy for patients with borderline personality disorder and drug-dependence. *American Journal of Addictions, 8*, 279–292.

Link, B.G., & Steuve, A. (1994). Psychotic symptoms and the violent/illegal behavior of mental patients compared to community controls. In J. Monahan & H. J. Steadman (Eds.), *Violence and mental disorder: Developments in risk assessment* (137–159). Chicago: University of Chicago Press.

Lipsey, M.W. (1992). Juvenile delinquency treatment: A meta-analytic inquiry into the variablilty of effects. In T.D. Cook, H. Cooper, D.S. Corday, H. Hartmann, L.V. Hedges, R.J. Light, T.A. Louis, & F. Mosteller (Eds.), *Meta-analysis for explanation* (pp. 83–127). New York: Sage.

Lipsey, M.W., & Derzon, J.H. (1998). Predictors of violent or serious delinquency in adolescence and early adulthood: A synthesis of longitudinal research. In R. Loeber & D.P. Farrington (Eds.). *Serious and violent juvenile offenders: Risk factors and successful interventions* (pp. 86–105). Thousand Oaks, CA: Sage Publications.

Lipsitt, P.D., Lelos, D., & McGarry, L. (1971). Competency to stand trial: A screening instrument. *American Journal of Psychiatry, 128*, 104–109.

Lisak, D., & Roth, S. (1988). Motivational factors in nonincarcerated sexually aggressive men. *Journal of Personality and Social Psychology, 55*, 795–802.

Lochman, J.E., Whidby, J.M., & FitzGerald, D.P. (2000). Cognitive-behavioral assessment and treatment with aggressive children. In P.C. Kendall (Ed.), *Child and adolescent therapy: Cognitive-behavioral procedures* (2nd ed.). New York: Guilford.

Loeber, R., & Farrington, D.P. (Eds.). (1998). *Serious and violent juvenile offenders.* Thousand Oaks, CA: Sage Publications.

Loeber, R., & Farrington, D.P. (2000). Young children who commit crime: Epidemiology, developmental origins, risk factors, early interventions, and policy implications. *Development and Psychopathology, 12*, 737–762.

Loeber, R., Keenan, K., Lahey, B.B., Green, S.M., & Thomas, C. (1993). Evidence for developmentally based diagnoses of Oppositional Defiant Disorder and Conduct Disorder. *Journal of Abnormal Psychology, 100*, 379–390.

Loftus, E., & Palmer, J.C. (1974). Reconstructions of automobile destruction: An example of the interaction between language and memory. *Journal of Verbal Learning and Verbal Behavior, 12*, 585–589.

Loftus, E.F. (1975). Leading questions and the eyewitness report. *Cognitive Psychology, 7*, 560–572.

Loftus, E.F. (1979a). Reactions to blatantly contradictory information. *Memory and Cognition, 7*, 368–374.

Loftus, E.F. (1979b). The malleability of human memory. *American Scientist, 67*, 312–320.

Loftus, E.F. (1983). Silence is not golden. *American Psychologist, 38*, 564–572.

Loftus, E.F., Altman, D., & Geballe, R. (1975). Effects of questioning upon a witness' later recollections. *Journal of Police Science and Administration, 3*, 162–165.

Loftus, E.G., Miller, D.G., & Burns, H.J. (1978). Semantic integration of verbal information into a visual memory. *Journal of Experimental Psychology. Human Learning and Memory, 4*, 19–31.

Lombroso, C., & Ferrero, W. (1895). *The female offender*. Fisher Unwin, London.

London Family Court Clinic (1993). *Three years after the verdict: A longitudinal study of the social and psychological adjustment of child witnesses referred to the child witness project* (FVDS #4887-06-91-026). London, ON: London Family Court Clinic Inc.

Lonsway, K.A., & Fitzgerald, L.F. (1994). Rape myths: In review. *Psychology of Women Quarterly, 18*, 133–164.

Loo, R. (1994). Burnout among Canadian police managers. *The International Journal of Organizational Analysis, 2*, 406–417.

Loo, R. (2003). A meta-analysis of police suicide rates: Findings and issues. *Suicide and Life-Threatening Behavior, 33*, 313–335.

Looman, J. (2006). Comparison of two risk assessment instruments for sexual offenders. *Sexual Abuse: A Journal of Research and Treatment, 18*, 193–206.

Loos, M.E., & Alexander, P.C. (1997). Differential effects associated with self-reported histories of abuse and neglect in a college sample. *Journal of Interpersonal Violence, 12*, 340–360.

Lösel, F. & Schmucker, M. (2005). The effectiveness of treatment for sexual offenders: A comprehensive meta-analysis. *Journal of Experimental Criminology, 1*, 117–146.

Loucks, A.D., & Zamble, E. (2000). Predictors of criminal behavior and prison misconduct in serious female offenders. *Empirical and Applied Criminal Justice Review, 1*, 1–47.

Lowenkamp, C.T., Holsinger, A.M., & Latessa, E.J. (2001). Risk/need assessment, offender classification, and the role of childhood abuse. *Criminal Justice and Behavior, 28*, 543–563.

Lowry, P.E. (1996). A survey of the assessment center process in the public sector. *Public Personnel Management, 25*, 307–321.

Luo, B., Cheu, J.W., & Siegel, A. (1998). Cholecystokinin B receptors in the periaqueductal gray potentiate defensive rage behavior elicited from the medial hypothalamus of the cat. *Brain Research, 796*, 27–37.

Luus, C.A.E., & Wells, G.L. (1991). Eyewitness identification and the selection of distractors for lineups. *Law and Human Behavior, 15*, 43–57.

Luus, C.A.E., & Wells, G.L. (1994). The malleability of eyewitness confidence: Co-witness and perseverance effects. *Journal of Applied Psychology, 79*, 714–723.

Lykken, D.T. (1960). The validity of the guilty knowledge technique: The effects of faking. *Journal of Applied Psychology, 44*, 258–262.

Lykken, D.T. (1998). *A tremor in the blood. Uses and abuses of the lie detector*. New York: Plenum.

Lynam, D.R., Caspi, A., Moffitt, T.E., Loeber, R., & Stouthamer-Loeber, M. (2007). Longitudinal evidence that psychopathy scores in early adolescence predict adult psychopathy. *Journal of Abnormal Psychology, 116*, 155–165.

Maccoby, E.E., & Mnookin, R.H. (1992). *Dividing the child: Social and legal dilemmas of custody*. Cambridge: Harvard University Press.

MacCoun, R.J., & Kerr, N.L. (1988). Asymmetric influence in mock deliberation: Jurors' bias for leniency. *Journal of Personality and Social Psychology, 54*, 21–33.

MacDonald, J.M., Manz, P.W., Alpert, G.P., & Dunham, R.G. (2003). Police use of force: Examining the relationship between calls for service and the balance of police force and suspect resistance. *Journal of Criminal Justice, 31*, 119–127.

MacMillan, H.L. (2000). Child maltreatment: What we know in the year 2000. *Canadian Journal of Psychiatry, 45*, 702–709.

MacMillan, H.L., Fleming, J.E., Streiner, D.L., Lin, E., Boyle, M.H., Jamieson, E., Duku, E.K., Walsh, C.A., Wong, M.Y.Y., & Beardslee, W.R. (2001). Childhood abuse and lifetime psychopathology in a community sample. *American Journal of Psychiatry, 158*, 1878–1883.

Magdol, L., Moffitt, T.E., & Caspi, A. (1997). Gender differences in partner violence in a birth cohort of 21-year-olds: Bridging the gap between clinical and epidemiological approaches. *Journal of Consulting and Clinical Psychology, 65*, 68–78.

Malinosky-Rummell, R., & Hansen, D.J. (1993). Long-term consequences of childhood physical abuse. *Psychological Bulletin, 114*, 68–79.

Malpass, R.S., & Devine, P.G. (1981). Eyewitness identification: Lineup instructions and the absence of the offender. *Journal of Applied Psychology, 66*, 482–489.

Mann, S., Vrij, A., & Bull, R. (2004). Detecting true lies: Police officers' ability to detect suspects' lies. *Journal of Applied Psychology, 89*, 137–149.

Manzoni, P., Brochu, S., Fischer, B., & Rehm, J. (2006). Determinants of property crime among illicit opiate users outside of treatment across Canada. *Deviant Behavior, 27*, 351–376.

Marcus, K.D., Lyons Jr., P.M., & Guyton, M.R. (2000). Studying perceptions of juror influence In Vivo: A social relations analysis. *Law and Human Behavior, 24*, 173–186.

Mark, V.H., & Ervin, F.R. (1970). *Violence and the brain*. New York: Harper and Row.

Marlatt, G.A., & Gordon, J.R. (Eds.) (1985). *Relapse prevention: Maintenance strategies in the treatment of addictive behaviors*. New York: Guilford.

Marques, J.K. (1999). How to answer the questions "Does sexual offender treatment work?" *Journal of Interpersonal Violence, 14*, 437–451.

Marshall, W.L. (1999). Current status of North American assessment and treatment programs for sexual offenders. *Journal of Interpersonal Violence, 14*, 221–239.

Marshall, W.L., Anderson, D., & Champagne, F. (1997). Self-esteem and its relationship to sexual offending. *Psychology, Crime and Law, 3*, 161–186.

Marshall, W.L., & Barbaree, H.E. (1988). An outpatient treatment program for child molesters. *Annals of the New York Academy of Sciences, 528,* 205–214.

Marshall, W.L., & Barbaree, H.E. (1990). An integrated theory of the etiology of sexual offending. In W.L. Marshall & D.R. Laws, *Handbook of sexual assault: Issues, theories, and treatment of the offender* (pp. 257–275). New York: Plenum Press.

Marshall, W.L., Barbaree, H.E., & Fernandez, Y.M. (1995). Some aspects of social competence in sexual offenders. *Sexual Abuse: Journal of Research and Treatment, 7,* 113–127.

Marshall, W.L., Eccles, A., & Barbaree, H.E. (1991). The treatment of exhibitionists: A focus on sexual deviance versus cognitive and relationship features. *Behavior Research and Therapy, 29,* 129–135.

Marshall, W.L., & Fernandez, Y.M. (2003). Sexual preferences are they useful in the assessment and treatment of sexual offenders? *Aggression and Violent Behavior, 8,* 131–143.

Martinson, R. (1974). What works? Questions and answers about prison reform. *The Public Interest, 35,* 22–54.

Masten, A.S., Best, K.M., & Garmezy, N. (1990). Resilience and development: Contributions from the study of children who overcome adversity. *Development and Psychopathology, 2,* 425–444.

Maume, M.O., Ousey, G.C., & Beaver, K. (2005). Cutting the grass: A reexamination of the link between marital attachment, delinquent peers and desistance from marijuana use. *Journal of Quantitative Criminology, 21,* 27–53.

McCann, J.T. (1998). A conceptual framework for identifying various types of confessions. *Behavioral Sciences and the Law, 16,* 441–453.

McCloskey, M., & Egeth, H. (1983). Eyewitness identification: What can a psychologist tell a jury? *American Psychologist, 38,* 550–563.

McCloskey, M., & Zaragoza, M. (1985). Misleading post event information and memory for events: Arguments and evidence against memory impairment hypothesis. *Journal of Experimental Psychology: General, 114,* 1–16.

McCormick, C.T. (1972). *Handbook of the law of evidence* (2nd ed.). St. Paul, MN: West.

McCraty, R., Tomasino, D., Atkinson, M., & Sundram, J. (1999). *Impact of the HeartMath self-management skills program on physiological and psychological stress in police officers.* Boulder Creek, CA: HeartMath Research Center, Institute of HeartMath.

McCreary, D.R., & Thompson, M.M. (2006). Development of two reliable and valid measures of stressors in policing: The Operational and Organizational Police Stress Questionnaires. *International Journal of Stress Management, 13,* 494–518.

McDaniel, M.A., Whetzel, D.L., Schmidt, F.L., & Maurer, S.D. (1994). The validity of employment interviews: A comprehensive review and meta-analysis. *Journal of Applied Psychology, 79,* 599–616.

McDonagh, D., Taylor, K., & Blanchette, K. (2002). Correctional adaptation of dialectical behaviour therapy (DBT) for federally sentenced women. *Forum on Corrections, 14,* 36–39.

McFatter, R.M. (1986). Sentencing disparity. *Journal of Applied Social Psychology, 16,* 150–164.

McGurk, B.J., & McDougall, C. (1981). A new approach to Eysenck's theory of criminality. *Personality and Individual Differences, 2,* 338–340.

McKenna, P.F. (2002). *Police powers I.* Toronto: Prentice Hall.

McMahon, M. (1999). Battered women and bad science: The limited validity and utility of battered women syndrome. *Psychiatry, Psychology, and Law, 6,* 23–49.

McMahon, R.J. (1994). Diagnosis, assessment, and treatment of externalizing problems in children: The role of longitudinal data. *Journal of Consulting and Clinical Psychology, 62,* 901–917.

McNiel, D.E., & Binder, R.L. (1994). The relationship between acute psychiatric symptoms, diagnosis, and short-term risk of violence. *Hospital and Community Psychiatry, 45,* 133–137.

McNiel, D.E., Sandberg, D.A., & Binder, R.L. (1998). The relationship between confidence and accuracy in clinical assessment of psychiatric patients' potential for violence. *Law and Human Behavior, 22,* 655–669.

McQuinston-Surrett, D., Malpass, R.S., & Tredoux, C.G. (2006). Sequential vs. simultaneous lineups: A review of methods, data, and theory. *Psychology, Public Policy, and Law, 12,* 137–169.

Meadow, R. (1977). Munchausen syndrome by proxy: The hinterland of child abuse. *Lancet, 2,* 343–345.

Meehl, P.E. (1954). *Clinical vs. statistical prediction.* Minneapolis: University of Minnesota Press.

Meissner, C.A., & Brigham, J.C. (2001). Thirty years of investigating the own-race bias in memory for faces: A meta-analytic review. *Psychology, Public Policy, and Law, 7,* 1–35.

Meissner, C.A., & Russano, M.B. (2003). The psychology of interrogations and false confessions: Research and recommendations. *The Canadian Journal of Police and Security Services: Practice, Policy and Management, 1,* 53–64.

Meissner, D. (2000, March 5). Reena Virk murder trial set to begin this week. *Canadian Press.* Retrieved May 12, 2004, from http://acmi.canoe.ca/CNEWSLaw0003/13_virk6.html.

Melchers, R. (2003). Do Toronto police engage in racial profiling? *Canadian Journal of Criminology and Criminal Justice, 45,* 347–366.

Meloy, J.R. (1997). Predatory violence during mass murder. *Journal of Forensic Sciences, 42,* 326–329.

Melton, G., Petrila, J., Poythress, N.G., & Slobogin, C. (1997). Competency to stand trial. In *Psychological evaluations for* the court: A handbook for mental health professionals and lawyers (2nd ed., pp. 119–155). New York: Guilford Press.

Melton, H.C. (1999). Police response to domestic violence. *Journal of Offender Rehabilitation, 29*, 1–21.

Memon, A., & Bull, R. (1991). The cognitive interview: Its origins, empirical support, evaluation and practical implications. *Journal of Community and Applied Social Psychology, 1*, 291–307.

Memon, A., & Gabbert, G. (2003). Improving the identification accuracy of senior witnesses: Do prelineup questions and sequential testing help? *Journal of Applied Psychology, 88*, 341–347.

Memon, A., & Shuman, D.W. (1998). Juror perception of experts in civil disputes: The role of race and gender. *Law and Psychology Review, 22*, 179–197.

Memon, A., Vrij, A., & Bull, R. (2003). *Psychology and law: Truthfulness, accuracy, and credibility*. London, UK: Jossey-Bass.

Menard, S., & Huizinga, D. (1989). Age, period, and cohort size effects on self-reported alcohol, marijuana, and polydrug use: Results from the National Youth Survey. *Social Science Research, 18*, 174–194.

Mental Health, Law, and Policy Institute, Department of Psychology, Simon Fraser University. (2007). SFU—Mental Health Law and Policy Institute. Retrieved April 12, 2007, from http://www.sfu.ca/mhlpi.

Merton R.K. (1938). Social structure and anomie. *American Sociological Review, 3*, 672–682.

Messman-Moore, T.L., & Long, P.J. (2003). The role of childhood sexual abuse sequelae in the sexual revictimization of women: An empirical review and theoretical reformulation. *Clinical Psychology Review, 23*, 537–571.

Miethe, T.D., & Drass, K.A. (1999). Exploring the social context of instrumental and expressive homicides: An application of qualitative comparative analysis. *Journal of Quantitative Criminology, 15*, 1–21.

Miller, H.A. (2001). *M-FAST: Miller Forensic Assessment of Symptoms Test and professional manual*. Odessa, FL: Psychological Assessment Resources.

Miller, H.A. (2005). The *Miller-Forensic Assessment of Symptoms Test* (M-FAST): Test generalizability and utility across race, literacy, and clinical opinion. *Criminal Justice and Behaviour, 32*, 591–611.

Miller, A.R., & Rosenfeld, J.P. (2004). Response-specific scalp distributions in deception detection and ERP correlates of psychopathic personality traits. *Journal of Psychophysiology, 18*, 13–26.

Millis, J.B., & Kornblith, P.R. (1992). Fragile beginnings: Identification and treatment of postpartum disorders. *Health and Social Work, 17*, 192–199.

Millon, C.M. (1987). Concordance among Borderline personality disorder measures and the predictivity of their clinical attributes. *Dissertation Abstracts International, 47*, 50–61.

Mills, J.F., Jones, M.N., & Kroner, D.G. (2005). An examination of the generalizability of the LSI-R and VRAG probability bins. *Criminal Justice and Behavior, 32*, 565–585.

Mischel, W. (1968). *Personality and assessment*. New York: Lawrence Erlbaum.

Mitchell, K.J., Finkelhor, D., & Wolak, J. (2001). Risk factors for and impact of online sexual solicitation of youth. *Journal of the American Medical Association, 285*, 3011–3014.

Mitchell, K.J., Livosky, M., & Mather, M. (1998). The weapon focus effect revisited: The role of novelty. *Legal and Criminological Psychology, 3*, 287–303.

Mitchell, T.L., Haw, R.M., Pfeifer, J.E., & Meissner, C.A. (2005). Racial bias in mock juror decision-making: A meta-analytic review of defendant treatment. *Law and Human Behavior, 29*, 621–637.

Moffitt, T.E. (1993). Adolescence-limited and life-course persistent antisocial behaviour: A developmental taxonomy. *Psychological Review, 100*, 674–701.

Moffitt, T.E., Caspi, A., Harrington, H., & Milne, B.J. (2002). Males on the life-course persistent and adolescence limited antisocial pathways: Follow-up at age 26 years. *Development and Psychopathology, 14*, 179–207.

Moffitt, T.E., & Henry, B. (1989). Neurological assessment of executive functions in self-reported delinquents. *Developmental and Psychopathology, 1*, 105–118.

Mojtabai, R. (2006). Psychotic-like experiences and interpersonal violence in the general population. *Social Psychiatry and Psychiatric Epidemiology, 451*, 183–190.

Monahan, J. (1981). *Predicting violent behavior: An assessment of clinical techniques*. Beverly Hills, CA: Sage.

Monahan, J., & Steadman, H.J. (1994). *Violence and mental disorder: Developments in risk assessment*. Chicago: University of Chicago Press.

Monahan, J., Steadman, H.J., Appelbaum, P., Grisso, T., Mulvey, E. P., Roth, L., Robbins, P.C., Banks, S., & Silver, E. (2006). Classification of Violence Risk. *Behavioral Sciences and the Law, 24*, 721–730.

Monahan, J., Steadman, H.J., Appelbaum, P.S., Robbins, P.C., Mulvey, E.P., Silver, E., et al. (2000). Developing a clinically useful actuarial tool for assessing violence risk. *British Journal of Psychiatry, 176*, 312–319.

Monahan, J., Steadman, H.J., Robbins, P.C., Appelbaum, P., Banks, S., Grisso, T., Heilbrun, K., Mulvey, E.P., Roth, L., & Silver, E. (2005). An actuarial model of violence risk assessment for persons with mental disorders. *Psychiatric Services, 56*, 810–815.

Moran, R. (1985). The modern foundation for the insanity defense: The cases of James Hadfield (1800) and Daniel M'Naughten (1843). *Annals of the American Academy of Political and Social Science, 477*, 31–42.

Morgan, P. (1975). *Child care: Sense and fable*. London: Temple Smith.

Mossman, D. (1994). Assessing predictions of violence: Being accurate about accuracy. *Journal of Consulting and Clinical Psychology, 62*, 783–792.

Motiuk, L., & Nafekh, M. (2001). Using reintegration potential at intake to better identify safe release candidates. *Forum on Corrections Research, 13*, 11–13.

Motiuk, L.L., & Porporino, F.J. (1991). *The prevalence, nature, and severity of mental health problems among federal male inmates in Canadian penitentiaries* (Research Report No. 24). Ottawa: Correctional Service of Canada.

Motiuk, L., & Vuong, B. (2005). *Homicide, sex, robbery and drug offenders in federal corrections: An end-of-2004 review*. Research Brief B-37, Correctional Service Canada.

Motiuk, L.L., & Serin, R.C. (2001). *Compendium 2000 on effective correctional programming*. Ottawa: Correctional Service of Canada.

Munsterberg, H. (1908). *On the witness stand*. Garden City, New York: Doubleday.

Murphy, J.M. (1976). Psychiatric labelling in cross-cultural perspective: Similar kinds of behaviour appear to be labelled abnormal in diverse cultures. *Science, 191*, 1019–1028.

Murrie, D.C., Boccaccini, M.T., McCoy, W. & Cornell, D.G. (2007). Diagnostic labels in juvenile court: How do descriptions of psychopathy and conduct disorder influence judges? *Journal of Clinical Child and Adolescent Psychology, 36*, 288–291.

Murrie, D.C., Cornell, D.G., Kaplan, S., McConville, D., & Levy-Elkon, A. (2004). Psychopathy scores and violence among juvenile offenders: A multi-measure study. *Behavioral Sciences and the Law, 22*, 49–67.

Murrie, D.C., Cornell, D.G. & McCoy, W. (2005). Psychopathy, conduct disorder, and stigma: Does diagnostic language affect juvenile probation officer recommendations. *Law and Human Behavior, 29*, 323–342.

Myers, B., Latter, R., & Abdollahi-Arena, M.K. (2006). The court of public opinion: Lay perceptions of polygraph testing. *Law and Human Behavior, 30*, 509–523.

Myers, B., Rosol, A., & Boelter, E. (2003). Polygraph evidence and juror judgments: The effects of corroborating evidence. *Journal of Applied Psychology, 35*, 948–962.

Myers, W.C., Scott, K., Burgess, A.W., & Burgess, A.G. (1995). Psychopathology, biopsychosocial factors, crime characteristics, and classification of 25 homicidal youths. *Journal of the American Academy of Child and Adolescent Psychiatry, 34*, 1483–1489.

Nafekh, M. (2003). Using proxy measures for correctional research [Electronic version]. *Forum on Corrections Research, 15*, 41–43.

Nafekh, M. & Motiuk, L. (2002). *The Statistical Information on Recidivism—Revised 1 (SIR-R1) Scale: A psychometric examination* (Research Report R-126). Ottawa: Correctional Service Canada.

Narby, D.J., Cutler, B.L., & Moran, G. (1993). A meta-analysis of the association between authoritarianism and jurors' perceptions of defendant culpability. *Journal of Applied Psychology, 78*, 34–42.

National Crime Prevention Council. (1995). *Risk or threat to children*. Ottawa: National Crime Prevention Council.

National Crime Prevention Council. (1997). *Preventing crime by investing in families and communities: Promoting positive outcomes in youth twelve- to eighteen-years-old*. Ottawa: National Crime Prevention Council.

National Parole Board. (2006). *2005–2006 performance monitoring report*. Ottawa: National Parole Board.

National Parole Board. (2007a). History of parole in Canada—Part 1: The beginning of parole in Canada. Retrieved April 16, 2007, from http://www.npb-cnlc.gc.ca/about/part1_e.htm.

National Parole Board. (2007b). Parole: Contributing to public safety. Retrieved April 16, 2007, from http://www.npb-cnlc.gc.ca/infocntr/parolec/contribe.htm.

National Parole Board. (2007c). Parole decision-making. Myths and realities. Retrieved April 16, 2007, from http://www.npb-cnlc.gc.ca/infocntr/myths_reality_e.htm.

National Research Council. (2003). *The polygraph and lie detection*. Washington, DC: National Academies Press.

Navon, D. (1990). How critical is the accuracy of eyewitness memory? Another look at the issue of lineup diagnosticity. *Journal of Applied Psychology, 75*, 506–510.

Nazroo, J. (1995). Uncovering gender differences in the use of marital violence: The effect of methodology. *Sociology, 29*, 475–494.

Nemeth, M. (1996, May 20). Joudrie not guilty. *Maclean's*. Retrieved from July 1, 2007, http://thecanadianencyclopedia.com/index.cfm?PgNm=TCE&Params=M1ARTM001067.

Newhill, C.E., Mulvey, E.P., & Lidz, C.W. (1995). Characteristics of violence in the community by female patients seen in a psychiatric emergency service. *Psychiatric Services, 46*, 785–789.

Newman, J.P., Brinkley, C.A., Lorenz, A.R., Hiatt, K.D., & MacCoon, D.G. (2007). Psychopathy as psychopathology: Beyond the clinical utility of the Psychopathy Checklist-Revised. In H. Hervé & J.C. Yuille (Eds.). *The psychopath: Theory, research and practice* (pp. 173–206). Mahway, NJ: Erlbaum.

Ng, W., & Lindsay, R.C.L. (1994). Cross-race facial recognition: Failure of the contact hypothesis. *Journal of Cross-Cultural Psychology, 25*, 217–232.

Nicholls, T.L., Brink, J., Desmarais, S.L., Webster, C. D., & Martin, M. (2006). The Short-Term Assessment of Risk and Treatability (START): A prospective validation study in a forensic psychiatric sample. *Assessment, 13,* 313–327.

Nicholls, T.L., Ogloff, J.R.P., & Douglas, K.S. (2004). Assessing risk for violence among male and female civil psychiatric patients: The HCR-20, PCL:SV, and VSC. *Behavioral Sciences and the Law, 22,* 127–158.

Nichols, T.R., Graber, J.A., Brooks-Gunn, J., & Botvin, G.J. (2006). Sex differences in overt aggression and delinquency among urban minority middle school students. *Applied Developmental Psychology, 27,* 78–91.

Nicholson, R.A., & Kugler, K. (1991). Competent and incompetent criminal defendants: A quantitative review of comparative research. *Psychological Bulletin, 109,* 355–370.

Niedermeier, K.E., Horowitz, I.A., & Kerr, N.L. (1999). Informing jurors of their nullification power: A route to a just verdict or judicial chaos? *Law and Human Behavior, 23,* 331–351.

Nietzel, M.T. (1979). *Crime and its modification: A social learning perspective.* Oxford: Pergamon.

Nisbett, R.E., & Wilson, T.D. (1977). Telling more than we can know: Verbal reports on mental processes. *Psychological Review, 84,* 231–259.

Note. (1953). Voluntary false confessions: A neglected area in criminal investigation. *Indiana Law Review, 28,* 374–392.

Nuffield, J. (1982). *Parole decision-making in Canada.* Ottawa: Solicitor General of Canada.

Nunes, K.L., Firestone, P., Bradford, J.M., Greenberg, D.M., & Broom, I. (2002). A comparison of modified versions of the Static-99 and the Sex Offender Risk Appraisal Guide. *Sexual Abuse: A Journal of Research and Treatment, 14,* 253–269.

Nunes, K.L., Firestone, P., Wexler, A., Jensen, T.L., & Bradford, J.M. (2007). Incarceration and recidivism among sexual offenders. *Law and Human Behavior, 31,* 305–318.

Nunes, K.L., Hanson, K., Firestone, P., Moulden, H.M., Greenberg, D.M., & Bradford, J. M. (2007). Denial predicts recidivism for some sexual offenders. *Sexual Abuse: A Journal of Research and Treatment, 19,* 91–106.

Oberlander, L.B., & Goldstein, N.E. (2001). A review and update on the practice of evaluating Miranda comprehension. *Behavioral Sciences and the Law, 19,* 453–471.

O'Bryant, S.E., & Lucas, J.A. (2006). Estimating the predictive value of the test of memory malingering: An illustrative example for clinicians. *The Clinical Neuropsychologist, 20,* 533–540.

Odeh, M.S., Zeiss, R.A., & Huss, M.T. (2006). Cues they use: Clinicians' endorsement of risk cues in predictions of dangerousness. *Behavioral Sciences and the Law, 24,* 147–156.

Odgers, C.L., & Moretti, M.M. (2002). Aggressive and antisocial girls: Research update and challenges. *International Journal of Forensic Mental Health, 1,* 103–119.

Odgers, C.L., Moretti, M., & Reppucci, N.D. (2005). Examining the science and practice of violence risk assessment with female adolescents. *Law and Human Behavior, 29,* 7–27.

Odgers, C.L., Reppucci, N.D., & Moretti, M.M. (2005). Nipping psychopathy in the bud: An examination of the convergent, predictive, and theoretical utility of the PCL-YV among adolescent girls. *Behavioral Sciences and the Law, 23,* 743–763.

Office of Juvenile Studies and Delinquency Prevention. (1992). *Juvenile justice bulletin: OJJDP update on statistics.* Washington, DC: Office of Juvenile Studies and Delinquency Prevention.

Offord, D.R., Boyle, M.H., Szatmari, P., Rae Grant, J.L., Links, P.S., Cadman, D.T., Byles, J.A., Crawford, J.W., Blum, H.M., Byrne, C., Thomas, H., & Woodward, C.A. (1987). Ontario Child Health Study: II Six month prevalence of disorder and rates of service utilization. *Archives of General Psychiatry, 44,* 832–836.

Offord, D.R., Lipman, E.L., & Duku, E.K. (2001). Epidemiology of problem behaviour up to age 12 years. In R. Loeber & D.P. Farrington (Eds.), *Child delinquents* (pp. 95–134). Thousand Oaks, CA: Sage Publications.

Ofshe, R.J. (1989). Coerced confessions: The logic of seemingly irrational action. *Journal of Cultic Studies, 6,* 1–15.

Ofshe, R.J., & Leo, R.A. (1997). The social psychology of police interrogation: The theory and classification of true and false confessions. *Studies in Law, Politics, and Society, 16,* 189–251.

Ofshe, R.J., & Watters, E. (1994). *Making monsters: False memories, psychotherapy, and sexual hysteria.* New York: Charles Scribner's.

Ogloff, J.R.P. (Ed.). (2002). *Taking psychology and law into the 21st century.* New York: Kluwer Academic.

Ogloff, J.R.P., & Cronshaw, S.F. (2001). Expert psychological testimony: Assisting or misleading the trier of fact. *Canadian Psychology, 42,* 87–91.

Ogloff, J.R.P., Schweighofer, A., Turnbull, S., & Whittemore, K. (1992). Empirical research and the insanity defense: How much do we really know? In J.R.P. Ogloff (Ed.), *Psychology and law: The broadening of the discipline* (pp. 171–210). Durham, NC: Carolina Academic Press.

Ogloff, J.R.P., & Vidmar, N. (1994). The effect of pretrial publicity on jurors: A study to compare the relative effects of television and print media in a child sex abuse case. *Law and Human Behavior, 18,* 507–525.

Ogloff, J.R.P., Wallace, D.H., & Otto, R.K. (1991). Competencies in the criminal process. In D. K. Kagehiro & W.S. Laufer (Eds.), *Handbook of psychology and law* (pp. 343–360). New York: Springer Verlag.

O'Hara, M.W. (1995). Childbearing. In M.W. O'Hara, R.C. Reiter, S.R. Johnson, A. Milburn, & J. Engeldinger (Eds.).

Psychological aspects of women's reproductive health (pp. 26–48). New York: Springer Publishing Co.

Olczak, P.V., Kaplan, M.F., & Penrod, S. (1991). Attorneys' lay psychology and its effectiveness in selecting jurors: Three empirical studies. *Journal of Social Behavior and Personality, 6,* 431–452.

Olio, K.A., & Cornell, W.F. (1998). The façade of scientific documentation: A case study of Richard Ofshe's analysis of the Paul Ingram case. *Psychology, Public Policy, and Law, 4,* 1182–1197.

Olver, M.E., & Wong, S.C.P. (2006). Psychopathy, sexual deviance, and recidivism among sex offenders. *Sexual Abuse: A Journal of Research and Treatment, 18,* 65–82.

O'Malley, M., & Wood, O. (2003). Cruel & unusual: The law and Latimer. *CBC News Online.* Retrieved September 5, 2007, from http://www.cbc.ca/news/background/latimer.

O'Neill, M.L., Lidz, V., & Heilbrun, K. (2003). Adolescents with psychopathic characteristics in a substance abusing cohort: Treatment process and outcomes. *Law and Human Behavior, 27,* 299–313.

Ontario Human Rights Commission. (2007). The existence of racial profiling. Retrieved January 28, 2007, from http://www.ohrc.on.ca/english/consultations/racial-profiling-report_4.shtml.

Orchard, T.L., & Yarmey, A.D. (1995). The effects of whispers, voice-sample duration, and voice distinctiveness on criminal speaker identification. *Applied Cognitive Psychology, 9,* 249–260.

O'Toole, M. (2007). Psychopathy as a behavior classification system for violent and serial crime scenes. In H. Hervé & J.C. Yuille (Eds.). *The psychopath: Theory, research and practice* (pp. 301–325). Mahway, NJ: Erlbaum.

Otto, R., & Heilbrun, K. (2002). The practice of forensic psychology: A look toward the future in light of the past. *American Psychologist, 57,* 5–19.

Paglia, A., & Schuller, R.A. (1998). Jurors' use of hearsay evidence: The effects of type and timing of instructions. *Law and Human Behavior, 22,* 501–518.

Palys, T.S., & Divorski, S. (1986). Explaining sentencing disparity. *Canadian Journal of Criminology, 28,* 347–362.

Pankratz, L. (1988). Malingering on intellectual and neuropsychological measures. In R. Rogers (Ed.), *Clinical assessment of malingering and deception* (1st ed., pp. 168–192). New York: Guilford Press.

Paolucci, E., Genuis, M., & Violato, C. (2001). A meta-analysis of the published research on the effects of child sexual abuse. *Journal of Psychology, 135,* 17–36.

Parker, A.D., & Brown, J. (2000). Detection of deception: Statement Validity Analysis as a means of determining truthfulness or falsity of rape allegations. *Legal and Criminological Psychology, 5,* 237–259.

Parker, J. (1995). Age differences in source monitoring of performed and imagined actions. *Journal of Experimental Child Psychology, 60,* 84–101.

Parker, J.G., & Asher, S.R. (1987). Peer relations and later personal adjustment: Are low accepted children at risk? *Psychological Bulletin, 102,* 357–389.

Parliament, L., & Yarmey, A.D. (2002). Deception in eyewitness identification. *Criminal Justice and Behavior, 29,* 734–746.

Parwatikar, S.D., Holcomb, W.R., & Menninger, K.A., II. (1985). The detection of malingered amnesia in accused murders. *Bulletin of American Academy of Psychiatry and Law, 13,* 97–103.

Patrick, C.J. (2006). *Handbook of Psychopathy.* New York: Guilford Press.

Patrick, C.J., Bradley, M.M., & Lang, P.J. (1993). Emotion in the criminal psychopath: Startle reflex modulation. *Journal of Abnormal Psychology, 102,* 82–92.

Patrick, C.J., & Iacono, W.G. (1989). Psychopathy, threat, and polygraph test accuracy. *Journal of Applied Psychology, 74,* 347–355.

Patrick, C.J., & Iacono, W.G. (1991). Validity of the control question polygraph test: The problem of sampling bias. *Journal of Applied Social Psychology, 76,* 229–238.

Patrick, C.P. (2007). Getting to the heart of psychopathy. In H. Hervé & J.C. Yuille (Eds.). *The psychopath: Theory, research and practice* (pp. 207–252). Mahway, NJ: Erlbaum.

Patterson, G.R., Reid, J.B., & Dishion, T.J. (1998). *Antisocial boys.* Eugene, OR: Castalia.

Paul, G.L., & Lentz, R.J. (1977). *Psychosocial treatment of chronic mental patients: Milieu versus social learning programs.* Cambridge, MA: Harvard University Press.

Pavlidis, I., Eberhardt, N.L., & Levine, J.A. (2002). Seeing though the face of deception. *Nature, 415,* 35.

Pearson, F.S., Lipton, D.S., & Cleland, C.M. (November 20, 1996). *Some preliminary findings from the CDATE project.* Paper presented at the Annual Meeting of the American Society of Criminology, Chicago.

Pence, E., & Paymar, M. (1993). *Education groups for men who batter: The Duluth model.* New York: Springer Publishing Co.

Pennington, N., & Hastie, R. (1986). Evidence evaluation in complex decision making. *Journal of Personality and Social Psychology, 51,* 242–258.

Pennington, N., & Hastie, R. (1988). Explanation-based decision making: Effects of memory structure on judgement. *Journal of Experimental Psychology: Learning, Memory, and Cognition, 14,* 521–533.

Penrod, S.D., & Cutler, B. (1995). Witness confidence and witness accuracy: Assessing their forensic relation. *Psychology, Public Policy, and Law, 1,* 817–845.

Penrod, S.D., & Heuer, L. (1997). Tweaking commonsense: Assessing aids to jury decision making. *Psychology, Public Policy, and Law, 3*, 259–284.

Perez, D.A., Hosch, H.M., Ponder, B., & Trejo, G.C. (1993). Ethnicity of defendants and jurors as influences on jury decisions. *Journal of Applied Social Psychology, 23*, 1249–1262.

Peters, M. (2001). Forensic psychological testimony: Is the courtroom door now locked and barred? *Canadian Psychology, 42*, 101–108.

Peterson, C., & Biggs, M. (1997). Interviewing children about trauma: Problems with "specific" questions. *Journal of Traumatic Stress, 10*, 279–290.

Peterson, C., & Grant, M. (2001). Forced-choice: Are forensic interviewers asking the right questions? *Canadian Journal of Behavioural Science, 2001*, 112–127.

Pfeifer, J., & Hart-Mitchell, R. (2001). Evaluating the effect of healing lodge residency on adult offenders. Canadian Institute for Peace, Justice and Security, University of Regina.

Pham, T.H., Ducro, C., Marghem, B., & Réveillère, C. (2005). Prediction of recidivism among prison inmates and forensic patients in Belgium. *Annales Médico Psychologiques, 163*, 842–845.

Phillips, H.K., Gray, N.S., MacCulloch, S.I., Taylor, J., Moore, S.C., Huckle, P., & MacCulloch, M.J. (2005). Risk assessment in offenders with mental disorders: Relative efficacy of personal demographic, criminal history and clinical variables. *Journal of Interpersonal Violence, 20*, 833–847.

Picard, A., (2003, July 22). Grieving mother's farewell: "Adieu, my little flower." *The Globe and Mail*. Retrieved April 30, 2004, from http://www.globeandmail.com.

Pickel, K.L. (1998). Unusualness and threat as possible causes of weapon focus. *Memory, 6*, 277–295.

Pickel, K.L. (1999). The influence of context on the "weapon focus" effect. *Law and Human Behavior, 23*, 299–311.

Pinizzotto, A.J., & Davis, E.F. (1992). *Killed in the line of duty*. Washington, DC: Department of Justice, FBI Uniform Crime Reporting Program.

Pinizzotto, A.J., & Finkel, N.J. (1990). Criminal personality profiling: An outcome and process study. *Law and Human Behavior, 14*, 215–233.

Piquero, A.R., Blumstein, A., Brame, R., Haapanen, R., Mulvey, E.P., & Nagin, D.S. (2001). Assessing the impact of exposure time and incapacitation on longitudinal trajectories of criminal offending. *Journal of Adolescent Research, 16*, 54–74.

Piquero, A.R., & Chung, H.L. (2001). On the relationships between gender, early onset, and the seriousness of offending. *Journal of Criminal Justice, 29*, 189–206.

Pithers, W.D., Martin, G.R., & Cumming, G.F. (1989). Vermont Treatment Program for Sexual Aggressors. In R.D. Laws (Ed.), *Relapse prevention with sex offenders* (pp. 292–310). New York: Guilford Press.

Platz, S.J., & Hosch,.M. (1988). Cross-racial/ethnic eyewitness identification: A field study. *Journal of Applied Social Psychology, 18*, 972–984.

Polak, A., & Harris, P. L. (1999). Deception by young children following noncompliance. *Developmental Psychology, 35*, 561–568.

Pollina, D.A., Dollins, A.B., Senter, S.M., Krapohl, D.J., & Ryan, A.H. (2004). Comparison of polygraph data obtained from individuals involved in mock crime and actual criminal investigations. *Journal of Applied Psychology, 89*, 1099–1105.

Pollock, P.H. (1999). When the killer suffers: Post-traumatic stress reactions following homicide. *Legal and Criminological Psychology, 4*, 185–202.

Pope, H.G., Jonas, J.M., & Jones, B. (1982). Factitious psychosis: Phenomenology, family history, and long-term outcome of nine patients. *American Journal of Psychiatry, 139*, 1480–1483.

Porporino, F. J., & Motiuk, L. L. (1995). The prison careers of mentally disordered offenders. *International Journal of Law and Psychiatry, 18*, 29–44.

Porter, S., & Birt, A.R. (2001). Is traumatic memory special? A comparison of traumatic memory characteristics with memory for other emotional life experiences. *Applied Cognitive Psychology, 15*, S101–S117.

Porter, S., Birt, A., & Boer, D.P. (2001). Investigation of the criminal and conditional release profiles of Canadian federal offenders as a function of psychopathy and age. *Law and Human Behavior, 25*, 647–661.

Porter, S., Campbell, M.A., Stapleton, J., & Birt, A.R. (2002). The influence of judge, target, and stimulus characteristics on the accuracy of detecting deceit. *Canadian Journal of Behavioural Science, 34*, 172–185.

Porter, S., Fairweather, D., Drugge, J., Hervé, H., Birt, A., & Boer, D.P. (2000). Profiles of psychopathy in incarcerated sexual offenders. *Criminal Justice and Behavior, 27*, 216–233.

Porter, S., Woodworth, M., & Birt, A. (2000). Truth, lies, and videotape: An investigation of the ability of federal parole officers to detect deception. *Law and Human Behavior, 24*, 643–658.

Porter, S., Woodworth, M., Earle, J., Drugge, J., & Boer, D. (2003). Characteristics of sexual homicides committed by psychopathic and nonpsychopathic offenders. *Law and Human Behavior, 27*, 459–470.

Poulson, R.L. (1990). Mock juror attribution of criminal responsibility: Effects of race and the guilty but mentall ill

(GBMI) verdict option. *Journal of Applied Social Psychology, 20*, 1596–1611.

Pozzulo, J.D., & Balfour, J. (2006). The impact of change in appearance on children's eyewitness identification accuracy: Comparing simultaneous and elimination lineup procedures. *Legal and Criminological Psychology, 11*, 25–34.

Pozzulo, J.D., & Crescini, C. (2007). Preschoolers' person description and identification accuracy: A comparison of the simultaneous and elimination lineup procedures. Unpublished manuscript.

Pozzulo, J.D., Dempsey, Corey, S., Girardi, A., Lawandi, A., & Aston, C. (in press). Can a lineup procedure designed for child witnesses work for adults?: Comparing simultaneous, sequential, and elimination lineup procedures. *Journal of Applied Social Psychology.*

Pozzulo, J.D., & Lindsay, R.C.L. (1998). Identification accuracy of children versus adults: A meta-analysis. *Law and Human Behavior, 22*, 549–570.

Pozzulo, J.D., & Lindsay, R.C.L. (1999). Elimination lineups: An improved identification procedure for child eyewitnesses. *Journal of Applied Psychology, 84*, 167–176.

Pozzulo, J.D., & Warren, K.L. (2003). Descriptions and identifications of strangers by youth and adult eyewitnesses. *Journal of Applied Psychology, 88*, 315–323.

Prentky, R.A., Burgess, A.W., Rokous, F., Lee, A., Hartman, C., Ressler, R. & Douglas, J. (1989). Serial vs. solo sexual homicide: The role of fantasy. *American Journal of Psychiatry, 146*, 887–891.

Prentky, R.A., Knight, R.A., Lee, A.F.S., & Cerce, D.D. (1995). Predictive validity of lifestyle impulsivity for rapists. *Criminal Justice and Behavior, 22*, 106–128.

Pryke, S., Lindsay, R.C.L., Dysart, J.E., & Dupuis, P. (2004). Multiple independent identification decisions: A method of calibrating eyewitness identifications. *Journal of Applied Psychology, 89*, 73–84.

Public Safety and Emergency Preparedness Canada. (2006). *Corrections and conditional release statistical overview: Annual report 2006.* Public Safety and Emergency Preparedness Canada.

Pugh, G. (1985a). The California Psychological Inventory and police selection. *Journal of Police Science and Administration, 13*, 172–177.

Pugh, G. (1985b). Situation tests and police selection. *Journal of Police Science and Administration, 13*, 31–35.

Putnam, F.W. (2003). Ten-year research update review: Child sexual abuse. *Journal of the American Academy of Child Adolescent Psychiatry, 42*, 269–278.

Pynes, J., & Bernardin, H.J. (1992). Entry-level police selection: The assessment centre is an alternative. *Journal of Criminal Justice, 20*, 41–52.

Quinsey, V.L. (2002). Evolutionary theory and criminal behaviour. *Legal and Criminological Psychology, 7*, 1–13.

Quinsey, V.L., & Ambtman, R. (1979). Variables affecting psychiatrists' and teachers' assessments of the dangerousness of mentally ill offenders. *Journal of Consulting and Clinical Psychology, 47*, 353–362.

Quinsey, V.L., Chaplin, T.C., & Upfold, D. (1984). Sexual arousal to nonsexual violence and sadomasochistic themes among rapists and non-sex-offenders. *Journal of Consulting and Clinical Psychology, 52*, 651–657.

Quinsey, V.L., & Earls, C.M. (1990). The modification of sexual preferences. In W.L. Marshall & D.R. Laws, *Handbook of sexual assault: Issues, theories, and treatment of the offender* (pp. 279–295). New York: Plenum Press.

Quinsey, V.L., Harris, G.T., Rice, M.E., & Cormier, C. (1998). *Violent offenders: Appraising and managing risk.* Washington, DC: American Psychological Association.

Quinsey, V.L., Harris, G.T., Rice, M.E., & Lalumière, M.L. (1993). Assessing the treatment efficacy in outcome studies of sex offenders. *Journal of Interpersonal Violence, 8*, 512–523.

Quinsey, V.L., Khanna, A., & Malcolm, P.B. (1998). A retrospective evaluation of the regional treatment centre sex offender treatment program. *Journal of Interpersonal Violence, 13*, 621–644.

Quinsey, V.L., & Lalumière, M. L. (1995). Evolutionary perspectives on sexual offending. *Sexual Abuse: Journal of Research and Treatment, 7*, 301–315.

Quinsey, V.L., & Maguire, A. (1983). Offenders remanded for a psychiatric examination: Perceived treatability and disposition. *International Journal of Law and Psychiatry, 6*, 193–205.

Quinsey, V.L., Rice, M.E., & Harris, G.T. (1995). Actuarial prediction of sexual recidivism. *Journal of Interpersonal Violence, 10*, 85–105.

Ramirez, D., McDevitt, J., & Farrell, A. (2000). *A resource guide on racial profiling data collection systems: Promising practice and lessons learned.* Washington, DC: U.S. Department of Justice.

Rankin, J., Quinn, J., Shephard, M., Simmie, S., & Duncanson, J. (2002, October 20). Police target black drivers. *Toronto Star*, p. A1.

Raskin, D.C., & Hare, R.D. (1978). Psychopathy and detection of deception in a prison population. *Psychophysiology, 15*, 126–136.

Raskin, D.C., Honts, C.R., & Kircher, J.C. (1997). The scientific status of research on polygraph techniques: The case for polygraph tests. In D.L. Faigman, D. Kaye, M.J. Saks, & J. Sanders (Eds.), *Modern scientific evidence: The law and science of expert testimony* (pp. 565–582). St. Paul, MN: West.

Rasmussen, L.A., Burton, J.E., & Christopherson, B.J. (1992). Precursors to offending and the trauma outcome process in sexually reactive children. *Journal of Child Sexual Abuse, 1*, 33–48.

Ratner, P.A. (1998). Modeling acts of aggression and dominance as wife abuse and exploring their adverse health effects. *Journal of Marriage and the Family, 60*, 453–465.

Read, J.D. (1999). The recovered/false memory debate: Three steps forward, two steps back? *Expert Evidence, 7,* 1–24.

Read, J.D., Connolly, D.A., & Welsh, A. (2006). An archival analysis of actual cases of historic child sexual abuse: A comparison of jury and bench trials. *Law and Human Behavior, 30,* 259–285.

Rees, L.M., Tombaugh, T.N., Gansler, D.A., & Moczynski, N.P. (1998). Five validation experiments of the Test of Malingered Memory (TOMM). *Psychological Assessment, 10,* 10–20.

Reifman, A., Gusick, S.M., & Ellsworth, P.C. (1992). Real jurors' understanding of the law in real cases. *Law and Human Behavior, 16,* 539–554.

Reinhart, M.A. (1987). Sexually abused boys. *Child Abuse and Neglect, 11,* 229–235.

Reiser, M. (1982). *Police psychology: Collected papers.* Los Angeles, CA: LEHI.

Reiser, M. (1989). Investigative hypnosis. In D. Raskin (Ed.), *Psychological methods in criminal investigation and evidence* (pp. 151–190). New York: Springer.

Resick, P.A. (1993). The psychological impact of rape. *Journal of Interpersonal Violence, 8,* 223–255.

Resnick, P.J. (1969). Child murder by parents: A psychiatric review of filicide. *American Journal of Psychiatry, 126,* 325–334.

Resnick, P.J. (1970). Murder of the newborn: A psychiatric review of neonaticide. *American Journal of Psychiatry, 126,* 1414–1420.

Resnick, P.J. (1997). Malingered psychosis. In R. Rogers (Ed.), *Clinical assessment of malingering and deception,* 2nd ed. (pp. 47–67). New York: Guilford Press.

Ressler, R.K., Burgess, A.W., Douglas, J.E., Hartman, C.R., & D'Agostino, R.B. (1986). Sexual killers and their victims: Identifying patterns through crime scene analysis. *Journal of Interpersonal Violence, 1,* 288–308.

Reuter, R.P. (1995, July 25). Consider "9 days of deceit" prosecutors urge Smith jury. *Toronto Star,* p. A4.

Rice, M.E., & Harris, G.T. (1990). The predictors of insanity acquittal. *International Journal of Law and Psychiatry, 13,* 217–224.

Rice, M.E., & Harris, G.T. (1992). A comparison of criminal recidivism among schizophrenic and nonschizophrenic offenders. *International Journal of Law and Psychiatry, 15,* 397–406.

Rice, M.E., & Harris, G.T. (1997a). Cross validation and extension of the Violence Risk Appraisal Guide with child molesters and rapists. *Law and Human Behavior, 21,* 231–241.

Rice, M.E., & Harris, G.T. (1997b). The treatment of mentally disordered offenders. *Psychology, Public Policy, and Law, 3,* 126–183.

Rice, M.E., Harris, G.T., & Cormier, C.A. (1992). An evaluation of a maximum security therapeutic community for psychopaths and other mentally disordered offenders. *Law and Human Behaviour, 16,* 399–412.

Rice, M.E., Harris, G.T., Lang, C., & Cormier, C. (2006). Violent sex offenses: How are they best measured from official records? *Law and Human Behavior, 30,* 525–541.

Richards, H.J., Casey, J.O., & Lucente, S.W. (2003). Psychopathy and treatment response in response to incarcerated female substance abusers. *Criminal Justice and Behavior, 30,* 251–276.

Rind, B., Jaeger, M., & Strohmetz, D.B. (1995). Effect of crime seriousness on simulated jurors' use of inadmissible evidence. *Journal of Social Psychology, 135,* 417–424.

Risin, L.I., & Koss, M.P. (1987). The sexual abuse of boys: Prevalence and descriptive characteristics of childhood victimizations. *Journal of Interpersonal Violence, 2,* 309–323.

Roberts, A.R. (1996). Battered women who kill: A comparative study of incarcerated participants with a community sample of battered women. *Journal of Family Violence, 11,* 291–304.

Roberts, J.V. (1991). Sentencing reform: The lessons of psychology. *Canadian Psychology, 32,* 466–477.

Roberts, J.V., & Birkenmayer, A. (1997). Sentencing in adult provincial courts. *Juristat, 17.*

Roberts, J.V., & Melchers, R. (2003). The incarceration of Aboriginal offenders: Trends from 1978 to 2001. *Canadian Journal of Criminology and Criminal Justice, 45,* 211–242.

Robins, L.N. (1986). The consequences of conduct disorder in girls. In D. Olweus, J. Block, & M. Radke-Yarrow (Eds.), *Development of antisocial and prosocial behavior* (pp. 385–408). New York: Academic Press.

Robinson, D. (1989). *Forum on Corrections Research (Correctional Service Canada), 1,* 12–22.

Rockett, J.L., Murrie, D.C., & Boccaccini, M.T. (2007). Diagnostic labeling in juvenile justice settings: Do psychopathy and conduct disorder findings influence clinicians? *Psychological Services, 4,* 107–122

Roebers, C.M., Bjorklund, D.F., Schneider, W., & Cassel, W.S. (2002). Differences and similarities in event recall and suggestibility between children and adults in Germany and the United States. *Experimental Psychology, 49,* 132–140.

Roesch, R., Eaves, D., Sollner, R., Normandin, M., & Glackman, W. (1981). Evaluating fitness to stand trial: A comparative analysis of fit and unfit defendants. *International Journal of Law and Psychiatry, 4,* 145, 157.

Roesch, R., Ogloff, J.R.P., Hart, S.D., Dempster, R.J., Zapf, P.A., & Whittemore, K.E. (1997). The impact of Canadian Criminal Code changes on remands and assessments of fitness to stand trial and criminal responsibility in British Columbia. *Canadian Journal of Psychiatry, 42,* 509–514.

Roesch, R., Zapf, P.A., Eaves, D., & Webster, C.D. (1998). *The Fitness Interview Test* (rev. ed.). (Available from the Mental

Health Law, and Policy Institute, Simon Fraser University, Burnaby British Columbia, Canada, V5A 1S6.)

Rogers, R. (1984). *Rogers Criminal Responsibility Assessment Scales*. Psychological Assessment Resources. Odessa, FL.

Rogers, R. (1986). *Conducting insanity evaluations*. New York: Van Nostrand Reinhold.

Rogers, R. (1988). Structured interviews and dissimulation. In R. Rogers (Ed.), *Clinical assessment of malingering and deception* (1st ed., pp. 250–268). New York: Guilford Press.

Rogers, R. (1990). Models of feigned mental illness. *Professional Psychology, 21,* 182–188.

Rogers, R. (1997). Structured interviews and dissimulation. In R. Rogers (Ed.), *Clinical assessment of malingering and deception* (2nd ed., pp. 301–327). New York: Guilford Press.

Rogers, R., Bagby, R.M., & Dickens, S.E. (1992). *Structured Interview of Reported Symptoms (SIRS) and professional manual*. Odessa, FL: Psychological Assessment Resources.

Rogers, R., & Ewing, C.P. (1992). The measurement of insanity: Debating the merits of the R-CRAS and its alternatives. *International Journal of Law and Psychiatry, 15,* 113–123.

Rogers, R., Jackson, R.L., Sewell, K.W., & Salekin, K.L. (2005). Detection strategies for malingering: A confirmatory factor analysis of the SIRS. *Criminal Justice and Behavior, 32,* 511–525.

Rogers, R., & Sewell, K.W. (1999). The R-CRAS and insanity evaluations: A reexamination of construct validity. *Behavioral Sciences and the Law, 17,* 181–194.

Rogers, R., Sewell, K.W., & Goldstein, A.M. (1994). Explanatory models of malingering: A prototypical analysis. *Law and Human Behavior, 18,* 543–552.

Rogers, R., Sewell, K.W., Martin, M.A., & Vitacco, J.J. (2003). Detection of feigned mental disorders: A meta-analysis of the MMPI-2 and malingering. *Assessment, 10,* 160–177.

Rogers, R., Ustad, K.L., & Salekin, R.T. (1998). Convergent validity of the Personality Assessment Inventory: A study of emergency referrals in a correctional setting. *Assessment, 5,* 3–12.

Rosenberg, D.A. (1987). A web of deceit: A literature review of Munchausen syndrome by proxy. *Child Abuse & Neglect, 11,* 547–563.

Rosenfeld, B. (2003). Recidivism in stalking and obsessional harassment. *Law and Human Behavior, 27,* 251–265.

Rosenfeld, B. (2004). Violence risk factors in stalking and obsessional harassment: A review and preliminary meta-analysis. *Criminal Justice and Behavior, 31,* 9–36.

Rosenfeld, J.P., Angell, A., Johnson, M., & Qian, J. (1991). An ERP-based, control-question lie detector analog: Algorithms for discriminating effects within individuals' average waveforms. *Psychophysiology, 38,* 319–335.

Rosenfeld, J.P., Nasman, V.T., Whalen, R., Cantwell, B., & Mazzeri, L. (1987). Late vertex positivity in event-related potentials as a guilty knowledge indicator: A new method of lie detection. *Polygraph, 16,* 223–231.

Rosenfeld, J.P., Soskins, M., Bosh, G., & Ryan, A. (2004). Simple, effective countermeasures to P300-based tests of detection of concealed information. *Psychophysiology, 41,* 205–219.

Rosenfeld, J.P., Sweet, J.L., Chuang, J., Ellwanger, J., & Song, L. (1996). Detection of simulated malingering using forced choice recognition enhanced with event-related potential recording. *Neurophysiology, 120,* 163–179.

Rosenhan, D.J., Eisner, S.L., & Robinson, R.J. (1994). Notetaking can aid juror recall. *Law and Human Behavior, 18,* 53–61.

Rosenhan, D.L. (1973). On being sane in insane places. *Science, 179,* 250–257.

Rossmo, D.K. (1995). Place, space and police investigations: Hunting serial violent criminals. In J.E. Eck & D. Weisburd (Eds.), *Crime and place* (pp. 217–235). Monsey, NY: Criminal Justice Press.

Rossmo, D.K. (2000). *Geographic profiling*. Boca Raton, FL: CRC Press.

Rossmo, D.K. (2005). Cognitive heuristics or shortcuts to failure: Response to Snook et al. *Applied Cognitive Psychology, 19,* 65–654.

Rotenberg, K.J., Hewlet, M.G., & Siegwart, C.M. (1998). Principled moral reasoning and self-monitoring as predictors of jury functioning. *Basic and Applied Social Psychology, 20,* 167–173.

Rothbaum, B.O., Foa, E.B., Riggs, D., Murdock, T., & Walsh, W. (1992). A prospective examination of post-traumatic stress disorder in rape victims. *Journal of Traumatic Stress, 5,* 455–475.

Royal Canadian Mounted Police. (2007). Preparatory guide for RCMP regular member selection interview. Retrieved May 25, 2007, from http://www.rcmp-grc.gc.ca/recruiting/rmsig_e.pdf.

Royal Commission on Aboriginal Peoples. (1996). *Bridging the cultural divide: A report on Aboriginal people and criminal justice and Canada*. Ottawa: Ministry of Supply and Services Canada.

Ruby, C.L., & Brigham, J.C. (1997). The usefulness of the criteria-based content analysis technique in distinguishing between truthful and fabricated allegations: A critical review. *Psychology, Public Policy, and Law, 3,* 705–727.

Rudolph, K.D., & Asher, S.R. (2000). Adaptation and maladaptation in the peer system: Developmental processes and outcomes. In A.J. Sameroff, M. Lewis, & S.M. Miller (Eds.), *Handbook of developmental psychopathology* (2nd ed., pp. 157–175). New York: Kluwer Academic/Plenum Publishers.

Rugge, T. (2006). *Risk assessment of male Aboriginal offenders: A 2006 perspective*. Ottawa, Ontario: Public Safety and Emergency Preparedness Canada.

Rutherford, M.J., Alterman, A.I., Cacciola, J.S., & McKay, J.R. (1997). Validity of the psychopathy checklist-revised in male methadone patients. *Drug and Alcohol Dependence*, 44, 143–149.

Rutter, M. (1979). Protective factors in children's responses to stress and disadvantage. In M.W. Kent & J.E. Rolf (Eds.), *Primary Prevention of Psychopathology, Vol. 3: Social Competence in Children* (pp. 49–74). New England: University Press of New England.

Rutter, M. (1988). *Studies of psychosocial risk: The power of longitudinal data*. Cambridge, MA: Cambridge University Press.

Rutter, M. (1990). Psychosocial resilience and protective mechanisms. In J. Rolf, A.S. Masten, D. Cicchetti, K. Nuechterlein, & S. Weintraub (Eds.), *Risk and protective factors in the development of psychopathology* (pp. 181–214). Cambridge, MA: Cambridge University Press.

Rutter, M. (Ed.). (1995). *Psychosocial disturbances in young people: Challenges for prevention*. Cambridge, MA: Press Syndicate of the University of Cambridge.

Ryan, G., Miyoshi, T.J., Metzner, J.L., Krugman, R.D., & Fryer, G.E. (1996). Trends in a national sample of sexually abusive youths. *Journal of the American Academy of Child and Adolescent Psychiatry*, 35, 17–25.

Saks, M.J., & Marti, M.W. (1997). A meta-analysis of the effects of jury size. *Law and Human Behavior*, 21, 451–466.

Salekin, R.T. (2002). Factor-analysis of the Millon Adolescent Clinical Inventory in a juvenile offender population: Implications for treatment. *Journal of Offender Rehabilitation*, 34, 15–29.

Salekin, R.T., Rogers, R., & Machin, D. (2001). Psychopathy in youth: Pursuing diagnostic clarity. *Journal of Youth and Adolescence*, 30, 173–195.

Salekin, R.T., Rogers, R., & Sewell, K.W. (1996). A review and meta-analysis of the Psychopathy Checklist and Psychopathy Checklist-Revised: Predictive validity of dangerousness. *Clinical Psychology: Science and Practice*, 3, 203–215.

Salekin, R.T., Rogers, R., & Sewell, K.W. (1997). Construct validity of psychopathy in female offender sample: A multitrait-multimethod evaluation. *Journal of Abnormal Psychology*, 106, 576–585.

Salekin, R.T., Rogers, R., Ustad, K.L., & Sewell, K.W. (1998). Psychopathy and recidivism among female inmates. *Law and Human Behavior*, 22, 109–128.

Sanders, B.A. (2003). Maybe there's no such thing as a "good cop": Organizational challenges in selecting quality officers. *Policing: An International Journal of Police Strategies and Management*, 26, 313–328.

Sandys, M., & Dillehay, R.C. (1995). First ballot votes, predeliberation dispositions and final verdicts in jury trials. *Law and Human Behavior*, 19, 175–195.

Saslove, H., & Yarmey, A.D. (1980). Long-term auditory memory: Speaker identification. *Journal of Applied Psychology*, 65, 111–116.

Saunders, D.G. (2001). Developing guidelines for domestic violence offenders: What can we learn from related fields and current research? In R.A. Geffner & A. Rosenbaum (Eds.), *Domestic violence offenders: Current interventions, research, and implications for policies and standards* (pp. 235–248). New York: Haworth.

Saunders, D.G. (2002). Are physical assaults by wives and girlfriends a major social problem? A review of the literature. *Violence Against Women*, 8, 1424–1448.

Saunders, J.W.S. (2001). Experts in court: A view from the bench. *Canadian Psychology*, 42, 109–118.

Saunders, P., & Thompson, J. (2002, Feb. 7). The missing women of Vancouver. *CBC News Online*. Retrieved July 23, 2003, from http://www.cbc.ca/news/features/bc_missingwomen.html.

Saywitz, K., Goodman, G.S., Nicholas, E., & Moan, S. (1991). Children's memories of physical examinations involving genital touch: Implications for reports of child sexual abuse. *Journal of Consulting and Clinical Psychology*, 59, 682–691.

Saywitz, K.J., & Snyder, L. (1996). Narrative elaboration: Test of a new procedure for interviewing children. *Journal of Consulting and Clinical Psychology*, 64, 1347–1357.

Scheck, B. Neufeld, P., & Dwyer, J. (2000). *Actual innocence*. Garden City, NY: Doubleday.

Schmidt, F., McKinnon, L., Chattha, H.K., & Brownless, K. (2006). Concurrent and predictive validity of the *Psychopathy Checklist: Youth Version* across gender and ethnicity. *Psychological Assessment*, 18, 393–401.

Schneider, E.M. (1986). Describing and changing: Women's self-defence work and the problem of expert testimony on battering. *Women's Rights Law Reports*, 9, 195–222.

Schneider, R.D., Bloom, H., & Heerema, M. (2007). *Mental health courts: Decriminalizing the mentally ill*. Toronto: Irwin Law.

Schuller, R.A. (1992). The impact of battered woman syndrome evidence on jury decision processes. *Law and Human Behavior*, 16, 597–620.

Schuller, R.A. (1995). Expert evidence and hearsay: The influence of "secondhand" information on jurors' decisions. *Law and Human Behavior*, 19, 345–362.

Schuller, R.A., & Cripps, J. (1998). Expert evidence pertaining to battered women: The impact of gender and timing of testimony. *Law and Human Behavior*, 22, 17–31.

Schuller, R.A., & Hastings, P. (1996). Trials of battered women who kill: The impact of alternative forms of expert evidence. *Law and Human Behavior*, 20, 167–187.

Schuller, R.A., & Hastings, P.A. (2002). Complainant sexual history evidence: Its impact on mock jurors' decisions. *Psychology of Women Quarterly*, 26, 252–261.

Schuller, R.A., & Ogloff, J.R.P. (2001). *Introduction to psychology and law: Canadian perspectives*. Toronto: University of Toronto Press.

Schuller, R.A., & Rzepa, S. (2002). Expert testimony pertaining to battered woman syndrome: Its impact on jurors' decisions. *Law and Human Behavior, 26*, 655–673.

Schuller, R.A., Smith, V.L., & Olson, J.M. (1994). Jurors' decisions in trials of battered women who kill: The role of prior beliefs and expert testimony. *Journal of Applied Social Psychology, 24*, 316–337.

Schuller, R.A., Terry, D., & McKimmie, B. (2005). The impact of expert testimony on jurors' decisions: Gender of the expert and testimony complexity. *Journal of Applied Social Psychology, 6*, 1266–1280.

Schwartz, D., Dodge, K.A., Coie, J.D., Hubbard, J.A., Cillessen, A.H.N., Lemerise, E.A., & Bateman, H. (1998). Social-cognitive and behavioral correlates of aggression and victimization in boys' play groups. *Journal of Abnormal Child Psychology, 26*, 431–440.

Scogin, F., Schumacher, J., Gardner, J., & Chaplin, W. (1995). Predictive validity of psychological testing in law enforcement settings. *Professional Psychology: Research and Practice, 26*, 68–71.

Seagrave, D., & Grisso, T. (2002). Adolescent development and the measurement of juvenile psychopathy. *Law and Human Behavior, 26*, 219–239.

Sear, L., & Williamson, T. (1999). British and American interrogation strategies. In D.V. Canter and L.J. Alison (Eds.), *Interviewing and deception* (pp. 67–81). Aldershot: Ashgate Publishing.

Seligman, M.E. (1975). *Helplessness: On depression, development, and death*. San Francisco, CA: W.H. Freeman.

Seltzer, R. (2006). Scientific jury selection: Does it work? *Journal of Applied Social Psychology, 36*, 2417–2435.

Serin, R.C. (1991). Psychopathy and violence in criminals. *Journal of Interpersonal Violence, 6*, 423–431.

Serin, R.C., & Amos, N.L. (1995). The role of psychopathy in the assessment of dangerousness. *International Journal of Law and Psychiatry, 18*, 231–238.

Seto, M.C., & Barbaree, H.E. (1999). Psychopathy, treatment behavior, and sex offender recidivism. *Journal of Interpersonal Violence, 14*, 1235–1248.

Seymour, T.L., Seifert, C.M., Shafto, M.G., & Mosmann, A.L. (2000). Using response time measures to assess "guilty knowledge." *Journal of Applied Psychology, 85*, 30–37.

Shackelford, T.K., & Mouzos, J. (2005). Partner killing by men in cohabiting and marital relationships: A comparative, cross-national analysis of data from Australia and the United States. *Journal of Interpersonal Violence, 20*, 1310–1324.

Shaw, D.S., Keenan, K., & Vondra, J.I. (1994). Developmental precursors of externalizing behaviour: Ages 1 to 3. *Developmental Psychology, 30*, 355–364.

Shaw, J.S., III (1996). Increases in eyewitness confidence resulting from postevent questioning. *Journal of Experimental Psychology: Applied, 12*, 126–146.

Shaw, J.S., III, & McClure, K.A. (1996). Repeated postevent questioning can lead to elevated levels of eyewitness confidence. *Law and Human Behavior, 20*, 629–654.

Shaw, M. (1994). Women in prison: A literature review. *Forum on Corrections Research, 6*, 13–18.

Sheehan, P.W., & Tilden, J. (1984). Real and simulated occurrences of memory distortion in hypnosis. *Journal of Abnormal Psychology, 93*, 47–57.

Sheehan, R., & Cordner, G.W. (1989). *Introduction to police administration* (2nd ed.). Cincinnati, OH: Anderson Publishing Co.

Sheldon, D.H., & Macleod, M.D. (1991). From normative to positive data: Expert psychological evidence re-examined. *Criminal Law Review, 811.*

Sheldon, W.H. (1949). *Varieties of delinquent youths: A psychology of constitutional differences*. New York: Harper & Row.

Shepherd, J.W. (1981). Social factors in face recognition. In G. Davies, H. Ellis, & J. Shepherd (Eds.), *Perceiving and remembering faces* (pp. 55–79). London: Academic Press.

Shepherd, J.W., Deregowski, J.B. (1981). Races and faces: A comparison of the responses of Africans and Europeans to faces of the same and different races. *British Journal of Social Psychology, 20*, 125–133.

Sheridan, M.S. (2003). The deceit continues: An updated literature review of Munchausen syndrome by proxy. *Child Abuse & Neglect, 27*, 431–451.

Sherman, L.W., & Berk, R.A. (1984). The specific deterrent effects of arrest for domestic assault. *American Sociological Review, 49*, 261–272.

Sherman, L.W., Schmidt, J.D., & Rogan, D.P. (1992). *Policing domestic violence: Experiments and dilemmas*. New York: Free Press.

Shover, N., & Thompson, C.Y. (1992). Age differential expectations, and crime desistance. *Criminology, 30*, 89–104.

Siegal, L., & Senna, J. (1994). *Juvenile delinquency: Theory, practice and law* (5th ed.). St. Paul, MN: West Publishing Company.

Silver, E. (2006). Understanding the relationship between mental disorder and violence: The need for a criminological perspective. *Law and Human Behavior, 30*, 685–706.

Simourd, D.J. (2004). Use of dynamic risk/need assessment instruments among long-term incarcerated offenders. *Criminal Justice and Behavior, 31*, 306–323.

Simourd, D.J., & Malcolm, P.B. (1998). Reliability and validity of the Level of Service Inventory-Revised among federally incarcerated sex offenders. *Journal of Interpersonal Violence, 13*, 261–274.

Simourd, D.J., Hoge, R.D., Andrews, D.A., & Leschied, A.W. (1994). An empirically based typology of male young offenders. *Canadian Journal of Criminology, 36*, 447–461.

Simourd, L., & Andrews, D.A. (1994). Correlates of delinquency: A look at gender differences. *Forum on Corrections Research*, 6, 26–31.

Sin, L. (2006, December 6). By the numbers. *Ottawa Citizen*, p. A3.

Sioui, R., & Thibault, J. (2001). *Pertinence of cultural adaptation of Reintegration Potential Reassessment (RPR) scale to Aboriginal context.* Research Report No. R-109. Ottawa: Correctional Service Canada.

Sioui, R., & Thibault, J. (2002). Examining reintegration potential for Aboriginal offenders. *Forum on Corrections Research*, 14, 49–51.

Sjöstedt, G., & Langström, N. (2002). Assessment of risk for criminal recidivism among rapists: A comparison of four different measures. *Psychology, Crime & Law*, 8, 25–40.

Skeem, J.L., Mulvey, E.P., Odgers, C., Schubert, C., Stowman, S., Gardner, W., & Lidz, C. (2005). What do clinicians expect? Comparing envisioned and reported violence for male and female patients. *Journal of Consulting and Clinical Psychology*, 73, 599–609.

Skilling, T.A., Quinsey, V.L., & Craig, W.M. (2001). Evidence of a taxon underlying serious antisocial behavior in boys. *Criminal Justice and Behavior*, 28, 450–470.

Skinner, B.F. (1974). *About behaviorism*. London: Cape.

Slone, A.E., Brigham, J.C., & Meissner, C.A. (2000). Social and cognitive factors affecting the own-race bias in Whites. *Basic and Applied Social Psychology*, 22, 71–84.

Smith, C., & Thornberry, T.P. (1995). The relationship between childhood maltreatment and adolescent involvement in delinquency. *Criminology*, 33, 451–481.

Smith, C.A., Ireland, T.O., & Thornberry, T.P. (2005). Adolescent maltreatment and its impact on young adult antisocial behavior. *Child Abuse & Neglect*, 29, 1099–1119.

Smith, D.A., Visher, C.A., & Davidson, L.A. (1984). Equity and discretionary justice: The influence of race on police arrest decisions. *Journal of Criminal Law and Criminology*, 75, 234–249.

Smith, D.W., Letourneau, E.J., Saunders, B.E., Kilpatrick, D.G., Resnick, H.S., & Best, C.L. (2000). Delay in disclosure of childhood rape: Results from a national survey. *Child Abuse & Neglect*, 24, 273–287.

Smith, G.P. (1997). Assessment of malingering with self-report measures. In R. Rogers (Ed.), *Clinical assessment of malingering and deception* (2nd ed., pp. 351–372). New York: Guilford Press.

Smith, G.P., & Borum, R. (1992). Detection of malingering in a forensic sample: A study of the M test. *Journal of Psychiatry and Law*, 20, 505–514.

Smith, M.D. (1990). Patriarchal ideology and wife beating: A test of a feminist hypothesis. *Violence and Victims*, 5, 257–273.

Smith, V.L. (1991). Impact of pretrial instruction on jurors' information processing and decision making. *Journal of Applied Psychology*, 76, 220–228.

Snook, B., Eastwood, J., Gendreau, P., Goggin, C., & Cullen, R.M. (2007). Taking stock of criminal profiling: A narrative review and meta-analysis. *Criminal Justice and Behavior*, 34, 437–453.

Snook, B., Taylor, P.J., & Bennell, C. (2004). Geographic profiling: The fast, frugal and accurate way. *Applied Cognitive Psychology*, 18, 105–121.

Snook, B., Zito, M., Bennell, C., & Taylor, P. J. (2005). On the complexity and accuracy of geographic profiling strategies. *Journal of Quantitative Criminology*, 21, 1–26.

Söchting, I., Fairbrother, N., & Koch, W. J. (2004). Sexual assault of women: Prevention efforts and risk factors. *Violence Against Women*, 10, 73–93.

Sommers, S.R., & Ellsworth, P.C. (2001). White juror bias: An investigation of prejudice against Black defendants in the American courtroom. *Psychology, Public Policy, and Law*, 7, 201–229.

Sonkin, D.J., Martin, D., & Walker, I.E. (1985). *The male batterer: A treatment approach*. New York: Springer.

Soothill, K., Harman, J., Francis, B., & Kirby, S. (2005). Identifying future repeat danger from sexual offenders against children: A focus on those convicted and those strongly suspected of such crime. *The Journal of Forensic Psychiatry & Psychology*, 16, 225–247.

Spanos, N.P., DuBreuil, S.C., & Gwynn, M.I. (1991–1992). The effects of expert testimony concerning rape on the verdicts and beliefs of mock jurors. *Imagination, Cognition, and Personality*, 11, 37–51.

Spanos, N.P., Myers, B., DuBreuil, S.C., & Pawlak, A.E. (1992–1993). The effects of polygraph and eyewitness testimony on the beliefs and decisions of mock jurors. *Imagination, Cognition, and Personality*, 12, 103–113.

Sparwood Youth Assistance Program. (2007). Sparwood youth assistance program. Retrieved May 25, 2007, from http://www.sparwood.bc.ca/syap-out.htm.

Spiegel, D., & Spiegel, H. (1987). Forensic uses of hypnosis. In I.B. Weiner & A.K. Hess (Eds.), *Handbook of forensic psychology* (pp. 474–498). New York: John Wiley & Sons.

Sporer, S.L. (1996). Psychological aspects of person descriptions. In S. Sporer, R. Malpass, G. Köehnken (Eds.), *Psychological issues in eyewitness identification* (pp. 53–86). Mahwah, New Jersey: Erlbaum.

Sporer, S.L. & Schwandt, B. (2006). Paraverbal indicators of deception: A meta-analytic synthesis. *Applied Cognitive Psychology*, 20, 421–446.

Sporer S.L., & Schwandt, B. (2007). Moderators of non-verbal indicators of deception: A meta-analytic synthesis. *Psychology, Public Policy, and Law*, 13, 1–34.

Sporer, S.L., & Penrod, S.D., Read, D., & Cutler, B.L. (1995). Choosing confidence and accuracy: A meta-analysis of the confidence-accuracy relations in eyewitness identification studies. *Psychological Bulletin*, 118, 315–327.

Sprott, J.B., & Doob, A. (1997). Fear, victimization, and attitudes to sentencing, the courts, and the police. *Canadian Journal of Criminology, 39,* 275–291.

Stack, S. (1997). Homicide followed by suicide: An analysis of Chicago data. *Criminology, 35,* 435–453.

Stadtland, C., Hollweg, M., Kleindienst, N., Dietl, J., Reich, U., & Nedopil, N. (2005). Risk assessment and prediction of violent and sexual recidivism in sex offenders: Long-term predictive validity of four assessment instruments. *The Journal of Forensic Psychiatry & Psychology, 16,* 92–108.

Stanton, J., & Simpson, A. (2002). Filicide: A review. *International Journal of Law and Psychiatry, 25,* 1–14.

Statistics Canada, Health Statistics Division (1999). Divorces, 1996 and 1997, cat. no. 84F0213XPB Ottawa: Statistics Canada.

Statistics Canada (2003a). Table: Court, youth cases by decision (total all decisions). Retrieved February 1, 2007, from http://www40.statcan.ca/l01/cst01/legal25a.htm.

Statistics Canada (2003b). Table: Court, youth cases by type of sentence, by province and territory (Canada). Retrieved February 2, 2007, from http://www40.statcan.ca/l01/cst01/legal40a.htm.

Statistics Canada. (2003c, June 20). Youth court statistics. *The Daily.* Retrieved June 10, 2004, from http://www.statcan.ca/Daily/English/030620/d030620d.htm.

Statistics Canada. (2004a, March 12). Youth court statistics. *The Daily.* Retrieved from July 1, 2007, from http://www.statcan.ca/Daily/English/040312/d040312c.htm.

Statistics Canada (2004b, October 13). Youth custody and community services. *The Daily.* Retrieved February 2, 2007, from http://www.statcan.ca/Daily/English/041013/d041013c.htm.

Statistics Canada. (2005a). CANSIM Table 252-0030: Youth court survey, number of cases by type of decision, annual, 1991 to 2003, cat. no. 85-002-X. Retrieved from http://www.statcan.ca/Daily/English/050624/d050624c.htm.

Statistics Canada (2005b, December 1). Youth correctional services: Key indicators. *The Daily.* Retrieved February 2, 2007, from http://www.statcan.ca/Daily/English/051201/d051201a.htm.

Statistics Canada. (2006a). *Family violence in Canada: A statistical profile.* Ottawa: Minister of Industry.

Statistics Canada. (2006b, November 8). Homicides, 2005. *The Daily.* Retrieved May 10, 2007, from http://www.statcan.ca/Daily/English/061108/d061108b.htm.

Statistics Canada (2006c). Report on the demographic situation in Canada 2003 and 2004, cat. no. 91-209-X1E.

Statistics Canada. (2007). Table: Population reporting an Aboriginal identity, by age group, by province and territory. Retrieved May 2, 2007, from http://www40.statcan.ca/l01/cst01/demo40a.htm.

Steadman, H.J. (2000). From dangerousness to risk assessment of community violence: Taking stock at the turn of the century. *Journal of the American Academy of Psychiatry and the Law, 28,* 265–271.

Steadman, H.J., & Cocozza, J. (1974). *Careers of the criminally insane.* Lexington, Mass: Lexington Books.

Steadman, H.J., McGreevy, M.A., Morrissey, J.P., Callahan, L.A., Robbins, P.C., & Cirincione, C. (1993). *Before and after Hinckley: Evaluating insanity defense reform.* New York: Guilford Press.

Steadman, H.J., Monahan, J., Appelbaum, P.S., Grisso, T., Mulvey, E.P., Roth, L.H., et al. (1994). Designing a new generation of risk assessment research. In J. Monahan & H. J. Steadman (Eds.), *Violence and mental disorder: Developments in risk assessment* (297–318). Chicago: University of Chicago Press.

Steadman, H.J., Mulvey, E.P., Monahan, J., Robbins, P.C., Appelbaum, P.S., Grisso, T., Roth, L.H., & Silver, E. (1998). Violence by people discharged from acute psychiatric inpatient facilities and by others in the same neighborhoods. *Archives of General Psychiatry, 55,* 393–401.

Steadman, H.J., Silver, E., Monahan, J., Appelbaum, P.S., Robbins, P.C., Mulvey, E.P., Grisso, T., Roth, L.H., & Banks, S. (2000). A classification tree approach to the development of actuarial violence risk assessment tools. *Law and Human Behavior, 24,* 83–100.

Steblay, N.M. (1992). A meta-analytic review of the weapon focus effect. *Law and Human Behavior, 16,* 413–424.

Steblay, N.M. (1997). Social influence in eyewitness recall: A meta-analytic review of lineup instruction effects. *Law and Human Behavior, 21,* 283–298.Steblay, N.M., Besirevic, J., Fulero, S.M., & Jimenez-Lorente, B. (1999). The effects of pretrial publicity on juror verdicts: A meta-analytic review. *Law and Human Behavior, 23,* 219–235.

Steblay, N.M., Besirevic, J., Fulero, S., & Jimenez-Lorente, B. (1999). The effects of pretrial publicity on juror verdicts: A meta-analytic review. *Law and Human Behaviour, 23,* 219–235.

Steblay, N.M. & Bothwell, R.B. (1994). Evidence for hypnotically refreshed testimony: The view from the laboratory. *Law and Human Behavior, 18,* 635–651.

Steblay, N.M., Dysart, J., Fulero, S., & Lindsay, R.C.L. (2001). Eyewitness accuracy rates in sequential and simultaneous lineup presentations: A meta-analytic comparison. *Law and Human Behavior, 25,* 459–474.

Steblay, N.M., Dysart, J.E., Fulero, S., & Lindsay, R.C.L. (2003). Eyewitness accuracy rates in police showup and lineup presentations: A meta-analytic comparison. *Law and Human Behavior, 27,* 523–540.

Stein, K. (2001). *Public perceptions of crime and justice in Canada: A review of opinion polls.* Ottawa: Department of Justice Canada.

Stein, M., Koverola, C., Hanna, C., Torchia, M., & McClarry, B. (1997). Hippocampal volume in woman victimized by childhood sexual abuse. *Psychological Medicine*, *27*, 951–959.

Stellar, M. (1989). Recent developments in statement analysis. In J.C. Yuille (Ed.), *Credibility assessment* (pp. 135–154). Dordrecht, the Netherlands: Kluwer.

Stern, W. (1910). Abstracts of lectures on the psychology of testimony and on the study of individuality. *American Journal of Psychology*, *21*, 270–282.

Stevens, D.J. (1994). Predatory rapists and victim selection techniques. *Social Science Journal*, *31*, 421–433.

Stewart, E. (2000). The comparative constitution of twinship: Strategies and paradoxes. *Twin Research*, *3*, 142–147.

Storm, J., & Graham, J.R. (2000). Detection of coached general malingering on the MMPI-2. *Psychological Assessment*, *12*, 158–165.

Stouthamer-Loeber, M., Wei, E., Loeber, R., & Masten, A.S. (2004). Desistance from persistent serious delinquency in the transition to adulthood. *Development and Psychopathology*, *16*, 897–918.

Strand, S., & Belfrage, H. (2001). Comparison of HCR-20 scores in violent mentally disordered men and women: Gender differences and similarities. *Psychology, Crime, & Law*, *7*, 71–79.

Strand, S., Belfrage, H., Fransson, G., & Levander, S. (1999). Clinical and risk management factors in risk prediction of mentally disordered offenders—more important than historical data? A retrospective study of 40 mentally disordered offenders assessed with the HCR-20 violence risk assessment scheme. *Legal and Criminological Psychology*, *4*, 67–76.

Straus, M.A. (1977). Wife beating: How common and why? *Victimology*, *2*, 443–458.

Straus, M.A. (1979). Measuring family conflict and violence: The Conflict Tactics Scale. *Journal of Marriage and the Family*, *41*, 75–88.

Straus, M.A. (1990). Measuring intrafamily conflict and violence: The Conflict Tactics (CTS) Scales. In M. Straus & R. Gelles (Eds.), *Physical violence in American families: Risk factors and adaptations to violence in 8,145 families* (pp. 29–47). New Brunswick, NJ: Transaction.

Straus, M.A., Gelles, R. J., & Steinmetz, S. (1980). *Behind closed doors: Violence in the American family*. Garden City, NY: Anchor/Doubleday.

Straus, M.A., Hamby, S.L., Boney-McCoy, S., & Sugarman, D.B. (1996). The revised Conflict Tactics Scales (CTS2): Development and preliminary psychometric data. *Journal of Family Issues*, *17*, 283–316.

Strier, F. (1999). Whither trial consulting? Issues and projections. *Law and Human Behavior*, *23*, 93–115.

Strömwall, L.A., Hartwig, M., & Granhag, P.A. (2006). To act truthfully: Nonverbal behaviour and strategies during a police interrogation. *Psychology, Crime & Law*, 12, 207–219.

Sue, S., Smith, R.E., & Caldwell, C. (1973). Effects of inadmissible evidence on the decisions of simulated jurors: A moral dilemma. *Journal of Applied Social Psychology*, *3*, 345–353.

Sundby, S.E. (1997). The jury as critic: An empirical look at how capital juries perceive expert and lay testimony. *Virginia Law Review*, *83*, 1109–1188.

Supreme Court of Canada. (2007). Supreme Court of Canada: About the Court. Retrieved May 1, 2007, from http://www.scc-csc.gc.ca/AboutCourt/index_e.asp.

Sutherland, E.H. (1939). *Principles of criminology*. Philadelphia: J.B. Lippincott Company.

Swanson, J.W. (1994). Mental disorder, substance abuse, and community violence: An epidemiological approach. In J. Monahan & H. J. Steadman (Eds.), *Violence and mental disorder: Developments in risk assessment* (101–137). Chicago: University of Chicago Press.

Swanson, J.W., Borum, R., Swartz, M.S., & Monahan, J. (1996). Psychotic symptoms and disorders and the risk of violent behavior in the community. *Criminal Behavior and Mental Health*, *6*, 317–338.

Swanson, J.W., Borum, R., Swartz, M.S., Hiday, V.A., Wagner, H.R., & Burns, B.J. (2001). Can involuntary outpatient commitment reduce arrests among persons with severe mental illness? *Criminal Justice and Behavior*, *28*, 156–189.

Swanson, J.W., Holzer, C.E., Ganju, V.K., & Jono, R.T. (1990). Violence and psychiatric disorder in the community: Evidence from the epidemiologic catchment area surveys. *Hospital and Community Psychiatry*, *41*, 761–770.

Sykes, J.B. (Ed.). (1982). *The Concise Oxford Dictionary* (7th ed.). Oxford: Oxford University Press.

Szymanski, L.A., Devlin, A.S., Chrisler, J.C., & Vyse, S.A. (1993). Gender role and attitudes toward rape in male and female college students. *Sex Roles*, *29*, 37–57.

Talwar, V., & Lee, K. (2002). Emergence of white-lie telling in children between 3 and 7 years of age. *Merrill-Palmer Quarterly*, *48*, 160–181.

Tanford, J.A. (1992). The law and psychology of jury instructions. In J.R.P. Ogloff (Ed.), *Law and psychology: The broadening of the discipline* (pp. 305–329). Durham, NC: Carolina Academic Press.

Taylor, A., & Bennell, C. (2006). Operational and organizational police stress in an Ontario police department: A descriptive study. *Canadian Journal of Police and Security Services*, *4*, 223–234.

Taylor, S.P., & Sears, J.D. (1988). The effects of alcohol and persuasive social pressure on human physical aggression. *Aggressive Behavior*, *14*, 237–243.

Teasdale, B., Silver, E., & Monahan, J. (2006). Gender, threat/control-override delusions and violence. *Law and Human Behavior*, *30*, 649–658.

Technical Working Group for Eyewitness Evidence. (1999). *Eyewitness evidence: A guide for law enforcement.* Washington, DC: United States Department of Justice, Office of Justice Programs. NCJ 178240. Available at: www.ojp.usdoj.gov.

Temrin, H., Buchmayer, S., & Enquist, M. (2000). Step-parents and infanticide New data contradict evolutionary predictions. *Proceedings of the Royal Society of London, Series B: Biological Sciences, 267,* 943–945.

Teplin, L.A. (1984). Criminalizing mental disorder: The comparative arrest rate of the mentally ill. *American Psychologist, 39,* 784–803.

Teplin, L.A. (1986). *Keeping the peace: The parameters of police discretion in relation to the mentally disordered.* Washington, DC: U.S. Department of Justice.

Teplin, L.A. (2000). *Keeping the peace: Police discretion and mentally ill persons. National Institute of Justice Journal,* July, 8–15.

Teplin, L.A. Abram, K.M., & McClelland, G.M. (1994). Does psychiatric disorder predict violent crime among released jail detainees? *American Psychologist, 49,* 335–342.

Teplin, L.A., Abram, K.M., & McClelland, G.M. (1996). Prevalence of psychiatric disorders among incarcerated women I. Pretrial jail detaninees. *Archives of General Psychiatry, 53,* 505–512.

Terman, L.M. (1917). A trial of mental and pedagogical tests in a civil service examination for policemen and firemen. *Journal of Applied Psychology, 1,* 17–29.

Terrance, C. & Matheson, K. (2003). Undermining reasonableness: Expert testimony in a case involving a battered woman who kills. *Psychology of Women Quarterly, 27,* 37–45.

Test, M.A., (1992). Training in community living. In R.P Liberman (Ed.), *Handbook of psychiatric rehabilitation* (pp. 153–170). New York: Macmillan.

The Guardian. (October 28, 1988). Police set up unit for stress crisis.

Thierry, K.L., Lamb, M.E., Orbach, Y., & Pipe, M. (2005). Developmental differences in the function and use of anatomical dolls during interviews with alleged sexual abuse victims. *Journal of Counsulting and Clinical Psychology, 73,* 1125–1134.

Thonney, J., Kanachi, M., Sasaki, H., & Hatayama, T. (2005). Eye blinking as a lie-detection index in an emotionally arousing context. *Tohoku Psychologica Folia, 64,* 58–67.

Thornberry, T.P., & Jacoby, J.E. (1979). *The criminally insane: A community follow-up of mentally ill offenders.* Chicago, IL: University of Chicago Press.

Thornhill, R., & Palmer, C.T. (2000). *A natural history of rape: Biological bases of sexual coercion.* Cambridge, MA: MIT Press.

Tibbetts, J. (2003, July 21). Divorce courts shift to parallel parenting. *Ottawa Citizen,* p. A5.

Tjaden, P., & Thoennes, N. (1998). *Stalking in America: Findings from the National Violence Against Women Survey.* Washington, DC: American Psychological Association.

Tjaden, P.G., & Thoennes, N. (2001). Coworker violence and gender: Findings from the National Violence Against Women Survey. *American Journal of Preventive Medicine, 20,* 85–89.

Tolan, P., & Thomas, P. (1995). The implications of age of onset for delinquency risk: II. Longitudinal data. *Journal of Abnormal Child Psychology, 23,* 157–181.

Tolman, R.M., & Weisz, A. (1995). Coordinated community intervention for domestic violence: The effects of arrest and prosecution on recidivism of woman abuse perpetrators. *Crime and Delinquency, 41,* 481–495.

Tombaugh, T.N. (1996). *Test of Malingered Memory (TOMM).* Toronto: Multi-Health Systems.

Tombaugh, T.N. (2002). The Test of Memory Malingering (TOMM) in forensic psychology. *Journal of Forensic Neuropsychology, 2,* 69–96.

Trevethan, S., Crutcher, N., & Rastin, C.J. (2002). *An examination of healing lodges for federal offenders in Canada. Research Report.* Ottawa: Correctional Service Canada.

Trevethan, S., Moore, J.P., & Allegri, N. (2005). *The "In Search of Your Warrior" program for Aboriginal offenders: A preliminary evaluation.* Ottawa: Correctional Service Canada.

Trevethan, S., Moore, J., & Rastin, C.J. (2002). A profile of Aboriginal offenders in federal facilities and serving time in the community. *Forum on Corrections Research, 14,* 17–19.

Trevethan, S., Moore, J., Auger, S., MacDonald, M. & Sinclair, J. (2002). Childhood experiences affect Aboriginal offenders. *Forum on Corrections Research, 14,* 7–9.

Trevethan, S., Tremblay, S., & Carter, J. (2000). *The overrepresentation of Aboriginal people in the justice system.* Ottawa: Canadian Centre for Justice Statistics.

Trice, A.D., & Lamb, M. (1996). Sex-role orientation among incarcerated women. *Psychological Reports, 79,* 92–94.

Trocme, N., Fallon, B., MacLaurin, B., Daciuk, J., Felstiner, C., Black, T., Tonmyr, L., Blackstock, C., Barter, K, Turcotte, D., & Cloutier, R., (2005). Canadian Incidence Study of Reported Child Abuse and Neglect 2003: Major Findings. Ottawa: Minister of Public Works and Government Services Canada, 2005.

Trupin, E.W., Stewart, D.G., Beach, B., & Boesky, L. (2002). Effectiveness of a Dialectical Behaviour Therapy Program for incarcerated female juvenile offenders. *Child and Adolescent Mental Health, 7*(3), 121–127.

Turtle, J.W., Lindsay, R.C.L., & Wells, G.L. (2003). Best practice recommendations for eyewitness evidence procedures: New ideas for the oldest way to solve a case. *The Canadian Journal of Police and Security Services, 1,* 5–18.

Turvey, B. (2002). *Criminal profiling: An introduction to behavioral evidence analysis* (2nd ed.). San Diego, CA: Academic Press.

Tversky, A., & Kahneman, D. (1981). The framing of decisions and the psychology of choice. *Science, 211,* 453–458.

Tweed, R.G., & Dutton, D.G. (1998). A comparison of impulsive and instrumental subgroups of batters. *Violence and Victims, 13,* 217–230.

Urbaniok, F., Noll, T., Grunewald, S, Steinbach, J., & Endrass, J. (2006). Prediction of violent and sexual offences: A replication study of the VRAG in Switzerland. *The Journal of Forensic Psychiatry & Psychology, 17,* 23–31.

U.S. Bureau of Justice Statistics. (2005). *Contacts between police and the public: Findings from the 2002 national survey.* Washington, DC: U.S. Bureau of Statistics.

U.S. Department of Justice (2001). *Internet crimes against children.* Office for victims of Crime Bulletin. Washington, DC: Author.

Uggen, C. (1999). Ex-offenders and the conformist alternative: A job quality model of work and crime. *Social Problems, 46,* 127–151.

Ullman, S.E., & Knight, R.A. (1993). The efficacy of women's resistance strategies in rape situations. *Psychology of Women Quarterly, 17,* 23–38.

Ulmer, J.T. (1997). Social worlds of sentencing: Court communities under sentencing guidelines. Albany, NY: State University of New York Press.

Vallée, B. (1998). *Life and death with Billy.* Toronto: Random House.

Valliant, P.M., Furac, C.J., & Antonowicz, D.H. (1994). Attitudes toward sex offenders by female undergraduate students enrolled in a psychology program. *Social Behavior and Personality, 22,* 105–110.

Van Koppen, P.J., & Lochun, S.K. (1997). Portraying perpetrators: The validity of offender descriptions by witnesses. *Law and Human Behavior, 21,* 661–685.

Vance, J.P. (2001). Neurobiological mechanisms of psychosocial resiliency. In J.M. Richman & M.W. Fraser (Eds.), *The context of youth violence: Resilience, risk, & protection* (pp. 43–81). Westport, CN: Praeger.

Vandiver, D.M., & Teske, R.J. (2006). Juvenile female and male sex offenders: A comparison of offender, victim and judicial processing characteristics. *International Journal of Offender Therapy and Comparative Criminology, 50,* 148–165.

Varendonck, J. (1911). Les temoignages d'enfants dans un proces retentisaant. *Archives de Psycholgie, 11,* 129–171.

Viding, E., Blair, R.J., Moffitt, T.E. & Plomin, R. (2005). Evidence for substantial genetic risk for psychopathy in 7-year-olds. *Journal of Child Psychology and Psychiatry and Allied Disciplines, 46,* 592–597.

Viljoen, J.L., Roesch, R., Ogloff, J.R.P., & Zapf, P.A. (2003). The role of Canadian psychologists in conducting fitness and criminal responsibility evaluations. *Canadian Psychology, 44,* 369–381.

Viljoen, J.L. & Zapf, P.A. (2002). Fitness to stand trial evaluations: A comparison of referred and non-referred defendants. *International Journal of Forensic Mental Health, 1,* 127–138.

Vingoe, F.J. (1995). Beliefs of British law and medical students compared to expert criterion group on forensic hypnosis. *Contemporary Hypnosis, 12,* 173–187.

Violanti, J.M., Marshall, J.R., & Howe, B. (1985). Stress, coping and alcohol use: The police connection. *Journal of Police Science and Administration, 31,* 106–110.

Violanti, J.M., Vena, J.E., & Marshall, J.R. (1986). Disease risk and mortality among police officers: New evidence and contributing factors. *Journal of Police Science and Administration, 14,* 17–23.

Vitale, J.E., Smith, S.S., Brinkely, C.A., & Newman, J.P. (2002). The reliability and validity of the Psychopathy Checklist-Revised in a sample of female offenders. *Criminal Justice and Behavior, 29,* 202–231.

Vizard, E., & Trantor, M. (1988). Helping young children to describe experiences of child sexual abuse: General issue. In A. Bentovim, A., Elton, J. Hilderbrand, M. Tranter, & E. Vizard (Eds.). *Child sexual abuse within the family: Assessment and treatment* (pp. 84–104). Bristol, UK: John Wright.

Vrij, A. (1994). The impact of information and setting on detection of deception by police detectives. *Journal of Nonverbal Behavior, 18,* 117–127.

Vrij, A. (1995). Behavioural correlates of deception in simulated police interview. *Journal of Psychology: Interdisciplinary and Applied, 129,* 15–29.

Vrij, A. (1998). Nonverbal communication and credibility. In A. Memon, A. Vrij, & R. Bull (Eds.), *Psychology and law: Truthfulness, accuracy, and credibility* (pp. 32–58). London: McGraw-Hill.

Vrij, A. (2000). *Detecting lies and deceits: The psychology of lying and the implications for professional practice.* Chichester, England: John Wiley & Sons.

Vrij, A. (2005). Criteria-Based Content Analysis: A qualitative review of the first 37 studies. *Psychology, Public Policy, and Law, 11,* 3–41.

Vrij, A., Akenhurst, L., Soukara, S., & Bull, R. (2002). Will the truth come out?: The effect of deception, age, status, coaching, and social skills on CBCA scores. *Law and Human Behavior, 26,* 261–284.

Vrij, A., Edward, K., Roberts, K.P., & Bull, R. (2000). Detecting deceit via analysis of verbal and nonverbal behaviour. *Journal of Nonverbal Behaviour, 24,* 239–263.

Vrij, A., & Mann, S. (2001). Who killed my relative? Police officers' ability to detect real-life high-stake lies. *Psychology, Crime, and Law, 7,* 119–132.

Vrij, A. & Mann, S. (2006). Criteria-Based Content Analysis: An empirical test of its underlying processes. *Psychology, Crime, & Law, 12,* 337–349.

Vrij, A., & Semin, G.R. (1996). Lie experts' beliefs about non-verbal indicators of deception. *Journal of Nonverbal Behavior, 20*, 65–80.

Wadsworth, M.E.J. (1976). Delinquency, pulse rates, and early emotional deprivation. *British Journal of Criminology, 16*, 245–256.

Wagstaff, G.F., MacVeigh, J., Boston, R., Scott, L., Brunas-Wagstaff, J., & Cole, J. (2003). Can laboratory findings on eyewitness testimony be generalized to the real world? An archival analysis of the influence of violence, weapon presence, and age on eyewitness accuracy. *The Journal of Psychology, 137*, 17–28.

Waite, S., & Geddes, A. (2006). Malingered psychosis leading to involuntary psychiatric hospitalization. *Australian Psychiatry, 14*, 419–421.

Wakefield, H., & Underwager, R. (1998). Coerced or nonvoluntary confessions. *Behavioral Sciences and the Law, 16*, 423–440.

Walker, L. (1979). *The battered woman*. New York: Harper Perennial.

Walker, L.E. (1984). *The battered woman syndrome*. New York: Springer.

Walker, L.E. (1993). Battered woman as defendants. In N.Z. Hilton (Ed.), *Legal response to wife assault: Current trends and evaluation* (pp. 233–257). Thousand Oaks, CA: Sage.

Walker, S., & Katz, C.M. (2001). *The police in America* (4th ed.). New York: McGraw Hill, Inc.

Wallace, H.S. (1993). Mandatory minimums and the betrayal of sentencing reform: A legislative Dr. Jekyll and Mr. Hyde. *Federal Probation, 57*, 9.

Walma, M.W., & West. L. (2002). *Police powers and procedures*. Toronto: Emond Montgomery Publications Limited.

Walters, G.D. (2003). Predicting institutional adjustment and recidivism with the psychopathy checklist factor scores: A meta-analysis. *Law and Human Behavior, 27*, 541–558.

Waltz, J., Babcock, J.C., Jacobson, N.S., & Gottman, J.M. (2000). Testing a typology of batterers. *Journal of Consulting and Clinical Psychology, 68*, 658–669.

Ward. T., & Siegert, R. (2002). Rape and evolutionary psychology: A critique of Thornhill and Palmer's theory. *Aggression and Violent Behavior, 7*, 145–168.

Warick, J. (1997, November 29). Power in the spirit: Okimaw Ohci Healing Lodge. *The Saskatchewan Star Phoenix*, p. C1.

Warick, J. (2003 July, 5). Saskatchewan considers racially balanced juries. *Ottawa Citizen*, p. A16.

Warren, J.L., Burnette, M., South, C.S., Chauhan, P., Bale, R., & Friend, R. (2002). Personality disorders and violence among female prison inmates. *Journal of the American Academy of Psychiatry and the Law, 30*, 502–509.

Warren, J.L., Burnette, M., South, C.S., Chauhan, P., Bale, R., Friend, R., & Van Patten, I. (2003). Psychopathy in women: Structural modelling and co-morbidity. *International Journal of Law and Psychiatry, 26*, 223–242.

Warren, J.L., South, S.C., Burnette, M.L., Rogers, A., Friend, R., Bale, R., & Van Patten, I. (2005). Understanding the risk factors for violence and criminality in women: The concurrent validity of the PCL-R and HCR-20. *International Journal of Law and Psychiatry, 28*, 269–289.

Waschbusch, D.A. (2002). A meta-analytic examination of comorbid hyperactive-impulsive-attention problems and conduct problems. *Psychological Bulletin, 128*, 118–150.

Waschbusch, D.A., Porter, S., Carrey, N., Kazmi, S.O., Roach, K.A., & D'Amico, D.A. (2004). Investigation of the heterogeneity of disruptive behaviour in elementary-age children. *Canadian Journal of Behavioural Science, 36*, 97–112.

Wasserman, G.A., & Saracini, A.M. (2001). Family risk factors and interventions. In R. Loeber, & D.P. Farrington (Eds.), *Child delinquents: Development, intervention, and service needs* (pp. 165–190). Thousand Oaks, CA: Sage.

Webster, C.D., & Jackson, M.A. (Eds.). (1997) *Impulsivity: Theory, assessment, and treatment*. New York: Guilford.

Webster, C.D., Douglas, K., Eaves, D., & Hart, S. (1997). *HCR-20: Assessing risk for violence, Version 2*. Burnaby, British Columbia: Simon Fraser University and Forensic Psychiatric Services Commission of British Columbia.

Webster, C.D., Menzies, R.S., Butler, B.T., & Turner, R.E. (1982). Forensic psychiatric assessment in selected Canadian cities. *Canadian Journal of Psychiatry, 27*, 455–462.

Webster, C.D., Martin, M.L., Brink, J., Nicholls, T.L., & Middleton, C. (2004). *Manual for the Short-Term Assessment of Risk and Treatability (START), Version 1.0 (consultation ed.)*. St. Joseph's Healthcare Hamilton, Ontario – Forensic Psychiatric Services Commission: Port Coquitlam, British Columbia.

Webster, C.D., Nicholls, T.L., Martin, M., Desmarais, S.L., & Brink, J. L. (2006). Short-Term Assessment of Risk and Treatability (START): The case for a new structured professional judgment scheme. *Behavioral Sciences and the Law, 24*, 747–766.

Weiler, B.L. & Widom, C.S. (1996). Psychopathy and violent behaviour in abused and neglected young adults. *Criminal Behaviour and Mental Health, 6*, 253–271.

Weinshenker, N.J., & Siegel, A. (2002). Bimodial classification of aggression: Affective defense and predatory attack. *Aggression and Violent Behavior, 7*, 237–250.

Weiss, W.U., Davis, R., Rostow, C., & Kinsman, S. (2003). The MMPI-2 L scale as a tool in police selection. *Journal of Police and Criminal Psychology, 18*, 57–60.

Wells, G.L. (1978). Applied eyewitness- testimony research: System variables and estimator variables. *Journal of Personality and Social Psychology, 12*, 1546–1557.

Wells, G.L. (1993). What do we know about eyewitness identification? *American Psychologist, 48*, 553–571.

Wells, G.L., & Bradfield, A.L. (1998). "Good, you identified the suspect": Feedback to eyewitnesses distorts their reports of the witnessing experience. *Journal of Applied Psychology, 83*, 366–376.

Wells, G.L., Leippe, M.R., & Ostrom, T.M. (1979). Guidelines for empirically assessing the fairness of a lineup. *Law and Human Behavior, 3*, 285–293.

Wells, G.L., Malpass, R.S., Lindsay, R.C.L., Turtle, J.W., & Fulero, S.M. (2000). From the lab to the police station: A successful application of eyewitness research. *American Psychologist, 55*, 581–598.

Wells, G.L., & Olson, E.A. (2003). Eyewitness testimony. *Annual Psychology Review, 54*, 277–295.

Wells, G.L., Rydell, S.M., & Seelau, E.P. (1993). On the selection of distractors for eyewitness lineups. *Journal of Applied Psychology, 78*, 835–844.

Wells, G.L., Small, M., Penrod, S., Malpass, R.S., Fulero, S.M., & Brimacombe, C.A.E. (1998). Eyewitness identification procedures: Recommendations for lineups and photo spreads. *Law and Human Behavior, 22*, 603–647.

Wells, G.L., & Turtle, J.W. (1986). Eyewitness identification: The importance of lineup models. *Psychological Bulletin, 99*, 320–329.

Werner, E.E., & Smith, R.S. (1992). *Overcoming the odds: High-risk children from birth to adulthood.* Ithaca, NK: Cornell University Press.

Wetter, M.W., & Corrigan, S.K. (1995). Providing information to clients about psychological tests: A survey of attorneys' and law students' attitudes. *Professional Psychology: Research and Practice, 26*, 474–477.

Whipple, G.M. (1909). The observer as reporter: A survey of "the psychology of testimony." *Psychological Bulletin, 6*, 153–170.

Whipple, G.M. (1910). Recent literature on the psychology of testimony. *Psychological Bulletin, 7*, 365–368.

Whipple, G.M. (1911). The psychology of testimony. *Psychological Bulletin, 8*, 307–309.

Whipple, G.M. (1912). The psychology of testimony and report. *Psychological Bulletin, 9*, 264–269.

White, M.D. (2001). Controlling police discretion to use deadly force: Re-examining the importance of administrative policy. *Crime and Delinquency, 47*, 131–151.

White, W.S. (1997). False confessions and the constitution: Safeguards against untrustworthy confessions. *Harvard Civil Rights-Civil Liberties Law Review, 32*, 105–131.

Widom, C., & Ames, M. (1994). Criminal consequences of childhood sexual victimization. *Child Abuse and Neglect, 18*, 303–318.

Widom, C.S. (1989a). Does violence beget violence? A critical examination of the literature. *Psychological Bulletin, 106*, 2–28.

Widom, C.S. (1989b). The cycle of violence. *Science, 244*, 160–166.

Wigmore, J.H. (1909). Professor Munsterberg and the psychology of testimony. *Illinois Law Review, 3*, 399–434.

Williams, K., & Houghton, A. (2004). Assessing risk of domestic violence reoffending: A validation study. *Law and Human Behavior, 28*, 437–455.

Williams, S.L. & Frieze, I.H. (2005). Patterns of violent relationship, psychological distress, and marital satisfaction in national sample of men and women. *Sex Roles, 52*, 771–785.

Williamson, S., Hare, R.D., & Wong, S. (1987). Violence: Criminal psychopaths and their victims. *Canadian Journal of Behavioral Science, 19*, 454–462.

Williamson, S., Harpur, T., & Hare, R. (1991). Abnormal processing of affective words by psychopaths. *Psychophysiology, 28*, 260–273.

Wilson, J.Q., & Herrnstein, R. J. (1985). *Crime and human nature.* New York: Simon and Schuster.

Wilson, M., & Daly, M. (1993). Spousal homicide risk and estrangement. *Violence and Victims, 8*, 3–16.

Wilson, M., Daly, M., & Daniele, A. (1995). Familicide: The killing of spouse and children. *Aggressive Behavior, 21*, 275–291.

Wilson, P., Lincoln, R., & Kocsis, R. (1997). Validity, utility and ethics of profiling for serial violent and sexual offenders. *Psychiatry, Psychology and Law, 4*, 1–12.

Winfield, L. (1994). *NCREL Monograph: Developing resilience in urban youth.* NCREL: Urban Education Monograph Series.

Wong, S.C.P., & Gordon, A. (2006). The validity and reliability of the violence risk scale: A treatment-friendly violence risk assessment tool. *Psychology, Public Policy, and Law, 12*, 279–309.

Woodsworth, M., & Porter, S. (1999). Historical foundations and current applications of criminal profiling in violent crime investigations. *Expert Evidence, 7*, 241–264.

Woodworth, M., & Porter, S. (2002). In cold blood: Characteristics of criminal homicides as a function of psychopathy. *Journal of Abnormal Psychology, 111*, 436–445.

Worling, J.R., & Curwen, T. (2000). Adolescent sexual offender recidivism: Success of specialized treatment and implications for risk prediction. *Child Abuse and Neglect, 24*, 965–982.

Wortley, S., & Tanner, J. (2005). Inflammatory rhetoric? Baseless accusations? A response to Gabor's critique of racial profiling research in Canada. *Canadian Journal of Criminology and Criminal Justice, 47*, 581–610.

Wright, A.M., & Holliday, R.E. (2007). Enhancing the recall of young, young-old, and old-old adults with cognitive interviews. *Applied Cognitive Psychology, 21*, 19–43.

Wrightsman, L.S. (2001). *Forensic psychology.* Belmont, CA: Wadsworth.

Yarmey, A.D. (2001). Expert testimony: Does eyewitness memory research have probative value for the courts? *Canadian Psychology, 42*, 92–100.

Yarmey, A.D., Jacob, J., & Porter, A. (2002). Person recall in field settings. *Journal of Applied Social Psychology, 32*, 2354–2367.

Yarmey, A.D., & Jones, H.P.T. (1983). Is the psychology of eyewitness identification a matter of common sense? In S. Lloyd-Bostock & B.R. Clifford (Eds.), *Evaluating witness evidence* (pp. 13–40). Chichester, UK: John Wiley & Sons.

Yarmey, A.D., & Yarmey, M.J. (1997). Eyewitness recall and duration estimates in field settings. *Journal of Applied Social Psychology, 27*, 330–344.

Yarmey, A.D., Yarmey, M.J., & Yarmey, A.L. (1996). Accuracy of eyewitness identifications in showups and lineups. *Law and Human Behavior, 20*, 459–477.

Yllo, K., & Straus, M. (1990). Patriarchy and violence against wives: The impact of structural and normative factors. In M. Straus & R. Gelles (Eds.), *Physical violence in American families* (pp. 383–399). New Brunswick, NJ: Transaction.

Yuille, J.C., Hunter, R., Joffe, R., & Zaparniuk, J. (1993). Interviewing children in sexual abuse cases. In G. Goodman, B. Bottoms, (Eds.), *Child victims, child witnesses: Understanding and improving testimony* (pp. 95–115). New York: Guilford Press.

Yurchesyn, K.A., Keith, A., & Renner, K.E. (1992). Contrasting perspectives on the nature of sexual assault provided by a service for sexual assault victims and by the law courts. *Canadian Journal of Behavioral Science, 24*, 71–85.

Zamble, E., & Quinsey, V.L. (1997). *The criminal recidivism process.* Cambridge: Cambridge University Press.

Zanis, D.A., Mulvaney, F., Coviello, D., Alterman, A.I., Savitz, B., & Thompson, W. (2003). The effectiveness of early parole to substance abuse treatment facilities on 24-month criminal recidivism. *Journal of Drug Issues, 33*, 223–236.

Zapf, P., & Roesch, R. (1998). Fitness to stand trial: Characteristics of remands since the 1992 criminal code amendments. *Canadian Journal of Psychiatry, 43*, 287–293.

Zill, N., Morrison, D.R., & Coiro, M.J. (1993). Long-term effects of parental divorce on parent-child relationships, adjustment, and achievement in young adulthood. *Journal of Family Psychology, 7*, 91–103.

Zinger, I., & Forth, A.E. (1998). Psychopathy and Canadian criminal proceedings: The potential for human rights abuses. *Canadian Journal of Criminology, 40*, 237–276.

Zingraff, M.T., Leiter, J., Johnsen, M.C., & Myers, K.A. (1994). The mediating effect of good school performance on the maltreatment delinquency relationship. *Journal of Research in Crime and Delinquency, 31*, 62–91.

Zoucha-Jensen, J.M., & Coyne, A. (1993). The effects of resistance strategies on rape. *American Journal of Public Health, 83*, 1633–1634.

Credits

Text Credits

p. 10, Ceci, S.J. & Bruck, M. (1993). Suggestibility of the child witness: A historical review and synthesis. *Psychological Bulletin*, 113, 403–439. (p. 406) © 1993 by the American Psychological Association. Adapted with permission. **p. 28**, Excerpt from Recruiting Unit, Vancouver Police Department website: http://www.city.vancouver.bc.ca/police/recruiting/jobpre.htm. © 2007 Vancouver Police Department. Reprinted with permission. **p. 34**, Doerner, W.G. (1997). The utility of the oral interview board in selecting police academy admissions. *Policing: An International Journal of Police Strategy and Management*, 20, 777–785. Adapted with permission of Emerald Group Publishing Limited http://www.emeraldinsight.com. **p. 37**, Adapted from Pynes, J. & Bernardin, H.J. (1992). Entry-level police selection: The assessment centre is an alternative. *Journal of Criminal Justice*, 20, 41–52, © 1992, with permission of Elsevier. **p. 41**, Teplin, L.A. (2000). Keeping the peace: Police discretion and mentally ill persons. *National Institute of Justice Journal*, July, 8–15. **p. 44**, Walma, M.W. & West. L. (2002). *Police powers and procedures*. Toronto, ON: Emond Montogomery Publications Limited. Reprinted with permission. **p. 45**, Canadian Association of Chiefs of Police. (2000). The National Use of Force Framework.www.cacp.ca/english/committees/download.asp?id=170. Reprinted with permission of CACP. **p. 53**, McCraty, R., Tomasino, D., Atkinson, M., & Sundram, J. (1999). *Impact of the HeartMath self-management skills program on physiological and psychological stress in police officers*. Boulder Creek, CA: HeartMath Research Center. © 1999 Institute of HeartMath. Adapted with permission. **p. 58**, Wakefield, H. & Underwager, R. (1998). Coerced or nonvoluntary confessions. *Behavioral Sciences and the Law*, 16, 423–440. (p. 428). © 1998 John Wiley & Sons Limited. Reproduced with permission. **p. 71**, Kassin, S.M. & Kiechel, K.L. (1996). The social psychology of false confessions: Compliance, internalization, and confabulation. *Psychological Science*, 7(3), 125–128. Reprinted with permission. **p. 81**, Kocsis, R.N. Irwin, H.J., Hayes, A.F. & Nunn, R. (2000). Expertise in psychological profiling: A comparative assessment. Journal of Interpersonal Violence, 13, 311–331. © 2000 by Sage Publications. Reprinted by permission of Sage Publications. **p. 100–101**, National Research Council (2003). *The polygraph and its detection*. Washington, DC: National Academies Press. Reprinted with permission. **p. 133**, Geiselman, R.E., Fisher, R.P., MacKinnon, D.P., & Holland, H.L. (1986). Enhancement of eyewitness memory with the cognitive interview. *American Journal of Psychology*, 99, 385–401. From American Journal of Psychology © 1986 by the Board of Trustees of the University of Illinois. Used with permission of the University of Illinois Press. **p. 134**, From Fisher, R.P., & Geiselman, R.E., Memory-enhancing techniques for investigative interviewing, 1992. Courtesy of Charles C. Thomas Publisher, Ltd., Springfield, Illinois. **p. 168**, Saywitz, K.J., & Snyder, L. (1996). Narrative Elaboration: Test of a new procedure for interviewing children. *Journal of Consulting and Clinical Psychology*, 64, 1347–1357 © 1996 by the American Psychological Association. Reprinted with permission. **pp. 173–174**, Bala, N., Lindsay, R.C.L., Lee, K., & Talwar, V. (September, 2000). The legal competence of child witnesses: Assessing present practices and the need for law reform. Presentation at the Faculty of Law, Queen's University. Kingston, Ontario, Canada. Available at http://qsilver.queensu.ca/law/witness/childcompsept20001_files/frame.htm. Used with permission. **p. 182**, From MacMillan, H.L. (2000). Child maltreatment: What we know in the year 2000. *Canadian Journal of Psychiatry*, 45, p. 704. Reprinted with permission of the Canadian Psychiatric Association. **p. 200,** Material reprinted with the express permission of "CANWEST NEWS SERVICE," a CanWest Partnership. **p. 217**, Kluwer Academic Publishers, *Law and Human Behavior*, 22, 17–31, 1998, p. 24, Expert evidence pertaining to battered women: The impact of gender and timing of testimony, Schuller, R.A., & Cripps, J. © 1998 American Psychology-Law Society/Division 41 of the American Psychological Association: with kind permission of Springer Science and Business Media. Reprinted with permission of the authors. **pp. 225–226**, Ackerman, M.J. *Forensic Psychological Assessment*. © 1999 John Wiley & Sons. Reprinted with permission of John Wiley & Sons, Inc. **p. 227**, Viljoen, J.L. & Zapf, P.A. (2002).

Photo Credits

Case and Legislation Index

Barefoot v. Estelle, 463 U.S. 880 (1983), **344**

Baxstrom v. Herald, 383 U.S. 107 (1966), **343**

Bill C-30. (1991). *An Act to amend the Criminal Code (Mental Disorder) and to amend the National Defense Act and Young Offender Act in consequence thereof* (as passed by the House of Commons November 21, 1991). Ottawa: Queen's Printer., **221, 222, 232, 236**

Bill C-41. (1995). *An Act to amend the Criminal Code of Canada (Sentencing)*. Ottawa, ON: Queen's Printer., **255, 394**

Bill C-72. (1995). *An Act to amend the Criminal Code (Self-Induced Intoxication)*. Ottawa: Queen's Printer., **240**

Bill C-106. (1986). Proposed Amendments (YOA). Ottawa: Queen's Printer., **372**

Bill C-15A. (2002). *An Act to amend the Criminal Code and to amend other Acts (protecting children from sexual exploitation)*. Ottawa: Queens Printer., **183**

Brian's Law. (Mental Health Legislative Reform). 2000. S.O. 2000, c. 9 (formerly Bill 68), online: Ontario Legislative Library http://www.ontla.on.ca/library/bills/68371.htm, **234**

Brown v. Board of Education, 347 U.S. 483 (1954), **12**

Brown v. Mississippi, 297 U.S. 278 (1936), **57**

Canada Evidence Act, R.S.C. (1985), (2006), s.16.1, **172, 176, 177**

Canadian Charter of Rights and Freedoms, **39, 43, 61, 178, 221, 230, 232**

Canadian Foundation for Children, Youth, and the Law v. Canada (Attorney General) (2004) 234 D.L.R. (4th) 257, **178**

Corrections and Conditional Release Act (1992), c. 20, s. 80, **394**

Corrections and Conditional Release Act (1992), c. 20, s. 81; 1995, c. 42, s. 21, **394, 400**

Criminal Code, R.S.C. (1985), C-46, s. 2; 1992, c. 20, s. 216, c. 51, s. 32, **222**

Criminal Code, R.S.C. (1985), C-46, s. 16; 1985, c. 27(1st Supp.), s. 185(F); 1991, c. 43, s. 2, **233, 235**

Criminal Code, R.S.C. (1985), C-46, s. 34(1), **390**

Criminal Code, R.S.C. (1985), C-46, s. 34(2), **390**

Criminal Code, R.S.C. (1985), C-46, s. 143, **289**

Criminal Code, R.S.C. (1985), C-46, s. 172, **183**

Criminal Code, R.S.C. (1985), C-46, s. 272; 1995, c. 39, s. 145, **191**

Criminal Code, R.S.C. (1985), C-46, s. 276; 1992, c. 38, s. 2, **214**

Criminal Code, R.S.C. (1985), C-46, s. 343; 1995, c. 44, s. 302, **190–191**

Criminal Code, R.S.C. (1985), C-46, s. 433; 1990, c. 15, s.1, **191**

Criminal Code, R.S.C. (1985), C-46, s. 469; c. 27 (1st Supp.), s. 62; 2000, c. 24, s. 44, **190**

Criminal Code, R.S.C. (1985), C-46, s. 473, **190**

Criminal Code, R.S.C. (1985), C-46, s. 553; c. 27 (1st Supp.), s. 104; 1992, c. 1, s. 58; 1994, c. 44, s. 57; 1995, c. 22, s. 2; 1996, c. 19, s. 72; 1997, c. 18, s. 66; 1999, c. 3, s. 37; 2000, c. 25, s. 4, **190**

Criminal Code, R.S.C. (1985), C-46, s. 599; c. 1 (4th Supp.), s. 16, **197**

Criminal Code, R.S.C. (1985), C-46, s. 649; 1998, c. 9, s. 7, **203**

Criminal Code, R.S.C. (1985), C-46, s. 672.1; 1991, c. 43, s. 4, **223**

Criminal Code, R.S.C. (1985), C-46, s. 672.15; 1991, c. 43, s. 4, **222**

Criminal Code, R.S.C. (1985), C-46, s. 672.22; 1991, c. 43, s. 4, **222**

Criminal Code, R.S.C. (1985), C-46, s. 672.23(2); 1991, c. 43, s. 4, **222**

Criminal Code, R.S.C. (1985), C-46, s. 672.28; 1991, c. 43, s. 4, **230**

Criminal Code, R.S.C. (1985), C-46, s. 672.29; 1991, c. 43, s. 4, **230**

Criminal Code, R.S.C. (1985), C-46, s. 672.33; 1991, c. 43, s. 4, **230**

Criminal Code, R.S.C. (1985), C-46, s. 672.47; 1991, c. 43, s. 4, **230**

Criminal Code, R.S.C. (1985), C-46, s. 672.54; 1991, c. 43, s. 4, **235–236**

Criminal Code, R.S.C. (1985), C-46, s. 672.58; 1991, c. 43, s. 4, **229**

Criminal Code, R.S.C. (1985), C-46, s. 672.81; 1991, c. 43, s. 4, **236**

Criminal Code, R.S.C. (1985), C-46, s. 718.1, **254**

Criminal Code, R.S.C. (1985), C-46, s. 718.2(e), **254, 394, 395**

Criminal Code, R.S.C. (1985), C-46, s. 745, **327**

Criminal Code, R.S.C. (1985), C-46, s. 753.1, **256**

Criminal Code, R.S.C. (1985), C-46, s. 787; c. 27 (1st Supp.), s. 171, **190**

Criminal Lunatics Act (1800), 39 & 40 Geo.III, c. 94 (U.K.), **232**

Daubert v. Merrell Dow Pharmaceuticals, Inc., 509 U.S. 579 (1993), **22, 101**

Dixon v. Attorney General of Commonwealth of Pennsylvania, 325 F. Supp. 966 (M.D. Pa. 1971), **343**

Employee Polygraph Protection Act of 1988, Pub. L. 100-347, 102 Stat. 646, 29 U.S.C. 2001-2009., **92**

Ernst v. Quinonez (2003), O.J. No. 3781 (Ont. Sup. Ct.), **43**

Estelle v. Smith, 451, US 454 (1981), **347**

Foto v. Jones (1974), 45 D.L.R. (3d) 43, **110**

Frye v. United States, 293 F. 1013 (1923), **91, 101**

Frye v. United States, 293 F. 1013 (DC Cir.1923), **22**

Health Care Consent Act, R.S.O. (1996), c. 2, Sched. A, s. 25, **229, 234**

Jackson v. Indiana (1972), 406 U.S. 715, **230**

Jenkins v. United States, 307 F.2d 637 (D.C. Court of Appeals, 1962), **12**

Juries Act, R.S.O. (1990), J.3; S.O. 1994, c. 27; 1997, c. 4, **192**

Juvenile Delinquents Act (1908), c. 40, **371**

Kumho Tire Company v. Carmichael, 526 U.S. 137 (1999), **23, 101**

Mallard v The Queen, WASCA 296 (2003), **102**

Mental Health Act, R.S.O. (1990), c. M.7; 2000, c. 9, s. 33.1, **234**

Miranda v. Arizona, 384 U.S. 336 (1966), **60**

Neil v. Biggers, 409 U.S. 188 (1972), **147, 152**

Police Services Act, R.S.O. (1990), c. P.15, **43**

R. v. Andrade (1985), 18 C.C.C. 3d 41 (Ont. CA), **205**

R. v. Balliram (2003), 173, C.C.C. (3d) 547, (Ont. SC), **221**

R. v. Barrett (1993), 82 C.C.C. (3d) 266 (Ont. CA), **64**

R. v. Beland (1987), 2 S.C.R. 398, **102**

R. v. Brown (2002), 48 C.R. (5th) 291 (Ont. S.C.J.), **85**

R. v. Brown (2005), S.J. No. 43, **196**

R. v. Budai, Gill, & Kim (2001), 154 C.C.C. (3d) 289, **197**

R. v. Darrach (2000), 2 S.C.R. 443, **214**

R. v. Daviault (1994), 93 C.C.C. 3d 21, **240**

R. v. Demers (2004), 2 S.C.R. 489, 2004 SCC 46, **230**

R. v. Gayme, (1991), 7 C.R.D. 725, **214**

R. v. Gill (2002), B.C.J. No. 1473, **197**

R. v. Gladue (1999), 1 S.C.R. 688, **13, 394, 395**

R. v. Guess (1998), B.C.J. No. 1989, **197**

R. v. Hoilett (1999), 136 C.C.C. (3d) 449, **63**

R. v. Hubbert (1975), 29 C.C.C. (2d) 279, 31 C.R.N.S. 27, 11 O.R. (2d) 464 (C.A.), **13**

R. v. Kliman, (1998), No. 49 B.C.J. (Quicklaw), **136**

R. v. Latimer, (2001), 1 S.C.R. 3, **201**

R. v. Lavallee (1990), 1 S.C.R. 852, **13**

R. v. Levogiannis (1993), 4 S.C.R. 475, 160 N.R. 1, 25 C.R. (4th) 325, 85 C.C.C. (3d) 327, 18 C.R.R. (2d) 242, **13**

R. v. Lyons (1987), 44 D.L.R. (4th) 193, **344**

R. v. Marquard (1993), 25 C.R. (4th) (S.C.C.), **173**

R. v. McIntosh and McCarthy, (1997), 117 C.C.C. 56 (B.C.C.A.), **152**

R. v. McIntosh and McCarthy (1997), 117 C.C.C. (3d) 385 (Ont. C.A.), **24**

R. v. Mcleod (2005), ABQB 946, **199**

R. v. McNaughton (1843), 8 Eng. Rep. 718, **230**

R. v. M.J.S. (2000), Alta.P.C. 44, **67**

R. v. Mohan (1994), 89 C.C.C. (3d) 402 (S.C.C.), **13, 23**

R. v. Morgentaler (1988), 1 S.C.R. 30, **201**

R. v. Nepoose (1991), 85 Alta. LR (2d) 8 (Q.B.), **195**

R. v. Oickle (2000), S.C.C. 38, **13, 62**

R. v. Parks (1992), 2 S.C.R. 871, **238**

R. v. Poulin, (2002), 169 C.C.C. (3d) 378, **178**

R. v. Prichard, (1836), 7. Car, **221**

R. v. S. (R. D.), (1997), 3 S.C.R. 484, **110**

R. v. Seaboyer (1991), 2 S.C.R. 577, **214**

R. v. Sherratt (1991), 1 S.C.R. 509, **195**

R. v. Sophonow (1986), 50 CR (3d) 193 (Man. CA), **154**

R. v. Sophonow, (No. 2) (1986), 25 C.C.C. (3d) 415, **13, 152**

R. v. Sterling (1995), 102 C.C.C. (3d) 481, **161**

R. v. Stone (1999), 2 S.C.R. 290, **238**

R. v. Swain (1991), 63 C.C.C. (3d) 481 (S.C.C.), **13, 230, 232**

R. v. Symes (2005), O.J. No. 6041, **184**

R. v. Taylor, (1992), 77 C.C.C. (3d) 551 (Ont. C.A.), **222**

R. v. Turnball et al. (1976), 63 Cr. App. R. 132, **152**

R. v. Williams (1998), 1 S.C.R. 1128, **13**

Re Moore and the Queen, 10 C.C.C. (3d) 306 (1984), **344**

Roe v. Wade (1973), 410 U.S. 113, **201**

Smith v. Jones, (1999) 1 S.C.R. 455, **340**

Starson v. Swayze (1999), O.J. No. 4483, **229**

Starson v. Swayze (2003), 1 S.C.R. 722, **229**

State v. Driver, 88 W.Va. 479, 107 S.E. 189 (1921), **11, 12**

State v. Harrington, 659 N. W. 2d 509 (2003), **105**

Stovall v. Denno. 388 U.S. 293 (1967), **143**

U.S. v. Scheffer, 140L. Ed. 2d 413 (1998), **101**

W. v. Egdell [1990] 1 All England Reports 835, **340**

Wenden v. Trikha (1991), 116 A.R. 81 (Q.B.), **13**

Wilkins v. Maryland State Police, No. CCB-93-468 (1999), **86**

Winko v. British Columbia (1999), 2 S.C.R. 625, **233**

Young Offenders Act, R.S.C. (1985), Y-1, s. 3, **372**

Young Offenders Act, R.S.C. (1985), Y-1, s. 4, **372**

Young Offenders Act, R.S.C. (1985), Y-1, s. 16, **372**

Young Offenders Act, R.S.C. (1985), Y-1, s. 20; R.S., 1985, c. 27 (1st Supp.), s. 187, c. 24 (2nd Supp.), s. 14, c. 1 (4th Supp.), s. 38; 1992, c. 11, s. 3; 1993, c. 45, s. 15; 1995, c. 19, s. 13, c. 22, ss. 16, 17, 25, c. 39, s. 178, **372**

Youth Criminal Justice Act (2002), c. 1, **373**

Youth Criminal Justice Act (2002), c. 1, s. 3, **373**

Youth Criminal Justice Act (2002), c. 1, s. 7, **373**

Youth Criminal Justice Act (2002), c. 1, s. 10, **373**

Youth Criminal Justice Act (2002), c. 1, s. 38(2)(c), **373**

Youth Criminal Justice Act (2002), c. 1, s. 42, **373**

Youth Criminal Justice Act (2002), c. 1, s. 61, **373**

Youth Criminal Justice Act (2002), c. 1, s. 141(10), **230**

Name Index

A

Abdollahi, M. K., 48
Abel, G. G., 288
Abotsay, Sereena, 200
Abram, K. M., 242
Adams, Randall Dale, 347
Adler, F., 385
Adonis, Dimitri, 90
Ainsworth, P. B., 30, 31
Aitken, C. C. G., 77
Akers, R. L., 14
Alarid, L. F., 385
Aldridge, M. L., 314
Alexander, D. A., 50
Alison, L. J., 80
Allan, W. D., 313
Allegri, N., 401
Alpert, G. P., 42
Alterman, A. I., 353
Amos, N. L., 351
Anderson, M., 282
Andrews, D. A., 265, 358, 393
Anshel, M. H., 52
Arboleda-Florez, Dr. J., 238
Archer, J., 278
Arditi, J. A., 186
Arenburg, Jeffrey, 233–234
Arnold, Terry, 155
Ascione, F. R., 283
Atkinson, J. L., 297
Atkinson, M., 49, 52, 53
Aubrey, M., 282
Auger, S., 397

B

Babcock, J. C., 287
Babiak, Paul, 328
Bagby, R. M., 115
Bala, Professor Nicholas, 174, 176, 177
Balfour, J., 171
Ball, B. C., 313
Ball, E. M., 352
Bandura, Albert, 16, 281, 379
Banks, Russell, 100
Baranovski, Matti, 210
Barbaree, H. E., 294
Barefoot, Thomas, 344
Barnard, G. W., 120
Barnhardt, J., 102

Baron, E., 199
Barry, C. T., 329
Bartol, A. M., 3, 11, 12
Bartol, C. R., 3, 11, 12
Batterman-Faunce, J. M., 163
Baxstrom, Johnnie, 343
Beach, B., 394
Beaumont, R., 313
Beck, K. A., 180
Becker, J. V., 288
Bekerian, D. A., 134
Belfrage, S., 389
Belknap, J., 393
Ben-Porath, Y. S., 115
Benda, B. B., 386, 388
Benedek, D. M., 313
Benedek, E. P., 313
Benitto, Jackie "Benny," 189
Bennell, C., 47, 48, 84
Bennett, E. A., 215
Bennett, L. W., 287
Berk, R. A., 285, 286
Bernardin, H. J., 36–37
Bernardo, Paul, 317
Besirevic, J., 196
Best, C. L., 137
Bianchi, Kenneth, 317
Bianchini, K. J., 121
Bilby, C., 303
Binder, R. L., 345
Binet, Alfred, 8–9
Birch, D. E., 339
Birkenmayer, A., 254, 259
Birt, A. R., 109, 136, 328
Birt, A., 108
Bittner, E., 40
Blair, R. J., 332
Blanchette, K., 388, 393
Bland, R. C., 241
Blatchford, C., 180
Blonigen, D. M., 332
Bodin, S. D., 329
Boe, R., 402
Boer, D. P., 328
Boesky, L., 394
Boney-McCoy, S., 279
Bonnie, R. J., 222
Bonta, J. L., 243, 256, 265, 338, 356, 358, 388, 398
Boothby, J., 365

Borduin, C. M., 354
Borum, R., 365
Boston, R., 139
Bowen, E., 287
Bowlby, John, 14
Bradfield, A. L., 148
Bradford, J. M., 299
Brame, B., 377
Brantingham, Paul, 83
Brigham, J. C., 6, 149, 165
Brinkley, C. A., 333
Brittan, R. R., 15
Broeders, A. P. A., 146
Brooks, Adrian, 198
Brooks, Neil, 152, 154
Brooks-Gordon, B., 303
Broom, I., 303
Brothers, L. T., 352
Brown, D., 169
Brown, Decovan "Dee," 85
Brown, G. R., 278
Brown, J. M., 49, 50
Brown, Jeffrey, 196
Brown, S. L., 328, 353
Browne, A., 388, 391
Browne, K. D., 314
Bruck, M., 8, 10, 160
Brunas-Wagstaff, J., 139
Brunton, M., 15
Brussel, Dr. James, 74–75
Buckley, J. P., 58
Bull, R., 108, 139
Bundy, Theodore (Ted), 316
Buono, Angelo, 317
Burgess, A. G., 313
Burgess, A. W., 73, 289–290, 313
Burgess, Ann, 347
Burgess, Anthony, 300
Burke, R. J., 52
Burrow, J. D., 392–393
Burton, V. S., Jr., 385
Butler, B. T., 222
Buttell, F., 278
Bynum, T., 392–393

C

Cabanaugh, M. M., 285, 287–288
Caldwell, C., 207
Caldwell, M. F., 331
Call, C., 287

Campbell, D., 234
Campbell, E. A., 49, 50
Campbell, J. C., 314, 392
Campbell, M. A., 109, 331
Canter, D. V., 320
Canter, David, 76, 77
Cares, A. C., 278
Carlson, S. R., 332
Carney, M., 278
Carriere, D., 256
Carroll, J. S., 196
Casey, J. O., 389
Caspi, A., 331
Cattell, James McKeen, 8
Ceci, S. J., 8, 10, 160, 169
Cerri, A. M., 98
Chaiken, J. M., 353
Chaiken, M. R., 353
Chalmers, J. C., 311
Chaplin, W., 35–36
Chapman, J. P., 345
Chapman, L. J., 345
Chapman, M. T., 166
Chen, Jennifer, 1
Chicvara, C. L., 142
Cho, Seung-Hui, 321–322
Chung, Christopher, 199
Cirincione, C., 243
Clark, Kenneth, 12
Clark-Robbins, P. C., 243
Cleckley, Hervey, 323, 324, 334
Clements, C. B., 365
Cochrane, Lee, 210
Cochrane, R. E., 29, 35
Cocozza, J., 343
Cohen, A. J., 380
Coiro, M. J., 186
Cole, J., 139
Collins, S. A., 49
Conlon, Gerry, 66
Connolly, D. A., 137
Cook, S., 146
Cooper, J., 215
Copson, G., 79
Corder, B. F., 313
Cordner, G. W., 38, 39
Cormier, C. A., 329
Cormier, R. B., 356
Cornell, D. G., 116, 313, 330
Cornell, W. F., 68
Cortina, L. M., 290–291
Cortoni, F., 298
Cory, Peter, 154
Coulson, G., 389
Coviello, D., 353

Coyne, A., 293
Crawford, M., 314
Cripps, J., 217, 218
Cronshaw, S. F., 20
Crosby, R. D., 113
Crutcher, N., 261, 401–402
Cullen, F. T., 265, 385
Cunningham, P. B., 354
Cunningham-Rathner, J., 288
Cutler, B. L., 142, 212

D

Dagenais, Bob, 375
Dahmer, Jeffrey, 316
Daly, M., 312, 314
Darby, P. J., 313
Darrach, Andrew, 214
Daviault, Henri, 240
Davies, G., 139, 169
Davies, Justice Barry, 197
Davis, E. F., 333
Day-Lewis, Daniel, 66
Dean, C. W., 285
Decaire, M. W., 5
DeFronzo, J., 317
DeKeseredy, W. S., 279
DeLeon, P. H., 223
DeLillo, Don, 100
DeLoache, J. S., 163
Delveaux, K., 393
Dennett, J. L., 134
DePaulo, B. M., 104, 105, 106, 107, 108
Devine, D. J., 213
Diamond, S. S., 258
Ditta, A., 317
Dobash, R. E., 280
Dobash, R., 280
Dodge, Kenneth A., 377, 379
Doerner, W. G., 33–34
Donchin, E., 102
Doob, A. N., 207, 272
Dooley, Marcia, 179, 180
Dooley, Randal, 179–180
Dooley, Tony, 179–180
Dotson, L. A., 352
Douglas, John E., 73
Douglas, Kevin, 349
Dowden, C., 353, 393
Drass, K. A., 315
Drugge, J., 328
Drummond, Edward, 230–232
Dubé, Sylvie, 178
DuBreuil, S. C., 213
Duffy, John, (a.k.a. Railway Rapist), 76
Dunham, R. G., 42

Dupuis, P., 147
Dutton, D. G., 314
Dutton, D., 278, 281
Dwyer, J., 65
Dysart, J. E., 143, 145, 147

E

Earle, J., 328
Easterbrook, J. A., 150
Eastman, O., 80
Eaves, Derek, 349
Ebbesen, E. G., 151
Eberhardt, N. L., 98
Edens, J. F., 330
Edmonon, Dean, 196
Eisendrath, S. J., 112
Eisner, S. L., 205
Ekman, P., 104, 108, 117
Elaad, E., 97
Elbogen, E. B., 346
Ellard, Kelly, 198
Ellerby, L. A., 400
Elliott, D., 352
Ellsworth, P. C., 143, 208, 209
Empster, R. J., 222
Ennis, B. J., 343
Epstein, J. A., 105
Ernst, Edward, 43
Ervin, F. R., 15
Ewaschuck, Eugene, 180
Ewing, C. P., 282, 391
Eysenck, Hans J., 16–17, 18

F

Fairbrother, N., 293
Fairweather, D., 328
Faller, K. C., 298
Farias, Mohadaseh, 276
Farkas, G. M., 223
Farrington, D. P., 352
Farrington, D., 332
Farwell, Lawrence A., 102, 105
Faulder, Joseph Stanley, 347
Faver, C., 283
Felson, R. B., 278
Finkel, N. J., 76
Finkelhor, D., 183, 294–295, 297, 388
Finn, P., 46, 47
Firestone, P., 299
Fisher, E., 288
Fisher, R. P., 129, 133–134, 142
Fitzgerald, L. F., 289
Fleming, J. A. E., 98
Flett, H., 287
Flin, R., 169

Flynn, C. P., 283
Foa, E. B., 290
ForsterLee, L., 205
Forth, A. E., 328
Frank, M. G., 108, 117
Franke, W. D., 49
Frederick, R. I., 113
Freud, Sigmund, 14
Frey, Marnie, 200
Frick, P. J., 329
Friesen, W. V., 104
Frieze, I. H., 278
Fritz, G., 297
Frye, James, 101
Fulero, S. M., 143, 145, 148, 196
Fyfe, J.J., 44

G

Gabbert, G., 149
Gabor, T., 261
Gacy, John Wayne, 318
Gale, Judy, 327
Ganis, G., 103
Gansler, D. A., 121
Gardner, J., 35
Garmezy, N., 381
Gartner, R., 314
Gaudet, F. J., 257
Geiselman, R. E., 133–134
Gelles, R. J., 285, 288
Gellespie, C., 390
Gendreau, P., 263, 264, 265, 359
George the III, 232
Giese, Keith, 109
Gilchrist, E., 287
Gill, Peter, 197
Gillig, P. M., 282
Ginton, A., 97
Glickman, Harry, 189
Golding, Dr. Stephen, 228
Goldstein, A. M., 114, 149
Goldstein, C. C., 61
Gondolf, E. W., 284, 288
Gonzalez, R., 143
Goodman, G. S., 163
Gorey, K., 288
Gorzalka, B. B., 289
Graham, J. R., 121
Granhag, P. A., 106
Grann, M., 362, 367
Grant, M., 161
Green, C. E., 287
Greenberg, D. M., 298–299
Greve, K. W., 121
Grieve, R., 162

Grigsby, M., 282
Grigson, Dr. James, 344, 347
Grisso, T., 222
Groth, A. N., 292, 293, 294
Grove, W., 346
Guay, J. P., 292
Guay, Joseph-Albert, 317
Gudjonsson, Dr. Gisli H., 65–66, 68, 69
Guess, Gillian, 197
Gumpert, C. H., 367
Gusick, S. M., 208
Guyton, M. R., 212
Gwynn, M. I., 213

H

Hadfield, James, 232
Haggard, U., 367
Haizlip, T. M., 313
Hall, G. C. N., 295
Hamby, S. L., 279
Hamilton, G., 392
Haney, Craig, 6
Haney, J., 388
Hankins, G. C., 120
Hann, R. G., 356
Hannon, L., 317
Hans, Valerie P., 207, 216
Hansen, D. J., 182
Hanson, R. Karl, 243, 298, 303, 362, 363
Hare, Dr. Robert, 100, 323, 324, 325, 326, 327, 328, 334
Harman, W. G., 356
Harpur, T., 334
Harrington, Terry, 105
Harris A. J., 363
Harris, A., 256
Harris, D., 85, 86
Harris, Grant T., 244, 295, 329, 352
Harris, P. L., 111
Hart, Stephen D., 222, 339, 349, 361
Hart-Mitchell, R., 401
Hartke, K. L., 313
Hartman, C. R., 73
Hartwig, M., 106
Hastie, R., 209, 210, 211
Hastings, Patricia A., 214, 216
Hauptman, Bruno Richard, 65, 146
Haw, R. M., 212
Hawk, G. L., 116
Hayes, A. F., 81
Heilbrun, K., 331
Hemphill, J. F., 326
Hendrickse, W., 315
Henggeller, S. W., 354
Henry, B., 377

Hervé, H., 328
Hess, A. K., 21
Heuer, L., 205, 206
Hewlet, M. G., 212
Hiatt, K. D., 333
Hickey E. W., 317, 318, 319
Hillbrand, M., 353
Hilton, N. Z., 366
Hinckley, John, Jr., 19
Hinz, P. N., 49
Hirsch, H. R., 35
Hirschell, D., 285
Hirschi, T., 15
Hirschman, R., 295
Hodgins, S., 243
Hogarth, J., 257
Hoge, R. D., 265
Holland, H. L., 133–134
Hollin, C., 16
Holmes, R. M., 320
Holmes, S. T., 320
Holmstrom, L. L., 289
Holtfreter, K., 389
Holtzworth-Monroe, A., 284
Homolka, Karla, 317
Honts, C. R., 98
Horowitz, I. A., 201, 205, 213
Horselenberg, R., 72
Hosch, H. M., 151, 212
Houghton, A., 362
Howitt, D., 73
Hughes, Kevin, 105
Hughes, M., 162
Hunter, S., 199
Hurrell, J. J., 49
Hurshman-Corkum, Jane (Stafford), 277, 390
Hutchinson, I. W., 285

I

Iacono, Dr. William G., 95, 96, 98, 99, 100, 101, 103, 117
Inbau, F. E., 58
Ingram, Paul, 67–68
Innes, G., 50
Inwald, R. E., 35
Irving, B. L., 50
Irwin, H. J., 81
Izzett, R. R., 213

J

Jack the Ripper, 316
Jackson, Mark, 56
Jackson, R. L., 120
Jacob, J., 139

Jacobs, P. A., 15
Jacoby, J. E., 343
Jansen, N. J. M., 146
Jayne, B. C., 58
Jimenez-Lorente, B., 196
Joesbury, Andrea, 200
Johnson, R., Jr., 102
Johnson, Suzanne Killinger, 311
Johnston, J. C., 397
Jonas, J. M., 116
Jones, B., 116
Jones, H. P. T., 24
Josephs, S., 72
Joudrie, Dorothy, 238
Joudrie, Earl, 238
Junginger, J., 354
Jungman, M., 97

K

Kaplan, M. F., 193
Kaplan, S., 330
Kashani, J. H., 313
Kashy, D. A., 105
Kask, K., 139
Kassin, Dr. Saul M., 61, 62, 64,
    65, 67–68, 71, 71t, 72, 151,
    154, 207
Katz, C. M., 42
Katz, R. S., 385–386
Kebbell, M. R., 132
Kehoe, Andrew, 316
Kelley, K., 279
Kelly, Allison, 370
Kemp, R., 145
Kendall-Tackett, K. A., 183
Kendell, R. E., 311
Kennedy, M. A., 289
Keppel, R. D., 321
Kerr, N. L., 196, 201, 211
Kerry, G., 314
Kerstholt, J. H., 146
Kiechel, K. L., 71, 71t, 72
Kilpatrick, D. G., 137
Kim, D., 346
Kindrat, Jeffrey, 196
King, Rodney, 41
KIngsbury, S. J., 315
Kircher, J. C., 98, 99
Kirkendol, S. E., 104–105
Klassen, D., 354
Kliman, Michael, 135–136
Knight, R. A., 292, 293
Koch, W. J., 293
Kocsis, R. N., 81
Konecni, V. J., 151

Koons, B. A., 392–393
Koss, M. P., 288–289, 297
Kozel, F. A., 103
Koziol-McLain, J., 314
Kramer, G. P., 196
Kraut, R. E., 107
Kristianson, C. M., 388
Kroes, W. H., 49
Kroner, D. G., 360
Kropp, P. R., 361
Krueger, R. F., 332
Kubiak, S. B., 290–291
Kugler, K., 226
Kuhn, J., 163

L

Lalumičre, M., 295
Lamb, M. E., 163
Lambert, M. T., 315
Lamberth, J., 86
LaPrairie, C., 397, 398
Larson, John, 92
Lassiter, G. D., 104
Latimer, J., 223, 234
Latimer, Robert, 201
Latimer, Tracy, 201
Laurier, Sir Wilfrid, 266
Law, M., 243
Lawrence, A., 223, 234
LeBlanc, M., 366
Lee, K., 111, 174
Lee, M. Y., 287
Lees-Haley, P. R., 113
Leginski, W., 213
Leichtman, M. D., 169
Leippe, M. R., 152
Lépine, Marc, 316, 321, 322
Leslie, D., 288
Letourneau, E. J., 137
Levine, J. A., 98
Levy-Elkon, A., 330
Leyton, James, 27
Lidz, V., 331
Lieberman, J. D., 208
Lindberg, A., 166
Lindberg, M., 166
Lindbergh, Charles, 65–66, 146
Lindbergh, Charles, Jr., 66
Lindsay, D. S., 136
Lindsay, Dr. Rod C. L., 138, 140,
    142, 143, 144, 147, 150, 170,
    171, 172, 174
Link, B. G., 353–354
Litwack, T. R., 343
Lochun, S. K., 138

Loeber, R., 331
Loftus, Elizabeth F., 130, 135, 136, 155
Lombroso, Cesare, 385
Long, P. J., 183
Lonsway, K. A., 289
Loo, Dr. Robert, 50, 51
Lorenz, A. R., 333
Lorenzo, Paul, 249
Lösel, F., 303
Loucks, A. D., 389
Lucas, J. A., 121
Lucente, S. W., 389
Luus, C. A. E., 140
Lykken, D. T., 94, 99, 101
Lynam, D. R., 331
Lyons, P. M., Jr., 212

M

MacCoon, D. G., 333
MacCoun, R. J., 211
MacDonald, J. M., 42
MacDonald, M., 397
MacKinnon, D. P., 133–134
MacMillan, H. L., 182
MacVeigh, J., 139
Maguin, E., 387
Malinosky-Rummell, R., 182
Malloy, K., 282
Malpass, R. S., 148
Mann, S., 108, 109
Manz, P. W., 42
Marcus, K. D., 212
Margolis, B. L., 49
Mariani, Meir, 210
Mark, V. H., 15
Marques, J. K., 301
Marshall, J. R., 49
Marshall, Joanne, 337
Marshall, W. L., 294–295
Marston, William, 91, 92, 101
Marti, M. W., 210–211
Martin, Dominic, 178
Martin, R., 138
Marzolf, D. P., 163
Mauro, R., 209
McCarthy, Paul, 24
McClelland, G. M., 242
McClemont, W. F., 15
McCloskey, K., 282
McConville, D., 330
McCoy, W., 330
McCraty, R., 49, 52, 53
McCreary, D. R., 47
McDougall, C., 18
McFatter, R. M., 256, 258–259, 260

McGhee, Curtis, 105
McGurk, B. J., 18
McIntosh, Owen, 24
McKenna, P. F., 37
McKimmie, B., 215
McLachlin, Beverley, 252
McLeod, Germaine, 199
McNaughton, Daniel, 230–232
McNiel, D. E., 345
McPherson, M., 400–401
Meadow, R., 112
Meehl, Paul, 346, 347
Meissner, C. A., 64, 149, 212
Melchers, R., 394
Melton, H. C., 41
Melville, M. M., 15
Memon, A., 149, 151, 215
Menendez, Erik, 194
Menendez, Lyle, 194
Menzies, Robert S., 222, 349
Merckelbach, H., 72
Merton, R. K., 15
Messman-Moore, T. L., 183
Metesky, George, 75
Michaud, René, 375
Miethe, T. D., 315
Miller, A. R., 99
Miller, B., 387
Mills, J. F., 360
Mitchell, T. L., 212
Mittelman, M., 288
Moan, S., 163
Moczynski, N. P., 121
Moffitt, T. E., 331, 332, 377
Mojtabai, R., 354
Monahan, John, 243, 343, 344, 345
Moore, J., 396, 397, 399
Moran, G., 212
Morash, M., 389, 392–393
Morgan, K., 80
Morgentaler, Dr. Henry, 201
Morris, Errol, 347
Morrison, D. R., 186
Morton-Bourgon, K. E., 362
Motiuk, L.L., 242, 262, 388
Moulden, H. M., 299
Mouzos, J., 314
Mudgett, Herman Webster, 316
Mulvaney, F., 353
Munsterberg, Hugo, 10–11
Murdock, T., 290
Murphy, J. M., 323
Murrie, D. C., 330
Myers, B., 102
Myers, W. C., 313

N
Nafekh, M., 388
Nagin, D. A., 377
Narby, D. J., 212
Nemeth, M., 238
Neufeld, P., 65
Newman, J. P., 333
Newman, R., 223
Newman, S. C., 241
Ng, W., 150
Nicholas, E., 163
Nicholson, R. A., 226
Niedermeier, K. E., 201, 202
Nisbett, R. E., 199
Northrop, L. C., 35
Nunes, K. L., 299
Nunn, R., 81

O
O'Bryant, S. E., 121
O'Connor, W. A., 354
O'Neill, M. L., 331
O'Sullivan, M., 108
O'Toole, M., 333
Ofshe, Dr. Richard J., 64, 68
Ogloff, Dr. James R. P., 18, 19–20, 180, 222, 234
Oickle, Richard, 62
Olczak, P. V., 193
Olio, K. A., 68
Olson, Clifford, 316, 327
Olson, J. M., 217
Orbach, Y., 163
Orchard, T. L., 146
Orn, H., 241

P
Palmer, J. C., 130
Pang, B., 388
Papin, Georgina, 200
Parks, Kenneth, 238
Parliament, L., 110
Patrick, Dr. Christopher J., 95, 96, 98, 99, 100, 104, 117, 332
Patterson, Jeremy, 249
Pavlidis, I., 98
Peel, Robert, 230, 232
Peluso, Lucy, 125, 126
Pembroke, M., 143
Pennington, N., 209, 210, 211
Penrod, S. D., 148, 193, 205, 206, 210, 211
Perez, D. A., 212
Peterson, C., 161

Petrie, Mike, 200
Pfeifer, J. E., 212, 401
Pfeifer, R. L., 108
Phillips, Dr. George, 74
Picard, A., 179
Pickel, K. L., 151
Pickton, Robert William, 197, 199, 200, 316
Pike, G., 145
Pinizzotto, A. J., 76, 333
Pipe, M-E., 169
Pipe, M., 163
Platz, C. L., 311
Plomin, R., 332
Polak, A., 111
Pollina, D. A., 97
Pollock, P. H., 315
Ponder, B., 212
Pope, H. G., 116
Porporino, F. J., 242
Porter, A., 139
Porter, S., 74, 76, 108, 109, 136, 315, 328, 331, 351
Posner, Dr. Paul, 229
Poulin, Lucille, 178
Pozzulo, J. D., 169, 170, 171, 172
Prentky, R. A., 320
Prochnow, J., 317
Pryke, S., 147
Puente, Dorothea, 318
Pugh, G., 30
Putnam, F. W., 183
Pynes, J., 36–37

Q
Quas, J. A., 163
Quinsey, Dr. Vernon, 295, 296, 364

R
Rainbow, L., 80
Raskin, D. C., 98, 99
Rastin, C. J., 396, 399, 401
Read, J. D., 136, 137
Reagan, Ronald, 19
Rees, L. M., 121
Reid, J. C., 313
Reid, John E., 58
Reifman, A., 208
Reisig, M. D., 389
Reno, Janet, 153
Resnick, H. S., 137
Resnick, P. J., 118, 119
Ressler, R. K., 73, 78
Rice, Marnie E., 244, 295, 329, 352
Richards, H. J., 389

Riddlesberger. M., 163
Ridgeway, David, (a.k.a. Green River Killer), 316
Riggs, D., 290
Risin, L. I., 297
Ritchie, Peter, 200
Roach, Jason, 307
Robbins, L., 120
Roberts, A. R., 392
Roberts, Professor Julian V., 253, 254, 256, 257, 259, 260, 270, 394
Robie, C., 287
Robinson, R. J., 205
Roesch, Dr. Ron, 222, 223–224, 226, 227–228, 227–228
Rogan, D. P., 285
Rogers, Richard, 113, 114, 115, 235, 389
Rollins, R., 313
Rosenberg, D. A., 112
Rosenfeld, B., 355
Rosenfeld, J. P., 99
Rosenham, David L., 116, 118
Rosenhan, D. J., 205
Rossmo, Dr. Kim, 83–84, 83
Roszko, James, 316
Rotenberg, K. J., 212
Rothbaum, B. O., 290
Rowland, M. D., 354
Ruby, C. L., 165
Russano, M. B., 64
Rutter, M., 381
Ryan, G., 295
Rzepa, S., 391

S

Saks, M. J., 210
Salekin, R. T., 113, 331, 389
Sales, B. D., 208
Samsock, D., 166
Sandberg, D. A., 345
Santor, D., 331
Saunders, B. E., 137
Saunders, J. W. S., 287–288
Savitsky, K., 61
Savitz, B., 353
Saywitz, K. J., 167, 169
Saywitz, K., 163
Scalora, M. J., 346
Scheck, B., 65
Schmidt, F. L., 35
Schmidt, J. D., 285
Schmucker, M., 303

Schoenwald, S. K., 354
Schuller, Dr. Regina A., 18, 214, 215, 216–217, 215–217, 218, 391
Schumacher, J., 35
Schwandt, B., 107
Schweer, John, 105
Schweighofer, A., 234
Scogin, F., 35
Scott, K., 313
Scott, L., 139
Sebold, J., 287
Seguin, D. G., 213
Seligman, Martin, 390
Sellers, C. S., 14
Semin, G. R., 108
Semrau, Dr. Stanley, 327
Senna, J., 39
Serin, R. C., 262, 351
Sewell, K. W., 114, 389
Shackelford, T. K., 314
Sheehan, R., 38, 39
Sheldon, W. H., 15
Sheridan, M. S., 112
Sherman, L. W., 285, 286
Shipman, Dr. Harold, 318
Shover, N., 366
Shuman, D. W., 215
Siegal, L., 39
Siegert, R., 294–295
Siegwart, C. M., 212
Silver, E., 363
Silver, James, 232
Simmons, J. L., 366
Simpson, A., 310
Simpson, O. J., 190, 194
Sin, L., 200
Sinclair, J., 397
Sinclair, S. D., 50
Singh, Monica, 220
Sioui. R., 398, 401
Sitaker, M., 282
Skeem, J., 331
Skinner, B. F., 16
Slade, Michael, 84
Small, M., 148
Smith, Brian, 233, 234
Smith, D. W., 137
Smith, Jason, 159
Smith, M. D., 280
Smith, M., 80
Smith, R. E., 207
Smith, Susan, 109, 110
Smith, V. L., 208, 217
Snook, B., 84–85

Snyder, L., 167, 169
Söchting, I., 293
Sommers, S. R., 207
Sophonow, Thomas, 13, 154, 155
Spanos, N. P., 213
Sporer, S. L., 107, 166
Sprott, J. B., 272
Stafford, Billy, 390
Stanton, J., 310
Stapleton, J., 109
Starson, Scott, (a.k.a. Schutzman, Scott Jeffery,), 229
Steadman, H. J., 243, 343, 344, 345
Steblay, N., 143, 145, 196
Stein, K., 264, 271
Stellar, M., 164, 165
Stephenson, M., 303
Sterling, Linda, 161
Sterling, Ronald, 161
Sterling, Travis, 161
Stern, William, 8–9
Steuve, A., 353
Stevenson-Robb, Y., 169
Steves, Jason, 43
Stewart, D. G., 394
Stewart, Martha, 194
Stoll, K., 297
Stone, Bert, 238–239
Stone, J. I., 104
Stoops, C., 287
Stoppel, Barbara, 154, 155
Storm, J., 121
Stouthamer-Loeber, M., 331
Strand, E. B., 283, 360
Strand, S., 389
Straus, M. A., 279, 280
Strömwall, L. A., 106
Stuart, G. L., 284
Sue, S., 207
Sugarman, D. B., 279
Sukel, H. L., 215
Sundby, S. E., 215
Sundram, J., 49, 52, 53
Sutcliffe, Peter, (a.k.a. Yorkshire Ripper), 73, 83
Sutherland, E. H., 15
Sutterfield, T., 392
Swanson, J. W., 353, 354
Swayze, Dr. Ian, 229
Symes, Kenneth, 184

T

Talwar, V., 111, 174
Tanford, J. A., 208

Tarrant, A., 169
Taylor, A., 47, 48
Taylor, P. J., 84
Templeton, R., 326
Teplin, L. A., 40, 41, 242
Terman, Lewis, 28
Terry, D., 215
Teske, R. J., 298
Tett, R. P., 29, 35
Thibault, J., 398, 401
Thierry, K. L., 163
Thoennes, N., 279
Thomas, S. W., 166
Thompson, C. Y., 366
Thompson, M. M., 47
Thompson, W., 353
Thornberry, T., 343
Thornton, David, 363
Tjaden, P. G., 279
Tolman, R. M., 285
Tomasino, R., 49, 52, 53
Tombaugh, T. N., 121
Tomkins, A. J., 346
Tomz, J. E., 46, 47
Towell, N., 145
Trejo, D. C., 212
Tremblay, Dr. Richard E., 377, 378
Trevethan, S., 396, 397, 399, 400,
  401–402
Trocme, N., 180, 182
Trupin, E. W., 394
Tubb, V., 151
Turnbull, S., 234
Turner, R. E., 222
Turtle, J. W., 153

U
Uken, A., 287
Ullman, S. E., 293
Ulmer, J. T., 257
Underwager, R., 58
Undeutsch, Udo, 164
Unruh, Howard, 316
Ustad, K. L., 113, 389

V
Van Amelsvoort, A. G., 146
Van Koppen, P. J., 138
Van Rybroek, J., 331
Vandecreek, L., 29, 35
Vandiver, D. M., 298
Varendonck, Julian, 10
Vena, J. E., 49
Viding, E., 332
Viljoen, J. L., 226, 227
Violanti, J. M., 49
Virk, Reena, 198
von Schrenck-Notzing, Albert, 10, 125
Vrij, A., 106, 108, 109

W
Wagner, N., 297
Wagstaff, G. F., 132, 139
Wakefield, H., 58
Walker, Lenore G., 50, 390, 391
Walker, S., 42
Wallace-Capretta, S., 388, 398
Walma, M. W., 38, 43, 44
Walsh, W., 290
Walter, R., 321
Ward, T., 294
Warren, Chief Justice Earl, 12
Warren, J. L., 389
Warren, K. L., 169
Webber, Carrie, 159
Webber, L., 138
Webster, Dr. Christopher D., 222, 314,
  348, 349, 365
Wedin, I., 362
Weiler, B. L., 333
Weisz, A., 285
Wells, Gary L., 140, 141, 142
Wells, H., 303
Welsh, A., 137
Wentink, N., 320
West, L., 38, 43, 44
White, M. D., 44
White, W. S., 64

Whittemore, K. E., 222, 234
Wickett, J., 393
Widom, C. S., 333, 352
Wigmore, John Henry, 11
Wilding, J., 146
Williams, A. L., 346
Williams, Justice James W., 200
Williams, K., 362
Williams, L. M., 183
Williams, S. L., 278
Williamson, S., 326, 334
Wilson, M., 312, 314
Wilson, Mona, 200
Wilson, T. D., 199
Wolfe, Brenda, 200
Wong, S., 326
Woodworth, M., 74, 76, 108,
  315, 328
Wrightsman, L. S., 65, 67
Wundt, Wilhelm, 8, 10
Wuornos, Aileen, 318
Wyer, M. M., 105
Wynkoop, T. F., 113

Y
Yarmey, A. L., 143
Yarmey, Dr. A. Dan, 24, 110, 138,
  139, 143, 146, 152
Yarmey, M. J., 138, 143
Yates, Andrea, 311, 312
Yllo, K., 280
Young, D., 352
Yuille, Dr. John, 136, 161, 164, 165,
  166, 167

Z
Zamble, E., 364, 389
Zanis, D. A., 353
Zapf, P. A., 222, 223, 226, 227–228
Zeisel, H., 258
Zhu, J., 102
Zill, N., 186
Zinger, I., 256, 265
Zoucha-Jensen, J. M., 293

Subject Index

A

ABFP. *See* American Board of Forensic Psychology (ABFP)
Aboriginal correction programs, 399–400
Aboriginal healing lodges, 384, 400
  example of, 401
Aboriginal Legal Services, Toronto, 395
Aboriginal offenders,
  history, 394
  reasons for, 397
  recidivism of, 398
  risk factors for, 397–398
  statistics, 395, 396, 396f, 396t
  treatment for, 399, 400, 401
Aboriginal peoples,
  in criminal justice system, 384–385
  statistics, 402
absolute discharge, 235, 236, 255, 256
absolute judgment (by witness), 142
acquired immune deficiency syndrome (AIDS), 201
Action for Child Protection procedure, 166
actuarial prediction (in risk assessment), 346
actus reus (wrongful deed), 221
adaptive coping skills (for stress), 52, 53f
Addiction Research Foundation, Toronto, 349
ADHD. *See* attention-deficit hyperactivity disorder (ADHD)
adjournment of trial, 198
administrative tribunals, 251
admissibility, 22, 23
adult risk factors (for Aboriginal offenders), 397–398
AIDS. *See* acquired immune deficiency syndrome (AIDS)
Alberta Court of Appeal, 13
Alberta Court of Queen's Bench, 13
American Bar Association Gavel Awards Competition, 228
American Board of Forensic Psychology (ABFP), 2
American Polygraph Association, 91
American Psychiatric Association (APA), 112, 347
American Psychological Association, 12, 99

American Psychology-Law Society (AP-LS), 2, 18, 20
Amnesty International, 51
anatomically detailed dolls, 163
  use of, 164
anger rapist, 292
animal maltreatment,
  battered women and, 283
anterograde amnesia, 121
Anti-Slavery International, 51
antisocial batterer, 284
antisocial behaviour, 14, 16
  theories on youth, 377–379
antisocial personality disorder (APD), 325, 326f, 376
Antisocial Process Screening Device (APSD), 329, 331
AP-LS. *See* American Psychology-Law Society (AP-LS)
APA. *See* American Psychiatric Association (APA)
APD. *See* antisocial personality disorder (APD)
APSD. *See* Antisocial Process Screening Device (APSD)
assessment centres, 36
  situational tests in, 37
attention-deficit hyperactivity disorder (ADHD), 376, 377, 379
automatism (as defence), 238, 239
  example cases of, 238–239
  NCRMD and, 240
  processes for, 238–240
autonomic nervous systems (ANS), 17

B

B.C.'s Violence Against Women in Relationships Policy, 41, 44
backfire effect, 207
battered woman syndrome (BWS), 216–217, 390, 391
  animal maltreatment and, 283
  characteristics of, 391–392
  example of, 390
  myths of, 281–283
Baxstrom study, 343
biological theories (to explain antisocial youth), 377
biological theories (to explain female criminality), 385

biosocial theory of crime, 16
Birmingham Six (case of), 69, 70
black sheep effect (in juries), 211, 212
Boston Legal, 190
Brain Fingerprinting Laboratories, 105
brain fingerprinting, 105
brainwashing, 68
Brian's Law (Mental Health Legislative Reform). 2000. S.O. 2000, c. 9 (formerly Bill 68), 234
British Columbia Court of Appeal, 177
broad-based approach (to jury selection), 193–194
Burnt Bones, 84
BWS. *See* battered woman syndrome (BWS)

C

CACP. *See* Canadian Association of Chiefs of Police (CACP)
CAI. *See* Competency to Stand Trial Assessment Instrument (CAI)
Cambridge Study in Delinquent Development, 332
CAMR. *See* Centre for Addiction and Mental Health (CAMR) (prev. Clarke Institute of Psychiatry), Toronto
Canadian Association of Chiefs of Police (CACP), 46
Canadian Charter of Rights and Freedoms, 39, 43, 61, 178, 221, 232, 372
Canadian Foundation for Children, Youth, and the Law, 178
Canadian Human Rights Commission (1981), 383
Canadian Journal of Behavioural Science, 270
Canadian Journal of Criminology, 270
Canadian Police College, 91
Canadian Psychological Association (CPA), 18, 20, 144, 296, 339
Canadian Security Intelligence Service (CSIS), 92
Canadian Sentencing Commission, 270
capital punishment, 213, 312
  in Canada, 263
  verdicts, 330f
capping (mental illness), 236

Cardiff University, Wales, 324
case-specific approach (to jury selection), 194
CBSA. *See* criterion-based content analysis (CBSA)
CCRA. *See* Corrections and Conditional Release Act (CCRA) (1993)
CD. *See* conduct disorder (CD)
CEGEP. *See* Collège d'enseignement général et professionne (CEGEP)
Center for Geospatial Intelligence and Investigation, Department of Criminal Justice, Texas State University, 83
Centre for Addiction and Mental Health (CAMR) (prev. Clarke Institute of Psychiatry), Toronto, 229, 349
Centre for Children and Families in the Justice System, 174
Centre for Investigative Psychology (CIP), University of Liverpool, 76
challenge for cause (in jury selection), 192–198
    cases, 198–199
change of venue (for trials), 197–198
child custody, 184
    joint, 185
    legal history of, 185
child emotional maltreatment, 177, 178
Child Maltreatment Section (CMS), Health Canada, 177, 179
child maltreatment, 177–178, 179, 180–181
    categories of, 177–178
    risk factors for, 182
child molester, 291
    extra-familial, 291
    fixated, 293
    intra-familial, 291
    regressed, 293–294
    sex-force, 294
    sex-pressure, 294
    types of, 293–294
child neglect, 177, 178–179
child physical abuse, 177
    Canadian case, 180
    effects of, 182
child sexual abuse, 177, 380
    effects of, 183
    risk factors for, 182*t*
Child Witness Project, 174
child witnesses, 159
    court changes for, 175–176
    culprit descriptions by, 169

direct questioning of, 161–162
free recall by, 160, 161
identification procedure for, 171, 172
interview methods, 164, 165–168, 167*t*, 169
lineups and, 170–171
negative attitudes to, 160
recognition by, 170
see also anatomically detailed dolls
suggestibility in, 162
testifying in court, 172–173, 174–175
childhood risk factors (for Aboriginal offenders), 397–398
Children's Aid Society, 177, 180, 339
chromosomal theory of crime, 15
CIP. *See* Centre for Investigative Psychology (CIP), University of Liverpool
City College, New York City, 12
City of Vancouver Police Department, 28
CJOH television station, Ottawa, 233
Clarke Institute of Psychiatry. *See* Centre for Addiction and Mental Health (CAMR) (prev. Clarke Institute of Psychiatry), Toronto
Clarke Sex History Questionnaire, 298
classic trait model of personality, 79
Classification of Violence Risk (software program), 358
clinical factors (in violence/antisocial prediction), 353–354
clinical forensic psychologists, 4
    licensing of, 4
clinical risk factors (in violence/antisocial prediction), 350
Clockwork Orange, A, 300
CMS. *See* Child Maltreatment Section (CMS), Health Canada
cognitive ability tests, 34, 35
cognitive and social skills training, 382
cognitive distortion (sex offender), 299
cognitive interview, 133
    components of, 133–134
    enhanced, 134
cognitive theories (to explain antisocial youth), 377–379
cognitive-behavioural group therapy, 286
Collège d'enseignement général et professionne (CEGEP), 322
Columbia University, New York, 8

Columbine High School, 316
communicating with counsel, 222
community service, 255, 256
community treatment order, 245
competency inquiry, 172
    questions for, 173–174
Competency Screening Test (CST), 225
Competency to Stand Trial Assessment Instrument (CAI), 225
Competency to Stand Trial, 228
compliance, 68–69
conditional discharge, 235, 236, 255, 256
conditional sentence, 255, 256
conduct disorder (CD), 376, 377, 380
    treatment for, 382–383
confabulation (in confession), 72
confessions, 62
    disputed, 64–65
    retracted, 64–65
    see also false confessions
confidentiality, limits of, 339, 340
Conflict Tactics Scale (CTS), 277, 278
    criticisms of, 278–279
constitutional theory of crime, 15
constructing and validating (police selection instruments), 30, 31
Consulting Psychology Research Award, 228
contextual risk factors (in violence/antisocial prediction), 349–350, 354–355
Continental Drift, 100
conversation management (interview method), 64
coping-relapse model of criminal recidivism, 364
corporal punishment, 178
correctional interventions, 264–265
Correctional Service Canada (CSC), 268, 356, 384, 386, 389, 394, 400
Corrections and Conditional Release Act (CCRA) (1993), 394
Court Martial Appeal Court, 252
court system (Canadian), 249–250
    structure of, 250, 251–252, 251*f*
CPA. *See* Canadian Psychological Association (CPA)
CQT. *See* polygraph tests, control question test (CQT)
Creating Choices: Report of the Task Force on Federally Sentenced Women (1990), 384
Crime and Personality, 16

crime, theories of, 14, 15
  biological, 15
  learning, 14–16
  personality, 14, 16–17, 18
  psychoanalytic, 14
  see also individual theories
  sociological, 15
Criminal Justice in Canada: A Reader, 270
criminal profiling, 73
  ambiguity difficulties of, 80
  construction, 76
  deductive method of, 76–77
  definitions of, 73–74
  FBI and, 74, 75, 77, 78, 320
  history of, 74–75
  inductive method of, 77
  organized-disorganized model, 77–78t,
    79, 320
  professional accuracy of,
    81–82, 81t
  RCMP and, 75–76
  see also investigative psychology
  theory of, 79–80
  validity of, 78–79
criteria (psychology), 21
criterion-based content analysis (CBSA),
  164, 165–166
cross-race effect (on witnesses), 149
CSC. *See* Correctional Service
  Canada (CSC)
CSI (television series), 1
CSIS. *See* Canadian Security Intelligence
  Service (CSIS)
*CST. See Competency Screening
  Test (CST)*
CTS. See Conflict Tactics Scale (CTS)
cue-utilization hypothesis, 150
culprit, 139
cycle-of-violence theory, 390, 391

D

Dalhousie University, 349
dangerous offender designation, 256
Dannemora State Hospital for the
  Criminally Insane, 343
date rape, 213
Daubert criteria, 23
DBT. *See* Dialectical behaviour
  therapy (DBT)
death penalty. *See* capital punishment
deception detection, 60–61
  accuracy of, 107–108, 109t
  ethics of research into, 116, 117
  in children, 111–112

in witnesses, 109–110
  vocal and non-verbal clues to,
    104–107, 107t
deception disorders, 112–114
defensiveness, 114
denial (sex offender), 298–299
deoxyribonucleic acid (DNA), 95, 200,
  209, 215
  exoneration cases, 153, 153t
Department of Psychology, University
  of Minnesota, 100
deviant sexual interests, 300–301
Devlin Report (1976), 152
*Diagnostic and Statistical Manual of
  Mental Disorders*, (3rd ed.) (1980)
  (DSM-III), 386
*Diagnostic and Statistical Manual of
  Mental Disorders*, (4th ed.) (1994)
  (DSM-IV), 112, 114, 290,
  326f, 376
Diagnostic Interview Schedule, 386
Dialectical behaviour therapy
  (DBT), 393
differential association theory
  of crime, 15
direct-question recall, 128
dispositional risk factors (in violence/
  antisocial prediction), 349
  demographics of, 350
  personality characteristics of,
    351, 352
diversion (to treatment program),
  244–245, 372
divorce, 184
  child access, 184
  effects on children, 185–186
Dixon study, 343
DNA. *See* deoxyribonucleic acid (DNA)
domestic disturbance exercise, 37
domestic violence, 41, 276–277
  animal maltreatment and, 283
  BWS and, 281–283
  criminal justice response to, 285
  gender-based, 278
  numbers involved in, 279–280, 280t
  studies of deterrence effects of arrest
    on, 285–286, 286f
  theories, 280, 281
*DSM-III. See Diagnostic and Statistical
  Manual of Mental Disorders,
  (3rd ed.) (1980) (DSM-III)*
*DSM-IV. See Diagnostic and Statistical
  Manual of Mental Disorders,
  (4th ed.) (1994) (DSM-IV)*

Duluth Domestic Abuse Intervention
  Project, Minnesota. *See* Duluth
  model (feminist psychoeducational
  group therapy) of intervention
Duluth model (feminist psychoeducational
  group therapy) of intervention,
  286, 287
duty to warn, 339
dynamic risk factors (in violence/
  antisocial prediction), 348
dyscontrol theory of crime, 15
dysphoric/borderline batterer, 284

E

École Polytechnique, Montreal, 316, 322
Edmonton Remand Centre, 241,
  241t, 243
elimination lineup (for children),
  171, 172
empathy training (for sex offenders), 299
Employee Protection Act (1988), 92
epistemology (psychology), 21
ERPs. *See* event-related potentials
  (ERPs) (in polygraph tests)
estimator variables (in eyewitness
  studies), 128
European Journal of Criminology, 270
event-related potentials (ERPs)
  (in polygraph tests), 98, 102–103
exhibitionists, 291
experimental forensic psychologists, 5, 6
expert witness,
  battered women and, 216–215, 217
  challenges for, 20–22
  criteria for, 13, 22–23, 24
  first in US, 12
  first, 10
  functions, 20
  juries and, 215
explanation (story) models of juries,
  209–210
externalizing problems (youth), 375
extrajudicial measures, 373
extroversion (personality), 16–17
*Eyewitness Evidence: A Guide for Law
  Enforcement*, 153
eyewitness interviews, 129
  cognitive, 133, 134
  recall of culprit, 138
  supportive procedures for, 132–133
eyewitness testimony, 8–9, 13, 125
  confidence and accuracy of,
    147–148
  memory and, 126

public views on, 152–153, 154
reliability of, 151–152
research into, 127, 128
Eysenck Personality Questionnaire, 18

F

fabricating, 160
factitious disorder, 112, 113
faint hope clause, 327
false confessions, 60, 64–65
   coerced-compliant, 66, 68
   coerced-internalized, 67–68
   consequences of, 72–73
   frequency of, 65
   laboratory analysis of, 70–71—72
   see also confessions
   types of, 65
   voluntary, 65–66
false memory syndrome, 135
   traumatic events and, 135–136
familial protective factors (for youth
   behavioural problems), 381
familial risk factors (of youth behavioural
   problems), 380
familicide, 312
*Family violence in Canada: A statistical
   profile* (2006), 280
family-only batterer, 284
FBI Crime Classification Manual, 313
FBI serial murder model, 320
FBI. *See* Federal Bureau of Investigation
   (FBI)
Federal Bureau of Investigation
   (FBI), 73, 83
   Behavioral Sciences Unit, 75
   criminal profiling and, 74, 75, 77
Federal Court of Appeal, 252
Federal Court of Canada, 252
female offenders, 383
   Aboriginal, 385
   borderline personality disorder
     and, 393
   data on, 386, 387
   history, 383–384
   risk factors for, 388–389
   statistics, 384–385, 385t
   theories, 385–386
   treatment for, 392–393
   victimization rates for, 387–388
femicide, 313–314
feminist pathways research, 386
filicide, 309
   maternal, 310
   paternal, 312

fines, 255, 257
Finkelhor's theory of child
   molesting, 294
FIT-R. See Fitness Interview Test
   Revised (FIT-R)
fitness evaluation, 222
   defendant numbers referred for,
     222–223, 223t
   defendants referred to, 226–228,
     227, 227t
   events following the, 230–231
   instruments for, 224, 225, 226
   practitioners for, 223
Fitness Interview Test Revised (FIT-R),
   224, 227, 228
fitness standard (for trial), 221–222
   processes in, 231f
   raising issue of, 222
fitness treatment, 229
fMRI. *See* functional magnetic
   resonance imaging (fMRI)
focus groups (for jury-eligible
   respondents), 195
forensic anthropology, 5
forensic chemistry, 5
forensic entomology, 5
forensic linguistics, 5
forensic ondontology, 5
forensic pathology, 5
forensic psychiatry, 4
forensic psychologists,
   roles of, 3–4, 5, 6
forensic psychology,
   compared to forensic psychiatry, 4
   definitions of, 2–3
   history of, 8, 9, 10, 11, 12–13
   popular media view of, 1
functional magnetic resonance imaging
   (fMRI), 103
fundamental principle of
   sentencing, 254

G

Gallup Poll, 86
GCS. *See Gudjonsson Compliance
   Scale (GCS)*
gender theory (to explain female
   criminality), 386
general acceptance test, 22
general deterrence, 253
*General Statistical Information on
   Recidivism (GSIR) scale*, 356,
   388–389
general violent/antisocial batterer, 284

Geographic Profiling Section, Vancouver
   Police Department, 83
Geographic Profiling, 84
geographic profiling, 82, 83
   systems, 83–85
GKT. *See* polygraph tests, guilty
   knowledge test (GKT)
Gladue Court, 394, 395
Gough Dissimulation Scale (Ds), 120
Green River serial murder case
   (Washington State), 82
ground truth (in polygraph
   tests), 95
GSIR. *See General Statistical Information
   on Recidivism (GSIR) scale* GSS1.
   *See Gudjonsson Suggestibility Scale
   (GSS1)*
Gudjonsson Compliance Scale (GCS),
   68–69
   use of, 69
*Gudjonsson Suggestibility Scale
   (GSS1)*, 69
   use of, 69

H

Handbook of Psychopathy, 100
*Hare Psychopathy Checklist - Revised
   (PCL-R)*, 323, 324, 327, 328,
   329, 333, 389
*Hare Psychopathy Checklist: Screening
   Version (PCL:SV)*, 332, 357
Harvard University, 10
*HCR-20 Structured Guide for the
   Assessment of Violence Risk*,
   349, 359–360, 367, 389
HCSA. *See* historic child sex abuse
   (HCSA)
HeartMath stress management
   program, 52
heuristics, 84
Hillside Stranglers, 317
historic child sex abuse (HCSA),
   136, 137, 138
   judge alone trial results, 137
   jury trial results, 137
historical factors (in violence/antisocial
   prediction), 352–353
   childhood abuse as, 352
   past behaviour as, 352
   past failures as, 352
   starting age as, 352
HIV. *See* human immunodeficiency
   virus (HIV)
homeowner complaint, 37

homicide, 307–308
  biomodal classification of, 315
  BWS and, 389–390
  by juveniles, 313
  multiple (serial), 316–317
  psychopaths and, 327
  PTSD and, 315
  spousal, 313–314
  statistics, 309, 309f
  types, 308
human immunodeficiency virus
      (HIV), 201
Humm-Wadsworth Temperament Scale, 29
hung jury, 210, 211
hypnosis, 132–133, 155

I

ICT. *See Iterative Classification
      Tree (ICT)*
idiographic approaches (to law), 21
IFI. *See Interdisciplinary Fitness
      Interview (IFI)*
illusory correlation (in risk assessment),
      345
impartiality (of juries), 195, 196
  Canadian example of, 197
  methods for improving likelihood of,
      197–198
  threats to, 196–197
imprisonment, 255, 256
In the Name of the Father, 66
inadmissible evidence, 207
  disregarding of, 207
Incidence Study of Reported Child Abuse
      and Neglect (2nd., Canadian)
      (2003), 179
individual protective factors (for youth
      behavioural problems), 381
individual risk factors (of youth
      behavioural problems), 379–380
infanticide, 308
  mental illness and, 310–311
insanity,
  assessing, 235
  defence, 12–13, 232
  defendant numbers claiming,
      234–235, 234t
  definition of, 232
  plea, 312
  standard of, 232, 233
instigators (in domestic assault), 281
Institute of Psychiatry, London, 69
instrumental (predatory) aggression, 315
inter-rater reliability (of interviewers),
      33–34

Interdisciplinary Fitness Interview (IFI),
      225–226
internalization (in confession), 72
internalizing problems (youth), 375
Internet,
  sex solicitation over, 183, 184
intimate partner violence, 277
intoxication (as defence), 240
investigative psychology, 76
investigator bias (interrogation), 61, 62
Inwald Personality Inventory (IPI), 35
Iowa State Penitentiary, 105
IRA. *See Irish Republican Army (IRA)*
Irish Republican Army (IRA), 69
Iterative Classification Tree (ICT),
      357–358

J

Jack the Ripper murder case, 74
JDA. *See Juvenile Delinquents
      Act (JDA) (1908)*
job analysis (police agency), 30, 31
John Howard Society, 255, 263, 268
Joint Missing Women Task Force
      (Vancouver), 200
Journal of Applied Psychology, 144
JPO. *See juvenile probation officer (JPO)*
judge's instructions (to juries), 208
  reform of, 208
Judging the Jury, 216
juries,
  aids for, 205–206
  attitudes of, 213
  behaviour studies, 202, 203–204
  characteristics of, 195
  confidentiality of, 203
  decision-making models of, 208–209,
      210
  deliberations of, 204, 210
  demographic variables of,
      193, 211, 212
  effect of defendant's characteristics
      on, 213
  effect of victim's characteristics
      on, 214
  expert witnesses and, 215
  field studies of, 204
  function of, 199–200, 201–202
  impartiality of, 195, 196, 197
  in British Columbia, 192
  in Ontario, 192
  inadmissible evidence and, 207
  judge's instructions to, 208
  lawyers and selection of, 193, 194
  note taking by, 205–206

  offences tried by, 190–191
  payment, 193
  personality traits of, 212–213
  questioning by, 206
  representativeness of, 195
  scientific selection of, 193–195
  selection of, 189–190, 191, 193
  sequestered, 193
  verdict prediction of, 211, 212, 213
  verdicts, 210–211
Jury Act (provincial and territorial), 191
jury nullification, 200, 201–202
  examples of, 201
jury summons, 191
juvenile delinquency, 11, 12, 14
Juvenile Delinquents Act (JDA)
      (1908), 371, 371t, 372
juvenile probation officer (JPO), 330

K

knowledge (psychology), 21
knowledge, skills, and abilities (KSAs),
      30, 31, 33, 36
known-groups design (malingering
      research), 117

L

Larry King Live, 190
latitude (psychology), 21
Law and Human Behavior, 216
Law and Order, 190
Law Reform Commission of Canada
      (1976), 232
Law Reform Commission of Canada
      (1984), 308
law,
  differences between psychology
      and, 21
  nature of, 21
leading question, 130–131
learned helplessness, 329, 390
Leipzig, Germany, 8
leniency bias (of jurors), 210
*Level of Service Inventory - Revised
      (LSI-R)*, 358–359, 365, 389
lineups, 128
  accuracy of identification in, 140
  biases, 145
  child witnesses and, 170–171
  distractors (or foils), 140
  fair, 140
  format, 142, 144
  identification guidelines, 153–154
  implications of identification
      in, 141

multiple independent, 147
photo arrays and, 141–142
reasons for, 139–140
see also showup
sequential, 142
simultaneous, 142
target-absent, 140–141
target-present, 140
linkage blindness (in serial crime
investigations), 75
Liquor Licensing Board, 251
London Family Court Clinic, 174
long-term offender designation, 256
Los Angels Police Department
(LAPD), 29
*LSI-R. See Level of Service Inventory-
Revised (LSI-R)*

M

M test (for malingering), 113–114
*M-FAST. See Miller-Forensic Assessment
of Symptoms Test (M-FAST)
MacArthur Competence Assessment
Tool - Criminal Adjudication
(MacCAT-CA),* 224–226, 357
*MacArthur Violence Risk
Assessment Study,* 345 *MacCAT-
CA. See MacArthur Competence
Assessment Tool - Criminal
Adjudication (MacCAT-CA)
Maclean's* magazine, 51
magnetic resonance imaging (MRI), 183
Making Sense of Sentencing, 270
male batterers,
treatments for, 286–288
types of, 284–285
malingered amnesia, 121
detection methods, 121
malingering, 113–114
explanatory models for, 114
psychosis detection., 119–121
psychosis, 85–116, 118, 118*t*, 119
research, 115
Malleus Maleficarum, 74
mandatory charging policies, 285
mandatory minimum sentences
(MMS), 261, 261*t*
Manitoba Court of Appeal, 13
Manitoba Risk-Needs Scale, 398
manslaughter, 308
Martensville babysitting case, 161
Maryland State Police, 86
Mask of Sanity, The, 323, 324
mass murder, 316–317, 321–322
in Canada, 321, 322

*Massachusetts Treatment Center Rapist
Typology (MTC: R3),* 328
Massachusetts Treatment Center, 291
masturbatory satiation, 300
mathematical models of juries, 209
maturation,
offending and, 366
maximization techniques
(interrogation), 60
memory impairment hypothesis, 131
memory,
delayed recall, 135
difference in recall between
children and adults, 162
estimator recognition variables,
148–150
eyewitness testimony and, 126
hypnotically-refreshed, 132
recall, 126, 129
recognition, 126–127, 139
stages, 127*f*
mens rea (criminal intent), 221
Mental Disorder Project, 232
mental health courts, 245
effectiveness of, 246
objectives of, 245
mental illness,
defendants with, 241, 242
infanticide and, 310–311
offences committed by people
with, 244
recidivism of people with, 244
see also schizophrenia
treatment of defendants with,
244, 245
violence and, 243, 353–354
Mental, Health, Law, Policy Institute
(MHLPI), 6
methodology (psychology), 21
*Miller-Forensic Assessment of Symptoms
Test (M-FAST),* 120
Millon Clinical Multiaxial Inventory, 314
minimization (sex offender), 298
minimization techniques
(interrogation), 60
*Minnesota Multiphasic Personality
Inventory (MMPI),* 35, 365
*Minnesota Multiphasic Personality
Inventory (MMPI-2),* 120
*Minnesota Multiphasic Personality
Inventory, version 2 (MMPI-2),* 35
Miranda rights, 60–61
problems with, 61
misinformation acceptance
hypothesis, 131

misinformation effect, 130–131
reasons for, 131–132
*MMPI-2. See Minnesota Multiphasic
Personality Inventory, version 2
(MMPI-2)
MMPI. See Minnesota Multiphasic
Personality Inventory (MMPI)*
MMS. *See* mandatory minimum
sentences (MMS)
mock jury trials, 195
Mohan criteria, 23
problems with, 24
Monash University, Melbourne,
Australia, 19
MST. *See* multisystemic therapy (MST)
*MTC: R3. See Massachusetts Treatment
Center Rapist Typology (MTC: R3)*
multisystemic therapy (MST), 382–383
Munchausen syndrome by proxy
(MBP), 112
Munchausen syndrome, 112
murder,
first-degree, 308
second-degree, 308
Murderous Minds on Trial, 327

N

Nancy Grace, 190
narrative elaboration interview
procedure, 167–168, 169
National Advisory Commission on
Criminal Justice Standards and
Goals in the United States
(1973), 29
National Center for the Analysis of
Violent Crime, 75
National Parole Board (NPB), 242, 251,
266, 267, 268, 269, 270, 337, 338,
341, 356
National Survey on Children (U.S., 1976,
1981, 1987), 186
National Use-of-Force Model (Canada),
45, 44
National Violence Against Women Survey
(2006), 291
NCRMD. *See* Not Criminally
Responsible by Reason of Mental
Disorder (NCRMD)
need principle (of correctional
intervention), 264
neonaticide, 310, 312
neuroticism, 16–17
New York City's Mad Bomber case, 74
New York Police Department (NYPD),
44, 74

nomothetic approaches, 21
Northwestern University, Chicago, 11, 216
Not Criminally Responsible by Reason of Mental Disorder (NCRMD), 230, 233, 239, 241
  automatism and, 240
  defendants claiming, 234, 235
  dispositions after finding, 235–237, 237f
  example case of, 233–234
  recidivism rates of those, 244
Nova Scotia Court of Appeal, 110
NPB. See National Parole Board (NPB)

O

observational learning, 281
occupational stressors (police), 47
ODD. See oppositional defiant disorder (ODD)
offences (in Canada), 190–191
offenders with mental illness, 40
Okimaw Ohci Healing Lodge, Maple Creek, Saskatchewan, 385, 401
On the Witness Stand, 10
Ontario Child Health Study (1987), 376
Ontario Court of Appeal, 14, 63, 152, 201, 222, 229
Ontario Mental Health Centre, Penetanguishene, 233
Ontario Review Board, 229
Ontario Superior Court of Justice, 178, 229
Ontario Supreme Court, 85
open-ended recall (free narrative), 128
Operational Police Stress Questionnaire, 47
oppositional defiant disorder (ODD), 370, 376
Organizational Police Stress Questionnaire, 47
organizational stressors (police), 47
other-race effect (on witnesses), 149
Oxford University, 270

P

parallel parenting, 185
parent training programs, 382
parole, 265–272
  day, 268
  decision making myths, 267
  decision making, 266, 267
  factors effecting public opinion on, 272
  full, 268

public opinion surveys on, 270—271
  revocation, 269f, 270f
  risk assessment and, 341
  see also statutory release
  studies in effectiveness of, 269
  types, 268
parricide, 313
pathway model of child sexual abuse, 294–295
patriarchy, 280, 281
PCL-R. See Hare Psychopathy Checklist - Revised (PCL-R)
PCL:SV. See Hare Psychopathy Checklist: Screening Version (PCL:SV)
PCL:YV. See Psychopathy Checklist: Youth Version (PCL:YV)
PEACE interrogation model, 64
pedophile, 291
Penetanguishene Mental Health Centre, Ontario, 296
penile phallometry, 300
Performance Monitoring Report, 269
personality tests, 35
photo arrays, 141–142
physiognomic homogeneity, 149
polarization (of jurors), 210
police discretion, 37, 38
  areas of usage of, 39–40, 41–42
  control of, 43–44
  departmental policies and, 44
  domestic violence and, 41
  factors influencing, 42–43
  necessity of, 38–39
  use-of-force situations and, 42
  youth crime and, 39
Police Foundation, Washington DC, 83
police interrogations, 57
  courts and, 62–63
  problems with, 57–58
  procedural safeguards during, 60–61
  recent procedure changes to, 64
  see also Reid model of interrogation
  video recording of, 64
police selection, 28, 33
  history of, 28–29
  in Canada, 30
  in US, 29
  interview, 33–34
  psychological tests in, 34, 35, 36
  stages, 30, 31, 32–33
  validation of, 31–33
Police Services Act (1990) (Canada), 43

police stress, 46
  consequences of, 49, 50
  job performance and, 50–51
  managing, 52–54
  physical problems from, 49–50
  preventing, 51–52
  psychological problems from, 50
  sources of, 46–47, 48
  suicide and, 51
polygraph disclosure tests, 92
polygraph tests, 30, 62, 90–91
  accuracy assessment of, 95–97, 98
  admissibility of, 101–102
  applications for, 92
  brain-based, 102, 103–104
  confessions and, 95
  control question test (CQT), 92–93, 93t, 93–95, 96, 96t, 98, 99, 101
  countermeasures to, 98
  effects on jury, 102
  expert opinion on, 99, 99t, 101
  guilty knowledge test (GKT), 94–95, 96, 97, 98, 99, 101, 103
  in Canada, 91, 92
  origins of, 91
  psychopaths and, 99
  relevant/irrelevant test, 92
post-event information effect, 130
post-traumatic stress disorder (PTSD), 290
  homicide and, 315
post-trial interviews (of juries), 203
postpartum (period after childbirth), blues, 310–311
  depression, 311, 312
  psychosis, 311, 312
Pottawattamie County Attorney, 105
power rapist, 292
PPI. See Psychopathic Personality Inventory (PPI)
prima facie case, 230
principles (psychology), 21
Prison for Women, Kingston, Ontario, 383–384
probation, 255, 256
profiling. See criminal profiling; geographic profiling; racial profiling
protective factors (reduce antisocial behaviour), 365
psychology and the law, 7
  differences, 21
psychology in the law, 7
Psychology of Harry Potter, The, 100
psychology of the law, 7–8

Psychopathic Personality Inventory (PPI), 332
Psychopathy Checklist: Youth Version (PCL:YV), 329, 331
psychopathy, 323
    APD and, 325, 326f
    assessment of, 323–324
    cognitive and affective models of, 333–334
    environmental factors of, 332
    example of, 327
    family and, 332–333
    genetic factors of, 332
    labelling, 329–330
    law enforcement and, 333
    recidivism rates for, 351, 352
    sexual violence and, 328
    treatment, 328–329
    violence and, 326, 328
    youth traits, 329–330
psychoticism, 16
    violence and, 354
PTSD. *See* post-traumatic stress disorder (PTSD)
Public Opinion, Crime, and Criminal Justice, 270
Public Safety and Emergency Preparedness Canada (2006), 385t
Public Service Commission of Canada, 51

Q

Queen's University, Kingston, Ontario, 144, 177, 296, 349

R

R-CRAS. See Rogers Criminal Responsibility Assessment Scales (R-CRAS)
racial bias (of juries), 211–212
racial profiling, 85, 86–87
    in Canada, 85–87
Rape Empathy Scale, 299
rape shield provisions, 214
rape trauma syndrome, 289–290
rape,
    effects, 289–290
    myths, 289, 290
    psychological consequences of, 290–291
    resisting, 293
    see also sexual assault
Rapid Risk Assessment for Sex Offence Recidivism (RRASOR), 362, 363

rapists, 291
    psychopathic, 328
    types of, 291–293
RCMP Police Aptitude Test (RPAT), 30, 34
RCMP Regular Member Selection Interview, 33
RCMP. *See* Royal Canadian Mounted Police (RCMP)
reactive (affective) aggression, 315
reasonable doubt, 206
recidivism,
    process, 364f
    statistics, 356
regulators (in domestic assault), 281
rehabilitation, 264–265
Reid model of interrogation, 58–59, 64, 67
    basis of, 59
    problems with, 60–62
    stages of, 59
    techniques of, 59–60
relapse prevention (RP) (sexual offender), 301, 302
relational theory (on female criminality), 386
relative judgment (by witness), 142
reparations, 253, 255
representativeness (of juries), 195
resilient children, 381
resolution conference, 39
responsivity principle (or correctional intervention), 265
restitution, 255
retroactive memory falsification, 10
retrograde amnesia, 121
Review Boards, 233, 236
    Ontario, 233
Revised Rapist Typology, Version 3, The (MTC:R3), 291–292
Rigel computer system, 83
risk assessment, 338
    actuarial instruments, 356–358
    approaches to, 346–348
    base rate in, 342–343
    by mental health practitioners, 343–344
    child protection context, 339
    civil context, 339, 340
    components, 338–339
    criminal context, 339, 340–341
    definition, 338
    errors in, 345–346
    factor types in, 348
    gender bias in, 346

history, 343–344
    instruments for, 355, 358
    methodological issues in, 344–345
    outcomes, 341, 342, 342t
    parole release and, 341
    sentencing and, 341
    theory, 363
    use of, 365–366
risk factors (in violence/antisocial prediction), 348
    important, 349–350
    in youth, 379–380
    stalking and, 355
risk principle (of correctional intervention), 264–265
Rogers Criminal Responsibility Assessment Scales (R-CRAS), 235
Roman Catholic Church, 74
Royal Canadian Mounted Police (RCMP), 51, 83, 316, 327
    criminal profiling and, 75–76 Royal Ottawa Hospital, 234 RP. *See* relapse prevention (RP) (sexual offender)
RRASOR. See Rapid Risk Assessment for Sex Offence Recidivism (RRASOR)
Rwanda war-crime trial, 144

S

sadistic rapist, 292
Salem witch trials (1692), 160
SARA. See Spousal Assault Risk Assessment (SARA)
Saskatchewan Court of Appeal, 196
Saskatchewan Federal Institution., 327
Saskatchewan Justice Department, 196
SCC. *See* Supreme Court of Canada (SCC)
schizophrenia, 220, 221, 234, 241, 242, 243, 244, 353, 356, 357
    paranoid, 233
    treatment for, 245
school risk factors (of youth behavioural problems), 380
Science, 116
Scotland Yard, 76, 83
self-defence, 389–390
    court decisions, 391
sentencing disparity, 257
    reducing, 260
    sources of, 258
    studies of, 258, 259
    unwarranted, 258

sentencing process, 253
  achieving goals of, 261–262, 263–264
  factors affecting decisions in, 256–257
  factors effecting public opinion on, 272
  fundamental principle in, 254
  guidelines for, 260, 261
  options in, 254, 255–256
  principles of, 254
  purposes of, 253–254
  risk assessment in., 341
sequestered jurors, 193
serial murder, 316
  characteristics, 317–318
  comfort, 320
  female, 318, 318t
  lust, 320
  mission-oriented, 320
  power/control, 320
  reasons for, 319
  statistics, 317, 318t
  typologies of, 320–321
  visionary, 320
serotonin-reuptake inhibitors (SSRIs), 301
sexual assault,
  definition, 289
  instruments for predicting, 361, 362–363
  psychopathy and, 328
  see also rape
  statistics for, 288–289
  theories of, 294–295
sexual offenders,
  adolescent, 295
  classification of, 291
  effectiveness of psychological treatment, 301, 303
  female, 296–298
  perceptions of, 291
  treatment of, 298–301
Shark, 190
Shipley Institute of Living Scale (SILS), 36
Short-Term Assessment of Risk and Treatability (START), 365
showup, 144–145
Silence of the Lambs, The, 1
Simon Fraser University (SFU), 6, 19, 83, 228, 349
simulation design (malingering research), 115, 117
simulation studies (in sentencing disparity), 258, 259

SIRS. See Structured Interview of Reported Symptoms (SIRS)
situational test, 36
Six Factor Personality Questionnaire, 30
60 Minutes, 105
social compliance, 162
social control theory of crime, 15
social learning theory of crime, 15–281, 379
social risk factors (of youth behavioural problems), 380
social theories (to explain antisocial youth), 379
social theories (to explain female criminality), 385
social/external protective factors (for youth behavioural problems), 381
Society for Psychophysiological Research, 99
Society for the Psychological Studies of Social Issues, 228
Society for the Scientific Study of Psychopathy, 100
sociological theories (to explain female criminality), 385
sociopathic batterer, 284
somatoform disorders, 113
source misattribution hypothesis, 131
Sparwood Youth Assistance Program (SYAP), 39
specific deterrence, 253
SPJ. See structured professional judgment (SPJ) (in risk assessment)
Spousal Assault Risk Assessment (SARA), 361–362
spousal assault, 380
  instruments for predicting, 361–362, 369
  see also homicide, spousal
spree murder, 317
SSRIs. See serotonin-reuptake inhibitors (SSRIs)
stalking, 355
Stanford University, 229
Stanford-Binet intelligence test, 28
START. See Short-Term Assessment of Risk and Treatability (START)
statement validity analysis (SVA), 164, 165, 166, 169
static (historical) risk factors (in violence/antisocial prediction), 349
Static-99 scale, 363
Statistics Canada Violence Against Women Survey (1993), 279
Statistics Canada, 280, 309, 374, 402

statutory release, 268
  risk assessment and, 341
step-wise interview (for children), 166–167, 167t
strain theory of crime, 15
Structured Interview of Reported Symptoms (SIRS), 119–120
structured professional judgment (SPJ) (in risk assessment), 348
substance abuse problems, 300
  criminal behaviour prediction and, 353
suggestibility, 8–9, 68–69
Supreme Court of British Columbia, 197, 200
Supreme Court of Canada (SCC), 13, 62, 102, 110, 178, 201, 214, 229, 230, 232, 233, 238, 252, 340, 394, 395
  characteristics of juries, 195
Supreme Court of Iowa, 105
surveillance records (for identification), 145–146
suspect, 139
SVA. See statement validity analysis (SVA)
Symptom Validity Test (SVT), 121
system variables (in eyewitness studies), 128
systematic disparity (of sentencing), 257, 258

T

Tax Court of Canada, 252
TCO. See threat/control override (TCO) symptoms (of psychosis)
Technical Working Group for Eyewitness Evidence (1999), 152, 153
telephone surveys (for jury-eligible respondents), 194
temporary absence (parole), 268
Test of Memory Malingering (TOMM), 121
testimony,
  children's, 8, 10, 13
  expert, 10, 12, 13, 20, 22–23, 24
  see also eyewitness testimony
theory of maternal deprivation, 14
Thin Blue Line, The, (documentary), 347
threat/control override (TCO) symptoms (of psychosis), 354
thrill murderer, 320
Time magazine, 378
Toronto Police Service, 86

Toronto Raptors basketball team, 85
trauma-control model of serial murder,
   319, 319f
Treatise on Evidence, 11
trial records, 203
trial simulation, 203–204
truth bias, 107
typical batterer, 285

U

*U. S. Bureau of Statistics Police Public
   Contact Survey* (2005), 42
U. S. President's Commission on Law
   Enforcement and Administration
   of Justice (1970), 29
U. S. Supreme Court, 12, 22, 23, 147,
   201, 343, 344
unanimous verdicts, 210
*Understanding Public Attitudes to Criminal
   Justice*, 270
Underworld, 100
unfit to stand trial, 221
United Nations' Convention of the
   Rights of he Child, 178, 183
United States National Research
   Council (NRC), 101, 107
United States Supreme Court, 101, 230
University of Alabama Law Enforcement
   Academy, 36
University of Alberta, 144, 324, 325
University of British Columbia, 6, 19,
   161, 289, 323, 324, 349
University of Calgary, 19, 100
University of California, Santa Cruz,
   6, 68
University of Guelph, 24
University of Illinois, 228
University of Lethbridge, 51
University of London, England, 378
University of Massachusetts,
   Amherst, 294

University of Montreal, 378
University of Nebraska, Lincoln, 19
University of Saskatchewan, 19
University of Toronto, 270, 349
University of Western Ontario,
   216, 311, 324
unstructured clinical judgment (in risk
   assessment), 346
   example of, 347
unsystematic disparity (of
   sentencing), 258
unusualness, 150–151
use-of-force situations, 42
   continuum model, 44
uxoricide, 314

V

vagueness (psychology), 22, 23
Verdict with Paula Todd, The, 190
VICLAS. *See* Violent Crime Linkage
   Analysis System (VICLAS)
Victorian Institute of Forensic Mental
   Health, 19
Violence Against Woman Survey
   (1996), 282
Violence Risk Appraisal Guide (VRAG),
   346, 356–357, 365–366
Violence Risk Scale (VRS), 360–361
Violent Crime Linkage Analysis System
   (VICLAS), 75–76
Virginia Polytechnic Institute and
   State University (Virginia Tech),
   316, 322
voice identification, 146
   factors affecting, 146
voice-stress analysis, 107
voir dire (jury selection questioning), 194
voyeurs, 291
VRAG. *See Violence Risk Appraisal Guide*
   (VRAG)
VRS. *See Violence Risk Scale (VRS)*

W

Wahpeton Healing Lodge,
   Saskatchewan, 401
walk-by, 145
weapon focus phenomenon, 150
Western Australian Court of Criminal
   Appeal, 102
white lies, 111–112
Winnipeg Police Service, 155
witness probing exercise, 37
work simulation exercise, 37

Y

YCJA. *See* Youth Criminal Justice Act
   (YCJA) (2003)
YOA. *See* Young Offenders Act (YOA)
   (1984)
York University, 216
Yorkshire Ripper serial murder
   investigation, 73, 82–83
Young Offenders Act (YOA) (1984),
   372–373, 373t
young offenders, 371
   history of, 371, 371t, 372, 373,
      373t, 374t
youth crime, 39
   adolescent onset trajectory of,
      376–377
   assessment of, 375–376
   behaviour disorder rates for, 376
   childhood onset trajectory of,
      376–377
   protective factors for, 381
   resilience to, 381
   risk factors for, 350, 379–380
   statistics, 374, 374t
   theories, 377–379
   treatments for, 382–383
Youth Criminal Justice Act (YCJA)
   (2003), 373, 374, 374t
Youth Psychopathic Inventory, 332